Science and Technology Today

Readings for Writers

SCIENCE
AND
TECHNOLOGY
TODAY

Readings for Writers

Nancy R. MacKenzie
Mankato State University

St. Martin's Press

NEW YORK

Editor: Nancy Lyman
Associate editor: Clare Payton
Managing editor: Patricia Mansfield-Phelan
Project editor: Erica Appel
Production supervisor: Alan Fischer
Art director: Sheree Goodman
Text design: Andy Zutis
Cover design: Michael Jung
Cover art: Cliff Pickover

Library of Congress Catalog Card Number: 94-65183

9 8 7 6 5
f   e   d   c   b   a

For information, write:
St. Martin's Press, Inc.
175 Fifth Avenue
New York, NY 10010

ISBN: 0-312-09692-5

Acknowledgments

Baumrind, Diana. "Some Thoughts on the Ethics of Research." *American Psychologist,* volume 19(6), 1964, pages 421–432. Copyright 1964 by the American Psychological Association. Reprinted by permission.

Begley, Sharon. "Is Science Censored?" from *Newsweek,* Sept. 14, 1992. Copyright © 1992, Newsweek Inc. All rights reserved. Reprinted by permission.

Bolter, Jay David. "The Network Culture." From *Writing Space: The Computer, Hypertext, and the History of Writing* by Jay David Bolter. Reprinted by permission of Lawrence Erlbaum Associates, Inc. and the author.

Bradbury, Ray. "The Veldt." Reprinted by permission of Don Congdon Associates, Inc. Copyright © 1950, renewed 1977 by Ray Bradbury.

Brown, Jr., George E. "Technology's Dark Side," originally published in *The Chronicle of Higher Education,* June 30, 1993. Permission granted by Rick E. Borchelt, Press Secretary for Committee on Science, Space, and Technology, U.S. House of Representatives.

Calandra, Alexander. "Angels on a Pin." Copyright Alexander Calandra, Professor of Physics, Washington University, St. Louis, MO 63110. 1968, 1993.

Carson, Rachel. "The Obligation to Endure" from *Silent Spring* by Rachel Carson. Copyright © 1962 by Rachel L. Carson, © renewed 1990 by Roger Christie. Reprinted by permission of Houghton Mifflin Co. All rights reserved.

Cowan, Ruth Schwartz. "From Virginia Dare to Virginia Slims: Women and Technology in America Life." From *Technology and Culture,* vol. 20, no. 4, October 1979. Reprinted with the permission of The University of Chicago Press and the author.

DeMarinis, Rick. "Weeds." Reprinted from *Under the Wheat,* by Rick DeMarinis, by permission of the University of Pittsburgh Press. Copyright © 1986 by Rick DeMarinis.

Dorner, Marjorie. "Pulling Contest." Originally published in *Winter Roads, Summer Fields* by Marjorie Dorner. Copyright © 1992 by Marjorie Dorner. Reprinted with the permission of Milkweed Editions.

Ehrenreich, Barbara. "Science, Lies and The Ultimate Truth." Copyright 1991 Time Inc. Reprinted by permission.

Acknowledgments and copyrights are continued at the back of the book on pages 530–531, which constitute an extension of the copyright page. It is a violation of the law to reproduce these selections by any means whatsoever without the written permission of the copyright holder.

Preface

To inquire, to experiment, to observe, to read, to debate, to write: these are the pursuits of scientists, engineers, researchers, explorers, doctors, writers—indeed of all educated, thoughtful persons. *Science and Technology Today: Readings for Writers* is designed to provide a context and some working materials for these pursuits.

The genesis of this collection comes from the belief that all of us as members of today's society need to be aware of the issues and implications of scientific and technological developments. This book assumes that intelligent awareness may be achieved by thoughtful reading, critical analysis, open discussion, and focused writing on issues and practices in scientific and technological fields that affect us all. The purpose of this text, then, is to provide a rich and varied collection of readings which are lively, provocative, and challenging to students who are both inside and outside of the science and technology disciplines. To that end this anthology gathers the writing of engineers, research scientists, fiction writers, physicians, naturalists, journalists, teachers, and others who offer insights and perspectives ranging from literary to journalistic to scholarly.

The authors represented here encourage the student to analyze and question some common assumptions about science, technology, and writing: Scientists are notoriously bad writers; good writing requires passion, intuition, inspiration, or genius; science deals with facts and certainty; the scientific method enables one to discover the truth; improved technology brings a better quality of life; girls aren't good at math or science; "[L]iterary intellectuals [stand] at one pole—at the other scientists. . . . between the two a gulf of mutual incomprehension" (C. P. Snow).

The scholarly articles, editorials, personal essays, fiction, and drama collected here offer alternatives to stereotypical notions. Scientists show a sophisticated understanding of the rhetorical dimension of all writing. All of the authors prove that good writing is produced not by relying on inspiration, but by attending to detail, striving for clarity, and taking into consideration the audience's needs. Some of the writers argue convincingly that science, like all knowledge, is a human construct, reflecting not so much objective reality as a set of observations agreed upon by the scientific community. Even many scientists now acknowledge that the traditional notion of the scientific method is not a reliable formula. Studies show that females are good at math and science, but that many women entering the professions of science and technology will encounter prejudice when their colleagues are predominantly male. And finally, the gulf between science and the humanities is narrowing as we all come to share the overriding concerns of how technology shapes our lives (and deaths), our common culture, and our physical environment.

The Readings and Organization

The readings are arranged into eight thematic chapters, to help students tackle some of the complicated issues pertaining to technology and science, issues such as the causal relationship between technology and social culture; the role of science and technology in today's health care system; and recognition of the environmental risks attached to controlling nature with technology. The book's flexible organization allows instructors to pick and choose among topics or individual selections within each topic, according to pedagogical needs and preferences.

In addition to creating a foundation for provocative discussion and writing, the selections themselves provide excellent examples of the methods students will need for their own writing, such as summary, paraphrase, quotation, argument, and the like. Some of these pieces arouse the emotions, while others conform to a tightly reasoned structure. Some of these writings enthrall the reader with the power of figurative language, while others illustrate the utilitarian value of plain language.

They all, however, dispel that notion that scientists are notoriously bad writers; indeed, these selections illustrate just how powerful the writing from the scientific community can be. In addition, the choice of reading selections aims to achieve the kind of balance seldom found in anthologies of this sort.

- ☐ **Science and technology.** The selections examine both today's pressing issues in science *and* the recent dilemmas surrounding our technological progress. The relationship between the two has become so symbiotic that they deserve equal consideration.
- ☐ **Women and men.** This collection seeks to give female and male writers the equal status they deserve. With nearly half the selections written by women, *Science and Technology Today* strives to provide the best balance available in such readers.
- ☐ **Essays and imaginative literature.** In addition to the forty-four essays, the book contains eight pieces of fiction and one play, further dispelling the myth of "literary intellectuals at one pole – at the other scientists. . . ."

Pedagogical Features

No doubt the most exciting classrooms are those in which the students determine the focus and direction, with (minimal) helpful guidance from the instructor. In such a classroom, a reader can enhance the experience by including some biographical background on the authors, along with a variety of suggestions for discussing and writing about the reading selections. The apparatus in this text was created on several key pedagogical principles: that writing can be a means of learning; that reading, thinking, talking, and writing are interconnected; and that encouraging students to explore ideas and resist stereotypes leads to increased student authority.

The strong pedagogical apparatus seeks to enrich the students' knowledge of the subject matter while illustrating the exciting complications of the relevant issues. Students learn to struggle with questions that do not have answers, to identify problems that do not yet have solutions, and to resist stereotypes about science and technology.

Six elements surround each reading selection with materials for achieving these goals:

- ☐ **Biographical Headnotes** precede every selection, with material on the writer's background along with previous important works and achievements, providing a context for getting the student started on the reading.
- ☐ **Questions to Consider** are intended to function as critical thinking prompts before a student begins to read. They give a focus—not a bias or programmed approach—for the student who may initially need a reference point.
- ☐ **Discussion Questions** follow each reading and are designed to emphasize the important interplay between lively classroom talk and critical analysis. These questions first address the content and issues as a whole, then move to rhetorical and technical concerns, providing equal attention to the "what" and "how" of writing.
- ☐ **Journal Entries** allow students to explore ideas presented in the reading and/or write about related experiences they have had but may not be ready to share with the class or form into an essay. For this purpose students can be encouraged to create either a private journal or a writer's notebook.
- ☐ **Writing Projects** offer opportunities for both a further exploration of the issues presented and careful analysis of the writer's strategies. Thus, these projects call for written responses to difficult but enduring questions, research reports for gathering more information, interview assignments for culling opinions on various subjects, as well as traditional essays analyzing the form and style of the author's piece. This duality among the writing assignments allows instructors to use the text according to the emphasis of their courses—whether a content-driven issues course or a composition course.
- ☐ **Collaborative Projects,** a unique feature to science readers, unite two or more students in an in-depth and often creative study of the controversies at hand. Collaborative observations and research investigations as well as collaborative writing and on-line writing

projects give students the chance to interact and practice first hand the social construction of knowledge. Students are then encouraged to report their research methodology as well as their conclusions to the class, as a way of lending authority to their newfound knowledge.

Each of the eight thematic chapters ends with **Making Connections** questions, which ask students to reach conclusions about the broader implications involved in the thematic concerns. Suggested writing projects give them ample opportunity to compare the authors and the ideas presented in the chapter (or elsewhere).

An extensive **Instructor's Manual** provides further background on the selections and more suggestions for classroom discussion and analysis. Introductory questions are given for each thematic chapter; helpful hints appear at every turn. Also included in the Instructor's Manual are two student essays, complete with outlines, drafts, revisions, and comments from the instructor. The apparatus is carefully explained and includes special attention to collaborative work as well as group work. Overall, instructors will find a wealth of material for fully utilizing this book.

Acknowledgments

I am indebted to the many people who collaborated with me to make this book. I owe the most to my children, Philip and Fiona, who encouraged me, tolerated my preoccupation, and helped me in countless ways, from keeping track of telephone messages to photocopying manuscript pages to proofreading. Thanks also go to my sister, Shirley K Rose, who frequently reminded me that "every writing project is agony."

Two student assistants contributed abundant time, energy, and insightful suggestions. Kelly Schmidt tracked down elusive names, titles, and dates for the headnotes; drafted and revised portions of the apparatus; and, most important, suggested strategies for dealing with various difficulties. Aaron Guggemos was enthusiastic and tireless as he read and critiqued numerous essays, came up with discussion questions, and kept the permissions file accurate and complete.

My colleagues at other institutions who served as manuscript reviewers were outstanding. Their review comments were thorough, insightful, specific, helpful, and encouraging; one could not ask for anything more. My deep appreciation goes to Victoria Aarons, Trinity University; Elizabeth Bell, University of South Carolina–Aiken; Kurt Eisen, Tennessee Technological University; Keith Hjortshoj, Cornell University; David Jolliffe, The University of Illinois at Chicago; Jimmie Killingsworth, Texas A & M University; JoJane Marshall, West Los Angeles College; Bruce Maylath, University of

Memphis; Vicky McMillan, Colgate University; James Norman, DeVry Institute of Technology; Barry Pegg, Michigan Technological University; Carolyn Ross, Stanford University; Michael Strickland, Guilford College; and Terry Zawacki, George Mason University.

Acknowledgment is also due to my colleagues and students at Mankato State University. Administrative support along with personal encouragement and some wonderful ideas were provided by Jane F. Earley. Kathy Hurley and Terry Flaherty were also generous with advice and personal support. I am especially grateful to my colleagues Roger Sheffer and Richard Robbins, who allowed me to rely on their extensive knowledge of contemporary fiction and poetry, suggested titles and authors, and even went so far as to find copies of works for me and hunt down addresses for permission correspondence. Secretarial assistance from Patti Wolle, Sharon Evans, and Bonnie Fralish was very helpful and generously given.

Students in my classes over the past several years played a major role in making this book, as they participated in classroom testing of the readings, discussion questions, and writing assignments.

Finally, of course, the book would not have been made without the exceptional professional dedication of everyone at St. Martin's Press. Cathy Pusateri was largely responsible for getting this book started. The book's primary editor is Clare Payton, who deserves the credit for making the book what it is. Her hard work and deep commitment to the project encompassed negotiating permissions as well as having a hand in organizing the entire book and revising all of the apparatus. Throughout the process she has shared with me her excitement about the project and been generous with encouragement. I also wish to thank Nancy Lyman, who made countless administrative decisions, and Erica Appel, for her careful attention in guiding the manuscript through production.

Contents

2
Applying Technology 62

5
Healing with Technology   283

7

Considering Ethical Dilemmas

8
Writing to Construct Science and Technology 461

Rhetorical Contents

Analogy

Argument

Cause and Effect

Classification

Comparison and Contrast

Definition

Description

Dialogue and Monologue

Example

Humor

Narration

Process

Science and Technology Today

Readings for Writers

1

Defining Science

 Does scientific endeavor excite you? Scientific research can indeed be exciting. This chapter includes an excerpt from C. P. Snow's novel *The Search* (1958) in which a young scientist describes his own sensations when engaged in scientific problem solving: "Whatever I was doing, I was not at rest unless it was taking me towards the problem; and even then it was an unsettled rest, like lying in a fever half-way to sleep." Here is a scientist who is not just enthusiastic about his work but obsessed with his quest for scientific knowledge.

Not everyone, however, considers scientific problem solving to be a spellbinding endeavor. Cynthia Ozick gives scientific inquiry a venerable status when she refers to it as "God's work." Then she retreats from expressing an awestruck attitude by describing science as a discipline that is "fragmented, in hot pursuit of split ends." Ozick does not go so far as to say that scientific pursuits are trivial, only that science is a "multidivergent venture—dozens and dozens of disciplines, each one nearly a separate nation with its own governance. . . ."

Thus we speak of *the sciences*, rather than *science*—even classifying them into the hard versus the soft sciences, or the physical versus the life sciences. It is not easy to define science in a manner acceptable to those who have a vested interest in it.

Nevertheless, various scientists and writers have attempted to capture the essence of science in a definition, as demonstrated by the essays in this chapter. Writing half a century ago, George Orwell identified the two most common meanings of science: "Science is generally taken as meaning either (a) the exact sciences, such as chemistry, physics, etc., or (b) a method of thought which obtains verifiable results by reasoning logically from observed fact."

It is up to you to decide whether either of these definitions fully expresses the complexity of the scientific enterprise. By reading this chap-

1

ter you may come to agree with Orwell that these definitions merely represent a level of scientific understanding that many people are content to accept. Or you may decide that during the last half of the twentieth century we have become more sophisticated in both our understanding of science and the demands we make of it.

The critical need to reach an understanding of what characterizes scientific study and to recognize its importance to our society is not new. Thomas Henry Huxley, writing at the end of the nineteenth century, addressed this issue. Huxley believed, as many science teachers do today, that everyone should possess a working knowledge of the scientist's investigative approach, which is commonly referred to as the scientific method.

In the scientific method of induction, one derives general principles by examining particular instances. Huxley argued that this method was not the sole property of the scientist, but that it represented a common way of forming conclusions based on experience. Huxley's essay in this chapter was adapted from a talk he gave to a working-class audience. In it Huxley uses an analogy to illustrate that scientists employ the same methods to reach conclusions that we all use on a daily basis. He pointed out that if you take a bite out of a hard green apple and find it sour, and then upon subsequent tasting of hard green apples you discover that they are all sour, you can conclude that hard green apples are sour. This conclusion represents logical reasoning based upon your own observations.

This example, although memorable and appropriate for Huxley's audience, fails to illustrate the complexities of much modern scientific inquiry. Analogies and examples can be effective teaching tools, but oversimplification will not help. Unfortunately, the scientific method is often taught in a manner that is both simplistic and rigid.

There is concern today about a general lack of scientific literacy in our culture. Studies show that many children start out in life being curious about science. But by the time they reach third grade, at least half of them seem no longer interested in science; by eighth grade, 80 percent say they don't like science. Many blame the schools for teaching science in the wrong way. Nobel prize–winning physicist Leon Lederman says that our schools take "naturally curious, natural scientists and manage to beat that curiosity right out of them."

How were you taught science in elementary school or high school? Were you ever involved in a science fair? If so, your understanding of what science is and how it operates was probably shaped by that experience. The science fair is a valid and effective means of introducing students to the field. But you may recall that your project was evaluated on the basis of how well you followed a prescribed approach. Your report probably had to be presented in a standard format: hypothesis, methodology, findings, interpretation, and conclusion. In fact, elementary students today can purchase science fair presentation boards with these headings already printed on them. The implied message is clear: only one approach is legitimate.

Some people question these assumptions, however. Alexander Calandra, a physics teacher, has written the story "Angels on a Pin" about a student who challenges his teacher's by-the-book teaching methods. The student knows what exam answer the teacher expects, but he gives a different answer—it is not wrong, but neither is it the expected answer. Should the student's answer count? You'll have a chance to consider the issue in this chapter.

Our culture continues to promote the belief that science is objective, impartial, and factual. Science teachers proceed as if by teaching the scientific method they provide students with access to incontrovertible scientific truths.

Not all scientists view their work in this way, however. Over the past thirty years or so, research based on close observation of how scientists actually work (as opposed to how they report they have worked) demonstrates that what comes to be accepted as a "scientific fact" is most often the result of consensus among those in the scientific community. And it is as much a matter of fact *making* as fact *finding*, because scientists rely on more than logic and evidence alone to persuade each other of what should qualify as scientific knowledge. Having been influenced by these social constructionist theories of science and her own experience as a practicing physicist, Evelyn Fox Keller explains in her essay how she came to see that "cultural norms and values can, indeed have, helped define the success and shape the growth of science."

So we see that during the twentieth century our understanding of the nature of science has changed in some ways, and in other ways scientific activity goes on much as it did before. One thing that has not changed much is the scarcity of women and minorities in prominent or influential positions in science. Shirley Tilghman's essay provides evidence that sexism and racism continue to be prevalent in scientific disciplines today. She explains that science, like other disciplines, reflects our cultural biases.

As you read, talk, and write about the essays in this chapter, construct your own definition of science. Consider how responsible you think each of us is for understanding and influencing the scope and consequences of current scientific practice.

Reference

Sharon Begley et al., "Rx for Learning: There's No Secret about How to Teach Science," *Newsweek*, 9 April 1990.

Cynthia Ozick

Science and Letters: God's Work—And Ours

Cynthia Ozick *(b. 1928), born and raised in New York City, has written both essays and fiction on the tension between scientists and humanists. In the essay that follows, which was originally published in the* New York Times Book Review *in 1987, Ozick takes an up-to-date look at the lack of understanding between literary writers and scientists that C. P. Snow addressed in his extremely controversial essay "The Two Cultures"* (New Statesman, *October 6, 1956). Snow, a novelist and a scientist, saw himself as a member of a learned society that had divided itself into two separate cultures, with the sciences standing in opposition to the arts and humanities. Writing twenty-eight years after the publication of Snow's expanded treatment of the two-cultures debate,* The Two Cultures: And a Second Look *(1959), Ozick rejects the old debate, asserting that both the science and letters communities have changed significantly during the past three decades. Ozick's work, noted for its strong personal voice and demonstrated literary expertise, includes a collection of short fiction,* The Pagan Rabbi and Other Stories *(1971); a novel,* The Cannibal Galaxy *(1983); and a collection of essays,* Metaphor and Memory *(1989), in which the following essay appears under the title "Crocodiled Moats in the Kingdom of Letters."*

Questions to Consider

☐ As you read, try to determine what prompted Ozick to write this essay so long after the two-culture debate had died down. Why did she bring it up again almost thirty years later?

☐ Given Ozick's title, whom do you think she includes in "ours"?

For constantly I felt I was moving among two groups—comparable in intelligence, identical in race, not grossly different in social origin, earning about the same incomes, who had almost ceased to communicate at all, who in intellectual, moral and psychological climate had so little in common that . . . one might have crossed an ocean.

—C. P. SNOW,
"The Two Cultures and the Scientific Revolution"

DISRAELI in his novel "Sybil" spoke of "two nations," the rich and the poor. After the progress of more than a century, the phrase (and the reality) remains regrettably apt. But in the less than three decades since C. P. Snow proposed his "two cultures" thesis – the gap of incomprehension between the scientific and literary elites – the conditions of what we still like to call culture have altered so drastically that Snow's arguments are mostly dissolved into pointlessness. His compatriot and foremost needler, the Cambridge critic F. R. Leavis, had in any case set out to flog Snow's hypothesis from the start. Snow, he said, "rides on an advancing swell of cliché," "doesn't know what literature is" and hasn't "had the advantage of an intellectual discipline of any kind." And besides – here Leavis emitted his final boom – "there is only one culture."

In the long run both were destined to be mistaken – Leavis perhaps more than Snow. In 1959, when Snow published "The Two Cultures," we had already had well over a hundred years to get used to the idea of science as a multidivergent venture – dozens and dozens of disciplines, each one nearly a separate nation with its own governance, psychology, entelechy. It might have been possible to posit, say, a unitary medical culture in the days when barbers were surgeons; but in recent generations we don't expect our dentist to repair a broken kneecap, or our orthopedist to practice cardiology. And nowadays we are learning that an ophthalmologist with an understanding of the cornea is likely to be a bit shaky on the subject of the retina. Engineers are light-years from astrophysicists. Topology is distinct from topography, paleobotany from paleogeology, particle physics from atomic. In reiterating that scientific culture is specialist culture – who doesn't know this? – one risks riding an advancing swell of cliché. Yet science, multiplying, fragmented, in hot pursuit of split ends, is in a way a species of polytheism, or, rather, animism: every grain of matter, every path of conceptualization, has its own ruling spirit, its differentiated lawgiver and traffic director. Investigative diversity and particularizing empiricism have been characteristic of science since – well, since alchemy turned into physical chemistry (and lately into superconductivity); since the teakettle inspired the locomotive; since Icarus took off his wax wings to become Pan Am; since Archimedes stepped out of his tub into Einstein's sea.

Snow was in command of all this, of course – he was pleased to identify himself as an exceptional scientist who wrote novels – and still he chose to make a monolith out of splinters. Why did he do it? In order to have one unanimity confront another. While it may have been a polemical contrivance to present a diversiform scientific culture as unitary, it was patently not wrong, thirty years ago, to speak of literary culture as a single force or presence. That was what was meant by the peaceable word "humanities." And it was what Leavis meant, too, when he growled back at Snow that one culture was all there was worth having. "Don't mistake me," Leavis pressed, "I am not preaching that we should defy, or try to reverse, the accelerating movement of external civilization (the phrase sufficiently explains itself, I hope) that is determined by advancing technology. . . . What I *am* saying is that such a concern is not enough – disastrously not enough." Not enough, he argued, for "a human future . . . in full intelligent possession of its full humanity." For Leavis, technology was the mere outer rind of culture, and the job of literature (the hot core at the heart of culture) was not to oppose science but to humanize it. Only in Snow's wretchedly deprived mind did literature stand apart from science; Snow hardly understood what literature was *for*. And no wonder; Snow's ideas about literary intellectuals came, Leavis sneered, from "the reviewing in the Sunday papers."

It has never been easy to fashion a uniform image of science – which is why we tend to say "the sciences." But until not very long ago one could take it for granted (despite the headlong decline of serious high art) that there was, on the humanities side, a concordant language of sensibility, an embracing impulse toward integration, above all the conviction of human connectedness – even if that conviction occasionally partook of a certain crepuscular nostalgia we might better have done without. Snow pictured literature and science as two angry armies. Leavis announced that there was only one army, with literature as its commander in chief. Yet it was plain that both Leavis and Snow, for all their antagonisms, saw the kingdom of letters as an intact and enduring power.

This feeling for literary culture as a glowing wholeness – it *was* a feeling, a stirring, a flush of idealism – is now altogether dissipated. The fragrant term that encapsulated it – belles-lettres – is nearly archaic and surely effete: it smacks of leather tooling for the moneyed, of posturing. But it was once useful enough. Belles-lettres stood for a binding thread of observation and civilizing emotion. It signified not so much that letters are beautiful as that the house of letters is encompassingly humane and undivisive, no matter how severally its windows are shaped, or who looks out or in. Poets, scholars, journalists, librarians, novelists, playwrights, art critics, philosophers, historians, political theorists and all the rest may have inhabited different rooms, differently furnished, but it was indisputably one house with a single roof and plenty of connecting doors and passageways. And sometimes – so elastic and compressive was the humanist principle – poet, scholar, essayist, philosopher, etc., all lived side by side in the same head. Seamlessness (even if only an illusion) never implied locked and separate cells.

And now? Look around. Now "letters" suggest a thousand enemy camps, "genres" like fortresses, professions isolated by crocodiled moats. The living tissue of intuition and inference that nurtured the commonalty of the humanities is ruptured by an abrupt invasion of specialists. In emulation of the sciences? But we don't often hear of astronomers despising molecular biologists; in science, it may be natural for knowledge to run, like quicksilver, into crannies.

In the ex-community of letters, factions are in fashion, and the business of factions is to despise. Matthew Arnold's mild and venerable dictum, an open-ended, open-armed, definition of literature that clearly intends a nobility of inclusiveness – "the best that is known and thought in the world" – earns latter-day assaults and jeers. What can all that mean now but "canon," and what can a received canon mean but reactionary, racist, sexist, elitist closure? Politics presses against disinterestedness; all categories are suspect, no category is allowed to display its wares without the charge of enslavement by foregone conclusion and vested interest. What Arnold called the play of mind is asked to show its credentials and prove its legitimacy. "Our organs of criticism," Arnold complained in 1864 (a period as uninnocent as our own), "are organs of men and parties having practical ends to serve, and with them those practical ends are the first thing and the play of mind the second."

And so it is with us. The culture of the humanities has split and split and split again, always for reasons of partisan ascendancy and scorn. Once it was not unusual for writers—Dreiser, Stephen Crane, Cather, Hemingway!—to turn to journalism for a taste of the workings of the world. Today novelists and journalists are alien breeds reared apart, as if imagination properly belonged only to the one and never to the other; as if society and instinct were designed for estrangement. The two crafts are contradictory even in method; journalists are urged to tell secrets in the top line; novelists insinuate suspensefully, and wait for the last line to spill the real beans. Dickens, saturated in journalism, excelled at shorthand; was a court reporter; edited topical magazines.

In the literary academy, Jacques Derrida has the authority that Duns Scotus had for medieval scholastics—and it is authority, not literature, that mainly engages faculties. In the guise of maverick or rebel, professors kowtow to dogma. English departments have set off after theory, and use culture as an instrument to illustrate doctrinal principles, whether Marxist or "French Freud." The play of mind gives way to signing up and lining up. College teachers were never so cut off from the heat of poets dead or alive as they are now; only think of the icy distances separating syllables by, say, Marianne Moore, A. R. Ammons, May Swenson or Amy Clampitt from the papers read at last winter's Modern Language Association meeting—viz., "Written Discourse as Dialogic Interaction," "Abduction, Transference, and the Reading Stage," "The Politics of Feminism and the Discourse of Feminist Literary Criticism."

And more: poets trivialize novelists, novelists trivialize poets. Both trivialize critics. Critics trivialize reviewers. Reviewers report that they *are* critics. Short-story writers assert transfigurations unavailable to novelists. Novelists declare the incomparable glories of the long pull. Novelizing estheticians, admitting to literature no claims of moral intent, ban novelizing moralists. The moralists condemn the estheticians as precious, barren, solipsist. Few essayists essay fiction. Few novelists hazard essays. Dense-language writers vilify minimalists. Writers of plain prose ridicule complex sentences. Professors look down on commercial publishers. Fiction writers dread university presses. The so-called provinces envy and despise the provinciality of New York. New

York sees sour grapes in California and everywhere else. The so-called mainstream judges which writers are acceptably universal and which are to be exiled as "parochial." The so-called parochial, stung or cowardly or both, fear all particularity and attempt impersonation of the acceptable. "Star" writers—recall the International PEN Congress in New York last year—treat lesser-knowns as invisible, negligible. The lesser-knowns, crushed, disparage the stars.

And even the public library, once the unchallenged repository of the best that is known and thought, begins to split itself off, abandons its mandate and rents out Polaroid cameras and videotapes, like some semiphilanthropic Crazy Eddie. My own local library, appearing to jettison the basic arguments of the age, flaunts shelf after shelf prominently marked Decorating, Consumer Power, How-To, Cookery, Hooray for Hollywood, Accent on You, What Makes Us Laugh and many more such chitchat categories. But there are no placards for Literature, History, Biography; and Snow and Leavis, whom I needed to moon over in order to get started on this essay, were neither one to be had. (I found them finally in the next town, in a much smaller if more traditionally bookish library.)

Though it goes against the grain of respected current belief to say so, literature is really *about* something. It is about us. That may be why we are drawn to think of the kingdom of letters as a unity, at least in potential. Science, teeming and multiform, is about how the earth and the heavens and the microbes and the insects and our mammalian bodies are constructed, but literature is about the meaning of the finished construction. Or, to set afloat a more transcendent vocabulary: science is about God's work; literature is about our work. If our work lies untended (and what is our work but aspiration?), if literary culture falls into a heap of adversarial splinters—into competing contemptuous clamorers for turf and mental dominance—then what will be left to tell us that we are one human presence?

To forward that strenuous telling, Matthew Arnold (himself now among the jettisoned) advised every reader and critic to "try and possess one great literature, at least, besides his own; and the more unlike his own, the better." Not to split off from but to add on to the kingdom of letters: so as to uncover its human face.

An idea which—in a time of ten thousand self-segregating literary technologies—may be unwanted, if not obsolete.

Discussion Questions

1. What are some examples of Ozick's use of figurative language (metaphor, simile, sensory imagery) that you found particularly apt? What effect does she achieve with figurative language?

2. What denotations (literal definitions) and connotations (suggestive implications) do you associate with the term *belles-lettres*? How many class members agree with Ozick that *belles-lettres* is a "fragrant term," one that "smacks of leather tooling for the moneyed, of posturing"?

3. What do you think Ozick's point is in saying that "science, multiplying, fragmented, in hot pursuit of split ends, is in a way a species of polytheism, or, rather, animism. . ."? What does this phrase mean? Do you agree with her description of science? Why or why not?

4. Ozick points out what she considers a serious problem when she asks, "If literary culture falls into a heap of adversarial splinters – into competing contemptuous clamorers for turf and mental dominance – then what will be left to tell us that we are one human presence?" How does Ozick illustrate the seriousness of this problem? Do you agree with her? Why or why not?

Journal Entry

Write down your immediate response to the notion of science as God's work. Explore your own beliefs and biases regarding the distinction between, or the interplay of, religion and science.

Writing Projects

1. Write an essay directed toward elementary teachers, who often teach both language arts and science. Explain why it is important for them to present science and literature as disciplines of equal prestige so that young students do not grow up viewing one as superior to the other.

2. Write an essay exploring why you think Ozick emphasized a connection between God and science, and explaining what you think Ozick means by "God's work." Discuss why you do, or do not, agree with Ozick; share your thoughts on whether scientists are likely to view their work with a religious attitude.

Collaborative Projects

1. Working with a partner, write two essays, each one in response to Writing Project 2. One partner could write an essay using the journalist's style that Ozick mentions whereby the writer "tell(s) secrets in the top line." The other partner could write an essay using the literary style, waiting "for the last line to spill the real beans." Or you might write both essays together.

2. Ozick describes the difficulty she had in finding a library that carried copies of works by Snow and Leavis; instead, she found shelf after shelf marked

"How-To," "Consumer Power," "Accent on You." Working with one or two classmates, visit your community library and a local (nonuniversity) bookstore. Survey what kinds of books are most numerous and most prominently displayed. Present to the class your findings and conclusions about your community's reading interests and its views on the function of libraries and bookstores.

George Orwell

What Is Science?

George Orwell *(1903–1950), the pen name of Eric Arthur Blair, was an esteemed British novelist, social critic, and journalist. Orwell was born in Bengal, where his father was an agent in the British colonial administration of India. The family returned to England, where Orwell attended private school and graduated from Eton in 1921. Orwell's writing represents a model of clear, direct, and morally forceful exposition. He achieved status in the literary canon with two political novels:* Animal Farm *(1945), a masterpiece of political satire; and* 1984 *(1949), a fictional polemic against totalitarianism. "What Is Science?" was originally published in 1945 in the* Tribune, *a British Socialist weekly to which Orwell was a regular contributor. Here the author seeks to define science and goes on to explain why he believes there is resistance to his definition.*

Questions to Consider

☐ This essay was published in 1945 shortly after the United States dropped the atomic bomb on Japan. How do you suppose the public's interest in the scientific development of weapons produced during wartime influenced both Orwell's and his readers' views of the role of science?

☐ While you read this example of journalistic writing, consider whether Orwell displays any bias (positive or negative) toward scientists or toward writers. Is Orwell's approach here in keeping with what you expect journalists to do?

I N last week's *Tribune*, there was an interesting letter from Mr. J. Stewart Cook, in which he suggested that the best way of avoiding the danger of a "scientific hierarchy" would be to see to it that every member of the general public was, as far as possible, scientifically educated. At the same time, scientists should be brought out of their isolation and encouraged to take a greater part in politics and administration.

As a general statement, I think most of us would agree with this, but I notice that, as usual, Mr. Cook does not define science, and merely implies in passing that it means certain exact sciences whose experiments can be made under laboratory conditions. Thus, adult education tends "to neglect scientific studies in favor of literary, economic and social subjects," economics and sociology not being regarded as branches of science, apparently. This point is of great importance. For the word science is at present used in at least two meanings, and the whole question of scientific education is obscured by the current tendency to dodge from one meaning to the other.

Science is generally taken as meaning either (a) the exact sciences, such as chemistry, physics, etc., or (b) a method of thought which obtains verifiable results by reasoning logically from observed fact.

If you ask any scientist, or indeed almost any educated person, "What is science?" you are likely to get an answer approximating to (b). In everyday life, however, both in speaking and in writing, when people say "science" they mean (a). Science means something that happens in a laboratory: the very word calls up a picture of graphs, test-tubes, balances, Bunsen burners, microscopes. A biologist, an astronomer, perhaps a psychologist or a mathematician, is described as a "man of science": no one would think of applying this term to a statesman, a poet, a journalist or even a philosopher. And those who tell us that the young must be scientifically educated mean, almost invariably, that they should be taught more about radioactivity, or the stars, or the physiology of their own bodies, rather than that they should be taught to think more exactly. ←

This confusion of meaning, which is partly deliberate, has in it a great danger. Implied in the demand for more scientific education is the claim that if one has been scientifically trained one's approach to *all* subjects will be more intelligent than if one had had no such training. A scientist's political opinions, it is assumed, his opinions on sociological questions, on morals, on philosophy, perhaps even on the arts, will be more valuable than those of a layman. The world, in other words, would be a better place if the scientists were in control of it. But a "scientist," as we have just seen, means in practice a specialist in one of the exact sciences. It follows that a chemist or a physicist, as such, is politically more intelligent than a poet or a lawyer, as such. And, in fact, there are already millions of people who do believe this.

But is it really true that a "scientist," in this narrower sense, is any likelier than other people to approach non-scientific problems in an objective way? There is not much reason for thinking so. Take one simple test – the ability to withstand nationalism. It is often loosely said that "Science is international," but in practice the scientific workers of all countries line up behind their own governments with fewer scruples than are felt by the writers and the artists. The German scientific community, as a whole, made no resistance to Hitler. Hitler may have ruined the long-term prospects of German science, but there were still plenty of gifted men to do the necessary research on such things as synthetic oil, jet planes, rocket projectiles and the atomic bomb. Without them the German war machine could never have been built up.

On the other hand, what happened to German literature when the Nazis came to power? I believe no exhaustive lists have been published, but I imagine that the number of German scientists – Jews apart – who voluntarily exiled themselves or were persecuted by the régime was much smaller than the number of writers and journalists. More sinister than this, a number of German scientists swallowed the monstrosity of "racial science." You can find some of the statements to which they set their names in Professor Brady's *The Spirit and Structure of German Fascism.*

But, in slightly different forms, it is the same picture everywhere. In England, a large proportion of our leading scientists accept the structure of capitalist society, as can be seen from the comparative freedom with which they are given knighthoods, baronetcies and even peerages. Since Tennyson, no English writer worth reading – one might, perhaps, make an exception of Sir Max Beerbohm – has been given a title. And those English scientists who do not simply accept the *status quo* are frequently Communists, which means that, however intellectually scrupulous they may be in their own line of work, they are ready to be uncritical and even dishonest on certain subjects. The fact is that a mere training in one or more of the exact sciences, even combined with very high gifts, is no guarantee of a humane or sceptical outlook. The physicists of half a dozen great nations, all feverishly and secretly working away at the atomic bomb, are a demonstration of this.

But does all this mean that the general public should *not* be more scientifically educated? On the contrary! All it means is that scientific education for the masses will do little good, and probably a lot of harm, if it simply boils down to more physics, more chemistry, more biology, etc. to the detriment of literature and history. Its probable effect on the average human being would be to narrow the range of his thoughts and make him more than ever contemptuous of such knowledge as he did not possess: and his political reactions would probably be somewhat less intelligent than those of an illiterate peasant who retained a few historical memories and a fairly sound aesthetic sense.

Clearly, scientific education ought to mean the implanting of a rational, sceptical, experimental habit of mind. It ought to mean acquiring a *method* – a method that can be used on any problem that one meets – and not simply piling up a lot of facts. Put it in those words, and the apologist of scientific education will usually agree. Press him further, ask him to particularize, and somehow it always turns out that scientific education means more attention to the exact sciences, in other words – more *facts*. The idea that science means a way of looking at the world, and not simply a body of knowledge, is in practice strongly resisted. I think sheer professional jealousy is part of the reason for this. For if science is simply a method or an attitude, so that anyone whose thought-processes are sufficiently rational can in some sense be described as a scientist – what then becomes of the enormous prestige now enjoyed by the chemist, the physicist, etc. and his claim to be somehow wiser than the rest of us?

A hundred years ago, Charles Kingsley described science as "making nasty smells in a laboratory." A year or two ago a young industrial chemist informed me, smugly, that he "could not see what was the use of poetry." So the pendulum swings to and fro, but it does not seem to me that one attitude is any better than the other. At the moment, science is on the up-grade, and so we hear, quite rightly, the claim that the masses should be scientifically educated: we do not hear, as we ought, the counter-claim that the scientists themselves would benefit by a little education. Just before writing this, I saw in an American magazine the statement that a number of British and American physicists refused from the start to do research on the atomic bomb, well knowing what use would be made of it. Here you have a group of sane men in the middle of a world of lunatics. And though no names were published, I think it would be a safe guess that all of them were people with some kind of general cultural background, some acquaintance with history or literature or the arts—in short, people whose interests were not, in the current sense of the word, purely scientific.

Discussion Questions

1. Characterize the structure and tone of Orwell's essay. As an essay, is it more journalistic than literary or vice versa? On what do you base your assessment?

2. What methods of exposition and illustration does Orwell use to develop his definition of science? Are his methods effective? Why or why not?

3. Does this essay, written almost fifty years ago, seem out-of-date or still applicable? If you find it relevant today, why do you think Orwell's ideas still apply to our current culture? What elements seem no longer accurate?

4. Do you believe science is a way of looking at the world, or is it a body of knowledge? What is the difference between these two definitions? Can science be both?

5. Do you agree that the general public should be more scientifically educated? Why or why not? Do you believe that scientists should be more educated about nonscientific issues and knowledge? Why or why not? Which is more important: to increase the scientific understanding of the public, or to increase the type and depth of a scientist's knowledge outside the scientific domain—in the arts and politics, for example?

Journal Entry

There is concern today that Americans lack scientific literacy. Explain why you do, or do not, consider yourself to be scientifically literate. If you think you need to be more literate about scientific subjects, how do you plan to acquire that knowledge?

Writing Projects

1. Write an essay, to be directed to a group of scientists, entitled "Too Much Science Education Can Be Harmful." Respond to Orwell's assertion that "scientific education for the masses will do little good, and probably a lot of harm, if it simply boils down to more physics, more chemistry, more biology, etc. . . ."

2. Orwell says that the call for more science education is based on a belief that the scientifically trained person is more likely to approach all learning, and thus all decisions in daily life, in a more intelligent, logical way than the nonscientifically trained person. Write an essay in which you explain why you agree or disagree with Orwell's reservations about this belief.

Collaborative Project

Working with one or two partners, construct a definition of science based on research. The definition should illustrate how the field of science differs from the humanities. One or two of your team members might conduct primary research—for example, by interviewing science professionals (teachers and other experts) as well as professionals in the humanities, or by watching professionals in both fields at work. Another team member might do secondary research, including surveys of textbooks and college curriculum catalogs. Or your team could all gather the data and write the definition together. Share your definition with the class.

Thomas Henry Huxley

How a Scientist Thinks

Thomas Henry Huxley *(1825–1895), a British scientist, educator, and prolific essay-ist, wrote on science education and natural history. Many of his essays defended Darwin's theories in particular, earning him the designation of "Darwin's bulldog." Born into a large family that had very little money, Huxley did not receive formal schooling after the age of 10. Self-educated, he was only 26 when he became a Fellow of the Royal Society. In addi-tion to writing extensively, Huxley was a popular lecturer and skilled debater who spoke frequently on the controversial subject of evolution. Collections of his essays, such as* Science and Education *(1893),* Darwinia *(1896), and* Autobiography and Selected Essays *(1909), attest to Huxley's interest in educating the general public about science. In "How a Scientist Thinks," which was first delivered as a lecture to an audience of working-class laborers, Huxley argues that the thought processes used by scientists are not unique to the field of science. Scientists use the common processes of induction and deduction that we all use daily, but the scientists' investigations require more careful and extensive verification.*

Questions to Consider

☐ Huxley's essay describes a thinking process. As you read, consider how he has, or has not, used the process of induction himself.

☐ As you read, note elements of structure and features of style commonly as-sociated with oral rather than written delivery. What evidence do you see of the author's adapting his examples to his working-class audience?

THE method of scientific investigation is nothing but the expression of the necessary mode of working of the human mind. It is simply the mode at which all phenomena are reasoned about, rendered precise and exact. There is no more difference, but there is just the same kind of dif-ference, between the mental operations of a man of science and those of an or-dinary person, as there is between the operations and methods of a baker or of a butcher weighing out his goods in common scales, and the operations of a chemist in performing a difficult and complex analysis by means of his balance and finely graduated weights. It is not that the action of the scales in the one case, and the balance in the other, differ in the principles of their construction or manner of working; but the beam of one is set on an infinitely finer axis than the other, and of course turns by the addition of a much smaller weight.

You will understand this better, perhaps, if I give you some familiar example. You have all heard it repeated, I dare say, that men of science work by means of induction and deduction, and that by the help of these operations, they, in a sort of sense, wring from Nature certain other things, which are called natural laws, and causes, and that out of these, by some cunning skill of their own, they build up hypotheses and theories. And it is imagined by many, that the operations of the common mind can be by no means compared with these processes, and that they have to be acquired by a sort of special apprenticeship to the craft. To hear all these large words, you would think that the mind of a man of science must be constituted differently from that of his fellow men; but if you will not be frightened by terms, you will discover that you are quite wrong, and that all these terrible apparatus are being used by yourselves every day and every hour of your lives.

There is a well-known incident in one of Molière's plays, where the author makes the hero express unbounded delight on being told that he had been talking prose during the whole of his life. In the same way, I trust, that you will take comfort, and be delighted with yourselves, on the discovery that you have been acting on the principles of inductive and deductive philosophy during the same period. Probably there is not one here who has not in the course of the day had occasion to set in motion a complex train of reasoning, of the very same kind, though differing of course in degree, as that which a scientific man goes through in tracing the causes of natural phenomena.

A very trivial circumstance will serve to exemplify this. Suppose you go into a fruiterer's shop, wanting an apple, — you take up one, and, on biting it, you find it is sour; you look at it, and see that it is hard and green. You take up another one, and that too is hard, green, and sour. The shopman offers you a third; but, before biting it, you examine it, and find that it is hard and green, and you immediately say that you will not have it, as it must be sour, like those that you have already tried.

Nothing can be more simple than that, you think; but if you will take the trouble to analyze and trace out into its logical elements what has been done by the mind, you will be greatly surprised. In the first place you have performed the operation of induction. You found that, in two experiences, hardness and greenness in apples went together with sourness. It was so in the first case, and it was confirmed by the second. True, it is a very small basis, but still it is enough to make an induction from; you generalize the facts, and you expect to find sourness in apples where you get hardness and greenness. You found upon that a general law that all hard and green apples are sour; and that, so far as it goes, is a perfect induction. Well, having got your natural law in this way, when you are offered another apple which you find is hard and green, you say, "All hard and green apples are sour; this apple is hard and green, therefore this apple is sour." That train of reasoning is what logicians call a syllogism, and has all its various parts and terms, – its major premiss, its minor premiss and its conclusion. And, by the help of further reasoning, which, if drawn out, would have to be exhibited in two or three other syllogisms, you arrive at your final determination, "I will not have that apple." So that, you see, you have, in the first place, established a law by induction, and upon that you have founded a deduction, and reasoned out the special particular case. Well now, suppose, having got your conclusion of the law, that at some time afterwards, you are discussing the qualities of apples with a friend: you will say to him, "It is a very curious thing, – but I find that all hard and green apples are sour!" Your friend says to you, "But how do you know that?" You at once reply, "Oh, because I have tried them over and over again, and have always found them to be so." Well, if we were talking science instead of common sense, we should call that an experimental verification. And, if still opposed, you go further, and say, "I have heard from the people in Somersetshire and Devonshire, where a large number of apples are grown, that they have observed the same thing. It is also found to be the case in Normandy, and in North America. In short, I find it to be the universal experience of mankind wherever attention has been directed to the subject." Whereupon, your friend, unless he is a very unreasonable man, agrees with you, and is convinced that you are quite right in the conclusion you have drawn. He believes, although perhaps he does not know he believes it, that the more extensive verifications are, – that the more frequently experiments have been made, and results of the same kind arrived at, – that the more varied the conditions under which the same results are attained, the more certain is the ultimate conclusion, and he disputes the question no further. He sees that the experiment has been tried under all sorts of conditions, as to time, place, and people, with the same result; and he says with you, therefore, that the law you have laid down must be a good one, and he must believe it.

In science we do the same thing; – the philosopher exercises precisely the same faculties, though in a much more delicate manner. In scientific inquiry it becomes a matter of duty to expose a supposed law to every possible kind of verification, and to take care, moreover, that this is done intentionally, and not left to a mere accident, as in the case of the apples. And in science, as in common life, our confidence in a law is in exact proportion to the absence of variation in the result of our experimental verifications. For instance, if you let go your grasp of an article you may have in your hand, it will immediately fall to the ground. That is a very common verification of one of the best established laws of nature – that of gravitation. The method by which men of science establish the existence of that law is exactly the same as that by which we have established the trivial proposition about the sourness of hard and green apples. But we believe it in such an extensive, thorough, and unhesitating manner because the universal experience of mankind verifies it, and we can verify it ourselves at any time; and that is the strongest possible foundation on which any natural law can rest.

So much, then, by way of proof that the method of establishing laws in science is exactly the same as that pursued in common life. Let us now turn to another matter (though really it is but another phase of the same question), and that is, the method by which, from the relations of certain phenomena, we prove that some stand in the position of causes towards the others.

I want to put the case clearly before you, and I will therefore show you what I mean by another familiar example. I will suppose that one of you, on coming down in the morning to the parlor of your house, finds that a tea-pot and some spoons which had been left in the room on the previous evening are gone, – the window is open, and you observe the mark of a dirty hand on the window-frame, and perhaps, in addition to that, you notice the impress of a hob-nailed shoe on the gravel outside. All these phenomena have struck your attention instantly, and before two seconds have passed you say, "Oh, somebody has broken open the window, entered the room, and run off with the spoons and the tea-pot!" That speech is out of your mouth in a moment. And you will probably add, "I know there has; I am quite sure of it!" You mean to say exactly what you know; but in reality you are giving expression to what is, in all essential particulars, an hypothesis. You do not *know* it at all; it is nothing but an hypothesis rapidly framed in your own mind. And it is an hypothesis founded on a long train of inductions and deductions.

What are those inductions and deductions, and how have you got at this hypothesis? You have observed in the first place, that the window is open; but by a train of reasoning involving many inductions and deductions, you have probably arrived long before at the general law – and a very good one it is – that windows do not open of themselves; and you therefore conclude that something has opened the window. A second general law that you have arrived at in the same way is, that tea-pots and spoons do not go out of a window spontaneously, and you are satisfied that, as they are not now where you left them, they have been removed. In the third place, you look at the marks on the window-sill, and the shoe-marks outside, and you say that in all previous experience the former kind of mark has never been produced by anything else but the hand of a human being; and the same experience shows that no other animal but man at present wears shoes with hob-nails in them such as would produce the marks in the gravel. I do not know, even if we could discover any of those "missing links" that are talked about, that they would help us to any other conclusion! At any rate the law which states our present experience is strong enough for my present purpose. You next reach the conclusion that, as these kinds of marks have not been left by any other animal than man, or are liable to be formed in any other way than a man's hand and shoe, the marks in question have been formed by a man in that way. You have, further, a general law, founded on observation and experience, and that, too, is, I am sorry to say, a very universal and unimpeachable one, – that some men are thieves; and you assume at once from all these premises – and that is what constitutes your hypothesis – that the man who made the marks outside and on the window-sill, opened the window, got into the room, and stole your tea-pot and spoons. You have now arrived at a *vera causa*; – you have assumed a cause which, it is plain, is competent to produce all the phenomena you have observed. You can explain all these phenomena only by the hypothesis of a thief. But that is a hypothetical conclusion, of the justice of which you have no absolute proof at all; it is only rendered highly probable by a series of inductive and deductive reasonings.

I suppose your first action, assuming that you are a man of ordinary common sense, and that you have established this hypothesis to your own satisfaction, will very likely be to go off for the police, and set them on the track of the burglar, with the view to the recovery of your property. But just as you are starting with this object, some person comes in, and on learning what you are about, says, "My good friend, you are going on a great deal too fast. How do you know that the man who really made the marks took the spoons? It might have been a monkey that took them, and the man may have merely looked in afterwards." You would probably reply, "Well, that is all very well, but you see it is contrary to all experience of the way tea-pots and spoons are abstracted; so that, at any rate, your hypothesis is less probable than mine." While you are talking the thing over in this way, another friend arrives, one of the good kind of people that I was talking of a little while ago. And he might say, "Oh, my dear sir, you are certainly going on a great deal too fast. You are most presumptuous. You admit that all these occurrences took place when you were fast asleep, at a time when you could not possibly have known anything about what was taking place. How do you know that the laws of Nature are not suspended during the night? It may be that there has been some kind of supernatural interference in this case." In point of fact, he declares that your hypothesis is one of which you cannot at all demonstrate the truth, and that you are by no means sure that the laws of Nature are the same when you are asleep as when you are awake.

Well, now, you cannot at the moment answer that kind of reasoning. You feel that your worthy friend has you somewhat at a disadvantage. You will feel perfectly convinced in your own mind, however, that you are quite right, and you say to him, "My good friend, I can only be guided by the natural probabilities of the case, and if you will be kind enough to stand aside and permit me to pass, I will go and fetch the police." Well, we will suppose that your journey is successful, and that by good luck you meet with a policeman; that eventually the burglar is found with your property on his person, and the marks correspond to his hand and to his boots. Probably any jury would consider those facts a very good experimental verification of your hypothesis, touching the cause of the abnormal phenomena observed in your parlor, and would act accordingly.

Now, in this supposititious case, I have taken phenomena of a very common kind, in order that you might see what are the different steps in an ordinary process of reasoning, if you will only take the trouble to analyze it carefully. All the operations I have described, you will see, are involved in the mind of any man of sense in leading him to a conclusion as to the course he should take in order to make good a robbery and punish the offender. I say that you are led, in that case, to your conclusion by exactly the same train of reasoning as that which a man of science pursues when he is endeavoring to discover the origin and laws of the most occult phenomena. The process is, and always must be, the same; and precisely the same mode of reasoning was employed by Newton and Laplace in their endeavors to discover and define the causes of the movements of the heavenly bodies, as you, with your own common sense, would employ to detect a burglar. The only difference is, that the nature of the inquiry being more abstruse, every step has to be most carefully watched, so that there may not be a single crack or flaw in your hypothesis. A flaw or crack in many of the hypotheses of daily life may be of little or no moment as affecting the general correctness of the conclusions at which we may arrive; but, in a scientific inquiry, a fallacy, great or small, is always of importance, and is sure to be in the long run constantly productive of mischievous if not fatal results.

Do not allow yourselves to be misled by the common notion that an hypothesis is untrustworthy simply because it is an hypothesis. It is often urged, in respect to some scientific conclusion, that, after all, it is only an hypothesis. But what more have we to guide us in nine-tenths of the most important affairs of daily life than hypotheses, and often very ill-based ones? So that in science, where the evidence of an hypothesis is subjected to the most rigid examination, we may rightly pursue the same course. You may have hypotheses, and hypotheses. A man may say, if he likes, that the moon is made of green cheese: that is an hypothesis. But another man, who has devoted a great deal of time and attention to the subject, and availed himself of the most powerful telescopes and the results of the observations of others, declares that in his opinion it is probably composed of materials very similar to those of which our own earth is made up: and that is also only an hypothesis. But I need not tell you that there is an enormous difference in the value of the two hypotheses. That one which is based on sound scientific knowledge is sure to have a corresponding value; and that which is a mere hasty random guess is likely to have but little value. Every great step in our progress in discovering causes has been made in exactly the same way as that which I have detailed to you. A person observing the occurrence of certain facts and phenomena asks, naturally enough, what process, what kind of operation known to occur in Nature applied to the particular case, will unravel and explain the mystery? Hence you have the scientific hypothesis; and its value will be proportionate to the care and completeness with which its basis had been tested and verified. It is in these matters as in the commonest affairs of practical life: the guess of the fool will be folly, while the guess of the wise man will contain wisdom. In all cases, you see that the value of the result depends on the patience and faithfulness with which the investigator applies to his hypothesis every possible kind of verification.

Discussion Questions

1. How does Huxley's use of the second-person perspective ("you") affect the style and tone of his essay?

2. How do you rate the effectiveness of Huxley's overall argument? How successful is Huxley in choosing individual examples to illustrate that the differences between the thought processes of a scientist and those of a nonscientist are just a matter of degree?

3. In what ways does this essay seem dated in terms of both style and content? In what ways is it still surprisingly current, even though it was written almost a century ago?

4. What effect, if any, does Huxley's consistent reference to scientists and other professionals as "he" have on your response to the ideas in this essay? Given the era in which Huxley wrote, do you think he considered the potential effect of his consistent use of the male pronoun?

Journal Entry

With Huxley's discussion of forming and testing a hypothesis in mind, keep a personal log for a specific period of time—say, 48 hours—noting any hypotheses you form during your normal daily routine. Do you test your hypotheses? How? What insights and conclusions do you reach about the usefulness of hypothetical thinking?

Writing Projects

1. Write an essay defining one (or more) of the following terms: *syllogism, induction, deduction, verification.* Write for readers who have not been introduced to the elements of formal argument. Make your definition of the abstract terms you select as concrete and specific as possible. Imitating Huxley's use of the hard green apples example, develop your definitions through the use of at least one extended example for each key term.

2. Select a hypothesis of interest to you (for example, the hypothesis that a variety of violent, impulsive behaviors, including suicide, are associated with low levels of the brain chemical serotonin). Trace whatever verification has been attempted by professional researchers working with that hypothesis.

What facts did they assume at the outset? How were those facts confirmed or disproved? What discoveries did they make?

Collaborative Project

With a partner, conduct a short, informal survey to determine whether Americans believe that scientists conduct their work in ways that are significantly different from the way other experts work. Each of you could use a different survey instrument—for example, one a written questionnaire and the other an oral one—as a means of experimenting with various approaches to collecting data. Write an article analyzing your findings and drawing conclusions about both your findings and the usefulness of your methodology.

C. P. Snow

The Moment

Charles Percy Snow *(1905–1980) conducted scientific research at Cambridge University and wrote novels, including* The Light and the Dark *(1948),* A Time of Hope *(1950), and* The Affair *(1960). Working alongside both scientists and literary colleagues, Snow became concerned about what he saw as a gulf between the "two cultures." He found that his colleagues from the two fields viewed each other with hostility, dislike, and a lack of understanding. The following excerpt is from a chapter entitled "The Moment" in Snow's novel* The Search *(written in 1934, revised in 1958). Snow explained that he revised this novel partly because of the reactions provoked by his "Two Cultures" essay (published in* New Statesman *on October 6, 1956). Snow set out in* The Search *to provide for the general reader an account of what it was like to be a working scientist. In this excerpt a young scientist recounts how he thinks and feels—literally, the physical sensations he experiences—about his work.*

Questions to Consider

☐ As you read, watch for what may seem like stereotypes today. Do you think the author uses them deliberately to make a point, or unconsciously because he believes in them? Consider, too, whether your perception would be different if you had read the selection at the time it was written.

☐ Traditionally, novels are structured around a central character who must deal with a conflict. What kind of conflict does the central character in this excerpt experience? Watch how the conflict serves as a suspenseful focal point in the excerpt.

I T was in that mood, mixed of pleasure at being able to thrust into my work and distress at altering my life with Audrey, that I arrived in Cambridge one cold wet April afternoon.

I was driven by discontent more completely into science than I had been since my first term of research. In the first month I discovered that I had never had such opportunities for work before. Research in Cambridge was on a different scale from anything I had ever seen. There were more great figures than junior lecturers in London. And some of the figures were among the greatest.

By now I was used to men who had made their contributions to the structure of modern science; the day when I had been excited at hearing Austin lecture was very far away. But I recaptured some of that old thrill when I saw Rutherford walking underneath the arch of the Cavendish. As I watched him, I remembered the first time I heard his name, when Luard broke out and inspired me with the news of the nuclear atom, when I was in the lowest form at school, twelve years before; it was strange to see a man whose name had become part of my mind.

Before I had been a term in Cambridge, I heard him announce another of the great Cavendish discoveries; the rumor had been running around the laboratories for days, and now I sat in the crowded lecture-room and heard the first authoritative news. In a week it would be told to the Royal Society and published for the world in a month or two: but it made the blood go faster to be told, as though in private, something which had never been heard before and which would alter a great part of our conception of the atom. We were all asking ourselves: how soon are we going to be able to disintegrate atoms as we wish?

I shall not easily forget those Wednesday meetings in the Cavendish. For me they were the essence of all the *personal* excitement in science; they were romantic, if you like, and not on the plane of the highest experience I was soon to know; but week after week I went away through the raw nights with east winds howling from the fens down the old streets, full of a glow that I had seen and heard and been close to the leaders of the greatest movement in the world. The lecture-room, packed from the top gallery to the floor, from the bottom row where professors sat to the ceiling where the degree-students took notes feverishly: the lantern, which, as seemed ironically appropriate in the most famous centre of experimental science, was always giving out: the queer high stretch of excitement that bound us all at times, so that we laughed for relief at every shadow of a joke: the great men. It is all so vivid that even now I can hear the words and feel the same response. There was Rutherford himself; Niels Bohr, the Socrates of atomic science, who talked to us amiably one night in his Danish-English for something like two and a half hours; Dirac, of whom I heard it prophesied very early that he would be another Newton; Kapitza, with a bizarre accent and an unreproducible genius; Eddington, who made some of his Carroll-like jokes; and all the rest, English, Americans, Germans, Russians, who were in atomic physics at the time when the search was hottest.

At those meetings I made some of the friends who were to be important to me later: Constantine and Lüthy I remember meeting on the same night, when W. L. Bragg had given the talk and we three had stayed behind to ask him questions. I had seen Constantine's tawny mane of hair often in the streets, and I heard reports of his eccentric ability. I liked him at sight, but somehow or other I did not see much of him till afterwards. Lüthy was a polite young Bavarian of about my own age, in Cambridge for a couple of terms. He was very useful to me from the start. Looking back, I think I was abler than he, even at the time; I was certainly more original, had more ideas and wider scope; but he had a capacity for detailed scientific criticism and a formal background of physics that I altogether lacked. I suppose he was much the better trained.

Urged on in the atmosphere of science, helped and criticized by Lüthy and some others, and spurred by the success of their researchers, I made great roads into my own work. By Christmas I had done more in eight months than in nearly two years in London. The clue to the structure of the organic group still eluded me; I felt, irritatedly, that the generalization was almost in my hands, and yet I kept missing it. Lüthy's quick destructive mind wrecked my tentative ideas as soon as I built them up. So, after a few weeks in Cambridge, I left the bigger problem on one side and started on a side-line; and this went so well, and opened up so many speculations worth testing, that I was busy on it for the best part of a year. In that time I published two substantial papers, and had another more ambitious one in hand. I was now getting the name, quite widely, of a very promising young man: in my own subjects there were not many English rivals; I was asked to contribute to all the conferences on crystallography; my personal future was near to being comfortably determined for the next four or five years. My College was one of the few in Cambridge which elect Fellows as the result of an open competition; I was eligible to send in a thesis as soon as I took my doctorate, and my tutor Merton and Macdonald both told me there was no room for doubt.

"I shall be one referee and the other is an admirer of yours," said Macdonald. "They can't get out of taking you." More urbanely, Merton said the same thing: "A good many factors come into Fellowship elections as a rule, you know. But in competitive fellowships ability is peculiarly difficult to ignore except by the rather irregular process of altering the referees' reports. And even with someone more deplorably disreputable than yourself, my dear Miles, a majority would disapprove of such an action."

It was comforting to know that I should be secure for a while. Although I had schooled myself to wait until the end of two years at Cambridge before I thought seriously of position or money, for some time it had not been easy to put these things aside. Myself apart, I was worried by the thought of Audrey. Also, my parents were getting old, and I might have to help keep them. With the future temporarily assured, I turned eagerly once more to the problem which had enticed me for so long.

Now, however, I was in a very different mood to tackle it. I had done enough for place and reputation, and I could afford to gamble on what might be a barren chase. The structure of the organic group was not going to come out easily, I knew; I might very well be wasting a year or more, from the point of view of my career; but my career had been sound enough, and now I was working on something which I could allow to envelop me completely, simply for its own sake, in a way I had not yet known. So strong was this feeling that when I was beginning the work I often kept away from the laboratory for a day, as though my research were a pleasure of which I could, if I pleased, deprive myself. Working on my other problems – my bread-and-butter problems, as it were – I could not waste a day without a twist of uneasiness. Now I was on a piece of work I supremely wanted to do, it was natural to leave it when I was tired, to come back to it when I wished, until I was swept on beyond prudence and ambition and made to think and work and discover until the passion was drained out of me.

There was another reason which gave me far more hope of seeing my way into these molecules at last. I had gained a good deal of experience and technique in research; I had sharpened my mind on Lüthy and the rest, and broadened it on Macdonald's metaphysical schemes; and perhaps more important, I was full of confidence. If I had an idea, it would stand a chance; even if it seemed improbable, it would be looked into; for I had learned by now that more than one of my less likely ideas had worked. This confidence would have been a dangerous state of mind to begin some routine work: I might easily have been careless, simply because my luck had kept coming off. But for work which no one had dared to touch, I had to start with something like an exaggerated belief in myself. I have often thought I was quite unpardonably confident at the time – but perhaps tackling a difficult job was the least objectionable way of showing it.

Almost as soon as I took up the problem again, it struck me in a new light. All my other attempts have been absurd, I thought: if I turn them down and make another guess, then what? The guess didn't seem probable; but none of the others was any good at all. According to my guess, the structure was very different from anything one could have imagined; but that must be true, since the obvious structure didn't fit any of my facts. Soon I was designing structures with little knobs of plasticine for atoms and steel wires to hold them together; I made up the old ones, for comparison's sake, and then I built my new one, which looked very odd, very different from any structure I had ever seen. Yet I was excited – "I think it works," I said, "I think it works."

For I had brought back to mind some calculations of the scattering curves, assuming various models. None of the values had been anything like the truth. I saw at once that the new structure ought to give something much nearer. Hurriedly I calculated: it was a long and tiresome and complicated piece of arithmetic, but I rushed through it, making mistakes through impatience and having to go over it again. I was startled when I got the answer: the new model did not give perfect agreement, but it was far closer than any of the others. So far as I remember, the real value at one point was 1.32, my previous three models gave 1.1, 1.65 and 1.7, and the new one just under 1.4. "I'm on it, at last," I thought. "It's a long shot, but I'm on it at last."

For a fortnight I sifted all the evidence from the experiments since I first attacked the problem. There were a great many tables of figures, and a pile of X-ray photographs (for in my new instrument in Cambridge I was using a photographic detector); and I had been through most of them so often that I knew them almost by heart. But I went through them again, more carefully than ever, trying to interpret them in the light of the new structure. "If it's right," I was thinking, "then these figures ought to run up to a maximum and then run down quickly." And they did, though the maximum was less sharp than it should have been. And so on through experiments which represented the work of over a year; they all fitted the structure, with an allowance for a value a shade too big here, a trifle too small there. There were obviously approximations to make, I should have to modify the structure a little, but that it was on the right lines I was certain. I walked to my rooms to lunch one morning, overflowing with pleasure; I wanted to tell someone the news; I waved violently to a man whom I scarcely knew, riding on a bicycle. I thought of sending a wire to Audrey, but decided to go and see her on the following day instead: King's Parade seemed a particularly admirable street, and young men shouting across it were all admirable young men. I had a quick lunch; I wanted to bask in satisfaction, but instead I hurried back to the laboratory so that I could have it all finished with no loose ends left, and then rest for a while. I was feeling the after-taste of effort.

There were four photographs left to inspect. They had been taken earlier in the week and I had looked over them once. Now they had to be definitely measured and entered, and the work was complete. I ran over the first, it was everything I expected. The structure was fitting even better than in the early experiments. And the second: I lit a cigarette. Then the third: I gazed over the black dots. All was well – and then, with a thud of the heart that shook me, I saw behind each distinct black dot another fainter speck. The bottom had fallen out of everything: I was wrong, utterly wrong. I hunted round for another explanation: the film might be a false one, it might be a fluke experiment; but the look of it mocked me: far from being false, it was the only experiment where I had arrived at precisely the right conditions. Could it be explained any other way? I stared down at the figures, the sheets of results which I had forced into my scheme. My cheeks flushing dry, I tried to work this new photograph into my idea. An improbable assumption, another improbable assumption, a possible experimental error – I went on, fantastically, any sort of criticism forgotten. Still it would not fit. I was wrong, irrevocably wrong. I should have to begin again.

Then I began to think: If I had not taken this photograph, what would have happened? Very easily I might not have taken it. I should have been satisfied with my idea: everyone else would have been. The evidence is overwhelming, except for this. I should have pulled off a big thing. I should be made. Sooner or later, of course, someone would do this experiment, and I should be shown to be wrong: but it would be a long time ahead, and mine would have been an honorable sort of mistake. On my evidence I should have been right. That is the way everyone would have looked at it.

I suppose, for a moment, I wanted to destroy the photograph. It was all beyond my conscious mind. And I was swung back, also beyond my conscious mind, by all the forms of—shall I call it "conscience"—and perhaps more than that, by the desire which had thrown me into the search. For I had to get to what I myself thought was the truth. Honor, comfort and ambition were bound to move me, but I think my own desire went deepest. Without any posturing to myself, without any sort of conscious thought, I laughed at the temptation to destroy the photograph. Rather shakily I laughed. And I wrote in my note-book:

> Mar. 30: Photograph 3 alone has secondary dots, concentric with major dots. This removes all possibility of the hypothesis of structure B. The interpretation from Mar. 4–30 must accordingly be disregarded.

From that day I understood, as I never had before, the frauds that creep into science every now and then. Sometimes they must be quite unconscious: the not-seeing of facts because they are inconvenient, the delusions of one's own senses. As though in my case I had not seen, because my unconscious self chose not to see, the secondary ring of dots. Sometimes, more rarely, the fraud must be nearer to consciousness; that is, the fraud must be realized, even though the man cannot control it. That was the point of my temptation. It could only be committed by a man in whom the scientific passion was weaker for the time than the ordinary desires for place or money. Sometimes it would be done, impulsively, by men in whom no faith was strong; and they could forget it cheerfully themselves and go on to do good and honest work. Sometimes it would be done by a man who reproached himself all his life. I think I could pick out most kinds of fraud from among the mistakes I have seen; after that afternoon I could not help being tolerant toward them.

For myself, there was nothing left to do but start again. I looked over the entry in my note-book; the ink was still shining, and yet it seemed to have stood, final, leaving me no hope, for a long time. Because I had nothing better to do, I made a list of the structures I had invented and, in the end, discarded. There were four of them now. Slowly, I devised another. I felt sterile. I distrusted it; and when I tried to test it, to think out its properties, I had to force my mind to work. I sat until six o'clock, working profitlessly; and when I walked out, and all through the night, the question was gnawing at me: "What is this structure? Shall I ever get it? Where am I going wrong?"

I have never had two sleepless nights together before that week. Fulfillment deferred had hit me; I had to keep from reproaching myself that I had already wasted months over this problem, and now, just as I could consolidate my work, I was on the way to wasting another year. I went to bed late and heard the Cambridge clocks, one after another, chime out the small hours. I would have ideas with the uneasy clarity of night, switch on my light, scribble in my note-book, look at my watch, and try to sleep again; I would rest a little and wake up with a start, hoping that it was morning, to find that I had slept for twenty minutes: until I lay awake in a grey dawn, with all my doubts pressing in on me as I tried with tired eyes to look into the future. "What is the structure? What line must I take?" And then, as an under-theme, "Am I going to fail at my first big job? Am I always going to be a competent worker doing little problems?" And another, "I shall be twenty-six in the winter: I ought to be established. But shall I be getting anywhere?" My ideas, that seemed hopeful when I got out of bed to write them, were ridiculous when I saw them in this cold light.

This went on for three nights, until my work in the daytime was only a pretence. Then there came a lull, when I forgot my worry for a night and slept until mid-day. But, though I woke refreshed, the questions began to whirl round again in my mind. For days it went on, and I could find no way out. I walked twenty miles one day, along the muddy fenroads between the town and Ely, in order to clear my head; but it only made me tired, and I drank myself to sleep. Another night I went to a play, but I was listening not to the actors' words, but to others that formed themselves inside me and were giving me no rest.

While my nerves were still throbbing with work that was getting nowhere, Audrey came up for the week-end. As soon as she met me on the platform, she said:

"You're very worried. And pale. What's gone wrong?"

"Nothing," I said.

"Can't I leave you a fortnight without seeing you look like death?" she said.

We tried to meet each week-end, but she was living at home now, and her father often expected her to entertain his guests.

"I'm quite well," I replied.

We walked towards the gate. She said nothing. I talked on: "But what's the news? I'm rather out of touch. Anything happened in the world? Have you read anything since I saw you?"

I went on until we got into a taxi; then she said:

"Stop that."

I murmured; she took my hand.

"I'm not altogether a fool," she said. "And you've never been able to control your face. And there are lines here – and here – " She traced them, on my forehead and round my mouth – "Why, you're ten years older than when I saw you first."

"It's nearly four years," I said.

"Don't put me off." Her eyes were shining. "What's the matter?"

Although I half-resented it, I was grateful that she was taking me in hand.

"The work's not going too well," I said, and put my arm round her for comfort. "I found there was a hole in my idea."

"A fortnight ago you thought it was almost perfect."

"That was a fortnight ago." I could not help my voice going dulled.

"It's all wrong, now?"

"Quite wrong," I said. "As wrong as anything can be. And I can't see how I can put it right," I added.

She did not try to sympathize in words, but in the way she leaned against my shoulder and glanced up at me I gained more ease than I had had for many days.

"You'll do it, of course," she said at last.

"I'm not so certain," I said. "I might go on for years like this. Just fooling and not seeing any sort of way. It's not easy—"

The line had crept between her eyes.

"I wish I knew this stuff of yours," she burst out. "Then you could talk to me. And it might help a bit."

She was anxious, now. I said:

"Oh, never mind. Let's talk of other things. That'll take me away from it."

But even exchanging private thoughts with Audrey, hearing her say words that had become currency after long use, I still had moments when her voice and mine in reply sounded like noises in the outside world. Disturbing noises which I would get away from if I could. We sat in my rooms and she made me eat lunch and told me of Sheriff's latest affair, and how he had asked her to dinner and introduced his girl—"a little better than Miss Stanton-Browne, but they might be cousins," Audrey said. And she had had a letter from Hunt, who rarely wrote to either of us. He was still at his school, but seemed to be a little less disconsolate. "Why, I don't know," she said. And all the time those names . . . Sheriff . . . Hunt . . . would get mixed in structures that were dancing in my mind. I shook myself free for a while, and I was myself, talking to Audrey. Then she mentioned the Labour Party and my mind leapt to the association Labour Party—Macdonald—Macdonald, my professor—and so to my problem, and I was preoccupied once more.

In the middle of the afternoon Audrey said, suddenly: "It'll be good for you to get out of here for a bit. We'll go somewhere." Rather unwillingly I borrowed a car, and Audrey drove along the London road. I tried to talk, but I was glad when she said something which required no answer. There was a cold wind, but once as we stopped for a moment I caught a smell of spring: it gave me an empty nostalgia, for what I did not know, except some end to this.

We had tea at a village whose name I have forgotten: it must have been Baldock or Stevenage, I think. But I remember the room as sharply as the café where I read my newspaper this morning. It was a stiff, austerely clean little parlor, with hard chairs and round wooden tables; and pale sunshine fell across it on to a grate, where a few lumps of coal lay half burnt. Audrey's hair was the only warm color in the room. We ate hard little home-made cakes, and Audrey bit at hers firmly, in order to punctuate her views on her women friends.

"What can you do with most of them? What ever are they for? Except have their children and keep their houses, and make their men feel important because they've got a silly woman who believes what they say." She stopped.

"Most of these women haven't the intelligence of a penguin – and they're not as good to look at."

"Really beautiful women are quite as rare," I heard my own voice saying, "as really intelligent ones."

"I don't believe it," she said, "but I'd give anything to meet either after a morning with these – these incubators." She thought a moment.

"I suppose it's inevitable," she added. "I suppose women are meant to be incubators first and foremost. But it's a little strange they should glory in it so."

"Yes," I said, absently.

"I'm ashamed of it when it comes up in myself. And it does come up, you know. Sometimes I'm afraid I'm a real incubator at heart," she laughed. "My dear, when you're all upset like this, and paying no notice to anything I say I ought to get up and go out, if I had a decent independent spirit – but instead I can't help staying to look after you."

I started. My thoughts had stopped going back upon themselves. As I had been watching Audrey's eyes, an idea had flashed through the mist, quite unreasonably, illogically. It had no bearing at all on any of the hopeless attempts I had been making; I had explored every way, I thought, but this was new; and, too agitated to say even to myself that I believed it, I took out some paper and tried to work it out. Audrey was staring with intent eyes. I could not get very far. I wanted my results and tables. But everything I could put down rang true.

"An idea's just come to me," I explained, pretending to be calm. "I don't think there's anything in it. But there might be a little. But anyway I ought to try it out. And I haven't my books. Do you mind if we go back pretty soon?" I fancy I was getting up from the table, for Audrey smiled.

"I'm glad you had some excuse for not listening," she said.

She drove back very fast, not speaking. I made my plans for the work. It couldn't take less than a week, I thought. I sat hunched up, telling myself that it might be all wrong again; but the structure was taking shape, and a part of me was beginning to laugh at my caution. Once I turned and saw Audrey's profile against the fields; but after a moment I was back in the idea.

When I got out at the Cavendish gateway, she stayed in the car. "You'd better be alone," she said.

"And you?"

"I'll sit in Green Street." She stayed there regularly on her week-end visits. I hesitated. "It's – "

She smiled. "I'll expect you to-night. About ten o'clock," she said.

I saw very little of Audrey that week-end. When I went to her, my mind was active, my body tired, and despite myself it was more comfort than love I asked of her. I remember her smiling, a little wryly, and saying: "When this is over, we'll go away. Right away." I buried my head against her knees, and she stroked my hair. When she left me on the Monday morning, we clung to each other for a long time.

For three weeks I was thrusting the idea into the mass of facts. I could do nothing but calculate, read up new facts, satisfy myself that I had made no mistakes in measuring up the plates: I developed an uncontrollable trick of not being sure whether I had made a particular measurement correctly: repeating it: and then, after a day, the uncertainty returned, and to ease my mind I had to repeat it once more. I could scarcely read a newspaper or write a letter. Whatever I was doing, I was not at rest unless it was taking me towards the problem; and even then it was an unsettled rest, like lying in a fever half-way to sleep.

And yet, for all the obsessions, I was gradually being taken over by a calm which was new to me. I was beginning to feel an exultation, but it was peaceful, as different from wild triumph as it was from the ache in my throbbing nerves. For I was beginning to feel in my heart that I was near the truth. Beyond surmise, beyond doubt, I felt that I was nearly right; even as I lay awake in the dawn, or worked irritably with flushed cheeks, I was approaching a serenity which made the discomforts as trivial as those of someone else's body.

It was after Easter now and Cambridge was almost empty. I was glad; I felt free as I walked the deserted streets. One night, when I left the laboratory, after an evening when the new facts were falling into line and making the structure seem more than ever true, it was good to pass under the Cavendish! Good to be in the midst of the great days of science! Good to be adding to the record of those great days! And good to walk down King's Parade and see the Chapel standing against a dark sky without any stars!

The mingling of strain and certainty, of personal worry and deeper peace, was something I had never known before. Even at the time, I knew I was living in a strange happiness. Or, rather, I knew that when it was over I should covet its memory.

And so for weeks I was alone in the laboratory, taking photographs, gazing under the red lamp at films which still dripped water, carrying them into the light and studying them until I knew every grey speck on them, from the points which were testing my structures down to flaws and scratches on the surface. Then, when my eyes tired, I put down my lens and turned to the sheets of figures that contained the results, the details of the structure and the predictions I was able to make. Often I would say—if this structure is right, then this crystal here will have its oxygen atom 1.2 a.u. from the nearest carbon; and the crystal will break along this axis, and not along that; and it will be harder than the last crystal I measured, but not so hard as the one before, and so on. For days my predictions were not only vaguely right, but right as closely as I could measure.

I still possess those lists of figures, and I have stopped writing to look over them again. It is ten years and more since I first saw them and yet as I read:

PREDICTED	OBSERVED
1.435	1.44
2.603	2.603

and so on for long columns, I am warmed with something of that first glow.

At last it was almost finished. I had done everything I could; and to make an end of it I thought out one prediction whose answer was irrefutable. There was one more substance in the organic group which I could not get in England, which had only been made in Munich; if my general structure was right, the atoms in its lattice could only have one pattern. For any other structure the pattern would be utterly different. An X-ray photograph of the crystal would give me all I wanted in a single day.

It was tantalizing, not having the stuff to hand. I could write and get some from Munich, but it would take a week, and a week was very long. Yet there seemed nothing else to do. I was beginning to write in my clumsy scientist's German—and then I remembered Lüthy, who had returned to Germany a year ago.

I cabled to him, asking if he would get a crystal and photograph it on his instrument. It would only take him a morning at the most, I thought, and we had become friendly enough for me to make the demand on him. Later in the afternoon I had his answer: "I have obtained crystal will telegraph result tomorrow honored to assist. Lüthy." I smiled at the "honored to assist," which he could not possibly have left out, and sent off another cable: "Predict symmetry and distances. . . ."

Then I had twenty-four hours of waiting. Moved by some instinct to touch wood, I wanted to retract the last cable as soon as I had sent it. If—if I were wrong, no one else need know. But it had gone. And, nervous as I was, in a way I knew that I was right. Yet I slept very little that night; I could mock, with all the detached part of myself, at the tricks my body was playing, but it went on playing them. I had to leave my breakfast, and drank cup after cup of tea, and kept throwing away cigarettes I had just lighted. I watched myself do these things, but I could not stop them, in just the same way as one can watch one's own body being afraid.

The afternoon passed, and no telegram came. I was persuaded there was scarcely time. I went out for an hour, in order to find it at my rooms when I returned. I went through all the antics and devices of waiting. I grew empty with anxiety as the evening drew on. I sat trying to read; the room was growing dark, but I did not wish to switch on the light, for fear of bringing home the passage of the hours.

At last the bell rang below. I met my landlady on the stairs, bringing in the telegram. I do not know whether she noticed that my hands were shaking as I opened it. It said: "Felicitations on completely accurate prediction which am proud to confirm apologies for delay due to instrumental adjustments. Lüthy." I was numbed for a moment; I could only see Lüthy bowing politely to the postal clerk as he sent off the telegram. I laughed, and I remembered it had a queer sound.

Then I was carried beyond pleasure. I have tried to show something of the high moments that science gave to me; the night my father talked about the stars, Luard's lesson, Austin's opening lecture, the end of my first research. But this was different from any of them, different altogether, different in kind. It was further from myself. My own triumph and delight and success were there, but they seemed insignificant beside this tranquil ecstasy. It was as though I had looked for a truth outside myself, and finding it had become for a moment part of the truth I sought; as though all the world, the atoms and the stars, were wonderfully clear and close to me, and I to them, so that we were part of a lucidity more tremendous than any mystery.

I had never known that such a moment could exist. Some of its quality, perhaps, I had captured in the delight which came when I brought joy to Audrey, being myself content; or in the times among friends, when for some rare moment, maybe twice in my life, I had lost myself in a common purpose; but these moments had, as it were, the tone of the experience without the experience itself.

Since then I never quite regained it. But one effect will stay with me as long as I live; once, when I was young, I used to sneer at the mystics who have described the experience of being at one with God and part of the unity of things. After that afternoon, I did not want to laugh again; for though I should have interpreted the experience differently, I thought I knew what they meant.

Discussion Questions

1. Why does Snow include descriptions of the narrator's physical sensations that were caused by his work? For example, when the narrator studies the photographs, he is described as experiencing "a thud of the heart that shook me" and "my cheeks flush[ed] dry." What does Snow accomplish with this type of detail?

2. How does the author manage to keep the reader's interest while providing details of what might be considered rather dry scientific research? What narrative techniques does Snow use to describe the research in such a way that he tells a story rather than giving a report?

3. Why does the author include the conversation in which Audrey talks about her friends as "incubators"? What does it contribute to the overall story (or as much of the story as you have here)? What do you think of the narrator's gaining insight into his work at the same time Audrey pours out to him her own innermost feelings of discontent and concern for their future?

4. What are some examples of scientific competitiveness portrayed in this excerpt? How would you describe the narrator's attitude toward professional competition? If, indeed, scientists consider themselves to be only motivated by a desire to make a contribution to knowledge and to humankind in general—without profit—then why is getting the answer first and gaining personal credit so important to them?

5. Discuss what it means to be obsessed with one's work. Do you think Snow wants us to view the narrator's obsession as a good one or not? What aspects of the story support your view?

Journal Entry

The narrator writes of his own temptation to destroy a photograph that called into question his favorite theory. He says, "From that day I understood, as I never had before, the frauds that creep into science every now and then." Write about an incident in which you were tempted to commit some type of academic fraud or dishonesty. How easy would it have been to succumb to temptation? Is it possible that some of your colleagues may have already indulged in such deceit without suffering any consequences?

Writing Projects

1. Consider Snow's use of sexual metaphor ("thrust into my work," "ecstasy of success") to describe the narrator's work. Analyze the purpose and effect of this type of figurative language in Snow's selection.

2. Write an essay examining how Snow conveys the narrator's feelings of excitement about his work and his sense of awe at associating with the "great men of science." Describe your own response to the narrator. What do you think of his view of himself and the thrill he derives from his work? Explain why Snow's character describes his meetings with his colleagues as "romantic."

Collaborative Project

The narrator struggles with his own conscience and comes to a realization regarding the ways in which scientific research is vulnerable to fraud. Working with one or more classmates, read about a fraud in scientific research that was discovered and brought to light (see, for example, Barbara Ehrenreich's essay in Chapter 7). How was the fraud committed, discovered, and treated? Was anyone punished? If so, how? Report your findings and conclusions to the class.

Evelyn Fox Keller

Gender and Science: An Update

Evelyn Fox Keller (b. 1936), a mathematical biophysicist, feminist scholar, and philosopher of science, has written extensively on the nature of scientific thought. Her work has appeared in national and international scholarly journals in the fields of psychology, philosophy, and feminist theory. She has taught at New York University, Northeastern University, University of California at Berkeley, and is currently at the Massachusetts Institute of Technology. In the following excerpt from her book Secrets of Life, Secrets of Death (1993), Keller explores the idea that science and gender are both categories that are constructed on the basis of definitions and associations that we share as a culture. She examines closely the conflicts that arise in science because we consider it to have certain characteristics, such as objectivity, that suggest notions of gender and relative worth. Keller's other books include Reflections on Gender and Science (1985), which has been published in several languages; A Feeling for the Organism: The Life and Work of Barbara McClintock (1983); and Conflicts in Feminism (1990), co-edited with Marianne Hirsch.

Questions to Consider

☐ Before reading this selection, pause and consider why you believe a scientist's gender does, or does not, affect how that person conducts and interprets science.

☐ Ordinarily we do not expect scientific writing to include personal examples, but Keller draws from her personal life to support her general points about the nature of science. As you read, take note of your own response to Keller's personal examples.

The Meaning of Gender

Schemes for classifying human beings are necessarily multiple and highly variable. Different cultures identify and privilege different criteria in sorting people of their own and other cultures into groups: They may stress size, age, color, occupation, wealth, sanctity, wisdom, or a host of other demarcators. All cultures, however, sort a significant fraction of the human beings that inhabit that culture by sex. What are taken to be the principal indicators of sexual difference as well as the particular importance attributed to this difference undoubtedly vary, but, for fairly obvious reasons, people everywhere engage in the basic act of distinguishing people they call male from those they call female. For the most part, they even agree about who gets called what. Give or take a few marginal cases, these basic acts of categorization do exhibit conspicuous cross-cultural consensus: Different cultures will sort any given collection of adult human beings of reproductive age into the same two groups. For this reason, we can say that there is at least a minimal sense of the term "sex" that denotes categories given to us by nature.[1] One might even say that the universal importance of the reproductive consequences of sexual difference gives rise to as universal a preoccupation with the meaning of this difference.

But for all the cross-cultural consensus we may find around such a minimalist classification, we find equally remarkable cultural variability in what people have made and continue to make of this demarcation; in the significance to which they attribute it; in the properties it connotes; in the role it plays in ordering the human world beyond the immediate spheres of biological reproduction; even in the role it plays in ordering the nonhuman world. It was to underscore this cultural variability that American feminists of the 1970s introduced the distinction between sex and gender, assigning the term "gender" to the meanings of masculinity and femininity that a given culture attaches to the categories of male and female.[2]

The initial intent behind this distinction was to highlight the importance of nonbiological (that is, social and cultural) factors shaping the development of adult men and women, to emphasize the truth of Simone de Beauvoir's famous dictum, "Women are not born, rather they are made." Its function was to shift attention away from the time-honored and perhaps even ubiquitous question of the meaning of sexual difference (that is, the meanings of masculine and feminine), *to* the question of how such meanings are constructed. In Donna Haraway's words, "Gender is a concept developed to contest the naturalization of sexual difference" (1991:131).

Very quickly, however, feminists came to see, and, as quickly, began to exploit, the considerably larger range of analytic functions that the multipotent category of gender is able to serve. From an original focus on gender as a cultural norm guiding the psychosocial development of individual men and women, the attention of feminists soon turned to gender as a cultural structure organizing social (and sexual) relations between men and women,[3] and finally, to gender as the basis of a sexual division of cognitive and emotional labor that brackets women, their work, and the values associated with that work from culturally normative delineations of categories intended as "human"—objectivity, morality, citizenship, power, often even "human nature" itself.[4] From this perspective, gender and gender norms come to be seen as silent organizers of the mental and discursive maps of the social and natural worlds we simultaneously inhabit and construct—*even of those worlds that women never enter.*[5] This I call the symbolic work of gender; it remains silent precisely to the extent that norms associated with masculine culture are taken as universal.

The fact that it took the efforts of contemporary feminism to bring this symbolic work of gender into recognizable view is in itself noteworthy. In these efforts, the dual focus on women as subjects and on gender as a cultural construct was crucial. Analysis of the relevance of gender structures in conventionally male worlds only makes sense once we recognize gender not only as a bimodal term, applying symmetrically to men *and* women (that is, once we see that men too are gendered, that men too are made rather than born), but also as denoting social rather than natural kinds. Until we can begin to envisage the possibility of alternative arrangements, the symbolic work of gender remains both silent and inaccessible. And as long as gender is thought to pertain only to women, any question about its role can only be understood as a question about the presence or absence of biologically female persons.

This double shift in perception—first, from sex to gender, and second, from the force of gender in shaping the development of men and women to its force in delineating the cultural maps of the social and natural worlds these adults inhabit—constitutes the hallmark of contemporary feminist theory. Beginning in the mid 1970s, feminist historians, literary critics, sociologists, political scientists, psychologists, philosophers, and soon, natural scientists as well, sought to supplement earlier feminist analyses of the contribution, treatment, and representation of men and women in these various fields with an enlarged analysis of the ways in which privately held and publicly shared ideas about gender have shaped the underlying assumptions and operant categories in the intellectual history of each of these fields. Put simply, contemporary feminist theory might be described as "a form of attention, a lens that brings into focus a particular question: What does it mean to describe one aspect of human experience as 'male' and another as 'female'? How do such labels affect the ways in which we structure the world around us, assign value to its different domains, and in turn, acculturate and value actual men and women?" (Keller 1985:6).

With such questions as these, feminist scholars launched an intensive investigation of the traces of gender labels evident in many of the fundamental assumptions underlying the traditional academic disciplines. Their earliest efforts were confined to the humanities and social sciences, but by the late 1970s, the lens of feminist inquiry had extended to the natural sciences as well. Under particular scrutiny came those assumptions that posited a dichotomous (and hierarchical) structure tacitly modeled on the prior assumption of a dichotomous (and hierarchical) relation between male and female—for example, public/private; political/personal; reason/feeling; justice/care; objective/subjective; power/love, and so on. The object of this endeavor was not to reverse the conventional ordering of these relations, but to undermine the dichotomies themselves—to expose to radical critique a worldview that deploys categories of gender to rend the fabric of human life and thought along a multiplicity of mutually sanctioning, mutually supportive, and mutually defining binary oppositions.

Feminism and Science

But if the inclusion of the natural sciences under this broad analytic net posed special opportunities, it also posed special difficulties, and special dangers, each of which requires special recognition. On the one hand, the presence of gender markings in the root categories of the natural sciences and their use in the hierarchical ordering of such categories (for example, mind and nature; reason and feeling; objective and subjective) is, if anything, more conspicuous than in the humanities and social sciences. At the same time, the central claim of the natural sciences is precisely to a methodology that transcends human particularity, that bears no imprint of individual or collective authorship. To signal this dilemma, I began my first inquiry into the relations between gender and science (Keller 1978) with a quote from George Simmel, written more than sixty years ago:

> The requirements of . . . correctness in practical judgments and objectivity in theoretical knowledge . . . belong as it were in their form and their claims to humanity in general, but in their actual historical configuration they are masculine throughout. Supposing that we describe these things, viewed as absolute ideas, by the single word "objective," we then find that in the history of our race the equation objective = masculine is a valid one (cited in Keller 1978:409).

Simmel's conclusion, while surely on the mark as a description of a cultural history, alerts us to the special danger that awaits a feminist critique of the natural sciences. Indeed, Simmel himself appears to have fallen into the very trap that we are seeking to expose: In neglecting to specify the space in which he claims "validity" for this equation as a *cultural or even ideological space*, his wording invites the reading of this space as a biological one. Indeed, by referring to its history as a "history of our race" without specifying "our race" as late-modern, northern European, he tacitly elides the existence of other cultural histories (as well as other "races") and invites the same conclusion that this cultural history has sought to establish; namely, that "objectivity" is simultaneously a universal value and a privileged possession of the male of the species.

The necessary starting point for a feminist critique of the natural sciences is thus the reframing of this equation as a conundrum: How is it that the scientific mind can be *seen* at one and the same time as both male and disembodied? How is it that thinking "objectively," that is, thinking that is defined as self-detached, impersonal, and transcendent, is also understood as "thinking like a man"? From the vantage point of our newly "enlightened" perceptions of gender, we might be tempted to say that the equation "objective = masculine," harmful though it (like that other equation woman = nature) may have been for aspiring women scientists in the past, was simply a descriptive mistake, reflecting misguided views of women. But what about the views of "objectivity" (or "nature") that such an equation necessarily also reflected (or inspired)? What difference – for science, now, rather than for women – might such an equation have made? Or, more generally, what sort of work in the actual production of science has been accomplished by the association of gender with virtually all of the root categories of modern science over the three hundred odd years in which such associations prevailed? How have these associations helped to shape the criteria for "good" science? For distinguishing the values deemed "scientific" from those deemed "unscientific"? In short, what particular cultural norms and values has the language of gender carried into science, and how have these norms and values contributed to its shape and growth?

These, then, are some of the questions that feminist theory brings to the study of science, and that feminist historians and philosophers of science have been trying to answer over the last fifteen years. But, for reasons I have already briefly indicated, they are questions that are strikingly difficult to hold in clear focus (to keep distinct, for example, from questions about the presence or absence of women scientists). For many working scientists, they seem not even to "make sense."

One might suppose, for example, that once such questions were properly posed (that is, cleansed of any implication about the real abilities of actual women), they would have a special urgency for all practicing scientists who are also women. But experience suggests otherwise; even my own experience suggests otherwise. Despite repeated attempts at clarification, many scientists (especially, women scientists) persist in misreading the force that feminists attribute to gender ideology as a force being attributed to sex, that is, to the claim that women, for biological reasons, would do a different kind of science. The net effect is that, where some of us see a liberating potential (both for women *and* for science) in exhibiting the historical role of gender in science, these scientists often see only a reactionary potential, fearing its use to support the exclusion of women from science.[6]

The reasons for the divergence in perception between feminist critics and women scientists are deep and complex. Though undoubtedly fueled by political concerns, they rest finally neither on vocabulary, nor on logic, nor even on empirical evidence. Rather, they reflect a fundamental difference in mind-set between feminist critics and working scientists – a difference so radical that a "feminist scientist" appears today as much a contradiction in terms as a "woman scientist" once did.[7]

I need only recall my own trajectory from practicing scientist to feminist critic to appreciate the magnitude of difference between these two mind-sets, as well as the effort required to traverse that difference. In the hope that my experience, with its inevitable idiosyncrasies, might prove helpful in furthering our understanding of the more general problem, I offer a reconstruction of that trajectory.

From Working Scientist to Feminist Critic

I begin with three vignettes, all drawn from memory.

1965. In my first few years out of graduate school, I held quite conventional beliefs about science. I believed not only in the possibility of clear and certain knowledge of the world, but also in the uniquely privileged access to this knowledge provided by science in general, and by physics in particular. I believed in the accessibility of an underlying (and unifying) "truth" about the world we live in, and I believed that the laws of physics gave us the closest possible approximation of this truth. In short, I was well trained in both the traditional realist worldviews assumed by virtually all scientists and in the conventional epistemological ordering of the sciences. I had, after all, been trained, first, by theoretical physicists, and later, by molecular biologists. This is not to say that I lived my life according to the teachings of physics (or molecular biology), only that when it came to questions about what "really is," I knew where, and how, to look. Although I had serious conflicts about my own ability to be part of this venture, I fully accepted science, and scientists, as arbiters of truth. Physics (and physicists) were, of course, the highest arbiters.

Somewhere around this time, I came across the proceedings of the first major conference held in the United States on "Women and the Scientific Professions" (Mattfield and Van Aiken 1965) – a subject of inevitable interest to me. I recall reading in those proceedings an argument for more women in science, made by both Erik Erikson and Bruno Bettelheim, based on the invaluable contributions a "specifically female genius" could make to science. Although earlier in their contributions both Erikson and Bettelheim had each made a number of eminently reasonable observations and recommendations, I flew to these concluding remarks as if waiting for them, indeed forgetting everything else they had said. From the vantage point I then occupied, my reaction was predictable: To put it quite bluntly, I laughed. Laws of nature are universal – how could they possibly depend on the sex of their discoverers? Obviously, I snickered, these psychoanalysts know little enough about science (and by implication, about truth).

1969. I was living in a suburban California house and found myself with time to think seriously about my own mounting conflicts (as well as those of virtually all my female cohorts) about being a scientist. I had taken a leave to accompany my husband on his sabbatical, remaining at home to care for our two small children. Weekly, I would talk to the colleague I had left back in New York and hear his growing enthusiasm as he reported the spectacular successes he was having in presenting our joint work. In between, I would try to understand why my own enthusiasm was not only not growing, but actually diminishing. How I went about seeking such an understanding is worth noting: What I did was to go to the library to gather data about the fate of women scientists in general – more truthfully, to document my own growing disenchantment (even in the face of manifest success) as part of a more general phenomenon reflecting an underlying misfit between women and science. And I wrote to Erik Erikson for further comment on the alarming (yet somehow satisfying) attrition data I was collecting. In short, only a few years after ridiculing his thoughts on the subject, I was ready to at least entertain if not embrace an argument about women in, or out of, science based on "women's nature." Not once during that entire year did it occur to me that at least part of my disenchantment might be related to the fact that I was in fact not sharing in the *kudos* my colleague was reaping for our joint work.

1974. I had not dropped out of science, but I had moved into interdisciplinary, undergraduate teaching. And I had just finished teaching my first women's studies course when I received an invitation to give a series of "Distinguished Lectures" on my work in mathematical biology at the University of Maryland. It was a great honor, and I wanted to do it, but I had a problem. In my women's studies course, I had yielded to the pressure of my students and colleagues to talk openly about what it had been like, as a woman, to become a scientist. In other words, I had been persuaded to publicly air the exceedingly painful story of the struggle that had actually been[8] – a story I had previously only talked about in private, if at all. The effect of doing this was that I actually came to *see* that story as public, that is, of political significance, rather than as simply private, of merely personal significance. As a result, the prospect of continuing to present myself as a disembodied scientist, of talking about my work as if it had been done in a vacuum, as if the fact of my being a woman was entirely irrelevant, had come to feel actually dishonest.

I resolved the conflict by deciding to present in my last lecture a demographic model of women in science – an excuse to devote the bulk of that lecture to a review of the many barriers that worked against the survival of women as scientists, and to a discussion of possible solutions. I concluded my review with the observation that perhaps the most important barrier to success for women in science derived from the pervasive belief in the intrinsic masculinity of scientific thought. Where, I asked, does such a belief come from? What is it doing in science, reputedly the most objective, neutral, and abstract endeavor we know? And what consequences does that belief have for the actual doing of science?

In 1974 "women in science" was not a proper subject for academic or scientific discussion; I was aware of violating professional protocol. Having given the lecture – having "carried it off" – I felt profoundly liberated. I had passed an essential milestone.

Although I did not know it then, and wouldn't recognize it for another two years, this lecture marked the beginning of my work as a feminist critic of science. In it I raised three of the central questions that were to mark my research and writing over the next decade. I can now see that, with the concluding remarks of that lecture, I had also completed the basic shift in mind-set that made it possible to begin such a venture. Even though my views about gender, science, knowledge, and truth were to evolve considerably over the years to come, I had already made the two most essential steps: I had shifted attention from the question of male and female nature to that of *beliefs about* male and female nature, that is, to gender ideology. And I had admitted the possibility that such beliefs could affect science itself.

In hindsight, these two moves may seem simple enough, but when I reflect on my own history, as well as that of other women scientists, I can see that they were not. Indeed, from my earlier vantage point, they were unthinkable. In that mind-set, there was room neither for a distinction between sexual identity and beliefs about sexual identity (not even for the prior distinction between sex and gender upon which it depends), nor for the possibility that beliefs could affect science—a possibility that requires a distinction analagous to that between sex and gender, only now between nature and science. I was, of course, able to accommodate a distinction between belief and reality, but only in the sense of "false" beliefs—that is, mere illusion, or mere prejudice; "true" beliefs I took to be synonymous with the "real."

It seems to me that in that mind-set, beliefs per se were not seen as having any real force—neither the force to shape the development of men and women, nor the force to shape the development of science. Some people may "misperceive" nature, human or otherwise, but properly seen, men and women simply *are*, faithful reflections of male and female biology—just as science simply *is*, a faithful reflection of nature. Gravity has (or is) a force, DNA has force, but beliefs do not. In other words, as scientists, we are trained to see the locus of real force in the world as physical, not mental.

There is of course a sense in which they are right: Beliefs per se cannot exert force on the world. But the people who carry such beliefs can. Furthermore, the language in which their beliefs are encoded has the force to shape what others—as men, as women, and as scientists—think, believe, and, in turn, actually do. It may have taken the lens of feminist theory to reveal the popular association of science, objectivity, and masculinity as a statement about the social rather than natural (or biological) world, referring not to the bodily and mental capacities of individual men and women, but to a collective consciousness; that is, as a set of beliefs given existence by language rather than by bodies, and by that language, granted the force to shape what individual men and women might (or might not) do. But to see how such culturally laden language could contribute to the shaping of science takes a different kind of lens. That requires, first and foremost, a recognition of the social character (and force) of the enterprise we call "science," a recognition quite separable from—and in fact, historically independent of—the insights of contemporary feminism.

The Meaning of Science

Although people everywhere, throughout history, have needed, desired, and sought reliable knowledge of the world around them, only certain forms of knowledge and certain procedures for acquiring such knowledge have come to count under the general rubric that we, in the late twentieth century, designate as science. Just as "masculine" and "feminine" are categories defined by a culture, and not by biological necessity, so too, "science" is the name we give to a set of practices and a body of knowledge delineated by a community. Even now, in part because of the great variety of practices that the label "science" continues to subsume, the term defies precise definition, obliging us to remain content with a conventional definition—as that which those people we call scientists do.

What has compelled recognition of the conventional (and hence social) character of modern science is the evidence provided over the last three decades by historians, philosophers, and sociologists of science who have undertaken close examination of what it is that those people we call (or have called) scientists actually do (or have done).[9] Careful attention to what questions get asked, of how research programs come to be legitimated and supported, of how theoretical disputes are resolved, of "how experiments end" reveals the working of cultural and social norms at every stage.[10] Consensus is commonly achieved, but it is rarely compelled by the forces of logic and evidence alone. On every level, choices are (must be) made that are social *even as* they are cognitive and technical. The direct implication is that not only different collections of facts, different focal points of scientific attention, but also different conceptions of explanation and proof, different representations of reality, different criteria of success, are both possible and consistent with what we call science.

But if such observations have come to seem obvious to many observers of science, they continue to seem largely absurd to the men and women actually engaged in the production of science. In order to see how cultural norms and values can, indeed have, helped define the success and shape the growth of science, it is necessary to understand how language embodies and enforces such norms and values. This need far exceeds the concerns of feminism, and the questions it gives rise to have become critical for anyone currently working in the history, philosophy, or sociology of science. That it continues to elude most working scientists is precisely a consequence of the fact that their world-views not only lack but actually preclude recognition of the force of language on what they, in their day-to-day activity as scientists, think and do. And this, I suggest, follows as much from the nature of their activity as it does from scientific ideology.

NOTES

This essay is adapted from Keller (1990), with excerpts from Keller (1987).

1. A somewhat different view is given by Tom Laqueur (1990).
2. See, for example, Gayle Rubin (1975).
3. See, for example, Rubin (1975) and Catherine MacKinnon (1988).
4. In the most recent literature, discussions of gender have become yet more sophisticated as feminist scholars have begun to shift their focus away from the unifying force of gender norms within particular culturally homogeneous systems, to such inhomogeneities as class and race prevailing within ostensibly unitary cultures. But within the confines of those few worlds that can be said to be culturally homogeneous – such as, for example, the almost entirely white, upper and middle-class, predominantly Eurocentric world of modern science – analysis of the force of gender and gender norms remains relatively straightforward. Indeed, the very exclusivity of this tradition provides one of the few cases in which, precisely because of its racial and class exclusivity, the variables of race and class can be bracketed from the analysis. It must be remembered, however, that the concept of "gender" that appears in such an analysis is one that is restricted to a particular subset of "Western" culture.
5. See, for example, Sandra Harding (1986) for a useful summary of these multiple yet interacting meanings of the term gender.
6. Of course, scientists are not the only ones who persist in such a mistranslation; it is also made by many others, and even by some feminists who are not themselves scientists. It is routinely made by the popular press. The significant point here is that this mistranslation persists in the minds of most women scientists even after they are alerted to the (feminist) distinction between sex and gender.
7. Indeed, a striking number of those feminist critics who began as working scientists have either changed fields altogether or have felt obliged to at least temporarily interrupt their work as laboratory or "desk" scientists (I am thinking, for example, of [the late] Maggie Benston, Ruth Hubbard, Marian Lowe, Evelynn Hammonds, Anne Fausto-Sterling, and myself).
8. This story was subsequently published in Ruddick and Daniels's *Working It Out* (1977).
9. In large part, stimulated by the publication of Thomas S. Kuhn's *The Structure of Scientific Revolutions*, in 1962.
10. See, for example, Galison (1988); Pickering (1984); Shapin and Schaffer (1985); Smith and Wise (1989).

REFERENCES

Galison, P. "Between War and Peace." In *Science, Technology, and the Military*, edited by Everett Mendelsohn, Merritt Roe Smith, Peter Weingart. Dordrecht; Boston: Kluwer Academic Publishers, 1988. Mendelsohn, Smith & Weingart. (1988).
Haraway, D. *Simians, Cyborgs, and Women.* New York: Routledge, 1991.
Harding, S. *The Science Question in Feminism.* New York: Cornell Univ. Press, 1986.

Keller, E. F. "Physics and the Emergence of Molecular Biology." *J. Hist. Biol.* 23(3): 389–409, 1990.

——. "Working Scientists and Feminist Critics of Science." *Daedalus* 116(4): 77–91, 1987.

——. *Reflections on Gender and Science.* New Haven, CT: Yale Univ. Press, 1985.

——. "Gender and Science." *Psychoanalysis and Contemporary Thought* 1:409–33, 1978.

Kuhn, T. S. *The Structure of Scientific Revolutions.* Chicago: Univ. of Chicago Press, 1962.

Laqueur, T. *The Making of Sexual Difference.* Cambridge: Harvard Univ. Press, 1990.

MacKinnon, C. *Feminism Unmodified.* Cambridge: Harvard Univ. Press, 1988.

Mattfield, J. A. and C. E. Van Aiken, eds, *Women and the Scientific Professions.* Cambridge, MA: MIT Press, 1965.

Pickering, A. *Constructing Quarks.* Chicago: Univ. of Chicago Press, 1984.

Rubin, G. "The Traffic in Women: Notes on the 'Political Economy' of Sex." In *Toward an Anthropology of Women,* ed. R. R. Reiter. New York: Monthly Review Press, 1975.

Ruddick, S. and P. Daniels, eds. *Working It Out.* New York: Pantheon, 1977.

Shapin, S. and S. Schaffer. *Leviathan and the Air-Pump.* Princeton: Princeton Univ. Press, 1985.

Smith, C. and N. Wise. *Energy and Empire: A Biographical Study of Lord Kelvin.* Cambridge: Cambridge Univ. Press, 1989.

Discussion Questions

1. Given the overall organization and structure of this essay, how does Keller integrate the section that begins as follows: "I begin with three vignettes, all drawn from memory"? What is a vignette? Is this type of autobiography usually found in scientific writing? What does Keller seek to accomplish by presenting these vignettes?

2. Make a list of terms often used to describe scientific endeavor (terms such as *objective*). Record on the board the terms suggested by class members. What conclusions and interpretations do these terms suggest about how you and your classmates view scientific work? Which terms appeared on several students' lists? Are most of the terms positive or negative in tone? Does your group's list seem to be slanted toward terms that suggest more male or female personality traits?

3. The author reveals some conventional beliefs she once held about her profession. For example, she says she believed in the possibility of "clear and certain knowledge of the world" and an acceptance of "science and scientists as the arbiters of truth." Can you think of some additional conventionally held beliefs about science (or another professional area)? What are some reasons for challenging those conventions?

4. Keller asserts that "a 'feminist scientist' appears today as much a contradiction in terms as a 'woman scientist' once did." What are the implications of

this statement? Do you agree with the way in which Keller finds a fundamental conflict between the mind-set of feminist critics and of working scientists? Why or why not? If you do agree with Keller, why is this conflict important?

Journal Entries

1. Keller writes about how she came to see her discipline of study differently from how she had before and how this altered her view of herself and her relationship to her field. Write about an experience that caused you to view yourself, or others, in a new way. Have any of the readings in this volume caused you to alter your way of thinking about yourself or others – about scientists, for example?

2. Keller explains that while lecturing about the difficulties she faced as a woman scientist, she discovered that talking about her personal experience gave it public, even political, significance. Relate a personal experience that allowed you to enter the public dialogue on a social or cultural issue. How did your attitudes change? What did you do to act on your experience and knowledge?

Writing Projects

1. Write a stylistic analysis of how Keller employs certain tactics for particular effects. One element you could analyze is Keller's use of a number of extraordinarily long sentences (see, for example, the second sentence in paragraph 4 and the final sentence in paragraph 7). Or, follow her tone throughout, her diction or her point of view.

2. Write a research-based essay in which you trace how a scientist or some other scholar used personal experience to make a public, perhaps even a political, contribution to a body of knowledge. (Examples of scientists in this book who are appropriate for such study include Jane Goodall and Shirley Tilghman. Also, Cynthia Ozick uses her personal experience as the groundwork for writing about factions in the literary culture today.)

Collaborative Projects

1. Working with a partner or in a small group, prepare an annotated bibliography of works that address the issue of science and gender. Begin by looking at a sample of an annotated bibliography so that you have an idea of what your finished product should be like. Next, determine the format of the materials you will include in your bibliography – for example, books,

articles, audio tapes, films, and the like. Then obtain the assistance of a reference librarian in locating relevant sources. The librarian can demonstrate how to choose standard search terms and how to limit your search to a manageable number of sources. Present your bibliography to the class, along with a summary of your process in developing it.

2. Working with one or two partners, conduct some research to find out what special opportunities, or difficulties, there are for women scientists. Your research team could combine both primary research derived from interviews of women scientists and secondary research based on published accounts, both fiction and nonfiction. Interpret your findings and share an account of your research process with your classmates.

Shirley M. Tilghman

Science versus the Female Scientist

Shirley M. Tilghman *is a professor of molecular biology at Princeton University. "Science versus the Female Scientist," which is part one of a two-part article, appeared in* the New York Times *(January 1993) as an adaptation of Tilghman's presentation in October 1992 at the Olin Conference on Women and the Culture of Science at Washington University in St. Louis. Here Tilghman demonstrates that in some ways laboratory science is conducted today much like it was in the 1950s; there is still evidence of discrimination against women and minorities. Tilghman explains why discrimination continues to exist with little change and what that means for both women and science as well as society. Tilghman has published scientific articles on the subject of developmental genetics in journals such as* Nature *and* Science.

Questions to Consider

☐ Consider what assumptions about her audience lead Tilghman to begin with an ethical appeal.

☐ As you read, consider if you agree with Tilghman's criteria for assessing whether occurrences in scientific fields are advances or setbacks for women. What would you do differently from Tilghman, if anything, to establish criteria and assess the situation for women and minorities?

IN the last two years, we have witnessed a flurry of concern over the under-representation of women and minorities in science and engineering. The concern does not arise from a belated appreciation that women and minorities have been denied access to careers in science. Rather it comes from projections of a significant shortfall in scientists around the turn of the century, caused, at least in part, by the reduced number of white males choosing scientific careers.

This reminds me of the explanation given by a president of an all-male university for why he favored co-education. He explained that unless the institution admitted women, it would no longer be able to compete for the best

51

male students, who were being attracted to co-ed campuses. The inclusion of women, in his eyes, was a solution to a problem.

Likewise, today women and minorities are viewed as one solution to a manpower problem in the sciences. Despite the base underpinnings of the motive, this may be a unique opportunity to bring about a greater participation of women and minorities in science. In fact, many universities have commissioned studies on improving recruiting and retention of women students and faculty in science and engineering. Programs abound in government and the philanthropic community to encourage the inclusion of women and minorities.

What are the realistic prospects for these endeavors? First, we need to understand what has stood in the way of women in science.

You can look at the last 20 years in two ways, depending on whether you are an optimist or pessimist. The optimist sees that between 1966 and 1988, the percentage of women receiving science, medical or engineering degrees increased dramatically. In 1966, 23 percent of the bachelor's degrees in science were awarded to women; by 1988, that figure had risen to 40 percent. Women now compose 38 percent of medical school enrollments. As for science doctorates, women earned 9 percent of the total in 1966 and 27 percent in 1988.

The first thing a pessimist would find in the same 20-year span is that the increase in women in scientific and medical careers has not been steady. Most of the increase came in the 1970's, with very little progress after 1982. The second thing a pessimist would note is that the women who have been trained are not in leadership positions in proportion to their representation in the field. The most common response to this is that enough time has not passed for women graduates to have acquired the appropriate seniority. But this is not the case.

Finally, the pessimist would point out that the increases are the average of highly disparate disciplines and hide large differences between fields. For example, in psychology women receive more than half of new doctorates, while in engineering they earn just 7 percent. If you look carefully, almost no progress has been made in increasing the number of women practicing physics, mathematics and engineering in the last 50 years.

Physics and mathematics are clearly at one extreme. In the life sciences, a slightly different dynamic is at work. Fifty percent of bachelor's degrees in biology are awarded to women. There is a drop in graduate and medical schools, where 35 to 40 percent of the graduating classes are female.

Only then do women begin to disappear from the system. By almost every measure, postgraduate women in the life sciences are faring less well than their male colleagues. If one takes as a measure of success those who have reached the status of principal investigator of a National Institutes of Health grant, just 19 percent are women. Where are the other 19 percent who received M.D.'s and Ph.D.'s? They are in non-tenure-track positions in which they often cannot compete for research funds.

What the different experiences of women in the physical and life sciences tell us is that multiple forces are at work to retard the rate at which women enter the scientific work force. Yet I believe that the common thread is the role that culture plays in determining career choices for women.

The cultural issues begin with the low expectations that our education system sets on the performance of females in science, especially in physics and math. This culminates in the hierarchical culture of the laboratory, which evolved in the absence of females. This notion that cultural biases are at the basis of the problem is sobering, as cultures are difficult to change. However, if we indeed have to change the culture, we need to understand its underpinnings and where the pressure points lie.

Let's begin with education. A study by Joan Girgus for the Pew Charitable Trust Science Education Program revealed that differences in the two sexes can be detected as early as 9 years of age, when girls report fewer science-related experiences, such as looking through a telescope. By 13, girls are less likely than boys to read science articles and books, watch science shows or have science hobbies. The cues girls receive in these formative years are not always subtle. Mattel Inc. recently marketed a Barbie doll that says, "I hate math!" when poked in the stomach. I shudder to think what Ken says back!

Another example comes from the experience of a young assistant professor at Princeton. In high school, she obtained the highest grades in science. Shortly before graduation, her principal called her in and asked if she would be willing to forgo the traditional science award so that the second-ranked student, a male, could receive it. The explanation was that he would be better able to use it, as he was headed for a career in science. To the principal, it was inconceivable that this young woman would also consider such a career.

These are shocking stories, the more so because they occurred in the 1980's and 1990's, not the 1950's. This failure of our society, particularly our educators, to equate women with careers in science, and the propensity to discount their achievements when they persist with this ambition lies at the heart of the problem.

In universities, the trend of discouraging women from science careers continues. The number of declared freshman science majors of both sexes is three times the number who will actually graduate with a degree in science or engineering. However, the percentage decline is greater for women than men. The only exception to this is instructive: women's colleges lose far fewer of their science undergraduates to other fields. Surely this is telling us that in an environment that places high expectations on women's achievement, women flourish in science.

When questioned about their experiences as science majors, women at co-ed colleges complain of feelings of isolation in a large class of males, of being ignored by faculty and of not being taken seriously. Women who begin college well-qualified and strongly motivated lose their self-esteem.

I think the difference between the numbers who overcome these hurdles in the physical vs. the biological sciences is directly attributable to the number of women practicing each discipline. It is slowly becoming accepted that women make good biologists, and consequently women are no longer discouraged from following this path. Put another way, the rich tend to get richer. All but the most determined women will tend to gravitate to the environment which is most positive and rewarding, and that tends to be where other women have already led the way.

Discussion Questions

1. Tilghman's opening paragraphs link concern over the shortage of women and minorities in science and engineering to the larger problem of a reduced number of people choosing scientific careers. Why is that a problem? What would be the consequences of having fewer scientists and engineers in our culture?

2. Identify and evaluate what Tilghman implements to support her argument that despite the increased numbers of women in science today (compared to twenty years ago) it still does not provide a supportive environment for women.

3. What does Tilghman mean by *culture* when she says, "I believe that the common thread is the role that culture plays in determining career choices for women"? How is Tilghman's definition of culture similar to or different from Cynthia Ozick's (see pp. 6–7)? When you use the term *culture*, do you more often think of it in terms of sociology or the arts?

Journal Entry

In paragraph 12 Tilghman cites examples of young girls' behavior, such as a decrease in reading books about science, that illustrate how females become sensitive at an early age to cultural cues that science is not for them. Relate an experience from your own childhood in which you rejected some hobby or activity because you felt other people considered it inappropriate on account of your sex.

Writing Projects

1. Write an essay, to be directed to science faculty and curriculum planners, giving specific guidelines for addressing the complaints of female students who feel ignored or isolated in predominantly male classes. Suggest what can be done to combat the perception that they are not taken seriously, that faculty tend to disregard their ideas. You may have to interview members of the faculty and administration as well as students, male and female, who feel there is strong evidence to suggest that female students are not treated in the same way as male students. Develop a plan of action, one that either convincingly dismisses the accusations or offers constructive ways to change the classroom experience.

2. Write an essay examining the extent to which Tilghman strengthens her argument by presenting both a pessimistic and an optimistic interpretation of the same data. How does she structure her essay around these two perspectives?

Collaborative Project

Working with one or two partners, investigate some of the programs that Tilghman says are designed to promote science as a career for women. Evaluate the methods used in these programs and their success rate. Report your findings to the class. Suggest ways to improve the recruitment of women to scientific fields and ways to provide a more supportive environment for women who are already working in scientific fields.

Alexander Calandra

Angels on a Pin

Alexander Calandra *(b. 1911) is a physicist whose research interests include statistical techniques that are used in tests and measurements. A professor emeritus at Washington University in St. Louis, Calandra advocates integrating more science and math course work into the educational curriculum, from the elementary to the college level. Calandra has published essays and articles that seek to define science and examine society's general view of science from a historical perspective. In an essay entitled "What Is Science?" Calandra asserts that "the idea of a unique scientific methodology recently developed is a major delusion of our times." In the story reprinted here, "Angels on a Pin" (published first in* Saturday Review *in 1968), Calandra adapts a dramatic form of argument dating back at least to Plato and draws on his own experience as a teacher to produce a short, amusing dialogue between a teacher and a student. Among the serious issues addressed here are the limitations of test instruments and an acknowledgment of the role of persuasion and consensus in science.*

Questions to Consider

☐ As you read, consider how the author's construction of a dialogue between a teacher and a student advances the story with a minimum of explanation.

☐ As you read, do you find yourself identifying with the student portrayed here? Do you suppose your own teacher identifies with the student or with one or both of the teachers in this story?

S OME time ago, I received a call from a colleague who asked if I would be the referee on the grading of an examination question. He was about to give a student a zero for his answer to a physics question, while the student claimed he should receive a perfect score and would if the system were not set up against the student. The instructor and the student agreed to submit this to an impartial arbiter, and I was selected.

I went to my colleague's office and read the examination question: "Show how it is possible to determine the height of a tall building with the aid of a barometer."

The student had answered: "Take the barometer to the top of the building, attach a long rope to it, lower the barometer to the street, and then bring it up, measuring the length of the rope. The length of the rope is the height of the building."

I pointed out that the student really had a strong case for full credit, since he had answered the question completely and correctly. On the other hand, if full credit were given, it could well contribute to a high grade for the student in his physics course. A high grade is supposed to certify competence in physics, but the answer did not confirm this. I suggested that the student have another try at answering the question. I was not surprised that my colleague agreed, but I was surprised that the student did.

I gave the student six minutes to answer the question, with the warning that his answer should show some knowledge of physics. At the end of five minutes, he had not written anything. I asked if he wished to give up, but he said no. He had many answers to this problem; he was just thinking of the best one. I excused myself for interrupting him, and asked him to please go on. In the next minute, he dashed off his answer, which read:

"Take the barometer to the top of the building and lean over the edge of the roof. Drop the barometer, timing its fall with a stopwatch. Then, using the formula $S = \frac{1}{2}\, at^2$, calculate the height of the building."

At this point, I asked my colleague if *he* would give up. He conceded, and I gave the student almost full credit.

In leaving my colleague's office, I recalled that the student had said he had other answers to the problem, so I asked him what they were. "Oh, yes," said the student. "There are many ways of getting the height of a tall building with the aid of a barometer. For example, you could take the barometer out on a sunny day and measure the height of the barometer, the length of its shadow, and the length of the shadow of the building, and by the use of a simple proportion, determine the height of the building."

"Fine," I said. "And the others?"

"Yes," said the student. "There is a very basic measurement method that you will like. In this method, you take the barometer and begin to walk up the stairs. As you climb the stairs, you mark off the length of the barometer along the wall. You then count the number of marks, and this will give you the height of the building in barometer units. A very direct method.

"Of course, if you want a more sophisticated method, you can tie the barometer to the end of a string, swing it as a pendulum, and determine the value of 'g' at the street level and at the top of the building. From the difference between the two values of 'g,' the height of the building can, in principle, be calculated."

Finally, he concluded, there are many other ways of solving the problem. "Probably the best," he said, "is to take the barometer to the basement and knock on the superintendent's door. When the superintendent answers, you speak to him as follows: 'Mr. Superintendent, here I have a fine barometer. If you will tell me the height of this building, I will give you this barometer.'"

At this point, I asked the student if he really did not know the conventional answer to this question. He admitted that he did, but said that he was fed up with high school and college instructors trying to teach him how to think, to use the "scientific method," and to explore the deep inner logic of the subject in a pedantic way, as is often done in the new mathematics, rather than teaching him the structure of the subject. With this in mind, he decided to revive scholasticism as an academic lark to challenge the Sputnik-panicked classrooms of America.

————————————

Discussion Questions

1. Point out some specific passages in this story where the author economically yet effectively reveals the character and personality of both the student and the narrator. What techniques does he use: language, word choice, tone, pacing, point of view, or others?

2. What is the source of the "angels on a pin" reference? Why does the author link it to his story?

3. Do you think the student in this story should receive an exam score of zero, a perfect score, or a score somewhere in between? Support your view. What score do you think the author (who is not the same as the narrator) implies the student should receive?

Journal Entry

Write about a conflict in which you defied a teacher because you did not accept the teaching method being used. Why did you feel compelled to resist the teacher? What did you do? How did your teacher react? What happened as a consequence of your rebellion? If you did not act on your feelings of defiance, why not? What made you comply even though you did not agree?

Writing Projects

1. Although it is quite short, this story demonstrates an impressive range of rhetorical devices—for example, illustration, narrative, process, example, anecdote, and analogy. Analyze how these elements are integrated to develop the main idea. How does Calandra use them to discuss a serious issue while still entertaining the reader?

2. Write a letter addressed to the student in this story in which you respond to the validity of his various exam answers.

3. Write a conversation that might take place between these two physics teachers—the examiner and the colleague who served as arbiter in this story—in the faculty lounge after the exchange with the student.

Collaborative Project

Working with a partner, construct a dialogue modeled on the one in the story. Create a conversation in which the teacher and student engage in a conflict of ideas. You and your partner might work together, both writing both characters' lines. Or you could each assume a role and carry on a dialogue, which you tape record and then transcribe. Or you could each assume a role and carry on a dialogue by writing back and forth to each other on electronic mail. Then revise and polish your work together for a coherent whole.

Making Connections

1. In "Science and Letters: God's Work—And Ours," Cynthia Ozick points out that our culture has been unable to "fashion a uniform image of science." Consider your own definition and image of science. Compare it to other definitions of science with which you are familiar, either from this book or elsewhere. Share views with your classmates.

2. In "Science versus the Female Scientist," Shirley Tilghman says that the attitudes of many scientists toward their profession, particularly the view that science is an endeavor more suited to men than women, have not changed much in the last quarter of a century. Discuss any significant similarities between her portrayal of current scientific study and C. P. Snow's portrayal of it in "The Moment" that would support or refute Tilghman's assertion.

3. Both Cynthia Ozick and George Orwell divide educated people into two main categories, those trained in the sciences and those trained in the humanities. Point out any ways in which you find Ozick's and Orwell's categories in need of expansion to include additional important similarities or differences in training and professional outlook that characterize specialists in these two areas.

Suggested Writing Projects

1. In Alexander Calandra's story "Angels on a Pin," a student objects to his professor's pedantic method of teaching physics. What response do you think the precocious student in Calandra's story would have to Thomas Henry Huxley's essay? Write a dialogue between the student and Huxley illustrating the response each might have to the other's views.

2. C. P. Snow's writing style is noticeable for its long sentences, often comprised of lengthy, complicated independent clauses held together by a colon or semicolon. Today this would be considered a rather old-fashioned style, and some readers might have difficulty with it. Choose another writer in this chapter whose writing style is distinctive. The style need not be dense like Snow's; it might be striking for its colloquial nature, for example. Write an essay analyzing how either of the writers' styles complements (or fails to complement) the content and theme of his or her writing.

3. Evelyn Fox Keller, describing what she once felt about science in "Gender and Science: An Update," says that she believed in the "possibility of clear and certain knowledge provided by science," in the "accessibility of an underlying (and unifying) 'truth' about the world," and that she "accepted science, and scientists, as arbiters of truth." Write an essay in which you ex-

plore your own view of science and its role in providing an access to "truth." Examine the ways in which one or two other authors in this chapter define science in a manner that reflects Keller's view of science either before or after her consideration of gender issues caused her to change her mind. If your own thinking has been affected by any of the writings here, show how and why.

2

Applying Technology

 Our attitude toward technology has long been one of ambivalence. For example, a century and a half ago the development of the locomotive elicited mixed responses from many nineteenth-century thinkers. Henry David Thoreau retreated to Walden Pond to escape the encroachment of industrialism. As the intercontinental railroad neared completion, he warned his neighbors to beware: "We do not ride upon the rails; they ride upon us." For Thoreau, the railroad represented the tie between technology and commerce: each drove the other. He did not want to be driven by either.

Yet Walt Whitman glorified the locomotive as a "Fierce-throated beauty!" Excited by its noise and power, he exclaimed: "Thy trills of shrieks by rocks and hills return'd, / Launch'ed o'er the prairies wide . . . unpent and glad and strong."

Such a machine was a marvel to behold: noisy, fast, and powerful. Today we still marvel at technology, but, like Thoreau, we also fear it. We know that the products of technology make our lives easier and enable us to live longer. Machines help us work faster and more efficiently. But we also worry that machines might replace us. We wonder if the jobs we have now and the careers we are preparing for will be transformed, maybe even disappear, in the near future. Technological progress is viewed more warily than ever before. Like the characters in the short story "Pulling Contest" by Marjorie Dorner, we have seen technology change family businesses and entire ways of life.

At the root of our ambivalence toward technology is our anxiety that it may control us more than we control it. Witold Rybczynski writes an essay that seeks to reassure us that our fears are groundless: How can we fear that which we create? We are not creatures powerless against the tide of technological progress. We need not sit by the roadside waiting to see if technology will mow us down. We have the intelligence to design, produce, and market inventions that we want and need.

On the other hand, some people argue that we create particular technologies that allow us to accomplish quickly and efficiently tasks that we didn't need to do before we had the tools to do them. Robert Samuelson, who classifies technology into two categories – smart and stupid – laments that "computer mail has transformed idle chitchat into an all-day affair." Have you ever had a frustrating experience like going to the trouble of transferring the contents of your address book onto your personal computer only to have the computer break down? At such times your old, pocketsize address book doesn't seem like a completely outmoded tool.

Some scholars distrust technology not because it can be wasteful and expensive but because it arouses a desire we all have to exert power over others. In Sally Hacker's essay on the eroticism of technology, she explores how technology is used for the "eroticized domination and control of nature" and humans.

Advertising campaigns frequently equate machines and sex. Think of all the commercials you have seen in which a machine – say, an automobile – is shown with a seductively postured, scantily clad woman draped across it. The machine itself is sometimes described as "sexy."

Technology promises even more than satisfaction and gratification of desire. For some it promises solutions to major problems. Two authors who advocate the creation and application of new technology are Hajime Karatsu and Alvin Weinberg. Karatsu believes that technology has made a tiny nation like Japan into a world power. He links manufacturing productivity to economic growth, which in turn produces affluence leading to a better quality of life for an entire nation. Alvin Weinberg shows how technology makes life better because it can be used to address current social problems. Many of us believe that certain major social problems stem from self-centered or irrational human behavior. Although technology cannot prevent these kinds of problems, Weinberg believes it can provide what he terms a "technological fix."

In Chapter 1 we considered definitions of science. Here we consider definitions of technology. The term "technology" includes more than machinery and hardware; in fact, it also means techniques and methods. Neil Postman argues convincingly that language itself is a kind of technology, albeit an invisible one; indeed, its very invisibility as a technology imbues language with special power. Postman says that "in many respects, a sentence functions very much like a machine."

As students, your exposure to educational technology is not limited to computers and other electronic devices used in the classroom, although these are examples of some of the newest teaching tools. Educational technology also includes the teaching methods used by your professors, their grading systems, the means they use to determine whether you have fulfilled the requirements for obtaining a degree, and their approaches to fostering learning both within the classroom and beyond it, whether that be in the library or in the community at large.

These tools of learning are the technology of our age, which is often referred to as the "information age." We have moved beyond the "machine age" that frightened and awed nineteenth-century thinkers. We are speeding along the information superhighway. We are logging onto computer networks that allow us to cross continents in an instant. It is predicted that in the twenty-first century the average number of times a person will change careers — not just jobs — is seven. As technological advances require us to change careers, these same advances will provide us with the systems and tools needed to excel at different careers. We can look forward to enjoying an unprecedented measure of self-fulfillment through these explorations.

References

Henry Thoreau, "Walden." *The Portable Thoreau*, ed. Carl Bode. New York: Viking Press, 1964.

Walt Whitman, "To a Locomotive in Winter." *Walt Whitman: Leaves of Grass*, ed. Sculley Bradley and Harold W. Blodgett. New York: W. W. Norton, 1973.

Hajime Karatsu

Improving the Quality of Life through Technology

Hajime Karatsu *(b. 1919) teaches at the R & D (Research and Design) Institute of Tokai University. He was born in the People's Republic of China and moved to Japan in 1935. A recipient of Japan's prestigious Deming Prize in 1981, Karatsu has served various Japanese professional constituencies, including the Industrial Structural Council of the Ministry of International Trade and Industry, the Institute of Fifth Generation Computer Systems, and the Office Automation Committee of the Tokyo metropolitan government. He received an Industry Education Award from the Japanese Ministry of Education in 1984. His main area of study is statistical quality control. Karatsu's books include* System Engineering *(1970),* Marketing Science *(1974), and* Scenario of Japan *(1981). In the following essay, reprinted from* Globalization of Technology: International Perspectives *(1988), Karatsu explains what has made Japan rise from the devastation of World War II to become a superpower in a relatively short time: Japan has achieved affluence and strength through the development of industry.*

Questions to Consider

☐ Before reading this essay, consider your current perception of and attitude toward Japan. What stereotypes do you have?

☐ As you read, identify statements made by the author that might betray a Japanese bias.

☐ Notice that the author begins with statistics from published Harris polls. Why might he choose to do this? What do you expect to follow these statistics? As you read, notice whether your expectations are fulfilled.

I N a recent Harris poll, American manufacturing executives were asked which countries would pose the most serious competitive threat to American manufacturing over the next 5 years and in the year 2000 (*Business Week*, January 12, 1987). Sixty-nine percent of the executives answered that emerging countries such as Brazil, South Korea, and Taiwan would be America's chief competitors in the manufacturing sector over the next 5 years, and 76 percent responded that those countries would pose a threat to U.S. manufacturing in the year 2000. Only 29 percent of those who responded said that Japan would be a serious competitor over the next 5 years, and only 11 percent cited Japan for the year 2000.

These findings illustrate an interesting trend. In the past, a nation's competitive power was determined by its geographical size and population. Beginning in the eighteenth century, however, the industrial revolution changed the balance of power among nations, and today even a small nation can achieve affluence and economic strength through its industrial achievement.

In Southeast Asia, there are major differences between nations even though they are located in the same geographical region and are surrounded by similar natural conditions. Singapore has a high wage rate, second only to Japan in Asia, yet it is a tiny island comparable in size to Manhattan and has a population of 2.7 million people. It is also located in a tropical zone with few natural resources.

On the other hand, the people of other nations in Asia are still living at a primitive level. When we look carefully at statistical data on the status of each nation, we see the correlation between a country's economic standing and various indicators of the quality of life. High economic figures are indicative of the advanced state of industrialization of each nation.

Coping with Change through Technology

Just before the oil crisis of 1974, *The Limits to Growth*, a controversial report prepared for the Club of Rome, projected a very pessimistic scenario for the future of the global economy and industrialized nations in particular (Meadows et al., 1972). Given the atmosphere at that time—which included a general economic slowdown and the antipollution and antitechnology movement—the report had an enormous impact. It supported the theory, and more importantly the prevailing mood, that the global economy was headed for a period of decline. These influences contributed to a certain pessimism in many industrialized countries.

However, nations have demonstrated that they can cope with such conditions through the creativity of human beings. Faced with the oil crisis, Japan introduced innovative energy-saving technology into the steel industry, and today not a drop of oil is used in that sector. Japan has achieved an increase in its gross national product (GNP) of 2.7 times that at the time of the first oil crisis, while oil consumption has decreased to 80 percent of that in 1974.

Almost every industrialized nation instituted similar energy-saving measures. These efforts to eliminate energy losses in factories, automobiles, and elsewhere were successful in overcoming the energy price hikes. As a result of the new technology, decreased oil consumption has even forced oil producers to cut the price of oil.

Pollution in the industrialized areas of Japan, a by-product of the push for high economic growth, was another major problem in the 1970s. However, after a radical antiindustrialization movement became active, the Japanese government issued numerous antipollution laws. The strictest automobile emission regulations in the world were instituted in Japan in 1975, and cars that did not meet the emissions control specifications could not be sold in Japan. Such regulations were applied not only to automobiles but also in every factory. Consequently, the engineers working in the regulated sectors made great efforts to develop technologies within the framework of the new constraints.

As a result of those efforts, the air and water of Japan today have become clean again. It is said that half the budget to construct new ironworks plants was spent on energy-saving and antipollution devices. The average expenditure of the energy-saving/antipollution industry, which did not exist in Japan before the 1970s, is estimated to be $15 billion per year. Recently, these energy-saving and antipollution technologies have begun to be used all over the world, especially in Western Europe to eliminate pollution caused by acid rain.

Increasing the Economic Pie through Technology

The importance of a strong manufacturing base and the economic advantages of industrialization are well illustrated by Japan. Japan is one of the world's most crowded countries. With 2.7 percent of the world's population yet only 0.3 percent of the land area, Japan has few natural resources and is located on the fringe of the Asian continent, which is far from the world's main markets. Yet in 1986, Japan achieved a GNP of $2.3 trillion, 11 percent of the world's economic activity. The locomotive force of the Japanese economy is clear. It is technology. Many attempts to understand the basis of Japan's success, however, are marked by misconceptions. Some commentators say Japan has merely followed in the path of Western Europe and the United States or imitated ideas from developed nations and in this way moved ahead in manufacturing and other technologies. Some of these statements may be true, but my experience in the Japanese manufacturing sector since World War II has provided an insight into two key factors of Japan's success. The first factor is the way Japanese manufacturers develop new products through innovative technology. The second factor is the way the Japanese cope with and overcome problems that occur on the manufacturing shop floor.

In October 1985, I attended a conference in Toulouse, France, on advanced technology. During the conference, I wondered whether many Western Europeans understood the real meaning of advanced technology. When new technologies appear in the world, Western Europeans tend to apply them in complicated ways such as in space technology or missiles. Since these are difficult fields they seldom apply the advanced technologies in immediately practical ways. On the other hand, the Japanese make use of new technologies in whatever form seems to be easily applicable at the time.

Consider carbon fiber, for example. It is a highly innovative new material, lighter than aluminum and stronger than steel. Japanese manufacturers first used it for the shaft of golf clubs. Next they used it for fishing rods. And because they were using these new materials for simple products, even if some minor defects occurred, serious problems were avoided. After they perfected these production techniques for carbon fiber, Japanese companies used carbon fiber in more complex applications.

A more recent example is that of shape-memory alloy. In Japan, manufacturers started using this alloy in every possible field and explored many different product areas – such as air conditioners, eyeglass frames, and coffee makers. Consequently, Japan produces more of this alloy than any other country, 90 percent of the world total.

The most important strategy for using innovative technology is discovering and developing a new, profitable market. Technology should not stay at the idea stage; it should be converted into marketable products. Japanese firms are successful at commercializing new technologies because they select technologies with ready applications and move quickly in developing and manufacturing the product. A driving force in maintaining this commercialization strategy is severe competition among Japanese firms.

Another point is the difference in assumptions between Western European and Japanese engineers. If I talk with Western European engineers, their discussions tend to be "digital." They always think in terms of black or white and yes or no. This Cartesian way of thinking was quite effective in the natural sciences, where greater simplification is necessary to organize ambiguous data. However, production activity is not that simple.

Basically, manufacturing is a battle against thousands of different possible breakdowns and errors: mistakes in planning schedules, incorrect design, accidental mixture of materials, and so forth. Moreover, machines do not always work uniformly, and factory workers occasionally make mistakes. If these errors accumulate, the result will be a pile of defective goods. The lesson here is that it is easy to fail if you are not aware of all the "gray areas" of production.

We cannot predict where and how such errors will occur, however. Everyone in the factory must cooperate, looking for potential problems and taking care of them in order to prevent future problems. Japan's strategy for dealing with these issues is the total quality control (TQC) system.

Conclusion

Every nation has the potential for achieving a more affluent society by introducing technology and developing added value in manufactured goods. India succeeded in supplying food for its population, and projections are that India will even export food in the near future. On the other hand, even today 60 percent of the world's population subsists at a starvation level. Therefore, there should be cooperation and understanding among nations concerning the use of technology as a tool for achieving an improved standard of living for all people. Unfortunately, the fruits of technology are often treated too politically to be used to upgrade the quality of human life. Nations should strive to introduce technology for the purpose of improving tomorrow's quality of life.

REFERENCES

Business Week. January 12, 1987. BW/Harris executive poll: Manufacturing's rise depends on the dollar, p. 68.
Meadows, D. H., D. L. Meadows, J. Randers, and W. W. Behrens III. 1972. The Limits to Growth. New York: Universe Books.

Discussion Questions

1. Karatsu says that only 29 percent of those responding to a Harris poll in 1987 believed that "Japan would be a serious competitor over the next 5 years. . . ." If the same poll were conducted today, do you think the percentage of those who consider Japan a serious competitor would change? Would there be fewer, more, or the same as there were in 1987? How do Karatsu's arguments influence your opinion?

2. Karatsu states: "High economic figures are indicative of the advanced state of industrialization of each nation." What exactly does "advanced state of industrialization" mean? Do you agree with Karatsu that there is a direct positive correlation between high industrialization and a good quality of life? Explain your point of view.

3. In the concluding paragraph, the author asserts: "Therefore, there should be cooperation and understanding among nations concerning the use of technology as a tool for achieving an improved standard of living for all people." Why might someone agree with this statement? Why might someone disagree?

4. Is Karatsu's argument convincing? Where does he make his conclusive arguments? Do his data justify his conclusions?

Journal Entry

For you personally, how much does the quality of your life depend on the amount of money you have? To what extent does technology determine the quality of your own life? What connection do you see between technology, affluence, and comfort?

Writing Projects

1. What does the term *TQC* (total quality control) mean? Discuss the concept of TQC and its history. Where did it originate? How many companies in this country have implemented the concept? Has the administration at your college or university integrated any TQC concepts into the structure of your academic institution? Interview at least one person who understands and has implemented TQC in some way in his or her work. Include an analytical summary of this interview in your report.

2. Karatsu makes several references to the "antipollution and antitechnology movement." How does he link the idea of antipollution with antitechnology? Why does he create this juxtaposition? Analyze how the juxtaposition is relevant to his main argument.

Collaborative Project

Working with a partner, identify a group that is responsible for an antipollution and antitechnology movement in this country. Conducting your research jointly, investigate the history of the movement. How has it been successful in its efforts to affect business or government policy? What have been some of its obstacles? Then write two papers on your findings, either together or separately, each aimed at a different audience: for example, one for a profit-making corporation and one for representatives of the EPA (Environmental Protection Agency). Together, compare the goals that each of you had when writing. What did you want to prove? How did you use the raw data to support your statements? Compare the differences in presentation between the two papers. Which of these differences reflect the contrasting features of the two audiences?

Alvin M. Weinberg

Can Technology Replace Social Engineering?

Alvin M. Weinberg *(b. 1915) has received the President's Medal of Science, the Atoms for Peace Award, and the Enrico Fermi Award, among other honors. A physicist educated at the University of Chicago, Weinberg was an early leader in the research and development of large-scale atomic energy. He was part of the World War II Manhattan Project and then served as director of the Oak Ridge National Laboratory from 1955 to 1973. This article, first published in* University of Chicago Magazine *(1966), established a new term:* technological fix. *Some of the issues and technologies Weinberg discusses here may now seem dated. Nevertheless, his argument for using technology to combat social problems still deserves consideration. When social ills stem from insurmountable problems, treating the symptoms with technology is more practical than attempting to change human nature, Weinberg believes. Other works by Weinberg include* Reflections on Big Science *(1967),* The Second Nuclear Era *(1985), and* Nuclear Reactions: Science and Trans-Science *(1992).*

Questions to Consider

☐ Notice how far into this essay you proceed before you determine Weinberg's answer to the question posed by his title.

☐ In the past several decades some technological developments that Weinberg mentions, such as nuclear energy and the IUD (intrauterine device), have proven to be hazardous. Notice how Weinberg described them in 1966, and think about how our views have, or have not, changed.

D URING World War II, and immediately afterward, our federal government mobilized its scientific and technical resources, such as the Oak Ridge National Laboratory, around great technological problems. Nuclear reactors, nuclear weapons, radar, and space are some of the miraculous new technologies that have been created by this mobilization of federal effort. In the past few years there has been a major change in focus of much of our federal research. Instead of being preoccupied with technology, our government is now mobilizing around problems that are largely social. We are beginning to ask what can we do about world population, about the deterioration of our environment, about our educational system, our decaying cities, race relations, poverty. Recent administrations have dedicated the power of a scientifically oriented federal apparatus to finding solutions for these complex social problems.

Social problems are much more complex than are technological problems. It is much harder to identify a social problem than a technological problem: how do we know when our cities need renewing, or when our population is too big, or when our modes of transportation have broken down? The problems are, in a way, harder to identify just because their solutions are never clear-cut: how do we know when our cities are renewed, or our air clean enough, or our transportation convenient enough? By contrast, the availability of a crisp and beautiful technological *solution* often helps focus on the problem to which the new technology is the solution. I doubt that we would have been nearly as concerned with an eventual shortage of energy as we now are if we had not had a neat solution – nuclear energy – available to eliminate the shortage.

There is a more basic sense in which social problems are much more difficult than are technological problems. A social problem exists because many people behave, individually, in a socially unacceptable way. To solve a social problem one must induce social change – one must persuade many people to behave differently than they have behaved in the past. One must persuade many people to have fewer babies, or to drive more carefully, or to refrain from disliking blacks. By contrast, resolution of a technological problem involves many fewer individual decisions. Once President Roosevelt decided to go after atomic energy, it was by comparison a relatively simple task to mobilize the Manhattan Project.

The resolution of social problems by the traditional methods – by motivating or forcing people to behave more rationally – is a frustrating business. People don't behave rationally; it is a long, hard business to persuade individuals to forgo immediate personal gain or pleasure (as seen by the individual) in favor of longer term social gain. And indeed, the aim of social engineering is to invent the social devices – usually legal, but also moral and educational and organizational – that will change each person's motivation and redirect his activities along ways that are more acceptable to the society.

The technologist is appalled by the difficulties faced by the social engineer; to engineer even a small social change by inducing individuals to behave differently is always hard even when the change is rather neutral or even beneficial. For example, some rice eaters in India are reported to prefer starvation to eating wheat which we send to them. How much harder it is to change motivations where the individual is insecure and feels threatened if he acts differently, as illustrated by the poor white's reluctance to accept the black as an equal. By contrast, technological engineering is simple: the rocket, the reactor, and the desalination plants are devices that are expensive to develop, to be sure, but their feasibility is relatively easy to assess, and their success relatively easy to achieve once one understands the scientific principles that underlie them. It is, therefore, tempting to raise the following question: In view of the simplicity of technological engineering, and the complexity of social engineering, to what extent can social problems be circumvented by reducing them to technological problems? Can we identify Quick Technological Fixes for profound and almost infinitely complicated social problems, "fixes" that are within the grasp of modern technology, and which would either eliminate the original social problem without requiring a change in the individual's social attitudes, or would so alter the problem as to make its resolution more feasible? To paraphrase Ralph Nader, to what extent can technological *remedies* be found for social problems without first having to remove the *causes* of the problem? It is in this sense that I ask, "Can technology replace social engineering?"

The Major Technological Fixes of the Past

To better explain what I have in mind, I shall describe how two of our profoundest social problems – poverty and war – have in some limited degree been solved by the Technological Fix, rather than by the methods of social engineering. Let me begin with poverty.

The traditional Marxian view of poverty regarded our economic ills as being primarily a question of maldistribution of goods. The Marxist recipe for elimination of poverty, therefore, was to eliminate profit, in the erroneous belief that it was the loss of this relatively small increment from the worker's paycheck that kept him poverty-stricken. The Marxist dogma is typical of the approach of the social engineer: one tries to convince or coerce many people to forgo their short-term profits in what is presumed to be the long-term interest of the society as a whole.

The Marxian view seems archaic in this age of mass production and automation not only to us, but apparently to many Eastern bloc economists. For the brilliant advances in the technology of energy, of mass production, and of automation have created the affluent society. Technology has expanded our productive capacity so greatly that even though our distribution is still inefficient, and unfair by Marxian precepts, there is more than enough to go around. Technology has provided a "fix" – greatly expanded production of goods – which enables our capitalistic society to achieve many of the aims of the Marxist social engineer without going through the social revolution Marx viewed as inevitable. Technology has converted the seemingly intractable social problem of *widespread* poverty into a relatively tractable one.

My second example is war. The traditional Christian position views war as primarily a moral issue: if men become good, and model themselves after the Prince of Peace, they will live in peace. This doctrine is so deeply ingrained in the spirit of all civilized men that I suppose it is a blasphemy to point out that it has never worked very well – that men have not been good, and that they are not paragons of virtue or even of reasonableness.

Though I realize it is terribly presumptuous to claim, I believe that Edward Teller may have supplied the nearest thing to a Quick Technological Fix to the problem of war. The hydrogen bomb greatly increases the provocation that would precipitate large-scale war – and not because men's motivations have been changed, not because men have become more tolerant and understanding, but rather because the appeal to the primitive instinct of self-preservation has been intensified far beyond anything we could have imagined before the H-bomb was invented. To point out these things today, with the United States involved in a shooting war, may sound hollow and unconvincing; yet the desperate and partial peace we have now is much better than a full-fledged exchange of thermonuclear weapons. One cannot deny that the Soviet leaders now recognize the force of H-bombs, and that this has surely contributed to the less militant attitude of the USSR. One can only hope that the Chinese leadership, as it acquires familiarity with H-bombs, will also become less militant. If I were to be asked who has given the world a more effective means of achieving peace, our great religious leaders who urge men to love their neighbors and, thus, avoid fights, or our weapons technologists who simply present men with no rational alternative to peace, I would vote for the weapons technologist. That the peace we get is at best terribly fragile, I cannot deny; yet, as I shall explain, I think technology can help stabilize our imperfect and precarious peace.

The Technological Fixes of the Future

Are there other Technological Fixes on the horizon, other technologies that can reduce immensely complicated social questions to a matter of "engineering"? Are there new technologies that offer society ways of circumventing social problems and at the same time do *not* require individuals to renounce short-term advantage for long-term gain?

Probably the most important new Technological Fix is the Intra-Uterine Device for birth control. Before the IUD was invented, birth control demanded very strong motivation of countless individuals. Even with the pill, the individual's motivation had to be sustained day in and day out; should it flag even temporarily, the strong motivation of the previous month might go for naught. But the IUD, being a one-shot method, greatly reduces the individual motivation required to induce a social change. To be sure, the mother must be sufficiently motivated to accept the IUD in the first place, but, as experience in India already seems to show, it is much easier to persuade the Indian mother to accept the IUD once, than it is to persuade her to take a pill every day. The IUD does not completely replace social engineering by technology; and indeed, in some Spanish American cultures where the husband's manliness is measured by the number of children he has, the IUD attacks only part of the problem. Yet, in many other situations, as in India, the IUD so reduces the social component of the problem as to make an impossibly difficult social problem much less hopeless.

Let me turn now to problems which from the beginning have had both technical and social components – broadly, those concerned with conservation of our resources: our environment, our water, and our raw materials for production of the means of subsistence. The social issue here arises because many people by their individual acts cause shortages and, thus, create economic, and ultimately social, imbalance. For example, people use water wastefully, or they insist on moving to California because of its climate, and so we have water shortages; or too many people drive cars in Los Angeles with its curious meteorology, and so Los Angeles suffocates from smog.

The water resources problem is a particularly good example of a complicated problem with strong social and technological connotations. Our management of water resources in the past has been based largely on the ancient Roman device, the aqueduct: every water shortage was to be relieved by stealing water from someone else who at the moment didn't need the water or was too poor or too weak to prevent the steal. Southern California would steal from Northern California, New York City from upstate New York, the farmer who could afford a cloud-seeder from the farmer who could not afford a cloud-seeder. The social engineer insists that such shortsighted expedients have got us into serious trouble; we have no water resources policy, we waste water disgracefully, and, perhaps, in denying the ethic of thriftiness in using water, we have generally undermined our moral fiber. The social engineer, therefore, views such technological shenanigans as being shortsighted, if not downright immoral. Instead, he says, we should persuade or force people to use less water, or to stay in the cold Middle West where water is plentiful instead of migrating to California where water is scarce.

The water technologist, on the other hand, views the social engineer's approach as rather impractical. To persuade people to use less water, to get along with expensive water, is difficult, time-consuming, and uncertain in the extreme. Moreover, say the technologists, what right does the water resources expert have to insist that people use water less wastefully? Green lawns and clean cars and swimming pools are part of the good life, American style, . . . and what right do we have to deny this luxury if there is some alternative to cutting down the water we use?

Here we have a sharp confrontation of the two ways of dealing with a complex social issue: the social engineering way which asks people to behave more "reasonably," and the technologists' way which tries to avoid changing people's habits or motivation. Even though I am a technologist, I have sympathy for the social engineer. I think we must use our water as efficiently as possible, that we ought to improve people's attitudes toward the use of water, and that everything that can be done to rationalize our water policy will be welcome. Yet as a technologist, I believe I see ways of providing more water more cheaply than the social engineers may concede is possible.

⟶I refer to the possibility of nuclear desalination. The social engineer dismisses the technologist's simpleminded idea of solving a water shortage by transporting more water primarily because, in so doing, the water user steals water from someone else – possibly foreclosing the possibility of ultimately utilizing land now only sparsely settled. But surely water drawn from the sea deprives no one of his share of water. The whole issue is then a technological one; can fresh water be drawn from the sea cheaply enough to have a major impact on our chronically water-short areas like Southern California, Arizona, and the Eastern seaboard?

I believe the answer is yes, though much hard technical work remains to be done. A large program to develop cheap methods of nuclear desalting has been undertaken by the United States, and I have little doubt that within the next ten to twenty years we shall see huge dual-purpose desalting plants springing up on many parched seacoasts of the world. At first these plants will produce water at municipal prices. But I believe, on the basis of research now in progress at ORNL and elsewhere, water from the sea at a cost acceptable for agriculture – less than ten cents per 1,000 gallons – is eventually in the cards. In short, for areas close to the seacoasts, technology can provide water without requiring a great and difficult-to-accomplish change in people's attitudes toward the utilization of water.

The Technological Fix for water is based on the availability of extremely cheap energy from very large nuclear reactors. What other social consequences can one foresee flowing from really cheap energy eventually available to every country regardless of its endowment of conventional resources? Though we now see only vaguely the outlines of the possibilities, it does seem likely that from very cheap nuclear energy we shall get hydrogen by electrolysis of water, and, thence, the all important ammonia fertilizer necessary to help feed the hungry of the world; we shall reduce metals without requiring coking coal; we shall even power automobiles with electricity, via fuel cells or storage batteries, thus reducing our world's dependence on crude oil, as well as eliminating our air pollution insofar as it is caused by automobile exhaust or by the burning of fossil fuels. In short, the widespread availability of very cheap energy everywhere in the world ought to lead to an energy autarky in every country of the world; and eventually to an autarky in the many staples of life that should flow from really cheap energy.

Will Technology Replace Social Engineering?

I hope these examples suggest how social problems can be circumvented or at least reduced to less formidable proportions by the application of the Technological Fix. The examples I have given do not strike me as being fanciful, nor are they at all exhaustive. I have not touched, for example, upon the extent to which really cheap computers and improved technology of communication can help improve elementary teaching without having first to improve our elementary teachers. Nor have I mentioned Ralph Nader's brilliant observation that a safer car, and even its development and adoption by the auto company, is a quicker and probably surer way to reduce traffic deaths than is a campaign to teach people to drive more carefully. Nor have I invoked some really fanciful Technological Fixes: like providing air conditioners and free electricity to operate them for every black family in Watts on the assumption (suggested by Huntington) that race rioting is correlated with hot, humid weather; or the ultimate Technological Fix, Aldous Huxley's soma pills that eliminate human unhappiness without improving human relations in the usual sense.

My examples illustrate both the strength and the weakness of the Technological Fix for social problems. The Technological Fix accepts man's intrinsic shortcomings and circumvents them or capitalizes on them for socially useful ends. The Fix is, therefore, eminently practical and, in the short term, relatively effective. One does not wait around trying to change people's minds: if people want more water, one gets them more water rather than requiring them to reduce their use of water; if people insist on driving autos while they are drunk, one provides safer autos that prevent injuries even after a severe accident.

But the technological solutions to social problems tend to be incomplete and metastable, to replace one social problem with another. Perhaps the best example of this instability is the peace imposed upon us by the H-bomb. Evidently the pax hydrogenica is metastable in two senses: in the short term, because the aggressor still enjoys such an advantage; in the long term, because the discrepancy between have and have-not nations must eventually be resolved if we are to have permanent peace. Yet, for these particular shortcomings, technology has something to offer. To the imbalance between offense and defense, technology says let us devise passive defense which redresses the balance. A world with H-bombs and adequate civil defense is less likely to lapse into thermonuclear war than a world with H-bombs alone, at least if one concedes that the danger of the thermonuclear war mainly lies in the acts of irresponsible leaders. Anything that deters the irresponsible leader is a force for peace: a technologically sound civil defense therefore would help stabilize the balance of terror.

To the discrepancy between haves and have-nots, technology offers the nuclear energy revolution, with its possibility of autarky for haves and have-nots alike. How this might work to stabilize our metastable thermonuclear peace is suggested by the possible political effect of the recently proposed Israeli desalting plant. The Arab states I should think would be much less set upon destroying the Jordan River Project if the Israelis had a desalination plant in reserve that would nullify the effect of such action. In this connection, I think countries like ours can contribute very much. Our country will soon have to decide whether to continue to spend 5.5×10^9 per year for space exploration after our lunar landing. Is it too outrageous to suggest that some of this money be devoted to building huge nuclear desalting complexes in the arid ocean rims of the troubled world? If the plants are powered with breeder reactors, the out-of-pocket costs, once the plants are built, should be low enough to make large-scale agriculture feasible in these areas. I estimate that for $\$4 \times 10^9$ per year we could build enough desalting capacity to feed more than ten million new mouths per year (provided we use agricultural methods that husband water), and we would, thereby, help stabilize the metastable, bomb-imposed balance of terror.

Yet, I am afraid we technologists shall not satisfy our social engineers, who tell us that our Technological Fixes do not get to the heart of the problem; they are at best temporary expedients; they create new problems as they solve old ones; to put a Technological Fix into effect requires a positive social action. Eventually, social engineering, like the Supreme Court decision on desegregation, must be invoked to solve social problems. And, of course, our social engineers are right. Technology will never *replace* social engineering. But technology has provided and will continue to provide to the social engineer broader options, to make intractable social problems less intractable; perhaps, most of all, technology will buy time – that precious commodity that converts violent social revolution into acceptable social evolution.

Our country now recognizes and is mobilizing around the great social problems that corrupt and disfigure our human existence. It is natural that in this mobilization we should look first to the social engineer. But, unfortunately, the apparatus most readily available to the government, like the great federal laboratories, is technologically oriented, not socially oriented. I believe we have a great opportunity here; for, as I hope I have persuaded you, many of our seemingly social problems do admit of partial technological solutions. Our already deployed technological apparatus can contribute to the resolution of social questions. I plead, therefore, first for our government to deploy its laboratories, its hardware contractors, and its engineering universities around social problems. And I plead, secondly, for understanding and cooperation between technologist and social engineer. Even with all the help he can get from the technologist, the social engineer's problems are never really solved. It is only by cooperation between technologist and social engineer that we can hope to achieve what is the aim of all technologists and social engineers – a better society, and thereby, a better life, for all of us who are part of society.

Discussion Questions

1. To what extent do you consider the social problems Weinberg lists in his first paragraph (world population, environment, education, decaying cities, race relations, and poverty) still to be major problems almost thirty years

later? How would you change this list to reflect more of today's pressing social problems?

2. In the Questions to Consider preceding this selection, we identified nuclear energy and the IUD as two technological developments that have come to be seen as hazardous. What are some additional examples of technological research or products that were produced as a technological fix but ended up creating additional social problems?

3. Weinberg explains that the aim of social engineering is to invent "social devices—usually legal, but also moral and educational and organizational—that will change each person's motivation and redirect his activities" to produce a better society. Explain why you do, or do not, agree with Weinberg's definition of social engineering. What examples of social devices can you identify? How would you classify them: legal, moral, educational, or organizational?

4. Why do Weinberg and others prefer technological remedies rather than social engineering? What assumptions about human nature make a person inclined to prefer technological remedies?

Journal Entry

Discuss your attitude toward writing-related technological fixes. For example, the computer is a large-scale technological fix, with spell checkers, word finds, editing functions, and on-line dictionaries serving as small-scale examples. Do you rely on any of these fixes? How do they affect your writing?

Writing Projects

1. Describe and analyze your own experience with a technological fix. Feel free to expand on your journal response, or consider a technological fix in your home or dorm room, such as answering machines, call-waiting, call-identifying, or anything else you see around you. How has this technological fix changed your life? In what ways is life easier? What problems have arisen from the implementation of and dependence on this technological fix?

2. Analyze the rhetorical techniques Weinberg uses to be persuasive. For example, does he use definition, example, appeal to emotion, appeal to reason, cause and effect, or others? Which techniques do you consider most effective? Why?

Collaborative Project

In collaboration with one or more classmates, and drawing on ideas suggested by the preceding Writing Projects, conduct research into the ways in which technology has provided a technological fix but also inadvertently produced social problems. Measure the good against the harmful outcomes of selected uses of technology. Your writing team might focus on computer technology, with each team member investigating computer developments in his or her major field. For example, an engineering major could research CAD (computer-assisted design) technology; a journalism major might investigate how multimedia technology is changing the nature of the news business; and a business major could study how computer-generated projections are used by managers. Write a report on your findings and their implications.

Sally L. Hacker

Technology and Eroticism

Sally L. Hacker *(1938–1988), a sociology professor at Oregon State University at the time of her death, immersed herself in "people's sociology," which is a study of people in relation to society that seeks through knowledge and support to empower people who are without power. She developed innovative techniques for conducting research by listening carefully so that she could truly hear what people were saying as well as not saying, by becoming part of the social context she wanted to learn about, and by relying on her personal experience of a situation. She called her method "doing it the hard way." "Technology and Eroticism" is part of a series of Hacker's papers edited and introduced by Dorothy E. Smith and Susan M. Turner in* Doing It the Hard Way: Investigations of Gender and Technology *(1990). This fascinating piece uncovers the prevalence of passion and sexual energy in the rhetoric of engineering, a profession that purports to be rational and mechanistic.*

Questions to Consider

☐ There is disagreement in our culture about the meaning of the term *eroticism*. What does the term mean to you? Based on this essay's title, what do you expect it to explore?

☐ As you read, watch how Hacker sets the tone for this essay through the use of slang. What might be her reason for doing this?

Technology and Eroticism

THE EROTIC IN TECHNOLOGY

Let us consider the field of engineering, foregrounding the passionate context of this occupation. This field, the apparent epitome of cool rationality, is shot through with desire and excitement. Much of this excitement stirs the mind. It is as though an intricately shaped erotic expression finds its most creative outlet today in the design of technology. The contemporary images of eroticism and of machines and systems reflect the imagination of the designer. How could it be otherwise in any human venture?

As with any human and social activity, some care a lot and some don't give a damn. Technical skills and activities and erotic skills and activities leave some cold, but fire the imagination of many. The latter, rightly or wrongly, view the disinterested as alienated, pathological, or deficient in some way. The disinterested may view the aficionado as obsessed, either with sexuality or with technology (like Weizenbaum's programmer in *Computer Power and Human Reason* [1976]). When some men describe their feelings about technology, they often talk about God, glory, honor, and other noble sentiments. These are acceptable channels through which men can express transcendent desire. There is also, however, a lot of sexy, gendered talk about technology. This talk is heterosexual and male dominant. Gender discourse is yet another approved mode of expression for passionate feelings. The phallic and reproductive imagery of weapons systems has escaped no one (see . . . Hacker 1982; Easlea 1983; Cohn 1987; Edwards, forthcoming), including cartoonists in most any progressive publication. But that is hardly all there is. Both these modes of expression signal "off limits" to most women, and to many men and women with their own, different form of passion for science, technology, and eroticism. Relations of dominance and submission are also eroticized in gender-stratified societies (Valverde 1987), and shape the design of technological products and systems. Many note the grim connections between these phenomena under Fascism as men suppress the feared and envied feminine within themselves (Millett 1970; Griffin 1981; Theweleit 1987).

Samuel Florman (1976), the oft-cited apologist for technology as it is currently organized, a wealthy contractor, conveys his excitement with technology, the passionate relations between men and machine. Engineers, he says, have yet to express their own powerful feelings about technology. He gives examples, quoting from literature, the Bible, and so on, describing structures and fabrics and machines and tools with sensual delight:

> From Frank's "Panama Canal slashing its way through the tropical jungle: its gray sobriety is apart from the luxuriance of nature. Its willfulness is victor over a voluptuary world that will lift no vessels, that would bar all vessels"; from Kipling, on how the "Feed pump sobs and heaves"; Spender's airliner, "more beautiful and soft than any moth, with burring furred antennae . . . gently, broadly she falls"; McKenna's description of engineer meeting engine. "'Hello engine. I'm Jake Holman' he said under his breath. Jake Holman loved machinery in the way some other men love God, women and their country"; Longfellow's ship which "Feels the thrill of life along her keel" as she "leaps into the Ocean's arms!" Platonov's engineer who enters "into the very essence of the abstruse, inanimate mechanisms . . . actually feeling the degree of intensity of an electrical current as if it were a secret passion of his own"; the pilot who "Passed his fingers along a steep rib and felt the stream of life that flowed in it. . . . The engine's gentle current fraying its ice-cold rind into a velvety bloom." (pp. 133–39)

This is steamy stuff! But what about real live women? Florman cites the engineer who says, "I'm in love, Chief." He hears from his boss, "So was I once, but I shut myself up for three weeks and worked at an air machine. Grew so excited I forgot the girl. You try it" (p. 38). Florman explicitly acknowledges the safety and comfort of technology, the world of things and machines, compared with the confusion and conflict of the social world of human interaction. As above, the passion culturally ascribed to the erotic or sexual sphere often drives that of the technical. The technical is coyly eroticized, and, with it, the relations of dominance and submission, sometimes driven by violence and fear.

Some spoof this phenomenon and its trappings, as in Norman Spinrad's brilliant satire on Fascism and eroticism, the science fiction novel *The Iron Dream* (1972; compare Le Guin 1975). The novel contains no women, but is chock full of detailed descriptions of heel clicking and truncheon wielding, outrageous perceptions of the world and others, technologies as exaggerated extensions of the human form, and the peculiar intense interest in uniforms, never complete without the ubiquitous "bright shiny metal work."[1]

Valverde (1987) describes milder forms of the eroticization of domination, in which one simply desires to be overwhelmed by the erotic force and power of the other, not necessarily experiencing pain or humiliation in the process. These and other forms of eroticized power relations seem apparent in many older men/younger men scientific and technological scenarios, as in the frenzied social relations of high-tech production systems and products (Edwards 1985, 1986). Many young men in the field experience a special high in being driven to inhuman intensity and competition with their brothers by the older men of the tribe (Kidder 1981). (This of course may be characteristic of all, not merely technical disciplines.)

Inmates of various institutions – schools, prisons, monasteries, madhouses, and barracks – order themselves in proper space, time and motion, to prescribed muscle movement, posture, and attitude. These culturally approved techniques of control do the job more efficiently than any external authority. I have suggested elsewhere that these techniques, this "microphysics of power" (Foucault 1979, 139), may be easily observed today in the structure of the engineering classroom and curriculum. What I failed to note was the extent to which the techniques of constant examination and grading controlled professor more than student.

In that experience I learned how it felt, day by day, sometimes minute by minute, to encounter a subtle control, largely self-imposed, that affects both mind and body. I learned that many of the faculty were as turned off by the hidden curriculum as I, and felt it impaired the students' ability to learn to do good engineering. The overall impression was one of intense discipline – particularly over pleasures and the use of time. I also came to appreciate the special privileges, delights, and fascinations of the field and to understand the faculty I had interviewed earlier a little better. I saw how others reacted as well, friends and colleagues holding back from demands on my time now that they saw me as engaged in "important" work. Above all, I learned how engineering education is embedded in a context of rational criteria for the practice of engineering that is essential to leadership in bureaucratic organization—control of sensuality, emotions, passion, one's very physical rhythms. Dominance in such rationally ordered institutions is indeed inscribed on the body (Foucault 1979).

It is no surprise to find relations of dominance and submission an important part of the curriculum in our engineering classrooms (Snyder 1971). Bart Hacker (1987) shows the origins of engineering education in military institutions of the eighteenth century. Max Weber (1968) suggests that military institutions provide the model for discipline in all major social institutions. He notes that "military discipline gives birth to all discipline" and it has always in some way affected the structure of the state, the economy, and possibly the family. As Fatima Mernissi (1975) observes, without the control of men's eroticism, armies would be impossible.

Eighteenth- and nineteenth-century debates over the form of training of a new military and administrative leadership reveal many motives for the teaching of mathematics and science. These subjects would "cool the passions," "calm the fires of youth." "Math was used to educate gentlemen, not to train mathematicians" (Enroe 1981). The way these subjects were taught was also important. Rationalized examinations in mathematics and science, by which students were to be rejected or accepted, ranked, and placed, provided a filter against all but the most disciplined, or repressed, as Davis (1980) would have it.

Noble's *America by Design* (1977) shows the predominance of military institutions in the forming of engineering education, and the men in it, at the turn of this century. Public and vocational education soon followed. Military forms of discipline, standardization of "parts" (men), hierarchy and order pervaded university engineering and then spread to secondary education through programs such as vocational education. This process further strengthened that arid technical rationality built on suppressed emotion decried earlier by critical theorists and radical feminists.

Thus control of passion, particularly among men, shapes the organization of technology and technical education in fascinating form. It is but one note in the important theme (Kandiyoti 1984) that the first purpose of patriarchy is the control of most men by a few older men with power. And it is in our interest to continue to learn how we persuade and are persuaded to give up so much for so little. Some of us are seduced by gendered, stratified, and eroticized technologies—both machine and social technics of dominance.

THE TECHNICAL IN THE EROTIC

As men specialize in technology and its disciplines and relations of dominance, women are also specialized. As erotic passion may influence technology, so may technological exhilaration inform erotic activity. Eugene Ferguson (cited in Hounshell 1984) calls attention to the exhilaration technologists feel for their work, an intense pleasure and arousal at the core of technological development and innovation, captured most recently by Kidder (1981). Ferguson warns against too economistic an analysis of technology, and says we ignore the role of exhilaration in the organization of technology at our peril. I agree. Above, I have suggested ways in which gendered eroticism shapes its technology to fit. Here, I want to explore the masculine nature of technological exhilaration for its influence on the shape of eroticism.

Some may merely delight in the exercise of technique or skill, while remaining distant from passionate involvement in process or goals of others.[2] Homey examples of technological excitement as it influences erotic activities may be found in extensive directions for use of fashion, cosmetics, or sex toys; or in explicit suggestions for women to please their men, through techniques and technologies of clothing, scents, postures, or numerous social and physical accoutrements. Manuals for service workers in the sex industry (see Delacoste and Alexander 1987; McLeod 1982) and related service industries (Hochschild 1982) or prescriptive books for fundamentalist housewives, provide fascinating analyses of the technology of eroticism (see MacCannell and MacCannell 1987; Brownmiller 1984; Banner 1983). Comparative research would be rewarding (as well as fun) with the antierotic sex and hygiene manuals issued by the U.S. military, the first form of sex education for several generations of young men. These technologies of eroticism have been exchanged among women for centuries (Jones 1987). Erasmus in 1523 warned young men not to let their women gossip with married women, who would share these valuable skills of manipulation (Thompson 1965).

Rita Sabagh's (1983) ethnographic study of the "sex goddesses" in an L.A. mafia strip joint seems to provide a contemporary explication of the technologies of sexual power. One can tease, throw out a jerk, allow measured familiarities depending on tips, place one's cigarette near a favorite at the bar to indicate one's intent to return. However, in such a situation, the participant's attention is rarely captured by the overwhelmingly male-defined political and economic setting. One is more impressed by the moment-to-moment interpersonal power of women over the men who enter as customers.

Similarly, Valverde (1987, 40–41) describes the sexiest women in society, those who most skillfully maximize "feminine wiles," the passive power to grant and withhold. Such wily women exercise skills of timing and manipulation with such expertise that these politics of powerlessness, this passive power, "almost looks and feels like active power." Within a situation defined by others, it sometimes works.

Machine as well as social technics are seductive. In the passion to control desire, or shape it through technologies of discipline, one can become intrigued with transforming the body itself into a machine. The vulnerability of being human, especially female, in a world that increasingly prefers the flawless and mechanical (Noble 1984), is expressed in Haraway's (1985) brilliant essay on cyborgs. Perhaps the fear of punishment for freely expressing erotic capability encourages us, particularly men, to channel the energy safely toward the machine.[3]

In its most obvious and fetishistic mode, perhaps, technological exhilaration may fasten on the loving care and maintenance of S/M equipment and tools (Samois 1987). Intense concern for erotic skill and technique can be observed in conversations with managers in the sex industry (for example, the 1982 film *Not a Love Story*) or in the discourse of sex therapists (see English et al. 1982; Rubin 1984, 1987). The fascination with measurement appears in the practice of sex researchers who attach electrodes and rings to the penises of sex offenders viewing erotic material (Griffitt 1987), as if these objective data could give access to human thought and emotion.

There are, then, some striking interpenetrations of erotic and technological spheres. Examining one in light of the other can be both interesting and illuminating. We can explore in greater detail points of contact in debates over definitions and concepts, parallel theoretical concerns and related conclusions, and the strategies we adopt toward whatever it is we define as the social problems (Schneider 1985; Woolgar and Pawluch 1985a, 1985b; Pfohl 1985; Hazelrigg 1985) of technology and pornography/eroticism. The problems of one—technology or pornography—will not be alleviated in isolation from the other. The two are only apparently ideologically separated, and it is one of our most pleasurable tasks to degender and reunite technology and eroticism openly. Finally, I suggest that unexplored class differences among proponents of various arguments cloud the debates, and inhibit unified action necessary to deal effectively with antifeminist forces.

Concepts and Definitions in the Debates on Technology and Pornography

For the last several years, in the United States and elsewhere, feminists have debated and discussed and struggled to define sexuality, particularly eroticism, and a particular kind of eroticism, pornography (see Valverde 1987; Smith and Waisburg 1985, for annotated bibliography; Vance 1984; also Hacker et al. 1984).

Some feminists would eliminate pornography as it is produced, or as it is consumed. This view of pornography emphasizes women's and children's relative powerlessness in patriarchal society. Women's image in sexual material affects both men and women viewers, and is an instrument of gender domination socially constructed by men to maintain women's subordination to men's desires. From this perspective, less against sex than against violence, sex can be playful, gentle, rough, hetero- or homosexual, but should exclude relations of dominance and violence. Sexuality is best expressed in relationships of egalitarian community, or long-term relationships of mutual trust and commitment. Female imagery in pornography subverts the possibility of such egalitarian relationships. Pornography rouses prurient interest, demeans women or sexuality in general, eroticizes domination, and is morally offensive (Linden et al. 1982). As Andrea Dworkin (1979, 1983) says of the definitions: in patriarchal society, pornography is women; women are pornography.

A few, sometimes called sex radicals, say all of that is true, and they like it that way. They emphasize a person's right to choose her own type of hetero- or homosexual behavior, to work in or consume the products of the sex industry as any other, as a path to liberation from older, more puritanical stereotypes. Some activists oppose censorship and boycotts, speak to women workers in the sex industry, and demand greater protection of civil liberties of sex radicals. Efforts to block the production and consumption of pornography may undermine civil rights (Burstyn 1985). Any regulation of pornography may be extended to feminist and lesbian material, and women to workers in the sex industry. Still others say it is impossible to differentiate pornography from eroticism, except in the eye of each beholder. They argue against censorship and for increasing dialogue on sexuality. Sex can be playful, gentle, or violent, can include relations of dominance and submission, and can take place in superficial, temporary relations. For some, this is the only kind that is exciting, and feminism should also liberate our right to choose our own sexuality. They argue that antipornographer feminists went "over the heads of the [sex] workers," threatening their employment and dignity at work. Sex radicals answer arguments against the exploitation and brutalization of women and children by noting that any waged work is exploitive, that children's sexuality should not be repressed, and that the sex industry often offers the only escape route from even more violent and brutalizing families (Rubin 1984, 1987; Califia 1987; Delacoste and Alexander 1987; Constantine and Martinson 1981).

To sex radicals, antipornography feminists appear puritanical, antimale, and antisex, wanting to define a sanitized feminist sexuality for all. "Vanilla sex," the "missionary position of the women's movement" (Rubin 1987), soft, gentle sex in relationships of long-term commitment to others, "doesn't do a thing for my clit," as one puts it at a meeting of Leather and Lace (Los Angeles, 1983). Another asks why women get stuck with eroticism while "men get to do the interesting things, like violence and aggression." Games of domination, sadomasochistic role playing, are experienced as exciting. These practices provide a route out of restrictive, passive, erotic roles for women. Sex radicals themselves threaten to degender eroticism, claiming for women a participation, a style, formerly appropriate for men only. And interestingly, sex radical texts display something of the technocrats' compulsion for technique, with prescriptions for the proper care and use of sadomasochistic toys and tools (Samois 1987).

Interestingly, in a debate less familiar in feminist circles, similar questions surround the definition of technology. Some think technology refers merely to machinery (as sexuality might refer to genitals), while others insist it means the entire set of social relations within which the machinery is designed, developed, and used (Staudenmaier 1985). Some argue that technology is shaped by historical and material relations, even if totally socially constructed. The machine has no meaning outside that which we give it through interaction. Similarly, feminist scholars argue that all sexuality is socially constructed; there is no absolute, really "natural" sexuality other than that which is in our minds (Stimpson and Person 1980; Rich 1980; Ferguson et al. 1981).

Some define technology broadly as the organization of material and energy to accomplish work; the research has recently been extended by women's studies scholars to include household technology and the work of homemaking (Bose et al. 1984; Cowan 1983). It could be extended as well to work performed in the sex industry. Others say that this definition is much too broad and thus includes everything—a similar argument against defining sexuality as pleasure.

Occasionally, the legitimacy of the concepts themselves is called into question. As some suggest that the very concept of technology takes our attention off real power relations of class and productive forces (Noble 1984), so others suggest the concepts of pornography (Ehrenreich et al. 1986) and eroticism (Foucault 1979) do the same. The concepts themselves are diversions, distracting attention from the real issues: alliances, relationships of power and control. Some go so far as to say that technology studies may have been created for this purpose. Likewise, the pornography debate takes our minds off the economic and political subordination of women, and how difficult these conditions are to resist.

There is no single, parallel, negative term for a kind of technology that rouses prurient interest, demeans the powerless, eroticizes domination, or offends along a moral dimension. We could all think of technologies that fill this bill, such as the short hoe recently outlawed for migrant field workers, nuclear energy, or the fat American car; tools of torture, or weapons systems; chemical technologies for the exciting and often eroticized domination and control of nature (Hacker 1985). Many do describe such technologies as pornographic.

As with the sex radicals, there are those who agree, but like it that way. Some have described to me the beauties of napalm, difficult to understand without "being there": "You really have to see it in action to appreciate it." Or the excitement of watching weeds "grow themselves to death" in the search for chemical defoliants; the challenge to implant the embryo of a calf into the womb of a rabbit for cheaper transportation to a Third World country; or the curiosity to see whether a bioengineered calf will be too large for live birthing.

The only terms we have for technologies embodying hierarchical social relations are Lewis Mumford's (1967) "megamachine," or Langdon Winner's (1977) "autonomous technology." These seem somewhat bland terms for the technologies and social relations described above, which so specifically eroticize domination, as in tools and training designed to inflict pain on a helpless prisoner, perhaps for the erotic gratification of the captor. Bart Hacker has suggested coining another term, "pornotechnics," with which we could analyze, comparatively, "pornographics."

Similar political implications surround the definition of pornotechnics as of pornographics. For example, some of us may find our favorite forms of technological excitement classified as politically incorrect—the rides we love to scare ourselves with at the carnival, the fast cars and motorcycles of our young (and not so young) adulthood, the risks we willingly share with others in outdoor adventure, the chemicals we freely consume. Finally, it is not difficult to imagine who might be morally offended at the control by the working class, or by the enlisted soldiers, of certain "command" technologies (Noble 1985).[4]

In the debate over technology, too, one side addresses power held among those who research, design, implement, and distribute new technologies. People, even the earth itself, may often be the victim of such innovations. Activists argue for the elimination of industries from and for which these destructive technologies emerge. Technology can be playful, exciting, but not violent or set in social relations of dominance; it should emerge from democratic communities, within long-term relationships of mutual trust and commitment, in relations of caring for others and the natural world (Cooley 1982). The other side argues that a free expression of technological imagination benefits all. If everyone is allowed his or her free expression to invent, to create, to consume the technology of his or her choice, the wellsprings of human creativity will be unleashed, perhaps providing a way out of much of the existential alienation of the modern world. Activists oppose attempts to curb research and development, and argue greater freedom for the free play of invention (Florman 1981; Rybczynski 1983).

The parallels in these debates over strategy raise interesting questions for us, which return us to the issues of community and power. Do those in the environmental movement, for example, argue for a "vanilla technology"? Do they want a sanitized technology, cleansed of the excitement of danger and risk? Are they really antitechnology, modern Luddites, as their opponents claim, similar to the antisex, puritanical members of the antiporn feminists? Do they want to lead us back to the closed societies of the past, characterized by stagnation and informal moral and social control?

On the other hand, are those who argue for laissez-faire technology or eroticism really blind to the relations of power within which both are designed, developed, and distributed? Do they really believe that entry to the field is democratic and open to all? Will more women in engineering change the organization of technology? Will more women playing masculine games of eroticized dominance change the organization of eroticism? Are most of these arguments actually self-serving (to those who make their living through the Department of Defense, or the sex industry, or are dependent on others who do)?

Class Contradictions in the Debates on Technology and Eroticism

In the case of both technology and pornography, some of the debate, then, turns around the definitions: What is it? Who gets to define it? And, perhaps most important, who gets to define what as a social problem? But problems of class as well as gender are relevant.

Those who rule truly fear a working class in control of its own technology, or its own eroticism. The voluminous literature on the labor process documents the former. And here is a military example. Susan Douglas (1985) analyzes the U.S. Navy's adoption of radio communication, an adoption not welcomed by the previously independent heads of bureaus, and captains of ships, who were now in communication with central control while out to sea, coerced, coordinated, cajoled by the powers that be, helped by the disaster of the *Titanic*, to adopt this new technology. Among points of contention was whether or not enlisted men were to be trained as operators and allowed free, unmonitored use of the equipment. The strategy for adoption would be more successful if officers could be involved. The winning argument for officers came with the observation that unenlisted men used the equipment for irreverent comments about their work and supervisors, and to chat up their girlfriends back in port.

Studies of early twentieth-century working-class leisure (Peiss 1983) and sexuality (Bullough 1987; Money 1985) show excessive concern over urban youth pleasure in general, and masturbation in particular. Thus, the docile worker or woman is good; that worker or woman is dangerous who messes with his or her own equipment, one way or the other. Such fears led not only to the various youth club movements in the twenties, to control the troublesome energy of the immigrant youth (Pivar 1972; DuBois and Gordon 1984; Woloch 1984), but to such bizarre inventions as J. H. Kellogg's (as in cornflakes) "birdcage" device to be worn around the waist by young girls, to prevent masturbation (Kellogg 1882).

Unfortunately, within the working class itself, as Cockburn (1983, 1985) demonstrates, control over technology and technical skill is a core element of masculinity, defining one male worker against another and stratifying male workers. Control over technical skills is also a painful source of contradiction and division between men and women, as the working-class man and his union fail to include women in the technological enterprise. Feminine control by some over the exercise of erotic skills is equally potentially divisive among working-class women (Walker 1982) and is certainly a key to the division of man from woman.

The working-class man may gender eroticism and technology to the detriment of solidarity among working-class people. Realizing the problematics of defining class among women (Acker 1988), I want to focus on ways in which women's class background may encourage us to work against each other on these dimensions of technology and eroticism.

Middle-class and working-class men are seriously divided on the current organization of technology, its apparent threat to health and safety, its ability to provide the comfortable living we have come to expect, its implications for a democratic society. Middle-class and working-class women may be divided on eroticism for analogous reasons. Within the debate on pornography/eroticism, in my experience theoretical support for the sex radical position is often offered by socialist feminists, speaking for and to the working class. Such analyses oppose censorship or limits, in part because those limits would likely come down hard on feminist and homosexual/lesbian material, and on women workers in the sex industry. But most socialist feminists I know, even those working in laundries, factories, and restaurants, are upper-middle-class in origin.

On the other hand, though most of the radical feminists I know are indeed middle-class or professional, their origins are working-class. Many argue against pornography and violence against women, and are termed middle-class "cultural feminists" by their opposition. In the early 1980s, a legitimate concern for sexual violence and abuse of women and children led feminists (called "cultural feminists" by the Left opposition, to indicate a lack of material analysis) to a somewhat overdrawn picture of woman as victim and male sexuality as aggressive and dangerous. One strategy is to eliminate the pornographic stimulus for this. The practice following from such perspectives tends toward the politics of the powerless, seeking protectors.

Thus, an upper-middle-class socialist analysis of eroticism argues greater freedom and less restriction on sexual behavior, arguments that many working-class women may find appalling. On the other hand, the "middle-class feminist" fighting pornography and violence against women may speak more directly to the way in which working-class women construct sexual reality (Dworkin 1983).

This informal observation about the class origins of friends on either side of the debate led me to test the notion by questionnaire among 120 of my undergraduate students—a fair cross section of a large land-grant university, mostly but not entirely white and protestant, Pacific Northwest and therefore somewhat more socially conservative than East Coast or Midwest, half working-class in origin (plywood mills, food packing plants, clerical worker parents, with moderate to low income), and half middle- or upper-middle-class (professional, entrepreneurial with high incomes).

For several days, we discussed the two sides of the debate—sex radical and radical feminist, as I had experienced it during an ethnographic study in Los Angeles, in 1982 and 1983. In addition, five of us, feminists with different positions on these issues, met over potluck once a month to hash it out (Hacker et al. 1984) and try for as balanced a presentation as possible.

In response, the majority of students rejected both positions as too extreme, or wanted a position that incorporated what they considered to be the best of both. Of the 30 to 40 percent who did make a choice, the major difference was not by class, but by sex. Almost all those who chose the sex radical position were males. After sex, class did matter. Most of the young men and all of the women who chose this position were middle- and upper-class in origin. Working-class kids, and all working-class young women who chose one or the other position, chose the antipornography stance of the radical feminists.

In one question, I asked those who saw the sex industry as providing jobs like any other how they would react if their sons or daughters chose the profession, as managers or workers. Most of those who chose the sex radical position, the middle- or upper-class college young people, made it clear they had no prejudice against these professions – for other people's children. They stated it was unlikely their own would make such a choice.

Thus, socialist feminists who argue the sex radical position, and usually in the name of or for the benefit of the working-class woman, have missed the mark. Ideologies of decency and romance may be strongest among the working class (Snitow 1983; Vance 1983), accounting for the otherwise most puzzling support of antiwomen policies and politicians (see Dworkin 1983; the literature on romance novels, the literature on ideologies of working-class women).

Contradictions and Questions

We find ourselves caught in peculiar contradictions in the debates over pornography/eroticism and over technology. It is, of course, at these painful moments, when we find ourselves "of two minds" that we may withdraw, hang on to old comforts, familiar problems and discourses. Or possibly we may be able to break out of older habits and see the problem afresh. Are there any two spheres as greatly gendered as eroticism and technology? I suggest we ask the questions we are familiar with in one area or the other. Some examples:

☐ Some wonder whether either technology or eroticism/pornography is inherently good or evil, or whether the value merely lies in the eye of the beholder. Does the Buddha, as Robert Pirsig (1975) claims, rest as easily in the transistors of a computer as in the petals of the lotus? What, then, do we do with the knowledge that both computer and transistor but not lotus were designed and shaped by military needs? (See Smith 1985; Edwards 1985; Tirman 1984; Misa 1985.) If the artifacts of technology contain a politics, as Langdon Winner (1980) suggests, what about the technologies and practices of eroticism?

☐ Do we substitute violent for erotic imagery, and are the two fused in our culture at this moment? Do we substitute violent for playful technology, and are those activities confounded? How does the common person experience technology or eroticism?

☐ Should there be limits on the creative expression of either technology or eroticism? Set by whom? What would technology or eroticism look like, if freed from the context of domination and exploitation? How much of contemporary alienation is cause or effect of existing pornotechnic or pornographic relations? How much of the analysis flows directly from the writer's (including this one's) concrete experiences?

☐ What is our active, participative role as subjects in the construction of technology and eroticism in the activities of daily life? Even given that both are defined, designed, and shaped by a few for the many, how are we encouraged, seduced, to support these constrained meanings by taking part in technological or erotic activities so defined in the round of everyday activities? Is resistance on this level sufficient?

Both technology and eroticism show signs of a degendering transformation. Women do enter the crafts and engineering. This entry of women into new technologies threatens the masculinity of some craftsmen, while other men enter traditionally women's fields such as nursing (Cockburn 1983, 1985). A new eroticism legitimates a pouting, "feminine" style for men, and a tougher, teasing, "masculine" stance for women.[5]

Today, as engineering undergoes the deskilling and degradation familiar to older crafts, working-class women are encouraged to enter those aspects of engineering and computer science next most likely to suffer automation, such as drafting and design (Kraft and Dubroff 1983). In erotic activity, women are encouraged to be independent and aggressive, to depend less and less on men.

As Dworkin notes in *Right-Wing Women* (1983), women are not stupid. Even knowing that the old protections, economic and physical, do not work, there is at this point no alternative, short of a revolution in all major social institutions. And no revolutionary force at the moment is also feminist. The few support systems for women's economic and political independence dwindle, particularly in the working class. Thus it is especially important to explicate various ideologies, to see wherein we are confused about class perhaps, to examine closely those points at which we may be most easily manipulated by those with vested interests in maintaining hierarchical and patriarchal relations.[6]

Conclusion

A marvel of our experience is found in the different ways in which we delight each other and ourselves. The pleasures and delights of technology and eroticism do not need to be gendered. Men and women can enjoy the activities of either. The problem is neither technology nor pornography, but the deep and pervasive difference in power between, and limits on spheres appropriate for, men and women. But this means foregrounding, not burying the connections between technology and eroticism, for these are the processes most successful in mystifying the relations of power.

"Where there is strong eroticism, there is power," as Mariana Valverde (1987, 47) notes. But equality, not gendered power, can be eroticized without enveloping everything "in the soft mists of tenderness and harmony" (p. 43). An imbalance of power is woven into the social fabric of all civilized societies and is expressed in the social control of both technology and eroticism. We are born into a society with traditional and enduring institutions. In this chapter, I have tried to show how we also support these institutions by taking part in them in our everyday lives.

Most of us find at least some technology sexy, erotic, engendering some passion, strong feeling, comfort or pleasure. For some this will be the technology of dazzling weapons systems, with their speed, elegance, complexity, and power, or the high-science technologies of scientific, or even social scientific, research; for others, automobiles, motorcycles, or our own personal computers. Then there are the areas of traditional "women's technologies," perhaps called "women's" because of the absence of the elements of risk and danger, or the relatively small number of people influenced at once—cooking, language, photography, basket weaving, pottery, gardening, the technology of fashion or cosmetics. The contemporary images of eroticism and of machine and system reflect the imagination and desires of the designer. How could it or should it be otherwise in any human venture?

An imbalance of power and resources means, however, that the designs of both technology and eroticism primarily reflect the desires of a certain class of men. These designs will at times reflect the hostility and suspicion this dominant group has, for us, the subordinated group, and possibly for the natural world as well.

Ann Kaplan (1983) describes the "male gaze" in the construction of pornography. Men see, view, point, photograph, write. That gaze may idealize women or watch us with suspicion and hostility. Kaplan suggests that filmmakers, photographers, and authors could imagine both male and female gazes, which can lead to an unconscious delight in mutual gazing.

The fusion of eroticism and technical exhilaration need not be expressed in relations of dominance—firecrackers as opposed to firearms, for example; the Golden Gate Bridge's cables plucked like a harp; as in Henry Petroski's *To Engineer Is Human* (1985), playfully comparing the human body walking, turning, lifting a child, to the cranes, scaffolding, pulleys, and mechanics of building and engineering, to explain how much each of us knows "by nature." Sensual delights with texture, light, sound, taste, and smell inform the world of the infant as well as the sexual delights of one's own and others' flesh and form and energy.

But given our humanness, there are also the abuses of power of which we are capable. We have to figure out the best arrangements, structures, and processes to minimize such excess, those that bring out the best in us without expecting ever to eliminate the worst. This is what continuing revolution is all about.

Neither eroticism nor technology should be defined and shaped by a few. Neither should be difficult or expensive to experience for the many. An appropriate technology or eroticism, a democratic technics, could allow the vision and imagination of all to shape a new society. But these fine sentiments are not enough. Those in power do not of their own volition offer to share it with the powerless. And it will take more than willing and wishing our own way of constructing reality in our circumscribed areas of direct face-to-face contact. And so I return to the notion that to change relations in gender and technology, we will have to work together, often with people we don't like a lot, to change the relations of power in the community.

More has been suggested on appropriate technology communities than on appropriate erotic communities. One problem was and is that by choice we live in one of the three most highly mobile societies in the world. It appears that communities, cities, societies in rapid social change are those wherein we need most of all to build strong local and neighborly affinity groups, to develop our own technology and eroticism—this time not so cozy and intolerant of difference, not so class/taste/race based, more open. The same principles that we found could create community in the midst of rapid change before, and that often led to sharing of skills and techniques, to a more democratic technics, could also lead to greater freedom and creativity in erotic expression. These were not easy efforts, nor were they free of conflict.

I am not sure we have the luxury of returning to individual solutions. People in such communities making open decisions with each other, and openly helping children of the community to make decisions as they mature, should be able to approximate communities wherein work, as Marx puts it, is an act of freedom and a source of human creativity (see Street 1983). In that case, the organization of material and energy to accomplish work, embedded in relationships of democratic technics, might once again unite technology and eroticism, freed of the authoritarian dimension that has distorted both since military institutions emerged some 5,000 years ago.

NOTES

1. Those unfamiliar with military history museums may be amazed at the amount of space—most, in my recollection of museums in several different countries—devoted to fashion: case after case of jackets with ribbons and braids, hats with feathers and ornaments, boots, leather, much of it studded with some version of Spinrad's bright, shiny metal work, and all of it taken quite seriously, indeed. Spinrad was truly a man ahead of his time in the fashion world of S/M.

2. As Tom Lehrer (1981) suggests for Werner Von Braun, Georg Simmel (1984) claims for the flirt.

3. There is no denying that for many of us, such channeling is most pleasurable. I explored the seduction of the abstract and the mathematical in my ethnographic study of the engineering students. The pleasures are not unlike those of the empirical social sciences, or the abstraction of any professional discipline or calling, which offers a buffer against the demands of "women's work," unrewarded work in the community.

4. Some radio and film technologies are now possessed solely by the military. Twenty years ago, in Houston, we tried to buy infrared, heat-sensitive film equipment for our son to play with. He was fascinated by film and its related technology. Whether true or not, we were told such equipment could be purchased only by police or the military. I still experience a sense of rage at this incident. As a HAM operator, I am sensitive too, to the increasing military possession of frequencies and other technologies of communication.

5. As always there is greater freedom, less punishment for such cross-sex behavior in the upper middle class than in the working class. Analyses of causes of high school dropouts, or arrest rates, may well indicate these tendencies. Donald Black in *The Behavior of Law* (1976) notes such effects on children with one—insufficiently patriarchal family—parent.

6. Truly ethnic and urban experience will make a difference; Peiss (1983) observes that New York ethnic migrants have greatly varied traditions of heterosociality, Germans and Italians holding polar positions. Working-class women in those times and places may have played out a different, gutsier sexuality than today. But as Gordon notes, the working class in England has been extremely sexually conservative for decades. The picture that emerges from the histories of sexuality portray sex radicals in two lights. One picture shows us well-heeled men and opportunistic women of any class. Others, working- and middle-class radicals, organized around the sexual freedom of themselves and others, linked these to other struggles and issues and landed in jail for their efforts (Kansas City, nineteenth century). By and large today, evidence such as we have would suggest more sexual conservatism among the working class.

On the other issue the working class may be less likely to be critical of technology and technologists, suspicious in fact of environmental movements that show little concern for employment. I have been struck over and again by the strong beliefs in "progress" and positive attitudes toward technological change even among those whose jobs are most likely to be threatened.

References

Acker, Joan. 1988. "Class, Gender, and the Relations of Distribution." *Signs* 13: 473–97.

Banner, Lois W. 1983. *American Beauty*. New York: Alfred A. Knopf.

Black, Donald J. 1976. *The Behavior of Law*. New York: Academic Press.

Bose, Christine E., Philip L. Bereano, and Mary Malloy. 1984. "Household Technology and the Social Construction of Housework." *Technology and Culture* 25: 53–82.

Brownmiller, Susan. 1984. *Femininity*. New York: Linden Press/Simon & Schuster.

Bullough, Vern. 1987. "Technology for the Prevention of 'Les Maladies Produites par la Masturbation.'" *Technology and Culture* 28: 828–32.

Burstyn, Varda, ed. 1985. *Women against Censorship*. Vancouver, BC: Douglas & McIntyre.

Califia, Pat. 1987. "A Personal View of the History of the Lesbian S/M Community and Movement in San Francisco." *Coming to Power: Writings and Graphics in Lesbian S/M*, ed. members of Samois, 245–83. Boston: Alyson.

Cockburn, Cynthia (1983). *Brothers: Male Brothers and Technological Change*. London: Pluto.

———. 1985. *Machinery of Dominance: Women, Men and Technical Know-How*. London: Pluto.

Cohn, Carol. 1987. "Sex and Death in the Rational World of Defense Intellectuals." *Signs* 12: 687–718.

Constantine, Larry L., and Floyd M. Martinson, eds. 1981. *Children and Sex: New Findings, New Perspectives*. Boston: Little, Brown.

Cooley, Michael. 1982. *Architect or Bee? The Human/Technology Relationship*. Boston: South End.

Cowan, Ruth Schwartz. 1983. *More Work for Mother: The Ironies of Household Technology from the Open Hearth to the Microwave*. New York: Basic Books.

Davis, Chandler. 1980. "Where Did Twentieth-Century Mathematics Go Wrong?" Paper presented at the joint annual meetings of the Society for the History of Technology, History of Science Society, Philosophy of Science Association, and Society for the Social Study of Science, Toronto.

Delacoste, Frederique, and Priscilla Alexander, eds. 1987. *Sex Work: Writings by Women in the Sex Industry*. San Francisco and Pittsburgh: Cleis.

Douglas, Susan. 1985. "The Navy Adopts the Radio, 1899–1919." In *Military Enterprise and Technological Change: Perspectives on the American Experience*, ed. Merritt Roe Smith, 117–73. Cambridge: MIT Press.

DuBois, Ellen Carol, and Linda Gordon. 1984. "Seeking Ecstasy on the Battlefield: Danger and Pleasure in Nineteenth-Century Feminist Sexual Thoughts." In *Pleasure and Danger: Exploring Female Sexuality*, ed. Carole S. Vance, 31–49. Boston: Routledge & Kegan Paul.

Dworkin, Andrea. 1979. *Pornography: Men Possessing Women*. New York: Perigee.

———. 1983. *Right-Wing Women*. New York: Wideview/Perigee.

Easlea, Brian. 1983. *Fathering the Unthinkable: Masculinity, Scientists and the Nuclear Arms Race*. London: Pluto.

Edwards, Paul N. 1985. "Technologies of the Mind: Computers, Power, Psychology, and World War II" (Working Paper No. 2). Silicon Valley Research Group, University of California, Santa Cruz.

———. 1986. "Artificial Intelligence and High Technology War: The Perspective of the Formal Machine" (Working Paper No. 6). Silicon Valley Research Group, University of California, Santa Cruz.

Ehrenreich, Barbara, Elizabeth Hess, and Gloria Jacobs. 1986. *Remaking Love: The Feminization of Sex*. Garden City, NY: Anchor.

English, Deirdre, Amber Hollibaugh, and Gayle Rubin. 1982. "Talking Sex: A Conversation on Sexuality and Feminism." *Feminist Review* 11 (Summer): 40–52. (Reprinted from *Socialist Review* 58 [1981], 43–62.)

Enroe, Phillip C. 1981. "Cambridge University and the Adaptation of Analytics in Early 19th Century England." In *Social History of Nineteenth Century Mathematics*, eds. Herbert Mehrtens, Henk Bos, and Ivo Schneider, 135–48. Boston: Birkhauser.

Ferguson, Ann, Jacquelyn N. Zita, and Kathryn Pyne Addelson. 1981. "On 'Compulsory Heterosexuality and Lesbian Existence': Defining the Issues." *Signs* 7: 158–99.

Florman, Samuel. 1976. *The Existential Pleasures of Engineering.* New York: St. Martin's Press.

———. 1981. *Blaming Technology: The Irrational Search for Scapegoats.* New York: St. Martin's Press.

Foucault, Michel. 1979. *Discipline and Punish: The Birth of the Prison.* Trans. Alan Sheridan. New York: Vintage.

Griffin, Susan. 1981. *Pornography and Silence: Culture's Revolt against Nature.* New York: Harper & Row.

Griffitt, William. 1987. "Females, Males, and Sexual Responses." In *Females, Males, and Sexuality: Theories and Research,* ed. Kathryn Kelley, 141–73. Albany: State University of New York Press.

Hacker, Bart. 1982. "Imaginations in Thrall: The Social Psychology of Military Mechanization, 1919–1939." *Parameters* 12 (March): 50–61.

———. 1987. "'A Corps of Able Engineers' Military Institutions and Technical Education since the 18th Century." Paper presented at the annual meeting of the Society for the History of Technology, Durham, N.C.

Hacker, Sally L. 1985. "Doing It the Hard Way: Ethnographic Study of Ideology in Agribusiness and Engineering Classes." *Humanity and Society* 9: 123–41.

Hacker, Sally L., Eleen Baumann, Dorice Tentschoff, Jule Wind, and Sutree Irving. 1984. "Some Material and Ideological Bases of the Radical Sex Controversy." Paper presented at the annual meeting of the Society for the Study of Social Problems, San Antonio, Tex.

Haraway, Donna J. 1985. "A Manifesto for Cyborgs: Science, Technology, and Socialist Feminism in the 1980s." *Socialist Review* 80: 65–107.

Hazelrigg, Lawrence E. 1985. "Were It Not for Words." *Social Problems* 32: 234–37.

Hochschild, Arlie Russell. 1982. "Emotional Labor in the Friendly Skies." *Psychology Today* 16 (June), 13–15.

Hounshell, David A. 1984. *From the American System to Mass Production, 1800–1932: The Development of Manufacturing Technology in the United States.* Baltimore: Johns Hopkins University Press.

Jones, Ann Rosalind. 1987. "Nets and Bridles: Early Modern Conduct Books and Sixteenth-Century Women's Lyrics." In *The Ideology of Conflict: Essays on Literature and the History of Sexuality,* eds. Nancy Armstrong and Leonard Tennehouse, 39–71. New York: Methuen.

Kandiyoti, Deniz. 1984. "Women and Society." Address on women and development presented at Oregon State University, Corvallis.

———. 1977. Men and Women of the Corporation. New York: Basic Books.

Kaplan, E. Ann. 1983. "Is the Gaze Male?" In *Powers of Desire: The Politics of Sexuality,* eds. Ann Snitow, Christine Stansell, and Sharon Thompson, 309–27. New York: Monthly Review Press.

Kellogg, J. H. 1882. *Ladies' Guide in Health and Disease: Girlhood, Maidenhood, Wifehood, Motherhood.* Battle Creek, MI: Modern Medicine Publishing Co.

Kidder, Tracy. 1981. *The Soul of a New Machine.* New York: Avon.

Kraft, Philip, and Steven Dubroff. 1983. "Software Workers Survey." *Computer World,* Nov., 3, 5, 6, 8–13.

LeGuin, Ursula K. 1975. *The Dispossessed.* New York: Avon.

Lehrer, Tom. 1981. *Too Many Songs by Tom Lehrer with Not Enough Drawings by Ronald Searle.* New York: Pantheon.

Linden, Robin Ruth, Darlene R. Pagano, Diana E. H. Russell, and Susan Leigh Star, eds. 1982. *Against Sadomasochism: A Radical Feminist Analysis.* East Palo Alto, Calif.: Frog in the Well.

MacCannell, Dean, and Juliet Flower MacCannell. 1987. "The Beauty System." In *The Ideology of Conflict: Essays on Literature and the History of Technology,* eds. Nancy Armstrong and Leonard Tennenhouse, 206–38. New York: Methuen.

McLeod, Eileen. 1982. *Women Working: Prostitution Now.* London: Croom Helm.

Mernissi, Fatima. 1975. *Beyond the Veil: Male-Female Dynamics in a Modern Muslim Society.* Cambridge, Mass.: Schenckman.

Millett, Kate. 1970. *Sexual Politics.* Garden City, N.Y.: Doubleday.

Misa, Thomas J. 1985. "Military Needs, Commercial Realities, and the Development of the Transistor, 1948–1958." In *Military Enterprise and Technological Change: Perspectives on the American Experience,* ed. Merritt Roe Smith, 253–87. Cambridge: MIT Press.

Money, John. 1985. *The Destroying Angel: Sex, Fitness and Food in the Legacy of Degeneracy Theory, Graham Crackers, Kellogg's Corn Flakes and American Health History.* Buffalo, N.Y.: Prometheus.

Mumford, Lewis. 1967. *The Myth of the Machine.* Vol. 1, *Technics and Human Development.* New York: Harcourt Brace Jovanovich.

Noble, David F. 1977. *America by Design: Science, Technology and the Rise of Corporate Capitalism.* New York: Alfred A. Knopf.

———. 1984. *Forces of Production: A Social History of Industrial Automation.* New York: Alfred A. Knopf.

———. 1985. "Command Performance: A Perspective on Military Enterprise and Technological Change." In *Military Enterprise and Technological Change: Perspectives on the American Experience,* ed. Merritt Roe Smith, 329–46. Cambridge: MIT Press.

Peiss, Kathy. 1983. "'Charity Girls' and City Pleasures: Historical Notes on Working-Class Sexuality, 1880–1920." In *Powers of Desire: The Politics of Sexuality,* eds. Ann Snitow, Christine Stansell, and Sharon Thompson, 74–87. New York: Monthly Review Press.

Petroski, Henry. 1985. *To Engineer Is Human: The Role of Failure in Successful Design.* New York: St. Martin's Press.

Pfohl, Stephen. 1985. "Toward a Sociological Deconstruction of Social Problems." *Social Problems* 32: 228–32.

Pirsig, Robert M. 1975. *Zen and the Art of Motorcycle Maintenance.* New York: Bantam.

Pivar, David J. 1972. *Purity Crusade: Sexual Morality and Social Control, 1868–1900.* Westport, Conn.: Greenwood.

Rich, Andrienne. 1980. "Compulsory Heterosexuality and Lesbian Existence." *Signs* 5: 631–60.

Rubin, Gayle. 1984. "Thinking Sex: Notes for a Radical Theory of the Politics of Sexuality." In *Pleasure and Danger: Exploring Female Sexuality,* ed. Carole S. Vance, 267–319. Boston: Routledge & Kegan Paul.

———. 1987. "The Leather Menace: Comments on Politics and S/M." In *Coming to Power: Writings and Graphics on Lesbian S/M,* ed. members of Samois, 194–229. Boston: Alyson.

Rybczynski, Witold. 1983. *Taming the Tiger: The Struggle to Control Technology.* New York: Viking.

Sabagh, Rita. 1983. "Fiscal Relationships in an Urban Strip Club." Paper presented at the annual meeting of the Pacific Sociological Association, San Jose, California.

Samois, Members of, eds. 1987. *Coming to Power: Writings and Graphics in Lesbian S-M.* Boston: Alyson.

Schneider, Joseph W. 1985. "Defining the Definitional Perspective on Social Problems." *Social Problems* 32: 232–34.

Simmel, Georg. 1984. "Flirtation." In *Georg Simmel: On Women, Sexuality, and Love,* trans. Guy Oakes, 133–52. New Haven, Conn.: Yale University Press. (Original work published 1923.)

Smith, Margaret, and Barbara Waisburg. 1985. *Pornography: A Feminist Survey.* Toronto: Boudicca.

Snitow, Ann Barr. 1983. "Mass Market Romance: Pornography for Women Is Different." In *Powers of Desire: The Politics of Sexuality,* eds. Ann Snitow, Christine Stansell, and Sharon Thompson. New York: Monthly Review Press.

Snyder, Benson R. 1971. *The Hidden Curriculum.* New York: Alfred A. Knopf.

Spinrad, Norman. 1972. *The Iron Dream.* New York: Avon.

Staudenmaier, John M. 1985. *Technology's Storytellers: Reweaving the Human Fabric.* Cambridge: Society for the History of Technology and MIT Press.

Stimpson, Catharine R., and Ethel Spector Person, eds. 1980. *Women: Sex and Sexuality.* Chicago: University of Chicago Press.

Street, John. 1983. "Socialist Arguments for Industrial Democracy." *Economic and Industrial Democracy* 4: 519–39.

Theweleit, Klaus. 1987. *Male Fantasies.* Vol. 1, *Women, Floods, Bodies, History.* Trans. Stephen Conway, with Rita Carter and Chris Turner. Minneapolis: University of Minnesota Press.

Thompson, Craig R., trans. 1965. *The Colloquies of Erasmus.* Chicago: University of Chicago Press.

Tirman, John, ed. 1984. *The Militarization of High Technology.* Cambridge, Mass.: Ballinger.

Valverde, Mariana. 1987. *Sex, Power and Pleasure.* Toronto: Women's Press.

Vance, Carole S. 1983. "Gender Systems, Ideology, and Sex Research." In *Powers of Desire: The Politics of Sexuality,* eds. Ann Snitow, Christine Stansell, and Sharon Thompson, 371–84. New York: Monthly Review Press.

—— ed. 1984. *Pleasure and Danger: Exploring Female Sexuality.* Boston: Routledge & Kegan Paul.

Walker, Alice. 1982. *The Color Purple.* New York: Harcourt Brace Jovanovich.

Weber, Max. 1968. *Economy and Society: An Outline of Interpretive Sociology.* Trans. Ephraim Fischoff et al.; eds. Guenther Roth and Claus Wittich. New York: Bedminster.

Weizenbaum, Joseph. 1976. *Computer Power and Human Reason: From Judgement to Calculation.* San Francisco: W. H. Freeman.

Winner, Langdon. 1977. *Autonomous Technology: Technics-out-of-Control as a Theme in Political Thought.* Cambridge: MIT Press.

——. 1980. "Do Artifacts Have Politics?" *Daedalus* (Winter): 121–36.

Woloch, Nancy. 1984. *Women and the American Experience.* New York: Alfred A. Knopf.

Woolgar, Steve, and Dorothy Pawluch. 1985a. "Ontological Gerrymandering: The Anatomy of Social Problems Explanations." *Social Problems* 32: 214–27.

——. 1985b. "How Shall We Move Beyond Constructivism?" *Social Problems* 32: 159–62.

Discussion Questions

1. How would you describe Hacker's attitude toward her subject? Does she appeal to the reader's intellect or emotions, or both? Is her article likely to provoke a negative response? What might be her purpose in provoking such a response?

2. How are engineers usually portrayed in fiction, cartoons, and movies (that is, as good or bad characters, as introverts or extroverts, as socially adept or as nerds)? Are female engineers ever represented? How much do media portrayals of professional people influence your attitudes?

3. Hacker says that most of us find "some technology sexy, erotic, engendering some passion, strong feeling, some comfort or pleasure." Do you agree? What examples of technology do you find sexy? Which machines do you have strong feelings about—your car, motorcycle, computer? Which machines bring you comfort, either physical or psychological?

4. Hacker refers to a "microphysics of power" in the engineering curriculum. Do you agree with her interpretation of this phrase? Explain your answer. Do you see evidence of such control in your own major curriculum, engineering or otherwise?

Journal Entry

Respond to one or more of the questions Hacker poses in the "Contradictions and Questions" section of her essay.

Writing Projects

1. Further develop your response to the preceding Journal Entry item by integrating your analysis of secondary sources and adding examples from your own experience.

2. Hacker makes a connection between pornography and domination, between domination and eroticism, and between eroticism and technology. What is the connection? Write an essay assessing how she illustrates the connection. Can you think of additional ways in which pornography and technology are linked?

3. Analyze the eroticism of technology portrayed in the media. How do companies eroticize their products in order to sell them? Examine several examples of advertisements or other promotional materials from two or more

companies, and compare the tactics used. If you have the opportunity, create some illustrations or graphics on which you chart your points.

Collaborative Project

Working with a partner, conduct an informal survey of how people view technological achievements or technological products. For example, you might ask your acquaintances what machine they consider most important to their daily productivity. (You could compare their answers to your own response to the first Writing Project assignment for the Weinberg essay on page 79, or to your classmates' answers to Discussion Question 3 above.) Or you could ask ten people, selected at random, what individual comes to their minds as a great modern inventor. Ask them what qualifies this inventor to be considered great. How many people in your survey described their views in the terms Hacker mentions: for example, in terms of glory, honor, and other noble pursuits? Did the women surveyed express their views differently from the men? With your partner, write an article reporting your findings and analyzing to what extent your research did or did not confirm Hacker's argument about the general view of technology in our culture.

Witold Rybczynski

Controlling Technology Means Controlling Ourselves

Witold Rybczynski *(b. 1943) has written extensively about technology as a human activity. Rybczynski believes that "any attempt to control technology must take into account not only its mechanical nature, but its human nature as well." In this excerpt from his book* Taming the Tiger: The Struggle to Control Technology *(1983), Rybczynski illustrates how technological inventions reflect the overall culture and particular technological environment that fostered them. We create the machines, fashioning them after ourselves. Consequently, according to Rybczynski, we need not feel ourselves to be at the mercy of technology. A practicing architect and professor of architecture, Rybczynski has written recently on architecture and society, the psychological need for personal space, and the role of recreation in modern times. His other books include* The Most Beautiful House in the World *(1989),* Waiting for the Weekend *(1991), and* Looking Around: A Journey through Architecture *(1992).*

Questions to Consider

☐ What do you consider to be society's role in the invention, production, and dissemination of technological products? As you read, consider whether you subscribe to the views the author assumes his audience holds.

☐ Rybczynski asks: "We claim that we are afraid of becoming machinelike, but what if technology is actually humanlike?" Notice the examples Rybczynski uses to illustrate the humanlike characteristics of technology. Do you find these examples effective?

I T is obvious that technology is the result of technical activity by the inventor, but what may be less apparent, at least at first glance, is that any technological invention is also the product of the overall technical environment of which it is a part. The claw hammer must be anticipated by the activity of carpentry; the plow by that of agriculture. Or, to put it another way, the act of hammering precedes the invention of the hammer, just as the practice of agriculture precedes the plow. This is not to say that the activity will inevitably produce the required device, or that invention is always the result of need. The act of invention is much more haphazard and even more accidental than that. . . . But even if need does not, by itself, stimulate invention, one can at least say that without an existing technical milieu, an invention is unlikely to be recognized as useful, or, even if recognized, it is unlikely to be applied.

Inventions rely on earlier discoveries and previously known skills. Even an unprecedented invention such as the flying machine had its roots in the extensive experience of unpowered gliders already extant and in the independent development of the internal combustion engine. It was also no coincidence that the first powered flight was made by Orville Wright, a manufacturer of bicycles.

The invention of a technology does not, however, guarantee its immediate use. Aviation in the United States did not commence on a wide commercial scale until 1926, more than twenty years after the first successful flight at Kitty Hawk. While the Wright brothers were somewhat ahead of their European contemporaries, their counterparts in England, France, and Germany were the first to actually apply this new technology and to promote commercial, as well as military, aviation.

The time lag that occurs between the *invention* of a device and its *application* is a common feature of most technological development. The first bicycle, for instance, was patented in 1818, but the machine did not achieve popular success until more than fifty years later. Television was invented in 1920, but its first commercial application was in 1931, when the Columbia Broadcasting System began the first of a regular schedule of telecasts, and in most of the United States and Europe television was not widespread until after the Second World War.

The distinction between invention and application is an important one. Application depends on many external factors such as public acceptance, economic incentives that make it attractive to pursue the development of a technology, and the general level of technological development that surrounds and reinforces the invention. The popularity, not to mention the comfort, of the bicycle was greatly enhanced by a subsequent invention—the pneumatic tire. The existence of television is due not only to the successful experiments of Vladimir Zworykin, but also to the consumer society that made the rapid dissemination of the new device possible.

The German economist Gerhard Mensch gives an interesting example that illustrates the absence of inevitability in the application of new technological discoveries (*Stalemate in Technology*). The transistor and the holograph were both patented in the same year—1948—but thirty-four years later, while the transistor has developed into a multibillion-dollar industry, the holograph has remained very much on the sidelines. There are no holographic cinemas, no holographic billboards, no holographic teaching aids. It was not so much that holographic technology was not useful, but that, unlike the transistor or later the microprocessor, it did not fit into any estab lished area of technical activity. It has remained what Mensch termed an "unexploited technology."

Mensch's attempt to postulate a causal link between the application of technological inventions and fluctuating economic cycles is much less convincing. According to his theory, application occurs in "spurts" during periods of economic prosperity; between these bouts of innovation are what he calls "technological stalemates." When Mensch published his book in 1979 the Western world was still recovering from the Oil Crisis of six years before, and the economic conditions would have led one to expect a "stalemate" as far as technological innovation was concerned. In fact, while the Oil Crisis may have had a serious negative effect on the American economy, it also promoted a large number of new energy-conserving technologies. So successful was this unexpected reaction that only nine years later petroleum prices actually began to drop, some petroleum producers such as Mexico went into *de facto* bankruptcy, and the seemingly invincible oil cartel, the Organization of Petroleum Exporting Countries, seemed on the verge of collapse. Nor does Mensch's theory explain, as Martin Pawley has pointed out, why, in 1982 during a major economic recession, we are witnessing what many have called a "Communications Revolution," the result of the massive application of new technology in the field of telecommunications and computers.

Which all goes to show that while some investment capital must be available for the application of new technologies, the relationship between technological innovation and economics is hardly one of cause and effect. Just as technology is not governed by an internal imperative, neither is it ruled by a narrow set of economic conditions. This is not so surprising if one considers that the application of technology ultimately involves society as a whole, and that technology is not just a constraint on culture, it is itself a part of culture.

It is inaccurate to speak of a "technological invasion" of society, as if machines sprang fully formed from the imagination of their inventors onto an unsuspecting public. As the gap between invention and application demonstrates, a certain level of technical activity must be present in society for the successful application of technology to take place. The manufacture of the electric car has been feasible for some time—the first vehicle powered by a battery-charged electric motor was built only three years after the invention of the electric motor, in 1834—but we still await the large-scale commercialization of this technology as a passenger car. Sometimes it takes time to recognize the potential of a technological device. After the Second World War, the British operated captured Volkswagen automobile plants in occupied Germany. For a number of years they produced vehicles, but only for military use, and finally ceased production without any attempt to convert the plants to civilian use or to transplant the technology of the "Beetle" to Britain. Another technology acquired by the Allies was the Pier-Farben coal hydrogenation process which had been developed by the Germans to produce synthetic fuel from coal. This technol-

ogy was likewise ignored, and today the Pier-Farben process is used by only
one country—South Africa.

On the other hand, the success of the microcomputer industry is not just
due to the invention of the inexpensive microprocessor chip, but above all to
the presence of technically competent entrepreneurs who, while they did not
necessarily have the resources to invent technology, were better placed than
large, conservative corporations when it came to innovation. The result was
that in 1982, the 4.9 billion-dollar market in personal computers was still dominated by these newcomers rather than by the larger, established computer
manufacturers.

The importance of the pre-existence of technical activity to the successful
application of technology becomes especially clear if one examines what happens when technology has been introduced to societies that were largely untechnological. Here the cart frequently arrived before the horse, and technology was acquired without the presence of technical activity. The current
difficulties being experienced by almost all less-developed countries are due in
no small part to this condition.

The fashionable euphemism for the difficulty of implanting technology in
untechnological cultures is "technology transfer," but all this really means is
that when technology is taken out of the cultural context that produced it, its
application and use cannot be taken for granted. Technology transfer is sometimes described as a problem of the poor countries trying to acquire technology from the rich, but even in those less-developed countries that are wealthy
enough to purchase whatever technology they desire, the application of machines in a technological vacuum has not been without difficulty.

The limited success of technology in the less-developed countries indicates
that the presence of machines alone is not enough to make a society "technological." Conversely, if our own culture is technological, it is so not because
we have been overcome by technology, but rather because we have organized
ourselves in a certain way. While it may be difficult to accept, the fact is that
our technology is a symptom of our culture, not vice versa. For, as Heidegger
reminds us, technology is not only a means to an end: technology is a human
activity.

Technology begins not with the tool, but with the human imagination, and the
acts of imagining, inventing, and using tools and machines are human acts. So,
while technology is certainly artificial, it is also eminently natural. Moreover,
since technology is a *human* activity, it is thus a part of human culture and
hence reflects the human preoccupations of its time.

Inventions and innovations always occur in a social context. Lenses, for
example, were known to the Muslims as early as the tenth century, but their
first practical use was recorded in Europe four hundred years later. It should
not be a surprise that those who lived in a period that promoted literacy, secular literature, and, later, printing, should have found it necessary to invent

reading glasses. Three hundred years later, a more militaristic European culture once again used lenses in a new device – the telescope, whose main application was in target spotting for artillery. It was not any technical constraint that accounted for the lag between reading glasses and the telescope, but rather a change in human activities and interests.

Any attempt to control technology must take into account not only its mechanical nature, but its human nature as well. The engineers who designed the automobile assembly plant at Lordstown were very aware of the purpose of their technology – to produce cars as efficiently as possible – but they ignored the fact that assembling cars is also a human activity. Efficiency measured in purely mechanical terms produced a factory environment that was unacceptable to the workers. It is not a question of creating a "technology with a human face" (a catchy but misleading phrase), but rather of recognizing the human component present in all technology.

It is worth bearing the human factor in mind when considering the impact that automation is likely to have on employment in the near future. Adam Osborne, a computer engineer, has estimated that as many as 50 percent of all jobs held in 1978 in the United States could be eliminated in the next twenty-five years as the result of office and factory automation. Such a drastic change – which, should it occur, would truly qualify as a new Industrial Revolution – is by no means preordained. There are many ways in which society could deal with the new technology. Many nine-to-five jobs could be retained as social institutions, inefficient but culturally desirable. The medieval tradition of working at home could be revived, thus further promoting privatization and individualization. Or, with massive "robotization," the leisure society that sociologists have been predicting for the last fifty years could finally come to pass. The inoffensive computer chip could bring about any of these changes, but which one will actually occur will depend as much on how society chooses to organize itself as on the technology alone. Issues such as the re-definition of work in the home (including housework), the relationship between labor and management in the workplace, and adult access to education will have to be re-examined if the right technological choices are to be made.

An earlier communications innovation – the technology of paper-making and movable type – had a momentous effect on life in fifteenth-century Europe. Braudel estimated that during that century, the number of printed books increased from about twenty million to an astonishing two hundred million, with a consequent acceleration in the exchange of information and in the development of ideas (*Capitalism and Material Life 1400–1800*). The latter had a particularly marked effect on changes in philosophy (humanism), science (the Renaissance), and religion (the Reformation).

The printed book neatly illustrates a number of the points I have been trying to make in this chapter. While it was an object, it was above all a means to an end: the transmission of information. It was also the result of technical activity. Although neither paper-making nor movable type were European inventions – they had originated in China and Japan – their use in Europe in the early fourteenth century was linked to earlier technical developments. Particularly important were the use of waterpower and the knowledge of metallurgy; waterwheels were required for mass producing paper, while metallurgy made possible the rapid proliferation of typesetting (the first type was made by goldsmiths). But the printed book was also the result of another activity (technical in the broadest sense of the word): reading. The development of European paper-making, which preceded the invention of the printing press by more than a hundred years, was a response to the growing demand for books, which, before the introduction of paper, had to be handwritten on expensive parchment manufactured from animal skins. Movable type simply completed the process of making less expensive books available to larger numbers of people.

The printed book also demonstrates the human aspect of technology, for the essence of the book lay not in its printing but in the human activities of writing and reading. The technology of the book also opened possibilities for human insights and understanding that previously would have been impossible. Perhaps the computer will do the same, for it is not just that we are influenced by our tools and machines, but that in using them we are able to rediscover our environment, and ourselves.

Why then do we distrust technology? Why do we still insist on referring to modern technology as inhuman, or at least dehumanizing? Part of the difficulty seems to be that we have a confused attitude toward machines; we form quixotic attachments to old technologies that make it even harder for us to accept new ones. This romantic view generally ignores the disadvantages of old devices and describes previous technologies in idealized and often inaccurate terms. The picturesque medieval hamlet is appealingly portrayed in charming paintings, but the smell, the putrefaction and decay that were a part of that sewerless society are forgotten. Renaissance buildings are admired for their solidity, but their lack of even the most basic comforts goes unremembered. Beautiful, nineteenth-century sailing ships are romanticized, but the suffering and human misery that characterized the lives of their hapless crews are ignored. As a result, it is hardly surprising that we fail to understand why these "wonderful old devices" were replaced by "heartless modern technology."

Not a little of the difficulty that our culture experiences with new technology stems from this romantic posture. No sooner does a new technology come along than we suddenly discover previously unrecognized values in its antecedent. When the typewriter first became popular, it was still considered ill-mannered to use it for personal letters – they had to be written by hand. Today, the word processor is replacing the typewriter, but efficient, automated dot-matrix printers are not used for business letters because the result does not look as if it had been typewritten.

If machines such as old steam engines, hot-air balloons, or horse-drawn carriages are viewed more sentimentally than diesel generators, wide-body jets, and compact cars, it may be that, having lost their utility, they can now be seen as artistic, rather than scientific, objects. Literature and art have consistently emphasized the duality of the natural and the artificial, but the natural is elusive—as Thoreau found—so it has been necessary to classify older machines as being more "natural" than newer ones. This illogical schism makes it even more difficult to understand and to control new technological developments.

We claim that we are afraid of becoming machinelike, but what if technology is actually humanlike? We believe that mass production goes against "the laws of nature," whereas mass production is precisely how nature reproduces itself, whether it is in the production of seeds by plants or of ova by animals. As we learn more about the biological building blocks of the natural environment, we are coming to realize that the universe is, like a machine, made up of standardized, interchangeable parts.

We think that obsolescence is uniquely the product of technology, but Martin Pawley reminds us that "Short-life products are no more unnatural than short-life insects or fish, and none need be wasteful in an evolutionary sense." Indeed, he goes on to suggest that there is no reason why technological evolution, which thus far has been more or less haphazard, could not be brought under control by a kind of "product eugenics" which would draw on the genetic pool of scientific ideas to form effective chains of reusable products. If this seems farfetched, consider the numerous examples cited previously of technologies that have drawn on earlier, and apparently unrelated devices or have combined known machines in unexpected mutations.

Whether we control technology by directing its evolution, by choosing when and how to use it, or by deciding what significance it should have in our lives, we shall succeed only if we are able to accept what at first appears to be an impossible shift in our point of view: different as people and machines are, they exist not in two different worlds, but at two ends of the same continuum. Just as we have discovered that we are a part of the natural environment, and not just surrounded by it, so also we will find that we are an intimate part of the environment of technology. The auxiliary "organs" that extend our sight, our hearing, and our thinking really are an extension of our physical bodies. When we are able to accept this, we shall discover that the struggle to control technology has all along been a struggle to control ourselves.

Discussion Questions

1. Notice that Rybczynski uses a historical approach to his material. Is it interesting? Why might he consider this approach relevant? How does it shape his argument?
2. The author distinguishes between the invention and application of technol-

ogy. Why does he think the distinction is important? Do you agree? Are his examples of that distinction effective?

3. How does the overall technical environment affect the invention, development, and reception of technical products?

4. Do you agree with Rybczynski that we as a culture need to control ourselves in order to control technology? Do we need to be less technology dependent? If so, what can you do as an individual, or as part of a group, to alter human behavior so that we are less dependent on technology?

Journal Entries

1. The author notes that the technology of today's information age is reviving the "medieval tradition of working at home." Do you see yourself working successfully at home, receiving instructions and submitting your work via modem and fax? Do you like working in a comfortable but solitary setting like home, without the social structure of an office? Why? What kind of work both appeals to you and lends itself to the home setting?

2. Think of a machine, or any manufactured product, that you use regularly but that you did not need until you discovered that such a product existed. Discuss your own habits and attitudes toward this machine, which you did not need or miss as long as you did not know it existed.

Writing Projects

1. Why do people tend to romanticize older technology? Think of one or more examples of machines that have been replaced or surpassed with new technology yet retain a certain romantic fascination for us (for example, large sailing vessels, locomotives, horse-drawn plows, and the like). Discuss both the romantic and the unromantic elements. Are there any aspects of these machines that we now overlook because of nostalgia?

2. Write an essay exploring the author's integration of the evolutionary process into his account of technological progress. Keeping in mind Rybczynski's discussion of the societal impact of the invention of printing, develop the evolution metaphor by tracing the cultural impact of a modern machine.

Collaborative Project

Working with a partner, identify common examples of resistance to technology. For example, some people distrust computers; some people cannot seem to learn to program their videocassette recorders. Observe people around you and talk to your acquaintances. Analyze specific examples of people resisting new technology; look for examples of how they embrace new technology as well. Discuss in class your conclusions about why people embrace certain types of technology while rejecting others.

Marjorie Dorner

Pulling Contest

Marjorie Dorner *(b. 1942) teaches English at Winona State University in Minnesota, where she also writes mystery novels and short stories. Some of her books include* Nightmare *(1987), which was adapted as the television movie* Don't Touch My Daughter; Family Closets *(1989); and* Blood Kin *(1992). This story is from* Winter Roads, Summer Fields *(1992), a collection of engaging short stories set in midwestern farm country depicting family life that is shaped by both the natural environment and technology. In "Pulling Contest," Dorner portrays the conflicts and successes that unite three generations of a family struggling for economic survival as they attempt to adjust their farming business to contemporary conditions. The story transcends its regional setting in its treatment of complex family relationships.*

Questions to Consider

☐ Notice how the author establishes the characterization of Luke Sensbauer in the opening paragraph by describing his appearance, his clothing in particular. As you continue through the story, take note of the techniques Dorner uses to portray her other characters as well.

☐ Think about how technology is portrayed as you read this story. Notice what fictional strategies Dorner uses to show the mixed feelings the farmers have toward technological advances.

LUKE Sensbauer was diffusing some of his anger by pounding as hard as he could on the metal feeder bin. The pounding was a signal for the calves all over the twenty-acre pasture to come to this shady corner for their food supplement ration. Luke was an old man, over seventy, but he still stood straight, his shoulders squared as if he were daring something to take him on, and the arm that swung the stick against the feeder did not tire easily. Only his clothes showed that he couldn't be a young farmer, for no one else would wear the baggy overalls and the wide-brimmed straw hat, though it was still possible to buy these things at the Farmers' Trading Company in the village. Luke Sensbauer seldom wore anything else and considered the modern caps very close to useless as protection against the summer sun. As for the tight-fitting jeans that his grandsons wore, and even his son, Tom, who was almost fifty and ought to know better, well, Luke was sure they were positively dangerous for farm work where it was important to be able to move your legs freely.

He liked calves, liked just to look at them, especially when they were a few months old and frisked around the pasture. His favorites were the Holstein-Hereford mix, with their smaller, blunter bodies and their nicely shaped heads. Nowadays, Holstein heifers were bred to a Hereford bull for their first calves because the lower birth weight made for easier labor. Later, the same cows would have Holstein calves to grow up into dairy cattle. Well, Luke thought, the Ag schools must be good for something, after all, because in his own days he'd often seen both heifer and calf die because of a difficult birth, especially if the labor started at night when there was no one around to help. And these little guys were really cute too, with Holstein markings and, usually, the reddish color of their papa. Watching them running toward him, Luke forgot for a moment and felt a little more cheerful.

He was angry partly with his grandson, Dennis, for what the boy had said to Tom, and partly with himself for standing there listening in when he should just have walked back out of the barn and gone about his business; he hated sneakiness of any kind and he felt as if he'd been sneaky, eavesdropping like that. He also felt betrayed. He actually turned the word over in his mind a couple of times, "betrayed." Because he'd always liked Denny best of all his grandsons, had the highest hopes for him. And he'd thought that the boy liked him too, appreciated the help he tried to give him in learning his way around farming. But there Denny was, standing in the silo shed doorway, saying those awful things to his father, when Luke had come into the barn from the east-side doors and had stopped short, unnoticed, to listen.

"I know all that, Dad, but I just wish you could get him off my back. He rides me all the time, like I was some kind of lazy hired hand or something."

"Come on, it's not that bad," Tom had answered from inside the silo shed where Luke couldn't even see him.

"It sure as hell is," Denny said, raising his voice even louder. "He bosses me all the time, and he acts like I don't know diddly about farming when he doesn't even know how to drive half the machinery we got."

"Well, he does know a lot about farming, young fella, and don't you forget it. I won't have you sassing your grandpa."

"I don't sass him. I never get to say anything at all to him because he just keeps on and on about how he used to do this and he used to do that."

"Well, he can't help it that times have changed. He likes to talk about the times when his ways were everybody's ways. You're family, so it doesn't hurt you to listen."

"But he's like that to all the hands, Dad. You wonder why we can't keep a herdsman for more than six months? It's because Grandpa is always after them too. You know what he said to Dan last year? He said, 'I guess you smart Ag school boys don't know everything, do you?'"

Inside the silo shed, Tom had chuckled softly.

"Listen, Denny. Dan left us because he finally got enough money together for a farm of his own, not because Pa ran him off."

"Well, you gotta talk to him anyway, Dad, because he's making me crazy."

Making him crazy. Hadn't he, Luke, taught that kid to ride a bicycle when his older brothers ignored him and Tom didn't have time for him? Hadn't he taken that kid to his silly high school football games and even stayed to cheer for him? And now he was making him crazy. Betrayed.

At the midday meal, Luke spoke to no one except to mutter "thanks" when Betsy, his daughter-in-law, passed him some food. He finished before the others and stalked back outside. Tom found him in the shade under the maple tree.

"So, how does the corn look to you, Pa?"

Luke gave him a sideways glance. So they were going to sneak up on it, were they?

"It looks great. Those hybrids are wonderful things, but we could use another good rain."

"Yeah, it's been a little dry lately."

There was a little pause, so Luke decided to take the offensive.

"You should quit that barn cleaner business and tend just to this farm, Tom."

"What makes you say that?" He looked really stunned.

"I don't know," Luke shrugged. "I'm getting too old to make it all run while you're gone most of the time."

"Has Denny been saying anything to you?"

"No, Denny doesn't say much to me." He couldn't keep the aggrieved note out of his voice.

"Listen, Pa. You know I got to keep turning a profit on the barn cleaner thing just to make the interest payments on all this." He made a sweeping gesture that took in barn, fields, cattle, and machinery. "And we got to have something to fall back on when the farm has a bad year."

Luke just grunted.

"And what's all this about you being too old, anyway? What brought this on? You're as hale as a hickory tree."

"Maybe it's just my ways is too old. All these big modern toys are beyond me."

"You been fighting with Denny, Pa?"

"No!" He said it a little too loud. "But that kid is getting to be a smart aleck."

"He's not a kid, Pa. He's twenty years old and he pulls his weight."

"You mean riding around the fields in that oversized buggy you call a combine, with its air-conditioning and that damned rock music so loud the

Tomcheks can hear it clear the other side of the back forty? He could wreck the underside of that eighty-thousand-dollar rig and never know it, while he's deafening himself in comfort."

"If he hit something serious, the hydraulic system would lift the blades out of the way, and the warning light on the panel would come on."

Luke, who'd never ridden inside the combine, was stunned into silence for a moment by this piece of information. But it only seemed to make him more angry when he spoke again.

"I don't think it's natural, Tom. He can be in the field all day and he don't even get dirty. If he's fixing to be a real farmer, he should get some of his land on himself while he's working it."

"Whose rule is that, Pa? Where is that written down? You know that Denny really cares about the place, is interested in taking it over someday. We couldn't make farmers out of the other two, you remember. We lost them to the city and the paper mills, so we got to be glad that Denny takes an interest. Well, don't we?"

Luke turned his face away and gave no answer.

"Look here, Pa," Tom said, more gently. "I guess you and Denny are going through some rocky times right now, but what's most important here is that we keep this place moving along, and we got to work together for that. This is a family business, after all. It belongs to all of us."

"It ain't mine anymore," Luke said. "I'm just somebody who lives here."

"Now cut that crap, Pa," Tom said sharply. "This is Sensbauer land and it has been for more than a hundred years. You are the oldest Sensbauer around, so of course it's your farm."

"You got the deed."

"Yeah, and Denny will have it after me, if he wants it, but it'll still be my farm too."

Luke had developed a habit of deferring to Tom's opinions, and he couldn't help but see the reason in what he said now. When Luke spoke again, it was in a softened tone.

"It's just that everything is so changed. Farming used to be fun, and now it's just big business."

Tom laughed, a short, snorting laugh.

"Jesus, your memory is beginning to go, isn't it?" he said. "Cast your mind back, Pa. Farming was never fun. It was always damned hard work, even if you could love it like we did. And it was always a business, a family business, like I said before. What else is it when you make your living out of what you own?"

"Of course, that's true," Luke said. He was trying to be fair. "But you know what I mean. Some of these guys go only for the profit and loss. They don't really care about the land or about the life."

"Sure, there's guys like that. But they ain't us."

"But so much of it is slipping away. Jake Himrich had to sell his place for a golf course. And now you tell me them foreign investors want to buy Bill Seidl's farm for a tax write-off and then just let it lay there, going to weeds."

"Florida investors, Pa, not foreign investors."

Luke blinked twice, his face impassive.

"Same difference," he said at last.

Tom smiled broadly and touched his father's shoulder.

"Well, they ain't got us yet, Pa, and if we stick together, they won't get us ever."

Luke smiled back and then they both watched the fields for a while.

"I gotta go to Marshfield tomorrow to look at the new line of cleaner equipment," Tom said. "Denny is entering his mini-tractor in his first pulling contest over at Davister's. I'd like to see him drive, and I think he feels kinda bad that I won't be there. Maybe you could go along to see how he does."

"Uh," Luke grunted. It could have meant either "yes" or "no."

In the late afternoon sunshine, Luke stood outside the machine shed, having an argument with himself, readjusting the straw hat each time he changed sides. On the one hand, Tom was right about Denny's interest in the place, and probably he, Luke, was sometimes too hard on the boy, who, to give him his just due, was really a good kid. And it would be a shame if the boy had to go to Davister's track without his family backing him. On the other hand, this mini-tractor business was downright silly, and the boy had said some disrespectful things, even some untrue things, that very morning. Luke would never have dared to say such things about his own grandfather, because nobody would have allowed them to be said.

But as soon as he thought about his grandfather, Luke had to suppress the smile that began to turn up the corners of his mouth. The old man had lived to be ninety-four and was considered a genuine "character" for three counties around. And so he had been. He'd come from Germany as a boy not much older than Denny and had taken on the enormous task of clearing the eighty-acre farm that still formed the center of the present Sensbauer land. Having coped with that one high-risk change, he firmly resisted all other change for the rest of his life. He stubbornly refused to learn English, considered the earliest cars a passing fancy, and regarded air travel as a tool of the devil. When his son, Luke's father, had installed a telephone in the farmhouse, he had grumbled bitterly that it was *"ein verdammtes Ding,"* a damned thing. Only a few months later did the family learn from puzzled neighbors and relatives that the old man had learned one English sentence that he could use when the rest of the family was out of the house and the ringing of the phone was finally too much for him to stand. He would snatch down the receiver and bellow into the speaker, "Dis is Heinrich Sensbauer; you vant to talk to me, you come to mein house." Then he would hang up.

Well, Luke thought to himself, maybe his grandfather wasn't the only one who had trouble with change. He settled his hat more firmly onto his head and walked into the machine shed. He wanted to be fair, after all.

Denny was painting black stripes onto the white fenders of his mini-tractor, the finishing touches before tomorrow's contest. With his cousin, Bob Heim, Denny had built the engine and put together the frame of the machine he'd named "the Gambler," and he was very proud of it. To Luke, the tractor looked like some oversized toy, its large rear wheels coming only just above Denny's waist, the front wheels looking like they'd come off a baby buggy. All of the exposed engine was painted silver, and the chrome exhaust pipes, which pointed straight up on either side of the manifold, were not much taller than Luke.

Denny was concentrating on keeping the flow of paint even between the two strips of masking tape, but he'd seen his grandfather come into the shed. He was a nice-looking boy, Luke thought, well built and clean-shaven, but his blond hair was too long, almost in his eyes, and those jeans – any tighter and he wouldn't be able to bend over. Luke walked all around the little tractor before speaking.

"Where's the radiator?" he asked.

"Doesn't have a radiator," Denny said without looking up.

"What cools the engine, then?"

"Nothing cools the engine. It only runs for two or three minutes, so it just gets hot. It can cool down later. A radiator would add too much weight."

Luke snorted.

"It can only run for two minutes and it's the size of a calf. What a waste of money and gas."

"It doesn't use gas," Denny said, cool as well water. "It runs on alcohol."

"Sounds dangerous."

"It is. That's why I got this fire extinguisher built in here." He leaned over to pat the bright red cylinder.

Luke frowned, his already-creased brow folding over itself as a knot of fear twisted in his stomach. His own brother had died in a fire.

"What the hell is this thing good for, anyway?" he growled. "Now, mind you, I think a pulling contest is a good thing. We always had 'em, first with horses and later with tractors. But we used to have some purpose for 'em, to test our animals or our machines, the same ones we used every day on the farm. There was some practical purpose to the whole thing."

Denny looked up for a second, the brush hanging from his hand, and his face was half-amused, half-scornful.

"Come on, Grandpa. A contest is a contest. It ain't about 'practical.' It's about seeing who can win."

"But we didn't waste time and money building toys like this."

"I got the time and the money is mine," Denny said coldly and went back to painting.

"Just so you don't kill yourself over the fool thing."

After a long pause, Luke made another circuit around the Gambler and reached out to trace his finger over some of the wiring.

"You better not touch anything, Grandpa," Denny said without looking up. "Bob had to drive all the way to Kenosha for some of those parts."

"Really? How far is that?"

"Almost three hours."

"I mean, how many miles is it?" Luke said, irritation coming back into his voice.

Denny looked up with the kind of blank expression he sometimes had when his grandfather said something he couldn't see the sense of.

"I don't know. You could look at a map or something, I guess." His voice was calm as he bent to his painting once more.

Again, an uncomfortable pause followed, and Luke folded his arms inside his overall bib.

"Yes, sir," Luke said at last. "Pulling contests really used to be something. The horses were the best. We used to talk about the contest weeks ahead of time. Every Sunday after church, we'd cross the road to Smeester's tavern and try to find out about all the teams."

"Smeester's?" Denny looked up in surprise. "The same tavern that's there now?"

"Sure, the same building. Different owner now, of course, and it's all changed inside. Oh, you should have seen it in my day. It had a polished floor and a pressed tin ceiling. You don't see that—"

"I thought you were going to tell me about the horse pulling contests."

Luke had a stunned look on his face. Then he snapped, "You're the one who asked me about Smeester's, aren't you?"

"Sorry," Denny murmured, and Luke decided it was best to go on as if Smeester's hadn't been mentioned.

"We'd have 'em at the fairgrounds, make a real picnic out of it. George Sacker would bring his stone boat and we'd load on the stones, not too many at first, and then every team had a turn. Gradually, we'd pile on more and more stones and the teams would start to get eliminated. That was the real test of strength, not like them computerized sleds you got nowadays."

"They're not computerized, for God's sake. It's just simple hydraulics. The more the weight moves forward, the harder it is to pull the sled. And the weight can be measured exactly."

"Well, next year, they'll be computerized for sure. Anyway, like I was saying, towards the end, when there were only about four teams left, the pile of stones was higher than the horses. You shoulda seen 'em, leaning into the harnesses, practically digging themselves down to China with them big hooves, muscles standing out in their necks."

"Sounds kinda hard on the horses."

"No, no. They was bred to pull, liked it. Peter Kollross had a pair of silver Belgians that was beautiful to look at. They won almost every year, till Pete sold 'em off to buy his first tractor."

"Did you ever win, Grandpa?"

"Nope. Came close a coupla times, but my team wasn't as big as them Belgians."

"Big isn't always best," Denny said, patting the wheel next to him and smiling slyly at his grandfather.

"Hmph," Luke snorted, but it was hard to tell what he meant because he smiled afterwards.

It was a hot day and the temporary bleachers were already full by the time Luke got to Davister's track. Denny had taken the pickup around behind a barrier where other drivers would help him unload his mini-tractor. Luke found himself a place to stand along a snow fence that had been set up to mark off the track from the field around it. Off to his left was a stand with a microphone and loudspeaker.

Ron Davister had sold off most of his land for a housing development, but he still had about fifteen acres where he raised saddle horses for sale. And he had set aside this place behind his barn for tractor pulling contests. The track was a quarter-mile path cut out of the sod. The dirt was raked smooth for the start of the truck pulling, which came first.

Luke thought the customized trucks looked ridiculous, the pickup bodies perched high above wheels so huge and so wide-set that the fenders couldn't possibly cover them. The trucks were painted in bright colors and covered with advertisements for local businesses and garages. When the first truck was hooked up to the weighted sled and set into roaring motion, it was clear what the day was going to be like. The truck's whirring tires bit into the dry ground, sending clouds of reddish brown dust twenty feet into the air. The wind was from the northeast, sending the clouds straight over the spectators.

Luke got a few muffled laughs out of the trucks. Twice, the flashy, bucking machines pranced up to the sled only to have their drive shafts ripped out several seconds later, before they'd pulled the sled fifteen feet.

"Damned idjits," Luke said to no one in particular, feeling very satisfied.

The full-size tractors came next and this was something Luke could enjoy despite the buildup of grit in his nose and mouth. Some of the tractors were vintage models, old John Deeres whose two huge cylinders gave them that familiar "putt-putt" sound, and even an old Oliver 88 just like the one Luke had once owned. Olivers were good tractors, Luke thought happily, and he was pleased when the 88 won second prize in its class.

The mini-tractors were last because this was the most popular event, and Denny would be the last contestant because he was a late entrant. By that time, the track would be as torn up as it could get. Luke began to feel depressed again. The sun was hot on his shoulders. Someone touched his arm, and when he turned, he saw Denny holding out a sweating bottle of beer.

"Thought you could use this," Denny said and was walking back through the crowd before Luke could think of what he wanted to say to the boy.

Luke drained the beer before the announcer had finished naming the first contestant in this last competition. The mini-tractor, painted bright red, was towed out onto the track by Lloyd Liebeck's pickup. Luke remembered what Denny had said about the engines running for only two or three minutes without radiators, so he guessed they couldn't be started at all until they were ready to begin pulling. The pickup bounced off to the side of the track and a towrope was stretched between the little tractor and the sled. The driver's head was hidden inside a motorcycle helmet with a dark windscreen across the face. Someone shouted, "Tear 'em up, Hank," and a pattering of applause spread through the bleachers just before the engine started with a sound like a small explosion. The big wheels began to spin instantly and the whole front part of the tractor bucked up into the air like a rearing horse. In a few seconds, the engine was making a high-pitched screaming sound and the tractor had disappeared in a cloud of brown dirt. The cloud moved forward, fast enough at first, and then slower and slower as the weight moved toward the front of the sled. Finally, the little front wheels dropped out of the cloud and the noise stopped as abruptly as it had begun.

Men rushed toward the machine, one to mark the place where the wheels had dropped, one to unhook the towline, and one to record the weight. The crowd was still applauding while the pickup truck towed the mini-tractor off the track. It had been a good first run, hard to beat, the announcer said, as a tractor dragged the sled back to its starting position.

One by one, the mini-tractors were announced, their names taken from country and western songs or just from local taverns which had sponsored them, their drivers representing both families Luke had known all his life and names he'd never heard before. Each time the expectant hush was broken by the screaming engine, and each time the dirt whirled upward as if a bomb had erupted from under the ground. Some of the tractors bucked to a stop almost as soon as they started, their customized engines hopelessly flooded. Others churned forward almost to the marks made by the first entry, excitement building in the crowd each time one came close.

Luke found himself caught up in the excitement, urging some of the tractors forward just because their drivers were named Kollross or Ashenbrenner. After the sixth entry, he took out his big, white pocket handkerchief and held it over his mouth and nose, for he was beginning to think he might choke to death before Denny's turn came around. The eighth tractor started out sluggishly, its wheels seeming to move in slow motion. Suddenly the driver threw his arms in front of his face as a liquid began spraying up from the engine; it was the alcohol fuel. The crowd gasped as little flashes of fire danced over the hot surface of the engine wherever drops of alcohol landed. Two men rushed forward with fire extinguishers already fogging the air in front of them, and the fires were instantly killed. The driver waved gamely, though a bit sheepishly, to cheering spectators as his tractor was towed away. Luke lifted his handkerchief back to his mouth, but his grime-encircled eyes had grown nar-. row and worried.

Finally, the announcer was saying, "And the last entry is newcomer Dennis Sensbauer on the Gambler, built by the driver and his cousin, Robert Heim." The tractor appeared, and Luke felt a flash of irritation when he saw that the white fenders had already been coated by the drifting dust, making the tractor look a little shabby. Denny sat rigidly upright, his bare hands clutching the steering wheel as if he was already urging the tractor forward. He had pushed his hair up inside a billed cap bearing the name of the garage where Bob worked. The sled rope was attached and the tow truck moved away. Luke pressed the edges of the handkerchief against the sides of his face until he could feel his teeth beginning to hurt.

Denny's right hand moved and the engine exploded into sound, the wheels churning, the front end bucking. Then Denny disappeared into the cloud of dirt as all the other drivers had done. The sled moved surprisingly quickly at first and the crowd, dazed into silence by three hours of heat and dirt and noise, began to stir a little. As the sled started to slow, the screaming of the engine became louder, and a sudden gust of wind let everyone have a brief glimpse of the back wheels, still churning madly, the rubber treads clawing down into the trenches made by the other tractors. The noise of the crowd began to build. Luke had neither moved nor made a sound.

Now the tone of the engine began to come down as the numbers of revolutions slowed toward the inevitable stall. But still the sled inched forward, and still the cloud of dust crept toward the announcer's stand. The sound of the motor had quieted enough so that the cheering from the bleachers rose above it. The tractor was moving so slowly now that the cloud of dust was shrinking around it. By the time the engine growled to a stop and the front wheels fell to the ground for the last time, the dust had cleared enough so everyone could see that Denny had passed the marks made by the first tractor.

The crowd noise was almost deafening and the announcer's voice over the loudspeaker had an hysterical ring to it. Luke let go of his own face for the first time since Denny's tractor had come out onto the track. His voice was just a hollow croak as he tried to shout with the crowd, so he snatched his big straw hat off his head and threw it to the ground. Then, because that somehow didn't seem enough, he danced up and down on the hat, smashing the crown level with the brim, trampling all of the pale straw into the swirling dust.

Denny had jumped down to see for himself where his wheels were being marked. Now he stood up straight, grabbed his cap in his right hand, and waved it at the bleachers. Then he lifted both of his arms above his head, dancing in a half circle until he could see Luke against the snow fence. The boy's hair was plastered against his head. Upward from the line of his cap, his pale forehead gleamed in the afternoon sun; below the line, his face was dark brown, completely covered in dirt. With his arms still aloft, he began to run toward his grandfather, whose own arms were now thrust out in front of him, the soiled handkerchief dangling unnoticed from his right hand.

Discussion Questions

1. How does Dorner show us that Luke and Denny are very different kinds of farmers? What are some of the ways in which they differ from each other? Along with these differences, what similarities do you see between this grandfather and grandson?

2. What narrative techniques (for example, description, tone, point of view, sentence structure, figures of speech) does Dorner use to convey the excitement of the tractor pull?

3. What do you see as the essential differences between the views Denny and his grandfather hold on the tractor pulling contest? Which of them do you agree with? Given the author's title for this story, do you see the pulling contest being used to develop a theme?

4. Why do you think humans resist change, technological or otherwise? What family conflicts have you been a part of that stemmed from one person wanting to embrace change while another resisted?

Journal Entries

1. Following Dorner's example, write a passage of dialogue in which two of your own family members or friends carry on a discussion that involves disagreement. Assign each speaker dialogue, as if you were writing a play, that illustrates how the characters feel about each other and how they think about the topic of disagreement.

2. Recall an incident or conversation in which you and someone older, such as a parent or grandparent, argued over the old way of doing things versus the new way. What happened? How was the conflict resolved?

Writing Projects

1. Conflict is a major element in most short stories. Write an essay examining the source and type of conflict in this story. When is it resolved, and how? Do you think the conflict is presented and resolved effectively?

2. How does Dorner's "Pulling Contest" illustrate through fiction a wide range of attitudes toward technology, without explicitly siding with one particular view? What fictional techniques make Dorner more successful than the authors of nonfiction pieces who use exposition and argument? What advantages does Dorner have?

3. Write an essay analyzing your research into the recent history of farming in America. How have developments in technology over the past fifty years changed farming? How have farm machines changed? Do farmers spend more or less time in the field than they used to? Have machines made farming more or less profitable than it used to be? How many of today's farms are family operations?

Collaborative Project

Working with a partner, compare and contrast a contest that involves technology with one that does not. You might each write about a different contest. Or you could both study various contests together. Do you have difficulty finding a contest that is not at least indirectly affected by technology? (For example, most sporting events involve the use of equipment, even if only a ball or a stick, that is manufactured in a certain way for optimum usefulness.) Write a paper explaining which contest you consider the most valid or the most exciting: the one that is directly dependent on machines or the one that centers mostly on the human participants.

Robert J. Samuelson

Technology in Reverse

Robert J. Samuelson *(b. 1945) writes a biweekly column for* Newsweek *in which he analyzes socioeconomic issues. He also writes a syndicated column for the* Washington Post, Los Angeles Times, *and* Boston Globe, *among others. Samuelson has earned many journalism awards, including the national Headliner Award in 1992 and 1987, and the Gerald Loeb Award in 1994, 1986, and 1983. In this article (from the July 20, 1992, issue of* Newsweek*) Samuelson illustrates what he considers to be the unnecessary status consciousness and economic waste that technology sometimes encourages.*

Questions to Consider

☐ As you read, notice Samuelson's tone. How does he achieve this tone? How does it affect you?

☐ Samuelson structures his essay around a two-part classification: useful and wasteful examples of technology. Notice what kinds of examples he selects and how he illustrates usefulness versus wastefulness.

LET me introduce you to retarded technology. It's the opposite of advanced technology. Advanced technology enables us to do useful new things or to do old things more efficiently. By contrast, retarded technology creates new and expensive ways of doing things that were once done simply and inexpensively. Worse, it encourages us to do things that don't need doing at all. It has made waste respectable, elaborate, alluring and even fun.

Just the other week, *Newsweek* reported a boom in electronic books. The idea is to put books onto discs that you can plug into your customized book-displaying computer. Here's a swell idea of retarded technology. On the one hand, you can buy a $900 or $9,000 book-reading computer that you can feed with $20 discs of your favorite books. It's cumbersome. If you take it to the beach, it gets clogged with sand. You can't use it as a pillow. If it slips off the kitchen counter, it smashes.

On the other hand, you can buy an old-fashioned book. It's cheaper, more mobile, less fragile and more durable. You can lend it, even to casual friends. If you don't like it, you can stop reading without hating yourself for ever buying it. Losing it is not a traumatizing event.

The pro-technology comeback is that computers will someday compress entire libraries onto chips or discs and, thereby, open vast vistas of information to almost anyone. The trouble with this is arithmetic and common sense. A school library with 2,000 books can theoretically serve 2,000 readers simultaneously. A school library with one computer terminal that can call up 200,000 books can serve only one reader at a time. The computer creates a bottleneck. Sure, the library can buy more computers, but they're costlier and bulkier than books. Finally, there's common sense: do most people really need access to, say, the entire collection of the New York Public Library?

Here's another example of technology racing backward: the video press release. In my business, we're bombarded with press releases for products, politicians and policies. And now there are promotional videos. Instead of a 10-cent press release that took two days to prepare and 29 cents to mail, I get a $4.50 tape that cost $2 to mail and two months to prepare. I can read standard press releases in 10 or 15 seconds before tossing 99 percent of them. But the videos get tossed immediately. To view them would require finding a VCR and wasting five to 10 minutes watching. Sorry, no sale. The video costs more and does less.

I am not about to argue that all technology is bad. Heavens, no. Ours is an era of conspicuous technological upheaval. But the purported gains of new technology—rising incomes, greater productivity—seem to elude us. Somehow, the paradox must be explained. One theory holds that we're still in the primitive stages of, say, the computer revolution, whose full benefits will soon burst upon us. Maybe. (A corollary is that techno-dopes like me are holding back progress.)

But to this theory, I would add the notion of retarded technology. Yup, the gains from new technologies are plentiful and real. But the benefits are being crudely offset by a lot of technology-inspired waste. Technology is often misused because the reasons people embrace it can be fairly frivolous. To wit:

☐ **Social Status.** Suppose your brother in Honolulu gets a car phone. He might even need it for work. Can you then be without one? Obviously not. Need isn't an issue. (Since 1985, the number of cellular subscribers has leaped from 340,000 to about 8 million.)

☐ **Adult Play.** New machines are often grown-up toys, successors to Legos and dolls. A woman I know well (my wife) recently exulted after creating invitation cards on her personal computer. (I dared not ask how long this took.) "I know I could have gone out and bought Hallmark cards," she says. "But I'm so proud of myself. I'm thrilled." In the office, computer mail has transformed idle chitchat into an all-day affair.

☐ **The Mount Everest Effect.** Every new technology inspires the temptation to see what it will do—no matter how inane or time-consuming the task. This is the technological equivalent of "We're climbing that mountain because it's there." Hence, the video press release. Entire areas of academic life (political science, economics and even history) are now increasingly given over to number crunching. Computers allow numbers to be easily crunched; so they are. Genuine thought is discouraged. The same thought-deadening process afflicts American managers.

The survival of stupid technology is ordained by ego and money. New technologies often require a hefty investment. Once investments are made, they can't easily be unmade. To do so would be embarrassing. Old and inexpensive ways of doing things are eliminated to help pay for new and expensive methods. Retarded technology becomes institutionalized and permanent.

This is routinely denied, because people won't admit they're frivolous or wasteful. One survey of cellular-phone owners found that 87 percent said their phones raised their productivity by an average of 36 percent. More than half (54 percent) said the phone had improved their marriages. Imagine if these gains were generalized to the entire population: our economy's output would instantly leap from $6 trillion to $8 trillion; divorce rates would plunge, and "family values" would triumph. What we need are cellular subsidies so everyone can have one.

The beat goes on. Apple Computer recently announced Newton, the first of a generation of handheld "personal digital assistants." Newton will, Apple says, recognize your handwriting when you scribble something on its small display screen. This seems impressive. You scrawl "Joe Smith," and Newton calls up "Joe Smith" from its memory and tells you Joe's phone number and anything else you've put in Joe's tiny file. Just like a Rolodex.

Hey, maybe a Rolodex is better. It's cheaper. How about a standard notebook or address book? They already accept handwriting. Even fancy address books cost only $15 or $20. Apple says Newton (which will also act as a pager and send messages over phone lines) will be priced "well under $1,000." It should be a smashing success.

Discussion Questions

1. Do you accept the author's key terms – *smart* and *stupid* – as he applies them to technology? As a culture, do you think we are more interested in advanced or retarded technology? Why?

2. Evaluate the author's presentation of the pros and cons of electronic books. Are there advantages or disadvantages he overlooks? Does he clearly prefer one over the other? What, in his essay, alerts you to this?

3. How does Samuelson appeal to our common sense? Do you find this appropriate and effective? Why do you agree, or disagree, with his illustrations of common sense?

4. Based on your experience at work or school, would you agree or disagree with Samuelson that "computer mail has transformed idle chitchat into an all-day affair"? What about phone mail? Has it enabled you to work more or less efficiently than you used to? How has it affected your social life, if at all?

5. Samuelson says we need government subsidies so that everyone can afford a cellular phone. Is he being straightforward or sarcastic? How can you tell?

Journal Entry

Come up with some of your own examples of technology that fit into the author's two categories. In your own home, which kind is most prevalent?

Writing Projects

1. Write an essay supporting Samuelson's assertion that some technology has made waste "respectable, elaborate, alluring and even fun."

2. Argue against Samuelson's thesis about the wastefulness of some kinds of technology. Consider what kind of readers are likely to agree with Samuelson and what kind are more likely to agree with you.

Collaborative Project

First *estimate* the reading grade level of this essay. Then *measure* it against a readability test, such as The Gunning Fog Index, by calculating its reading difficulty on the basis of the number of syllables per word, words per sentence, and sentences per paragraph. Your instructor can give you a readability measurement formula to use, or you can find instructions for calculating readability in most technical writing textbooks. Or you could work with a partner who knows how to use text-scanning software to scan Samuelson's article from this book into your own word processing program, and then measure its readability by using the calculation tools of your software. Does the readability level, as determined by the particular test you used, match your assessment of the essay's readability? How do paragraph and sentence length affect readability in this piece? How would you describe the readability and style of a sentence that begins with "Yup" (paragraph 7)?

Neil Postman

Invisible Technologies

Neil Postman *challenges traditional assumptions about technology in his controversial book* Technopoly: The Surrender of Culture to Technology *(1992). According to Postman, the term* technopoly *describes a society in which technology is produced as an end in itself rather than as a means to an end. This excerpt from* Technopoly *defines some of our "invisible technologies" and identifies some of the dangers inherent in their use. Postman is chair of the Department of Communication Arts at New York University, where he received the Distinguished Professor Award in 1989. The National Council of Teachers of English awarded him the George Orwell Award for Clarity in Language in 1986 for his book* Amusing Ourselves to Death *(1985). Postman has written seventeen books, including* Teaching as a Subversive Activity *(with Charles Weingartner, 1969), which brought him to prominence in the 1960s and 1970s as the voice of radical reform in education;* Teaching as a Conserving Activity *(1979); and* Conscientious Objections *(1988).*

Questions to Consider

☐ Postman asserts that "our most powerful ideological instrument is the technology of language itself." As you read, notice the methods Postman uses to explain and support his argument.

☐ To whom is Postman writing? Do you think he considers his audience to be pro-technology or anti-technology?

IF we define ideology as a set of assumptions of which we are barely conscious but which nonetheless directs our efforts to give shape and coherence to the world, then our most powerful ideological instrument is the technology of language itself. Language is pure ideology. It instructs us not only in the names of things but, more important, in what things can be named. It divides the world into subjects and objects. It denotes what events shall be regarded as processes, and what events, things. It instructs us about time, space, and number, and forms our ideas of how we stand in relation to nature and to each other. In English grammar, for example, there are always subjects who act, and verbs which are their actions, and objects which are acted upon. It is a rather aggressive grammar, which makes it difficult for those of us who must use it to think of the world as benign. We are obliged to know the world as made up of things pushing against, and often attacking, one another.

Of course, most of us, most of the time, are unaware of how language does its work. We live deep within the boundaries of our linguistic assumptions and have little sense of how the world looks to those who speak a vastly different tongue. We tend to assume that everyone sees the world in the same way, irrespective of differences in language. Only occasionally is this illusion challenged, as when the differences between linguistic ideologies become noticeable by one who has command over two languages that differ greatly in their structure and history. For example, several years ago, Susumu Tonegawa, winner of the 1987 Nobel Prize in Medicine, was quoted in the newspaper *Yomiuri* as saying that the Japanese language does not foster clarity or effective understanding in scientific research. Addressing his countrymen from his post as a professor at MIT in Cambridge, Massachusetts, he said, "We should consider changing our thinking process in the field of science by trying to reason in English." It should be noted that he was not saying that English is better than Japanese; only that English is better than Japanese for the purposes of scientific research, which is a way of saying that English (and other Western languages) have a particular ideological bias that Japanese does not. We call that ideological bias "the scientific outlook." If the scientific outlook seems natural to you, as it does to me, it is because our language makes it appear so. What we think of as reasoning is determined by the character of our language. To reason in Japanese is apparently not the same thing as to reason in English or Italian or German.

To put it simply, like any important piece of machinery—television or the computer, for example—language has an ideological agenda that is apt to be hidden from view. In the case of language, that agenda is so deeply integrated into our personalities and world-view that a special effort and, often, special training are required to detect its presence. Unlike television or the computer, language appears to be not an extension of our powers but simply a natural expression of who and what we are. This is the great secret of language: Because it comes from inside us, we believe it to be a direct, unedited, unbiased, apolitical expression of how the world really is. A machine, on the other hand, is outside of us, clearly created by us, modifiable by us, even discardable by us; it is easier to see how a machine re-creates the world in its own image. But in many respects, a sentence functions very much like a machine, and this is nowhere more obvious than in the sentences we call questions.

As an example of what I mean, let us take a "fill-in" question, which I shall require you to answer exactly if you wish full credit:

Thomas Jefferson died in the year ___ .

Suppose we now rephrase the question in multiple-choice form:

Thomas Jefferson died in the year (a) 1788   (b) 1826
(c) 1926   (d) 1809.

Which of these two questions is easier to answer? I assume you will agree with me that the second question is easier unless you happen to know precisely the year of Jefferson's death, in which case neither question is difficult. However, for most of us who know only roughly when Jefferson lived, Question Two has arranged matters so that our chances of "knowing" the answer are greatly increased. Students will always be "smarter" when answering a multiple-choice test than when answering a "fill-in" test, even when the subject matter is the same. A question, even of the simplest kind, is not and can never be unbiased. I am not, in this context, referring to the common accusation that a particular test is "culturally biased." Of course questions can be culturally biased. (Why, for example, should anyone be asked about Thomas Jefferson at all, let alone when he died?) My purpose is to say that the structure of any question is as devoid of neutrality as is its content. The form of a question may ease our way or pose obstacles. Or, when even slightly altered, it may generate antithetical answers, as in the case of the two priests who, being unsure if it was permissible to smoke and pray at the same time, wrote to the Pope for a definitive answer. One priest phrased the question "Is it permissible to smoke while praying?" and was told it is not, since prayer should be the focus of one's whole attention; the other priest asked if it is permissible to pray while smoking and was told that it is, since it is always appropriate to pray. The form of a question may even block us from seeing solutions to problems that become visible through a different question. Consider the following story, whose authenticity is questionable but not, I think, its point:

Once upon a time, in a village in what is now Lithuania, there arose an unusual problem. A curious disease afflicted many of the townspeople. It was mostly fatal (though not always), and its onset was signaled by the victim's lapsing into a deathlike coma. Medical science not being quite so advanced as it is now, there was no definite way of knowing if the victim was actually dead when burial appeared seemly. As a result, the townspeople feared that several of their relatives had already been buried alive and that a similar fate might await them. How to overcome this uncertainty was their dilemma.

One group of people suggested that the coffins be well stocked with water and food and that a small air vent be drilled into them, just in case one of the "dead" happened to be alive. This was expensive to do but seemed more than worth the trouble. A second group, however, came up with a less expensive and more efficient idea. Each coffin would have a twelve-inch stake affixed to the inside of the coffin lid, exactly at the level of the heart. Then, when the coffin was closed, all uncertainty would cease.

The story does not indicate which solution was chosen, but for my purposes the choice is irrelevant. What is important to note is that different solutions were generated by different questions. The first solution was an answer to the question, How can we make sure that we do not bury people who are still alive? The second was an answer to the question, How can we make sure that everyone we bury is dead?

Questions, then, are like computers or television or stethoscopes or lie detectors, in that they are mechanisms that give direction to our thoughts, generate new ideas, venerate old ones, expose facts, or hide them. In this chapter, I wish to consider mechanisms that act like machines but are not normally thought of as part of Technopoly's repertoire. I must call attention to them precisely because they are so often overlooked. For all practical purposes, they may be considered technologies – technologies in disguise, perhaps, but technologies all the same.

Aside from language itself, I don't suppose there is a clearer example of a technology that doesn't look like one than the mathematical sign known as zero. A brief word about it may help to illuminate later examples.

The zero made its way from India to Europe in the tenth century. By the thirteenth century, it had taken hold of Western consciousness. (It was unknown to the Romans and the classical Greeks, although analogous concepts were known to Babylonian mathematicians of the Hellenistic period.) Without the zero, you will find it difficult to perform any of the calculations that are quite simple to do with it. If you should try multiplying MMMMMM by MMDCXXVI, you will have this point confirmed. I have been told, by the way, that such a calculation *can* be done, but the process is so laborious that the task is unlikely to be completed, a truth that did not escape the notice of medieval mathematicians. There is, in fact, no evidence that Roman numerals were ever used, or intended to be used, for calculation. For that purpose, mathematicians used an abacus, and between the tenth and thirteenth centuries, a struggle of sorts took place between abacists, who wrote Roman numerals but calculated with the abacus, and algorists, who used Hindu numerals employing the zero sign. The objection raised by the abacists was that the zero registered the *absence* of a power of ten, which no Roman numeral did, and which struck them as philosophically and perhaps aesthetically offensive. After all, the zero is a sign that affects values of numerals wherever it occurs but has no value in itself. It is a sign about signs, whose very etymology, via "cipher" from the Hindu word for "void," suggests the idea of "nothingness." To the abacists, it was a bizarre idea to have a sign marking "nothing," and I fear that I would have sided with the abacists.

I speak of the zero for two reasons: First, to underscore that it is a kind of technology that makes both possible and easy certain kinds of thoughts which, without it, would remain inaccessible to the average person. If it does not exactly have an ideology, it contains, at least, an idea. I have previously alluded to the technology of using letters or numbers to grade students' papers, and to the Greek discovery of the technology of alphabetization: like the use of zero, these are examples of how symbols may function like machines in creating new mind-sets and therefore new conceptions of reality. Second, the use of the zero and, of course, the Hindu numbering system of which it was a part made possible a sophisticated mathematics which, in turn, led to one of the most powerful technologies now in use: statistics.

Statistics makes possible new perceptions and realities by making visible large-scale patterns. Its uses in science are too well known to warrant notice here, except to remark that if, as the physicists tell us, the world is made up of probabilities at the level of subatomic particles, then statistics is the only means by which to describe its operations. Indeed, the uncertainty principle ensures that in the nature of things physics is unable to do more than make statistical predictions.

Of course, it is possible that physicists conceive of the world as probabilistic *because* statistics was invented. But that is not the question I wish to pursue here. A more practical question is, To what extent has statistics been allowed entry to places where it does not belong? . . .

In a culture that reveres statistics, we can never be sure what sort of nonsense will lodge in people's heads. The only plausible answer to the question why we use statistics for such measurements [as intelligence tests] is that it is done for sociopolitical reasons whose essential malignancy is disguised by the cover of "scientific inquiry." If we believe that blacks are dumber than whites, and that this is not merely our opinion but is confirmed by objective measures, then we can believe we have an irreproachable authority for making decisions about the allocation of resources. This is how, in Technopoly, science is used to make democracy "rational."

Polling is still another way. Just as statistics has spawned a huge testing industry, it has done the same for the polling of "public opinion." One may concede, at the start, that there are some uses of polling that may be said to be reliable, especially if the case involves a greatly restricted question such as, Do you plan to vote for X or Y? But to say a procedure is reliable is not to say it is useful. The question is as yet undecided whether knowledge of voter trends during a political campaign enriches or demeans the electoral process. But when polls are used to guide public policy, we have a different sort of issue altogether.

I have been in the presence of a group of United States congressmen who were gathered to discuss, over a period of two days, what might be done to make the future of America more survivable and, if possible, more humane. Ten consultants were called upon to offer perspectives and advice. Eight of them were pollsters. They spoke of the "trends" their polling uncovered; for example, that people were no longer interested in the women's movement, did not regard environmental issues as of paramount importance, did not think the "drug problem" was getting worse, and so on. It was apparent, at once, that these polling results would become the basis of how the congressmen thought the future should be managed. The ideas the congressmen had (all men, by the way) receded to the background. Their own perceptions, instincts, insights, and experience paled into irrelevance. Confronted by "social scientists," they were inclined to do what the "trends" suggested would satisfy the populace.[1]

It is not unreasonable to argue that the polling of public opinion puts democracy on a sound and scientific footing. If our political leaders are supposed to represent us, they must have some information about what we "believe." In principle, there is no problem here. The problems lie elsewhere, and there are at least four of them.

The first has to do with the forms of the questions that are put to the public. I refer the reader to the matter of whether it is proper to smoke and pray at the same time. Or, to take a more realistic example: If we ask people whether they think it acceptable for the environment to continue to be polluted, we are likely to come up with answers quite different from those generated by the question, Do you think the protection of the environment is of paramount importance? Or, Do you think safety in the streets is more important than environmental protection? The public's "opinion" on almost any issue will be a function of the question asked. (I might point out that in the seminar held by the congressmen, not one asked a question about the questions. They were interested in results, not in how these were obtained, and it did not seem to occur to them that the results and how they are obtained are inseparable.)

Typically, pollsters ask questions that will elicit yes or no answers. Is it necessary to point out that such answers do not give a robust meaning to the phrase "public opinion"? Were you, for example, to answer "No" to the question "Do you think the drug problem can be reduced by government programs?" one would hardly know much of interest or value about your opinion. But allowing you to speak or write at length on the matter would, of course, rule out using statistics. The point is that the use of statistics in polling changes the meaning of "public opinion" as dramatically as television changes the meaning of "political debate." In the American Technopoly, public opinion is a yes or no answer to an unexamined question.

Second, the technique of polling promotes the assumption that an opinion is a thing inside people that can be exactly located and extracted by the pollster's questions. But there is an alternative point of view, of which we might say, it is what Jefferson had in mind. An opinion is not a momentary thing but a process of thinking, shaped by the continuous acquisition of knowledge and the activity of questioning, discussion, and debate. A question may "invite" an opinion, but it also may modify and recast it; we might better say that people do not exactly "have" opinions but are, rather, involved in "opinioning." That an opinion is conceived of as a measurable thing falsifies the process by which people, in fact, do their opinioning; and how people do their opinioning goes to the heart of the meaning of a democratic society. Polling tells us nothing about this, and tends to hide the process from our view.

Which leads to the third point. Generally, polling ignores what people know about the subjects they are queried on. In a culture that is not obsessed with measuring and ranking things, this omission would probably be regarded as bizarre. But let us imagine what we would think of opinion polls if the questions came in pairs, indicating what people "believe" and what they "know" about the subject. If I may make up some figures, let us suppose we read the following: "The latest poll indicates that 72 percent of the American public believes we should withdraw economic aid from Nicaragua. Of those who expressed this opinion, 28 percent thought Nicaragua was in central Asia, 18 percent thought it was an island near New Zealand, and 27.4 percent believed that 'Africans should help themselves,' obviously confusing Nicaragua with Nigeria. Moreover, of those polled, 61.8 percent did not know that we give economic aid to Nicaragua, and 23 percent did not know what 'economic aid' means." Were pollsters inclined to provide such information, the prestige and power of polling would be considerably reduced. Perhaps even congressmen, confronted by massive ignorance, would invest their own understandings with greater trust.

The fourth problem with polling is that it shifts the locus of responsibility between political leaders and their constituents. It is true enough that congressmen are supposed to represent the interests of their constituents. But it is also true that congressmen are expected to use their own judgment about what is in the public's best interests. For this, they must consult their own experience and knowledge. Before the ascendance of polling, political leaders, though never indifferent to the opinions of their constituents, were largely judged on their capacity to make decisions based on such wisdom as they possessed; that is, political leaders were responsible for the decisions they made. With the refinement and extension of the polling process, they are under increasing pressure to forgo deciding anything for themselves and to defer to the opinions of the voters, no matter how ill-informed and shortsighted those opinions might be. . . .

Before leaving the subject of the technology of statistics, I must call attention to the fact that statistics creates an enormous amount of completely useless information, which compounds the always difficult task of locating that which is useful to a culture. This is more than a case of "information-overload." It is a matter of "information-trivia," which has the effect of placing all information on an equal level. No one has expressed this misuse of a technology better than the *New Yorker* magazine cartoonist Mankoff. Showing an attentive man watching television news, Mankoff has the newscaster saying, "A preliminary census report indicates that for the first time in our nation's history female anthropologists outnumber male professional golfers." When statistics and computers are joined, volumes of garbage are generated in public discourse. Those who have watched television sports programs will know that Mankoff's cartoon is, in fact, less of a parody than a documentary. Useless, meaningless statistics flood the attention of the viewer. Sportscasters call them "graphics" in an effort to suggest that the information, graphically presented, is a vital supplement to the action of the game. For example: "Since 1984, the Buffalo Bills have won only two games in which they were four points ahead with less than six minutes to play." Or this: "In only 17 percent of the times he has pitched at Shea Stadium has Dwight Gooden struck out the third and fourth hitters less than three times when they came to bat with more than one runner on base."[2] What is one to do with this or to make of it? And yet there seems to be a market for useless information. Those who read *USA Today*, for example, are offered on the front page of each issue an idiotic statistic of the day that looks something like this: "The four leading states in banana consumption from 1980 through 1989 are Kansas, North Dakota, Wyoming, and Louisiana. Oddly, Nevada, which was ninth in 1989, fell to twenty-sixth last year, which is exactly where it ranks in kiwi consumption."[3]

It is surprising how frequently such blather will serve as the backbone of conversations which are essentially meaningless. I have heard New Yorkers, with a triumphant flourish, offer out-of-towners the statistic that New York City is only eighth in the nation in per-capita violent crimes and then decline to go outside because it was past 6:00 P.M.

I do not say, of course, that all such statistical statements are useless. If we learn that one out of every four black males between the ages of twenty and thirty has spent some time in prison, and that the nation's expenditure for the education of black children is 23 percent less than it is for white children, we may have some statistical facts that will help us to see a cause-and-effect relationship, and thereby suggest a course of action. But statistics, like any other technology, has a tendency to run out of control, to occupy more of our mental space than it warrants, to invade realms of discourse where it can only wreak havoc. When it is out of control, statistics buries in a heap of trivia what is necessary to know.

And there is another point, which in fact is the core of this chapter. Some technologies come in disguise. Rudyard Kipling called them "technologies in repose." They do not look like technologies, and because of that they do their work, for good or ill, without much criticism or even awareness. This applies not only to IQ tests and to polls and to all systems of ranking and grading but to credit cards, accounting procedures, and achievement tests. It applies in the educational world to what are called "academic courses," as well. A course is a technology for learning. I have "taught" about two hundred of them and do not know why each one lasts exactly fifteen weeks, or why each meeting lasts exactly one hour and fifty minutes. If the answer is that this is done for administrative convenience, then a course is a fraudulent technology. It is put forward as a desirable structure for learning when in fact it is only a structure for allocating space, for convenient record-keeping, and for control of faculty time. The point is that the origin of and raison d'être for a course are concealed from us. We come to believe it exists for one reason when it exists for quite another. . . .

It is necessary to understand where our techniques come from and what they are good for; we must make them visible so that they may be restored to our sovereignty.

NOTES

1. The occasion, in the spring of 1990, was a retreat outside of Washington, D.C. The group of twenty-three Democratic congressmen was led by Richard Gephardt.
2. I have, of course, made up these ridiculous statistics. The point is, it doesn't matter.
3. See the preceding note.

Discussion Questions

1. Review Postman's examples of invisible technologies. Think of some additional examples. What are the positive and negative aspects of both sets of examples?

2. Do you share Postman's concern about the use and abuse of statistics? Why or why not? How often do you use statistics to support your arguments? Do you consider yourself to be knowledgeable about the interpretations of statistics? Why or why not?

3. Postman says, "A question, even of the simplest kind, is not and can never be unbiased." What does he mean? Do you agree? Give examples to support your view.

4. Does Postman seem to think our elected representatives in government should follow their own judgment and experience, or that they should go along with public opinion as determined by pollsters? How does Postman support his views on this matter? Is his support convincing? Explain.

Journal Entries

1. While reading the newspaper and watching television over the course of several days, compile a list of the useless statistics you find. Explain whether you find these trivial statistics potentially harmful or simply entertaining.

2. Recall a personal experience involving an invisible technology. Feel free to stretch Postman's definition of invisible technology. Then explain why your examples fit the definition, and tell whether your experience was one of growth or disappointment.

Writing Projects

1. Postman discusses the way in which legislators are often confronted with statistics and polling during the decision-making process. Write an essay to

a group of legislators or other policy makers in which you explain the hidden hazards of using statistics and polling in the political arena. Include an analysis of the types of questions often asked in political polls, and provide examples of the kind of questions you think should be asked but usually are not.

2. Explain why Postman discusses the mathematical sign of a zero as an example of technology. Evaluate his presentation of this example. Using Postman's discussion as a basis, develop your own example of a technology — either an explicit or an invisible one — that has created "new mind-sets and therefore new conceptions of reality."

Collaborative Projects

1. Cartoons use humor to convey a range of attitudes and emotions toward any number of concepts and practices, including statistics and technology. Working with a classmate, assemble a collection of cartoons related to technology and/or statistics; see, for example, Gary Larson's "The Far Side" cartoons. Observe how the point of the cartoon relies on a combination of verbal and visual modes. Show the rest of your class your findings and analysis of the cartoons' humor.

2. Study Postman's examples of biased questions. Then, working with a classmate, find or create your own examples to illustrate the concept of a biased question. You might think of a topic about which you would like to conduct an opinion poll. Working with a partner, each of you could phrase questions about the same subject differently so as to elicit opposing responses. Or you could study questions as they are phrased in textbooks. Compare how two different texts present material on the same subject, and determine whether their discussion questions reflect different interpretations of the subject. Report to the class on your findings and methodology.

Making Connections

Questions to Discuss

1. Rank the seven writers in this chapter from the least to the most in favor of developing and using technology. Discuss your rankings and explain how each writer stands in relation to the others.

2. Do you see significant connections between Robert Samuelson's views on modern technology and Witold Rybczynski's ideas on why we tend to resist some new products of technology and romanticize certain older ones? Looking at Samuelson's and Rybczynski's examples, and drawing on your own experience, do you see any patterns in the specific kinds of machines that we resist as well as those we embrace? For example, do we adapt more quickly to machines that provide speed and power but less quickly to machines that increase convenience while requiring time to master them?

3. Defining key terms is one of the strategies writers use when they seek to persuade their audience to a certain way of thinking, or simply to provide their audience with new information. Some common approaches to definition include the following: formal definitions, etymological background, examples and illustrations, or synonyms. Select two or three essays from this chapter and analyze the authors' approaches to defining key terms. Compare and contrast, for example, Robert Samuelson's methods of defining "smart" and "stupid" technology, Alvin Weinberg's method of defining a "technological fix," and Neil Postman's construction of a definition of "technologies in repose."

Suggested Writing Projects

1. Hajime Karatsu and Witold Rybczynski discuss at some length the cause-and-effect relationship between a country's technology and its economy. Write an essay comparing and contrasting their views and how they support them. Explain which view you think best describes the relationship between technology and economics in the United States.

2. Which selections were written by authors to audiences they saw as needing to be persuaded to change their minds, or at least to consider technology in a new way? Write an essay analyzing the rhetorical techniques those authors employed in their attempt to persuade the audience to consider a different view.

3. The effects of technology on humans are discussed by most of the authors in this chapter. Select two or three of the readings and write an essay responding to the way in which each of the authors presents the probable effects of technology on us. Feel free to incorporate discussion of effects that you consider important but that the authors did not address.

3

Practicing Science

 "Every great advance in science has issued from a new audacity of imagination," according to John Dewey (1859–1952), a noted American philosopher and educator. If Dewey was right, scientists must proceed boldly – even impudently – to form concepts and theorems that deal creatively with reality. This chapter presents scientists who work in such a way.

Typically, scientists describe their work as requiring close, accurate observation along with precise, detailed record keeping. We expect scientists to test their assumptions, resist oversimplification, refrain from making hasty generalizations, and offer abundant support for their conclusions.

We tend not to recognize the role that intuition and imagination play in the scientist's work. Perhaps the idea of a scientist using imagination suggests a person less grounded in reality, whereas we typically visualize the scientist working in the midst of microscopes, test tubes, and Bunsen burners. Yet conducting scientific research is not limited to carrying out laboratory experiments according to rigid rules that allow no room for following hunches and listening to one's intuition. If it were, Loren Eiseley would not have been drawn to the way in which Darwin displayed an "intuitive sensitivity to the life of other creatures about him."

Nevertheless, scientists do not usually write about their emotional or intuitive responses to their work. After reading reports of scientific research one might conclude that science is an entirely orderly, logical, even predictable process. Scientific reports imply that the scientist goes into the laboratory or out into the field to collect data, which he or she carefully tests and analyzes. Then the scientist draws a logical conclusion and thereby discovers a scientific fact.

From conducting scientific experiments yourself, you have probably realized that science is not particularly orderly and that scientific facts do not actually lie hidden, avoiding discovery. Anthropological studies of how science is practiced, such as *Laboratory Life* by Bruno Latour and Steve Woolgar, portray the scientific laboratory as a "system of fact construction" whereby scientific knowledge is "fabricated from disorder and chaos." Indeed, evidence suggests that science is a creative process, not a mechanical one.

This chapter presents various perspectives on the practice of science. In the first essay, Loren Eiseley thrusts the reader into the midst of conflicting scientific methods. He identifies two diametrically opposed approaches to interpreting the natural world: Charles Darwin's, which was suffused with what Eiseley terms "a sense of the holy"; and Sigmund Freud's, which Eiseley considers "cold, clinical, and reserved." Adding an ironic dimension to Eiseley's essay is his description of a scientist like Darwin, whose work aroused tremendous religious controversy, as a man of reverence.

Next, Lewis Thomas tackles the weighty issue of scientific hubris, an attitude of arrogance and conceit. His essay explores the biases in our culture that account for an intolerant view of scientists' pride in themselves and their work, particularly when it seeks to unveil the mysteries of nature.

An excerpt from Mary Shelley's novel *Frankenstein* further highlights the societal and personal consequences of scientific hubris. Being critical of the Romantic idealism of her day, Shelley created an allegory to portray the dangers inherent in scientific realization of an abstract ideal. Dr. Frankenstein comes to regret his prideful attempts to "become greater than his nature will allow."

There follows an excerpt from Thomas Kuhn's landmark work, *The Structure of Scientific Revolutions.* This book has been largely responsible for debunking the myth of science as a steady, logical process of accumulating specialized knowledge. Kuhn's excerpt defines two closely related key terms, *normal science* and *paradigms,* both of which suggest that scientific practice is based on "particular coherent traditions" to which working scientists are committed. These traditions come to be overturned as a consequence of periodic revolutions in scientific thought.

Such revolutions often begin with a subtle but definite resistance from an individual scientist to accepted notions in the scientific community. Jane Goodall is one such scientist. Goodall, who has worked with chimpanzees in Gombe National Park for more than thirty years, antagonized the community of anthropological experts when she first referred to chimpanzees in human terms.

Just as Goodall's colleagues favored certain ways of referring to their research subjects, all scientists conduct their work according to professional biases. As a group they believe that certain methods, theories, and types of equipment are better than the ones they have rejected. Scientists sometimes allow their work to be influenced by their personal prejudices. Stephen Jay Gould, in an incisive historical account, outlines how a particular example of research was used to provide biological justification for racial prejudice.

An essay by O. B. Hardison, Jr., concludes the chapter; it takes a broad, humanistic view of scientific practice. Fascinated by the way in which Darwin described his research, Hardison illustrates how Darwin was closely attuned to the richness of both nature and language. Hardison compares the writing of nineteenth-century poet Oliver Wendell Holmes in "The Chambered Nautilus" to Darwin's description of the La Plata woodpecker, claiming Darwin's writing to be the more gracefully poetic.

From the writers presented in this chapter we gain insights into the human dimension of the scientific enterprise. Scientists seek to gather and interpret data objectively, but sometimes, unbeknown to themselves, their personal biases intrude. Successful scientists rely on their instruments but also follow their instincts and intuition. Throughout it all, they work as a community to construct useful facts and impose order upon chaos.

References

John Dewey, *The Quest for Certainty*. London: G. Allen & Unwin, 1930.
Bruno Latour and Steve Woolgar, *Laboratory Life: The Social Construction of Scientific Facts*. Beverly Hills: Sage Publications, 1979.

Loren Eiseley

Science and the Sense of the Holy

Loren Eiseley *(1907–1977), who served as curator of the University Museum and pro-*
fessor of anthropology at the University of Pennsylvania, was recognized for his literary
achievement in 1971 with his election to the National Institute of Arts and Letters. A natu-
ralist, poet, scientist, and humanist, Eiseley had a distinguished career; among his writings
are several well-respected essay collections treating scientific subjects in a meditative manner.
In this excerpt from The Star Thrower *(1978), Eiseley classifies scientists into two cate-*
gories: those who appreciate the mystery of the natural world, as did Charles Darwin, and
those who concentrate on the clinical, as did Freud. Eiseley's essays, which are appreciated
for their poetic quality as well as for the way in which they make scientific material accessible
to a wide audience, were published in scientific journals, such as American
Anthropologist, *as well as in* Harper's. *Other books by Eiseley include* The Immense
Journey *(1957) and* Notes of an Alchemist *(1972).*

Questions to Consider

☐ Notice how Eiseley's analogy at the beginning of this essay helps shape the
emphasis and structure of the piece.

☐ Eiseley uses comparison and contrast as a structural device in this essay.
What or who is being compared? Consider whether Eiseley reveals any
bias through his use of classification.

WHEN I was a young man engaged in fossil hunting in the Nebraska
badlands I was frequently reminded that the ravines, washes, and
gullies over which we wandered resembled the fissures in a giant
exposed brain. The human brain contains the fossil memories of its past—
buried but not extinguished moments—just as this more formidable replica
contained deep in its inner stratigraphic convolutions earth's past in the shape
of horned titanotheres and stalking, dirk-toothed cats. Man's memory erodes
away in the short space of a lifetime. Jutting from the coils of the earth brain
over which I clambered were the buried remnants, the changing history, of the
entire age of mammals—millions of years of vanished daylight with their ac-
companying traces of volcanic outbursts and upheavals. It may well be asked
why this analogy of earth's memory should so preoccupy the mind of a scien-

tist as to have affected his entire outlook upon nature and upon his kinship with – even his concern for – the plant and animal world about him.

Perhaps the problem can best be formulated by pointing out that there are two extreme approaches to the interpretation of the living world. One was expressed by Charles Darwin at the age of twenty-eight; one by Sigmund Freud in his mature years. Other men of science have been arrayed on opposite sides of the question, but the eminence of these two scholars will serve to point up a controversy that has been going on since science arose, sometimes quietly, sometimes marked by vitriolic behavior, as when a certain specialist wedded to his own view of the universe hurled his opponent's book into his wastebasket only to have it retrieved and cherished by a graduate student who became a lifelong advocate of the opinions reviled by his mentor. Thus it is evident that, in the supposed objective world of science, emotion and temperament may play a role in our selection of the mental tools with which we choose to investigate nature.

Charles Darwin, at a time when the majority of learned men looked upon animals as either automatons or creatures created merely for human exploitation, jotted thoughtfully into one of his early journals upon evolution the following observation:

"If we choose to let conjecture run wild, then animals, our fellow brethren in pain, disease, suffering and famine – our slaves in the most laborious works, our companions in our amusements – they may partake of our origin in one common ancestor – we may be all netted together."

What, we may now inquire, is the world view here implied, one way in which a great scientist looked upon the subject matter that was to preoccupy his entire working life? In spite of the fact that Darwin was, in his later years, an agnostic, in spite of confessing he was "in thick mud" so far as metaphysics was concerned, the remark I have quoted gives every sign of that feeling of awe, of dread of the holy playing upon nature, which characterizes the work of a number of naturalists and physicists down even to the present day. Darwin's remark reveals an intuitive sensitivity to the life of other creatures about him, an attitude quite distinct from that of the laboratory experimentalist who is hardened to the infliction of pain. In addition, Darwin's final comment that we may be all netted together in one gigantic mode of experience, that we are in a mystic sense one single diffuse animal, subject to joy and suffering beyond what we endure as individuals, reveals a youth drawn to the world of nature by far more than just the curiosity to be readily satisfied by the knife or the scalpel.

If we turn to Sigmund Freud by way of contrast we find an oddly inhibited reaction. Freud, though obviously influenced by the elegant medical experimenters of his college days, groped his way alone, and by methods not subject to quantification or absolute verification, into the dark realms of the subconscious. His reaction to the natural world, or at least his feelings and intuitions about it, are basically cold, clinical, and reserved. He of all men recognized what one poet has termed "the terrible archaeology of the brain." Freud states that "nothing once constructed has perished, and all the earlier stages of development have survived alongside the latest." But for Freud, convinced that childhood made the man, adult reactions were apt to fall under the suspicion of being childhood ghosts raised up in a disguised fashion. Thus, insightful though he could be, the very nature of his study of man tended to generate distrust of that outgoing empathy we observed in the young Darwin. "I find it very difficult to work with these intangible qualities," confessed Freud. He was suspicious of their representing some lingering monster of childhood, even if reduced in size. Since Freud regarded any type of religious feeling—even the illuminative quality of the universe—as an illusion, feelings of awe before natural phenomena such as that manifested by Darwin were to him basically remnants of childhood and to be dismissed accordingly.

In *Civilization and Its Discontents* Freud speaks with slight condescension of a friend who claimed a sensation of eternity, something limitless, unbounded—"oceanic," to use the friend's expression. The feeling had no sectarian origin, no assurance of immortality, but implied just such a sense of awe as might lie at the root of the religious impulse. "I cannot," maintained Freud, "discover this 'oceanic' impulse in myself." Instead he promptly psychoanalyzes the feeling of oneness with the universe into the child's pleasure ego which holds to itself all that is comforting; in short, the original ego, the infant's ego, included everything. Later, by experience, contended Freud, our adult ego becomes only a shrunken vestige of that far more extensive feeling which "expressed an inseparable connection . . . with the external world."

In essence, then, Freud is explaining away one of the great feelings characteristic of the best in man by relegating it to a childhood atavistic survival in adult life. The most highly developed animals, he observes, have arisen from the lowest. Although the great saurians are gone, the dwarfed crocodile remains. Presumably if Freud had completed the analogy he would have been forced to say that crocodilian adults without awe and with egos shrunken safely into their petty concerns represented a higher, more practical evolutionary level than the aberrant adult who persists in feelings of wonder before which Freud recoiled with a nineteenth-century mechanist's distaste, although not without acknowledging that this lurking childlike corruption might be widespread. He chose to regard it, however, as just another manifestation of the irrational aspect of man's divided psyche.

Over six decades before the present, a German theologian, Rudolf Otto, had chosen for his examination what he termed *The Idea of the Holy (Das Heilige)*. Appearing in 1917 in a time of bitterness and disillusionment, his book was and is still widely read. It cut across denominational divisions and spoke to all those concerned with that *mysterium tremendum*, that very awe before the universe which Freud had sighed over and dismissed as irrational. I think it safe to affirm that Freud left adult man somewhat shrunken and misjudged—misjudged because some of the world's scientists and artists have been deeply affected by the great mystery, less so the child at one's knee who frequently has to be disciplined to what in India has been called the "opening of the heavenly eye."

Ever since man first painted animals in the dark of caves he has been responding to the holy, to the numinous, to the mystery of being and becoming, to what Goethe very aptly called "the weird portentous." Something inexpressible was felt to lie behind nature. The bear cult, circumpolar in distribution and known archaeologically to extend into Neanderthal times, is a further and most ancient example. The widespread beliefs in descent from a totemic animal, guardian helpers in the shapes of animals, the concept of the game lords who released or held back game to man are all part of a variety of a sanctified, reverent experience that extends from the beautiful rock paintings of South Africa to the men of the Labradorean forests or the Plains Indian seeking by starvation and isolation to bring the sacred spirits to his assistance. All this is part of the human inheritance, the wonder of the world, and nowhere does that wonder press closer to us than in the guise of animals which, whether supernaturally as in the caves of our origins or, as in Darwin's sudden illumination, perceived to be, at heart, one form, one awe-inspiring mystery, seemingly diverse and apart but derived from the same genetic source. Thus the *mysterium* arose not by primitive campfires alone. Skins may still prickle in a modern classroom.

In the end, science as we know it has two basic types of practitioners. One is the educated man who still has a controlled sense of wonder before the universal mystery, whether it hides in a snail's eye or within the light that impinges on that delicate organ. The second kind of observer is the extreme reductionist who is so busy stripping things apart that the tremendous mystery has been reduced to a trifle, to intangibles not worth troubling one's head about. The world of the secondary qualities—color, sound, thought—is reduced to illusion. The *only* true reality becomes the chill void of ever-streaming particles.

If one is a biologist this approach can result in behavior so remarkably cruel that it ceases to be objective but rather suggests a deep grain of sadism that is not science. To list but one example, a recent newspaper article reported that a great urban museum of national reputation had spent over a half-million dollars on mutilating experiments with cats. The experiments are too revolting to chronicle here and the museum has not seen fit to enlighten the public on the knowledge gained at so frightful a cost in pain. The cost, it would appear, lies not alone in animal suffering but in the dehumanization of those willing to engage in such blind, random cruelty. The practice was defended by museum officials, who in a muted show of scientific defense maintained the right to study what they chose "without regard to its demonstrable practical value."

This is a scientific precept hard to override since the days of Galileo, as the official well knew. Nevertheless, behind its seamless façade of probity many terrible things are and will be done. Blaise Pascal, as far back as the seventeenth century, foresaw our two opposed methods. Of them he said: "There are two equally dangerous extremes, to shut reason out, and to let nothing else in." It is the reductionist who, too frequently, would claim that the end justifies the means, who would assert reason as his defense and let that *mysterium* which guards man's moral nature fall away in indifference, a phantom without reality.

"The whole of existence frightens me," protested the philosopher Søren Kierkegaard; "from the smallest fly to the mystery of the Incarnation, everything is unintelligible to me, most of all myself." By contrast, the evolutionary reductionist Ernst Haeckel, writing in 1877, commented that "the cell consists of matter . . . composed chiefly of carbon with an admixture of hydrogen, nitrogen and sulphur. These component parts, properly united, produce the soul and body of the animated world, and suitably nourished become man. With this single argument the mystery of the universe is explained, the Deity annulled and a new era of infinite knowledge ushered in." Since these remarks of Haeckel's, uttered a hundred years ago, the genetic alphabet has scarcely substantiated in its essential intricacy Haeckel's carefree dismissal of the complexity of life. If anything, it has given weight to Kierkegaard's wary statement or at least heightened the compassionate wonder with which we are led to look upon our kind.

"A conviction akin to religious feeling of the rationality or intelligibility of the world lies behind all scientific work of a high order," says Albert Einstein. Here once more the eternal dichotomy manifests itself. Thoreau, the man of literature, writes compassionately, "Shall I not have intelligence with the earth? Am I not partly leaves and vegetable mould myself?" Or Walt Whitman, the poet, protests in his *Song of Myself:* "whoever walks a furlong without sympathy walks to his own funeral drest in a shroud."

> "Magnifying and applying come I" – he thunders –
> "Outbidding at the start the old cautious hucksters . . .
> Not objecting to special revelations, considering a curl of smoke or a hair
> on the back of my hand just as curious as any revelation."

Strange, is it not, that so many of these voices are not those of children, but those of great men – Newton playing on the vast shores of the universe, or Whitman touched with pity or Darwin infused with wonder over the clambering tree of life. Strange, that all these many voices should be dismissed as the atavistic yearnings of an unreduced childlike ego seeking in "oceanic" fashion to absorb its entire surroundings, as though in revolt against the counting house, the laboratory, and the computer.

Discussion Questions

1. Why do you suppose the author chose to use the first person singular point of view in the opening paragraph and then switched to the first person plural in the second paragraph? What effect does this have on the reader?

2. Early in the essay, Eiseley asserts that in the "supposed objective world of science, emotion and temperament may play a role. . . ." Why is this an important observation? Do you agree with Eiseley? How does the author support his assertion?

3. What does Eiseley mean by a "sense of the holy" in this essay? Do you agree that some scientific study is best conducted with a "sense of the holy"? If you agree, give an example.

4. Eiseley lends authority to his arguments by citing various scientists, philosophers, and literary writers. Which of the writers he quotes are familiar to you? What kind of knowledge does he anticipate you to have? How much does he rely on your knowledge? Suggest other writers or scientists whose work would be relevant to Eiseley's discussion.

Journal Entries

1. Write an account, similar to Eiseley's description, of an experience in your own life when you became aware of the power of nature and were awed by it.

2. Most people have heard of Freud by the time they graduate from high school. Nevertheless, after reading Eiseley's passage you might wish to read about Freud in an encyclopedia or biographical dictionary if you have not read about his work or theories elsewhere. Then discuss your response to Eiseley's presentation of Freud. Do you agree that Freud is an appropriate example for Eiseley's category of reductionist scientists?

Writing Projects

1. What are some of Eiseley's most effective figures of speech (that is, analogies, metaphors, and similes)? What makes them striking? What is your response to them? Write an essay in which you analyze Eiseley's use of figurative language to prompt a response from the reader as well as to structure his argument.

2. Examine the attitudes and beliefs behind some scientists' insistence that they should be given financial support to study whatever they deem interesting "without regard to its demonstrable practical value." Why would someone oppose this view? Why is this argument important? How can it be resolved?

Collaborative Project

Working with a partner, research some of the beliefs and myths of an ancient culture that demonstrate how the reverence for animals is part of that culture's general sense of wonder toward the natural world. Read some of its myths and religious literature. Look at images in its art and artifacts. Include in your report an analysis of how the many different products in the culture express its sense of the holy in the natural world.

Lewis Thomas

The Hazards of Science

Lewis Thomas's (1913–1993) writing earned him the unofficial title of "poet laureate of twentieth-century medical science." He began writing essays for the New England Journal of Medicine in 1971; during his career he published more than 200 articles in medical and science journals. He won the National Book Award for his collection of essays entitled The Lives of a Cell (1974) and the American Book Award for his essay collection The Medusa and the Snail (1979), from which the following essay is taken. When Thomas was honored with the Albert Lasker Public Service Award in 1989, the jury said his writings "have converted countless nonscientists into appreciative spectators and supporters of biomedical research." Thomas specialized in cancer research; from 1973 to 1980 he was director of the Memorial Sloan-Kettering Cancer Center in New York City, one of the foremost cancer hospitals in the world. Ironically, he died from Waldenstrom's disease, a rare form of cancer named after one of his friends, Jan Waldenstrom of Sweden. Widely admired for his literary style, Thomas displayed a long-standing commitment to connecting the sciences and the humanities. Thomas's other books include his memoirs, The Youngest Science: Notes of a Medicine Watcher (1983) and The Fragile Species (1992). In "The Hazards of Science" Thomas explains why he considers scientific hubris, as displayed by scientists and nonscientists alike, to be a serious danger.

Questions to Consider

☐ Before you begin, look up the term *hubris* in a dictionary if it is not already familiar.

☐ Watch how Thomas structures his essay around the definition of a key term. How does he expand his definition and further his argument?

THE code word for criticism of science and scientists these days is "hubris." Once you've said that word, you've said it all; it sums up, in a word, all of today's apprehensions and misgivings in the public mind—not just about what is perceived as the insufferable attitude of the scientists themselves but, enclosed in the same word, what science and technology are perceived to be doing to make this century, this near to its ending, turn out so wrong.

"Hubris" is a powerful word, containing layers of powerful meaning, derived from a very old word, but with a new life of its own, growing way beyond the limits of its original meaning. Today, it is strong enough to carry the full weight of disapproval for the cast of mind that thought up atomic fusion and fission as ways of first blowing up and later heating cities as well as the attitudes which led to strip-mining, offshore oil wells, Kepone, food additives, SSTs, and the tiny spherical particles of plastic recently discovered clogging the waters of the Sargasso Sea.

The biomedical sciences are now caught up with physical science and technology in the same kind of critical judgment, with the same pejorative word. Hubris is responsible, it is said, for the whole biological revolution. It is hubris that has given us the prospects of behavior control, psychosurgery, fetal research, heart transplants, the cloning of prominent politicians from bits of their own eminent tissue, iatrogenic disease, overpopulation, and recombinant DNA. This last, the new technology that permits the stitching of one creature's genes into the DNA of another, to make hybrids, is currently cited as the ultimate example of hubris. It is hubris for man to manufacture a hybrid on his own.

So now we are back to the first word again, from "hybrid" to "hubris," and the hidden meaning of two beings joined unnaturally together by man is somehow retained. Today's joining is straight out of Greek mythology: it is the combining of man's capacity with the special prerogative of the gods, and it is really in this sense of outrage that the word "hubris" is being used today. This is what the word has grown into, a warning, a code word, a shorthand signal from the language itself: if man starts doing things reserved for the gods, deifying himself, the outcome will be something worse for him, symbolically, than the litters of wild boars and domestic sows were for the ancient Romans.

To be charged with hubris is therefore an extremely serious matter, and not to be dealt with by murmuring things about antiscience and antiintellectualism, which is what many of us engaged in science tend to do these days. The doubts about our enterprise have their origin in the most profound kind of human anxiety. If we are right and the critics are wrong, then it has to be that the word "hubris" is being mistakenly employed, that this is not what we are up to, that there is, for the time being anyway, a fundamental misunderstanding of science.

I suppose there is one central question to be dealt with, and I am not at all sure how to deal with it, although I am quite certain about my own answer to it. It is this: are there some kinds of information leading to some sorts of knowledge that human beings are really better off not having? Is there a limit to scientific inquiry not set by what is knowable but by what we *ought* to be knowing? Should we stop short of learning about some things, for fear of what we, or someone, will do with the knowledge? My own answer is a flat no, but I must confess that this is an intuitive response and I am neither inclined nor trained to reason my way through it.

There has been some effort, in and out of scientific quarters, to make re-combinant DNA into the issue on which to settle this argument. Proponents of this line of research are accused of pure hubris, of assuming the rights of gods, of arrogance and outrage; what is more, they confess themselves to be in the business of making live hybrids with their own hands. The mayor of Cambridge and the attorney general of New York have both been advised to put a stop to it, forthwith.

It is not quite the same sort of argument, however, as the one about limit-ing knowledge, although this is surely part of it. The knowledge is already here, and the rage of the argument is about its application in technology. Should DNA for making certain useful or interesting proteins be incorporated into *E. coli* plasmids or not? Is there a risk of inserting the wrong sort of toxins or hazardous viruses, and then having the new hybrid organisms spread be-yond the laboratory? Is this a technology for creating new varieties of pathogens, and should it be stopped because of this?

If the argument is held to this level, I can see no reason why it cannot be settled, by reasonable people. We have learned a great deal about the handling of dangerous microbes in the last century, although I must say that the oppo-nents of recombinant-DNA research tend to downgrade this huge body of in-formation. At one time or another, agents as hazardous as those of rabies, psit-tacosis, plague, and typhus have been dealt with by investigators in secure laboratories, with only rare instances of self-infection of the investigators them-selves, and no instances at all of epidemics. It takes some high imagining to postulate the creation of brand-new pathogens so wild and voracious as to spread from equally secure laboratories to endanger human life at large, as some of the arguers are now maintaining.

But this is precisely the trouble with the recombinant-DNA problem: it has become an emotional issue, with too many irretrievably lost tempers on both sides. It has lost the sound of a discussion of technological safety, and be-gins now to sound like something else, almost like a religious controversy, and here it is moving toward the central issue: are there some things in science we should not be learning about?

There is an inevitably long list of hard questions to follow this one, begin-ning with the one which asks whether the mayor of Cambridge should be the one to decide, first off.

Maybe we'd be wiser, all of us, to back off before the recombinant-DNA issue becomes too large to cope with. If we're going to have a fight about it, let it be confined to the immediate issue of safety and security, of the recombi-nants now under consideration, and let us by all means have regulations and guidelines to assure the public safety wherever these are indicated or even sug-gested. But if it is possible let us stay off that question about limiting human knowledge. It is too loaded, and we'll simply not be able to cope with it.

By this time it will have become clear that I have already taken sides in the matter, and my point of view is entirely prejudiced. This is true, but with a qualification. I am not so much in favor of recombinant-DNA research as I am opposed to the opposition to this line of inquiry. As a longtime student of infectious-disease agents I do not take kindly the declarations that we do not know how to keep from catching things in laboratories, much less how to keep them from spreading beyond the laboratory walls. I believe we learned a lot about this sort of thing, long ago. Moreover, I regard it as a form of hubris-in-reverse to claim that man can make deadly pathogenic microorganisms so easily. In my view, it takes a long time and a great deal of interliving before a microbe can become a successful pathogen. Pathogenicity is, in a sense, a highly skilled trade, and only a tiny minority of all the numberless tons of microbes on the earth has ever been involved itself in it; most bacteria are busy with their own business, browsing and recycling the rest of life. Indeed, pathogenicity often seems to me a sort of biological accident in which signals are misdirected by the microbe or misinterpreted by the host, as in the case of endotoxin, or in which the intimacy between host and microbe is of such long standing that a form of molecular mimicry becomes possible, as in the case of diphtheria toxin. I do not believe that by simply putting together new combinations of genes one can create creatures as highly skilled and adapted for dependence as a pathogen must be, any more than I have ever believed that microbial life from the moon or Mars could possibly make a living on this planet.

But, as I said, I'm not at all sure this is what the argument is really about. Behind it is that other discussion, which I wish we would not have to become enmeshed in.

I cannot speak for the physical sciences, which have moved an immense distance in this century by any standard, but it does seem to me that in the biological and medical sciences we are still far too ignorant to begin making judgments about what sorts of things we should be learning or not learning. To the contrary, we ought to be grateful for whatever snatches we can get hold of, and we ought to be out there on a much larger scale than today's, looking for more.

We should be very careful with that word "hubris," and make sure it is not used when not warranted. There is a great danger in applying it to the search for knowledge. The application of knowledge is another matter, and there is hubris in plenty in our technology, but I do not believe that looking for new information about nature, at whatever level, can possibly be called unnatural. Indeed, if there is any single attribute of human beings, apart from language, which distinguishes them from all other creatures on earth, it is their insatiable, uncontrollable drive to learn things and then to exchange the information with others of the species. Learning is what we do, when you think about it. I cannot think of a human impulse more difficult to govern.

But I can imagine lots of reasons for trying to govern it. New information about nature is very likely, at the outset, to be upsetting to someone or other. The recombinant-DNA line of research is already upsetting, not because of the dangers now being argued about but because it is disturbing, in a fundamental way, to face the fact that the genetic machinery in control of the planet's life can be fooled around with so easily. We do not like the idea that anything so fixed and stable as a species line can be changed. The notion that genes can be taken out of one genome and inserted in another is unnerving. Classical mythology is peopled with mixed beings – part man, part animal or plant – and most of them are associated with tragic stories. Recombinant DNA is a reminder of bad dreams.

The easiest decision for society to make in matters of this kind is to appoint an agency, or a commission, or a subcommittee within an agency to look into the problem and provide advice. And the easiest course for a committee to take, when confronted by any process that appears to be disturbing people or making them uncomfortable, is to recommend that it be stopped, at least for the time being.

I can easily imagine such a committee, composed of unimpeachable public figures, arriving at the decision that the time is not quite ripe for further exploration of the transplantation of genes, that we should put this off for a while, maybe until next century, and get on with other affairs that make us less discomfited. Why not do science on something more popular, say, how to get solar energy more cheaply? Or mental health?

The trouble is, it would be very hard to stop once this line was begun. There are, after all, all sorts of scientific inquiry that are not much liked by one constituency or another, and we might soon find ourselves with crowded rosters, panels, standing committees, set up in Washington for the appraisal, and then the regulation, of research. Not on grounds of the possible value and usefulness of the new knowledge, mind you, but for guarding society against scientific hubris, against the kinds of knowledge we're better off without.

It would be absolutely irresistible as a way of spending time, and people would form long queues for membership. Almost anything would be fair game, certainly anything to do with genetics, anything relating to population control, or, on the other side, research on aging. Very few fields would get by, except perhaps for some, like mental health, in which nobody really expects anything much to happen, surely nothing new or disturbing.

The research areas in the greatest trouble would be those already containing a sense of bewilderment and surprise, with discernible prospects of upheaving present dogmas.

It is hard to predict how science is going to turn out, and if it is really good science it is impossible to predict. This is in the nature of the enterprise. If the things to be found are actually new, they are by definition unknown in advance, and there is no way of telling in advance where a really new line of inquiry will lead. You cannot make choices in this matter, selecting things you think you're going to like and shutting off the lines that make for discomfort. You either have science or you don't, and if you have it you are obliged to accept the surprising and disturbing pieces of information, even the overwhelming and upheaving ones, along with the neat and promptly useful bits. It is like that.

The only solid piece of scientific truth about which I feel totally confident is that we are profoundly ignorant about nature. Indeed, I regard this as the major discovery of the past hundred years of biology. It is, in its way, an illuminating piece of news. It would have amazed the brightest minds of the eighteenth-century Enlightenment to be told by any of us how little we know, and how bewildering seems the way ahead. It is this sudden confrontation with the depth and scope of ignorance that represents the most significant contribution of twentieth-century science to the human intellect. We are, at last, facing up to it. In earlier times, we either pretended to understand how things worked or ignored the problem, or simply made up stories to fill the gaps. Now that we have begun exploring in earnest, doing serious science, we are getting glimpses of how huge the questions are, and how far from being answered. Because of this, these are hard times for the human intellect, and it is no wonder that we are depressed. It is not so bad being ignorant if you are totally ignorant; the hard thing is knowing in some detail the reality of ignorance, the worst spots and here and there the not-so-bad spots, but no true light at the end of any tunnel nor even any tunnels that can yet be trusted. Hard times, indeed.

But we are making a beginning, and there ought to be some satisfaction, even exhilaration, in that. The method works. There are probably no questions we can think up that can't be answered, sooner or later, including even the matter of consciousness. To be sure, there may well be questions we can't think up, ever, and therefore limits to the reach of human intellect which we will never know about, but that is another matter. Within our limits, we should be able to work our way through to all our answers, if we keep at it long enough, and pay attention.

I am putting it this way, with all the presumption and confidence that I can summon, in order to raise another, last question. Is this hubris? Is there something fundamentally unnatural, or intrinsically wrong, or hazardous for the species in the ambition that drives us all to reach a comprehensive understanding of nature, including ourselves? I cannot believe it. It would seem to me a more unnatural thing, and more of an offense against nature, for us to come on the same scene endowed as we are with curiosity, filled to over-brimming as we are with questions, and naturally talented as we are for the asking of clear questions, and then for us to do nothing about it or, worse, to try to suppress the questions. This is the greater danger for our species, to try to pretend that we are another kind of animal, that we do not need to satisfy our curiosity, that we can get along somehow without inquiry and exploration and experimentation, and that the human mind can rise above its ignorance by simply asserting that there are things it has no need to know. This, to my way of thinking, is the real hubris, and it carries danger for us all.

Discussion Questions

1. Why does Thomas allude to classical mythology? What mixed beings, part man and part animal or plant, can you recall from classical mythology? What was unhappy about their circumstances? Who was to blame? How does Thomas's reference to such beings strengthen his argument?

2. Thomas suggests that accusations of hubris are misdirected at scientists, that they reflect "a fundamental misunderstanding of science." What is this misunderstanding? Do you agree or not? Why?

3. Thomas raises the idea that certain kinds of knowledge are best left unrevealed and unpublished. Do you agree or disagree that it is better not to know some things? Why? How does Thomas convey his thoughts on this?

4. Do you agree with Thomas that as a culture we have a tendency to appoint committees to be in charge of what can and cannot be researched? Do you think there are significant problems with this approach?

Journal Entry

Answer one or more of the following questions: Have you ever been guilty of hubris? Have you been unjustly accused of hubris? How did you feel? What is an example of an unacceptable act of hubris? When is hubris ever acceptable? What is the distinction between hubris and the egotistic drive that leads to great accomplishments?

Writing Projects

1. Write an essay examining how Thomas develops his main argument. For example, at one point Thomas says, "By this time it will have become clear that I have already taken sides in the matter. . ." How far into his essay has he gone when he admits he is biased? How does he proceed after noting his own prejudice? Does he present a fully developed, though largely subjective, treatment? Or is his presentation weakened by his flaunting of his own bias?

2. Thomas says we are just now conducting science that is serious enough to enable us to discover how much we don't know, and that this discovery depresses us. What does he mean? How do scientific discoveries lead to depression? Where does hubris fit in? Does hubris motivate scientists (or any of us) to action that is more likely to depress or to exhilarate?

Collaborative Project

Thomas says that contrary to what some people fear, the risk of researchers harming themselves or others by letting toxins escape from secure laboratories is minimal. With a partner, investigate one or two recent developments that make scientific research safer to the researcher than it used to be. What role does technology play? What machines are used to examine or collect data while protecting the researcher from possible infection or other dangers? Your reference librarian can assist you in locating scientific journals, science research handbooks, and specialized encyclopedias with current information on this topic. Present your investigative research in a written report for science majors.

Mary Shelley

Frankenstein (Chapter 4)

Mary Shelley *(1797–1851) is most well known for creating Dr. Frankenstein and his monster. Mary Shelley was the daughter of Mary Wollstonecraft, who wrote* Vindication of the Rights of Woman *(1792), and William Godwin, a famous political philosopher and anarchist. While she was a teenager, she eloped with the poet Percy Bysshe Shelley. When she was 19 years old, her novel* Frankenstein *(1818) became a bestseller. Nevertheless, the book received negative reviews stemming in part from the fact that the author was a young woman. Variously described as the "most enduring ghost story of all time" and the "precursor to the existential thriller,"* Frankenstein *has become part of our cultural mythology, and it remains popular today. The story of a young scientist seduced by pride and ambition to create a new life form is a fable with contemporary relevance. In Chapter 4 of Shelley's novel, Dr. Frankenstein steeps himself in his scientific study and contemplates how he will create life and thus become like a god.*

Questions to Consider

☐ *Frankenstein* is well known as a ghost story, horror tale, and thriller – all designations suggesting a certain tone and atmosphere. As you read, notice what techniques of fiction the author employs to establish these atmospheric elements.

☐ How old were you when you first heard of Frankenstein? When did you first realize that Frankenstein was the name of the scientist, not the monster?

FROM this day natural philosophy, and particularly chemistry, in the most comprehensive sense of the term, became nearly my sole occupation. I read with ardor those works, so full of genius and discrimination, which modern inquirers have written on these subjects. I attended the lectures and cultivated the acquaintance of the men of science of the university, and I found even in M. Krempe a great deal of sound sense and real information, combined, it is true, with a repulsive physiognomy and manners, but not on that account the less valuable. In M. Waldman I found a true friend. His gentleness was never tinged by dogmatism, and his instructions were given with an air of frankness and good nature that banished every idea of pedantry. In a thousand ways he smoothed for me the path of knowledge and made the most abstruse inquiries clear and facile to my apprehension. My application was at first fluctuating and uncertain; it gained strength as I proceeded and soon became so ardent and eager that the stars often disappeared in the light of morning whilst I was yet engaged in my laboratory.

As I applied so closely, it may be easily conceived that my progress was rapid. My ardor was indeed the astonishment of the students, and my proficiency that of the masters. Professor Krempe often asked me, with a sly smile, how Cornelius Agrippa went on? whilst M. Waldman expressed the most heartfelt exultation in my progress. Two years passed in this manner, during which I paid no visit to Geneva, but was engaged, heart and soul, in the pursuit of some discoveries which I hoped to make. None but those who have experienced them can conceive of the enticements of science. In other studies you go as far as others have gone before you, and there is nothing more to know; but in a scientific pursuit there is continual food for discovery and wonder. A mind of moderate capacity which closely pursued one study must infallibly arrive at great proficiency in that study; and I, who continually sought the attainment of one object of pursuit and was solely wrapped up in this, improved so rapidly that at the end of two years I made some discoveries in the improvement of some chemical instruments, which procured me great esteem and admiration at the university. When I had arrived at this point and had become as well acquainted with the theory and practice of natural philosophy as depended on the lessons of any of the professors at Ingolstadt, my residence there being no longer conducive to my improvements, I thought of returning to my friends and my native town, when an incident happened that protracted my stay.

One of the phenomena which had peculiarly attracted my attention was the structure of the human frame, and, indeed, any animal endued with life. Whence, I often asked myself, did the principle of life proceed? It was a bold question, and one which has ever been considered as a mystery; yet with how many things are we upon the brink of becoming acquainted, if cowardice or carelessness did not restrain our inquiries. I revolved these circumstances in my mind and determined thenceforth to apply myself more particularly to those branches of natural philosophy which relate to physiology. Unless I had been animated by an almost supernatural enthusiasm, my application to this study would have been irksome and almost intolerable. To examine the causes of life, we must first have recourse to death. I became acquainted with the science of anatomy, but this was not sufficient; I must also observe the natural decay and corruption of the human body. In my education my father had taken the greatest precautions that my mind should be impressed with no supernatural horrors. I do not ever remember to have trembled at a tale of superstition or to have feared the apparition of a spirit. Darkness had no effect upon my fancy, and a churchyard was to me merely the receptacle of bodies deprived of life, which, from being the seat of beauty and strength, had become food for the worm. Now I was led to examine the cause and progress of this decay and forced to spend days and nights in vaults and charnel-houses. My attention was fixed upon every object the most insupportable to the delicacy of the human feelings. I saw how the fine form of man was degraded and wasted; I beheld the corruption of death succeed to the blooming cheek of life; I saw how the worm inherited the wonders of the eye and brain. I paused, examining and analyzing all the minutiae of causation, as exemplified in the change from life to death, and death to life, until from the midst of this darkness a sudden light broke in upon me — a light so brilliant and wondrous, yet so simple, that while I became dizzy with the immensity of the prospect which it illustrated, I was surprised that among so many men of genius who had directed their inquiries towards the same science, that I alone should be reserved to discover so astonishing a secret.

Remember, I am not recording the vision of a madman. The sun does not more certainly shine in the heavens than that which I now affirm is true. Some miracle might have produced it, yet the stages of the discovery were distinct and probable. After days and nights of incredible labor and fatigue, I succeeded in discovering the cause of generation and life; nay, more, I became myself capable of bestowing animation upon lifeless matter.

The astonishment which I had at first experienced on this discovery soon gave place to delight and rapture. After so much time spent in painful labor, to arrive at once at the summit of my desires was the most gratifying consummation of my toils. But this discovery was so great and overwhelming that all the steps by which I had been progressively led to it were obliterated, and I beheld only the result. What had been the study and desire of the wisest men since the creation of the world was now within my grasp. Not that, like a magic scene, it all opened upon me at once: the information I had obtained was of a nature rather to direct my endeavors so soon as I should point them towards the object of my search than to exhibit that object already accomplished. I was like the Arabian who had been buried with the dead and found a passage to life, aided only by one glimmering and seemingly ineffectual light.

I see by your eagerness and the wonder and hope which your eyes express, my friend, that you expect to be informed of the secret with which I am acquainted; that cannot be; listen patiently until the end of my story, and you will easily perceive why I am reserved upon that subject. I will not lead you on, unguarded and ardent as I then was, to your destruction and infallible misery. Learn from me, if not by my precepts, at least by my example, how dangerous is the acquirement of knowledge and how much happier that man is who believes his native town to be the world, than he who aspires to become greater than his nature will allow.

When I found so astonishing a power placed within my hands, I hesitated a long time concerning the manner in which I should employ it. Although I possessed the capacity of bestowing animation, yet to prepare a frame for the reception of it, with all its intricacies of fibers, muscles, and veins, still remained a work of inconceivable difficulty and labor. I doubted at first whether I should attempt the creation of a being like myself, or one of simpler organization; but my imagination was too much exalted by my first success to permit me to doubt of my ability to give life to an animal as complex and wonderful as man. The materials at present within my command hardly appeared adequate to so arduous an undertaking, but I doubted not that I should ultimately succeed. I prepared myself for a multitude of reverses; my operations might be incessantly baffled, and at last my work be imperfect: yet when I considered the improvement which every day takes place in science and mechanics, I was encouraged to hope my present attempts would at least lay the foundations of future success. Nor could I consider the magnitude and complexity of my plan as any argument of its impracticability. It was with these feelings that I began the creation of a human being. As the minuteness of the parts formed a great hindrance to my speed, I resolved, contrary to my first intention, to make the being of a gigantic stature; that is to say, about eight feet in height, and proportionably large. After having formed this determination and having spent some months in successfully collecting and arranging my materials, I began.

No one can conceive the variety of feelings which bore me onwards, like a hurricane, in the first enthusiasm of success. Life and death appeared to me ideal bounds, which I should first break through, and pour a torrent of light into our dark world. A new species would bless me as its creator and source; many happy and excellent natures would owe their being to me. No father could claim the gratitude of his child so completely as I should deserve theirs. Pursuing these reflections, I thought that if I could bestow animation upon lifeless matter, I might in process of time (although I now found it impossible) renew life where death had apparently devoted the body to corruption.

These thoughts supported my spirits, while I pursued my undertaking with unremitting ardor. My cheek had grown pale with study, and my person had become emaciated with confinement. Sometimes, on the very brink of certainty, I failed; yet still I clung to the hope which the next day or the next hour might realize. One secret which I alone possessed was the hope to which I had dedicated myself; and the moon gazed on my midnight labors, while, with unrelaxed and breathless eagerness, I pursued nature to her hiding-places. Who shall conceive the horrors of my secret toil as I dabbled among the unhallowed damps of the grave or tortured the living animal to animate the lifeless clay? My limbs now tremble, and my eyes swim with the remembrance; but then a resistless and almost frantic impulse urged me forward; I seemed to have lost all soul or sensation but for this one pursuit. It was indeed but a passing trance, that only made me feel with renewed acuteness so soon as, the unnatural stimulus ceasing to operate, I had returned to my old habits. I collected bones from charnel-houses and disturbed, with profane fingers, the tremendous secrets of the human frame. In a solitary chamber, or rather cell, at the top of the house, and separated from all the other apartments by a gallery and staircase, I kept my workshop of filthy creation: my eyeballs were starting from their sockets in attending to the details of my employment. The dissecting room and the slaughter-house furnished many of my materials; and often did my human nature turn with loathing from my occupation, whilst, still urged on by an eagerness which perpetually increased, I brought my work near to a conclusion.

The summer months passed while I was thus engaged, heart and soul, in one pursuit. It was a most beautiful season; never did the fields bestow a more plentiful harvest or the vines yield a more luxuriant vintage: but my eyes were insensible to the charms of nature. And the same feelings which made me neglect the scenes around me caused me also to forget those friends who were so many miles absent, and whom I had not seen for so long a time. I knew my silence disquieted them, and I well remembered the words of my father: "I know that while you are pleased with yourself you will think of us with affection, and we shall hear regularly from you. You must pardon me if I regard any interruption in your correspondence as a proof that your other duties are equally neglected."

I knew well therefore what would be my father's feelings, but I could not tear my thoughts from my employment, loathsome in itself, but which had taken an irresistible hold of my imagination. I wished, as it were, to procrastinate all that related to my feelings of affection until the great object, which swallowed up every habit of my nature, should be completed.

I then thought that my father would be unjust if he ascribed my neglect to vice or faultiness on my part, but I am now convinced that he was justified in conceiving that I should not be altogether free from blame. A human being in perfection ought always to preserve a calm and peaceful mind and never to allow passion or a transitory desire to disturb his tranquillity. I do not think that the pursuit of knowledge is an exception to this rule. If the study to which you apply yourself has a tendency to weaken your affections and to destroy your taste for those simple pleasures in which no alloy can possibly mix, then that study is certainly unlawful, that is to say, not befitting the human mind. If this rule were always observed; if no man allowed any pursuit whatsoever to interfere with the tranquillity of his domestic affections, Greece had not been enslaved, Caesar would have spared his country, America would have been discovered more gradually, and the empires of Mexico and Peru had not been destroyed.

But I forget that I am moralizing in the most interesting part of my tale, and your looks remind me to proceed.

My father made no reproach in his letters and only took notice of my silence by inquiring into my occupations more particularly than before. Winter, spring, and summer passed away during my labors; but I did not watch the blossom or the expanding leaves—sights which before always yielded me supreme delight—so deeply was I engrossed in my occupation. The leaves of that year had withered before my work drew near to a close, and now every day showed me more plainly how well I had succeeded. But my enthusiasm was checked by my anxiety, and I appeared rather like one doomed by slavery to toil in the mines, or any other unwholesome trade than an artist occupied by his favorite employment. Every night I was oppressed by a slow fever, and I became nervous to a most painful degree; the fall of a leaf startled me, and I shunned my fellow creatures as if I had been guilty of a crime. Sometimes I grew alarmed at the wreck I perceived that I had become; the energy of my purpose alone sustained me: my labors would soon end, and I believed that exercise and amusement would then drive away incipient disease; and I promised myself both of these when my creation should be complete.

Discussion Questions

1. Would you describe Frankenstein as a sympathetic character? Do his actions and thoughts cause you to turn away from him? Explain your reaction.

2. What methods does Shelley use to convey Frankenstein's emotional state, particularly at the point when he succeeds in creating life?

3. Writers often manipulate the setting of their stories to convey atmosphere or to alert the reader to the significance of certain events. Why does Shelley have Frankenstein comment on the fact that he hardly noticed the lovely summer weather while he was busy collecting body parts from the charnel houses? What does Shelley want us to learn about Frankenstein's personality and activities?

4. Although Frankenstein acknowledges his desire to discover "the principle of life," he states that it is a question others have avoided. He argues that "cowardice and carelessness" should not restrain one's inquiries. Do you think it is ever wise to leave certain questions unexplored? Would it be an act of cowardice to turn away from questions that might cause further difficulty for oneself or harm to others?

Journal Entry

Agree or disagree with this statement from Shelley's second paragraph: "In other studies [besides science] you go as far as others have gone before you, and there is nothing more to know; but in a scientific pursuit there is continual food for discovery and wonder."

Writing Projects

1. Analyze how Frankenstein reacts to his new-found knowledge and power to create human life. What practical difficulties did he face and how did he view them? What were his beliefs about the benefits to humankind of his creation of life? Remember that Frankenstein is Shelley's creation. How does she manipulate her character to illustrate a point? What is Shelley's main message?

2. Discuss the way in which Frankenstein describes his study at the university. What was his attitude toward his reading and the professors he knew during his first two years there? Describe any similarities between Frankenstein's cultivation of great "men of science" and the narrator's view of his colleagues in C. P. Snow's "The Moment" from Chapter 1 (pp. 25–27). What is your own view of the way in which Frankenstein's teachers supervised his study? Are they to be held responsible in any way for Frankenstein's hubristic creation of life?

Collaborative Projects

1. Working with one or two partners, view as many *Frankenstein* films as you can. Concentrate mainly on the section of the story you just read. Present an oral analysis to the class, showing film clips if possible, of the historical development of the Frankenstein story in movie form. Compare the different treatments of the Frankenstein character, particularly his attitude toward his own actions.

2. Working with your classmates, present a panel discussion of the moral issues raised by Shelley's story. Draw parallels with modern research in such areas as in vitro fertilization, gene splicing, or organ transplants. Focusing on the ethical issues involved, point out similarities to the issues Frankenstein ignored until it was too late.

Thomas S. Kuhn

The Route to Normal Science

Thomas Kuhn *(b. 1922) was trained as a physicist but switched to studying the history of science, an area in which he has revolutionized scientific thought. Kuhn has taught at Harvard University, the University of California at Berkeley, Princeton University, and the Massachusetts Institute of Technology. "The Route to Normal Science" is from his landmark book,* The Structure of Scientific Revolutions *(1962). In it Kuhn introduces and defines his central ideas of "paradigm" and "paradigm shift," which are ways of viewing knowledge both within and beyond the field of science. He provides examples of how paradigms operate, as well as how and why they shift. It is through establishing a paradigm, according to Kuhn, that an area of research proclaims itself a legitimate science. Kuhn's other works include* The Copernican Revolution *(1957),* The Essential Tension *(1977), and* Black-Body Theory and the Quantum Discontinuity *(1987).*

Questions to Consider

☐ Notice how Kuhn uses various forms of definition to explain his key term *paradigm.*

☐ Throughout his book Kuhn employs a series of aphorisms (short statements of general truths). As you read this excerpt, watch how he uses them and how they help clarify his argument.

IN this essay, "normal science" means research firmly based upon one or more past scientific achievements, achievements that some particular scientific community acknowledges for a time as supplying the foundation for its further practice. Today such achievements are recounted, though seldom in their original form, by science textbooks, elementary and advanced. These textbooks expound the body of accepted theory, illustrate many or all of its successful applications, and compare these applications with exemplary observations and experiments. Before such books became popular early in the nineteenth century (and until even more recently in the newly matured sciences), many of the famous classics of science fulfilled a similar function. Aristotle's *Physica*, Ptolemy's *Almagest*, Newton's *Principia* and *Opticks*, Franklin's *Electricity*, Lavoisier's *Chemistry*, and Lyell's *Geology*—these and many other works served for a time implicitly to define the legitimate problems and methods of a research field for succeeding generations of practitioners. They were able to do so because they shared two essential characteristics. Their achievement was sufficiently unprecedented to attract an enduring group of adherents away from competing modes of scientific activity. Simultaneously, it was sufficiently open-ended to leave all sorts of problems for the redefined group of practitioners to resolve.

Achievements that share these two characteristics I shall henceforth refer to as "paradigms," a term that relates closely to "normal science." By choosing it, I mean to suggest that some accepted examples of actual scientific practice – examples which include law, theory, application, and instrumentation together – provide models from which spring particular coherent traditions of scientific research. These are the traditions which the historian describes under such rubrics as "Ptolemaic astronomy" (or "Copernican"), "Aristotelian dynamics" (or "Newtonian"), "corpuscular optics" (or "wave optics"), and so on. The study of paradigms, including many that are far more specialized than those named illustratively above, is what mainly prepares the student for membership in the particular scientific community with which he will later practice. Because he there joins men who learned the bases of their field from the same concrete models, his subsequent practice will seldom evoke overt disagreement over fundamentals. Men whose research is based on shared paradigms are committed to the same rules and standards for scientific practice. That commitment and the apparent consensus it produces are prerequisites for normal science, i.e., for the genesis and continuation of a particular research tradition.

Because in this essay the concept of a paradigm will often substitute for a variety of familiar notions, more will need to be said about the reasons for its introduction. Why is the concrete scientific achievement, as a locus of professional commitment, prior to the various concepts, laws, theories, and points of view that may be abstracted from it? In what sense is the shared paradigm a fundamental unit for the student of scientific development, a unit that cannot be fully reduced to logically atomic components which might function in its stead? . . . answers to these questions and to others like them will prove basic to an understanding both of normal science and of the associated concept of paradigms. That more abstract discussion will depend, however, upon a previous exposure to examples of normal science or of paradigms in operation. In particular, both these related concepts will be clarified by noting that there can be a sort of scientific research without paradigms, or at least without any so unequivocal and so binding as the ones named above. Acquisition of a paradigm and of the more esoteric type of research it permits is a sign of maturity in the development of any given scientific field.

If the historian traces the scientific knowledge of any selected group of related phenomena backward in time, he is likely to encounter some minor variant of a pattern here illustrated from the history of physical optics. Today's physics textbooks tell the student that light is photons, i.e., quantum-mechanical entities that exhibit some characteristics of waves and some of particles.

Research proceeds accordingly, or rather according to the more elaborate and mathematical characterization from which this usual verbalization is derived. That characterization of light is, however, scarcely half a century old. Before it was developed by Planck, Einstein, and others early in this century, physics texts taught that light was transverse wave motion, a conception rooted in a paradigm that derived ultimately from the optical writings of Young and Fresnel in the early nineteenth century. Nor was the wave theory the first to be embraced by almost all practitioners of optical science. During the eighteenth century the paradigm for this field was provided by Newton's *Opticks*, which taught that light was material corpuscles. At that time physicists sought evidence, as the early wave theorists had not, of the pressure exerted by light particles impinging on solid bodies.[1]

These transformations of the paradigms of physical optics are scientific revolutions, and the successive transition from one paradigm to another via revolution is the usual developmental pattern of mature science. It is not, however, the pattern characteristic of the period before Newton's work, and that is the contrast that concerns us here. No period between remote antiquity and the end of the seventeenth century exhibited a single generally accepted view about the nature of light. Instead there were a number of competing schools and subschools, most of them espousing one variant or another of Epicurean, Aristotelian, or Platonic theory. One group took light to be particles emanating from material bodies; for another it was a modification of the medium that intervened between the body and the eye; still another explained light in terms of an interaction of the medium with an emanation from the eye; and there were other combinations and modifications besides. Each of the corresponding schools derived strength from its relation to some particular metaphysic, and each emphasized, as paradigmatic observations, the particular cluster of optical phenomena that its own theory could do most to explain. Other observations were dealt with by *ad hoc* elaborations, or they remained as outstanding problems for further research.[2]

At various times all these schools made significant contributions to the body of concepts, phenomena, and techniques from which Newton drew the first nearly uniformly accepted paradigm for physical optics. Any definition of the scientist that excludes at least the more creative members of these various schools will exclude their modern successors as well. Those men were scientists. Yet anyone examining a survey of physical optics before Newton may well conclude that, though the field's practitioners were scientists, the net result of their activity was something less than science. Being able to take no common body of belief for granted, each writer on physical optics felt forced to build his field anew from its foundations. In doing so, his choice of supporting observation and experiment was relatively free, for there was no standard set of methods or of phenomena that every optical writer felt forced to employ and explain. Under these circumstances, the dialogue of the resulting books was often directed as much to the members of other schools as it was to nature. That pattern is not unfamiliar in a number of creative fields today, nor is it incompatible with significant discovery and invention. It is not, however, the pattern of development that physical optics acquired after Newton and that other natural sciences make familiar today.

The history of electrical research in the first half of the eighteenth century provides a more concrete and better known example of the way a science develops before it acquires its first universally received paradigm. During that period there were almost as many views about the nature of electricity as there were important electrical experimenters, men like Hauksbee, Gray, Desaguliers, Du Fay, Nollett, Watson, Franklin, and others. All their numerous concepts of electricity had something in common—they were partially derived from one or another version of the mechanico-corpuscular philosophy that guided all scientific research of the day. In addition, all were components of real scientific theories, of theories that had been drawn in part from experiment and observation and that partially determined the choice and interpretation of additional problems undertaken in research. Yet though all the experiments were electrical and though most of the experimenters read each other's works, their theories had no more than a family resemblance.[3]

One early group of theories, following seventeenth-century practice, regarded attraction and frictional generation as the fundamental electrical phenomena. This group tended to treat repulsion as a secondary effect due to some sort of mechanical rebounding and also to postpone for as long as possible both discussion and systematic research on Gray's newly discovered effect, electrical conduction. Other "electricians" (the term is their own) took attraction and repulsion to be equally elementary manifestations of electricity and modified their theories and research accordingly. (Actually, this group is remarkably small—even Franklin's theory never quite accounted for the mutual repulsion of two negatively charged bodies.) But they had as much difficulty as the first group in accounting simultaneously for any but the simplest conduction effects. Those effects, however, provided the starting point for still a third group, one which tended to speak of electricity as a "fluid" that could run through conductors rather than as an "effluvium" that emanated from non-conductors. This group, in its turn, had difficulty reconciling its theory with a number of attractive and repulsive effects. Only through the work of Franklin and his immediate successors did a theory arise that could account with something like equal facility for very nearly all these effects and that therefore could and did provide a subsequent generation of "electricians" with a common paradigm for its research.

Excluding those fields, like mathematics and astronomy, in which the first firm paradigms date from prehistory and also those, like biochemistry, that arose by division and recombination of specialties already matured, the situations outlined above are historically typical. Though it involves my continuing to employ the unfortunate simplification that tags an extended historical episode with a single and somewhat arbitrarily chosen name (e.g., Newton or

Franklin), I suggest that similar fundamental disagreements characterized, for example, the study of motion before Aristotle and of statics before Archimedes, the study of heat before Black, of chemistry before Boyle and Boerhaave, and of historical geology before Hutton. In parts of biology – the study of heredity, for example – the first universally received paradigms are still more recent; and it remains an open question what parts of social science have yet acquired such paradigms at all. History suggests that the road to a firm research consensus is extraordinarily arduous.

History also suggests, however, some reasons for the difficulties encountered on that road. In the absence of a paradigm or some candidate for paradigm, all of the facts that could possibly pertain to the development of a given science are likely to seem equally relevant. As a result, early fact-gathering is a far more nearly random activity than the one that subsequent scientific development makes familiar. Furthermore, in the absence of a reason for seeking some particular form of more recondite information, early fact-gathering is usually restricted to the wealth of data that lie ready to hand. The resulting pool of facts contains those accessible to casual observation and experiment together with some of the more esoteric data retrievable from established crafts like medicine, calendar making, and metallurgy. Because the crafts are one readily accessible source of facts that could not have been casually discovered, technology has often played a vital role in the emergence of new sciences.

But though this sort of fact-collecting has been essential to the origin of many significant sciences, anyone who examines, for example, Pliny's encyclopedic writings or the Baconian natural histories of the seventeenth century will discover that it produces a morass. One somehow hesitates to call the literature that results scientific. The Baconian "histories" of heat, color, wind, mining, and so on, are filled with information, some of it recondite. But they juxtapose facts that will later prove revealing (e.g., heating by mixture) with others (e.g., the warmth of dung heaps) that will for some time remain too complex to be integrated with theory at all.[4] In addition, since any description must be partial, the typical natural history often omits from its immensely circumstantial accounts just those details that later scientists will find sources of important illumination. Almost none of the early "histories" of electricity, for example, mention that chaff, attracted to a rubbed glass rod, bounces off again. That effect seemed mechanical, not electrical.[5] Moreover, since the casual fact-gatherer seldom possesses the time or the tools to be critical, the natural histories often juxtapose descriptions like the above with others, say, heating by antiperistasis (or by cooling), that we are now quite unable to confirm.[6] Only very occasionally, as in the cases of ancient statics, dynamics, and geometrical optics, do facts collected with so little guidance from pre-established theory speak with sufficient clarity to permit the emergence of a first paradigm.

This is the situation that creates the schools characteristic of the early stages of a science's development. No natural history can be interpreted in the absence of at least some implicit body of intertwined theoretical and methodological belief that permits selection, evaluation, and criticism. If that body of belief is not already implicit in the collection of facts – in which case more than "mere facts" are at hand – it must be externally supplied, perhaps by a current metaphysic, by another science, or by personal and historical accident. No wonder, then, that in the early stages of the development of any science different men confronting the same range of phenomena, but not usually all the same particular phenomena, describe and interpret them in different ways. What is surprising, and perhaps also unique in its degree to the fields we call science, is that such initial divergences should ever largely disappear.

For they do disappear to a very considerable extent and then apparently once and for all. Furthermore, their disappearance is usually caused by the triumph of one of the pre-paradigm schools, which, because of its own characteristic beliefs and preconceptions, emphasized only some special part of the too sizable and inchoate pool of information. Those electricians who thought electricity a fluid and therefore gave particular emphasis to conduction provide an excellent case in point. Led by this belief, which could scarcely cope with the known multiplicity of attractive and repulsive effects, several of them conceived the idea of bottling the electrical fluid. The immediate fruit of their efforts was the Leyden jar, a device which might never have been discovered by a man exploring nature casually or at random, but which was in fact independently developed by at least two investigators in the early 1740's.[7] Almost from the start of his electrical researches, Franklin was particularly concerned to explain that strange and, in the event, particularly revealing piece of special apparatus. His success in doing so provided the most effective of the arguments that made his theory a paradigm, though one that was still unable to account for quite all the known cases of electrical repulsion.[8] To be accepted as a paradigm, a theory must seem better than its competitors, but it need not, and in fact never does, explain all the facts with which it can be confronted.

What the fluid theory of electricity did for the subgroup that held it, the Franklinian paradigm later did for the entire group of electricians. It suggested which experiments would be worth performing and which, because directed to secondary or to overly complex manifestations of electricity, would not. Only the paradigm did the job far more effectively, partly because the end of inter-school debate ended the constant reiteration of fundamentals and partly because the confidence that they were on the right track encouraged scientists to undertake more precise, esoteric, and consuming sorts of work.[9] Freed from the concern with any and all electrical phenomena, the united group of electricians could pursue selected phenomena in far more detail, designing much special equipment for the task and employing it more stubbornly and systematically than electricians had ever done before. Both fact collection and theory articulation became highly directed activities. The effectiveness and efficiency of electrical research increased accordingly, providing evidence for a societal version of Francis Bacon's acute methodological dictum: "Truth emerges more readily from error than from confusion."[10]

We shall be examining the nature of this highly directed or paradigm-based research in the next section, but must first note briefly how the emergence of a paradigm affects the structure of the group that practices the field. When, in the development of a natural science, an individual or group first produces a synthesis able to attract most of the next generation's practitioners, the older schools gradually disappear. In part their disappearance is caused by their members' conversion to the new paradigm. But there are always some men who cling to one or another of the older views, and they are simply read out of the profession, which thereafter ignores their work. The new paradigm implies a new and more rigid definition of the field. Those unwilling or unable to accommodate their work to it must proceed in isolation or attach themselves to some other group.[11] Historically, they have often simply stayed in the departments of philosophy from which so many of the special sciences have been spawned. As these indications hint, it is sometimes just its reception of a paradigm that transforms a group previously interested merely in the study of nature into a profession or, at least, a discipline. In the sciences (though not in fields like medicine, technology, and law, of which the principal *raison d'être* is an external social need), the formation of specialized journals, the foundation of specialists' societies, and the claim for a special place in the curriculum have usually been associated with a group's first reception of a single paradigm. At least this was the case between the time, a century and a half ago, when the institutional pattern of scientific specialization first developed and the very recent time when the paraphernalia of specialization acquired a prestige of their own.

The more rigid definition of the scientific group has other consequences. When the individual scientist can take a paradigm for granted, he need no longer, in his major works, attempt to build his field anew, starting from first principles and justifying the use of each concept introduced. That can be left to the writer of textbooks. Given a textbook, however, the creative scientist can begin his research where it leaves off and thus concentrate exclusively upon the subtlest and most esoteric aspects of the natural phenomena that concern his group. And as he does this, his research communiqués will begin to change in ways whose evolution has been too little studied but whose modern end products are obvious to all and oppressive to many. No longer will his researches usually be embodied in books addressed, like Franklin's *Experiments . . . on Electricity* or Darwin's *Origin of Species*, to anyone who might be interested in the subject matter of the field. Instead they will usually appear as brief articles addressed only to professional colleagues, the men whose knowledge of a shared paradigm can be assumed and who prove to be the only ones able to read the papers addressed to them.

Today in the sciences, books are usually either texts or retrospective reflections upon one aspect or another of the scientific life. The scientist who writes one is more likely to find his professional reputation impaired than enhanced. Only in the earlier, pre-paradigm, stages of the development of the various sciences did the book ordinarily possess the same relation to professional achievement that it still retains in other creative fields. And only in those fields that still retain the book, with or without the article, as a vehicle for research communication are the lines of professionalization still so loosely drawn that the layman may hope to follow progress by reading the practitioners' original reports. Both in mathematics and astronomy, research reports had ceased already in antiquity to be intelligible to a generally educated audience. In dynamics, research became similarly esoteric in the later Middle Ages, and it recaptured general intelligibility only briefly during the early seventeenth century when a new paradigm replaced the one that had guided medieval research. Electrical research began to require translation for the layman before the end of the eighteenth century, and most other fields of physical science ceased to be generally accessible in the nineteenth. During the same two centuries similar transitions can be isolated in the various parts of the biological sciences. In parts of the social sciences they may well be occurring today. Although it has become customary, and is surely proper, to deplore the widening gulf that separates the professional scientist from his colleagues in other fields, too little attention is paid to the essential relationship between that gulf and the mechanisms intrinsic to scientific advance.

Ever since prehistoric antiquity one field of study after another has crossed the divide between what the historian might call its prehistory as a science and its history proper. These transitions to maturity have seldom been so sudden or so unequivocal as my necessarily schematic discussion may have implied. But neither have they been historically gradual, coextensive, that is to say, with the entire development of the fields within which they occurred. Writers on electricity during the first four decades of the eighteenth century possessed far more information about electrical phenomena than had their sixteenth-century predecessors. During the half-century after 1740, few new sorts of electrical phenomena were added to their lists. Nevertheless, in important respects, the electrical writings of Cavendish, Coulomb, and Volta in the last third of the eighteenth century seem further removed from those of Gray, Du Fay, and even Franklin than are the writings of these early eighteenth-century electrical discoverers from those of the sixteenth century.[12] Sometime between 1740 and 1780, electricians were for the first time enabled to take the foundations of their field for granted. From that point they pushed on to more concrete and recondite problems, and increasingly they then reported their results in articles addressed to other electricians rather than in books addressed to the learned world at large. As a group they achieved what had been gained by astronomers in antiquity and by students of motion in the Middle Ages, of physical optics in the late seventeenth century, and of historical geology in the early nineteenth. They had, that is, achieved a paradigm that proved able to guide the whole group's research. Except with the advantage of hindsight, it is hard to find another criterion that so clearly proclaims a field a science.

NOTES

1. Joseph Priestley, *The History and Present State of Discoveries Relating to Vision, Light, and Colours* (London, 1772), pp. 385–90.

2. Vasco Ronchi, *Histoire de la lumière*, trans. Jean Taton (Paris, 1956), chaps. i–iv.

3. Duane Roller and Duane H. D. Roller, *The Development of the Concept of Electric Charge: Electricity from the Greeks to Coulomb* ("Harvard Case Histories in Experimental Science," Case 8; Cambridge, Mass., 1954); and I. B. Cohen, *Franklin and Newton: An Inquiry into Speculative Newtonian Experimental Science and Franklin's Work in Electricity as an Example Thereof* (Philadelphia, 1956), chaps. vii–xii. For some of the analytic detail in the paragraph that follows in the text, I am indebted to a still unpublished paper by my student John L. Heilbron. Pending its publication, a somewhat more extended and more precise account of the emergence of Franklin's paradigm is included in T. S. Kuhn, "The Function of Dogma in Scientific Research," in A. C. Crombie (ed.), "Symposium on the History of Science, University of Oxford, July 9–15, 1961," to be published by Heinemann Educational Books, Ltd.

4. Compare the sketch for a natural history of heat in Bacon's *Novum Organum*, Vol. VIII of *The Works of Francis Bacon*, ed. J. Spedding, R. L. Ellis, and D. D. Heath (New York, 1869), pp. 179–203.

5. Roller and Roller, *op. cit.*, pp. 14, 22, 28, 43. Only after the work recorded in the last of these citations do repulsive effects gain general recognition as unequivocally electrical.

6. Bacon, *op. cit.*, pp. 235, 337, says, "Water slightly warm is more easily frozen than quite cold." For a partial account of the earlier history of this strange observation, see Marshall Clagett, *Giovanni Marliani and Late Medieval Physics* (New York, 1941), chap. iv.

7. Roller and Roller, *op. cit.*, pp. 51–54.

8. The troublesome case was the mutual repulsion of negatively charged bodies, for which see Cohen, *op. cit.*, pp. 491–94, 531–43.

9. It should be noted that the acceptance of Franklin's theory did not end quite all debate. In 1759 Robert Symmer proposed a two-fluid version of that theory, and for many years thereafter electricians were divided about whether electricity was a single fluid or two. But the debates on this subject only confirm what has been said above about the manner in which a universally recognized achievement unites the profession. Electricians, though they continued divided on this point, rapidly concluded that no experimental tests could distinguish the two versions of the theory and that they were therefore equivalent. After that, both schools could and did exploit all the benefits that the Franklinian theory provided (*ibid.*, pp. 543–46, 548–54).

10. Bacon, *op. cit.*, p. 210.

11. The history of electricity provides an excellent example which could be duplicated from the careers of Priestley, Kelvin, and others. Franklin reports that Nollet, who at mid-century was the most influential of the Continental electricians, "lived to see himself the last of his Sect, except Mr. B.–his Eleve and immediate Disciple" (Max Farrand [ed.], *Benjamin Franklin's Memoirs* [Berkeley, Calif., 1949], pp. 384–86). More interesting, however, is the endurance of whole schools in increasing isolation from professional science. Consider, for example, the case of astrology, which was once an integral part of astronomy. Or consider the continuation in the late eighteenth and early nineteenth centuries of a previously respected tradition of "romantic" chemistry. This is the tradition discussed by Charles C. Gillispie in "The *Encyclopédie* and the Jacobin Philosophy of Science: A Study in Ideas and Consequences," *Critical Problems in the History of Science*, ed. Marshall Clagett (Madison, Wis., 1959), pp. 255–89; and "The Formation of Lamarck's Evolutionary Theory," *Archives internationales d'histoire des sciences*, XXXVII (1956), 323–38.

12. The post-Franklinian developments include an immense increase in the sensitivity of charge detectors, the first reliable and generally diffused techniques for measuring charge, the evolution of the concept of capacity and its relation to a newly refined notion of electric tension, and the quantification of electrostatic force. On all of these see Roller and Roller, *op. cit.*, pp. 66–81; W. C. Walker, "The Detection and Estimation of Electric Charges in the Eighteenth Century," *Annals of Science*, I (1936), 66–100; and Edmund Hoppe, *Geschichte der Elektrizität* (Leipzig, 1884), Part I, chaps. iii–iv.

Discussion Questions

1. Kuhn makes the following statement: "Men whose research is based on shared paradigms are committed to the same rules and standards for scientific practice." What does this statement mean? What are some examples of key rules and standards that scientists share?

2. From where does Kuhn draw the examples to explain and support his points? Can these examples be easily understood by the nonscientist? Why or why not?

3. What do you learn about the history of science from this excerpt? Why is a knowledge of the history of science important? Does writing about the history of science require a different writing style than that used in accounts of current scientific discoveries?

4. Identify and discuss the importance of some paradigms in your particular field of study.

Journal Entry

In this selection, Kuhn is primarily interested in scientific paradigms. But the concept of a paradigm, or model, can be applied to one's personal as well as professional life. Think of a model of behavior that a group of people you know have adopted. Write about the advantages and disadvantages of being guided by paradigms on a personal level.

Writing Projects

1. Analyze how Kuhn's definition of such key terms as *normal science* and *paradigm* goes beyond simply conveying information to form the basis of an argument.

2. Kuhn says that those who resist an established paradigm end up being excluded. Investigate the career of a scientist, or other thinker, who resisted an established paradigm. What were his or her reasons for resistance? What happened to his or her work? Review the scientist's career in a written analysis.

Collaborative Projects

1. Kuhn explains that increased specialization follows the establishment of a paradigm and that such specialization manifests itself through journal articles, or even entire journals, devoted to a particular scientific principle or method. Working with a partner, identify paradigms that seem to underlie the content and makeup of selected journals in your field. What theories, people, or methods are most often included? Do you know of any that are consistently excluded? Report your findings and conclusions to colleagues in your field.

2. Kuhn explains the role of science textbooks in establishing and preserving "normal science." Working with a partner, review two or more of the leading textbooks in a scientific field at the college level. Compare their presentations of one or two important scientific achievements and at least one key scientist. You could create comparison charts to illustrate the differences. Or write a comparison analysis together.

Jane Goodall

The Mind of the Chimpanzee

Jane Goodall *(b. 1934) has lived and worked in Africa since she was 18 years old. An anthropologist known worldwide for her more than thirty years of work with chimpanzees in the Gombe Stream National Park of Tanzania, Goodall spent part of her career serving in Kenya as an assistant to Louis Leakey, a famous paleontologist and anthropologist. Goodall was one of the first to conduct long-term research on chimpanzees in their natural habitat. Her work is distinguished by her close-up, detailed observations of individual chimps. In the following excerpt from her book* Through a Window *(1990), she tells of the resistance she met from science colleagues when she talked of the chimpanzees' minds, describing them in human terms, both emotionally and intellectually. Many of Goodall's colleagues believed that the mind was the distinguishing factor separating humans from other mammals, that we are the only so-called intelligent creatures. Goodall's writing is popular in part because her subject is chimpanzees, which arouse our curiosity and interest, but also because she writes warmly and informatively about a subject with which she is obviously fascinated. Other books by Goodall include* My Friends, the Wild Chimpanzees *(1967),* Grub, the Bush Baby *(with Hugo Van Lawick–Goodall, 1972), and* The Chimpanzee *(1992).*

Questions to Consider

☐ As you read, notice how Goodall juxtaposes the series of scenes and emotions that range from grief over her husband's death, to being kissed by a chimp, to being snubbed at a professional conference.

☐ Watch how Goodall characterizes the chimps Flo, Greybeard, and Lucy.

OFTEN I have gazed into a chimpanzee's eyes and wondered what was going on behind them. I used to look into Flo's, she so old, so wise. What did she remember of her young days? David Greybeard had the most beautiful eyes of them all, large and lustrous, set wide apart. They somehow expressed his whole personality, his serene self-assurance, his inherent dignity—and, from time to time, his utter determination to get his way. For a long time I never liked to look a chimpanzee straight in the eye—I assumed that, as is the case with most primates, this would be interpreted as a threat or at least as a breach of good manners. Not so. As long as one looks with gentleness, without arrogance, a chimpanzee will understand, and may even return the look. And then—or such is my fantasy—it is as though the eyes are windows into the mind. Only the glass is opaque so that the mystery can never be fully revealed.

I shall never forget my meeting with Lucy, an eight-year-old home-raised chimpanzee. She came and sat beside me on the sofa and, with her face very close to mine, searched in my eyes—for what? Perhaps she was looking for signs of mistrust, dislike, or fear, since many people must have been somewhat disconcerted when, for the first time, they came face to face with a grown chimpanzee. Whatever Lucy read in my eyes clearly satisfied her for she suddenly put one arm round my neck and gave me a generous and very chimp-like kiss, her mouth wide open and laid over mine. I was accepted.

For a long time after that encounter I was profoundly disturbed. I had been at Gombe for about fifteen years then and I was quite familiar with chimpanzees in the wild. But Lucy, having grown up as a human child, was like a changeling, her essential chimpanzeeness overlaid by the various human behaviors she had acquired over the years. No longer purely chimp yet eons away from humanity, she was man-made, some other kind of being. I watched, amazed, as she opened the refrigerator and various cupboards, found bottles and a glass, then poured herself a gin and tonic. She took the drink to the TV, turned the set on, flipped from one channel to another then, as though in disgust, turned it off again. She selected a glossy magazine from the table and, still carrying her drink, settled in a comfortable chair. Occasionally, as she leafed through the magazine she identified something she saw, using the signs of ASL, the American Sign Language used by the deaf. I, of course, did not understand, but my hostess, Jane Temerlin (who was also Lucy's "mother"), translated: "That dog," Lucy commented, pausing at a photo of a small white poodle. She turned the page. "Blue," she declared, pointing then signing as she gazed at a picture of a lady advertising some kind of soap powder and wearing a brilliant blue dress. And finally, after some vague hand movements—perhaps signed mutterings—"This Lucy's, this mine," as she closed the magazine and laid it on her lap. She had just been taught, Jane told me, the use of the possessive pronouns during the thrice weekly ASL lessons she was receiving at the time.

The book written by Lucy's human "father," Maury Temerlin, was entitled *Lucy, Growing Up Human*. And in fact, the chimpanzee is more like us than is any other living creature. There is close resemblance in the physiology of our two species and genetically, in the structure of the DNA, chimpanzees and humans differ by only just over one percent. This is why medical research uses chimpanzees as experimental animals when they need substitutes for humans in the testing of some drug or vaccine. Chimpanzees can be infected with just about all known human infectious diseases including those, such as hepatitis B and AIDS, to which other non-human animals (except gorillas, orangutans and gibbons) are immune. There are equally striking similarities between humans and chimpanzees in the anatomy and wiring of the brain and nervous system, and—although many scientists have been reluctant to admit to this—in social behavior, intellectual ability, and the emotions. The notion of an evolutionary continuity in physical structure from pre-human ape to modern man has long been morally acceptable to most scientists. That the same might hold good for mind was generally considered an absurd hypothesis—particularly by those who used, and often misused, animals in their laboratories. It is, after all, convenient to believe that the creature you are using, while it may react in disturbingly human-like ways, is, in fact, merely a mindless and, above all, unfeeling, "dumb" animal.

When I began my study at Gombe in 1960 it was not permissible—at least not in ethological circles—to talk about an animal's mind. Only humans had minds. Nor was it quite proper to talk about animal personality. Of course everyone knew that they *did* have their own unique characters—everyone who had ever owned a dog or other pet was aware of that. But ethologists, striving to make theirs a "hard" science, shied away from the task of trying to explain such things objectively. One respected ethologist, while acknowledging that there was "variability between individual animals" wrote that it was best that this fact be "swept under the carpet." At that time ethological carpets fairly bulged with all that was hidden beneath them.

How naive I was. As I had not had an undergraduate science education I didn't realize that animals were not supposed to have personalities, or to think, or to feel emotions or pain. I had no idea that it would have been more appropriate to assign each of the chimpanzees a number rather than a name when I got to know him or her. I didn't realize that it was not scientific to discuss behavior in terms of motivation or purpose. And no one had told me that terms such as *childhood* and *adolescence* were uniquely human phases of the life cycle, culturally determined, not to be used when referring to young chimpanzees. Not knowing, I freely made use of all those forbidden terms and concepts in my initial attempt to describe, to the best of my ability, the amazing things I had observed at Gombe.

I shall never forget the response of a group of ethologists to some remarks I made at an erudite seminar. I described how Figan, as an adolescent, had learned to stay behind in camp after senior males had left, so that we could give him a few bananas for himself. On the first occasion he had, upon seeing the fruits, uttered loud, delighted food calls: whereupon a couple of the older males had charged back, chased after Figan, and taken his bananas. And then, coming to the point of the story, I explained how, on the next occasion, Figan had actually suppressed his calls. We could hear little sounds, in his throat, but so quiet that none of the others could have heard them. Other young chimps, to whom we tried to smuggle fruit without the knowledge of their elders, never learned such self-control. With shrieks of glee they would fall to, only to be robbed of their booty when the big males charged back. I had expected my audience to be as fascinated and impressed as I was. I had hoped for an exchange of views about the chimpanzee's undoubted intelligence.

Instead there was a chill silence, after which the chairman hastily changed the subject. Needless to say, after being thus snubbed, I was very reluctant to contribute any comments, at any scientific gathering, for a very long time. Looking back, I suspect that everyone was interested, but it was, of course, not permissible to present a mere "anecdote" as evidence for anything.

The editorial comments on the first paper I wrote for publication demanded that every *he* or *she* be replaced with *it*, and every *who* be replaced with *which*. Incensed, I, in my turn, crossed out the *its* and *whichs* and scrawled back the original pronouns. As I had no desire to carve a niche for myself in the world of science, but simply wanted to go on living among and learning about chimpanzees, the possible reaction of the editor of the learned journal did not trouble me. In fact I won that round: the paper when finally published did confer upon the chimpanzees the dignity of their appropriate genders and properly upgraded them from the status of mere "things" to essential Beingness.

However, despite my somewhat truculent attitude, I did want to learn, and I was sensible of my incredible good fortune in being admitted to Cambridge. I wanted to get my Ph.D., if only for the sake of Louis Leakey and the other people who had written letters in support of my admission. And how lucky I was to have, as my supervisor, Robert Hinde. Not only because I thereby benefited from his brilliant mind and clear thinking, but also because I doubt that I could have found a teacher more suited to my particular needs and personality. Gradually he was able to cloak me with at least some of the trappings of a scientist. Thus although I continued to hold to most of my convictions – that animals had personalities; that they could feel happy or sad or fearful; that they could feel pain; that they could strive towards planned goals and achieve greater success if they were highly motivated – I soon realized that these personal convictions were, indeed, difficult to prove. It was best to be circumspect – at least until I had gained some credentials and credibility. And Robert gave me wonderful advice on how best to tie up some of my more rebellious ideas with scientific ribbon. "You can't *know* that Fifi was jealous," he admonished on one occasion. We argued a little. And then: "Why don't you just say *If Fifi were a human child we would say she was jealous.*" I did.

It is not easy to study emotions even when the subjects are human. I know how I feel if I am sad or happy or angry, and if a friend tells me that he is feeling sad, happy or angry, I assume that his feelings are similar to mine. But of course I cannot know. As we try to come to grips with the emotions of beings progressively more different from ourselves the task, obviously, becomes increasingly difficult. If we ascribe human emotions to non-human animals we are accused of being anthropomorphic – a cardinal sin in ethology. But is it so terrible? If we test the effect of drugs on chimpanzees because they are biologically so similar to ourselves, if we accept that there are dramatic similarities in chimpanzee and human brain and nervous system, is it not logical to assume that there will be similarities also in at least the more basic feelings, emotions, moods of the two species?

In fact, all those who have worked long and closely with chimpanzees have no hesitation in asserting that chimps experience emotions similar to those which in ourselves we label pleasure, joy, sorrow, anger, boredom and so on. Some of the emotional states of the chimpanzee are so obviously similar to ours that even an inexperienced observer can understand what is going on. An infant who hurls himself screaming to the ground, face contorted, hitting out with his arms at any nearby object, banging his head, is clearly having a tantrum. Another youngster, who gambols around his mother, turning somersaults, pirouetting and, every so often, rushing up to her and tumbling into her lap, patting her or pulling her hand towards him in a request for tickling, is obviously filled with *joie de vivre*. There are few observers who would not unhesitatingly ascribe his behavior to a happy, carefree state of well-being. And one cannot watch chimpanzee infants for long without realizing that they have the same emotional need for affection and reassurance as human children. An adult male, reclining in the shade after a good meal, reaching benignly to play with an infant or idly groom an adult female, is clearly in a good mood. When he sits with bristling hair, glaring at his subordinates and threatening them, with irritated gestures, if they come too close, he is clearly feeling cross and grumpy. We make these judgements because the similarity of so much of a chimpanzee's behavior to our own permits us to empathize.

It is hard to empathize with emotions we have not experienced. I can imagine, to some extent, the pleasure of a female chimpanzee during the act of procreation. The feelings of her male partner are beyond my knowledge—as are those of the human male in the same context. I have spent countless hours watching mother chimpanzees interacting with their infants. But not until I had an infant of my own did I begin to understand the basic, powerful instinct of mother-love. If someone accidentally did something to frighten Grub, or threaten his well-being in any way, I felt a surge of quite irrational anger. How much more easily could I then understand the feelings of the chimpanzee mother who furiously waves her arm and barks in threat at an individual who approaches her infant too closely, or at a playmate who inadvertently hurts her child. And it was not until I knew the numbing grief that gripped me after the death of my second husband that I could even begin to appreciate the despair and sense of loss that can cause young chimps to pine away and die when they lose their mothers.

Empathy and intuition can be of tremendous value as we attempt to understand certain complex behavioral interactions, provided that the behavior, as it occurs, is recorded precisely and objectively. Fortunately I have seldom found it difficult to record facts in an orderly manner even during times of powerful emotional involvement. And "knowing" intuitively how a chimpanzee is feeling—after an attack, for example—may help one to understand what happens next. We should not be afraid at least to try to make use of our close evolutionary relationship with the chimpanzees in our attempts to interpret complex behavior.

Today, as in Darwin's time, it is once again fashionable to speak of and study the animal mind. This change came about gradually, and was, at least in part, due to the information collected during careful studies of animal societies in the field. As these observations became widely known, it was impossible to brush aside the complexities of social behavior that were revealed in species after species. The untidy clutter under the ethological carpets was brought out and examined, piece by piece. Gradually it was realized that parsimonious explanations of apparently intelligent behaviors were often misleading. This led to a succession of experiments that, taken together, clearly prove that many intellectual abilities that had been thought unique to humans were actually present, though in a less highly developed form, in other, non-human beings. Particularly, of course, in the non-human primates and especially in chimpanzees.

When first I began to read about human evolution, I learned that one of the hallmarks of our own species was that we, and only we, were capable of making tools. *Man the Toolmaker* was an oft-cited definition—and this despite the careful and exhaustive research of Wolfgang Kohler and Robert Yerkes on the tool-using and tool-making abilities of chimpanzees. Those studies, carried out independently in the early twenties, were received with scepticism. Yet both Kohler and Yerkes were respected scientists, and both had a profound understanding of chimpanzee behavior. Indeed, Kohler's descriptions of the personalities and behavior of the various individuals in his colony, published in his book *The Mentality of Apes*, remain some of the most vivid and colorful ever written. And his experiments, showing how chimpanzees could stack boxes, then climb the unstable constructions to reach fruit suspended from the ceiling, or join two short sticks to make a pole long enough to rake in fruit otherwise out of reach, have become classic, appearing in almost all textbooks dealing with intelligent behavior in non-human animals.

By the time systematic observations of tool-using came from Gombe those pioneering studies had been largely forgotten. Moreover, it was one thing to know that humanized chimpanzees in the lab could use implements: it was quite another to find that this was a naturally occurring skill in the wild. I well remember writing to Louis about my first observations, describing how David Greybeard not only used bits of straw to fish for termites but actually stripped leaves from a stem and thus *made* a tool. And I remember too receiving the now oft-quoted telegram he sent in response to my letter: "Now we must redefine *tool*, redefine *Man*, or accept chimpanzees as humans."

There were, initially, a few scientists who attempted to write off the termiting observations, even suggesting that I had taught the chimps! By and large, though, people were fascinated by the information and by the subsequent observations of the other contexts in which the Gombe chimpanzees used objects as tools. And there were only a few anthropologists who objected when I suggested that the chimpanzees probably passed their tool-using traditions from one generation to the next, through observations, imitation and practice, so that each population might be expected to have its own unique tool-using culture. Which, incidentally, turns out to be quite true. And when I described how one chimpanzee, Mike, spontaneously solved a new problem by using a tool (he broke off a stick to knock a banana to the ground when he was too nervous to actually take it from my hand) I don't believe there were any raised eyebrows in the scientific community. Certainly I was not attacked viciously, as were Kohler and Yerkes, for suggesting that humans were not the only beings capable of reasoning and insight.

The mid-sixties saw the start of a project that, along with other similar research, was to teach us a great deal about the chimpanzee mind. This was Project Washoe, conceived by Trixie and Allen Gardner. They purchased an infant chimpanzee and began to teach her the signs of ASL, the American Sign Language used by the deaf. Twenty years earlier another husband and wife team, Richard and Cathy Hayes, had tried, with an almost total lack of success, to teach a young chimp, Vikki, to talk. The Hayes's undertaking taught us a lot about the chimpanzee mind, but Vikki, although she did well in IQ tests, and was clearly an intelligent youngster, could not learn human speech. The Gardners, however, achieved spectacular success with their pupil, Washoe. Not only did she learn signs easily, but she quickly began to string them together in meaningful ways. It was clear that each sign evoked, in her mind, a mental image of the object it represented. If, for example, she was asked, in sign language, to fetch an apple, she would go and locate an apple that was out of sight in another room.

Other chimps entered the project, some starting their lives in deaf signing families before joining Washoe. And finally Washoe adopted an infant, Loulis. He came from a lab where no thought of teaching signs had ever penetrated. When he was with Washoe he was given no lessons in language acquisition—not by humans, anyway. Yet by the time he was eight years old he had made fifty-eight signs in their correct contexts. How did he learn them? Mostly, it seems, by imitating the behavior of Washoe and the other three signing chimps, Dar, Moja and Tatu. Sometimes, though, he received tuition from Washoe herself. One day, for example, she began to swagger about bipedally, hair bristling, signing *food! food! food!* in great excitement. She had seen a human approaching with a bar of chocolate. Loulis, only eighteen months old, watched passively. Suddenly Washoe stopped her swaggering, went over to him, took his hand, and molded the sign for *food* (fingers pointing towards mouth). Another time, in a similar context, she made the sign for *chewing gum*—but with *her* hand on *his* body. On a third occasion Washoe, apropos of nothing, picked up a small chair, took it over to Loulis, set it down in front of him, and very distinctly made the *chair* sign three times, watching him closely as she did so. The two food signs became incorporated into Loulis's vocabulary but the sign for chair did not. Obviously the priorities of a young chimp are similar to those of a human child!

When news of Washoe's accomplishments first hit the scientific community it immediately provoked a storm of bitter protest. It implied that chimpanzees were capable of mastering a human language, and this, in turn, indicated mental powers of generalization, abstraction and concept-formation as well as an ability to understand and use abstract symbols. And these intellectual skills were surely the prerogatives of *Homo sapiens*. Although there were many who were fascinated and excited by the Gardners' findings, there were many more who denounced the whole project, holding that the data was suspect, the methodology sloppy, and the conclusions not only misleading, but quite preposterous. The controversy inspired all sorts of other language projects. And, whether the investigators were sceptical to start with and hoped to disprove the Gardners' work, or whether they were attempting to demonstrate the same thing in a new way, their research provided additional information about the chimpanzee's mind.

And so, with new incentive, psychologists began to test the mental abilities of chimpanzees in a variety of different ways; again and again the results confirmed that their minds are uncannily like our own. It had long been held that only humans were capable of what is called "cross-modal transfer of information"—in other words, if you shut your eyes and someone allows you to feel a strangely shaped potato, you will subsequently be able to pick it out from other differently shaped potatoes simply by looking at them. And vice versa. It turned out that chimpanzees can "know" with their eyes what they "feel" with their fingers in just the same way. In fact, we now know that some other non-human primates can do the same thing. I expect all kinds of creatures have the same ability.

Then it was proved, experimentally and beyond doubt, that chimpanzees could recognize themselves in mirrors—that they had, therefore, some kind of self-concept. In fact, Washoe, some years previously, had already demonstrated the ability when she spontaneously identified herself in the mirror, staring at her image and making her name sign. But that observation was merely anecdotal. The proof came when chimpanzees who had been allowed to play with mirrors were, while anesthetized, dabbed with spots of odorless paint in places, such as the ears or the top of the head, that they could see only in the mirror. When they woke they were not only fascinated by their spotted images, but immediately investigated, with their fingers, the dabs of paint.

The fact that chimpanzees have excellent memories surprised no one. Everyone, after all, has been brought up to believe that "an elephant never forgets" so why should a chimpanzee be any different? The fact that Washoe spontaneously gave the name-sign of Beatrice Gardner, her surrogate mother, when she saw her after a separation of eleven years was no greater an accomplishment than the amazing memory shown by dogs who recognize their owners after separations of almost as long—and the chimpanzee has a much longer life span than a dog. Chimpanzees can plan ahead, too, at least as regards the immediate future. This, in fact, is well illustrated at Gombe, during the termiting season: often an individual prepares a tool for use on a termite mound that is several hundred yards away and absolutely out of sight.

This is not the place to describe in detail the other cognitive abilities that have been studied in laboratory chimpanzees. Among other accomplishments chimpanzees possess pre-mathematical skills: they can, for example, readily differentiate between *more* and *less*. They can classify things into specific categories according to a given criterion – thus they have no difficulty in separating a pile of food into *fruits* and *vegetables* on one occasion, and, on another, dividing the same pile of food into *large* versus *small* items, even though this requires putting some vegetables with some fruits. Chimpanzees who have been taught a language can combine signs creatively in order to describe objects for which they have no symbol. Washoe, for example, puzzled her caretakers by asking, repeatedly, for a *rock berry*. Eventually it transpired that she was referring to Brazil nuts which she had encountered for the first time a while before. Another language-trained chimp described a cucumber as a *green banana*, and another referred to an Alka-Seltzer as a *listen drink*. They can even invent signs. Lucy, as she got older, had to be put on a leash for her outings. One day, eager to set off but having no sign for *leash*, she signaled her wishes by holding a crooked index finger to the ring on her collar. This sign became part of her vocabulary. Some chimpanzees love to draw, and especially to paint. Those who have learned sign language sometimes spontaneously label their works, "This [is] apple" – or bird, or sweet-corn, or whatever. The fact that the paintings often look, to our eyes, remarkably unlike the objects depicted by the artists either means that the chimpanzees are poor draughtsmen or that we have much to learn regarding ape-style representational art!

People sometimes ask why chimpanzees have evolved such complex intellectual powers when their lives in the wild are so simple. The answer is, of course, that their lives in the wild are not so simple! They use – and need – all their mental skills during normal day-to-day life in their complex society. They are always having to make choices – where to go, or with whom to travel. They need highly developed social skills – particularly those males who are ambitious to attain high positions in the dominance hierarchy. Low-ranking chimpanzees must learn deception – to conceal their intentions or to do things in secret – if they are to get their way in the presence of their superiors. Indeed, the study of chimpanzees in the wild suggests that their intellectual abilities evolved, over the millennia, to help them cope with daily life. And now, the solid core of data concerning chimpanzee intellect collected so carefully in the lab setting provides a background against which to evaluate the many examples of intelligent, rational behavior that we see in the wild.

It is easier to study intellectual prowess in the lab where, through carefully devised tests and judicious use of rewards, the chimpanzees can be encouraged to exert themselves, to stretch their minds to the limit. It is more meaningful to study the subject in the wild, but much harder. It is more meaningful because we can better understand the environmental pressures that led to the evolution of intellectual skills in chimpanzee societies. It is harder because, in the wild, almost all behaviors are confounded by countless variables; years of observing, recording and analyzing take the place of contrived testing; sample size can often be counted on the fingers of one hand; the only experiments are nature's own, and only time—eventually—may replicate them.

In the wild a single observation may prove of utmost significance, providing a clue to some hitherto puzzling aspect of behavior, a key to the understanding of, for example, a changed relationship. Obviously it is crucial to see as many incidents of this sort as possible. During the early years of my study at Gombe it became apparent that one person alone could never learn more than a fraction of what was going on in a chimpanzee community at any given time. And so, from 1964 onwards, I gradually built up a research team to help in the gathering of information about the behavior of our closest living relatives.

Discussion Questions

1. How does Goodall's choice of descriptive phrases, such as "utter determination," "serene self-assurance," "inherent dignity," when discussing David Greybeard reveal her view of her subject? What does her decision to name the chimps reveal of her attitude toward them and toward her research?

2. What is the significance of Goodall's battle over pronoun usage (he/she/who versus it/which) in her paper submitted for publication?

3. What point was Goodall making by describing the scene in which Lucy fixed herself a gin and tonic, watched television, and made comments in sign language pertaining to a magazine she had selected? How did you feel as you visualized that scene from Goodall's description?

4. Goodall says that because she had not had an undergraduate science education she was naive and thus did not know animals "were not supposed to have personalities, or to think, or feel emotions or pain." Is she being straightforward or ironic? How can you tell? What point is she implying about the advantages versus the disadvantages of the standard education in science? Do you agree with her? Why or why not?

Journal Entry

Goodall says she is grateful to her professor for cloaking her with the "trappings of a scientist." Using specific examples, write about your own experience of acquiring the trappings of science, from this class or elsewhere.

Writing Projects

1. Explain why Goodall's adviser suggested she use language for rhetorical purposes by not saying "Fifi was jealous" but rather "If Fifi were a human child we would say she was jealous." What did Goodall gain by prefacing her statement with a qualitative phrase like this one? Analyze this and other examples in Goodall's essay in which language is manipulated for a similar motive or effect.

2. Goodall points out the traits and methods of the scientist, such as the practice of recording precisely and objectively. She also notes how scientists use empathy and intuition. Write an essay explaining what you consider to be the proper role of empathy and intuition in scientific research. What subjects lend themselves to an intuitive research approach? Is there a danger of losing crucial objectivity in certain kinds of research by allowing feelings of empathy to surface?

Collaborative Project

Although Jane Goodall's work is well known, for many people knowledge and attitudes toward chimpanzees, apes, and gorillas is acquired from mainstream movies. Working with one or two partners, construct a bibliography of movies about chimpanzees, apes, and gorillas. Write a paper analyzing the portrayal of these animals in popular movies and compare selected portrayals with Goodall's characterization (see, for example, *Gorillas in the Mist, Planet of the Apes, Every Which Way But Loose, King Kong, Tarzan, Project X, Monkey Business, The Monkey's Uncle,* and *Bedtime for Bonzo*). In your analysis include answers to the following questions: Who is most often the hero in these movies? Are the chimpanzees and gorillas portrayed as having human characteristics? Are they usually the star of the film or a foil for the main character? Are they portrayed as lovable, frightening, ridiculous, or in some other way? Are these movies mostly comedy or drama or something else? What is the basis of the appeal of these films? How many of them were box-office hits and why?

Stephen Jay Gould

"Blacks and Indians Treated as Separate, Inferior Species"

Stephen Jay Gould *(b. 1941) is a professor of zoology and curator of paleontology at Harvard University. A self-described "dinosaur nut" who claims that dinosaurs have now become "overexposed," Gould is a prolific author of both scientific works and essays for a wider audience. He is highly respected for his writing on evolutionary theory in particular. At the age of 39, Gould was among the twenty-one recipients of the first MacArthur Foundation Prize. This prestigious prize is awarded to those deemed to be outstanding, self-directed, and original thinkers. Gould's genius for making any scientific subject he selects interesting, informative, and accessible to a wide audience accounts, in part, for his large readership; his books have won numerous prizes. The following selection, excerpted from* The Mismeasure of Man *(1981), illustrates Gould's dedication to acknowledging fraud in science—even when undeliberate—and to showing how scientists can unwittingly reinforce racist stereotypes by proceeding from unquestioned assumptions. Gould writes a monthly column for* Natural History *magazine; many of his essays have been collected in books such as* The Panda's Thumb *(1980),* Hen's Teeth and Horse's Toes *(1983),* The Flamingo's Smile *(1985), and* Eight Little Piggies *(1993).*

Questions to Consider

☐ Before reading this excerpt, think about your criteria for determining if data are objective. Do you believe that any data can ever be completely objective?

☐ Gould distinguishes between deliberate attempts to defraud and unconscious skewing of research results. Do you distinguish between the two in terms of their consequences or your attitude toward the scientists who are guilty of either?

Order is Heaven's first law; and, this confessed,
Some are, and must be, greater than the rest.
—ALEXANDER POPE,
Essay on Man (1733)

A ppeals to reason or to the nature of the universe have been used throughout history to enshrine existing hierarchies as proper and inevitable. The hierarchies rarely endure for more than a few generations, but the arguments, refurbished for the next round of social institutions, cycle endlessly.

The catalogue of justifications based on nature traverses a range of possibilities: elaborate analogies between rulers and a hierarchy of subordinate classes with the central earth of Ptolemaic astronomy and a ranked order of heavenly bodies circling around it; or appeals to the universal order of a "great chain of being," ranging in a single series from amoebae to God, and including near its apex a graded series of human races and classes. To quote Alexander Pope again:

> Without this just gradation, could they be
> Subjected, these to those, or all to thee?
> ....
> From Nature's chain whatever link you strike,
> Tenth, or ten thousandth, breaks the chain alike.

The humblest, as well as the greatest, play their part in preserving the continuity of universal order; all occupy their appointed roles.

This book treats an argument that, to many people's surprise, seems to be a latecomer: biological determinism, the notion that people at the bottom are constructed of intrinsically inferior material (poor brains, bad genes, or whatever). Plato, as we have seen, cautiously floated this proposal in the *Republic*, but finally branded it as a lie.

Racial prejudice may be as old as recorded human history, but its biological justification imposed the additional burden of intrinsic inferiority upon despised groups, and precluded redemption by conversion or assimilation. The "scientific" argument has formed a primary line of attack for more than a century. In discussing the first biological theory supported by extensive quantitative data—early nineteenth-century craniometry—I must begin by posing a question of causality: did the introduction of inductive science add legitimate data to change or strengthen a nascent argument for racial ranking? Or did a priori commitment to ranking fashion the "scientific" questions asked and even the data gathered to support a foreordained conclusion?. . .

Samuel George Morton, a Philadelphia patrician with two medical degrees—one from fashionable Edinburgh—provided the "facts" that won worldwide respect for the "American school" of polygeny. Morton began his collection of human skulls in the 1820s; he had more than one thousand when he died in 1851. Friends (and enemies) referred to his great charnel house as "the American Golgotha."

Morton won his reputation as the great data-gatherer and objectivist of American science, the man who would raise an immature enterprise from the mires of fanciful speculation. Oliver Wendell Holmes praised Morton for "the severe and cautious character" of his works, which "from their very nature are permanent data for all future students of ethnology" (in Stanton, 1960, p. 96). The same Humboldt who had asserted the inherent equality of all races wrote:

> The craniological treasures which you have been so fortunate as to unite in your collection, have in you found a worthy interpreter. Your work is equally remarkable for the profundity of its anatomical views, the numerical detail of the relations of organic conformation, and the absence of those poetical reveries which are the myths of modern physiology (in Meigs, 1851, p. 48).

When Morton died in 1851, the *New York Tribune* wrote that "probably no scientific man in America enjoyed a higher reputation among scholars throughout the world, than Dr. Morton" (in Stanton, 1960, p. 144).

Yet Morton gathered skulls neither for the dilettante's motive of abstract interest nor the taxonomist's zeal for complete representation. He had a hypothesis to test: that a ranking of races could be established objectively by physical characteristics of the brain, particularly by its size. Morton took a special interest in native Americans. As George Combe, his fervent friend and supporter, wrote:

> One of the most singular features in the history of this continent, is, that the aboriginal races, with few exceptions, have perished or constantly receded, before the Anglo-Saxon race, and have in no instance either mingled with them as equals, or adopted their manners and civilization. These phenomena must have a cause; and can any inquiry be at once more interesting and philosophical than that which endeavors to ascertain whether that cause be connected with a difference in the brain between the native American race, and their conquering invaders (Combe and Coates, in review of Morton's *Crania Americana*, 1840, p. 352).

Moreover, Combe argued that Morton's collection would acquire true scientific value *only if* mental and moral worth could be read from brains: "If this doctrine be unfounded, these skulls are mere facts in Natural History, presenting no particular information as to the mental qualities of the people" (from Combe's appendix to Morton's *Crania Americana*, 1839, p. 275).

Although he vacillated early in his career, Morton soon became a leader among the American polygenists. He wrote several articles to defend the status of human races as separate, created species. He took on the strongest claim of opponents—the interfertility of all human races—by arguing from both sides. He relied on travelers' reports to claim that some human races—Australian aborigines and Caucasians in particular—very rarely produce fertile offspring (Morton, 1851). He attributed this failure to "a disparity of primordial organization." But, he continued, Buffon's criterion of interfertility must be abandoned in any case, for hybridization is common in nature, even between species belonging to different genera (Morton, 1847, 1850). Species must be redefined as "a primordial organic form" (1850, p. 82). "Bravo, my dear Sir," wrote Agassiz in a letter, "you have at last furnished science with a true philosophical definition of species" (in Stanton, 1960, p. 141). But how to recognize a primordial form? Morton replied: "If certain existing organic types can be traced back into the 'night of time,' as dissimilar as we see them now, is it not more reasonable to regard them as aboriginal, than to suppose them the mere and accidental derivations of an isolated patriarchal stem of which we know nothing?" (1850, p. 82). Thus, Morton regarded several breeds of dogs as separate species because their skeletons resided in the Egyptian catacombs, as recognizable and distinct from other breeds as they are now. The tombs also contained blacks and Caucasians. Morton dated the beaching of Noah's Ark on Ararat at 4,179 years before his time, and the Egyptian tombs at just 1,000 years after that—clearly not enough time for the sons of Noah to differentiate into races. (How, he asks, can we believe that races changed so rapidly for 1,000 years, and not at all for 3,000 years since then?) Human races must have been separate from the start (Morton, 1839, p. 88).

But separate, as the Supreme Court once said, need not mean unequal. Morton therefore set out to establish relative rank on "objective" grounds. He surveyed the drawings of ancient Egypt and found that blacks are invariably depicted as menials—a sure sign that they have always played their appropriate biological role: "Negroes were numerous in Egypt, but their social position in ancient times was the same that it is now, that of servants and slaves" (Morton, 1844, p. 158). (A curious argument, to be sure, for these blacks had been captured in warfare; sub-Saharan societies depicted blacks as rulers.)

But Morton's fame as a scientist rested upon his collection of skulls and their role in racial ranking. Since the cranial cavity of a human skull provides a faithful measure of the brain it once contained, Morton set out to rank races by the average sizes of their brains. He filled the cranial cavity with sifted white mustard seed, poured the seed back into a graduated cylinder and read the skull's volume in cubic inches. Later on, he became dissatisfied with mustard seed because he could not obtain consistent results. The seeds did not pack well, for they were too light and still varied too much in size, despite sieving. Remeasurements of single skulls might differ by more than 5 percent, or 4 cubic inches in skulls with an average capacity near 80 cubic inches. Consequently, he switched to one-eighth-inch-diameter lead shot "of the size called BB" and achieved consistent results that never varied by more than a single cubic inch for the same skull.

Morton published three major works on the sizes of human skulls—his lavish, beautifully illustrated volume on American Indians, the *Crania Americana* of 1839; his studies on skulls from the Egyptian tombs, the *Crania Aegyptiaca* of 1844; and the epitome of his entire collection in 1849. Each contained a table, summarizing his results on average skull volumes arranged by race. I have reproduced all three tables here (Tables 3-1 to 3-3). They represent the major contribution of American polygeny to debates about racial ranking. They outlived the theory of separate creations and were reprinted re-

TABLE 3-1   Morton's summary table of cranial capacity by race

RACE	N	INTERNAL CAPACITY (IN^3)		
		MEAN	LARGEST	SMALLEST
Caucasian	52	87	109	75
Mongolian	10	83	93	69
Malay	18	81	89	64
American	144	82	100	60
Ethiopian	29	78	94	65

peatedly during the nineteenth century as irrefutable, "hard" data on the mental worth of human races. . . . Needless to say, they matched every good Yankee's prejudice—whites on top, Indians in the middle, and blacks on the bottom; and, among whites, Teutons and Anglo-Saxons on top, Jews in the middle, and Hindus on the bottom. Moreover, the pattern had been stable throughout recorded history, for whites had the same advantage over blacks in ancient Egypt. Status and access to power in Morton's America faithfully reflected biological merit. How could sentimentalists and egalitarians stand against the dictates of nature? Morton had provided clean, objective data based on the largest collection of skulls in the world.

During the summer of 1977 I spent several weeks reanalyzing Morton's data. (Morton, the self-styled objectivist, published all his raw information. We can infer with little doubt how he moved from raw measurements to summary tables.) In short, and to put it bluntly, Morton's summaries are a patchwork of fudging and finagling in the clear interest of controlling a priori convictions. Yet—and this is the most intriguing aspect of the case—I find no evidence of conscious fraud; indeed, had Morton been a conscious fudger, he would not have published his data so openly.

TABLE 3-2   Cranial capacities for skulls from Egyptian tombs

PEOPLE	MEAN CAPACITY (IN^3)	N
Caucasian		
Pelasgic	88	21
Semitic	82	5
Egyptian	80	39
Negroid	79	6
Negro	73	1

TABLE 3-3   **Morton's final summary of cranial capacity by race**

RACE AND FAMILIES	N	CRANIAL CAPACITY (IN³)			
		LARGEST	SMALLEST	MEAN	MEAN
Modern Caucasian Group					
Teutonic family					
Germans	18	114	70	90 ⎱	
English	5	105	91	96 ⎬	92
Anglo-Americans	7	97	82	90 ⎰	
Pelasgic family	10	94	75	84	
Celtic family	6	97	78	87	
Indostanic family	32	91	67	80	
Semitic family	3	98	84	89	
Nilotic family	17	96	66	80	
Ancient Caucasian Group					
Pelasgic family	18	97	74	88	
Nilotic family	55	96	68	80	
Mongolian Group					
Chinese family	6	91	70	82	
Malay Group					
Malayan family	20	97	68	86 ⎱	85
Polynesian family	3	84	82	83 ⎰	
American Group					
Toltecan family					
Peruvians	155	101	58	75 ⎱	79
Mexicans	22	92	67	79 ⎰	
Barbarous tribes	161	104	70	84	
Negro Group					
Native African family	62	99	65	83 ⎱	83
American-born Negroes	12	89	73	82 ⎰	
Hottentot family	3	83	68	75	
Australians	8	83	63	75	

Conscious fraud is probably rare in science. It is also not very interesting, for it tells us little about the nature of scientific activity. Liars, if discovered, are excommunicated; scientists declare that their profession has properly policed itself, and they return to work, mythology unimpaired, and objectively vindicated. The prevalence of *unconscious* finagling, on the other hand, suggests a general conclusion about the social context of science. For if scientists can be honestly self-deluded to Morton's extent, then prior prejudice may be found anywhere, even in the basics of measuring bones and toting sums.

The Case of Indian Inferiority: *Crania Americana**

Morton began his first and largest work, the *Crania Americana* of 1839, with a discourse on the essential character of human races. His statements immediately expose his prejudices. Of the "Greenland esquimaux," he wrote: "They are crafty, sensual, ungrateful, obstinate and unfeeling, and much of their affection for their children may be traced to purely selfish motives. They devour the most disgusting aliments uncooked and uncleaned, and seem to have no ideas beyond providing for the present moment. . . . Their mental faculties, from infancy to old age, present a continued childhood. . . . In gluttony, selfishness and ingratitude, they are perhaps unequalled by any other nation of people" (1839, p. 54). Morton thought little better of other Mongolians, for he wrote of the Chinese (p. 50): "So versatile are their feelings and actions, that they have been compared to the monkey race, whose attention is perpetually changing from one object to another." The Hottentots, he claimed (p. 90), are "the nearest approximation to the lower animals. . . . Their complexion is a yellowish brown, compared by travellers to the peculiar hue of Europeans in the last stages of jaundice. . . . The women are represented as even more repulsive in appearance than the men." Yet, when Morton had to describe one Caucasian tribe as a "mere horde of rapacious banditti" (p. 9), he quickly added that "their moral perceptions, under the influence of an equitable government, would no doubt assume a much more favorable aspect."

Morton's summary chart (Table 3-1) presents the "hard" argument of the *Crania Americana.* He had measured the capacity of 144 Indian skulls and calculated a mean of 82 cubic inches, a full 5 cubic inches below the Caucasian norm (Figs. 3-1 and 3-2). In addition, Morton appended a table of phrenological measurements indicating a deficiency of "higher" mental powers among Indians. "The benevolent mind," Morton concluded (p. 82), "may regret the inaptitude of the Indian for civilization," but sentimentality must yield to fact. "The structure of his mind appears to be different from that of the white man, nor can the two harmonize in the social relations except on the most limited scale." Indians "are not only averse to the restraints of education, but for the

---

* This account omits many statistical details of my analysis. The complete tale appears in Gould, 1978.

FIGURE 3-1   The skull of an Araucanian Indian. The lithographs of this and the next figure were done by John Collins, a great scientific artist unfortunately unrecognized today. They appeared in Morton's *Crania Americana* of 1839.

most part are incapable of a continued process of reasoning on abstract subjects" (p. 81).

Since *Crania Americana* is primarily a treatise on the inferior quality of Indian intellect, I note first of all that Morton's cited average of 82 cubic inches for Indian skulls is incorrect. He separated Indians into two groups, "Toltecans" from Mexico and South America, and "Barbarous Tribes" from North America. Eighty-two is the average for Barbarous skulls; the total sample of 144 yields a mean of 80.2 cubic inches, or a gap of almost 7 cubic inches between Indian and Caucasian averages. (I do not know how Morton made this elementary error. It did permit him, in any case, to retain the conventional chain of being with whites on top, Indians in the middle, and blacks on the bottom.)

But the "correct" value of 80.2 is far too low, for it is the result of an improper procedure. Morton's 144 skulls belong to many different groups of Indians; these groups differ significantly among themselves in cranial capacity. Each group should be weighted equally, lest the final average be biased by unequal size of subsamples. Suppose, for example, that we tried to estimate average human height from a sample of two jockeys, the author of this book (strictly middling stature), and all the players in the National Basketball Association. The hundreds of Jabbars would swamp the remaining three and give an average in excess of six and a half feet. If, however, we averaged the

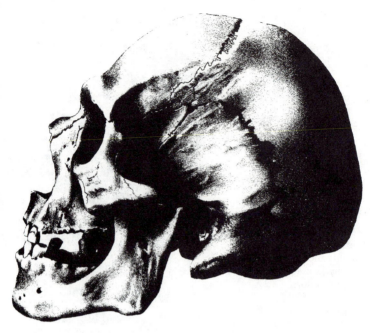

FIGURE 3-2   The skull of a Huron Indian. Lithograph by John Collins from Morton's *Crania Americana*, 1839.

averages of the three groups (jockeys, me, and the basketball players), then our figure would lie closer to the true value. Morton's sample is strongly biased by a major overrepresentation of an extreme group—the small-brained Inca Peruvians. (They have a mean cranial capacity of 74.36 cubic inches and provide 25 percent of the entire sample.) Large-brained Iroquois, on the other hand, contribute only 3 skulls to the total sample (2 percent). If, by the accidents of collecting, Morton's sample had included 25 percent Iroquois and just a few Incas, his average would have risen substantially. Consequently, I corrected this bias as best I could by averaging the mean values for all tribes represented by 4 or more skulls. The Indian average now rises to 83.79 cubic inches.

This revised value is still more than 3 cubic inches from the Caucasian average. Yet, when we examine Morton's procedure for computing the Caucasian mean, we uncover an astounding inconsistency. Since statistical reasoning is largely a product of the last one hundred years, I might have excused Morton's error for the Indian mean by arguing that he did not recognize the biases produced by unequal sizes among subsamples. But now we discover that he understood this bias perfectly well—for Morton calculated his high Caucasian mean by consciously eliminating small-brained Hindus from his sample. He writes (p. 261): "It is proper, however, to mention that but 3 Hindoos are admitted in the whole number, because the skulls of these people are probably smaller than those of any other existing nation. For example, 17 Hindoo heads give a mean of but 75 cubic inches; and the three received into the table are taken at that average." Thus, Morton included a large sub-sample of small-brained people (Inca Peruvians) to pull down the Indian average, but excluded just as many small Caucasian skulls to raise the mean of his own group. Since he tells us what he did so baldly, we must assume that Morton did not deem his procedure improper. But by what rationale did he keep Incas and exclude Hindus, unless it were the a priori assumption of a truly higher Caucasian mean? For one might then throw out the Hindu sample as truly anomalous, but retain the Inca sample (with the same mean as the Hindus, by the way) as the lower end of normality for its disadvantaged larger group.

I restored the Hindu skulls to Morton's sample, using the same procedure of equal weighting for all groups. Morton's Caucasian sample, by his reckoning, contains skulls from four subgroups, so Hindus should contribute one-fourth of all skulls to the sample. If we restore all seventeen of Morton's Hindu skulls, they form 26 percent of the total sample of sixty-six. The Caucasian mean now drops to 84.45 cubic inches, for no difference worth mentioning between Indians and Caucasians. (Eskimos, despite Morton's low opinion of them, yield a mean of 86.8, hidden by amalgamation with other subgroups in the Mongol grand mean of 83.) So much for Indian inferiority.

REFERENCES

Combe, G., and Coates, B. H. 1840. Review of *Crania Americana. American Journal of Science* 38: 341–375.

Gould, S. J. 1978. Morton's ranking of races by cranial capacity. *Science* 200: 503–509.

Meigs, C. D. 1851. *A memoir of Samuel George Morton, M.D.* Philadelphia: T. K. and P. G. Collins, 48pp.

Morton, S. G. 1839. *Crania Americana* or, a comparative view of the skulls of various aboriginal nations of North and South America. Philadelphia: John Pennington, 294pp.

——. 1844. Observations on Egyptian ethnography, derived from anatomy, history, and the monuments [separately reprinted subsequently as *Crania Aegyptiaca*, with title above as subtitle]. *Transactions of the American Philosophical Society* 9: 93–159.

——. 1847. Hybridity in animals, considered in reference to the question of the unity of the human species. *American Journal of Science* 3: 39–50, and 203–212.

——. 1849. Observations on the size of the brain in various races and families of man. *Proceedings of the Academy of Natural Sciences Philadelphia* 4: 221–224.

——. 1850. On the value of the word *species* in zoology. *Proceedings of the Academy of Natural Sciences Philadelphia* 5: 81–82.

———. 1851. On the infrequency of mixed offspring between European and Australian races. *Proceedings of the Academy of Natural Sciences Philadelphia* 5: 173–175.

Stanton, W. 1960. *The leopard's spots: scientific attitudes towards race in America 1815–1859.* Chicago: University of Chicago Press, 245pp.

Discussion Questions

1. What was Morton's hypothesis, and how did he go about testing it? What is Gould's assessment of Morton's methods of testing his hypothesis? How does Gould support his evaluation of Morton?

2. Gould provides quotations and summary to illustrate what an extensive and prestigious reputation Samuel Morton had. How do you account for so many intelligent, well-schooled men being in agreement with Morton's faulty interpretation of his findings?

3. What is the source of Gould's reference to "an American Golgotha"? What kind of attitude toward Morton's skull collection does Gould seem to have?

4. Why does Gould include Morton's tables? What points does Gould support by referring to Morton's tables? Do you think it was necessary to include these tables? Why or why not?

5. What are some ways by which researchers can guard against an unconscious lack of objectivity in the way they design experiments, collect data, and interpret data?

Journal Entry

Write an entry in which you explore your own attitude toward "unconscious finagling" in scientific research. Describe any instances in your own research when it occurred to you that you might be seeing things in a certain way because that is how you wanted or expected them to turn out. Explain what you did to decrease the likelihood of bias in your own interpretations.

Writing Projects

1. Gould begins his essay with the following statement: "Appeals to reason or to the nature of the universe have been used throughout history to enshrine existing hierarchies as proper and inevitable." In an essay, analyze how Gould supports his assertion. What kind of examples does he use? How much knowledge does he assume the reader has about the subject? What methods does he employ to convince the reader of the seriousness of his argument?

2. Using Gould's method as a guide, investigate another instance of scientific study skewed by racial prejudice. What evidence of bias did you discover? How did researcher bias affect the study? How did it affect the research subjects? How might the impact of researcher bias have been reduced?

Collaborative Project

Working with a partner from class, read Alexander Pope's *Essay on Man* (quoted at the beginning of Gould's essay) and *The Great Chain of Being* by Arthur O. Lovejoy. Analyze the examples and rationale used by Lovejoy and Pope. Summarize for your classmates the concept of the chain of being. You and your partner could construct a diagram to illustrate the chain analogy. Then explain how it relates to modern-day racial prejudice.

O. B. Hardison, Jr.

Charles Darwin's Tree of Life

Osborne Bennett Hardison, Jr. *(1928–1990) was a founding member of the Quark Club, a collection of humanists and scientists united in seeking cultural change. Hardison also directed the Folger Shakespeare Library in Washington, D.C., for many years. The recipient of numerous wards, he was honored with the Italian government's Cavaliere Ufficiale in 1974 and the Order of the British Empire in 1983. A professor, scholar, poet, and essayist, Hardison was frequently described as a "modern Renaissance man." Among his lively and varied works are the following:* Disappearing through the Skylight: Culture and Technology in the Twentieth Century *(1989), from which the following selection is excerpted;* The Enduring Moment *(1962), a book of criticism focused on the concept of praise in Renaissance literary theory; and* The Quest for Imagination *(1971), a collection of essays on aesthetic criticism of the twentieth century. In "Charles Darwin's Tree of Life," Hardison illustrates Darwin's ability to portray the beauty and complexity of the natural world through the energetic, vivid, and poetic use of language.*

Questions to Consider

☐ What does Hardison mean in his opening sentence when he says that Darwin's *The Origin of Species* represented the "culmination . . . and vindication of the Baconian tradition in science . . ."? Notice whether the remainder of Hardison's essay supports this statement.

☐ Hardison's writing style is noted for its clarity, vividness, and readability. Watch how he accomplishes this.

THE culmination and—for many Victorians—the vindication of the Baconian tradition in science was Charles Darwin's *The Origin of Species* (1859). Darwin acknowledges his debt to Bacon in his *Autobiography* (1876): "I worked on the true Baconian principles, and without any theory collected facts on a wholesale scale."

Wholesale is right. The book brings together twenty years of painstaking, minutely detailed observation ranging over the whole spectrum of organic life. Like Bacon, Darwin made little use of mathematics, although he had attempted (unsuccessfully) to deepen his mathematical knowledge while at

Cambridge. Nor was Darwin the sort of scientist whose observations depend on instruments. His four-volume study of barnacles – *Cirripedia* (1851–54) – uses microscopy frequently, but much of his best work could have been written entirely on the basis of direct observation.

As soon as it was published, *The Origin of Species* was recognized as one of those books that change history. Its reception was partly a tribute to the overwhelming wealth of detail it offers in support of the theory Darwin finally worked out to hold his enormous bundle of facts together and partly a case of powder waiting for a spark. Darwin was initially criticized for giving insufficient credit to his predecessors, and the third edition of *The Origin of Species* includes a list of important moments in the earlier history of the theory of evolution. It begins with Jean-Baptiste Lamarck, who proposed a generally evolutionary theory of biology in the *Histoire naturelle des animaux* (1815). Charles Lyell's *Principles of Geology* (1832) is not included in the list because it is not specifically evolutionary, but its analysis of the evidence of geological change over time was indispensable to Darwin. Using Lyell, he could be certain that the variations he observed among animals of the same species in the Galápagos Islands had occurred within a relatively short span of geologic time.

Another source mentioned in the list and the immediate stimulus to the publication of *The Origin of Species* was an essay by Alfred Russell Wallace entitled "On the Tendency of Varieties to Depart Indefinitely from the Original Type." Wallace sent this essay to Darwin in 1858, and it convinced Darwin that if he did not publish his own work he risked being anticipated. He acknowledges Wallace's paper in his introduction and admits in the *Autobiography* that it "contained exactly the same theory as mine." Again according to the *Autobiography*, it was Darwin's reading of Malthus that suggested, around 1838, that all species are locked in a remorseless struggle for survival.

In spite of these and other anticipations, *The Origin of Species* was an immediate sensation. By ignoring religious dogma and wishful thinking, Darwin was able to buckle and bow his mind to the nature of things and to produce the sort of powerful, overarching concept that reveals coherence in a vast area of experience that had previously seemed chaotic.

A modern reader can see a kinship between Darwin's passionate interest in all things living, beginning with his undergraduate hobby of collecting beetles, and the outburst of nature poetry that occurred in the Romantic period.

Darwin was unaware of this kinship. In the *Autobiography* he says that "up to the age of thirty, or beyond it, poetry of many kinds, such as the works of Milton, Gray, Byron, Wordsworth, Coleridge, and Shelley . . . gave me the greatest pleasure. . . . But now for many years I cannot endure to read a line of poetry." His *Journal of the Voyage of the Beagle* is filled with appreciative comments about tropical landscape and its animals and plants, but he remarks that natural scenery "does not cause me the exquisite delight which it formerly did." He is probably contrasting his own methodical descriptions of landscape with the romanticized landscapes of writers like Byron and painters like

Turner. He plays the role of Baconian ascetic collecting "without any theory . . . facts on a wholesale scale." His mind, he says (again in the *Autobiography*), has become "a kind of machine for grinding laws out of large collections of facts."

The idea that the mind is a machine that grinds laws out of facts echoes Bacon's injunction to use reason to "deliver and reduce" the imagination. The same asceticism is evident in Darwin's disparaging comments about his literary style. He believed he was writing dry scientific prose for other scientists, and John Ruskin, among others, agreed. Darwin was astounded, gratified, and a little frightened by his popular success.

No one can read Darwin today without recognizing that he was wrong about his style. As Stanley Edgar Hyman observes in *The Tangled Bank* (1962), both *The Voyage of the Beagle* and *The Origin of Species* are filled with passages that are beautiful and sensitive, whatever Darwin may have thought of them. The writing is effective precisely because it does not strain for the gingerbread opulence fashionable in mid-Victorian English prose. It has a freedom from pretense, a quality of authority, as moving as the natural descriptions in Wordsworth's *Prelude*. It is effective precisely because it stems from direct observation of the things and relationships that nature comprises. In addition to revealing a mind "buckled and bowed" to nature, it reveals a mind that has surrendered to the kaleidoscope of life around it. Consider the following comment on the life-styles of woodpeckers:

> Can a more striking instance of adaptation be given than that of a woodpecker for climbing trees and seizing insects in chinks in the bark? Yet in North America there are woodpeckers which feed largely on fruit, and others with elongated wings which chase insects on the wing. On the plains of La Plata, where hardly a tree grows, there is a woodpecker . . . which has two toes before and two behind, a long pointed tongue, pointed tail-feathers, sufficiently stiff to support the bird on a post, but not so stiff as in the typical woodpeckers, and a straight strong beak. . . . Hence this [bird] in all essential parts of its structure is a woodpecker. Even in such trifling characters as the colouring, the harsh tone of the voice, and undulatory flight, its close blood-relationship to our common woodpecker is plainly declared; yet . . . in certain large districts it does not climb trees, and it makes its nest in holes in banks! In certain other districts, however . . . this same woodpecker . . . frequents trees, and bores holes in the trunk for its nest.

Darwin was familiar with Audubon's *Birds of America*, and remarks that Audubon "is the only observer to witness the frigate-bird, which has all its four toes webbed, alight on the surface of the ocean." In spite of a possible touch of irony in this remark, the affinity between the two naturalists is striking. Darwin fixes things in the middle distance by means of words. The central device in his description of the La Plata woodpecker is detail: elongated wings, insects caught on the wing, two toes before and two behind, stiff tail, elongated beak, harsh voice, a nest in a hole in a bank. The accumulating details express close observation which is also loving observation. They create a thingly poetry, a poetry of the actual. . . .

In a similar way, Audubon fixes in images a nature that flaunts itself palpably and colorfully in the middle distance. In the process both Darwin and Audubon create an art of the actual.

A year before *The Origin of Species*, Oliver Wendell Holmes published "The Chambered Nautilus." It is a poem that attempts to fix a thing that is out there in the middle distance in verse:

> Year after year behold the silent toil
> That spread his lustrous coil;
> Still as the spiral grew,
> He left the past year's dwelling for the new,
> Stole with soft step its shining archway through, built up its idle door,
> Stretched in his last-found home, and knew the old no more.

Here, instead of the scientist becoming poet, the poet becomes a scientist. The problem is that the poem cannot forget it is art. It is more clumsy, finally, than Darwin's description of the La Plata woodpecker. Closer to Darwin are the photographs of Mathew Brady, the histories of Ranke and Burckhardt, and the novels of Balzac, George Eliot, and Turgenev.

Feeling is usually implicit in Darwin's prose but repressed. Facts are facts and poetry is poetry. Occasionally, however, Darwin allowed his feelings to bubble to the surface. The closing paragraph of *The Origin of Species* is a case in point. It describes a scene,

> . . . clothed with many plants of many kinds, with birds singing on the bushes, with various insects flitting about, and with worms crawling through the damp earth, and . . . these elaborately constructed forms, so different from each other, and dependent upon each other in so complex a manner, have all been produced by laws acting around us. . . . Thus, from the war of nature, from famine and death, the most exalted object which we are capable of conceiving, namely, the production of the higher animals, directly follows.

No passage is more obviously dominated by aesthetic feeling than Darwin's description of the variety of species created by the struggle for existence. The idea of the struggle is central to *The Origin of Species*. It involves a paradox that fascinated Darwin. Out of a silent but deadly struggle comes the infinitely varied and exotically beautiful mosaic of life:

> How have all these exquisite adaptations of one part of the organization to another part, and to the conditions of life, and of one organic being to another being, been perfected? We see these beautiful co-adaptations most plainly in the woodpecker and the mistletoe; and only a little less plainly in the humblest parasite which clings to the hairs of a quadruped or feathers of a bird; in the structure of the beetle which dives through the water; in the

plumed seed which is wafted by the gentlest breeze; in short we see beautiful adaptations everywhere and in every part of the organic world.

Exquisite, perfected, beautiful, humblest, plumed, gentlest. The world described by these adjectives is not cold, alien, or indifferent. It is a work of art. Nor is Darwin's prose the dispassionate, dry prose of a treatise devoted only to facts. Because it is the work of a naturalist, it pays close attention to detail. The parts are there because they are there in nature in the middle distance: the woodpecker, the mistletoe, the parasite clinging to the quadruped, the feathers of the bird, the water beetle, the plumed seed. They illustrate the harmonious relations created by the struggle for survival – "co-adaptation" is Darwin's word. The prose enacts these harmonies through elegantly controlled rhythms.

Darwin's language invites the reader to share experience as well as to understand it. *Exquisite, beautiful,* and *gentle* orient him emotionally at the same time that his attention is focused on the objects that give rise to the emotion – mistletoe, parasite, water beetle, plumed seed.

The passage flatly contradicts Darwin's statement in the *Autobiography* that his artistic sensitivity had atrophied by the time he was thirty. That he thought it did shows only that he believed with his contemporaries that science is science and art is art. The problem was in his psyche, not his prose. The tradition that science should be dispassionate and practical, that it is a kind of servitude to nature that demands the banishment of the humanity of the observer, prevented him from understanding that he was, in fact, responding to nature aesthetically and communicating that response in remarkably poetic prose. There is no detectable difference in this passage between a hypothetical figure labeled "scientific observer" and another hypothetical figure named "literary artist."

The most striking example of Darwin's artistry occurs in the "summary" of Chapter 3. The passage deals explicitly with the tragic implications of natural selection. It is a sustained meditation on a single image. The image – the Tree of Life – is practical because the branching limbs are a vivid representation of the branching pattern of evolution. However, the image is also mythic, an archetype familiar from Genesis and also from Egyptian, Buddhist, Greek, and other sources. In mythology, the Tree of Life connects the underworld and the heavens. It is the axis on which the spheres turn and the path along which creatures from the invisible world visit and take leave of earth. It is an ever-green symbol of fertility, bearing fruit in winter. It is the wood of the Cross on which God dies and the wood reborn that announces the return of life by sending out new branches in the spring. All of this symbolism is familiar from studies of archetypal and primitive imagery. Behind it is what Rudolf Otto calls, in *The Idea of the Holy*, the terrifying and fascinating mystery of things: *mysterium tremendum et fascinans.*

It is surprising to find a scientist, particularly a preeminent Victorian scientist and a self-avowed disciple of Bacon, using an archetypal image. Yet

Darwin's elaboration is both sensitive and remarkably full. Central to it is the paradox of life in death, and throughout, one senses the hovering presence of the *mysterium tremendum et fascinans:*

> The affinities of all the beings of the same class have sometimes been represented by a great tree. I believe this simile largely speaks the truth. The green and budding twigs may represent existing species; and those produced during former years may represent the long succession of extinct species. At each period of growth all the growing twigs have tried to branch out on all sides, and to overtop and kill the surrounding twigs and branches, in the same manner as species and groups of species have at all times overmastered other species in the great battle for life. . . . Of the many twigs which flourished when the tree was a mere bush, only two or three, now grown into great branches, yet survive and bear the other branches; so with the species which lived during long-past geological periods, very few have left living . . . descendants.
>
> From the first growth of the tree, many a limb and branch has decayed and dropped off; and all these fallen branches of various sizes may represent those whole orders, families, and genera which have now no living representatives, and which are known to us only in a fossil state. As we here and there see a thin, straggling branch springing from a fork low down in a tree, and which by some chance has been favored and is still alive on its summit, so we occasionally see an animal like the Ornithorhynchus or Lepidosiren, which in some small degree connects by its affinities two large branches of life, and which has apparently been saved from fatal competition by having inhabited a protected station. As buds give rise by growth to fresh buds, and these, if vigorous, branch out and overtop on all sides many a feebler branch, so by generation I believe it has been with the great Tree of Life, which fills with its dead and broken branches the crust of the earth, and covers the surface with its ever-branching and beautiful ramifications.

Darwin's music here is stately and somber. The central image is established at the beginning: a great tree green at the top but filled with dead branches beneath the crown. The passage becomes an elegy for all the orders of life that have perished since the tree began. Words suggesting death crowd the sentences: *overtopped, kill, the great battle for life, decayed, dropped off, fallen, no living representative, straggling branch, fatal competition.* As the passage moves toward its conclusion, a change, a kind of reversal, can be felt. Words suggesting life become more frequent: *alive, life, saved, fresh buds, vigorous.* The final sentence restates the central paradox in a contrast between universal desolation—"dead and broken branches [filling] the crust of the earth"—with images of eternal fertility—"ever-branching and beautiful ramifications."

In spite of the poetic qualities of *The Origin of Species*, the idea of science as the dispassionate observation of things is central to the Darwinian moment. Observation reveals truth; and once revealed, truth can be generalized.

The truths discovered by Darwin were applied almost immediately to sociology and political science. Herbert Spencer had coined the phrase "survival of the fittest" in 1852 in an article on the pressures caused by population growth entitled "A Theory of Population." Buttressed by the prestige of *The Origin of Species*, the concept of the survival of the fittest was used to justify laissez-faire capitalism. Andrew Carnegie remarked in 1900, "A struggle is inevitable [in society] and it is a question of the survival of the fittest." John D. Rockefeller added, "The growth of a large business is merely the survival of the fittest." Capitalism enables the strong to survive while the weak are destroyed. Socialism, conversely, protects the weak and frustrates the strong. Marx turned over the coin: socialism is a later and therefore a higher product of evolution than bourgeois capitalism. Being superior, it will replace capitalism as surely as warm-blooded mammals replaced dinosaurs.

Darwin also influenced cultural thought. To say this is to say that he changed not only the way the real was managed but the way it was imagined. The writing of history became evolutionary—so much so that historians often assumed an evolutionary model and tailored their facts to fit. The histories of political systems, national economies, technologies, machinery, literary genres, philosophical systems, and even styles of dress were presented as examples of evolution, usually interpreted to mean examples of progress from simple to complex, with simple considered good, and complex better.

And, of course, Darwin's theories were both attacked and supported in the name of religion. Adam Sedgwick, professor of geology at Cambridge, began the long history of attacks on Darwin when he wrote in "Objections to Mr. Darwin's Theory of the Origin of Species" (1860): "I cannot conclude without expressing my detestation of the theory, because of its unflinching materialism." Among the sins for which Darwin was most bitterly attacked was his argument that species are constantly coming into existence and dying, an argument that contradicts the fundamentalist reading of Genesis. He was also attacked for suggesting that struggle, including violent struggle, is ultimately beneficial, and that, by implication, the meek will not inherit the earth. Finally, he was attacked for suggesting that man is an animal sharing a common ancestor with the apes, an idea that is implicit in *The Origin of Species* and stated unequivocally in *The Descent of Man* (1871).

Darwin's conclusion to *The Origin of Species* is a summary of his vision. It has a strong emotional coloring even in its initial form. Perhaps because of the attacks, Darwin added the phrase "by the Creator" to the first revised (1860) and later editions of the book: "There is a grandeur in this view of life, with its several powers, having been originally breathed by the Creator into a few forms or into one; and that, whilst this planet has gone cycling on according to the fixed law of gravity, from so simple a beginning endless forms most beautiful and most wonderful have been, and are being evolved."

Whether the reference to God represents Darwin's personal view of religion is outside the scope of the present discussion. Probably it did not. At any rate the notion that God is revealed in evolution remains powerfully attractive today both to biologists and, as shown by Teilhard de Chardin's *The*

Phenomenon of Man (1955), to those attempting to formulate a scientific theology. More generally, in spite of his literary disclaimers, Darwin initiated a whole genre of writing, typified by the work today of Bertel Bager, Lewis Thomas, and Annie Dillard, which dwells on the intricate beauties of natural design.

Many of the applications of Darwin's ideas were, however, patently strained from the beginning. Time revealed the inadequacies of others. Social Darwinism is studied in history classes but is no longer a viable political creed. Evolutionary histories of this and that are still being written, but the approach has been shown to be seriously misleading in many applications. More fundamental, by the middle of the twentieth century Baconian empiricism was no longer adequate to the idea of nature that science had developed. Einstein and Heisenberg made it clear that mind and nature—subject and object—are involved in each other and not separate empires. An objective world that can be "observed" and "understood" if only the imagination can be held in check simply does not exist. Facts are not observations "collected . . . on a wholesale scale." They are knots in a net.

Discussion Questions

1. Hardison explains that Darwin made countless observations and then came up with a theory to "hold his enormous bundle of facts together." What is this scientific method called? How is it the same or different from what other scientists have described in this text?

2. In discussing how Darwin's writing style itself reflects the "co-adaptation" among living species, Hardison says that Darwin's "prose enacts these harmonies through elegantly controlled rhythms." What do you think Hardison means? How effective is his illustration?

3. Hardison devotes considerable space to showing the influence of other scientists' work on Darwin. What is Hardison's purpose in carefully tracing Darwin's debt to the previous scientific work in his field? What is he implying?

4. How many students in your class associate the phrase *survival of the fittest* with Darwin? Hardison points out that in fact it was Herbert Spencer who coined the term in 1852. Why do you suppose the term has become synonymous with Darwin's concept of co-adaptation?

5. Hardison says that the notion that a belief in God is consistent with the theory of evolution is an appealing one for both scientists and nonscientists. Do you also find this an appealing notion? Do you see a conflict between science and religion? If so, do you think the conflict can be resolved?

6. Contrast the current view of mind versus nature – or subject versus object – with the Baconian principle. Consider Hardison's statement that facts are not observed truths but "knots in a net." What does this metaphor mean?

Journal Entry

Hardison shows how Darwin viewed his own mind "as a kind of machine for grinding laws out of large collections of facts." What is your reaction to this notion? Do you view your own mind as a kind of machine with a particular function?

Writing Projects

1. Hardison quotes Bacon exhorting his colleagues to use "reason to 'deliver and reduce' imagination." What did Bacon mean? What definitions for his terms *reason* and *imagination* would have been in the forefront of Bacon's thinking, given his era? (Determining this may require you to do some research.) How are your definitions for these terms different from Bacon's? Analyze the connotations of *deliver* and *reduce* in Bacon's context and explain their significance. Do contemporary scientists think of themselves as engaged in delivering or reducing knowledge?

2. Hardison asserts that the reception of Darwin's *The Origin of Species* was a case of "powder waiting for a spark." Write an analytical report based on your research into the reception of Darwin's book. You will, of course, need to limit your search so that it is manageable. Consider setting chronological limits and focusing, for instance, on reviews and articles written during the first ten years after *Origin* was published in 1859.

3. Write a research paper in which you explain what Hardison means when he says that by "ignoring religious dogma and wishful thinking" Darwin was able to demonstrate "coherence in a vast area of experience that had previously seemed chaotic." Include consideration of ways in which Darwin was responsible for initiating what Kuhn refers to as a paradigm shift.

Collaborative Project

Working with one or two classmates, follow Hardison's suggestion of contrasting Darwin's description in *Journal of the Voyage of the Beagle* with landscape descriptions by Byron or paintings by Turner. Look at Darwin's landscape description in *Journal* to see if, indeed, it is as methodical and plain as Darwin himself claimed it to be. Analyze Byron's and Turner's work for elements representing the Romantic conventions of the times. How is Darwin's work similar to and different from the others'? Present your findings to the class; bring along examples of Byron's writing and Turner's painting.

Making Connections

Questions to Discuss

1. In "Science and the Sense of the Holy," Loren Eiseley classifies scientists into those who exhibit controlled awe and those who take a mechanical approach. Working with any selections from this text, choose two or three scientists and discuss which of Eiseley's categories best suit each one. Consider, for example, which category you think Jane Goodall fits into, based on "The Mind of the Chimpanzee." In which category would you place C. P. Snow and Lewis Thomas?

2. Stephen Jay Gould makes reference to scientists as well as poets with whom he thinks the reader will have some familiarity. His excerpt also includes several quotations from Alexander Pope's *Essay on Man*, published in 1733. Gould evidently assumes his readers possess a certain degree of general knowledge of both the arts and the sciences. Discuss one or two other writers from this chapter, or elsewhere in the text, who also make allusions to literature or philosophy that indicate they are knowledgeable and well read beyond their particular scientific discipline. How important do you think it is that authors treating scientific subjects also be knowledgeable about literature and that literary authors have a general understanding of scientific subjects?

3. The excerpt from Thomas Kuhn's "The Route to Normal Science" introduces the key concepts of paradigm and paradigm shift. Discuss how the selections by one or two of the other scientists in this text suggest they were challenging certain paradigms and might ultimately initiate a paradigm shift. Consider, in particular, Evelyn Fox Keller's and Jane Goodall's work.

4. To what extent would it be possible today to make significant contributions to science through the observation of living organisms without the use of specialized instruments (besides the microscope) or extensive mathematical knowledge, as did Darwin? Can science be conducted without technology today? Were Goodall, Gould, and Eiseley able to make contributions without relying on the latest high-tech instruments?

Suggested Writing Projects

1. In his discussion of Darwin's scientific method and style of writing about his findings, O. B. Hardison analyzes Darwin's poetic use of language to describe nature. Using Hardison's essay as a guide, analyze other scientists' writing in this text in terms of how diction, tone, and figurative language are used to present scientific information in a literary manner.

2. Hardison says that Darwin believed along with his contemporaries that

"science is science and art is art." Explain what you think this statement means, and discuss whether you agree with it. For examples, draw on Hardison's essay and others in this text, such as those by William Kittredge in Chapter 6 and Cynthia Ozick in Chapter 1.

3. Show connections between Mary Shelley's *Frankenstein* and Lewis Thomas's essay by discussing how each treats the concept of hubris. Both authors acknowledge that scientists sometimes attempt to take on the role of a god in their prideful attempts to shape nature. Describe the similarities and differences you see between Shelley's and Thomas's views regarding hubris, or between their views and those of other authors in this book.

4. Eiseley's selection begins with an analogy comparing the topography of the Nebraska Badlands to the convolutions of the human brain. Through the use of this analogy he is able both to illustrate an abstract concept and to structure his argument. Write an essay explaining how Eiseley develops his analogy, and compare it to the way in which another author from this chapter uses figurative language to illustrate his or her ideas.

4

Shaping Culture with Technology

 As you are no doubt well aware, technological innovation commands a central role in today's society. In your own life, you probably use technology to help you acquire a college education. For example, many students now use computers to write their papers for various courses. In a larger framework, electronic networks are actually reshaping the very nature of modern communication and influencing our culture. These networks, such as Internet and Bitnet, allow us to communicate immediately with audiences we may never actually see. Consequently, electronic writing has enlarged our opportunities for collaboration and reconstructed numerous intellectual communities.

This chapter examines several other key ways in which culture and technology shape each other. Jay David Bolter argues that "our culture is moving from a hierarchical social order to what we might call a 'network culture.'" In a hierarchical society we invest authority in certain institutions such as the government, the church, or the family. We rely on these institutions for ideologies and social order. But in a network culture we have more freedom to choose the institutions to which we will belong. As individuals we are no longer restricted by circumstances of birth or geography. We change jobs frequently, we move miles away from our parents, we change political parties, or we leave our church. We affiliate ourselves instead with others who have similar interests, income levels, and general tastes.

Reading Bolter's article may cause you to consider whether you think this is a positive change. We all need to weigh what is to be gained by having a network culture against what will be lost. Do we have more freedom? Is there more justice? Consider the issue of equity in the application of technological innovation. Do technological advances benefit everyone in the same way? To the same degree?

Ruth Schwartz Cowan's essay surveys four ways in which women's dependence on technology differs from men's. Technological developments that were meant to relieve some of the burdens women have shouldered as housewives and mothers have actually made *more* work for women, not less. Some women have escaped household drudgery only to enter the labor force and work at low-paying, tedious manufacturing jobs. However, Samuel Florman's essay provides a counter argument to Cowan's claim. Although he professes a limited sympathy for women who consider themselves to be excluded from technological contexts, Florman does admit the following: "Until women share in the understanding and creation of our technology—which is to say, until large numbers of women become engineers—they will suffer from a cultural alienation that ordinary power cannot cure."

Two short stories have been included in this chapter because they explore the role of technology in everyday life. Langston Hughes's story, set in the late 1950s and recounted through the eyes of a black man from Mississippi, reflects a skepticism felt by many then and now: that a technological innovation such as the atomic bomb would not provide equal protection for all the people whose safety it was designed to ensure. Hughes's character knows that blacks aren't welcome in the white folks' bomb shelters. Even today, we do not develop technology that is intended to be "integrated" into the entire population. In an unsettling science fiction short story, Ray Bradbury gives an allegorical warning of what happens when we forfeit human responsibilities to technological devices.

Even when the problems and inequities that accompany technological revolution are made evident, we continue to hail technology as the new frontier. Dorothy Nelkin faults the media for promoting technological discoveries without critically examining the side effects: "the dominant message conveyed is that the new development will give society the magic to cure economic or social ills."

George E. Brown, Jr., a member of the U.S. House of Representatives, has written an article that reveals the absence of this magic in certain technological advances. He points out just how market-driven technological development can be. Economic resources are always found to create technological solutions for those who can afford to pay for them, he notes. Furthermore, the solutions are usually convenient for affluent people. But technological approaches to preventing problems that are faced by poor people often go unexplored. One example is medical care. Treatment of underdeveloped lungs in infants is provided to those who can afford it, whereas prenatal care that would prevent underweight births among the poor is not adequately provided.

Overall, this chapter puts the spotlight on technological innovation. The purpose is not simply to fault those who create technology and those who use it. As members of a culture that is increasingly dependent on technological development, we all have a responsibility to assess its effects and to work for equity in its application.

Jay David Bolter

The Network Culture

Jay David Bolter's *(b. 1951) examination of the interrelationship between culture and computer technology has attracted considerable attention. Formerly a professor of classics at the University of North Carolina, Chapel Hill, Bolter is now a professor in the School of Literature, Communication, and Culture at Georgia Institute of Technology. He has written two books on computers,* Turning's Man *(1984) and* The Writing Space: The Computer, Hypertext, and the History of Writing *(1991), from which the following selection is taken. Bolter's scholarly articles have appeared in such journals as* Library Quarterly *and* Computers and Composition. *In "The Network Culture" Bolter explores the societal impact of today's web-like configuration of computer networks and argues in favor of the advantages this configuration could provide for social institutions, in contrast to the more conventional hierarchical structures that have dominated our lives thus far.*

Questions to Consider

☐ Before you begin reading, think about the computer's impact on cultural values and social roles in the United States. In what ways do you see our cultural values and social roles being shaped by computer technology? How have computers made your own life different in the last five years?

☐ This essay will be easier to follow if you find out what the following terms mean before you begin: *on-line, network, hypertext,* and *electronic writing space.*

O UR culture is itself a vast writing space, a complex of symbolic structures. Just as we write our minds, we can say that we write the culture in which we live. And just as our culture is moving from the printed book to the computer, it is also in the final stages of the transition from a hierarchical social order to what we might call a "network culture." For decades all forms of hierarchy have been disintegrating, as greater and greater freedom of action is granted to the individual. Much of this disintegration accords with the goals of liberal democracy: the diminishing of racial and religious segregation, for example. But whatever one thinks of the trend, no one can deny that an extremely powerful leveling force is at work in our society. It can be said that this leveling has always been a feature of American culture, that Tocqueville remarked on it one hundred and fifty years ago. The authors of

Habits of the Heart see today's "separation and individuation" as the culmination of a long historical process.

> [T]he colonists [to America] brought with them ideas of social obligation and group formation that disposed them to recreate in America structures of family, church, and polity that could continue . . . the texture of older European society. Only gradually did it become clear that every social obligation was vulnerable, every tie between individuals fragile. Only gradually did what we have called ontological individualism, the idea that the individual is the only firm reality, become widespread. (Bellah et al., 1985, p. 276)

Today the leveling has gone further than perhaps even Tocqueville could have imagined. Hierarchies in government, church, and family may retain status in law, but they have almost no moral authority. The vestigial hierarchies in our society, like the Catholic Church, are tolerated because they are completely misunderstood. (Thus many American Catholics seem to regard their hierarchy either as their representative government or as a quaint, decorative motif in their religious tradition.) The only great hierarchical force left is money, and today the possession of money creates and depends on no other distinctions. Among the richest people in America are athletes and celebrities who are often indistinguishable in education and tastes from the poorest Americans. We certainly do not think of rich people as better people. Instead, we use money to play at class, at hierarchical organizations that no one now takes seriously. However, the end of hierarchy is not the end of social structure. The individual may now be "the only firm reality," but that does not mean that individuals no longer form groups. They may well form more groups than ever, because they are free to associate and break off their associations as they please. Individuals now regularly join and quit jobs, neighborhoods, clubs, political parties and action committees, and even churches several times in their lives. These affiliations are all seen as voluntary, and they are horizontal rather than vertical. The network has replaced the hierarchy.

Sociologists may disagree over the causes of the networking of American culture. The point here is that our culture of interconnections both reflects and is reflected in our new technology of writing. With all these transitions, the making and breaking of social links, people are beginning to function as elements in a hypertextual network of affiliations. Our whole society is taking on the provisional character of a hypertext: it is rewriting itself for each individual member. We could say that hypertext has become the social ideal. No one now holds as an ideal the proposition that a child, if male, should follow his father into his profession or, if female, should emulate her mother, stay home, and raise a family. Instead the message is that a child (as an ontological individual) should be free to choose what he or she wishes to do in life. That freedom of choice includes everything: profession, family, religion, sexual preference, and above all the ability to change any of the options (in effect to rewrite one's life story) at almost any time. Admittedly, for many Americans this ultimate freedom is not available. But the ideal remains, and it is the ideal of a network culture.

When critics complain of a decline in social and political values, they are often complaining about the loss of hierarchy. What Christopher Lasch identifies as the "culture of narcissism" or Allan Bloom calls the "closing of the American mind" are manifestations of the breakdown of traditions in which civic duty was placed above radical individualism and in which certain kinds of learning were regarded as more important than others. What has been lost is the belief in the legitimacy of hierarchy itself. The critics' complaints are as predictable as are the forces that incline our society to ignore the complaints and continue to replace hierarchies with networks. The development of electronic writing can only serve both to clarify and to accelerate the present impulse for change.

Cultural Unity

One consequence of the networking of culture is the abandonment of the ideal of high culture (literature, music, the fine arts) as a unifying force. If there is no single culture, but only a network of interest groups, then there is no single favored literature or music. Nor is there a single standard of grammar or diction in writing. Elizabeth Eisenstein has argued convincingly that printing was a force for cultural unification during the centuries when the modern nation states were being formed. "Typography arrested linguistic drift, enriched as well as standardized vernaculars, and paved the way for the more deliberate purification and codification of all major European languages" (Eisenstein, 1979, vol. 1, p. 117). As we have seen, electronic writing has just the opposite effect. It opposes standardization and unification as well as hierarchy. It offers as a paradigm the text that changes to suit the reader rather than expecting the reader to conform to its standards.

This attitude is already widespread among readers in the late age of print. As our written culture becomes a vast hypertext, the reader is free to choose to explore one subnetwork or many, as he or she wishes. It is no longer convincing to say that one subject is more important than another. Today even highly educated readers, especially but not exclusively scientists, may know only one or a few areas well. Such ignorance of the shared textual tradition is in part the result of the specialization of the sciences that has been proceeding since the 17th century. But even the humanities are now utterly fragmented, so that a student of Latin literature may know nothing about Renaissance poetry or the 20th-century novel. Throughout the late age of print, however, there has been a lingering feeling of guilt about this situation – a call somehow to reestablish a core of textual knowledge that everyone must possess. The last vestige of this guilt can be heard in pleas for a canon of great authors, which we discussed in an earlier chapter. But the specialization has gone far too far to be recalled. In the sciences it is indispensable. In the humanities and social sciences it is institutionalized. The intellectual world is now defined by numerous "special interest groups" pulling this way and that—Marxists, neo-Freudians, deconstructionists, cognitive scientists, phenomenologists. All the groups are interconnected: some grew out of others, and each sends outrunners (links) into other camps. Thus, there are Christian Marxists, Marxist deconstructionists, phenomenological anthropologists, Lacanian psychoanalysts who write on literature, and so on. But an over-arching unification is no longer even the goal. In *After Virtue* Alasdair MacIntyre (1981), complaining about the fragmented state of moral philosophy, drew the following compelling analogy. Imagine an environmental catastrophe that causes human society to turn against modern science. Scientists are persecuted, and science texts are torn up or destroyed. Then imagine a later generation trying to reassemble these fragments ("half-chapters from books, single pages from articles, not always fully legible because torn and charred") into a single system. The result would be a mish-mash of incoherent theories and misunderstood facts. Of course, this disaster has not happened to modern science, but it is according to MacIntyre exactly what has happened to the great systems of moral philosophy (MacIntyre, 1981, pp. 2–3). For MacIntyre the disaster was the Enlightenment.

MacIntyre's analogy can be extended beyond moral philosophy to almost all fields today: each is an incomplete and disorganized hypertext that no one knows how to read in its entirety. But to call this fragmentation a disaster is to assume that unity is an achievable goal. What MacIntyre does not admit is that there is now no way out of this impasse. (It is certainly not possible to forget the lessons of the Enlightenment.) In fact, the fragmentation of our textual world is only a problem when judged by the standards of print technology, which expects the humanities, including metaphysics and ethics, to be relatively stable and hierarchically organized. What we have instead in the sciences is fruitful specialization and in the humanities a noisy collision of conflicting groups who in the end must agree to disagree. Anyone can enter or leave any group at any time or maintain a combination of interests and positions that characterize two or more camps.

In the late age of print, this situation must appear as chaos, because print holds up stability and order as its ideals. Even though printed materials are still the medium of expression for all these conflicting views, the unwritten assumption is that the disorder can eventually be set right. But in the context of electronic writing, nothing is more natural than the centrifugal disorder of our present cultural life. There is no conceptual problem (though many technical ones) in feeding all these conflicting texts into the computer and generating one vastly reticulated, self-contradictory hypertext. The computer provides the only kind of unity now possible in our culture: unity at the operational level. Hypertextual publication can accommodate all the mutually incomprehensible languages that the intellectual world now speaks, and this unification of technique must serve as the consolation for the lost unity of purpose.

Within the hypertextual libraries that are now being assembled, individual intellectual communities can retreat into their subnetworks and operate with as much or as little connection to each other as they desire. These communities may be large or small. Contemporary art, music, and literature have divided into several tiny elites and several huge popular movements, while most of the liberal arts are now pursued by relatively small groups of professionals. We have come to accept the fact that a new painting, a novel, or an essay will appeal only to one group of viewers or readers—that each person is free not only to dislike a new work, but simply to ignore it as irrelevant to his or her needs. Individuals today wander through an aesthetic supermarket picking out what interests them—atonal music, concrete poetry, science fiction films, situation comedies on television, or paperback romances. We are hard put to criticize any of these choices: they are simply questions of taste.

In the United States, the most thoroughly networked society, the distinction between high culture and popular culture has all but vanished. In place of the hierarchical organization in which high culture (poetry, "serious" novels, scholarly monographs) is valued above popular culture (doggerel, genre literature, how-to books), we have simply different subnetworks that appeal to different readers. None of the familiar indications of quality apply. In the age of print, a classic might be presented on high-quality paper and bound in cloth or leather, whereas a popular romance would appear in paperback with a suitably gaudy cover. In the electronic writing space, both texts will likely arrive on a diskette. The software for the romance may well be more sophisticated than the software that presents the "serious" fiction—for the same economic reasons that Hollywood's popular movies are often technologically more polished than European art films. The refusal to distinguish between high art and popular entertainment has long been a feature of American culture, but the computer as hypertextual network both ratifies and accelerates this trend. We can now see that American culture has been working for decades against the assumptions of the printed book and toward the freedom from top-down control provided by electronic writing. The computer is the ideal technology for the networking of America, in which hierarchical structures of control and interpretation break down into their component parts and begin to oscillate in a continuously shifting web of relations.

Cultural Literacy

Because of this shift from hierarchy to network, the debate over cultural unity takes its strangest turns here in the United States. Recent examples are the discussion of Allan Bloom's *The Closing of the American Mind* (Bloom, 1987) and E. D. Hirsch's *Cultural Literacy*. Hirsch's book is a particularly instructive case. Many readers took it as a call to return to the classics, to a fixed curriculum of works and authors that would make one culturally literate. But this was a misreading, as anyone can see from the first sentences of the Preface:

> To be culturally literate is to possess the basic information needed to thrive in the modern world. The breadth of that information is great, extending over the major domains of human activity from sports to science. It is by no means confined to "culture" narrowly understood as an acquaintance with the arts. Nor is it confined to one social class. (Hirsch, 1987, p. xiii)

Hirsch is no champion of culture in the traditional sense. For him cultural literacy is the ability to function effectively in our current world of reading and writing. His is an operational definition of literacy—what one needs to get by. Hirsch never demands deep knowledge of any subject: a literate person simply needs to touch the surface of a broad range of topics. At the end of his book, Hirsch gives a list of hundreds of topics that exemplifies the range needed for cultural literacy in contemporary America. Here is a passage from the t's: "Tutankhamen; Twain, Mark; Tweed, Boss; Tweedledum and Tweedledee; Twenty-third Psalm (text); Twinkle, Twinkle Little Star (text)" (p. 210). Here is the beginning of the v's: "vaccine, vacuum, vagina, valence, Valhalla, Valley Forge, valley of the shadow of death, value judgement, Van Allen Belt, Vancouver" (p. 211). Clearly Hirsch's definition of culture has nothing to do with high culture: it is simply anything that a reader might expect to encounter in a newspaper or magazine. Elements in Hirsch's list shoot off in all directions; they are linked not by any hierarchy of values, but by shared associations. Hirsch's alphabetized list reminds us of the eclecticism of the local bookstore, where in the section marked "Philosophy" Hegel is shelved next to Kahlil Gibran, Shirley MacLaine next to John Locke. A visit to the bookstore reminds us that there are no longer accepted principles by which pop culture and high culture can be separated. As in Hirsch's list, there is no hierarchy; all these printed products are of value simply because they will appeal to some group of paperback consumers.

From this perspective, cultural literacy does not require a knowledge of traditional texts; instead, it means access to the vocabulary needed to read and write effectively. And in fact this operational definition is now making cultural literacy almost synonymous with computer literacy. Both cultural and computer literacy simply mean access to information and the ability to add to the store of information. Increasingly, cultural literacy will require working with the computer, as the computer becomes the most important writing space in our culture. The cultural literates will be those who can use this new medium either for their work or for personal communication and expression. By this measure traditional scholars, who are at home in the world of printed books and conventional libraries, are relatively illiterate: they may not know how to work their way through an electronic network of information, certainly not how to write electronically for a contemporary audience.

This new definition of cultural literacy brings us back to the question of the canon of important works and authors. The idea of a relatively stable canon made sense in a culture dominated by printed books. The canon was also appropriate to a centralized educational system, in which everyone studied the same subjects and the same texts in order to be introduced into the standards of cultural life. But the notion of a standard has now collapsed, and the collapse is mirrored in the shift from the printed to the electronic writing space, in which a stable canon of works and authors is meaningless. No wringing of hands and no proposals for a renewed emphasis on the great authors of the past can do much to counter the trend toward a network culture, which is fostered not only by social preference, but also by the very medium of reading and writing that is coming to dominate the literacy of our society.

This prediction must seem bleak to those who still feel allegiance to the traditional culture of printed books. The loss is real; the hope for a cultural center based upon traditional texts must now be abandoned. But much of the loss has already occurred in the late age of print. The computer is only reinforcing the effects of centrifugal forces in the 20th century. More important, as we have seen from the outset, the end of traditional print literacy is not the end of literacy. The computer is simply the technology by which literacy will be carried into a new age.

The Electronic Hiding Place

There is another, more positive way to view the loss of a stable core for our culture. Although we do lose the satisfaction of belonging to a coherent cultural tradition, we gain the freedom to establish our own traditions in miniature. The computer offers people the opportunity to build liaisons with other readers and writers and to work in relative isolation from other such groups. A group does not need to convince a major publishing house of its importance or saleability; it can use electronic mail and diskettes to disseminate its materials. A group does not need to feel answerable to a cultural norm, but can pursue its own definition of literacy. This feature of electronic writing will be as useful to traditionalists as to the avant-garde. Scholars in esoteric subjects will be able to communicate and publish their results by fax machine or electronic mail. Unlike television, which promotes uniformity (even through the apparent diversity of cable and satellite stations), the microcomputer and the phone network really do permit special literacies to survive.

The computer is an ideal writing space for our networked society, because it permits every form of reading and writing from the most passive to the most active. A large group of users (perhaps the largest) will use the resources of the machine to shop, read the weather report, and play fantastic video games under the rubric of virtual reality. There will be a large market for the electronic equivalents of how-to books and interactive romances, science fiction, and the other genres. Small groups will read and write "serious" interactive fiction and non-fiction. Tiny networks of scholars will conduct esoteric studies in ancient and modern literature and languages. Hundreds or thousands of different interest groups from fundamentalist religion to space exploration will publish and read each other's messages and hypertexts – on commercial, academic, or governmental communication networks. Government and business will produce electronic documents by the billions. All these groups will be in contact at various levels for various purposes. In other words, the chaos of publication and communication in the late age of print will continue. The ideal of stability and cultural cohesion will largely disappear. Few will feel the need to assert such cohesion, since even the smallest group of writers and readers can function happily in its niche in the electronic network. The computer can in fact provide a quiet place for readers and writers to pursue such interests, relatively secure from the noise of what remains of shared cultural elements. The computer as a writing space can also be a place to hide from the sensory overload of the daily world of work and leisure and the other electronic media. In this space, all the various definitions of cultural literacy can survive, but no single definition can triumph at the expense of all others.

REFERENCES

Bellah, Robert N., Madsen, Richard, Sullivan, William M., Swidler, Ann, & Tipton, Steven M. (1985) *Habits of the heart: Individualism and commitment in American life*. Berkeley: University of California Press.
Bloom, Allan D. (1987) *The closing of the American mind.* New York: Simon and Schuster.
Eisenstein, Elizabeth. (1979) *The printing as an agent of change: Communications and cultural transformations in early-modern Europe* (Vols, 1–2). Cambridge: Cambridge University Press.
Hirsch, E. D., Jr. (1987) *Cultural literacy: What every American needs to know.* Boston: Houghton Mifflin.
MacIntyre, Alasdair. (1981) *After virtue: A study in moral theory.* Notre Dame, IN: University of Notre Dame Press.

Discussion Questions

1. How computer literate does Bolter assume his audience to be? Could a person who has never encountered hypertext follow Bolter's argument? Why?

2. Bolter sees a link between the concept of a hypertext and the way in which current American culture has been dividing itself into separate interest groups that interact with each other only as the need arises. Based on what you have learned about a hypertext network, what does the term *network*

culture mean? Do you think Bolter's analogy is fitting? Why does Bolter assert that hypertext has become the "social ideal" when many people do not know what hypertext is?

3. Discuss Bolter's utopian vision of the electronic writing space. What are the advantages he cites? What are some disadvantages he overlooks?

4. What does Bolter mean when he talks about the electronic hiding place? What do people hide from? Does his concept seem reasonable or merely ironic?

Journal Entry

Describe the qualities that make a book "good" to read. Explain how much you think the electronic writing space, hypertext in particular, will influence the pleasure you take in the act of reading.

Writing Projects

1. Analyze how Bolter defines and compares two important abstract ideas, the concept of a hierarchical order versus a network order. What forms of definition does he use? How does he make these concepts concrete? What kinds of examples does he include?

2. Discuss the general educational and social implications of the change from paper-based print text to on-line computer text. Writing for an audience that has had limited exposure to writing on-line, such as someone significantly older than you, explain the positive and negative aspects of having available to you only on-line text.

Collaborative Projects

1. Working with a partner, create definitions of *high culture* and *popular culture*. Then, together, produce a written comparison of the two concepts. Also explain why you agree or disagree with Bolter that the distinction between these two types of culture is disappearing.

2. Work in pairs (ideally, one of you will be familiar with hypertext) to create a HyperCard stack that is a short, interactive text. The stack should contain multiple linking options and may be based on any piece of literature you like. For example, you may create a stack that relates to a poem or popular song and incorporate graphics. You might link the lines of the poem or song together from separate cards or link concepts in the poem or song to other works by the same author or other works on the same topic.

3. With a partner, play an interactive fiction game (such as *Déjà Vu II: Lost in Las Vegas, Wishbringer,* or *Mortal Combat*). Report to the class on how the use of narrative makes interactive fiction different from other computer games. If you have the programming experience and considerable time, do a term project programming your own interactive fiction game; work with a class-mate.

Dorothy Nelkin

The Press on the Technological Frontier

Dorothy Nelkin *(b. 1933), a professor in both sociology and law at New York University, writes frequently and cogently on the impact of science and technology on society. Her scholarly interests range widely from the plight of migrant workers to morality and politics in military research. In the following excerpt from* Selling Science *(1987), Nelkin illustrates how the media has characterized scientific and technological developments as the major advancements for humankind. Yet Nelkin believes that the press has a responsibility to do more than simply sell science to the public; journalists ought to examine science critically and inform the public of any negative ramifications from scientific and technological development. Her other works include* The University and Military Research *(1972),* Science Textbook Controversies and the Politics of Equal Time *(1977), and* Dangerous Diagnostics *(with Laurence Tancredi, 1989).*

Questions to Consider

☐ Before reading this selection, consider to what extent you think the general population is influenced by the way in which the press shapes the "news." Do consumers of news reports, both written and televised, simply adopt the same attitudes toward events as the purveyors of the news, or do they approach the news more critically?

I N early 1982 *U.S. News and World Report* looked ahead to developments that could be expected in applied science and technology. The report talked of "breakthroughs" in many areas, of "startling" progress in space age communication, "radical changes" in medicine, "revolutionary" developments in agriculture, and the "far-reaching" effect of emerging technologies on the way all Americans live.[1] The images describing the application of scientific knowledge in this report are characteristic of the coverage of technology in the popular press. In article after article, extravagant claims are made about technological change; each new development promises a transformation of everyday life, whether for good or for ill. Conveyed in these reports is a sense of awe about the power of technology, resembling in some ways the presentation of science in the press. But there is a difference: whereas science appears in the press as an ultimate authority, technology appears as the cutting edge of history, as the new frontier.

The press frequently relocates this frontier, as technological advances occur in different fields or the novelty of an innovation wears thin. In the 1960s space had been the new frontier; the names of the space probes were Pioneer, Voyager, and Explorer. But space flights (until the Challenger accident) soon became routine—often in the news as much because of a misfire or because they include an occasional civilian among their astronauts as for their technological sophistication. In the 1980s frontier images appear instead in the news coverage of computer advances, biotechnology innovations, and the development of new medical techniques.

Every frontier has its dangers, even technological ones. Sometimes, as we shall see, the tenor of press reporting about a new development in technology is apocalyptic, especially when its implications appear to run against the current of prevailing public values or when extravagant claims of its promise are not realized. But the coverage of technology is mainly promotional; the dominant message conveyed is that the new development will give society the magic to cure economic or social ills. What is missing is a clear presentation of the role of technology and a clear assessment of its effects. Perhaps in no areas of technology is this promotional bias in reporting more apparent than in the coverage of computers and biotechnology.

Advertising High Technology

In the early 1970s the phrase "high technology" began to appear as a synonym for computer technology in specialized newspaper articles about investments in the computer industry. Today "high technology" has become a national symbol of progress, much like the space program a decade ago. As one reporter put it, "The term high technology has become as much a part of the political lexicon as motherhood, apple pie and the flag."[2]

Many of the hundreds of articles on high technology celebrate new computer developments as the "dawn of a new era," "the wave of the future," or "the force for revolutionary change." The images imply unlimited progress: "Experts believe that only economics and imagination limit the scope of computer technology: the revolution is real. . . . Every prediction is probably conservative."[3] Computer-based technologies will resolve medical problems and even provide social success; one computer article promotes "high tech ways to meet a man." Articles on, for example, stock prices, product sales, computer camps, career choices, college enrollment, and military strategies all make reference to developments in high technology as the new frontier.

The people who work in high technology are portrayed in these articles as pioneers and armed missionaries. A Minnesota computer consortium is "a pioneer in the midst of the high-technology prairie . . . blazing the trail for the educated around the world."[4] Scientists are "armed" with computers. Sometimes they are "gurus" or "apostles," and their followers, "converts." Boston's Route 128 is "East Mecca," California's Silicon Valley, "West Mecca." Their products are "man-made miracles" or "economic magic."[5]

The language in these articles is one of competition, struggle, and war – an imagery long used to promote science and technology. In November 1957 a cover story of *Newsweek* was called the "World War of Science – How We're Mobilizing to Win It." Science was "the front"; "supremacy" over the "growing army of Soviet scientists" was the goal.[6]

Today the imagery is similar; just as the Soviet Union is labeled an enemy on the political front, so Japan becomes the enemy in the technological arena. "The technological battle with the Japanese," a *Newsweek* article tells its readers, "is really an industrial equivalent to the East-West arms race."[7] The *Newsweek* cover of this issue shows a samurai warrior leaping out of a computer screen.

On the home front, local and regional newspapers typically portray high technology as the answer to revitalizing regional economies, and the inability to compete for high-tech industry as a problem. The *Kansas City Star* characterizes the desperate desire of cities to attract the computer industry: "Like an aging burlesque queen seeking the magic of silicone, the nation's older urban centers are trying for another whirl in the bright lights of prosperity. . . . This Burlesque Queen Needs More Bump and Grind."[8] Utah, according to the *Salt Lake Tribune*, suffers from an "image problem," related to temperance laws, that makes it hard to attract high-technology personnel.[9] However, in Alabama it is not the state's image, but the absence of a major research university, that creates "problems in the mind power race."[10]

Just as the press has tended to follow corporate advocacy by promoting computer education as the basis of science literacy, so it has uncritically adopted the corporate rhetoric in its coverage of high technology. By its frequent promotion of computer applications and its use of corporate sources of information on high-technology products, the press unreflectively accepts the assumptions of an aggressive industry seeking an expanded market. Articles appearing in the *Christian Science Monitor* during 1982, for example, described computers that supposedly provide reliable security systems, build appliances to simulate sight and hearing and even human thought, create art, track the course of acid rain, link prison inmates to a career, offer a way out of the recession, search for people lost in a desert, help officials cope with emergencies, analyze poems and prose, aid the poor, provide hands-on experience in analyzing chemicals, teach complex repair tasks, make complicated concepts interesting to kids, solve crime, aid in the running of a restaurant, turn oil into a renewable resource, and bolster local economies.

The inflated language of press reports on technological developments is strikingly similar to the language of "high-tech" ads in the magazines and newspapers in which these reports appear. Advertisers, for example, sell computers as "the cure for technophobia, the dreaded ego deflator," or as "the latest breakthrough." Frontier metaphors leap out of the computer employment ads: "Join Us in Charting New Territories"; "Technology That Knows No Limits"; "Our Sights Are Trained Just Over the Next Horizon at the Elusive Borderline Where Imagination and Technology Intermingle."[11]

Given the promotion of high technology in the press, it is no surprise that a wide range of other advertisers now employ technology metaphors to convey images of competence, precision, or prestige. For example, automobile ads, often printed on graph paper with engineering cutaways, visually and linguistically convey competence through reference to "laboratory testing," "impressive engineering credentials," and "state of the art research technology." Ads use language drawn from genetic engineering or computer engineering—"biomechanically engineered parts," "computerized, finite elements"—to suggest precision. An automobile music system is not just "high tech" but "higher tech for higher living." Even running shoes are "scientifically designed," reflecting the most "advanced biokinetic research" and incorporating "breakthroughs."

During the 1970s and early 1980s rare was the article in the popular press suggesting that high technology might not be the panacea advertised. By 1983, however, the failures of extravagant claims became defined as news, with reporters referring to high-technology expectations as a "cruel illusion" or "naive exaggeration." In March 1983 *Newsweek* revised its earlier oversell to mock the "visions of Atari Democrats who seem to believe that high-tech companies will be the country's economic salvation."[12] (That February Atari had laid off 1700 workers and shifted its manufacturing operation from Silicon Valley to Taiwan and Hong Kong.)

Some articles began to discuss problems that in fact had been evident all along. For example, a *New York Times* reporter pointed out that high technology can contribute to unemployment, create "mind stunting, mind dulling" jobs, and even encourage new forms of crime.[13] Others complained that high-tech industries may not produce the expected revenues to restore the eroding manufacturing base. In 1983 a Seattle journalist warned his readers: "Despite all the headlines of the past few years, this area will not become Silicon Valley 2 or Route 128 West."[14]

A mere two years later, however, the development of supercomputers—very large-scale computational systems—brought a new round of optimistic and promotional publicity. The press welcomed federally funded supercomputer centers as a symbol of the United States' technological muscle. Few articles questioned the effect that such concentrated allocation of resources would have on other areas of research. Most simply recorded the enthusiastic words of supercomputer advocates, who promise no less than a "second renaissance."[15]

As Star Wars robots compete with samurai warriors in a struggle for technological ascendance, there is relatively little critical analysis of the potential social and economic problems of a high-technology society, the problems of worker displacement, or the limited number of high-technology jobs. The promotional press provides little thoughtful reflection to temper oversell—until, of course, promises fail. . . .

Problems and Promises of the Technological Fix

In most popular press reports of high technology, promotional enthusiasm tends to overwhelm the undercurrent of ambivalence. But the coverage of those techniques that bear directly on problems of health is more ambivalent. Heralded by the press as panaceas and welcomed as affirmation that all problems can be solved, these advances also at times evoke deep skepticism, reflecting cultural, religious, and ethical concerns. This ambivalence is reflected in the coverage of organ transplantation.

Media coverage of transplant techniques began in the 1950s with reports in the press of, in the words of a 1958 *Life* article, a "revolutionary new stage of medicine . . . nearly ready to emerge from the research laboratory." This article, entitled "Science Nears a Goal: Bank of Vital Organs," portrayed transplantation as a technical solution to the most fundamental problems of life and death. The reporter predicted that "when kidneys can be transplanted, two kidneys will be a luxury."[16] A photograph in another *Life* article captured the motto on the door of a tissue bank: "Ex Morte Vita," "From Death, Life." There is "promise of a glowing future," claimed the caption.[17]

By 1968 the glowing future had arrived. Dr. Christiaan Barnard's heart transplant in Capetown, South Africa, that year stirred the public's imagination and attracted a flood of favorable and flamboyant reports. Journalists hailed Dr. Barnard's operation as a "surgical landmark," a pioneering venture comparable to space exploration. Barnard became a star; his work was described as a "milestone," a "revolutionary development bound to change our lives." Barely mentioned was the fact that his patient died soon after the operation.

After Barnard's "success," the press heralded America's early heart transplant operations with front-page headlines but few technical details. Emphasizing the heroic nature of transplantation, journalists underplayed the importance of the large technical and surgical team required to undertake complex transplant procedures. Primed by press releases from the participating medical centers, reporters also conveyed the misleading perception that the procedure was a miraculously effective solution for heart patients; they gave little attention to the patients' postoperative histories or their deaths. The transplant was a dramatic event; the aftermath ceased to be news.

By the early 1970s the coverage shifted, and the problems of organ transplantation became as newsworthy as the progress. Headlines announced

"Heart Transplant Future Looks Bleak," or "The Tragic Record of Heart Transplants: A New Report on an Era of Medical Failure." The press began to keep a box score of successes and failures of transplant operations, and publicized ongoing debates within the professional community, especially between the two Texas heart surgeons Denton Cooley and Michael DeBakey, who were respectively billed as "Texas Tornado and Dr. Wonderful." Reporters wrote of "transplant furor" and "medical rage," suggesting that the technique was hardly a panacea.[18]

Yet optimistic images once again dominated the coverage of the next technological fix, the artificial heart, in 1982. The first operation implanting the Jarvic-7 model in a human subject, Dr. Barney Clark, took place at the Utah Medical Center, where the hospital staff devoted a great deal of attention to media relations. In effect, this was scientific experimentation in a fishbowl. The center had invited the press, and reporters came, many remaining for the entire 112 days until Clark's death. The medical team included public relations experts who provided the journalists with technical details and even information on medical complications. However, according to *New York Times* reporter Lawrence Altman, much important information that would have served to better educate the public remained undisclosed.[19] Altman wanted to know how the patient was selected and the Jarvic-7 model chosen, and how the Institutional Review Board, set up to handle ethical dilemmas, had entered the deliberations. And he wanted to learn what scientific information was actually gained from the experiment. He argued that public relations control over the release of information limited the reporters' access to such potentially sensitive issues.

For the most part, journalist accounts of the operation were flamboyant and optimistic. They welcomed the human experiment as a "dazzling technical achievement," "an astounding medical advance," "the blazing of a new path," and a "medical milestone."[20] They said that researchers learned a lot from the experiment but said little about what was actually learned. They turned the patient into a hero: "This man is no different than Columbus or the pioneers who settled this valley. He is striking out into new territory."[21] Such frontier images mixed with military metaphors. Thus, technology became a "weapon in the conquest of heart disease." New drugs that facilitated the operation were "weapons in the counterattack" against the resistance of the immune system. The medical technologists were, of course, also heroes: "sleuths of the cardiovascular world," "men who race with death."[22]

Despite their enthusiasm, reporters in the Mormon-dominated region often expressed religious and moral doubts about the operation. They asked, for example: "It has been said that the heart is the symbol of love, site of life, habitat of the soul. Can it be replaced by a simple mechanical pump?" The *Salt Lake Tribune* reporter cited the answer from the director of the hospital's Division of Artificial Organs: "It's true that we may have palpitations, a rapid heart beat when we are in love, but this is secondary. If the owner of the artificial heart would find it pleasant to have these sensations, he can turn up the rate of the pump."[23]

Journalists reported briefly on the hospital's Institutional Review Board, but they had little material available on its deliberations and therefore on how the experiment was evaluated and policed. Thus they simply noted that its members had many sleepless nights while "wrestling" with the ethics of replacing a living heart.[24] Again, by focusing on the heroics of the procedure, the press avoided substantive questions that would inform readers about the process and the nature of the choices involved.

As the operation became more routine, some attention did turn to the high cost of the procedure and the related question of who should receive the heart, but coverage remained enthusiastic. A 1983 *New York Times* article on the conquest of heart disease called the mechanical heart a "breakthrough" and an "astounding medical advance." The attentive reader does learn that aspects of the technology are controversial, that scientific understanding is limited, and that "the road toward the conquest of heart disease still stretches beyond the horizon." Nonetheless, the reporter Harry Schwartz predicts, "Eventually, we will start clamoring to trade in our forty-year-old hearts at the very first hint of disease."[25]

In 1985 the public was once again deluged with reports, this time of William Schroeder's artificial heart implant at the Humana Institute. This coverage, orchestrated by a professional public relations team hired by the hospital, was more detailed and more technically sophisticated. However, the media mood changed with the short-term ups and downs of Schroeder's health; expressing promises and then dismay, the press provided readers with drama but little perspective.

The view of heart transplantation in the popular press has largely reflected reliance on interested advocates: most press reports have simply regurgitated their claims. The risk of unrealistic promotion of controversial procedures that follows from reliance on such sources was even more evident in the extensive press coverage of quite a different technology, estrogen replacement therapy (ERT). This coverage suggests that promotional efforts to influence the press are most effective when they converge with journalists' perceptions of prevailing social values; in this case, the popular fantasy of remaining forever young.

In 1963 articles began to appear in many newspapers and magazines proclaiming the virtues of estrogen replacement therapy—that is, the use of estrogen drugs to decrease the biological effects of menopause and aging.[26] ERT has been found to allay some of the symptoms of menopause and to reduce osteoporosis, the thinning of bone mass characteristic of postmenopausal women. But the press promoted estrogen theory, promising extraordinary benefits—even miracles. Typical headlines read: "Preventing Menopause," "Science Paints Bright Picture for Older Women." An Associated Press (AP) newswriter cited as fact a scientist's assertion that "there is no reason why they [women] should grow old." In 1964 the *Pittsburgh Post Gazette* promised a new era of youth for aging females. The article termed reluctance to prescribe estrogen "archaic," and claimed that "there is no scientific reason to object to its administration." The same story appeared in many women's magazines, where ERT was touted uncritically as an exciting new discovery, a scientific fact, a cure for growing old.[27]

Clearly the discovery of a pill that would keep women young forever was a newsworthy event. Reports of this discovery not only covered a subject of wide interest, but conveyed a message readers want to hear. The problem with this promotional reporting was that it ignored or underplayed the growing evidence indicating ERT's potential risk.

Who were the experts cited by reporters promoting ERT? The major source of information was Dr. Robert A. Wilson, a gynecologist, an active promoter of estrogen treatment, and the director of the Wilson Research Foundation. Funded by three drug firms, his foundation existed to publish and distribute reports and recommendations about specific products. Wilson had authored a paper in the October 1963 issue of the *Journal of the American Medical Association* that described experiments using estrogen drugs to postpone menopause, as well as a popular book called *Feminine Forever*.[28]

He and other scientists who were advocates of estrogen drugs minimized the risks that were increasingly apparent from cancer studies. They made sure that promotional materials on the rejuvenating effects of estrogen were mailed to newspapers and magazines throughout the country. They succeeded in attracting press attention. Articles promoting the therapy continued to appear despite a growing number of health warnings. An Associated Press report in 1965, called "Pills for Femininity," cited a physician: "It can preserve the femininity of 17 million postmenopausal females in the United States. It would cost far less than a cocktail."[29] A 1966 AP article publicized the claims of an unspecified "medic" who promised eternal youth to takers of the drug; the article criticized doctors who worried about the side effects as "impediments to keeping women young and lovely."[30] *Time* reported that estrogen was a "spring of youth," which would "ward off aging of the skin, breasts, and bones." *Look* in 1966 quoted Wilson as saying that "the vitality and freshness of the young girl need not fade at forty."[31]

In the late 1960s the press cited Dr. Robert A. Kistner, a professor of gynecology from Harvard Medical School, a regular consultant to drug companies, and a writer of popular books on ERT. Kistner was vocally critical of those studies that suggested a relationship between estrogen treatment and endometrial cancer, even in 1969 after the Food and Drug Administration (FDA) had issued warnings to that effect.[32]

The widely publicized U.S. Senate hearings on the safety of oral contraceptives in 1970 called attention to the side effects of estrogen drugs. The press responded, conveying the message that using estrogen for birth control could be harmful for health. But articles on using estrogen to postpone menopause selectively cited evidence to minimize the hazards of ERT and continued to emphasize its promise: "You can stop worrying about the menopause," said *McCall's* in 1971.[33] Still referring to Wilson's 1962 research, *Vogue* in 1974 promised "extra years of vitality," calling cancer worries "needless fear."[34] When a 1975 article in the *New England Journal of Medicine* linked ERT to increased risk of endometrial cancer, this was duly reported in the press, but so too were the persistent claims of ERT proponents. "When we drive the freeways we take a risk," a Beverly Hills gynecologist told Jane Brody of the *New York Times*.[35]

In December 1976 the public relations firm Hill and Knowlton proposed to Ayerst Laboratories, its client and a producer of estrogen drugs, a strategy for offsetting the warnings about the risk of endometrial cancer and for maintaining sales of estrogen replacement drugs. To "restore general perspective," and to "counteract unfavorable publicity" the firm recommended Ayerst contact science editors. When doing so, the firm stressed, "it is important to steer clear of attempting to promote the use of estrogens, and instead concentrate on the menopause. . . . The estrogen message can be effectively conveyed by discrete references to products that your doctors may prescribe."[36] . . . The press coverage of new technological developments plays on and probably encourages the public's desire for easy solutions to economic, social, and medical problems. Just as high technology is presented as the solution to international competition, so medical technologies are portrayed as solutions to problems of health. . . .

Even aging has a technological fix. Similar messages have recently been conveyed in the reporting on AIDS. The press has focused extensively on the search for a vaccine well before this technological solution is in sight, helping to divert public attention from the more immediate need to prevent the transmission of the disease.

As we have seen, this style of reporting often reflects the activities of aggressive sources of information, as well as press perceptions of what readers want to hear. Academic, industrial, and research institutions are eager to promote the latest technologies and therapeutic techniques, and many reporters simply convey their stories of success—especially if they fit with prevailing hopes or beliefs. Thus, failures lead easily to disillusionment, and the result is a tendency toward polarized reporting about technological developments. This tendency has become increasingly evident in the press coverage of technological risks.

NOTES

1. *U.S. News and World Report,* December 28, 1981; January 4, 1982.
2. *Salt Lake Tribune,* March 1983.
3. *U.S. News and World Report,* September 15, 1980.
4. *Christian Science Monitor,* June 9, 1982.
5. *Columbus Evening Dispatch,* January 23, 1983.
6. *Newsweek,* October 18, 1957.

7. *Newsweek*, August 9, 1982.

8. *Kansas City Star*, January 9, 1983.

9. *Salt Lake Tribune*, March 14, 1983.

10. *Birmingham Alabama News*, October 27, 1982.

11. Such advertisements appear, for example, in *New York Times* high-technology career supplements.

12. *Newsweek*, March 7, 1983, p. 67.

13. *New York Times*, September 18, 1983.

14. *Seattle Times*, January 9, 1983.

15. Kenneth Wilson, cited in *SIPIScope* 13, November/December 1985, p. 11.

16. *Life*, July 14, 1958.

17. *Life*, February 17, 1958.

18. See, for example, *Life*, September 17, 1971.

19. Lawrence K. Altman, "After Barney Clark: Reflections of a Reporter on Unsolved Issues," in Margery Shaw (ed.), *After Barney Clark* (Austin: University of Texas Press, 1984), pp. 113–128.

20. *New York Times*, December 3, 1982; and *Philadelphia Inquirer*, December 5, 1982.

21. *Salt Lake Tribune*, December 2, 1982.

22. *Salt Lake Tribune*, December 3, 1982.

23. *Salt Lake Tribune*, December 3, 1982.

24. *Salt Lake Tribune*, May 25, 1982.

25. In Harry Schwartz, "Towards the Conquest of Heart Disease," *New York Times Magazine*, March 27, 1983.

26. While writing this section, I discovered an excellent unpublished list of media reports and articles on ERT, compiled by Nancy T. Sommers, Princeton, New Jersey.

27. For example, see *San Diego Union*, December 13, 1964; *Pittsburgh Post Gazette*, November 10, 1964; and *Ladies' Home Journal*, January 1965.

28. Robert A. Wilson, "The Roles of Estrogen and Progesterone in Breast and Genital Cancer," *Journal of the American Medical Association*, 182, October 1962, pp. 327–331; and *Feminine Forever*, New York: M. Evans, 1966.

29. AP report, April 14, 1965, quoting Francis P. Rhoads.

30. AP report, January 29, 1966.

31. *Look*, January 11, 1966.

32. Robert Kistner developed his ideas in a popular book entitled *The Pill: Fact and Fallacies* (New York: Delacorte Press, 1969) and in the *Ladies' Home Journal* and other women's magazines in 1969.

33. *McCall's*, October 1971.

34. *Vogue*, January 1974.

35. *New York Times*, December 5, 1975.

36. Letter from Stanley Sauerhaft, Hill and Knowlton, to William Davis, Ayerst Laboratories, December 17, 1976.

Discussion Questions

1. What is your reaction to Nelkin's argument? Does it seem valid? Has she provided sound reasoning and reliable research? If so, where? If not, where do you find loopholes?

2. What is Nelkin's purpose in quoting single words and phrases from various newspaper accounts? Evaluate the effectiveness of this in strengthening her own argument.

3. If you agree with Nelkin that journalists are sometimes too easily awed by technological achievements, why do you think this is the case? Is it related to their having been trained in the arts rather than the sciences? Why would the press be reluctant to emphasize risks associated with technological breakthroughs?

4. To whom does Nelkin seem to be writing? What assumptions does she make about her audience's political attitudes, educational level, and familiarity with her topic?

Journal Entry

Write about the personal associations you have with one or more of the terms highlighted by Nelkin: *frontier, high technology,* or *progress,* for example. Try to estimate to what extent your understanding of these terms derives from the media.

Writing Projects

1. Write an essay responding to these questions: Do you agree with Nelkin's criticism of press coverage on technology? What role does Nelkin think we as consumers of mass media and technological products play in determining the kind of coverage of technology we receive? What do you think we can do to shape what information we receive?

2. Select a particular technological product or discovery (for example, a machine, a drug, or a medical procedure) that failed to fulfill its initial promise. Trace how the press initially presented the product and how the media later unraveled its complication or failure. Who was given credit initially for the product or discovery, and who was later blamed for its failure, if indeed it came down to those terms?

3. Write a research report based on review of the advertisements in several general interest magazines to determine what kinds of images are frequently used to present technological products. Analyze and draw conclusions from your findings about language, pictures, colors, and the like that seem to dominate the presentations. Examine news stories dealing with technology to determine whether these same images are prevalent there as well.

Collaborative Project

Working with a partner from class, find out what is the current status of organ transplants. How many are performed each year? What do they cost? How many are successful? How are the transplanting physicians viewed by the medical community? Who are today's heroes in this area? Analyze and interpret your findings, linking them to Nelkin's assessment of journalists' treatment of news about organ transplants and to related ideas that were raised in class discussion.

Langston Hughes

Radioactive Red Caps

Langston Hughes *(1902–1967) wrote poetry, plays, and fiction, and translated African poetry and folklore. He started publishing poetry in high school and later became active in organizing black theater companies in major cities, including Chicago. Hughes belonged to an influential group of artists who promoted the Harlem Renaissance in the late 1920s, a movement that emphasized both African heritage and contemporary life in Harlem. Hughes's early short stories were collected in* The Ways of White Folks *(1934). In 1942 he created the strikingly original character of Jesse B. Simple, a black working-class resident of Harlem. Hughes instituted a forum through which Simple, a cynically witty fellow speaking the colloquial language, and an educated, middle-class narrator carry on conversations about a variety of topics. In "Radioactive Red Caps," Simple and the narrator converse on the subject of blacks and the atomic bomb. The story first appeared in* The Best of Simple *(1961). Other collections by Hughes include* Simple Takes a Wife *(1952) and* Simple Stakes a Claim *(1957).*

Questions to Consider

☐ Based on the title alone, in what time period do you think this story is set? When was there a prevalent concern about radioactivity? Do you know what a Red Cap is?

☐ When you read this story, notice how you reach conclusions about the personalities, politics, and life-styles of the two speakers in this dialogue. On what evidence do you base these conclusions?

"**H**OW wonderful," I said, "that Negroes today are being rapidly integrated into every phase of American life from the Army and Navy to schools to industries—advancing, advancing!"

"I have not advanced one step," said Simple. "Still the same old job, same old salary, same old kitchenette, same old Harlem and the same old color."

"You are just one individual," I said. "I am speaking of our race in general. Look how many colleges have opened up to Negroes in the last ten years. Look at the change in restrictive covenants. You can live anywhere."

"You mean *try* to live anywhere."

234

"Look at the way you can ride unsegregated in interstate travel."

"And get throwed off the bus."

"Look at the ever greater number of Negroes in high places."

"Name me one making an atom bomb."

"That would be top-secret information," I said, "even if I knew. Anyway, you are arguing from supposition, not knowledge. How do you know what our top Negro scientists are doing?"

"I don't," said Simple. "But I bet if one was making an atom bomb, they would have his picture on the cover of *Jet* every other week like Eartha Kitt, just to make Negroes think the atom bomb is an integrated bomb. Then, next thing you know, some old Southern senator would up and move to have that Negro investigated for being subversive, because he would be mad that a Negro ever got anywhere near an atom bomb. Then that Negro would be removed from his job like Miss Annie Lee Moss, and have to hire a lawyer to get halfway back. Then they would put that whitewashed Negro to making plain little old-time ordinary bombs that can only kill a few folks at a time. You know and I know, they don't want no Negroes nowhere near no bomb that can kill a whole state full of folks like an atom bomb can. Just think what would happen to Mississippi. Wow!"

"Your thinking borders on the subversive," I warned. "Do you want to fight the Civil War over again?"

"Not without an atom bomb," said Simple. "If I was in Mississippi, I would be Jim Crowed out of bomb shelters, so I would need some kind of protection. By the time I got the N.A.A.C.P. to take my case to the Supreme Court, the war would be over, else I would be atomized."

"Absurd!" I said. "Bomb shelters will be for everybody."

"Not in Mississippi," said Simple. "Down there they will have some kind of voting test, else loyalty test, in which they will find some way of flunking Negroes out. You can't tell me them Dixiecrats are going to give Negroes free rein of bomb shelters. On the other hand, come to think of it, they might *have* to let us in to save their own skins, because I hear tell that in the next war everything that ain't sheltered will be so charged with atoms a human can't touch it. Even the garbage is going to get radioactive when the bombs start falling. I read last week in the *News* that, in case of a bombing, it will be a problem as to where to put our garbage, because it will be radioactive up to a million years. So you sure can't keep garbage around. If you dump it in the sea, it will make the fish radioactive, too, like them Japanese tunas nobody could eat. I am wondering what the alley cats will eat—because if all the garbage is full of atomic rays, and the cats eat the garbage, and my wife pets a strange cat, Joyce will be radioactive, too. Then if I pet my wife, what will happen to me?"

"You are stretching the long arm of coincidence mighty far," I said. "What is more likely to happen is, if the bombs fall, you will be radioactive long before the garbage will."

"That will worry white folks," said Simple. "Just suppose all the Negroes down South got atomized, charged up like hot garbage, who would serve the white folks' tables, nurse their children, Red Cap their bags, and make up their Pullman berths? Just think! Suppose all the colored Red Caps carrying bags on the Southern Railroad was atom-charged! Suitcases would get atomized, too, and all that is packed in them. Every time a white man took out his toothbrush to wash his teeth on the train, his teeth would get atom-charged. How could he kiss his wife when he got home?"

"I believe you are charged now," I said.

"No," said Simple, "I am only thinking how awful this atom bomb can be! If one fell up North in Harlem and charged me, then I went downtown and punched that time clock where I work, the clock would be charged. Then a white fellow would come along behind me and punch the time clock, and he would be charged. Then both of us would be so full of atoms for the next million years, that at any time we would be liable to explode like firecrackers on the Fourth of July. And from us, everybody else in the plant would get charged. Atoms, they tell me, is catching. What I read in the *News* said that if you even look at an atom bomb going off, the rays are so strong your eyes will water the rest of your life, your blood will turn white, your hair turn gray, and your children will be born backwards. Your breakfast eggs will no longer be sunny-side up, but scrambled, giving off sparks—and people will give off sparks, too. If you walk down the street, every doorbell you pass will ring without your touching it. If you pick up a phone, whoever answers it will be atomized. So if you know somebody you don't like, for example, just phone them—and you can really fix them up! That's what they call a chain reaction. I am getting my chain ready now—the first person I am going to telephone is my former landlady! When she picks up the phone, I hope to atomize her like a Japanese tuna! She will drive a Geiger counter crazy after I say, 'Hello!'"

"My dear boy," I said, "what makes you think you, of all people, would be able to go around transferring atomic radiation to others? You would probably be annihilated yourself by the very first bomb blast."

"Me? Oh, no," said Simple. "Negroes are very hard to annihilate. I am a Negro—so I figure I would live to radiate and, believe me, once charged, I will take charge."

"In other words, come what may, you expect to survive the atom bomb?"

"If Negroes can survive white folks in Mississippi," said Simple, "we can survive anything."

Discussion Questions

1. What is Simple's view of how racism tinges the development and use of technological products? What do you think of Simple's explanation?

2. Analyze Hughes's use of dialogue. For example, how does Hughes use dialogue to develop character? What differences in language do you find between the narrator and Simple? Consider diction, word choice, tone, and point of view in your analysis.

3. How does Hughes use humor to illustrate the theme of this story? Why do you think he adopts a humorous approach? How do you respond to his use of humor?

4. Which speaker is the protagonist (the main character who is also the hero) in this story? Does the other speaker represent the antagonist (the character who opposes the hero)? Do you think either speaker represents the author's personal views? Explain your answer.

Journal Entry

Imagine yourself denied entrance to a shelter of some kind on the basis of your skin color or some other physical characteristic. How would you feel? What arguments would you make in favor of being allowed to enter the shelter?

Writing Projects

1. Write an essay exploring the degree to which Simple's understanding of the effects of atomic radiation reflects a typical human reaction comprised of fear, speculation, and occasional exaggeration in the face of new weapons technology. How much of his view reflects his own time, situation, and character?

2. How does Hughes use dialogue to develop plot? Analyze how what one character says leads the other to respond in a way that furthers the story by creating a rising tension, a climactic moment, and a final resolution.

Collaborative Project

Working with a classmate, look for works that explore the issue of racial prejudice as it relates to scientific studies and technological production. One of you could investigate fictional treatments, and the other could research nonfiction articles and reports of studies. Ask a reference librarian to assist you in choosing search terms and databases for published fiction and nonfiction. In this text, authors who have treated the topic include Stephen Jay Gould (Chapter 3) and Sally Hacker (Chapter 2).

Samuel C. Florman

The Feminist Face of Antitechnology

Samuel C. Florman *(b. 1925), a member of the American Society of Civil Engineers and the American Society for Engineering Education, has won awards from the Stevens Institute of Technology for his books and articles on the relationship between technology and society. Florman was born in New York and received a B.A. from Dartmouth College and an M.A. from Columbia University. His books include* Engineering and the Liberal Arts *(1968),* The Existential Pleasures of Engineering *(1976), and* Blaming Technology *(1981), from which the following excerpt is taken. Florman points to feminists as the source of some of the antitechnology sentiments he has recently encountered, and he considers women themselves largely responsible for the relatively low number of female professionals working in technological companies.*

Questions to Consider

☐ Before reading this essay, think about what the term *antitechnology* means. Do you think antitechnology sentiments are prevalent today? If so, do you think they are more often held by women than men?

☐ While reading, consider who Florman sees as his audience and what his purpose is in writing this selection.

THE campus of Smith College in Northampton, Massachusetts, is one of the pleasantest places in the world to be on a sunny spring afternoon. The setting is so lovely, the academic atmosphere so tranquil, that when I arrived there on such an afternoon in April, I was totally captivated. The spell of the place, however, made me uneasy about my mission, which was to convince a few of the students at this premier, all-female liberal arts college that they ought to become engineers.

The mission, as it turned out, was destined to fail. Most bright young women today do not want to become engineers. At first hearing this might not seem to be a matter of grave consequence, but since engineering is central to the functioning of our society, its rejection as a career option by female stu-

238

dents raises the most profound questions about the relationship of women to technology, and about the objectives of the women's movement.

It is not generally recognized that at the same time that women are making their way into every corner of the work-world, less than 3 percent of the professional engineers in the nation are female. A generation ago this statistic would have raised no eyebrows, but today it is difficult to believe. The engineering schools, reacting to social and governmental pressures, have opened wide their gates and are zealously recruiting women. The major corporations, reacting to even more intense pressures, are offering attractive employment opportunities to nearly all women engineering graduates. According to the College Placement Council, engineering is the only field in which average starting salaries for women are higher than those for men. Tokenism is disappearing, according to the testimony of women engineers themselves. By every reasonable standard one would expect women to be attracted to the profession in large numbers. Yet less than 10 percent of 1980's 58,000 engineering degrees were awarded to women (compared to 30 percent in medicine, 28 percent in law, and 40 percent in the biological sciences). By 1984 the total may reach 15 percent, still a dismal figure when one realizes that more women than men are enrolled in American colleges. Unless this situation changes dramatically, and soon, the proportion of women engineers in practice, among more than 1.25 million males, will remain insignificant for many decades. While women are moving vigorously—assertively, demandingly—toward significant numerical representation in industry, the arts, and the other professions, they are, for reasons that are not at all clear, shying away from engineering.

At Smith I was scheduled to participate in a seminar entitled "The Role of Technology in Modern Society." The program called for a "sherry hour" before dinner, during which the speakers had an opportunity to talk informally with the students. In a stately paneled room the late-afternoon light sparkled on crystal decanters as we sipped our sherry from tiny glasses. The students with whom I conversed were as elegant as the surroundings, so poised, so *ladylike*. I found myself thinking, "These girls are not going to become engineers. It's simply not their style." The young women were not vapid in the way of country gentry. Far from it. They were alert and sensible, well-trained in mathematics and the sciences. I could imagine them donning white coats and conducting experiments in quiet laboratories. But I could not see them as engineers. It is a hopeless cause, I thought. They will not become engineers because it is "beneath" them to do so. It is a question of social class.

This was an intuitive feeling of the moment, although, when scrutinized, it made sociological sense. Traditionally, most American engineers have come from working-class families. In the words of a post-Sputnik National Science Foundation study, "Engineering has a special appeal for bright boys of lower and lower-middle-class origins."[1] Yet in many of the blue-collar families that have been such a fertile source for male engineers, the idea of a scientific education for women has not taken hold. Therefore, most of the young women who have the educational qualifications to become engineers are likely to come from the middle and upper classes. But the upper classes do not esteem a career in engineering: thus few women engineers.

We have inherited much of our class consciousness from England, and so it is with our attitude toward engineering, which the English have always considered rather a "navvy" occupation. Because engineering did not change from a craft to a profession until the mid-nineteenth century, and never shed completely its craftsman's image, it was fair game for the sneers of pretentious social arbiters. Herbert Hoover, a successful mining engineer before he became President, and something of a scholar who translated Agricola from the Latin, enjoyed telling about an English lady whom he met during the course of an Atlantic crossing. When, near the end of the voyage, Hoover told her that he was an engineer, the lady exclaimed, "Why, I thought you were a gentleman!" The fact that this anecdote is told and retold whenever conversation turns to the role of engineers in American society indicates how basic is the point that it illustrates.

It may not be realistic to expect women to break down class barriers that were created mostly by men. Yet feminists, if they are serious in their avowed purposes, should by now have taken the lead in changing this situation, encouraging the elite among educated young women to reevaluate their social prejudices. For until upper-class aversion to engineering is overcome, or until lower-class women take to studying the sciences in earnest, engineering will remain largely a male profession. And while this condition prevails, the feminist movement will be stalled, probably without even knowing it. For, in a manmade world, how can women achieve the equality they seek?

My view, needless to say, is not shared by the feminists of the United States. Judging by their literature, they seem to attach no particular importance to increasing female enrollment in engineering, perhaps because they are more concerned about battering on closed doors than they are about walking through those that are open. When they do consider the problem, it is not to question or criticize choices being made by women, but only to deplore the effect of external forces.

There is an entire literature devoted to explaining how engineering, and to a lesser degree science and mathematics, has developed a "male image." The terminology of this literature has been ringing in our ears for a long time—"sex role socialization," "undoing sex stereotypes," "self-fulfilling prophecy," and so forth. We know the facts by heart: girls learn early that it is not socially acceptable for them to play with trains and trucks. They learn from teachers that boys perform better than girls in math and science. A condition called "math anxiety" is attributed to these social pressures. As girls mature, they are persuaded by counselors and family that it is not feminine to enter traditionally male professions. They are afraid to compete with men or to let their intelligence show, lest they seem sexually less desirable. Finally, there is a shortage of "role models" with whom a young girl can identify.

Yes, yes, yes, of course, but these facts, which seemed so interesting and important a decade and more ago, are now stale. As the sociologists busy themselves collating their data and getting it published, the times invariably pass them by. After all, *The Feminine Mystique* was published in 1963, and the Equal Pay Act was enacted by Congress that same year. Since then a social revolution has taken place. Educated young women know well enough that they can become engineers. Surely the women who are planning to be biologists and doctors know that they could choose engineering instead, and those who are crowding into the fields of law, business, and journalism know that they could have opted for engineering if they had been willing to take a little calculus and physics. Women's magazines that once specialized in menus and sewing patterns are now overflowing with advice on how to compete in what used to be a man's world—how to dress, sit, talk, intimidate, and in general "make it." Engineering's purported male image is no longer an adequate explanation for female aversion to the profession.

It has been hypothesized that women avoid engineering because it has to do with technology, an aspect of our culture from which they recoil instinctively. Ruth Cowan, a historian at the State University of New York, has done research on the influence of technology on the self-image of the American woman.[2] The development of household appliances, for example, instead of freeing the housewife for a richer life as advertised, has helped to reduce her to the level of a maidservant whose greatest skill is consumerism. Factory jobs have attracted women to the workplace in roles they have come to dislike. Innovations affecting the most intimate aspects of women's lives, such as the baby bottle and birth-control devices, have been developed almost exclusively by men. Dependent upon technology, but removed from its sources and, paradoxically, enslaved by it, women may well have developed deep-seated resentments that persist even in those who consider themselves liberated.

If this situation does exist, we might expect that the feminists would respond to it as a challenge. The brightest and most ambitious women should be eager to bend technology, at long last, to their own will. But this is not happening. The feminists seem content to write articles assuring each other that they have the talent to fix leaky faucets.

Wherever the enemies of technology gather, women are to be found in large numbers. The transcendental movement that arose out of the counterculture of the 1960s—what Marilyn Ferguson has called *The Aquarian Conspiracy*—pits feminine sensitivity against a "macho" materialism. "Wherever the Aquarian Conspiracy is at work," writes Miss Ferguson, "women are represented in far greater numbers than they are in the establishment." This follows from basic physical and social realities: "Women are neurologically more flexible than men, and they have had cultural permission to be more intuitive, sensitive, feeling."[3]

Such an outlook not only explains why women are likely to be hostile to technology, but also raises the question of whether or not women are equipped biologically to excel in engineering. This is a theory that arouses such rancor that I hesitate to bring it up, and yet it must be confronted. The intellectual factor most closely related to achievement in science is spatial ability, the ability to manipulate objects mentally. Experiments have shown that males are, on average, better at this than females, and that this superiority appears to be related to levels of the male hormone testosterone.

It is a mistake, I think, to argue as some feminists do that there is no discernible difference between the male and female brain. It would be more sensible to say that because of substantial overlap in test scores, the differences that do exist are not practically significant when one considers a large group of potential engineers of both sexes. It would be better yet to point out that such differences as there are would serve to enrich the profession, since good engineering requires intuition and verbal imagination as well as mathematical adeptness and spatial ability. In their so-called weakness may be women's hidden strength.

This is considered to be a reactionary view, I learned to my sorrow when I proposed it to a female executive at RCA whose special interest is the careers of professional women. In response to my remark, she said, "I know that you mean well, but to tell a woman engineer that she has female intuition is like telling a black that he has rhythm."

Inevitably it occurred to me that anyone wondering why women do not become engineers would be well advised to learn something about the few women who *do* become engineers. So one day I took myself to the Engineering Societies Building, a large stone-and-glass structure overlooking the East River near the United Nations in New York City. In this stately edifice are housed most of the major professional societies that represent American engineers. On the third floor, past the imposing offices of the Engineering Foundation and the American Association of Engineering Societies, there is a single room that serves as the home of the Society of Women Engineers. The society, founded in 1959 by 50 women engineers, has grown from a membership of just a few hundred in 1970 to more than 9,000 in 1980. Still, compared to the other engineering societies, it seems pitifully small.

During my visit I browsed through a pile of career guidance pamphlets, newsletters full of recruiting ads from DuPont, Boeing, Ford, and IBM, and also a booklet telling about the society's achievement award, given annually since 1952. The winners of this award are talented women who have made contributions in many fields: solar energy, circuit analysis, metallurgy, missile launchers, rubber reclamation, computers, fluid mechanics, structural design, heat transfer, radio-wave propagation, and so on. Their undeniable ability adds poignancy to the fact that they and their fellow women engineers are so few that their overall contributions to the profession have been, in essence, negligible.

In some of the society's literature I discovered a series of autobiographical essays prepared by society members. In each of these life-stories there was evidence of relatively humble family origins and of success earned through struggle. I also came across photographs of student-chapter members, smiling young women, mostly from the Midwest, who seemed—was it my imagination?—not at all like the sophisticated young women I had met at Smith.

Of course, the students at Smith do not study engineering. Neither do the students—male or female—at Harvard and Yale, which venerable institutions closed their professional schools of engineering years ago (although they still have some courses in engineering science), and neither of which deigned to respond to a recent statistical questionnaire from the Society of Women Engineers. All the circumstantial evidence I could garner served to reinforce my ideas about the class origins of the problem.

Wanting more information, I visited Carl Frey, executive director of the American Association of Engineering Societies, that organization of organizations to which most of the major professional engineering societies belong. In his position at the top of the organization pyramid, Frey has long lived with the many discontents and disputes endemic to the sprawling, variegated profession: four-year colleges versus five- and six-year programs (what constitutes a professional education?); state licensing (is an engineer a professional without it?); salaries (why do lawyers make so much more than engineers?); prestige (why do scientists get all the credit for engineering achievement?); leadership (why are there so few engineers in elective office?); conservatism of the self-employed versus radicalism of the hired hands; conscience, responsibility, the environmental crisis. Frey could not survive in his position without a genial disposition and a calm sense of history. From his point of view, women in engineering is just one more problem that the profession will cope with in due time.

"I wouldn't get hung up on any fancy theories about class," Frey said, after I outlined my hypothesis. "It's harder and harder to tell who comes from what class, and things are changing so fast that I wouldn't rely on any old statistics you might have seen about the social origins of engineers."

"Well, how do you explain it?" I asked. "Why aren't more bright young women getting into engineering?"

"I think that it has to do with their perception of power. These kids today—the bright girls particularly—they want to be where the action is, where the sources of power are. They don't see engineers as the ones who have the say in our society. And, let's face it, to a great extent they're right. We may have the knowhow, but we don't have the power."

Perception of power. The phrase kept going through my mind. It had a nice ring to it, and it had the ring of truth as well. It did not seem to contradict my ideas about class so much as to encompass them, for what is the origin of class structure if not the desire to perpetuate power?

Every engineer knows that the profession is relatively powerless. Engineers do not make the laws; they do not have the money; they do not set the fashions; they have no voice in the media. It is one of the most irritating ironies of our time that intellectuals constantly complain about being in the grip of a technocratic elite that does not exist.

To the extent that today's young women are not fooled by such nonsense, they are deserving of credit. But if intelligent, energetic women reject engineering because of an all-consuming desire to sit on the thrones of power, then woe to us all in the age of feminism.

When the National Organization for Women was formed in 1966, its Statement of Purpose spoke of bringing women "into full participation in the mainstream of American society *now*, exercising all the privileges and responsibilities thereof in truly equal partnership with men." Yet judging from the way that most advantaged women are selecting their careers, they seem to be a lot more interested in the privileges than in the responsibilities. In this they are following the lead of those males who appear to be in control of our society—the lawyers, writers, politicians, and business managers. This is all very well, but somebody in our society has to design, create, fabricate, build—to *do*. A world full of coordinators, critics, and manipulators would have nothing in it but words. It would be a barren desert, totally devoid of *things*.

Feminist ideology, understandably adopting the values of the extant, i.e., male, establishment, is founded on a misapprehension of what constitutes privilege. The feminist leaders have made the deplorable mistake of assuming that those who work hard without public recognition, and for modest rewards, are necessarily being exploited. "Man's happiness lies not in freedom but in his acceptance of a duty," said André Gide. When the duty turns out to be work that is creative and absorbing, as well as essential, then those who had been patronized for being the worker bees are seen to be more fortunate than the queen.

Studies have shown that young engineers, women as well as men, pursue their career because it promises "interesting work." This is more important to them than money, security, prestige, or any of the other trappings of power. They seem to recognize that a fulfilling career does not have to consist of a continuous ego trip.

Although power, in the popular imagination, is identified with wealth and domination, there is another kind of power that lies beneath the surface of our petty ambitions, and that is the engineer's in full measure. It is the force that Henry Adams had in mind when he wrote of the dynamo and the Virgin. The power of the Virgin raised the medieval cathedrals, although, as Adams noted, the Virgin had been dead for a millennium and had held no real power even when she lived. For better or for worse, technology lies at the heart of our contemporary culture, and the technologist is akin to a priest who knows the secrets of the temple. In this sense, and in this sense only, those who speak of a technocratic elite are touching on a profound truth. Until women share in the understanding and creation of our technology—which is to say, until large numbers of women become engineers—they will suffer from a cultural alienation that ordinary power cannot cure.

The feminist movement means different things to different people. Many of its goals, such as mutual respect and equality before the law, can be achieved even if there are no women engineers. But the ultimate feminist dream will never be realized as long as women would rather supervise the world than help build it.

NOTES

1. Martin Trow, "Some Implications of the Social Origins of Engineers," *Scientific Manpower* (National Science Foundation), 1958.
2. Ruth Schwartz Cowan, "From Virginia Dare to Virginia Slims: Women and Technology in American Life," *Technology and Culture*, January 1979.
3. Marilyn Ferguson, *The Aquarian Conspiracy*, J. P. Tarcher, Inc. and St. Martin's Press, 1980, pp. 226 and 228.

Discussion Questions

1. Florman sets up an opposition between "us" and "them." Who, exactly, does Florman believe makes up the "us" and the "them" groups?

2. Florman says his mission was to convince women to go into engineering, but he felt his mission "was destined to fail." Why does Florman believe failure was inevitable? Do you believe someone else might have been more successful at this mission than Florman? Why or why not?

3. According to Florman, what should women be doing rather than writing "articles assuring each other that they have the talent to fix leaky faucets"? Do you agree with Florman? Why or why not?

4. How do you respond to Florman's presentation of experiments that he says prove men are superior to women in spatial ability because of testosterone?

Journal Entry

Florman says, "Every engineer knows that the profession is relatively powerless." Relate this view to several other professions and classify them according to whether you consider them to be powerful or relatively powerless. How much do you think the power of a profession, or lack thereof, influences people to choose that profession? Why would women and minorities consider the power factor in choosing a profession?

Writing Projects

1. Analyze Florman's underlying assumptions in this selection. Explain what you think he is implying with the following statement: "Judging by their [feminists'] literature, they seem to attach no particular importance to increasing female enrollment in engineering." What is Florman's argument? How does he present and develop it?

2. Analyze how the author's class consciousness affects his views as expressed in this essay. He directly links class with surroundings in his description of the paneled room in which he sipped sherry with students at Smith College. Why does he describe the setting in detail? What effect did the setting have on him? Do you think Florman's examples in support of his thesis that feminists are to blame for women's antitechnology sentiments are based solely on his one visit to Smith? Explain your answer.

Collaborative Projects

1. Working with a partner, interview a female engineer—one who has been employed for longer than five years, if possible—to see what the profession is like for women engineers today. Then, together, write a report interpreting your findings for engineering students, both male and female. Recommend actions that could be taken to improve the situation for women and for engineers in general, particularly in regard to the powerlessness issue raised by Florman.

2. Working with one or two partners, collect and analyze recruitment materials used by the engineering profession (both written and multimedia materials) to see how women are targeted and what recruitment approaches are used. Talk to a staff person in your admissions office and to those in charge of recruitment in your engineering department to gather information about recruitment of women and minorities into technology programs at your own institution. Present an analysis of your findings to your class, and make recommendations for improving the recruitment process at your school.

Ruth Schwartz Cowan

From Virginia Dare to Virginia Slims: Women and Technology in American Life

Ruth Schwartz Cowan (b. 1941), a professor of history at the University of New York at Stony Brook, has said that she is most pleased when readers find they come to see themselves more clearly through reading her work: "If scholarship doesn't illuminate life, why bother with it?" While researching her book on household technology, More Work for Mother: The Ironies of Household Technology from the Open Hearth to the Microwave *(1983), Cowan discovered that some home appliances actually create more housework for women rather than less. Her book explores how women continue to be bound and controlled by their "womanly" household duties. In the following article, originally published in 1979 in the journal* Technology and Culture, *Cowan classifies and compares men's and women's work.*

Questions to Consider

☐ Before you read this article, see how many machines, inventions, or technical processes you can think of that pertain solely to women. How much do you think the average person, either male or female, knows about the history of the development of these things or processes?

☐ As you read, notice how Cowan classifies the significant differences between men's and women's relationships to technology. Can you think of additional important differences?

W HEN this topic—women and technology in American life—was first proposed to me as an appropriate subject for a bicentennial retrospective, I was puzzled by it. Was the female experience of technological change significantly different from the male experience? Did the introduction of the railroads, or the invention of the Bessemer process, or the diffusion of the reaper have a differential impact on the male and female segments of the population? A careful reading of most of the available histories of

American technology (or of Western technology in general, for that matter) would not lead one to suspect that important differences had existed. Was my topic perhaps a nonsubject? I mulled over the matter for several months and eventually came to the conclusion that the absence of a female perspective in the available histories of technology was a function of the historians who wrote them and not of historical reality. There are at least four significant senses in which the relation between women and technology has diverged from that between men and technology. I shall consider each of them in turn and ask the reader to understand that what I will say below is intended in much the same spirit that many of the bicentennial retrospectives were intended – to be suggestive, but not definitive.

Women as Bearers and Rearers of Children

Women menstruate, parturate, and lactate; men do not. Therefore, any technology which impinges on those processes will affect women more than it will affect men. There are many such technologies, and some of them have had very long histories: pessaries, sanitary napkins, tampons, various intrauterine devices, childbirth anesthesia, artificial nipples, bottle sterilizers, pasteurized and condensed milks, etc. Psychologists suggest that those three processes are fundamentally important experiences in the psychosocial development of individuals. Thus, a reasonable student of the history of technology might be led to suppose that the history of technological intervention with those processes would be known in some detail.

That reasonable student would be wrong, of course. The indices to the standard histories of technology – Singer's, Kranzberg and Pursell's, Daumas's, Giedion's, even Ferguson's bibliography – do not contain a single reference, for example, to such a significant cultural artifact as the baby bottle. Here is a simple implement which, along with its attendant delivery systems (!), has revolutionized a basic biological process, transformed a fundamental human experience for vast numbers of infants and mothers, and been one of the more controversial exports of Western technology to underdeveloped countries – yet it finds no place in our histories of technology.

There is a host of questions which scholars might reasonably ask about the baby bottle. For how long has it been part of Western culture? When a mother's milk could not be provided, which classes of people used the bottle and which the wet-nurse, and for what reasons? Which was a more crucial determinant for widespread use of the bottle, changes in milk technology or changes in bottle technology? Who marketed the bottles, at what price, to whom? How did mothers of different social classes and ethnicities react to them? Can the phenomenon of "not enough milk," which was widely reported by American pediatricians and obstetricians in the 1920s and 1930s, be connected with the advent of the safe baby bottle? Which was cause and which effect?[1]

I could go on, using other examples and other questions, but I suspect that my point is clear: the history of the uniquely female technologies is yet to be written, with the single exception of the technologies of contraception.[2] This is also true, incidentally, of the technologies of child rearing, a process which is not anatomically confined to females but which has been more or less effectively limited to them by the terms of many unspoken social contracts. We know a great deal more about the bicycle than we do about the baby carriage, despite the fact that the carriage has had a more lasting impact on the transport of infants than the bicycle has had on the transport of adults. Although we recognize the importance of toilet training in personality formation, we have not the faintest idea whether toilet-training practices have been affected by the various technologies that impinge upon them: inexpensive absorbent fabrics, upholstered furniture, diaper services, wall-to-wall carpeting, paper diapers, etc. The crib, the playpen, the teething ring, and the cradle are as much a part of our culture and our sense of ourselves as harvesting machines and power looms, yet we know almost nothing of their history. The history of technology is, of course, a new field, and it is not surprising that its practitioners have ignored many of the female technologies. We do not usually think of women as bearers of technological change, nor do we think of the home as a technological locale (in part because women reside there). Both of these common assumptions are incorrect; Adam knew that, but his descendants have forgotten it.

Women as Workers

Women have been part of the market economy of this country from its earliest days. In the colonial period they tended cows, delivered babies, kept taverns, published newspapers, and stitched fancy clothes, among other things. During industrialization they tended looms, folded paper bags, packed cigars, helped with harvests, washed laundry, and stitched fancy clothes, among other things. With the advent of automation they punch cards, handle switchboards, pack cookies, teach school, tend the sick, and stitch fancy clothes, again among other things. All along they have been paid for their work, sometimes in land, sometimes in produce, sometimes in cash.

But women workers are different from men workers, and the differences are crucial, for the women themselves and for any analysis of the relation between women and the American technological order. The economic facts of life for women are almost on a deterministic par with the anatomic facts of life; they are so pervasive over time and place as to be almost universal truisms. There are three of them: (1) when doing the same work women are almost always paid less than men; (2) considered in the aggregate, women rarely do the same work as men (jobs are sex typed); and (3) women almost always consider themselves, and are considered by others, to be transient participants in the work force.[3]

These characteristics of women as workers predate industrialization; they were economic facts of life even before our economy was dominated by cash. Sex typing of jobs occurred in the earliest Jamestown settlements, even before the household economy had completely replaced the communal economy: unmarried or poor women worked as laundresses in return for a portion from the communal store; men who were not entitled to grants of land worked as cooks and bakers.[4] Unequal pay for equal work was also characteristic of the early settlements: adventurers who came to settle in Maryland were allotted 100 acres of land for every manservant they brought with them and 60 acres of land for every woman servant; unmarried free men in Salem and Plymouth were given allotments of land when they requested them, but, after the first few years of settlement, unmarried women were not; the first American effort to obtain equal economic rights for women may well have been the request made in 1619 by the Virginia House of Burgesses that husbands and wives be granted equal shares of land on the grounds that the work of each was equally crucial to the establishment of a plantation.[5] That women were regarded as transitory members of the work force even then is shown by many things: for example, the fact that when girl children were "put out" for indenture or apprenticeship the persons who received their work were rarely required to teach them a trade,[6] or the fact that women who owned and operated businesses in the colonial period were almost always widows of the men who had first established the business, who consciously advertised themselves as worthy of patronage on those grounds alone.[7] Parents of daughters did not expect that their girl children would need to know any occupation other than housework; young women expected that they might need to support themselves while unmarried but that gainful employment would become unnecessary and undesirable after marriage; married women expected not to be gainfully employed unless their husbands died or were disabled.

So it was, and so it continues to be—despite industrialization, unionization, and automation. The Equal Pay Act of 1964 attempted to legislate equal pay for equal work for women, but in 1973 it was still true that women were earning from 37.8 percent to 63.6 percent of what men in the same job classifications were earning.[8] Power technologies have eased and simplified thousands of jobs, yet the labor market is still dominated by sex-typed occupations, despite the fact that the worker's "strength" is no longer a relevant criterion. In the garment industry in New York, for example, men cut and women sew. Thus, when a manufacturer goes into the labor market to find employees, he or she enters one labor market, with its own price structure and its own supply-demand pattern, if searching for a skilled cutter—and a different labor market, with a price structure and a supply-demand pattern all *its* own, if looking for a skilled sewing-machine operator.[9] A fairly sophisticated statistical analysis of sex typing in the labor market has demonstrated that, although some job classifications shifted from being male dominated to being female dominated between 1900 and 1960 (ironically, none have gone the other way), the total amount of sex typing has not changed appreciably. In 1900, 66 percent of all employed women would have had to shift their jobs into male-dominated fields in order for the distribution of women and men in all fields to resemble chance; in 1960 that figure was 68.4 percent. (The corresponding figure, incidentally, for racial typing of jobs in 1960 was 46.8 percent.)[10]

And of course it is still true, as it was in colonial days, that women are not regarded, by themselves or by others, as permanent members of the work force. Young women do not invest in expensive training for themselves because they anticipate leaving the work force when they marry and have children. Employers are equally unwilling to invest in training women because they anticipate the same thing—and with some statistical basis for their suspicion; the labor force participation rates of females fall off sharply between the ages of 18 and 25, the years when most women marry and begin their families.[11] The cumulative result of these attitudes is that women prefer to place themselves in fairly unskilled, unresponsible, and, therefore, lower-paying positions, and employers are content to have them remain there.

These three characteristics of women as workers—the fact that they work for less, that many jobs are not open to them because of sex typing, and that they are transient members of the work force (and therefore difficult to organize and unionize)—should be of signal importance in any discussion of rates of technological change, although they are rarely considered in that context. We are accustomed to thinking about the price and availability of labor as one of the key determinants of rates of change in any given industry or any given locality, but we are not accustomed to thinking of the price and availability of labor as determined by the sex of the laborers. The ways in which the sex of workers interacts with technological change can be illustrated by two somewhat different cases.

The first is the cigar industry in the second half of the 19th century, a case in which technological change was accelerated by the availability of female workers.[12] During the middle decades of the century cigarmaking was localized in factories, but the product was entirely handmade by skilled male workers, most of them Spanish, Cuban, and German. In 1869 the New York cigarmakers went on strike, and in retaliation several manufacturers arranged for the immigration of Bohemian women who worked in the cigar trade in their native land. These women were not as skilled as the men they replaced; they used a simple molding tool to shape the cigar. They also were accustomed to working at home, which meant that they were amenable to the tenement system of manufacture, which was much cheaper for the employers. The women were effective in breaking the strike. In subsequent years more women cigarmakers immigrated as the cigar trade in Bohemia was disrupted by the Franco-Prussian War. There were other male cigarmakers' strikes in New

York and elsewhere during the 1870s and 1880s, the net effect of which was that some manufacturers converted entirely to the tenement system and others were induced to try some simple pieces of machinery (also of European origin) which could be operated by women. The women were laborers of choice because they knew the cigar trade yet were willing to work for less and had not been organized. As one New York cigar manufacturer put it in 1895: ". . . the handwork has almost entirely disappeared. The suction tables, which are in reality nothing else than wrapper cutting machines, are used as price cutters. More so, because there are only girls employed on them."[13]

A somewhat contrary case is that of the ladies' garment industry in the 20th century; here technological change seems to have been slowed by the presence of female workers.[14] Since the time that sewing machines were initially hooked up to central power supplies (steam or electricity) in the last quarter of the 19th century, there has been little technological change in the sewing process, despite the fact that the industry is highly competitive and despite the fact that there have been substantial changes in the technology of the processes that are auxiliary to sewing—namely, cutting and pressing. The sewing process could potentially be automated, but there appears to be little incentive for manufacturers to do this, partly because the expense would be very great and many of the companies are very small. Yet another reason stems from the fact that sewers are women, and sewing is work that women from traditional cultures like to do. The ladies' garment industry has been populated by successive waves of fairly skilled immigrant women of various sorts: American farm girls who came to the cities to escape rural life in the middle of the 19th century, then immigrant women from Italy and eastern Europe, then black women from the South, then Puerto Rican women, and now Chinese women. Although these women are skilled, and although their trade has been unionized successfully for many years, the wages paid to sewing-machine operators are, as one would expect, significantly lower than the wages paid to other skilled machine operators. As a consequence of this the technology of sewing has remained fairly static.

There is yet another sense in which the characteristics of women as workers have interacted with the technological order in this country—and here we confront one of the most firmly grounded shibboleths about the relation between women's work and technology. It is true that there has been a vast increase in the number of women in the work force in the past century, and during this time some occupations (such as clerical work) have almost completely changed sex. It is also true that during the same period of time power-driven machinery has entered many fields, requiring much less human energy to do work that was once hard to do. Acknowledging that these facts are true, historians and others have concluded that technological change has drawn women into the work force by opening fields of work that were previously closed because of the physical strength required to do the work. That conclusion appears to be almost entirely unwarranted. Women have replaced men in several occupations in which hard physical labor was not required before industrialization (e.g., cigarmaking); they have replaced men in some occupations in which no significant technological change occurred (e.g., schoolteaching); and they have replaced men in some occupations in which technological change made no difference to the physical labor involved (e.g., bookkeeping). In all of these cases the crucial factor is not physical labor but price; women replaced men because they worked for less.[15]

Alternatively, there are many trades in which work has been transformed by the introduction of new machines but in which women have not replaced men. Typesetting is a perfect example.[16] From the colonial period to the present there have always been a few women typesetters, but they have worked in the smallest shops, often shops that were family owned. Typesetting was generally an apprenticed trade in the 19th century, and women were not set to apprenticeships. In any event, it was widely believed that women could not do the work of typesetting efficiently because they were not able to carry the heavy type cases from the composing tables to the press. Women typesetters were occasionally used to break strikes or to cut wages, a practice which did not endear them to the typesetters' unions which were formed during the early decades of the century. In 1887 the linotype machine was introduced, and after that time the work of typesetting was not terribly much more difficult than the work of typewriting. Various modifications of that machine, and the more recent introduction of photographic processes, have made the work easier still—but men dominate the trade. The reasons for this are several: after women were admitted to the typesetters' unions, in the latter part of the 19th century, they had to agree to work for scale, which meant, of course, that employers had little interest in hiring them; following this the advent of protective labor laws meant that night work for women was very carefully regulated, which made it unfeasible for women to become typesetters since so much of the work is on newspapers. Thus technological change has been, at best, a mixed blessing for women. More jobs are open to them that they are fit (either biologically or socially) to perform, but many of those jobs are at the very lowest skill and salary levels and are likely to remain that way as long as women are willing, for whatever reasons, to work for less than men and to let themselves be treated as marginal members of the labor force.[17]

Women as Homemakers

Both men and women live in homes, but only women have their "place" there—and this is another one of those salient facts about women's lives which make their interaction with technology somewhat different from men's. The homes in which we live, the household implements with which we work, and the ways in which that work is organized have changed greatly over the years, but the character of that change and its impact upon the people who work in homes (predominantly women) have proved very difficult to gauge.

Some tasks have disappeared (e.g., beating rugs), but other tasks have replaced them (e.g., waxing linoleum floors). Some tasks are easier (e.g., laundering) but are done much more frequently; it takes less time and effort to wash and iron a sheet than it once did, but there are now vastly more sheets to be washed in each household each week. Some tasks have become demonstrably more time consuming and arduous over the years: shopping, for example.[18] Less work needs to be done at home because so many aspects of home production have been transferred to the marketplace (e.g., canning vegetables), but there are now fewer hands to do the work as there are fewer servants, fewer unmarried females living at home, and fewer children per family. An equivocal picture at best.[19]

But one point is worth making. Despite all the changes that have been wrought in housework, and there have been many, the household has resisted industrialization with greater success than any other productive locale in our culture.[20] The work of men has become centralized, but the work of women remains decentralized. Several million American women cook supper each night in several million separate homes over several million separate stoves—a specter which should be sufficient to drive any rational technocrat into the loony bin, but which does not do so for reasons I will discuss in a moment. Out there in the land of household work there are small industrial plants which sit idle for the better part of every working day; there are expensive pieces of highly mechanized equipment which only get used once or twice a month; there are consumption units which weekly trundle out to their markets to buy 8 ounces of this nonperishable product and 12 ounces of that one. There are also workers who do not have job descriptions, time clocks, or even paychecks.[21] Cottage industry is alive and well and living in suburbia.

Why? There is no simple answer to that question, but I would like to attempt a rough list of what some of the components of the answer might be, presenting them in no particular order and with no pretense of knowing the relative weight which should be attached to each, or the relative likelihood that some are causes and others effects. To start with, since the middle of the 19th century Americans have idealized the household as a place where men could retreat from the technological order: a retreat, by definition, should not possess the characteristics that one is trying to escape. Increased efficiency and modernity in the home have occasionally been advocated by domestic reformers, most of whom have been women (Catherine Beecher, Ellen Swallow Richards, Charlotte Perkins Gilman, Christine Frederick, and Lillian Gilbreth immediately come to mind), but the general public has been hostile to certain crucial concomitants of those ideas.[22] The farm kitchen has been the American mythic dream, not the cafeteria. In some households the latest and showiest equipment is purchased in order to demonstrate status, not efficiency; in such cases the housebound housewife is as much proof of status as the microwave oven that she operates. In other households status is not the issue, but modern equipment is used to free the housewife for labor which is not currently technology intensive (stripping furniture, planting vegetable gardens, chauffeuring children), and the end result is far from an increase in overall efficiency. Except for a very brief period in the 1920s, "Early American" has been, far and away, the most popular decor for American kitchens; our ambivalence on the issue of efficiency in the home is nowhere better symbolized than when a dishwasher is built into a "rustic" cabinet or a refrigerator is faced with plastic "wood" paneling. For long periods of time, on either side of the industrial revolution in housework (which can be roughly said to have occurred in the first three decades of this century), the maintenance of a fundamentally inefficient mode of household operation, requiring the full attention of the housewife for the better part of every single day, has been a crucial part of the symbolic quality of the individual American home.

Connected with this is the fact that, also since the middle of the 19th century, most Americans have regarded communalization of households as socialistic and therefore un-American. There have been repeated attempts at communalizing some of the household functions, especially during the first two decades of the 20th century—communal canneries, laundries, kitchens, and even nursery schools appeared in many communities—but they have all failed for want of a supportive community attitude.[23]

The implements invented or developed for the home have very special features which may set them apart from other implements. Many of them were initially developed, for example, not for home use, but for commercial use: the automatic washing machine, the vacuum cleaner, the small electric motor, and the refrigerator, for example.[24] Most of them were not developed by persons intimately connected with the work involved; inventors tend to be men and homemakers tend to be women. On top of this, many of the implements were marketed through the use of selling techniques that also had little relation to the work performed. These three factors lead to the hypothesis that the implements which have transformed housework may not have been the implements that housewives would have developed had they had control of the processes of innovation.

Thus, for reasons which may have been alternately economic, ideological, and structural, there was very little chance that American homes would become part of the industrial order in the same sense that American businesses have, because very few Americans, powerful or not powerful, have wished it so—and the ones who have wished it so have not been numerous enough or powerful enough to make a difference.

Women as Antitechnocrats

This brings me to a final and somewhat related point. For the better part of its cultural life, the United States has been idealized as the land of practicality, the land of know-how, the land of Yankee ingenuity. No country on earth has been so much in the sway of the technological order or so proud of its involvement in it. Doctors and engineers are central to our culture; poets and artists live on the fringes.

If practicality and know-how and willingness to get your hands dirty down there with the least of them are signatures of the true American, then we have been systematically training slightly more than half of our population to be un-American. I speak, of course, of women. While we socialize our men to aspire to feats of mastery, we socialize our women to aspire to feats of submission. Men are hard; women are soft. Men are meant to conquer nature; women are meant to commune with it. Men are rational, women irrational; men are practical, women impractical. Boys play with blocks; girls play with dolls. Men build; women inhabit. Men are active; women are passive. Men are good at mathematics; women are good at literature. If something is broken, daddy will fix it. If feelings are hurt, mommy will salve them. We have trained our women to opt out of the technological order as much as we have trained our men to opt into it.

This is probably just as much true today as it was in the heyday of the archetypically passive, romantic Victorian female. An interesting survey of American college girls' attitudes toward science and technology in the 1960s revealed that the girls were planning careers, but that they could not assimilate the notion of becoming engineers and—and this is equally revealing—that there was no single occupation that they thought their male contemporaries and their parents would be less pleased to have them pursue.[25]

Thus, women who might wish to become engineers or inventors or mechanics or jackhammer operators would have to suppress some deeply engrained notions about their own sexual identity in order to fulfill their wishes. Very few people have ever had the courage to take up such a fight. It is no wonder that women have played such minor roles in creating technological change; in fact, it is a wonder that there have been any female engineers and inventors at all.

Conversely, it may be true that the recent upsurge in "antiscience" and "antitechnology" attitudes may be correlated very strongly with the concurrent upsurge in women's political consciousness. This is not to say that all of the voices that have been raised against the SST and atomic power plants and experimentation on animals have been female, but only that a surprisingly large number of them have been. Ann Douglas has recently written a complex analysis of the "feminization" of American culture in the 19th century, in which she suggests that the "tough-minded" theological attitudes that had served as cornerstones of American ideology in the 17th and 18th centuries were watered down and whittled away in the 19th century by several generations of educated and literary women working in concert with similar generations of liberal male theologians.[26] Both groups, she argues, realized that they were excluded from the burgeoning capitalist economy that the older theology had produced; they resented this exclusion and so fought against the economy and the theology together. The temptation to push Douglas's analysis into the 20th century is almost irresistible. If we are experiencing a similar feminization of American culture today, it is the tough-minded ideology of the scientific-technocratic state that is the focus of current animus. Women have traditionally operated on the fringes of that state, so it is not surprising that they should resent it and, when given the opportunity, fight against it. Women have experienced science and technology as consumers, not as producers – and consumers, as every marketing expert knows, are an infuriatingly fickle population. Trained to think of themselves as the possessors of subjectivity, women can hardly be expected to show much allegiance to the flag of objectivity. As more and more women begin to play active and powerful roles in our political and economic life, we may be surprised to discover the behavioral concomitants of the unspoken hostility to science and technology that they are carrying with them into the political arena.

NOTES

1. The history of nursing practices in early modern Europe is surveyed in Edward Shorter (*The Making of the Modern Family* [New York, 1975], chap. 5), but developments since the appearance of pasteurized milk and sterile (or sterilizable) bottles are not considered.

2. Norman E. Hines (*A Medical History of Contraception* [Baltimore, 1936]) does not cover more recent developments. Linda Gordon (*Woman's Body, Woman's Right: A Social History of Birth Control in America* [New York, 1976]) focuses on ideas about birth control, but not on the devices themselves.

3. On the economics of workers, see Robert W. Smuts, *Women and Work in America* (New York, 1959), and Juanita Kreps, *Sex in the Marketplace: American Women at Work* (Baltimore, 1971).

4. Julia Cherry Spruill, *Women's Life and Work in the Southern Colonies* (Chapel Hill, N.C., 1938), p. 6.

5. Ibid., pp. 9–11; also Edith Abbott, *Women in Industry: A Study in American History* (New York, 1910) p. 11.

6. Abbott, pp. 30–32.

7. Spruill, pp. 263–64, 276, 280.

8. United States Department of Labor, *1975 Handbook on Women Workers*, Bulletin no. 297 (Washington, D.C., 1975), p. 130.

9. On sex typing of jobs, see Valerie Kincaid Oppenheimer, *The Female Labor Force in the United States*, Population Monograph Series, no. 5 (Berkeley, 1970).

10. Edward Gross, "Plus ça change . . . The Sexual Structure of Occupations over Time," *Social Problems* 16 (Fall 1968): 198–206, esp. p. 202.

11. Kreps, pp. 28–29.

12. Abbott, chap. 9.

13. Ibid., p. 263. Patricia Cooper, a graduate student in history at the University

of Maryland, College Park, will soon complete a dissertation on tobacco workers which extends and reinforces these conclusions.

14. This account is based on Elizabeth Faulkner Baker, *Technology and Women's Work* (New York, 1954), chap. 15.

15. Ibid., chaps. 13 and 17.

16. Ibid., pp. 170–77; Abbott, chap. 11.

17. Interest in women workers has revived in the last few years: see Judith A. McGaw, "Technological Change and Women's Work: Mechanization in the Berkshire Paper Industry, 1820–1855" (Ph.D. diss., New York University, 1977); Rosalyn Baxandall, Linda Gordon, and Susan Reverby, eds., *America's Working Women: A Documentary History* (New York, 1976); and Barbara Mayer Wertheimer, *We Were There: American Women Who Worked* (New York, 1977).

18. On time spent in housework, see JoAnn Vanek, "Keeping Busy: Time Spent in Housework, United States, 1920–1970" (Ph.D. diss., University of Michigan, 1973).

19. For an extended discussion of this topic see my papers, "The 'Industrial Revolution' in the Home: Household Technology and Social Change in the 20th Century," *Technology and Culture* 17 (January 1976): 1–22; and "Two Washes in the Morning, and a Bridge Party at Night: The American Housewife between the Wars," *Women's Studies* 3 (Winter 1976): 147–72.

20. On this point see Allison Ravetz, "Modern Technology and an Ancient Occupation: Housework in Present-Day Society," *Technology and Culture* 6 (Spring 1965): 256–60. Also, for a general history of housework, see Ann Oakley, *Woman's Work, the Housewife Past and Present* (New York, 1974).

21. For an extended discussion of the sociological meaning of this phenomenon, see Ann Oakley, *The Sociology of Housework* (London, 1974).

22. See Kathryn Kish Sklar, *Catherine Beecher: A Study in American Domesticity* (New Haven, Conn., 1973); Caroline Hunt, *The Life of Ellen H. Richards* (Boston, 1912); and Waida Gerhardt, "The Pros and Cons of Efficiency in the Household," *Journal of Home Economics* 18 (1928): 337–39.

23. Victor Papanek and James Hennessey speculate about how various implements would have to be redesigned for communal ownership in *How Things Don't Work* (New York, 1977), chap. 2.

24. Siegfried Giedion, *Mechanization Takes Command* (New York, 1948), pp. 556–606.

25. Alice Rossi, "Barriers to the Career Choice of Engineering, Medicine or Science among American Women," in *Women and the Scientific Professions*, ed. Jacqueline Mattfeld and Carol Van Aken (Cambridge, Mass., 1965).

26. Ann Douglas, *The Feminization of American Culture* (New York, 1977).

Discussion Questions

1. What is Cowan's reaction to the inequity and bias in women's versus men's technology? Do you agree with her analysis? Why or why not? What kind of change, if any, is needed in technology intended for women?

2. What is the tone of this essay? How does Cowan achieve her tone? Is it effective?

3. Cowan's argument is structured primarily around classification. How does she divide the categories? Would you divide them differently? What other rhetorical devices does she use to construct an argument?

4. Cowan says that historically women in America have considered themselves to be transient members of the labor force. To what extent is this perception still relevant? How many women in your class are preparing themselves for a job to "fall back on" or to make a second income when they are married, as opposed to preparing for a full-time career?

Journal Entry

Without pausing to think, jot down at least ten job titles or careers. Then mark each job with an "F" or "M" to indicate your perception of that job as being one for a female or male. Go over your list and evaluate your choices. Write down what you discovered about your own stereotypes.

Writing Projects

1. According to the author, women have replaced men in some jobs because they can operate machines as well as men and still be paid less. What kind of support does the author provide to document this statement? Is her support convincing? Incorporate into your essay examples you have witnessed or researched that support or refute Cowan's assertion.

2. Analyze Cowan's opening paragraph. What type of introduction is it? Note, in particular, the use of questions, use of the first person, and her forecasting of what is to follow. Try writing an alternate introduction. Then point out the differences between yours and the author's.

Collaborative Projects

1. Working with a partner, collect examples of grown-ups' "toys" — that is, products intended for leisure activities. How many of these products are technology based? Are the women's products more high-tech or less than the men's? What conclusions can you draw about the connection between technology and work, and technology and play? Analyze your findings and present them to your class.

2. Working with a partner, survey several toy stores to determine how the toys are arranged and marketed. Are the toys divided into boys' and girls' sections? How can you tell? What percentage of the toys are based on

"grown-up" technology, such as toy washing machines or toy guns? What percentage of the toys reflect strictly child-oriented technology? Name some toys that are not modeled on products used by adults. Are any of these intended for only girls or only boys? Which toys seem like they would be the most fun, the boys' or girls' toys? Share with your class your findings and related conclusions about the role of toys in affecting the future career goals of children.

Ray Bradbury

The Veldt

Ray Bradbury *(b. 1920) began writing at an early age and to date has completed more than five hundred stories, poems, plays, screenplays, and novels. A major author of science fiction, Bradbury enjoys a wide readership because his stories and novels supersede the limits usually suggested by the science fiction label. He seeks mainly to entertain the reader with stories involving people and complex social issues, rather than with futuristic gadgets and hardware. He has always incorporated social criticism into his fiction, starting with his first novel* Fahrenheit 451 *(1953). His short story collections are numerous and still popular. "The Veldt" was originally published as "The World the Children Made" in* The Saturday Evening Post *in 1950. Here Bradbury criticizes our culture's willingness to entrust ourselves to technology so precisely and so ominously that his message still resonates today.*

Questions to Consider

☐ How large a role do you think technology plays in child rearing today? Parents are often accused of not monitoring their children's television watching closely enough. Can you think of other examples of machines that have a significant impact on family life?

☐ Almost every short story revolves around a conflict of some sort. As you read, notice how conflict increases the tension in this story and raises the stakes for the characters.

G EORGE, I wish you'd look at the nursery."
"What's wrong with it?"
"I don't know."
"Well, then."
"I just want you to look at it, is all, or call a psychologist in to look at it."
"What would a psychologist want with a nursery?"
"You know very well what he'd want." His wife paused in the middle of the kitchen and watched the stove busy humming to itself, making supper for four.
"It's just that the nursery is different now than it was."
"All right, let's have a look."

They walked down the hall of their soundproofed, Happylife Home, which had cost them thirty thousand dollars installed, this house which clothed and fed and rocked them to sleep and played and sang and was good to them. Their approach sensitized a switch somewhere and the nursery light flicked on when they came within ten feet of it. Similarly, behind them, in the halls, lights went on and off as they left them behind, with a soft automaticity.

"Well," said George Hadley.

They stood on the thatched floor of the nursery. It was forty feet across by forty feet long and thirty feet high; it had cost half again as much as the rest of the house. "But nothing's too good for our children," George had said.

The nursery was silent. It was empty as a jungle glade at hot high noon. The walls were blank and two dimensional. Now, as George and Lydia Hadley stood in the center of the room, the walls began to purr and recede into crystalline distance, it seemed, and presently an African veldt appeared, in three dimensions; on all sides, in colors reproduced to the final pebble and bit of straw. The ceiling above them became a deep sky with a hot yellow sun.

George Hadley felt the perspiration start on his brow.

"Let's get out of the sun," he said. "This is a little too real. But I don't see anything wrong."

"Wait a moment, you'll see," said his wife.

Now the hidden odorophonics were beginning to blow a wind of odor at the two people in the middle of the baked veldtland. The hot straw smell of lion grass, the cool green smell of the hidden water hole, the great rusty smell of animals, the smell of dust like a red paprika in the hot air. And now the sounds: the thump of distant antelope feet on grassy sod, the papery rustling of vultures. A shadow passed through the sky. The shadow flickered on George Hadley's upturned, sweating face.

"Filthy creatures," he heard his wife say.

"The vultures."

"You see, there are the lions, far over, that way. Now they're on their way to the water hole. They've just been eating," said Lydia. "I don't know what."

"Some animal." George Hadley put his hand up to shield off the burning light from his squinted eyes. "A zebra or a baby giraffe, maybe."

"Are you sure?" His wife sounded peculiarly tense.

"No, it's a little late to be sure," he said, amused. "Nothing over there I can see but cleaned bone, and the vultures dropping for what's left."

"Did you hear that scream?" she asked.

"No."

"About a minute ago?"

"Sorry, no."

The lions were coming. And again George Hadley was filled with admiration for the mechanical genius who had conceived this room. A miracle of efficiency selling for an absurdly low price. Every home should have one. Oh, occasionally they frightened you with their clinical accuracy, they startled you, gave you a twinge, but most of the time what fun for everyone, not only your own son and daughter, but for yourself when you felt like a quick jaunt to a foreign land, a quick change of scenery. Well, here it was!

And here were the lions now, fifteen feet away, so real, so feverishly and startlingly real that you could feel the prickling fur on your hand, and your mouth was stuffed with the dusty upholstery smell of their heated pelts, and the yellow of them was in your eyes like the yellow of an exquisite French tapestry, the yellows of lions and summer grass, and the sound of the matted lion lungs exhaling on the silent noontide, and the smell of meat from the panting, dripping mouths.

The lions stood looking at George and Lydia Hadley with terrible green-yellow eyes.

"Watch out!" screamed Lydia.

The lions came running at them.

Lydia bolted and ran. Instinctively, George sprang after her. Outside, in the hall, with the door slammed, he was laughing and she was crying, and they both stood appalled at the other's reaction.

"George!"

"Lydia! Oh, my dear poor sweet Lydia!"

"They almost got us!"

"Walls, Lydia, remember; crystal walls, that's all they are. Oh, they look real, I must admit—Africa in your parlor—but it's all dimensional superreactionary, supersensitive color film and mental tape film behind glass screens. It's all odorophonics and sonics, Lydia. Here's my handkerchief."

"I'm afraid." She came to him and put her body against him and cried steadily. "Did you see? Did you *feel*? It's too real."

"Now, Lydia . . . "

"You've got to tell Wendy and Peter not to read any more on Africa."

"Of course—of course." He patted her.

"Promise?"

"Sure."

"And lock the nursery for a few days until I get my nerves settled."

"You know how difficult Peter is about that. When I punished him a month ago by locking the nursery for even a few hours—the tantrum he threw! And Wendy too. They *live* for the nursery."

"It's got to be locked, that's all there is to it."

"All right." Reluctantly he locked the huge door. "You've been working too hard. You need a rest."

"I don't know—I don't know," she said, blowing her nose, sitting down in a chair that immediately began to rock and comfort her. "Maybe I don't have enough to do. Maybe I have time to think too much. Why don't we shut the whole house off for a few days and take a vacation?"

"You mean you want to fry my eggs for me?"

"Yes." She nodded.

"And darn my socks?"

"Yes." A frantic, watery-eyed nodding.

"And sweep the house?"

"Yes, yes—oh, yes!"

"But I thought that's why we bought this house, so we wouldn't have to do anything?"

"That's just it. I feel like I don't belong here. The house is wife and mother now and nursemaid. Can I compete with an African veldt? Can I give a bath and scrub the children as efficiently or quickly as the automatic scrub bath can? I can not. And it isn't just me. It's you. You've been awfully nervous lately."

"I suppose I have been smoking too much."

"You look as if you didn't know what to do with yourself in this house, either. You smoke a little more every morning and drink a little more every afternoon and need a little more sedative every night. You're beginning to feel unnecessary too."

"Am I?" He paused and tried to feel into himself to see what was really there.

"Oh, George!" She looked beyond him, at the nursery door. "Those lions can't get out of there, can they?"

He looked at the door and saw it tremble as if something had jumped against it from the other side.

"Of course not," he said.

At dinner they ate alone, for Wendy and Peter were at a special plastic carnival across town and had televised home to say they'd be late, to go ahead eating. So George Hadley, bemused, sat watching the dining-room table produce warm dishes of food from its mechanical interior.

"We forgot the ketchup," he said.

"Sorry," said a small voice within the table, and ketchup appeared.

As for the nursery, thought George Hadley, it won't hurt for the children to be locked out of it awhile. Too much of anything isn't good for anyone. And it was clearly indicated that the children had been spending a little too much time on Africa. That sun. He could feel it on his neck, still, like a hot paw. And the lions. And the smell of blood. Remarkable how the nursery caught the telepathic emanations of the children's minds and created life to fill their every desire. The children thought lions, and there were lions. The children thought zebras, and there were zebras. Sun—sun. Giraffes—giraffes. Death and death.

That last. He chewed tastelessly on the meat that the table had cut for him. Death thoughts. They were awfully young, Wendy and Peter, for death thoughts. Or, no, you were never too young, really. Long before you knew what death was you were wishing it on someone else. When you were two years old you were shooting people with cap pistols.

But this—the long, hot African veldt—the awful death in the jaws of a lion. And repeated again and again.

"Where are you going?"

He didn't answer Lydia. Preoccupied, he let the lights glow softly on ahead of him, extinguished behind him as he padded to the nursery door. He listened against it. Far away, a lion roared.

He unlocked the door and opened it. Just before he stepped inside, he heard a faraway scream. And then another roar from the lions, which subsided quickly.

He stepped into Africa. How many times in the last year had he opened this door and found Wonderland, Alice, the Mock Turtle, or Aladdin and his Magical Lamp, or Jack Pumpkinhead of Oz, or Dr. Doolittle, or the cow jumping over a very real-appearing moon—all the delightful contraptions of a make-believe world. How often had he seen Pegasus flying in the sky ceiling, or seen fountains of red fireworks, or heard angel voices singing. But now, this yellow hot Africa, this bake oven with murder in the heat. Perhaps Lydia was right. Perhaps they needed a little vacation from the fantasy which was growing a bit too real for ten-year-old children. It was all right to exercise one's mind with gymnastic fantasies, but when the lively child mind settled on *one* pattern . . . ? It seemed that, at a distance, for the past month, he had heard lions roaring, and smelled their strong odor seeping as far away as his study door. But, being busy, he had paid it no attention.

George Hadley stood on the African grassland alone. The lions looked up from their feeding, watching him. The only flaw to the illusion was the open door through which he could see his wife, far down the dark hall, like a framed picture, eating her dinner abstractedly.

"Go away," he said to the lions.

They did not go.

He knew the principle of the room exactly. You sent out your thoughts. Whatever you thought would appear.

"Let's have Aladdin and his lamp," he snapped.

The veldtland remained; the lions remained.

"Come on, room! I demand Aladdin!" he said.

Nothing happened. The lions mumbled in their baked pelts.

"Aladdin!"

He went back to dinner. "The fool room's out of order," he said. "It won't respond."

"Or —— "

"Or what?"

"Or it *can't* respond," said Lydia, "because the children have thought about Africa and lions and killing so many days that the room's in a rut."

"Could be."

"Or Peter's set it to remain that way."

"*Set* it?"

"He may have got into the machinery and fixed something."

"Peter doesn't know machinery."

"He's a wise one for ten. That I.Q. of his —— "

"Nevertheless —— "

"Hello, Mom. Hello, Dad."

The Hadleys turned. Wendy and Peter were coming in the front door, cheeks like peppermint candy, eyes like bright blue agate marbles, a smell of ozone on their jumpers from their trip in the helicopter.

"You're just in time for supper," said both parents.

"We're full of strawberry ice cream and hot dogs," said the children, holding hands. "But we'll sit and watch."

"Yes, come tell us about the nursery," said George Hadley.

The brother and sister blinked at him and then at each other. "Nursery?"

"All about Africa and everything," said the father with false joviality.

"I don't understand," said Peter.

"Your mother and I were just traveling through Africa with rod and reel; Tom Swift and his Electric Lion," said George Hadley.

"There's no Africa in the nursery," said Peter simply.

"Oh, come now, Peter. We know better."

"I don't remember any Africa," said Peter to Wendy. "Do you?"

"No."

"Run see and come tell."

She obeyed.

"Wendy, come back here!" said George Hadley, but she was gone. The house lights followed her like a flock of fireflies. Too late, he realized he had forgotten to lock the nursery door after his last inspection.

"Wendy'll look and come tell us," said Peter.

"She doesn't have to tell *me*. I've seen it."

"I'm sure you're mistaken, Father."

"I'm not, Peter. Come along now."

But Wendy was back. "It's not Africa," she said breathlessly.

"We'll see about this," said George Hadley, and they all walked down the hall together and opened the nursery door.

There was a green, lovely forest, a lovely river, a purple mountain, high voices singing, and Rima, lovely and mysterious, lurking in the trees with colorful flights of butterflies, like animated bouquets, lingering on her long hair. The African veldtland was gone. The lions were gone. Only Rima was here now, singing a song so beautiful that it brought tears to your eyes.

George Hadley looked in at the changed scene. "Go to bed," he said to the children.

They opened their mouths.

"You heard me," he said.

They went off to the air closet, where a wind sucked them like brown leaves up the flue to their slumber rooms.

George Hadley walked through the singing glade and picked up something that lay in the corner near where the lions had been. He walked slowly back to his wife.

"What is that?" she asked.

"An old wallet of mine," he said.

He showed it to her. The smell of hot grass was on it and the smell of a lion. There were drops of saliva on it, it had been chewed, and there were blood smears on both sides.

He closed the nursery door and locked it, tight.

In the middle of the night he was still awake and he knew his wife was awake. "Do you think Wendy changed it?" she said at last, in the dark room.

"Of course."

"Made it from a veldt into a forest and put Rima there instead of lions?"

"Yes."

"Why?"

"I don't know. But it's staying locked until I find out."

"How did your wallet get there?"

"I don't know anything," he said, "except that I'm beginning to be sorry we bought that room for the children. If children are neurotic at all, a room like that ─ "

"It's supposed to help them work off their neuroses in a healthful way."

"I'm starting to wonder." He stared at the ceiling.

"We've given the children everything they ever wanted. Is this our reward ─ secrecy, disobedience?"

"Who was it said, 'Children are carpets, they should be stepped on occasionally'? We've never lifted a hand. They're insufferable ─ let's admit it. They come and go when they like; they treat us as if *we* were offspring. They're spoiled and we're spoiled."

"They've been acting funny ever since you forbade them to take the rocket to New York a few months ago."

"They're not old enough to do that alone, I explained."

"Nevertheless, I've noticed they've been decidedly cool toward us since."

"I think I'll have David McClean come tomorrow morning to have a look at Africa."

"But it's not Africa now, it's Green Mansions country and Rima."

"I have a feeling it'll be Africa again before then."

A moment later they heard the screams.

Two screams. Two people screaming from downstairs. And then a roar of lions.

"Wendy and Peter aren't in their rooms," said his wife.

He lay in his bed with his beating heart. "No," he said. "They've broken into the nursery."

"Those screams—they sound familiar."

"Do they?"

"Yes, awfully."

And although their beds tried very hard, the two adults couldn't be rocked to sleep for another hour. A smell of cats was in the night air.

"Father?" said Peter.

"Yes."

Peter looked at his shoes. He never looked at his father any more, nor at his mother. "You aren't going to lock up the nursery for good, are you?"

"That all depends."

"On what?" snapped Peter.

"On you and your sister. If you intersperse this Africa with a little variety—oh, Sweden perhaps, or Denmark or China —— "

"I thought we were free to play as we wished."

"You are, within reasonable bounds."

"What's wrong with Africa, Father?"

"Oh, so now you admit you have been conjuring up Africa, do you?"

"I wouldn't want the nursery locked up," said Peter coldly. "Ever."

"Matter of fact, we're thinking of turning the whole house off for about a month. Live sort of a carefree one-for-all existence."

"That sounds dreadful! Would I have to tie my own shoes instead of letting the shoe tier do it? And brush my own teeth and comb my hair and give myself a bath?"

"It would be fun for a change, don't you think?"

"No, it would be horrid. I didn't like it when you took out the picture painter last month."

"That's because I wanted you to learn to paint all by yourself, son."

"I don't want to do anything but look and listen and smell; what else *is* there to do?"

"All right, go play in Africa."

"Will you shut off the house sometime soon?"

"We're considering it."

"I don't think you'd better consider it any more, Father."

"I won't have any threats from my son!"

"Very well." And Peter strolled off to the nursery.

"Am I on time?" said David McClean.

"Breakfast?" asked George Hadley.

"Thanks, had some. What's the trouble?"

"David, you're a psychologist."

"I should hope so."

"Well, then, have a look at our nursery. You saw it a year ago when you dropped by; did you notice anything peculiar about it then?"

"Can't say I did; the usual violences, a tendency toward a slight paranoia here or there, usual in children because they feel persecuted by parents constantly, but, oh, really nothing."

They walked down the hall. "I locked the nursery up," explained the father, "and the children broke back into it during the night. I let them stay so they could form the patterns for you to see."

There was a terrible screaming from the nursery.

"There it is," said George Hadley. "See what you make of it."

They walked in on the children without rapping.

The screams had faded. The lions were feeding.

"Run outside a moment, children," said George Hadley. "No, don't change the mental combination. Leave the walls as they are. Get!"

With the children gone, the two men stood studying the lions clustered at a distance, eating with great relish whatever it was they had caught.

"I wish I knew what it was," said George Hadley. "Sometimes I can almost see. Do you think if I brought high-powered binoculars here and —— "

David McClean laughed dryly. "Hardly." He turned to study all four walls. "How long has this been going on?"

"A little over a month."

"It certainly doesn't *feel* good."

"I want facts, not feelings."

"My dear George, a psychologist never saw a fact in his life. He only hears about feelings; vague things. This doesn't feel good, I tell you. Trust my hunches and my instincts. I have a nose for something bad. This is very bad. My advice to you is to have the whole damn room torn down and your children brought to me every day during the next year for treatment."

"Is it that bad?"

"I'm afraid so. One of the original uses of these nurseries was so that we could study the patterns left on the walls by the child's mind, study at our leisure, and help the child. In this case, however, the room has become a channel toward — destructive thoughts, instead of a release away from them."

"Didn't you sense this before?"

"I sensed only that you had spoiled your children more than most. And now you're letting them down in some way. What way?"

"I wouldn't let them go to New York."

"What else?"

"I've taken a few machines from the house and threatened them, a month ago, with closing up the nursery unless they did their homework. I did close it for a few days to show I meant business."

"Ah, ha!"

"Does that mean anything?"

"Everything. Where before they had a Santa Claus now they have a Scrooge. Children prefer Santas. You've let this room and this house replace you and your wife in your children's affections. This room is their mother and father, far more important in their lives than their real parents. And now you come along and want to shut it off. No wonder there's hatred here. You can feel it coming out of the sky. Feel that sun. George, you'll have to change your life. Like too many others, you've built it around creature comforts. Why, you'd starve tomorrow if something went wrong in your kitchen. You wouldn't know how to tap an egg. Nevertheless, turn everything off. Start new. It'll take time. But we'll make good children out of bad in a year, wait and see."

"But won't the shock be too much for the children, shutting the room up abruptly, for good?"

"I don't want them going any deeper into this, that's all."

The lions were finished with their red feast.

The lions were standing on the edge of the clearing watching the two men.

"Now *I'm* feeling persecuted," said McClean. "Let's get out of here. I never have cared for these damned rooms. Make me nervous."

"The lions look real, don't they?" said George Hadley. "I don't suppose there's any way —— "

"What?"

"—that they could *become* real?"

"Not that I know."

"Some flaw in the machinery, a tampering or something?"

"No."

They went to the door.

"I don't imagine the room will like being turned off," said the father.

"Nothing ever likes to die—even a room."

"I wonder if it hates me for wanting to switch it off?"

"Paranoia is thick around here today," said David McClean. "You can follow it like a spoor. Hello." He bent and picked up a bloody scarf. "This yours?"

"No." George Hadley's face was rigid. "It belongs to Lydia."

They went to the fuse box together and threw the switch that killed the nursery.

The two children were in hysterics. They screamed and pranced and threw things. They yelled and sobbed and swore and jumped at the furniture.

"You can't do that to the nursery, you can't!"

"Now, children."

The children flung themselves onto a couch, weeping.

"George," said Lydia Hadley, "turn on the nursery, just for a few moments. You can't be so abrupt."

"No."

"You can't be so cruel."

"Lydia, it's off, and it stays off. And the whole damn house dies as of here and now. The more I see of the mess we've put ourselves in, the more it sickens me. We've been contemplating our mechanical, electronic navels for too long. My God, how we need a breath of honest air!"

And he marched about the house turning off the voice clocks, the stoves, the heaters, the shoe shiners, the shoe lacers, the body scrubbers and swabbers and massagers, and every other machine he could put his hand to.

The house was full of dead bodies, it seemed. It felt like a mechanical cemetery. So silent. None of the humming hidden energy of machines waiting to function at the tap of a button.

"Don't let them do it!" wailed Peter at the ceiling, as if he was talking to the house, the nursery. "Don't let Father kill everything." He turned to his father. "Oh, I hate you!"

"Insults won't get you anywhere."

"I wish you were dead!"

"We were, for a long while. Now we're going to really start living. Instead of being handled and massaged, we're going to *live*."

Wendy was still crying and Peter joined her again. "Just a moment, just one moment, just another moment of nursery," they wailed.

"Oh, George," said the wife, "it can't hurt."

"All right—all right, if they'll only just shut up. One minute, mind you, and then off forever."

"Daddy, Daddy, Daddy!" sang the children, smiling with wet faces.

"And then we're going on a vacation. David McClean is coming back in half an hour to help us move out and get to the airport. I'm going to dress. You turn the nursery on for a minute, Lydia, just a minute, mind you."

And the three of them went babbling off while he let himself be vacuumed upstairs through the air flue and set about dressing himself. A minute later Lydia appeared.

"I'll be glad when we get away," she sighed.

"Did you leave them in the nursery?"

"I wanted to dress too. Oh, that horrid Africa. What can they see in it?"

"Well, in five minutes we'll be on our way to Iowa. Lord, how did we ever get in this house? What prompted us to buy a nightmare?"

"Pride, money, foolishness."

"I think we'd better get downstairs before those kids get engrossed with those damned beasts again."

Just then they heard the children calling, "Daddy, Mommy, come quick—quick!"

They went downstairs in the air flue and ran down the hall. The children were nowhere in sight. "Wendy? Peter!"

They ran into the nursery. The veldtland was empty save for the lions waiting, looking at them. "Peter, Wendy?"

The door slammed.

"Wendy, Peter!"

George Hadley and his wife whirled and ran back to the door.

"Open the door!" cried George Hadley, trying the knob. "Why, they've locked it from the outside! Peter!" He beat at the door. "Open up!"

He heard Peter's voice outside, against the door.

"Don't let them switch off the nursery and the house," he was saying.

Mr. and Mrs. George Hadley beat at the door. "Now, don't be ridiculous, children. It's time to go. Mr. McClean'll be here in a minute and . . ."

And then they heard the sounds.

The lions on three sides of them, in the yellow veldt grass, padding through the dry straw, rumbling and roaring in their throats.

The lions.

Mr. Hadley looked at his wife and they turned and looked back at the beasts edging slowly forward, crouching, tails stiff.

Mr. and Mrs. Hadley screamed.

And suddenly they realized why those other screams had sounded familiar.

"Well, here I am," said David McClean in the nursery doorway. "Oh, hello." He stared at the two children seated in the center of the open glade eating a little picnic lunch. Beyond them was the water hole and the yellow veldtland; above was the hot sun. He began to perspire. "Where are your father and mother?"

The children looked up and smiled. "Oh, they'll be here directly."

"Good, we must get going." At a distance Mr. McClean saw the lions fighting and clawing and then quieting down to feed in silence under the shady trees.

He squinted at the lions with his hand up to his eyes.

Now the lions were done feeding. They moved to the water hole to drink.

A shadow flickered over Mr. McClean's hot face. Many shadows flickered. The vultures were dropping down the blazing sky.

"A cup of tea?" asked Wendy in the silence.

Discussion Questions

1. Why does Lydia Hadley blame their problems with the room, and with the house in general, on her husband? What human traits, either good or bad, does the husband embody? The wife? How does Bradbury create a story that clearly illustrates how abstract concepts such as pride, greed, and foolishness can destroy peoples' peace and security?

2. Consider how the nursery progressed from fairy tales to the African veldt. What is Bradbury demonstrating with this progression? Why do you think

Bradbury chose an African setting in which to portray the scenes of predatory behavior?

3. What does George mean when he says, "We've been contemplating our mechanical, electronic navels for too long"? Why does the author attribute this insight to George?

4. The psychologist is referred to in the very beginning of the story and appears again in the last scene. Why does Bradbury have the psychologist reject the importance of facts, offering instead "hunches" and "instinct"? How do you interpret the role of the psychologist—who is a social scientist—in the story? How does he contribute to or help resolve the conflict?

Journal Entry

Imagine you lived in the Hadleys' house, or one similar to it, and could conjure up the perfect room. Describe what it would be like. Be thorough, including all the technological aspects of your perfect room.

Writing Projects

1. This story is rich in imagery, with more attention being given to the sense of smell than is typical in short stories. Imagine you are writing for an audience of writers interested in developing this technique; analyze how Bradbury presents sensory images. Assess the effects of Bradbury's description on the reader and on the story itself.

2. Writing for an audience of engineers, examine how the author presents technology in this story. The technologically controlled home produces both benefits and dangers. Outline for engineers how they should produce technology for the home that is beneficial without having harmful side effects.

Collaborative Project

The author uses George and Lydia Hadley's conversations to provide some interpretation of the situation. Working with a partner, construct a conversation between the two children, Wendy and Peter, in which they discuss their feelings toward their parents and toward their life in the nursery. Each of you might play the role of one of the children, or you may choose to write both speakers' parts together.

George E. Brown, Jr.

Technology's Dark Side

George E. Brown, Jr. *(b. 1920), a Democratic representative from California, serves as chair of the House of Representatives Committee on Science, Space, and Technology. Long considered an advocate of scientific research, Brown has lately begun to voice alternative views. In an editorial for the* Los Angeles Times *(1993) he recently wrote: "The promise of science — a miracle cure — serves politicians, who always are looking for a tonic to sell to the public, and it serves scientists, who understandably seek to preserve their elevated positions in our culture. But it may not serve society as advertised." The essay that follows was published in the* Chronicle of Higher Education *in June 1993; it is adapted from a paper Brown presented at a science and technology policy colloquium sponsored by the American Association for the Advancement of Science. Here Representative Brown calls for an increased sense of responsibility to society as a whole as we develop and use technology.*

Questions to Consider

☐ Before reading this essay, consider whether you believe there is a dark side to technology. If so, what makes it dark? After you have read Brown's essay, consider whether you agree with his reason for viewing technology as having a dark side.

☐ The author begins by contrasting his own earlier attitudes toward technology with his increasing impatience with common breakdowns in technology. Watch how his personal reflections draw you into his argument.

WHEN I was a boy, it didn't perturb me that the radio took five minutes to warm up. Nor was I particularly bothered that I had to talk to an operator to place a telephone call. As a young man, I don't recall feeling irritated that a flight from New York to Europe took 22 hours and stopped in Gander and Shannon on the way to Paris. When I was in my 40's, I believe that I was perfectly satisfied with my black-and-white TV, my dial telephone, my electric typewriter, and even my slide rule.

Today, though, I'm less tolerant. I can't stand it when the remote gets buried under a pile of papers on my desk, and I have to get out of my chair to turn on the television. I can't stand it when my flight to Los Angeles is delayed by half an hour or when the fax machine in my district office is busy or — God forbid—when I lose the audio on a video-teleconference with Moscow. What I never dreamed of yesterday, I can't do without today. Invention often seems to be the mother of necessity, not vice versa.

We need to think more clearly about the role that technology is playing in modern society. The role of technological and economic development is often explained in a straightforward manner. A recent report by the Bush Administration's Council on Competitiveness stated: "Throughout America's history, technology has been a major driver of economic growth. . . . Because of our great technological strength, U.S. manufacturing has stood head and shoulders above other nations in world markets." The 1993 Economic Report of the President—one of the last documents issued by the Bush Administration—completed the argument: "Strong and sustained economic growth is the key to providing Americans with rising real incomes and the resources to meet their needs, desires, and aspirations."

I think there is considerable reason to reexamine this conventional, straightforward view of the relations between technology, economic growth, and quality of life. One concrete example is the recently documented decline in infant mortality in the United States. Although we still rank near the bottom of the list of industrialized nations in infant mortality, we have recently risen from number 22 to number 20. The improvement results primarily from technological innovations that allow for more effective treatment of underdeveloped lungs—a major source of death for premature and underweight infants.

But there is a dark side to our progress. As our overall infant mortality rate declined, the disparity between white and black infant mortality continued to increase. The benefit of the technologies that treat underdeveloped lungs is limited to those who can afford fine medical care.

No doubt technological development is an efficient, market-driven approach to this medical problem. But it can also displace more equitable—and cheaper—nontechnological solutions. Many premature and underweight births could be prevented by wider access to adequate prenatal care. We know how to provide this care; we just don't manage to deliver it to poor people.

Why does the market-driven approach follow the technological route, instead of the preventative route? Because there are more profits to be made in treating the premature infants of mothers who can afford medical care than in preventing the premature infants of mothers who cannot. Thus, the market-driven technological approach provides a solution to the medical problem that actually exacerbates societal inequity. Such cases are not rare.

Another example of how technology-led economic growth can contribute to social inequity is found in the increased use of computers in elementary and secondary science education. Wealthier school districts tend to benefit from this trend more than poor districts, since wealthier parents have computers at home that their children can use. The government plans to link the nation's grade schools to a national computer network over the next several years; meanwhile urban libraries can't afford to stay open or buy new books.

Disparity of opportunity is magnified by technology-driven forces. If you can't read, it won't do you much good to log on.

The current U.S. economic recovery offers a more general example. As we know, the current recovery is not generating many new jobs. It appears that increased profitability is being fueled in part by technological innovation, with no need for additional workers. In fact, companies are improving their profitability by *firing* workers. The economy is growing, the recession is ending, and corporations are behaving in an economically rational manner: adopting new technologies, increasing efficiency, decreasing payrolls, boosting profits.

Looking more broadly, we find that the global distribution of wealth has become increasingly concentrated in the past 30 years, in spite of significant worldwide economic growth. In 1960, those nations with the wealthiest 20 per cent of the world's population accounted for 70 per cent of the world's annual gross profit. In 1989, the concentration of profit in the wealthiest nations had grown to 83 per cent. Trade, commercial lending, domestic investment and savings, and foreign private investment show similar trends.

I realize that global patterns of income, wealth, and economic growth reflect the extraordinarily complex political economy of international relations. Yet the role of technology in these relations is always viewed as a plus. Technology-driven economic growth in the industrialized world is supposed to promote investment in less-developed countries. This investment then allows those nations to purchase technologies and take advantage of their cheap and abundant labor, in turn fueling their own economic development. Eventually, the conventional theory holds, the less-developed countries become sort of like us.

But how do we know that these simple relationships will hold up in a high-technology world, where human physical labor becomes increasingly irrelevant to the production of wealth? In a high-technology world, how do we know whether market incentives will serve to mitigate or magnify economic disparity?

Further, the ability of human beings to achieve a basic measure of human dignity does not depend on advanced technologies. A nation's capacity to provide food and nutrition, education and literacy, clean water, decent housing, and basic health care does not correlate with technological sophistication, great wealth, or operation of market economies. Nations such as Costa Rica, North Korea, China, Sri Lanka, Jamaica, Cuba, and the former Soviet Union all managed to relieve most of their population from the elemental struggle for survival. Other nations, especially in the oil-producing Middle East, have accumulated great wealth, but have been less successful in meeting basic human needs.

Once basic needs are met, satisfaction with our lives cannot be said to depend on the amount of things we acquire, use, and consume. If that were the case, modern U.S. society would be the happiest in history, an assertion that would be difficult to support.

In terms of the social contract, we justify more growth because it is supposedly the most efficient way to spread economic opportunity and social well-being. But I believe that this reasoning is simplistic and often specious. When economic growth does not lead to greater public good, we do not blame dumb objects—technologies. Rather, we blame imperfections in the market system. The sources of such market imperfections go by names such as collusion, monopoly, pollution, nationalism, protectionism, authoritarianism, injustice, and war. These imperfections may all be grouped under a category commonly known as "reality."

Suppose that we viewed economic markets as an imperfect artifact of human culture, instead of vice versa. In this context, we might first ask: What type of technology policy would best serve the goals of human culture, such as reduction of injustice and inequity? The role of markets in promoting an optimal distribution of technologies would then become subservient to more fundamental objectives.

What would a socially oriented technology policy look like? We know that good health and quality education for the vast majority of human beings can be provided with little technological assistance. This point is so basic that it sounds almost asinine: Clean water, a good diet, and exercise would provide most Americans with a long and healthy life. Well-trained and dedicated teachers are the key to good education. Yet the average life expectancy of a black male in our inner cities is less than in many of the poorest developing nations, and we continue to graduate students from high school who can barely read or do math. Technology-driven economic growth didn't cause these problems, but it may be making it more difficult to solve them.

A social-technology policy might actually proscribe some types of technological solutions to social problems. This is not as insane as it sounds. The Japanese do it in a limited way. By limiting automation in agriculture, for example, Japanese agribusiness companies accept the cost of reduced productivity in order to insure fuller employment for their work forces.

Other aspects of a social-technology policy might encourage the development of technologies that decentralize political power and economic resources, to minimize the control that large institutions have over the lives of individuals. The federal government has spent 50 years subsidizing research and development on nuclear fission and nuclear fusion, while largely neglecting research into a wide range of renewable and generally decentralized energy sources that could help the world meet its energy needs in a more flexible and equitable way. These include solar and hydrothermal energy and hydrogen-derived power. The reason we took the nuclear path is obvious: Those who had a stake in nuclear energy—be it economic, political, or intellectual—were those already in power. Perhaps we can learn from this mistake, which has implications for an almost incredible range of social and economic phenomena, from dependence on imported oil to deterioration of the environment.

If we are to reduce technology-driven concentration of power—that is, if we are to achieve a world at once more equitable and more just—we must recognize that technology is a means, not an end. There is no invisible hand that ministers to the wise and equitable application of technology. We must provide that guiding hand through a conscious process of democratic action. Science and technology can and must be advanced in concert with the search for more justice in our society.

In his book *Steady-State Economics*, first published more than 15 years ago, Herman Daly, an economist at the World Bank, wrote: "The usual objection to limiting growth, made ostensibly in the name of the poor, only illustrates the extent of [our spiritual] void because it views growth as an alternative to sharing, which is considered unrealistic. For the traditional religious attitude, there is such a thing as material sufficiency, and beyond that admittedly vague and historically changing amount, the goal of life becomes wisdom, enjoyment, cultivation of the mind and soul, and community. It may even be that community requires a certain degree of scarcity, without which cooperation, sharing, and friendship would have no organic reason to be, and hence community would atrophy. . . . The answer to a failure of brotherhood is not simply more growth but is to be found mainly in more sharing."

How can someone like me, who has spent the last 30 years of his life enmeshed in the hard-headed world of Washington politics, take such utopian notions seriously? For the past 50 years this nation has focused its resources on building weapons of inconceivable destructive power, and we have viewed the rest of the world as a chess board designed to play out our own ideological struggle. We propped up governments that murdered nuns, priests, nurses, and children, and we provided high-technology weaponry to dictatorships. We undercut democratically elected governments, in some instances to protect the profits of U.S. companies.

We turned a blind eye while our tactical allies acquired the components necessary to build nuclear weapons, and we condoned authoritarian government in the name of the free flow of oil. Our vision during the cold war was cynical in the extreme. "Mutual assured destruction" was a U.S. philosophy of international relations; the "Peacekeeper" was a ballistic missile armed with nuclear warheads.

Now the cold war is over, and our excuse for this behavior is gone. We need a new and better vision. Neither technology nor economics can answer questions of values. Is our path into the future to be defined by the literally mindless process of technological evolution and economic expansion, or by a conscious adoption of guiding moral precepts? Progress is meaningless if we don't know where we're going. Unless we try to visualize what is beyond the horizon, we will always occupy the same shore.

Discussion Questions

1. How would you describe the overall tone of this essay? In what ways is the tone suited to the original audience, which was a science and technology policy colloquium?

2. Notice how Brown's choice of examples draws you into his argument. Which was the most effective in causing you to question the conventional view of the positive connections between technology, economic growth, and enhanced quality of life?

3. Can you cite specific instances in the text in which Brown demonstrates that the use of technology leads to an increase in human dignity? Cite instances of the use of technology resulting in a loss of human dignity, either as described by Brown or from your own experience.

4. Brown asks, "What would a socially oriented technology policy look like?" What answers to his own question does Brown offer? Which answers do you find most convincingly presented? What answers to this question can you offer?

5. What does Brown gain by echoing at several points in his article what he assumes his audience may be thinking of his argument?

Journal Entry

Describe what you think is most influential in determining the quality of one's life. Does a good life depend on having plenty of money, on doing fulfilling work, on having a rich spiritual life, or what? To what extent is the factor you select dependent on, or at least influenced by, technology?

Writing Projects

1. Brown rejects the common notion that improving technology produces increased affluence. He says that the way in which technology is produced and used often discriminates against the poor rather than decreasing their poverty. What examples does he provide? Do you agree with Brown's view? What examples can you cite to support or refute Brown's argument? Do you think an engineer has a moral obligation to pursue equitable use and distribution of his or her own technological products?

2. Compose a long letter to the instructors in your university, presenting the students' perspective on the benefits and disadvantages of classroom technology (for example, computers, laser discs, VCRs, video cameras, TV, and film projectors) and of technological products in education beyond the individual classroom (for example, on-line library card catalogs, CD-ROM [compact disk read-only memory] reference works, electronic mail [e-mail],

and the like). How have machines such as these improved your access to information? How have they made the classroom experience more productive and enjoyable? How has such technology increased your financial burden in acquiring an education? You might work with a partner to conduct a poll or interview at least ten other students before you begin writing.

Collaborative Project

With a partner, find out what the Committee on Science, Space, and Technology of the U.S. House of Representatives, which is chaired by Representative Brown, is designed to accomplish. Ask the reference librarian if your library houses government documents. If not, where and how can government documents be obtained? What issues and projects is Brown's committee currently considering? How long has Brown chaired the committee? Trace the work of the committee under his leadership. What has been its primary focus and most significant accomplishments? You might work together throughout the research phase, or divide it between the two of you. Try to analyze your findings together, and prepare a report on your findings and conclusions for the class.

Making Connections

Questions to Discuss

1. Jay David Bolter writes in "The Network Culture" that there is "fruitful specialization" in the sciences today and a "noisy collision of conflicting groups" in the humanities. Explain why you agree or disagree with his view that this is a positive situation. Considering Cynthia Ozick's concern over the fashion for factions in literature today (see "Science and Letters: God's Work—And Ours" in Chapter 1), what do you think would be her response to Bolter's view of the humanities today?

2. George Brown's article, as its title indicates, stresses the dark side of technology. Why do Brown and other writers in this chapter, and Chapter 2, emphasize the negative consequences of technology? Can you think of additional harmful effects of technology that were not addressed by the writers here?

3. It would not be accurate to describe Brown as being completely against technological developments. What is technology's bright side, as portrayed by Brown and other writers in this chapter and elsewhere in this text? (See, for example, Hajime Karatsu and Witold Rybczynski in Chapter 2.) What other important benefits of technology come to mind that have not been treated here?

4. Share with classmates your experiences in reading (or creating your own) hypertext material. What do you think are the key differences between reading a normal book and reading hypertext? How is the amount of control the author has over the reader's experience different in hypertext than in a regular book? How might hypertext initiate what Thomas Kuhn terms a *paradigm shift* in the way that printed information is stored and accessed?

Suggested Writing Projects

1. Study representations of technology in the media, choosing one or more of the following: textbooks from other courses, general interest magazines, newspapers, television, radio, or movies. Determine if each reference to technology conveyed by language and images comes laden with gender associations, either male or female. Consider your findings in relation to points made by Dorothy Nelkin, Ruth Schwartz Cowan, and/or Sally Hacker regarding the pervasiveness of male-dominated imagery for scientific and technological subjects. Write an analysis of your conclusions based on your findings.

2. In "Radioactive Red Caps," Langston Hughes uses dialogue between two characters to make observations about people in general and about racist behavior in particular. Using Hughes's technique as an example, construct a dialogue between two fictional characters in which one expresses Samuel Florman's opinions as presented in "The Feminist Face of Antitechnology" while the other responds from a feminist point of view.

3. In Ray Bradbury's story "The Veldt," a family allows technology to take control of its life. Draw parallels between the way in which Bradbury portrays the interdependence between humans and technology and the ways in which other authors here, or in other chapters, present that same interdependence. Demonstrate which author paints the grimmest picture, and which the most optimistic. Explain where you think the line should be drawn between a beneficial dependence on technology and a harmful dependence. Support your conclusions with references to selections in this text.

5

Healing with Technology

 When and how should we use science and technology to aid us in the processes of conception and death? Who should profit financially from others' desire to engineer conception or postpone death? What role, if any, should government play in a person's decisions about these matters? These are a few of the issues explored by the writers in this chapter.

You may recall that Alvin Weinberg (Chapter 2) introduced us to the concept of the technological fix. In health care the technological fix—which encompasses drugs, life-support machines, and surgical procedures—is the most expensive yet sometimes least effective method of ensuring health. Other approaches, such as changes in life-style, can be far more effective because they are preventive.

However, some diseases (such as cancer) cannot always be "fixed" by means of medical knowledge or technological prowess. In her story "In the Cemetery Where Al Jolson is Buried," Amy Hempel explores the role of human compassion in treating illness. She also shows the fear and helplessness that surround an incurable disease, effectively illustrating how fear of death causes most of us to behave selfishly. At such times we scramble for a technological fix.

In fact, we often seek to control both death and birth—two of life's most natural events—with high-tech methods and machinery. We tend to behave as though death were a misfortune that we could avoid if only we could push scientific research to the limit, or if only we could learn to fully exploit technology's promise.

But death does not necessarily represent a failure on the part of medicine or medical experts. After all, as Daniel Callahan, author of the book *The Troubled Dream of Life* (1993), points out, death is a "permanent part of the human condition." On the one hand, our culture acknowledges the inevitability of death: we purchase cemetery plots, draw up wills, and learn about hospice programs. On the other hand, we spend billions of dollars on high-tech medical treatment that too often prolongs the suffering preceding an inevitable death.

Our use of technology to deny death is analyzed in an excerpt from Elisabeth Kübler-Ross's famous book, *On Death and Dying*. Kübler-Ross, a renowned thanotologist (a person who specializes in the psychological and sociological dimensions of death), asserts that even though scientific and technological advances in medicine have decreased the infant mortality rate and increased the average person's longevity, they have not decreased our society's fear of death. In fact, Kübler-Ross believes that our technology-driven modern hospitals are promoting an increasingly clinical, mechanistic, and impersonal approach on the part of healers themselves.

Human reproduction is another area that draws interest in the promise of scientific experimentation. The procedure of in vitro fertilization—which involves fertilizing eggs, developing them into partial embryos outside of the body, and then implanting them in the womb— is no longer uncommon. These techniques advanced considerably owing to the work of several scientists at George Washington University. In fact, in October 1993, Dr. Jerry Hall announced that he could create twins using in vitro techniques.

Although in vitro procedures are becoming more common and more advanced, they are not simple, risk-free, or inexpensive. Nor are they looked upon favorably by all experts in the medical community. Money is a key factor. Currently, in vitro technology costs anywhere from $7,000 to $20,000 per attempt, and many attempts are unsuccessful. Thus, it is a profitable business venture for some, with the burden of the cost being borne by the patients. Because the technology is experimental and funded largely by private enterprise, there is minimal federal regulation.

Two writers in this chapter consider how women's lives are affected by cultural attitudes toward the reproductive process. Ruth Hubbard's feminist critique highlights both technological and moral issues related to in vitro fertilization. She indicates her concern for the women who undergo in vitro treatment and thereby give over control of their bodies to the medical establishment. Hubbard also draws attention to the way in which fertility research often proceeds from the assumption that a woman's life is unfulfilled if she is unable to conceive.

Carol Tavris too is concerned for women's general welfare and is bothered by the way in which women become subservient to the medical system. She argues that attaching labels such as "premenstrual syndrome" to natural female processes can validate normal mood changes yet stigmatize women by suggesting that the effects of the processes represent symptoms of a disease. Tavris points out how the media targets women who experience premenstrual syndrome by blaming them for the ways in which their bodies function.

Finally, two essays explore the topic of discrimination. David L. Wheeler outlines various implications of genetic testing for inherited disease, including the possibility that it could be used to discriminate against company employees and health insurance clients. Randy Shilts, in an excerpt from his well-known AIDS chronicle, *And the Band Played On*, examines the connection between health problems and discriminatory policies.

All the readings in this chapter suggest that birth, life, and death will continue to be influenced by the interplay of politics with the technological application of scientific research.

Amy Hempel

In the Cemetery Where Al Jolson Is Buried

Amy Hempel's *(b. 1951) prize-winning short stories deftly combine humor and sadness to portray people surviving the personal and natural disasters of modern urban life, such as illness, divorce, and earthquake. Hempel was born in Chicago and moved to California to attend San Francisco State University; she later attended Columbia University. Her stories have appeared in* Vanity Fair, Harper's, Vogue, *and the* New York Times Magazine, *among others. A* New York Times Book Review *critic has described Hempel's stories as "tough-minded, original and fully felt." "In the Cemetery Where Al Jolson Is Buried" appeared in her first collection,* Reasons to Live (1985); *it illustrates Hempel's spare, controlled style as well as her compassionate humor in the face of bleakness and loss. Hempel's second collection,* At the Gates of the Animal Kingdom, *was published in 1990.*

Questions to Consider

☐ Based on the title, what do you expect this story to be about? After you have finished it, consider the appropriateness of the title.

☐ Think about what subjects you expect to see treated with humor in short stories and which ones you expect to see portrayed as sad or serious. As you read this story, consider whether Hempel portrays her subject in the typical way.

---

for Jessica

TELL me things I won't mind forgetting," she said. "Make it useless stuff or skip it."

I began. I told her insects fly through rain, missing every drop, never getting wet. I told her no one in America owned a tape recorder before Bing Crosby did. I told her the shape of the moon is like a banana—you see it looking full, you're seeing it end-on.

The camera made me self-conscious and I stopped. It was trained on us from a ceiling mount—the kind of camera banks use to photograph robbers. It played our image to the nurses down the hall in Intensive Care.

"Go on, girl," she said, "you get used to it."

I had my audience. I went on. Did she know that Tammy Wynette had changed her tune? Really. That now she sings "Stand By Your *Friends*"? Paul Anka did it too, I said. Does "You're Having *Our* Baby." He got sick of all that feminist bitching.

"What else?" she said. "Have you got something else?"

Oh yes. For her I would always have something else.

"Did you know when they taught the first chimp to talk, it lied? When they asked her who did it on the desk, she signed back Max, the janitor. And when they pressed her, she said she was sorry, that it was really the project director. But she was a mother, so I guess she had her reasons."

"Oh, that's good," she said. "A parable."

"There's more about the chimp," I said. "But it will break your heart."

"No thanks," she says, and scratches at her mask.

We look like good-guy outlaws. Good or bad, I am not used to the mask yet. I keep touching the warm spot where my breath, thank God, comes out. She is used to hers. She only ties the strings on top. The other ones—a pro by now—she lets hang loose.

We call this place the Marcus Welby Hospital. It's the white one with the palm trees under the opening credits of all those shows. A Hollywood hospital, though in fact it is several miles west. Off camera, there is a beach across the street.

She introduces me to a nurse as "the Best Friend." The impersonal article is more intimate. It tells me that *they* are intimate, my friend and her nurse.

"I was telling her we used to drink Canada Dry Ginger Ale and pretend we were in Canada."

"That's how dumb *we* were," I say.

"You could be sisters," the nurse says.

So how come, I'll bet they are wondering, it took me so long to get to such a glamorous place? But do they ask?

They do not ask.

Two months, and how long is the drive?

The best I can explain it is this—I have a friend who worked one summer in a mortuary. He used to tell me stories. The one that really got to me was not the grisliest, but it's the one that did. A man wrecked his car on 101 going south. He did not lose consciousness. But his arm was taken down to the wet bone—and when he looked at it—it scared him to death. I mean, he died.

So I didn't dare look any closer. But now I'm doing it—and hoping I won't be scared to death.

She shakes out a summer-weight blanket, showing a leg you did not want to see. Except for that, you look at her and understand the law that requires *two* people to be with the body at all times.

"I thought of something," she says. "I thought of it last night. I think there is a real and present need here. You know," she says, "like for someone to do it for you when you can't do it yourself. You call them up whenever you want—like when push comes to shove."

She grabs the bedside phone and loops the cord around her neck.

"Hey," she says, "the End o' the Line."

She keeps on, giddy with something. But I don't know with what.

"The giveaway was the solarium," she says. "That's where Marcus Welby broke the news to his patients. Then here's the real doctor suggesting we talk in the solarium. So I knew I was going to die.

"I can't remember," she says, "what does Kübler-Ross say comes after Denial?"

It seems to me Anger must be next. Then Bargaining, Depression, and so on and so forth. But I keep my guesses to myself.

"The only thing is," she says, "is where's Resurrection? God knows I want to do it by the book. But she left out Resurrection."

She laughs, and I cling to the sound the way someone dangling above a ravine holds fast to the thrown rope.

We could have cried then, but when we didn't, we couldn't.

"Tell me," she says, "about that chimp with the talking hands. What do they do when the thing ends and the chimp says, 'I don't want to go back to the zoo'?"

When I don't say anything, she says, "O.K.—then tell me another animal story. I like animal stories. But not a sick one—I don't want to know about all the Seeing Eye dogs going blind."

No, I would not tell her a sick one.

"How about the hearing-ear dogs?" I say. "They're not going deaf, but they are getting very judgmental. For instance, there's this golden retriever in Jersey, he wakes up the deaf mother and drags her into the daughter's room because the kid has got a flashlight and is reading under the covers."

"Oh, you're killing me," she says. "Yes, you're definitely killing me."

"They say the smart dog obeys, but the smarter dog knows when to *dis*obey."

"Yes," she says, "the smarter *anything* knows when to disobey. Now, for example."

She is flirting with the Good Doctor, who has just appeared. Unlike the Bad Doctor, who checks the I.V. drip before saying good morning, the Good Doctor says things like "God didn't give epileptics a fair shake." He awards himself points for the cripples he could have hit in the parking lot. Because the Good Doctor is a little in love with her he says maybe a year. He pulls a chair up to her bed and suggests I might like to spend an hour on the beach.

"Bring me something back," she says. "Anything from the beach. Or the gift shop. Taste is no object."

The doctor slowly draws the curtain around her bed.

"Wait!" she cries.

I look in at her.

"Anything," she says, "except a magazine subscription."

The doctor turns away.

I watch her mouth laugh.

What seems dangerous often is not—black snakes, for example, or clear-air turbulence. While things that just lie there, like this beach, are loaded with jeopardy. A yellow dust rising from the ground, the heat that ripens melons overnight—this is earthquake weather. You can sit here braiding the fringe on your towel and the sand will all of a sudden suck down like an hourglass. The air roars. In the cheap apartments onshore, bathtubs fill themselves and gardens roll up and over like green waves. If nothing happens, the dust will drift and the heat deepen till fear turns to desire. Nerves like that are only bought off by catastrophe.

"It never happens when you're thinking about it," she observed once.

"Earthquake, earthquake, earthquake," she said.

"Earthquake, earthquake, earthquake," I said.

Like the aviaphobe who keeps the plane aloft with prayer, we kept it up till an aftershock cracked the ceiling.

That was after the big one in '72. We were in college; our dormitory was five miles from the epicenter. When the ride was over and my jabbering pulse began to slow, she served five parts champagne to one part orange juice and joked about living in Ocean View, Kansas. I offered to drive her to Hawaii on the new world psychics predicted would surface the next time, or the next.

I could not say that now—next. *Whose* next? she could ask.

Was I the only one who noticed that the experts had stopped saying *if* and now spoke of *when*? Of course not; the fearful ran to thousands. We watched the traffic of Japanese beetles for deviation. Deviation might mean more natural violence.

I wanted her to be afraid with me, but she said, "I don't know. I'm just not."

She was afraid of nothing, not even of flying.

I have this dream before a flight where we buckle in and the plane moves down the runway. It takes off at thirty-five miles an hour, and then we're airborne, skimming the tree tops. Still, we arrive in New York on time. It is so pleasant. One night I flew to Moscow this way.

She flew with me once. That time she flew with me she ate macadamia nuts while the wings bounced. She knows the wing tips can bend thirty feet up and thirty feet down without coming off. She believes it. She trusts the laws of aerodynamics. My mind stampedes. I can almost accept that a battleship floats, and everybody knows steel sinks.

I see fear in her now and am not going to try to talk her out of it. She is right to be afraid.

After a quake, the six o'clock news airs a film clip of first-graders yelling at the broken playground per their teacher's instructions.

"*Bad* earth!" they shout, because anger is stronger than fear.

But the beach is standing still today. Everyone on it is tranquilized, numb or asleep. Teenaged girls rub coconut oil on each other's hard-to-reach places. They smell like macaroons. They pry open compacts like clamshells; mirrors catch the sun and throw a spray of white rays across glazed shoulders. The girls arrange their wet hair with silk flowers the way they learned in *Seventeen.* They pose.

A formation of low-riders pulls over to watch with a six-pack. They get vocal when the girls check their tan lines. When the beer is gone, so are they — flexing their cars on up the boulevard.

Above this aggressive health are the twin wrought-iron terraces, painted flamingo pink, of the Palm Royale. Someone dies there every time the sheets are changed. There's an ambulance in the driveway, so the remaining residents line the balconies, rocking and not talking, one-upped.

The ocean they stare at is dangerous, and not just the undertow. You can almost see the slapping tails of sand sharks keeping cruising bodies alive.

If she looked, she could see this, some of it, from her window. She would be the first to say how little it takes to make a thing all wrong.

There was a second bed in the room when I returned. For two beats I didn't get it. Then it hit me like an open coffin.

She wants every minute, I thought. She wants my life.

"You missed Gussie," she said.

Gussie is her parents' 300-pound narcoleptic maid. Her attacks often come at the ironing board. The pillowcases in that family are all bordered with scorch.

"It's a hard trip for her," I said. "How is she?"

"Well, she didn't fall asleep, if that's what you mean. Gussie's great — you know what she said? She said, 'Darlin' just keep prayin', down on your knees.'"

She shrugged. "See anybody good?"

"No," I said, "just the new Charlie's Angel. And I saw Cher's car down near the Arcade."

"Cher's car is worth *three* Charlie's Angels," she said, "What else am I missing?"

"It's earthquake weather," I told her.

"The best thing to do about earthquakes," she said, "is not to live in California."

"That's useful," I said. "You sound like Reverend Ike: 'The best thing to do for the poor is not be one of them.'"

We're crazy about Reverend Ike.

I noticed her face was bloated.

"You know," she said, "I feel like hell. I'm about to stop having fun."

"The ancients have a saying," I said. "'There are times when the wolves are silent; there are times when the moon howls.'"

"What's that, Navajo?"

"Palm Royale lobby graffiti," I said. "I bought a paper there. I'll read to you."

"Even though I care about nothing?" she said.

I turned to page three, to a UPI filler datelined Mexico City. I read her "Man Robs Bank with Chicken," about a man who bought a barbecued chicken at a stand down the block from a bank. Passing the bank, he got the idea. He walked in and approached a teller. He pointed the brown paper bag at her and she handed over the day's receipts. It was the smell of barbecue sauce that eventually led to his capture.

The story made her hungry, she said, so I took the elevator down six floors to the cafeteria and brought back all the ice cream she wanted. We lay side by side, adjustable beds cranked up for optimal TV viewing, littering the sheets with Good Humor wrappers, picking toasted almonds out of the gauze. We were Lucy and Ethel, Mary and Rhoda in extremis. The blinds were closed to keep light off the screen.

We watched a movie starring men we used to think we wanted to sleep with. Hers was a tough cop out to stop mine, a vicious rapist who went after cocktail waitresses.

"This is a good movie," she said, when snipers felled them both.

I missed her already; my straight man, my diary.

A Filipino nurse tiptoed in and gave her an injection. She removed the pile of Popsicle sticks from the nightstand—enough to splint a small animal.

The injection made us sleepy—me in the way I picked up her inflection till her mother couldn't tell us apart on the phone. We slept.

I dreamed she was a decorator, come to furnish my house. She worked in secret, singing to herself. When she finished, she guided me proudly to the door. "How do you like it?" she asked, easing me inside.

Every beam and sill and shelf and knob was draped in black bunting, with streamers of black crepe looped around darkened mirrors.

"I have to go home," I said when she woke up.

She thought I meant home to her house in the Canyon, and I had to say No, *home* home. I twisted my hands in the hackneyed fashion of people in pain. I was supposed to offer something. The Best Friend. I could not even offer to come back.

I felt weak and small and failed. Also exhilarated. I had a convertible in the parking lot. Once out of that room, I would drive it too fast down the coast highway through the crab-smelling air. A stop in Malibu for sangria. The music in the place would be sexy and loud. They would serve papaya and shrimp and watermelon ice. After dinner I would pick up beach boys. I would shimmer with life, buzz with heat, vibrate with health, stay up all night with one and then the other.

Without a word, she yanked off her mask and threw it on the floor. She kicked at the blankets and moved to the door. She must have hated having to pause for breath and balance before slamming out of Isolation, and out of the second room, the one where you scrub and tie on the white masks.

A voice shouted her name in alarm, and people ran down the corridor. The Good Doctor was paged over the intercom. I opened the door and the nurses at the station stared hard, as if this flight had been my idea.

"Where is she?" I asked, and they nodded to the supply closet.

I looked in. Two nurses were kneeling beside her on the floor, talking to her in low voices. One held a mask over her nose and mouth, the other rubbed her back in slow circles. The nurses glanced up to see if I was the doctor, and when they saw I wasn't, they went back to what they were doing.

"There, there, honey," they cooed.

On the morning she was moved to the cemetery, the one where Al Jolson is buried, I enrolled in a Fear of Flying class. "What is your worst fear?" the instructor asked, and I answered, "That I will finish this course and still be afraid."

I sleep with a glass of water on the nightstand so I can see by its level if the coastal earth is trembling or if the shaking is still me.

What do I remember? I remember only the useless things I hear – that Bob Dylan's mother invented Wite-out, that twenty-three people must be in a room before there is a fifty-fifty chance two will have the same birthdate. Who cares whether or not it's true? In my head there are bath towels swaddling this stuff. Nothing else seeps through.

I review those things that will figure in the retelling: a kiss through surgical gauze, the pale hand correcting the position of the wig. I noted these gestures as they happened, not in any retrospect. Though I don't know why looking *back* should show us more than looking *at*. It is just possible I will say I stayed the night. And who is there that can say I did not?

Nothing else gets through until I think of the chimp, the one with the talking hands.

In the course of the experiment, that chimp had a baby. Imagine how her trainers must have thrilled when the mother, without prompting, began to sign to the newborn. Baby, drink milk. Baby, play ball. And when the baby died, the mother stood over the body, her wrinkled hands moving with animal grace, forming again and again the words, Baby, come hug, Baby, come hug, fluent now in the language of grief.

Discussion Questions

1. How does the author portray death in this story? List several adjectives that describe how Hempel treats this serious issue. Why do you think she chose to portray death in this way?

2. What do you learn about the narrator from what she says and what she does? What do you learn about the narrator's friend from their conversations? From what the narrator says about her friend? How old are the two friends? What kind of friendship do they have? How do they feel about each other? Do their feelings toward each other change during the course of the story?

3. Which of the two main characters in this story did you find yourself sympathizing with? Why were you drawn to this character?

4. Modern physicians depend to a great extent on scientific research and machines to heal their patients. But their effectiveness as healers also depends on their "bedside manner." The characters here refer to the "Good Doctor" and the "Bad Doctor." What criteria does the patient use to distinguish between good and bad doctors? Does the narrator understand her friend's attitude toward her doctors?

5. Hempel's style is often praised for being "spare, minimalist, elliptical, and economical." Why is a spare or economical style considered praiseworthy? What do you think are the most striking elements of Hempel's style in this story?

Journal Entries

1. Assume you are the narrator and you have left your dying friend before she felt the visit was over. Describe your feelings about the visit. Explain why you felt you had to leave early. Tell how you feel about leaving and why.

2. Assume you are the patient in this story. Your friend cut short her visit, leaving earlier than you expected. Describe your feelings about the visit and about her leaving.

Writing Projects

1. Setting is an important element in any story. Do you see ways in which the setting in this story—a hospital close to the beach in California—is particularly significant? Analyze the setting, illustrating how it interrelates with other elements such as characterization and plot.

2. Write an essay explaining why you think the author brings in such issues as sexism in song lyrics, animals who assist people with disabilities, earthquakes, and chimps expressing grief through the use of sign language. How does the author integrate these ideas into the story? Are these topics integrated effectively?

Collaborative Project

Working with a partner, read some articles and interview at least one doctor or another health professional to determine what they think is their role in helping a patient deal with a terminal illness. Determine how doctors view themselves in terms of having power over other people's lives. Do they see themselves as figures of authority? How do doctors see themselves in relation to technology—that is, drugs, machines that run tests, or computer-guided operating procedures? Do they feel they must rely on the products of technology to extend their own power and authority?

Elisabeth Kübler-Ross

On the Fear of Death

Elisabeth Kübler-Ross *(b. 1926), a psychiatrist and internationally known thanatologist (a specialist on the physical, psychological, and sociological problems associated with death), was born in Switzerland, where she later practiced as a country doctor. She has explained that her postwar relief work in Europe, during which she saw the concentration camps, accounts for some of her preoccupation with death. She has written extensively about the ethical issues and fears related to dying; she is particularly concerned about how certain so-called advanced societies are attempting to create an increasingly greater distance from people who are dying, in an effort to deny death. Kübler-Ross instituted a teaching seminar at the Billings Hospital of the University of Chicago in 1965 and invited terminally ill patients to talk to the medical students. She found that the patients "welcomed a frank, unemotional, honest discussion and a sharing of their feelings." The excerpt that follows is from her book* On Death and Dying *(1969); her other books include* Death: The Final Stage *(1974),* Working It Through *(1982), and* AIDS *(1989). In this excerpt, "On the Fear of Death," Kübler-Ross recalls her childhood experiences with death and suggests that the modern setting of most deaths — the hospital — denies relatives and friends participation in their loved one's death, a participation that is beneficial to both the patient and the survivors.*

Questions to Consider

☐ Try to discern whom Kübler-Ross considers as her primary audience. Watch for sentences that identify a particular audience.

☐ How much influence do you believe doctors should have in determining the setting of their terminally ill patients' deaths? Do you believe doctors are qualified to decide when it is time for their patients to die, when to pull the plug from life-sustaining machinery? Are they morally entitled to make these decisions?

Let me not pray to be sheltered from dangers but to be fearless in facing them.
Let me not beg for the stilling of my pain but for the heart to conquer it.

Let me not look for allies in life's
battlefield but to my own strength.
Let me not crave in anxious fear to
be saved but hope for the patience to
win my freedom.
Grant me that I may not be a
coward, feeling your mercy in my
success alone; but let me find the grasp
of your hand in my failure.
RABINDRANATH TAGORE
Fruit-Gathering

E PIDEMICS have taken a great toll of lives in past generations. Death in infancy and early childhood was frequent and there were few families
who didn't lose a member of the family at an early age. Medicine has
changed greatly in the last decades. Widespread vaccinations have practically
eradicated many illnesses, at least in western Europe and the United States.
The use of chemotherapy, especially the antibiotics, has contributed to an
ever-decreasing number of fatalities in infectious diseases. Better child care and
education has effected a low morbidity and mortality among children. The
many diseases that have taken an impressive toll among the young and mid-
dle-aged have been conquered. The number of old people is on the rise, and
with this fact come the number of people with malignancies and chronic diseases associated more with old age.

Pediatricians have less work with acute and life-threatening situations as
they have an ever-increasing number of patients with psychosomatic distur-
bances and adjustment and behavior problems. Physicians have more people
in their waiting rooms with emotional problems than they have ever had before, but they also have more elderly patients who not only try to live with
their decreased physical abilities and limitations but who also face loneliness
and isolation with all its pains and anguish. The majority of these people are
not seen by a psychiatrist. Their needs have to be elicited and gratified by
other professional people, for instance, chaplains and social workers. It is for
them that I am trying to outline the changes that have taken place in the last
few decades, changes that are ultimately responsible for the increased fear of
death, the rising number of emotional problems, and the greater need for understanding of and coping with the problems of death and dying.

When we look back in time and study old cultures and people, we are impressed that death has always been distasteful to man and will probably always be. From a psychiatrist's point of view this is very understandable and
can perhaps best be explained by our basic knowledge that, in our unconscious, death is never possible in regard to ourselves. It is inconceivable for
our unconscious to imagine an actual ending of our own life here on earth,
and if this life of ours has to end, the ending is always attributed to a malicious

intervention from the outside by someone else. In simple terms, in our unconscious mind we can only be killed; it is inconceivable to die of a natural cause or of old age. Therefore death in itself is associated with a bad act, a frightening happening, something that in itself calls for retribution and punishment.

One is wise to remember these fundamental facts as they are essential in understanding some of the most important, otherwise unintelligible communications of our patients.

The second fact that we have to comprehend is that in our unconscious mind we cannot distinguish between a wish and a deed. We are all aware of some of our illogical dreams in which two completely opposite statements can exist side by side – very acceptable in our dreams but unthinkable and illogical in our wakening state. Just as our unconscious mind cannot differentiate between the wish to kill somebody in anger and the act of having done so, the young child is unable to make this distinction. The child who angrily wishes his mother to drop dead for not having gratified his needs will be traumatized greatly by the actual death of his mother – even if this event is not linked closely in time with his destructive wishes. He will always take part or the whole blame for the loss of his mother. He will always say to himself – rarely to others – "I did it, I am responsible, I was bad, therefore Mommy left me." It is well to remember that the child will react in the same manner if he loses a parent by divorce, separation, or desertion. Death is often seen by a child as an impermanent thing and has therefore little distinction from a divorce in which he may have an opportunity to see a parent again.

Many a parent will remember remarks of their children such as, "I will bury my doggy now and next spring when the flowers come up again, he will get up." Maybe it was the same wish that motivated the ancient Egyptians to supply their dead with food and goods to keep them happy and the old American Indians to bury their relatives with their belongings.

When we grow older and begin to realize that our omnipotence is really not so omnipotent, that our strongest wishes are not powerful enough to make the impossible possible, the fear that we have contributed to the death of a loved one diminishes – and with it the guilt. The fear remains diminished, however, only so long as it is not challenged too strongly. Its vestiges can be seen daily in hospital corridors and in people associated with the bereaved.

A husband and wife may have been fighting for years, but when the partner dies, the survivor will pull his hair, whine and cry louder and beat his chest in regret, fear and anguish, and will hence fear his own death more than before, still believing in the law of talion – an eye for an eye, a tooth for a tooth – "I am responsible for her death, I will have to die a pitiful death in retribution."

Maybe this knowledge will help us understand many of the old customs and rituals which have lasted over the centuries and whose purpose is to diminish the anger of the gods or the people as the case may be, thus decreasing the anticipated punishment. I am thinking of the ashes, the torn clothes, the veil, the *Klage Weiber* of the old days—they are all means to ask you to take pity on them, the mourners, and are expressions of sorrow, grief, and shame. If someone grieves, beats his chest, tears his hair, or refuses to eat, it is an attempt at self-punishment to avoid or reduce the anticipated punishment for the blame that he takes on the death of a loved one.

This grief, shame, and guilt are not very far removed from feelings of anger and rage. The process of grief always includes some qualities of anger. Since none of us likes to admit anger at a deceased person, these emotions are often disguised or repressed and prolong the period of grief or show up in other ways. It is well to remember that it is not up to us to judge such feelings as bad or shameful but to understand their true meaning and origin as something very human. In order to illustrate this I will again use the example of the child—and the child in us. The five-year-old who loses his mother is both blaming himself for her disappearance and being angry at her for having deserted him and for no longer gratifying his needs. The dead person then turns into something the child loves and wants very much but also hates with equal intensity for this severe deprivation.

The ancient Hebrews regarded the body of a dead person as something unclean and not to be touched. The early American Indians talked about the evil spirits and shot arrows in the air to drive the spirits away. Many other cultures have rituals to take care of the "bad" dead person, and they all originate in this feeling of anger which still exists in all of us, though we dislike admitting it. The tradition of the tombstone may originate in the wish to keep the bad spirits deep down in the ground, and the pebbles that many mourners put on the grave are leftover symbols of the same wish. Though we call the firing of guns at military funerals a last salute, it is the same symbolic ritual as the Indian used when he shot his spears and arrows into the skies.

I give these examples to emphasize that man has not basically changed. Death is still a fearful, frightening happening, and the fear of death is a universal fear even if we think we have mastered it on many levels.

What has changed is our way of coping and dealing with death and dying and our dying patients.

Having been raised in a country in Europe where science is not so advanced, where modern techniques have just started to find their way into medicine, and where people still live as they did in this country half a century ago, I may have had an opportunity to study a part of the evolution of mankind in a shorter period.

I remember as a child the death of a farmer. He fell from a tree and was not expected to live. He asked simply to die at home, a wish that was granted without question. He called his daughters into the bedroom and spoke with each one of them alone for a few moments. He arranged his affairs quietly, though he was in great pain, and distributed his belongings and his land, none of which was to be split until his wife should follow him in death. He also asked each of his children to share in the work, duties, and tasks that he had carried on until the time of the accident. He asked his friends to visit him once more, to bid goodbye to them. Although I was a small child at the time, he did not exclude me or my siblings. We were allowed to share in the preparations of the family just as we were permitted to grieve with them until he died. When he did die, he was left at home, in his own beloved home which he had built, and among his friends and neighbors who went to take a last look at him where he lay in the midst of flowers in the place he had lived in and loved so much. In that country today there is still no make-believe slumber room, no embalming, no false makeup to pretend sleep. Only the signs of very disfiguring illnesses are covered up with bandages and only infectious cases are removed from the home prior to the burial.

Why do I describe such "old-fashioned" customs? I think they are an indication of our acceptance of a fatal outcome, and they help the dying patient as well as his family to accept the loss of a loved one. If a patient is allowed to terminate his life in the familiar and beloved environment, it requires less adjustment for him. His own family knows him well enough to replace a sedative with a glass of his favorite wine; or the smell of a home-cooked soup may give him the appetite to sip a few spoons of fluid which, I think, is still more enjoyable than an infusion. I will not minimize the need for sedatives and infusions and realize full well from my own experience as a country doctor that they are sometimes life-saving and often unavoidable. But I also know that patience and familiar people and foods could replace many a bottle of intravenous fluids given for the simple reason that it fulfills the physiological need without involving too many people and/or individual nursing care.

The fact that children are allowed to stay at home where a fatality has struck and are included in the talk, discussions, and fears gives them the feeling that they are not alone in their grief and gives them the comfort of shared responsibility and shared mourning. It prepares them gradually and helps them view death as part of life, an experience which may help them grow and mature.

This is in great contrast to a society in which death is viewed as taboo, discussion of it is regarded as morbid, and children are excluded with the presumption and pretext that it would be "too much" for them. They are then sent off to relatives, often accompanied by some unconvincing lies of "Mother has gone on a long trip" or other unbelievable stories. The child senses that something is wrong, and his distrust in adults will only multiply if other relatives add new variations of the story, avoid his questions or suspicions, shower him with gifts as a meager substitute for a loss he is not permitted to deal with. Sooner or later the child will become aware of the changed family situation and, depending on the age and personality of the child, will have an unresolved grief and regard this incident as a frightening, mysterious, in any case very traumatic experience with untrustworthy grownups, which he has no way to cope with.

It is equally unwise to tell a little child who lost her brother that God loved little boys so much that he took little Johnny to heaven. When this little girl grew up to be a woman she never solved her anger at God, which resulted in a psychotic depression when she lost her own little son three decades later.

We would think that our great emancipation, our knowledge of science and of man, has given us better ways and means to prepare ourselves and our families for this inevitable happening. Instead the days are gone when a man was allowed to die in peace and dignity in his own home.

The more we are making advancements in science, the more we seem to fear and deny the reality of death. How is this possible?

We use euphemisms, we make the dead look as if they were asleep, we ship the children off to protect them from the anxiety and turmoil around the house if the patient is fortunate enough to die at home, we don't allow children to visit their dying parents in the hospitals, we have long and controversial discussions about whether patients should be told the truth—a question that rarely arises when the dying person is tended by the family physician who has known him from delivery to death and who knows the weaknesses and strengths of each member of the family.

I think there are many reasons for this flight away from facing death calmly. One of the most important facts is that dying nowadays is more gruesome in many ways, namely, more lonely, mechanical, and dehumanized; at times it is even difficult to determine technically when the time of death has occurred.

Dying becomes lonely and impersonal because the patient is often taken out of his familiar environment and rushed to an emergency room. Whoever has been very sick and has required rest and comfort especially may recall his experience of being put on a stretcher and enduring the noise of the ambulance siren and hectic rush until the hospital gates open. Only those who have lived through this may appreciate the discomfort and cold necessity of such transportation which is only the beginning of a long ordeal—hard to endure when you are well, difficult to express in words when noise, light, pumps, and voices are all too much to put up with. It may well be that we might consider more the patient under the sheets and blankets and perhaps stop our well-meant efficiency and rush in order to hold the patient's hand, to smile, or to listen to a question. I include the trip to the hospital as the first episode in dying, as it is for many. I am putting it exaggeratedly in contrast to the sick man who is left at home—not to say that lives should not be saved if they can be saved by a hospitalization but to keep the focus on the patient's experience, his needs and his reactions.

When a patient is severely ill, he is often treated like a person with no right to an opinion. It is often someone else who makes the decision if and when and where a patient should be hospitalized. It would take so little to remember that the sick person too has feelings, has wishes and opinions, and has—most important of all—the right to be heard.

Well, our presumed patient has now reached the emergency room. He will be surrounded by busy nurses, orderlies, interns, residents, a lab technician perhaps who will take some blood, an electrocardiogram technician who takes the cardiogram. He may be moved to X-ray and he will overhear opinions of his condition and discussions and questions to members of the family. He slowly but surely is beginning to be treated like a thing. He is no longer a person. Decisions are made often without his opinion. If he tries to rebel he will be sedated and after hours of waiting and wondering whether he has the strength, he will be wheeled into the operating room or intensive treatment unit and become an object of great concern and great financial investment.

He may cry for rest, peace, and dignity, but he will get infusions, transfusions, a heart machine, or tracheostomy if necessary. He may want one single person to stop for one single minute so that he can ask one single question—but he will get a dozen people around the clock, all busily preoccupied with his heart rate, pulse, electrocardiogram or pulmonary functions, his secretions or excretions but not with him as a human being. He may wish to fight it all but it is going to be a useless fight since all this is done in the fight for his life, and if they can save his life they can consider the person afterwards. Those who consider the person first may lose precious time to save his life! At least this seems to be the rationale or justification behind all this—or is it? Is the reason for this increasingly mechanical, depersonalized approach our own defensiveness? Is this approach our own way to cope with and repress the anxieties that a terminally or critically ill patient evokes in us? Is our concentration on equipment, on blood pressure our desperate attempt to deny the impending death which is so frightening and discomforting to us that we displace all our knowledge onto machines, since they are less close to us than the suffering face of another human being which would remind us once more of our lack of omnipotence, our own limits and failures, and last but not least perhaps our own mortality?

Maybe the question has to be raised: Are we becoming less human or more human? Though this book is in no way meant to be judgmental, it is clear that whatever the answer may be, the patient is suffering more—not physically, perhaps, but emotionally. And his needs have not changed over the centuries, only our ability to gratify them.

Discussion Questions

1. Did you like the prayer the author includes at the beginning? How is the prayer related to the thesis the author develops? What is the stylistic effect of beginning four lines of the prayer with the same phrase, "Let me not"?

2. What kinds of examples does the author use? Are they based mostly on

her reading and research, on her experience as a doctor, or on a combination? What is the effect of her using so many examples involving children?

3. At what point does the author begin to point out some of the problematic side effects of people living longer nowadays? What is her purpose in summarizing these consequences?

4. Within most families (ignoring those with health care, religious, and social services professionals), who ends up dealing with the infirmities and illnesses of family members? Are caregivers usually male or female family members?

5. Why does the author discuss the guilt experienced by survivors when someone dies? Who is likely to experience this guilt? Does the author's explanation seem convincing? Why or why not?

6. Compile a list of euphemisms connected with death, for example, "passed on," "kicked the bucket," "pushing up daisies." Discuss the various connotations (personal associations) of each. Then arrange them in some kind of order; for example, least to most comforting to those grieving a loved one's death. Why do people use euphemisms about death? What is the prevailing tone of the expressions you listed, and how do you account for it?

Journal Entries

1. The author says that unconsciously we all feel that "death is never possible in regard to ourselves." Does that seem valid to you? Write down thoughts about your own eventual death. Is it something you ever consider? Do you spend any time contemplating your old age?

2. Imagine you have a close friend or relative who is facing the impending death, or the recent death, of a family member, lover, or close friend. Write a letter to your friend in which you urge him or her to seek counseling and perhaps participate in a support group for those dealing with the death or terminal illness of someone close to them. Explain why you think it is important to seek help in dealing with grief and the other emotions associated with the death of a loved one.

Writing Projects

1. Write an essay in response to the author's ideas about allowing children to be present at the death of loved ones. Describe the extent to which you think children should participate in the care of a dying person and in the rituals of grieving and burial. Point out the factors that need to be considered in determining how much a child can handle.

2. The author suggests that our modern ways of dealing with death have some serious, negative side effects. Write an essay on death and dying in which you argue for changing some of our modern views and procedures for coping with death and dying. Explain how your proposed changes could be implemented.

Collaborative Projects

1. Working with a partner, research and write a report on hospice programs. What does the term *hospice* mean? Where did the concept originate? Are hospice programs available nationwide? Are they available in your community? If not, why aren't they? Conduct both library research and primary research, talking to health care and social services professionals as well as your own friends and neighbors who have had experience with hospice programs. Report on your findings, including an assessment of the benefits of hospice care to both the terminally ill and their families.

2. Working with a partner, research the customs associated with death and burial in a particular culture. You could work together; or one of you might find out the general features of the selected culture's customs, and the other trace the history of the death rituals of that culture. How have the death rituals changed over time? How have they remained the same? Or you and your partner might each choose different cultures to investigate, using these questions as a guide, and then compare your findings.

Ruth Hubbard

Test-Tube Babies: Solution or Problem?

Ruth Hubbard *(b. 1924) was the first woman in the sciences to be tenured at Harvard University. Her specialties include the biochemistry of vision and women's health. In the following essay, Hubbard impresses upon the reader a moral imperative regarding the use and development of fertility technology, alerting us to the suffering and cost that may ultimately fall on those who are themselves products of the technology. "Test-Tube Babies: Solution or Problem?" was adapted from a talk Hubbard gave at a meeting of the American Association for the Advancement of Science; it first appeared in* Technology Review *in 1980. In vitro technology has advanced considerably since Hubbard first published this article. In fact, the procedure has provoked strong reactions to announcements regarding the recent work being done with embryos. Even though fertility technology has become more complex, the initial questions and dilemmas pointed out by Hubbard—in particular the concerns of the women undergoing the treatment and the human beings produced as a result—have not been sufficiently addressed. Hubbard's other writings include* Women Look at Biology Looking at Women *(1979), edited with Mary Sue Henifen and Barbara Fried;* Genes and Gender II: Pitfalls in Research on Sex and Gender *(1979), edited with Marian Lowe; and* Nature: Rationalizations of Inequality *(1983). In her most recent work (written with her son Elijah Wald),* Exploding the Gene Myth *(1993), Hubbard expresses her deep concern over the misuse of genetics.*

Questions to Consider

☐ Before reading Hubbard's essay, consider your own knowledge and opinions about test-tube babies. How much do you know about the subject? How did you acquire your knowledge? Do you consider in vitro or other fertility procedures as having relevance to you personally?

☐ Notice Hubbard's definition of infertility presented in the second paragraph. As you read, consider why she provided this particular definition. Can you think of an alternative definition?

I N vitro fertilization of human eggs and the implantation of early embryos into women's wombs are new biotechnologies that may enable some women to bear children who have hitherto been unable to do so. In that sense, it may solve their particular infertility problems. On the other hand, this technology poses unpredictable hazards since it intervenes in the process of fertilization, in the first cell divisions of the fertilized egg, and in the implantation of the embryo into the uterus. At present we have no way to assess in what ways and to what extent these interventions may affect the women or the babies they acquire by this procedure. Since the use of the technology is only just beginning, the financial and technical investments it represents are still modest. It is therefore important that we, as a society, seriously consider the wisdom of implementing and developing it further.

According to present estimates, about 10 million Americans are infertile by the definition that they have tried for at least a year to achieve pregnancy without conceiving or carrying a pregnancy to a live birth. In about a third of infertile couples, the incapacity rests with the woman only, and for about a third of these women the problem is localized in the fallopian tubes (the organs that normally propel an egg from the ovary to the uterus or womb). These short, delicate tubes are easily blocked by infection or disease. Nowadays the most common causes of blocked tubes are inflammations of the uterine lining brought on by IUDs, pelvic inflammatory disease, or gonorrhea. Once blocked, the tubes are difficult to reopen or replace, and doctors presently claim only a one-in-three success rate in correcting the problem. Thus, of the 10 million infertile people in the country, about 600 thousand (or 6 percent) could perhaps be helped to pregnancy by in vitro fertilization. (These numbers are from Barbara Eck Menning's *Infertility: A Guide for the Childless Couple.* Prentice-Hall, 1977. Ms. Menning is executive director of Resolve, a national, nonprofit counseling service for infertile couples located in Belmont, Mass.)

Louise Brown, born in England in July, 1978, is the first person claimed to have been conceived in vitro. Since then, two other babies conceived outside the mother are said to have been born—one in England, the other in India. In none of these cases have the procedures by which the eggs were obtained from the woman's ovary, fertilized, stored until implantation, and finally implanted in her uterus been described in any detail. However, we can deduce the procedures from animal experimentation and the brief published accounts about the three babies.

The woman who is a candidate for in vitro fertilization has her hormone levels monitored to determine when she is about to ovulate. She is then admitted to the hospital and the egg is collected in the following way: a small cut is made in her abdomen; a metal tube containing an optical arrangement that allows the surgeon to see the ovaries and a narrow-bore tube (called a micropipette) are inserted through the cut; and the egg is removed shortly before it would normally be shed from the ovary. The woman is ready to go home within a day, at most.

When the procedure was first developed, women were sometimes given hormones to make them "superovulate"—produce more than one egg (the usual number for most women). But we do not know whether this happened with the mothers of the three "test-tube" babies that have been born. Incidentally, this superovulation reportedly is no longer induced, partly because some people believe it is too risky.

After the egg has been isolated, it is put into a solution that keeps it alive and nourishes it, and is mixed with sperm. Once fertilized, it is allowed to go through a few cell divisions and so begin its embryonic development—the still-mysterious process by which a fertilized egg becomes a baby. The embryo is then picked up with another fine tube, inserted through the woman's cervix, and flushed into the uterus.

If the uterus is not at the proper stage to allow for implantation (approximately 17 to 23 days after the onset of each menstruation) when the embryo is ready to be implanted, the embryo must be frozen and stored until the time is right in a subsequent menstrual cycle. Again, we do not know whether the embryos were frozen and stored prior to implantation with the two British babies; we are told that the Indian one was.

In sum, then, there is a need, and there is a technology said to meet that need. But as a woman, a feminist, and a biologist, I am opposed to using it and developing it further.

Health Risks

As a society, we do not have a very good track record in anticipating the problems that can arise from technological interventions in complicated biological systems. Our physical models are too simpleminded and have led to many unforeseen problems in the areas of pest control, waste disposal, and other aspects of what is usually referred to as the ecological crisis.

In reproductive biology, the nature of the many interacting processes is poorly understood. We are in no position to enumerate or describe the many reactions that must occur at just the right times during the early stages of embryonic development when the fertilized egg begins to divide into increasing numbers of cells, implants itself in the uterus, and establishes the pattern for the different organ systems that will allow it to develop into a normal fetus and baby.

The safety of this in vitro procedure cannot be established in animal experiments because the details and requirements of normal embryonic development are different for different kinds of animals. Nor are the criteria of "normalcy" the same for animals and for people. The guinea pigs of the research and implementation of in vitro fertilization will be:

- the women who donate their eggs,
- the women who lend their wombs (who, of course, need not be the same as the egg-donors; rent-a-wombs clearly are an option), and
- the children who are produced.

The greatest ethical and practical questions arise with regard to the children. They cannot consent to be produced, and we cannot know what hazards their production entails until enough have lived out their lives to allow for statistical analysis of their medical histories.

This example shows the inadequacy of our scientific models because it is not obvious how to provide "controls," in the usual scientific sense of the term, for the first generation of "test-tube" individuals; they will be viewed as "special" at every critical juncture in their lives. When I ask myself whether I would want to be a "test-tube person," I know that I would not like to have to add *those* self-doubts to my more ordinary repertory of insecurities.

A concrete example of a misjudgment with an unfortunate outcome that could not be predicted was the administration of the chemical thalidomide, a "harmless tranquilizer" touted as a godsend and prescribed to pregnant women, which resulted in the births of thousands of armless and legless babies. Yet there the damage was visible at birth and the practice could be stopped, though not until after it had caused great misery. But take the case of the hormone DES (diethyl stilbesterol), which was prescribed for pregnant women in the mistaken (though at the time honest) belief that it could prevent miscarriages. Some 15 years passed before many of the daughters of these women developed an unusual form of vaginal cancer. Both these chemicals produced otherwise rare diseases, so the damage was easy to detect and its causes could be sought. Had the chemicals produced more common symptoms, it would have been much more difficult to detect the damage and to pinpoint which drugs were harmful.

The important point is that both thalidomide and DES changed the environment in which these babies developed—in ways that could not have been foreseen and that we still do not understand. This happened because we know very little about how embryos develop. How then can we claim to know that the many chemical and mechanical manipulations of eggs, sperms, and embryos that take place during in vitro fertilization and implantation are harmless?

A Woman's Right?

The push toward this technology reinforces the view, all too prevalent in our society, that women's lives are unfulfilled, or indeed worthless, unless we bear children. I understand the wish to have children, though I also know many people—women and men—who lead happy and fulfilled lives without them. But even if one urgently wants a child, why must it be biologically one's own? It is not worth opening the hornet's nest of reproductive technology for the privilege of having one's child derive from one's own egg or sperm. Foster and adoptive parents are much needed for the world's homeless children. Why not try to change the American and international practices that make it difficult for people who want children to be brought together with children who need parents?

Advocates of this new technology argue that every woman has a right to bear a child and that the technology will extend this right to a group previously denied it. It is important to examine this argument and to ask in what sense women have a "right" to bear children. In our culture, many women are taught from childhood that we must do without lots of things we want—electric trains, baseball mitts, perhaps later an expensive education or a well-paying job. We are also taught to submit to all sorts of social restrictions and physical dangers—we cannot go out alone at night, we allow ourselves to be made self-conscious at the corner drugstore and to be molested by strangers or bosses or family members without punching them as our brothers might do. We are led to believe that we must put up with all this—and without grousing—because as women we have something beside which everything else pales, something that will make up for everything: we can have babies! To grow up paying all the way and then to be denied that child *is* a promise unfulfilled; that's cheating.

But I would argue that to promise children to women by means of an untested technology—that is being tested only as it is used on them and their babies—is adding yet another wrong to the burdens of our socialization. Take the women whose fallopian tubes have been damaged by an infection provoked by faulty IUDs. They are now led to believe that problems caused by one risky, though medically approved and administered, technology can be relieved by another, much more invasive and hazardous technology.

I am also concerned about the extremely complicated nature of the technology. It involves many steps, is hard to demystify, and requires highly skilled professionals. There is no way to put control over this technology into the hands of the women who are going to be exposed to it. On the contrary, it will make women and their babies more dependent than ever upon a high-technology, super-professionalized medical system. The women and their babies must be monitored from before conception until birth, and the children will have to be observed all their lives. Furthermore, the pregnancy-monitoring technologies themselves involve hazard. From the start, women are locked into subservience to the medical establishment in a way that I find impossible to interpret as an increase in reproductive freedom, rights, or choices.

Health Priorities

The final issue—and a major one—is that this technology is expensive. It requires prolonged experimentation, sophisticated professionals, and costly equipment. It will distort our health priorities and funnel scarce resources into a questionable effort. The case of the Indian baby is a stark illustration, for in that country, where many children are dying from the effects of malnutrition and poor people have been forcibly sterilized, expensive technologies are being pioneered to enable a relatively small number of well-to-do people to have their own babies.

In the United States, as well, many people have less-than-adequate access to such essential health resources as decent jobs, food and housing, and medical care when they need it. And here, too, poor women have been and are still being forcibly sterilized and otherwise coerced into *not* having babies, while women who can pay high prices will become guinea pigs in the risky technology of in vitro fertilization.

In vitro fertilization is expensive and unnecessary in comparison with many pressing social needs, including those of children who need homes. We must find better and less risky solutions for women who want to parent but cannot bear children of their own.

Discussion Questions

1. Identify Hubbard's thesis and notice where she states it. What kind of argument does she present (deductive, inductive, or other)?

2. Why do you think Hubbard describes herself as "a woman, a feminist, and a biologist" when she states outright that she is opposed to using and developing in vitro fertilization techniques?

3. One of Hubbard's arguments against developing the in vitro fertilization technology is that it makes women even more dependent on institutionalized medicine than they already are. Do you agree? Do you think Hubbard clearly and convincingly supports this point? Support your judgment.

4. As with any expensive and risky health procedure, the cost of in vitro fertilization is high. Should this procedure be routinely covered by health insurance? Keeping in mind that any money spent on fertility research is money not spent on some other type of health research, explain why you do, or do not, believe that fertility research deserves extensive funding. Who should decide where medical research dollars are allocated: politicians, research institutes, insurance companies, physicians, or voters?

Journal Entry

Do all women have the "right" to bear children? Should technology be used to ensure that right? Explore your thoughts in your journal.

Writing Projects

1. Analyze how this essay does, or does not, conform to the conventions of a research report in terms of organization, reference to sources, use of professional jargon, amount of definition and detail provided, and other relevant features.

2. Writing as a representative of women who are unable to bear children without in vitro fertilization and whose opportunities to adopt a child are limited, respond to Hubbard's arguments with your own arguments in favor of in vitro fertilization.

3. Since this article was published in 1980, some of the problems Hubbard forecasted have materialized. Developments in the area of in vitro fertilization have raised additional concerns. Conduct your own research into the scientific developments made since the publication of Hubbard's article. Analyze your research findings and consider the social as well as ethical dimensions of this fertility procedure. Report and interpret your findings and conclusions for a female audience.

Collaborative Project

In vitro fertilization has been the subject of various forums: articles in all kinds of publications, daytime television talk shows, even movies. Working with a partner, select two of these forums and write a comparison of their treatments. Focus your discussion on the differences in content and style of presentation between the two forums.

Carol Tavris

The Manufacture of "PMS"

Carol Tavris *(b. 1944) has written extensively on a variety of topics. Her nonfiction works include* The Longest War: Sex Differences in Perspective *(with Carol Wade, 1977);* Anger, the Misunderstood Emotion *(1982); and* The Mismeasure of Woman *(1992), from which the following essay is taken. The title of Tavris's book,* The Mismeasure of Woman, *alludes to Stephen Jay Gould's book,* The Mismeasure of Man *(see the author headnote in Chapter 3), in which he confronts those who abuse scientific knowledge in the interest of a racist political agenda. Tavris seeks to expose the prevalent bias in scientific research that tries to demonstrate that the physical and psychological suffering associated with the menstrual cycle stems from women's physiological nature. By labeling premenstrual tension as a syndrome or disease, medical researchers simultaneously promote sexist stereotypes and allow women to be stigmatized and drug companies and gynecologists to make money.*

Questions to Consider

☐ Judging from the title of this essay, to whom does Tavris wish to speak?

☐ Consider Tavris's opening sentence: "Let's start by trying to identify the problem." What is the style and tone of this sentence? As you read, evaluate the method Tavris uses to identify the problem.

LET'S start by trying to identify the problem. A small percentage of women report having particularly difficult emotional symptoms associated with the premenstrual phase. Some describe severe Jekyll-and-Hyde-like personality changes that recur cyclically and predictably. In my lifetime of knowing hundreds of women, I have never met such a Jekyll-and-Hyde-like female. But there is something compelling about the testimony of women themselves and of researchers who have observed their behavior clinically. A woman in one study described herself this way:

> Something seems to snap in my head. I go from a normal state of mind to anger, when I'm really nasty. Usually I'm very even tempered, but in these times it is as if someone else, not me, is doing all this, and it is very frightening.[1]

A larger percentage of women describe premenstrual mood changes, notably depression and irritability, that they swear occur as predictably as ragweed in spring. "Unbeknownst to me, my husband kept track of my irritability days in his office diary," one friend reports, "and he could predict like clockwork when I was within a week of my period."

Which group has the premenstrual syndrome? The Jekyll-and-Hyde phenomenon reflects an abnormality in degree, kind, and severity of symptoms. But many researchers, the media, and women themselves now confuse mood changes that are abnormal and occur in *few* women with mood changes that are normal for *all* women – and, as it turns out, for all men, too.

This confusion is apparent in virtually all contemporary discussions of PMS in the media. Most of the media today regard PMS as if it were a clearly defined disorder that most, if not all, women "suffer." For example, *Science News* called it "the monthly menace," and the *Orange County Register* called it "an internal earthquake." An article in *Psychology Today* began: "Premenstrual Syndrome (PMS) remains as baffling to researchers as it is troublesome to women." *Troublesome?* To *all* women, as implied? The article turns out to be about a study of 188 nursing students and tea factory workers in China. In the tea factory, "almost 80% suffered from PMS." *Suffered?* "Overall, nearly 74% rated their symptoms as mild, 24% as moderate and 3% said they were severe." In other words, for 97 percent of the women the symptoms of this "syndrome" were no big deal.

Likewise, an article in the *Baltimore Sun*, headlined "Why PMS Triggers Hunger," begins by asking "Why is it so hard to diet when you're suffering from premenstrual syndrome?" (There we are "suffering" again.) The answer turns out to have nothing at all to do with PMS, or, for that matter, with suffering. According to the research, women feel hungrier in the few days before menstruation because their metabolism has increased. This is normal, the article states: "Your body is working as it should, building up the uterine lining . . ." Working as it should? Then why am I suffering from a syndrome?

It's easy to understand the media's confusion, because the list of symptoms thought to characterize "PMS" doesn't leave much out. One popular paperback book offers a "complete checklist" of physical, behavioral, and emotional changes, including weight gain, eye diseases, asthma, nausea, blurred vision, skin disorders and lesions, joint pains, headaches, backaches, general pains, epilepsy, cold sweats and hot flashes, sleeplessness, forgetfulness, confusion, impaired judgment, accidents, difficulty concentrating, lowered school or work performance, lethargy, decreased efficiency, drinking or eating too much, mood swings, crying and depression, anxiety, restlessness, tension, irritability, and loss of sex drive.[2] That's just for starters. Other alleged symptoms include allergies, alcoholism, anemia, low self-esteem, problems with identity, and cravings for chocolate. Some physicians have specified as many as *150* different symptoms.

Mercy! With so many symptoms, accounting for most of the possible range of human experience, who wouldn't have "PMS"? Obviously, the more symptoms that are listed, the more likely that someone will have them, at least sometimes. This likelihood is increased in checklists that include mutually contradictory symptoms (such as "was less interested in sex" *and* "was more sexually active," or "had less energy" *and* "couldn't sit still") and the entire range of negative emotions ("irritable or angry," "sad or lonely," "anxious or nervous").[3] On these lists, there is no way you can't have some symptoms.

Because researchers themselves don't agree on whether they are talking about a problem that a few women experience or that all women experience, estimates of the prevalence of the syndrome range from 5 percent (women who are severely incapacitated) to 95 percent (the number of women who will experience, as one article put it, "one or more PMS symptoms sometime in their lives"). In one typical conference on "PMS—an important and widespread problem," sponsored by England's Royal Society of Medicine Services, participating physicians tried to determine the scope of the "widespread problem." One thought it affected "between 20% and 40% of women at some stage in their lives." Another said that "a very large proportion of women are aware of cyclical physical and mood changes, but probably fewer than 5% of them are sufficiently moved by these symptoms to seek medical help." A third said that "Probably all women at some time in their lives have disturbing premenstrual symptoms . . . [but only] 5–10% of women have clear-cut PMS."[4]

It's heartening to know, I suppose, how many experts are worried about the cost to the economy of all those millions and millions of sick women whose premenstrual symptoms keep them from doing whatever work they do. One newspaper reported that "PMS-related absenteeism is estimated to have cost industry $5 billion in 1979 . . . not counting women who are working but who aren't functioning as well because of PMS." A physician writing in the *Wall Street Journal* estimated that "the illness [of PMS] costs U.S. industry 8% of its total wage bill."[5] This is no wonder, because so many PMS symptoms interfere with a woman's ability to work: she suffers from "confusion," "has trouble concentrating," and is "forgetful," "uncoordinated," and "inefficient." Some PMS guidebooks advise women to turn to routine tasks at that time of the month, and leave the really hard thinking work to later. Most of the women I know couldn't afford this luxury.

In short, everywhere you look, you find agreement that PMS is a real disorder, a disease. There's a widespread sickness among women! Up to half of all women are sick every month! Nearly all of us are sick sometimes! We're slowing down the economy! How fortunate that men are running things!

Luckily, help is at hand, because PMS cures are a thriving business. Across the country, nutritionists, psychologists, nurses, physicians, and writers are promoting books, tapes, and seminars. (One typical tape, "PMS: A positive program to gain control," promises to help all those uncontrollable premenstrual women get hold of themselves.) Physicians are setting up PMS

Medical Groups, some funded by drug companies, for the specific treatment of premenstrual syndrome and, according to the promotion letter of one such center, its "disabling psychological symptoms [including] depression, mood swings, irritability, confusion, agoraphobia, panic attacks and alcoholism."[6] Many products have appeared to help women manage all these disabling symptoms. Good old Midol, "the menstrual specialist™," now offers Midol PMS, "the premenstrual specialist™." A product redundantly called "prēmsyn PMS" consists of "premenstrual syndrome caplets" which the sufferer is to "take at the first sign of PMS." These products consist of acetaminophen (an aspirin substitute, used in Tylenol), pamabrom (a diuretic), and pyrilamine maleate (a common ingredient in all pain relievers).

Natural remedies for PMS are equally popular. The health and nutrition magazines have jumped on the PMS bandwagon uncritically, offering medical, psychological, and homeopathic treatments for their confused, depressed premenstrual readers who are phobically stuck at home, drinking too much and shouting at the children. Health magazines have frequent news notes and features on PMS. "It *is* true that few women feel at their best during PMS," one item proclaimed, with no evidence for this assertion whatsoever; it went on to describe a study of sixty "PMS sufferers" who benefited from Vitamin E. Another report, titled "New Study Strengthens Link Between Caffeine and PMS," acknowledged that the "causes of PMS are not completely understood" and that "a cause-and-effect relationship between caffeine and PMS has not been firmly established." Nevertheless the article recommended that women stop drinking coffee and tea when they are premenstrual.[7]

In a nutrition magazine called *Delicious!*, the infelicitously named Jeffrey Bland, described as a "nutritional biochemist," advises women on how to "Break the cycle of monthly discomfort." Bland thinks that Judy Garland, Mary Todd Lincoln, and Queen Victoria were all victims of PMS—a rather cavalier reduction of their complicated and difficult lives to the menstrual cycle. (Retrospective diagnoses of famous people are easy, after all, since the "sufferers" can't object.) Undeterred by the lack of scientific validity regarding the variety and prevalence of symptoms, Bland has divided PMS into four subclasses and somehow calculated the alleged proportions of "PMS sufferers" in each one, offering the appropriate nutritional treatments for each. "PMS C" types, for example (for "craving"), should take Vitamin B-6, zinc, and vitamin C to control their "cravings" for sweets or salty foods.[8] Other *Delicious!* remedies include anemone pulsatilla, which may "relieve symptoms of weepiness and emotional sensitivity." Headlines in nutrition newsletters and magazines tell the story:

☐ "Premenstrual syndrome: coping with the enigma" (*Mayo Clinic Nutrition Letter*)
☐ "Pasta and potatoes prescribed for PMS" (*the Edell Health Letter*)
☐ "Oh! those menstrual blues: how to fight back" (*Teen Magazine*)

☐ "Nutrient therapy relieves pain of PMS" (*Better Nutrition*)
☐ "PMS? Let 'em eat carbs" (*Vegetarian Times*)

Perhaps these nutritionists should read *Cooking Light* magazine, which admitted that "No scientific evidence shows that any food, nutritional supplement, vitamin, or mineral effectively combats PMS." It couldn't resist adding, however, that "Many women are able to control their symptoms of premenstrual syndrome with proper diet, stress management, and regular exercise."[9] Jeffrey Bland, for one, agrees. Exercise, diet, and stress-reduction programs "may help many women reach their potential," he writes patronizingly, "– every day." So would a good job.

How did women manage before they knew they had a premenstrual syndrome? The story of how we got from then to now is an illuminating tale, for the idea that menstruation is a debilitating condition that makes women unfit for work has its own cycle: It comes and goes in phase with women's participation in the labor market.

In 1931, a gynecologist named Robert T. Frank created the term "Premenstrual Tension" in an article he published in *The Archives of Neurology and Psychiatry*. "The group of women to whom I refer," wrote Frank, "especially complain of a feeling of indescribable tension from ten to seven days preceding menstruation which, in most instances, continues until the time that the menstrual flow occurs. These patients complain of unrest, irritability, 'like jumping out of their skin' and a desire to find relief by foolish and ill considered actions."[10] Frank was concerned about the consequences of these ill-considered actions in the work force, because "employers of labor," he said, must "make provision for the temporary care of their employees," and some women suffer such severe symptoms that a couple of days of bed rest are necessary.

Before we evaluate what Frank was saying, let us consider when he was saying it. "It strikes me as exceedingly significant," observes anthropologist Emily Martin, "that Frank was writing immediately after the Depression, at a time when the gains women had made in the paid labor market because of World War I were slipping away."[11] It strikes me as significant, too, especially after reading Martin's account of how research findings about menstruation change over time, corresponding to women's role in the work force. At the start of World War II, for example, studies suddenly found that menstruation and "premenstrual tension" were not problems for working women. One researcher, who wrote in 1934 that menstruation was debilitating, changed her mind after the war began: "Any activity that may be performed with impunity at other times," she wrote in 1944, "may be performed with equal impunity during menstruation."[12]

But after World War II, the news changed again. The real mover and shaker on behalf of PMS was Katharina Dalton, a British physician, who throughout the 1950s wrote articles on the dangers of menstruation: "Effect of Menstruation on Schoolgirls' Weekly Work," "Menstruation and Crime," "Menstruation and Accidents," "Menstruation and Acute Psychiatric Illness," "The Influence of Mother's Menstruation on Her Child." Reading these articles is enough to make you agree that a person who menstruates is unfit to be a mother.

In the early 1950s, Dalton and a colleague coined the term "premenstrual syndrome" (to include all those women who had more symptoms than simply premenstrual tension), and in 1964 she published a book, *The Premenstrual Syndrome.*[13] The term stuck like lint. In the ensuing decades, PMS became an increasingly hot research topic, as I learned by doing a computer search:

Number of articles in medical and psychological journals on "PMS," Premenstrual Syndrome, and Premenstrual Tension, 1964 through 1989. (This list *omits* other menstrual-cycle research that did not use these terms or categories.)

	NUMBER OF ARTICLES IN:	
YEARS	MEDICAL JOURNALS	PSYCHOLOGICAL JOURNALS
1964	1	–
1965	16	–
1966–1967	67	8
1968–1969	84	9
1970–1971	74	5
1972–1973	87	9
1974–1975	114	16
1976–1977	146	20
1978–1979	128	16
1980–1981	148	25
1982–1983	187	36
1984–1985	218	77
1986–1987	260	107
1988–1989	305	120

As this table shows, research on PMS erupted in the 1970s, a decade when, as Martin observes, "women had made greater incursions into the paid work force for the first time without the aid of a major war."[14] The growing emphasis on PMS, she argues, fits the pattern of recent history: When women's participation in the labor force is seen as a threat instead of a necessity, menstruation becomes a liability.

The table tells another story as well: the coopting of "PMS" by biomedical researchers. Mary Brown Parlee, a psychologist who has been conducting excellent menstrual-cycle research for many years, observes that psychologists who were studying menstruation tended to focus on normal menstrual cycles. The big money, the big grants, increasingly went to the biomedical researchers, on the assumption that PMS was a disease or a physiological abnormality that was best studied by radioimmunoassays of gonadal hormones and by other new weapons in the medical arsenal.[15]

The move toward the medicalization of PMS was and is actively supported by drug companies, Parlee observes, which stand to make a great deal of money if every menstruating woman would take a few pills every month. Drug companies sponsor research conferences and "medical education" seminars on PMS, events, she says, "for which they actively and effectively seek media coverage."[16] It is to the drug companies' interest, she adds, if physicians and the public confuse the small minority of women who have premenstrual or menstrual problems with the majority who have normal, undrugworthy menstrual cycles.

Because of this confusion, researchers are now reduced to speaking of "clearcut" or "true" PMS to distinguish the small group of women who have severe premenstrual symptoms from those who have normal menstrual changes – and from those who have other disorders. In studies of women who come in or are referred for treatment for PMS and who keep a daily diary of their symptoms over several cycles, three groups emerge: women who have significant premenstrual symptoms but no psychological problems; a group whose major problem is depression, and whose depressive symptoms are aggravated by menstruation; and a group that proves not to have premenstrual problems although they believe they do. Women with a history of emotional disorders are overrepresented in the latter two categories.[17]

By 1987, PMS was enshrined as an official psychiatric disorder in the reference manual of the American Psychiatric Association, *The Diagnostic and Statistical Manual of Mental Disorders*, where it is called Late Luteal Phase Dysphoric Disorder, or LLPDD. LLPDD is supposed to apply to premenstrual symptoms that are severe enough to "seriously interfere with work or with usual social activities or relationships with others."[18] Even for women who have severe symptoms that are unrelated to existing emotional disorders, it is bizarre, and many researchers think detestable, to have such a diagnosis in a manual of *mental disorders*. If LLPDD is a medical condition, why is a psychiatric diagnosis necessary? Thyroid abnormalities cause mood and behavior changes, but we don't consider these physiologically based changes a psychiatric disorder. And if LLPDD reflects a psychological problem, such as depression, why is a medical diagnosis of "late luteal phase disphoric disorder" necessary? We might draw an analogy to a man who suffers from chronic anxiety. Several times a month, he plays racquetball, an exercise that raises his heartbeat and sets off an anxiety attack. The man's problem is anxiety, not racquetball; he does not have Post-Exercising Syndrome.

Because of the evidence of sloppy research and confusion over the prevalence, diversity, and nature of premenstrual changes, LLPDD was relegated to an appendix in the manual, in a section of diagnoses needing "further study." Nevertheless, there it sits, a convenient label for physicians and psychiatrists to use in diagnosing patients and in turn receiving insurance compensation.[19]

In the early 1970s, Parlee published a major review of the research that had been done to date on the effects of the menstrual cycle. She put "PMS" in quotation marks, in order to denote it as an odd or unusual concept that "was purportedly scientific but was not supported by data." In a recent speech she described what happened:

> A copy editor took out all the quotation marks, and with them the meaning I wanted to establish. I lost–was silenced–then in my effort to shape in a small way the scientific discourse about PMS. The processes through which "PMS" has come to mean what it does today are too powerful, too internally and mutually self-sustaining, for that meaning to be affected by the results of good science. . . . People–women, researchers, the media, drug company representatives–now use the term PMS as if it had a clearly understood and shared meaning; the only question is how to help women who "have" it. Thus PMS has become real. The quotation marks have been removed.[20]

Many institutions and individuals now benefit from the concept of PMS. Biomedical researchers, medical schools, and drug companies profit financially. Gynecologists, many of whom have closed their obstetrical services because of malpractice insurance costs, have lost a traditional source of income and are turning to new patient groups and new diagnoses for replenishment. Many psychiatrists have shifted from conducting long-term psychotherapy to prescribing short-term (repeatable) drug treatments. Indeed, obstetricians and psychiatrists are already engaged in turf wars over who is best suited to diagnose and treat all those women with premenstrual symptoms.

But the success of PMS is not entirely a conspiracy of big institutions, although, as Parlee says, if PMS didn't exist as a "psychologically disturbing, socially disruptive, biologically caused disease" they would have needed to invent it. (They did.) We must also ask why so many women have responded so favorably to the term and use it so freely. Parlee suggests that "the language of 'PMS' is a means by which many women can have their experiences of psychological distress, or actions they do not understand, validated as 'real' and taken seriously."[21] In that sense the language of PMS is empowering for women, she believes, because it gives a medical and social reality to experiences that were previously ignored, trivialized, or misunderstood.

Like all psychological diagnoses, then, PMS cuts two ways: It validates women, but it also stigmatizes them. Psychiatrist Leslie Hartley Gise directs a PMS program at Mt. Sinai Hospital in New York, yet she too is worried about the stigmatizing effects of making PMS a psychiatric diagnosis. "If even the rumor that Michael Dukakis had undergone treatment for depression could be held against him," Gise told an interviewer, "think of what a PMS diagnosis would mean for a woman seeking public office."[22] We've come full circle.

NOTES

1. Woman interviewed by Emily Martin, 1987, p. 132.

2. Judy Lever and Michael G. Brush, *Pre-menstrual Tension* (New York: Bantam, 1981).

3. For example, see "A Nightly Checklist for PMS," *American Health*, December 1989, p. 58.

4. The debate on nature and prevalence of "PMS" symptoms is in Fisher, 1987, pp. 1–2.

5. Cited in Peele, 1989, p. 141, and in Golub, 1988.

6. From an (undated) publicity letter to health professionals written by Joseph T. Martorano, M.D., Director of the "P.M.S. Medical Group: A Center for the Treatment of Premenstrual Syndrome" in New York. The letter announces that "PMS MEDICAL GROUP has been effectively treating thousands of women." That's a lot of sick women.

7. News item on Vitamin E, "The Oil of Relief," *American Health*, April 1988; on caffeine, "A Cuppa Trouble?", October 1989.

8. Jeffrey Bland, "Break the Cycle of Monthly Discomfort," *Delicious!*, March 1988, pp. 10–12.

9. "Relief for PMS Symptoms," *Cooking Light*, March/April 1988, p. 19.

10. Frank, 1931, p. 1054. On the concern of employers, p. 1053.

11. Martin, 1987, p. 118.

12. G. H. Seward's 1944 paper, "Psychological Effects of the Menstrual Cycle on Women Workers," quoted in Martin, 1987, p. 120.

13. Actually, Greene and Dalton introduced the term "premenstrual syndrome" in 1953, as an improvement over Frank's "premenstrual tension"; they wanted, they said, "to prevent missing the diagnosis when tension was absent or overshadowed by a more serious complaint." While acknowledging that "PMS covers a wide spectrum from normality to gross abnormality," Dalton nevertheless argues that "PMS does exist and has only one definition: it is a syndrome needing treatment." (Dalton, 1987, p. 135.)

14. Martin, 1987, p. 120. See also Laws, 1983, who argues that the emphasis on PMS was a direct response to the challenges of feminism; and Anne Fausto-Sterling (1985), among the first to sound the alarm against the growing PMS bandwagon.

15. Mary Brown Parlee, "The Science and Politics of PMS Research." Invited address presented at the annual meeting of the Association for Women in Psychology, Newport, R.I., 1989. See also Parlee, 1987.

16. Parlee, 1989. (See Note 15.)

17. See for example DeJong et al., 1985; Hammarback and Backstrom, 1989.

18. American Psychiatric Association, 1987, p. 369.

19. There is considerable confusion, among researchers and clinicians, as to whether PMS and LLPDD are the same or even related phenomena. Some researchers consider LLPDD to be a subset of the more severe symptoms of PMS; others think that PMS simply refers to normal menstrual changes, whereas LLPDD is a distinct disorder; others think the two labels refer to the same phenomenon. In practice, however, most of the studies attempting to confirm LLPDD as a diagnostic category use the same measures as studies of PMS do; and they lack criteria for degree of symptom severity, let alone criteria of "interference with work or relationships."

20. Parlee, 1989. (See Note 15.) The original paper she is referring to is Parlee, 1973.

21. Ibid.

22. Quoted in Lynn Payer, "Hell Week," *Ms.*, March 1989, pp. 28–31. Quote on p. 28.

REFERENCES

American Psychiatric Association (1987). *Diagnostic and statistical manual of mental disorders, Third Edition, Revised.* Washington, D.C.: American Psychiatric Association.

Dalton, Katharina (1987). What is this PMS? In M. R. Walsh (Ed.), *The psychology of women: Ongoing debates.* New Haven, CT: Yale University Press.

DeJong, R.; Rubinow, D. R.; Roy-Byrne, P.; Hoban, M. C.; Grover, G. N.; & Post, R. M. (1985). Premenstrual mood disorder and psychiatric illness. *American Journal of Psychiatry,* 142, 1359–1361.

Fausto-Sterling, Anne (1985). *Myths of gender: Biological theories about women and men.* New York: Basic Books.

Fisher, Hyman W. (Ed.) (1987). *The premenstrual syndrome.* London: Royal Society of Medicine Services.

Frank, Robert T. (1931). The hormonal causes of premenstrual tension. *Archives of Neurology and Psychiatry,* 26, 1053–1057.

Golub, Sharon (1988). A developmental perspective. In L. H. Gise (Ed.), *The premenstrual syndromes.* New York: Churchill Livingstone.

Greene, Raymond, & Dalton, Katharina (1953). The premenstrual syndrome. *British Medical Journal,* 1, 1007–1014.

Hammarback, S., & Backstrom, T. (1989). A demographic study in subgroups of women seeking help for premenstrual syndrome. *Acta Obstetrics & Gynecology Scandinavia,* 68, 247–253.

Laws, Sophie (1983). The sexual politics of pre-menstrual tension. *Women's Studies International Forum,* 6, 19–31.

Martin, Emily (1987). *The woman in the body: A cultural analysis of reproduction.* Boston: Beacon.

Parlee, Mary B. (1973). The premenstrual syndrome. *Psychological Bulletin,* 80, 454–465.

—— (1987). Media treatment of premenstrual syndrome. In B. E. Ginsburg & B. F. Carter (Eds.), *Premenstrual syndrome.* New York: Plenum.

Peele, Stanton (1989). *Diseasing of America: Addiction treatment out of control.* Lexington, MA: Lexington Books.

Discussion Questions

1. What reasons might Tavris have for trying to expose PMS as a manufactured disease?

2. What point is Tavris making by referring to the language used to describe PMS in newspaper accounts? Are the quotes she uses effective in providing support and illustration for her point? How so, or why not?

3. Why does Tavris distinguish between abnormal mood changes occurring in some women and normal mood changes that most women—as well as men—experience?

4. Do you consider Tavris's use of statistical data effective? Why? What criteria do you use in determining an author's legitimate and informative use of statistics?

5. What does Tavris offer women who experience very real pain each month? She says that the diagnosis of PMS both validates and stigmatizes women. What are the advantages and disadvantages of having a name and a list of recognized symptoms for the condition one is experiencing?

Journal Entry

Whether you are male or female, write about the first information you received regarding menstruation. Where did it come from? How old were you? What was your reaction to the information? If you are female, how do you think that experience influences your current thoughts about your own menstruation? If you are male, how do you think that experience influences the way you feel about women and menstruation in general? How does your knowledge affect your understanding of women?

Writing Projects

1. Write an analysis of Tavris's argument. What methods does she employ, or fail to use, to make a convincing argument? What are the sources of most of her data, and are they reliable? To what extent are her conclusions reasonable and valid?

2. Report on your investigation of both manufactured and natural remedies for PMS. How many different remedies did you find? What did the manufactured ones cost? Were they available without prescription? How many of your women acquaintances experience PMS? (You might consider conducting an informal survey.) What remedies have they used? What success rate do the various remedies have?

Collaborative Projects

1. With a partner, investigate various historical aspects of menstruation and the status of women (in terms of taboos, separation, or uncleanness) in our culture. Offer conclusions about how these attitudes affect modern treatment of PMS. Or the two of you might compare menstruation practices and beliefs in two cultures. Then draw conclusions about how attitudes toward menstruation reflect and determine general societal attitudes and treatment of women throughout the selected cultures.

2. With one or two classmates, jointly research attitudes in the American workplace toward menstruation (particularly PMS), tracing how attitudes have altered during the past thirty years. Write a report on how menstruation-related difficulties have been included in the way female employees have been portrayed. Have women's menstrual cycles been blamed for company problems? Why? Has publicity about PMS been used to prevent women from breaking through the "glass ceiling"?

David L. Wheeler

Scientists Worry about the Implications of Genetic Testing for Inherited Disease

David L. Wheeler *is a reporter for the* Chronicle of Higher Education, *where his primary beat is biomedical research. He received an advanced degree from the Columbia Graduate School of Journalism. Wheeler has won several New England Press Association awards for his coverage of economic and educational issues. His essay here first appeared in the* Chronicle of Higher Education *in August 1993. He aims to show how vulnerable genetic testing results are to misuse. Even when scientists and health care professionals behave responsibly, there are few counselors trained to assist individuals in deciding what to do with the information that genetic testing provides them.*

Question to Consider

☐ Do you think much about diseases you may have inherited? When an older relative becomes seriously ill, do you wonder if you may have inherited that disease gene? Would you take advantage of genetic testing for inherited disease if it were readily available?

A 33-year-old woman, from a family that had frequently been stricken by breast cancer, walked into a physician's office at the University of Michigan and made a dramatic announcement. The woman – call her Ms. X – told the physician, Barbara Weber, that three days later she was scheduled for drastic surgery – "a bilateral radical mastectomy."

"Is there anything you want to tell me?" she asked.

Dr. Weber and other scientists were seeking a genetic basis for the high incidence of breast cancer in Ms. X's family. Ms. X knew there was a chance that the researchers might have discovered if she was at risk for the disease. But if the scientists didn't know whether she carried a breast-cancer gene, she wanted go ahead with the surgery to avoid the suffering that had plagued other women in her family.

Checking the "Pedigree"

Dr. Weber, an assistant professor of internal medicine and the director of breast oncology at the university's hospital, knew that an analysis of the family had just been completed. A team of scientists had found a marker so close to the flawed gene that they knew, with 98 percent certainty, who had the gene and who did not. A genetic family tree, known to scientists as a "pedigree," flashed in Dr. Weber's mind. She was almost certain that Ms. X did not carry the genetic flaw and, after double-checking, told her she was not at risk for the inherited form of the disease.

Ms. X, who was visiting Dr. Weber's office with a sister who was there for chemotherapy, was elated and canceled her surgery. Later, however, she felt guilty that she had escaped the disease that had stricken two sisters and her mother.

The rapid pace of discoveries of the genetic defects that cause disease has raised fears among scientists and physicians that the health-care system is not ready to handle the knowledge it is about to receive.

"I am really concerned about how we are going to handle this on a large scale," says Francis S. Collins, a member of the team studying breast cancer and director of the National Center for Human Genome Research.

Tests already exist for a few disease genes, including the mutations that cause cystic fibrosis, a genetic flaw that one out of 25 Americans is believed to carry. But in 1993 the rate of gene identifications has picked up, particularly for diseases that strike after adolescence. This year alone, scientists have identified genes for Huntington's disease, a relatively rare but devastating neurological disorder, and an inherited form of "Lou Gehrig's disease," or amyotrophic lateral sclerosis.

Scientists have also found markers close to the genes for inherited forms of colon cancer and breast cancer and believe that if their research goes well, they might identify the actual genes within a few months. When a gene is identified, a test for its presence is immediately available.

Although the implications of genetic tests have been discussed for years among small circles of medical ethicists, the prospect of millions of patients' demanding to find out if they are at risk for common forms of cancer now concerns a larger group of scholars and scientists. No one knows how the public, physicians, hospitals, health-insurance companies, and researchers studying families with genetic disorders will react to the widespread availability of genetic tests.

Scientists caution that administering the tests they will find for many afflictions will be appropriate only for those likely to have the inherited forms of the diseases. Those who don't have relatives stricken by the disease probably shouldn't bother to take a test, scientists say. But they fear that even people without a family history of disease might also demand to be tested.

Dr. Collins is urging researchers who work with families that have inherited disease to begin studying how to deliver counseling, testing, and medical care. He and others considering the implications of genetic tests see a few key problems.

One of them is keeping test results confidential in an age when medical records have come close to becoming public. Another is the chance that genetic tests will turn the health-insurance industry upside down: Instead of insuring people against unexpected illness, health insurance could gradually turn into a prepayment plan for medical problems that are on their way. A third difficulty presented by genetic tests, a problem already on the horizon, is a shortage of trained counselors who can talk to patients about the pros and cons of genetic tests and can explain what the results mean.

"It Would Be Tough"

That job isn't always easy. The test for cystic fibrosis, for example, can only detect about 85 percent of the genetic flaws that cause the disease. Parents who test negative could still have a child with the disease.

The country now has about 1,100 genetic counselors, who study for two years and work for one more before they can be certified. But the counselors acknowledge that they wouldn't be able to meet the demand if large numbers of people sought genetic tests. "It would be tough," says Bea Leopold, executive director of the National Society of Genetic Counselors.

Dr. Collins says ways must be found to supplement one-on-one genetic counseling. Health-care professionals may sometimes have to explain genetic tests to groups, he says, and some counselors may have to develop expertise in just one disease. Interactive videodisks, which would allow patients to seek out information pertinent to them, could be used in some situations, he says.

Whatever form the counseling takes, patients will have to be told that it will be difficult to keep their test results completely confidential. That lack of privacy will affect families as well as individuals.

"Genetic tests don't just tell something about you but about your brothers and sisters and children and parents," says Ray Moseley, director of the medical humanities program at the University of Florida and the leader of a study on the effects of genetic testing on health, disability, and life insurance. Genetic tests, for instance, may accidentally prove that a man children call "daddy" isn't really their father.

Access for Insurance Companies

Mr. Moseley says another study showed that about 250 employees in a medium-sized hospital had access to medical records—a number that makes inadvertent disclosure of private information seem likely. He also notes that to be reimbursed for their health care, most Americans routinely sign forms giving health-insurance companies access to all of their medical records, which can include the results of genetic tests.

Under the current system, Mr. Moseley and others who have studied the problem say it is impossible to keep the results of genetic tests out of the hands of insurance companies. The companies may well use that information to drop coverage for those who are at risk for disease. Many physicians believe legislation will be required to make genetic tests confidential and to prevent health-insurance companies from excluding families with inherited disease.

Researchers who study such disease also must guard against breaches of confidentiality. A team of scientists who found a marker for an inherited form of colon cancer, for example, chose, in a paper they published in *Science*, to omit information about which family members carried it. One family in the study was from a rural area in New Zealand and the other was from Newfoundland.

Gloria M. Petersen, an assistant professor of epidemiology at the Johns Hopkins University who worked on the research, says the two families come from small, tight-knit towns where others know they were participating in research. A busybody from those towns could deduce who was who on the published family trees.

So far, even the families participating in the colon-cancer research have not been informed about who has the marker and who does not. Ms. Petersen says that until the exact gene responsible has been identified, the information should not be used as a diagnostic or predictive test, especially since all family members should be getting an annual examination regardless of their status. "I definitely think this is still in the realm of research," she says.

Paul Billings, an assistant clinical professor at the University of California at San Francisco who has studied genetic-testing issues for five years, believes scientists should be concerned about how the information they have gathered might be used. Dr. Billings has used advertisements in medical journals to gather case studies of what he calls "genetic discrimination." He is also writing up the results of a survey of 30,000 people contacted largely through organizations set up to help those with inherited disease.

Well-Founded Fears

Dr. Billings says his studies show that many people do not want to take genetic tests because they either don't want to know the results or believe such tests might make them vulnerable to discrimination by insurance companies, the military, or private employers. Genome-project scientists, he says, often assume that people will be interested in finding out about their genes, but many people may not be.

The fears of discrimination are well founded, Dr. Billings says. "We're not sure how common genetic discrimination is, but the fact that we can detect it with the crude instruments we have been using indicates it is fairly common."

Dr. Billings and his colleagues found that health-insurance companies frequently tell people who have relatives with inherited disease that they must take a genetic test to prove they are not at risk, or they will not be covered under a health-care plan. "This is economic coercion," Dr. Billings says.

Mr. Moseley of the University of Florida says that the federal government's effort to reform the nation's health-care system to guarantee health insurance for everyone may not reduce the problem of forced testing. The reforms, he says, will emphasize preventive health care, and taxpayers and federal officials may not look kindly on those who refuse to take genetic tests that could keep costs down by catching disease in its early stages.

The history of public health, adds Mr. Moseley, is littered with examples of recommended treatments, such as vaccinations, that quickly turn into requirements.

Concern over Preventive Care

Genetic tests also may exacerbate controversies over the best preventive care for particular diseases. In one family studied at the University of Michigan, Dr. Collins says, every adult woman found to be at risk for breast cancer opted for a mastectomy. "Before I got into this field I never thought this step would be so popular," he says. "We did nothing to encourage it."

Physicians disagree over how much tissue needs to be removed to prevent breast cancer and ovarian cancer, and reports have emerged of cancer occurring in remaining tissue even after the breasts or ovaries have been removed. "There are no epidemiological data on risk of breast cancer among women who have had prophylactic mastectomy," writes Mary-Claire King, a professor of molecular and cell biology at the University of California at Berkeley. A double mastectomy, reconstructive surgery, and removing a woman's ovaries to eliminate the risk of ovarian cancer can cost up to $40,000, a sum that many insurance companies may not want to pay.

Despite all the controversies over genetic tests and their potentially negative societal effects, scientists say that the identification of genes should eventually lead to better medical treatments.

The Michigan research team had to tell one woman who had already had a bilateral mastectomy years earlier to avoid breast cancer that she probably wasn't carrying the cancer gene. She ultimately came to terms with the decision she had made, considering the information she had at the time. But when they told another woman in the same family that she probably did have the gene for breast cancer, she agreed to have a mammogram on the same day. A tiny lump was identified, and she had surgery to remove it three days later. If the tumor hadn't been removed, the cancer would have progressed.

"We probably saved her life," says Dr. Collins.

Discussion Questions

1. To what well-known experts does Wheeler refer? To what sources? Based on these, do you consider his argument to be reliable and authoritative?

2. In writing for readers of the *Chronicle of Higher Education*, what assumptions did Wheeler probably make about their level of knowledge as well as interest in this subject? Does he seek mainly to inform, or to caution the reader, or to argue for a course of action?

3. Overall, does Wheeler seem in favor of or opposed to pursuing further advancements in the science of genetic testing? Explain. Do you agree with this stance?

4. What do you consider the most serious implications of genetic testing for inherited disease? Why?

5. Discuss the complications and possible solutions to the nonmedical problems associated with genetic testing that were mentioned by Wheeler. Take, for example, the potential problem of confidentiality. How would anyone guarantee that this information could be kept confidential? Think of other complications.

Journal Entry

Write a dialogue between two siblings who have just undergone genetic testing. One has been told by the physician that he or she has the gene and will most likely get the disease; the other sibling has been given the all-clear. What might these two have to say to each other?

Writing Projects

1. Drawing on your own thoughts and the class response to Discussion Question 4, write an essay exploring the most serious implications of genetic testing. Extend the discussion of problems suggested by Wheeler, or do further reading about additional negative implications that you have identified. Consider also any positive implications that Wheeler failed to mention or to which you believe he gave inadequate consideration.

2. Write an essay analyzing Wheeler's use of narrative in this selection about medical procedures. How do the examples and stories he uses help you to understand the issues involved? Extend your essay to include comparison of Wheeler's brief narratives with the more extensive use of narrative technique evident in a piece of fiction dealing with genetic testing.

Collaborative Project

Wheeler suggests providing patient information on genetic testing through the use of interactive videos (a computer-based video system that allows the user to direct the presentation). Working with a partner, design an interactive video presentation for patient use. Begin by learning how interactive video works. Then identify and organize the most pertinent information, keeping in mind that your audience may have very little knowledge of either the medical procedure or this instructional technology. If the interactive element overcomplicates the project for you, design a presentation for CD-ROM (Compact Disk Read-Only Memory, in which a disk stores information in digital form). Write a script for the program and create a couple of sample visuals.

Randy Shilts

Reunion

Randy Shilts *(1951–1994), prior to his death from AIDS, was a widely read journalist who won numerous awards, such as the Media Alliance Award for outstanding nonfiction author. "Reunion" is excerpted from Shilts' well-known chronicle of the AIDS epidemic,* And the Band Played On *(1987). This lengthy book, which was made into a motion picture by Home Box Office, is both an exposé and a tale of inspiration. Shilts brings to light the perspectives of hundreds of people involved in the issues surrounding AIDS: doctors, scientists, civil rights leaders, politicians, gay activists, and AIDS patients. In the following excerpt Shilts tells how the October 1986 "Surgeon General's Report on Acquired Immune Deficiency Syndrome," by Dr. C. Everett Koop, brought national attention to AIDS as a major health and social issue. Shilts's other books include* The Mayor of Castro Street: The Life and Times of Harvey Milk *(1982) and* Conduct Unbecoming: Gays and Lesbians in the U. S. Military *(1993), which is based on five years of interviews with 1,100 gay service people.*

Questions to Consider

☐ As you read, consider what reaction you think Shilts is hoping to evoke in his readers. What is his purpose?

☐ Notice the author's attitude toward the news media in general, and in particular toward its role in publicizing the need to take action against AIDS.

May 31, 1987
Washington, D.C.

A sticky mugginess hung over Washington the day they arrived. The temperature was trapped in the upper nineties, and the air dense with humidity. Occasionally, lightning flashed and conversation stopped expectantly; thunder lumbered through the heavens, then passed. There was to be no relief.

The heat induced a light nausea among even the most acclimatized natives. For the thousands crowding airport cab stands, shuttle buses, and hotel lobbies that afternoon – the scientists and researchers, public health officials and activists converging on the capital city – the oppression was palpable.

The occasion was the Third International Conference on Acquired Immunodeficiency Syndrome, co-sponsored by the World Health Organization and the U.S. Department of Health and Human Services. Though the conference, a successor to the first international symposium held in Atlanta in 1985, would feature state-of-the-art information on all things AIDS-related, the focus of world attention on this event had less to do with such substance than with the conference's timing. Something had happened in the last two or three months; the epidemic had finally hit home.

Dr. Michael Gottlieb had been correct two years earlier when he stood in that auditorium in Los Angeles and realized that everything would be different for the AIDS epidemic from that day on. It was commonly accepted now, among the people who had understood the threat for many years, that there were two clear phases to the disease in the United States: there was AIDS before Rock Hudson and AIDS after. The fact that a movie star's diagnosis could make such a huge difference was itself a tribute to the power the news media exerted in the latter portion of the twentieth century.

Attention to the epidemic waned only slightly in 1986. There were other celebrity AIDS patients now, but for all the media cachet, the disease remained fundamentally embarrassing. When Broadway's star choreographer-director Michael Bennett fell ill, he maintained he was suffering from heart problems. A spokesman for Perry Ellis insisted the famed clothing designer was dying of sleeping sickness. Lawyer Roy Cohn insisted he had liver cancer, even while he used his political connections to get on an experimental AIDS treatment protocol at the National Institutes of Health Hospital. Conservative fund-raiser Terry Dolan claimed he was dying of diabetes. When Liberace was on his deathbed, a spokesman maintained the pianist was suffering the ill effects of a watermelon diet. As these well-known gay men lied to protect their posthumous public images, it was the first professional athlete to contract AIDS, former Washington Redskin star Jerry Smith, who calmly stepped forward and told the truth.

Even while such stories gave news organizations fresh angles, there was one aspect to the epidemic that continued to elude intelligent investigation: the federal government's role in combating the virus. Congress continued its ritual of force-feeding AIDS funds to a reluctant Reagan administration. Funding levels increased dramatically, but within the executive branch of government, there seemed little excitement about launching anything like a coordinated attack on the disease. Initiatives for development of a vaccine and effective treatments puttered along at their usual speed.

Nor had the federal government launched anything resembling a coordinated AIDS prevention program. In late 1985, the CDC had actually stopped money from being spent on AIDS education when conservatives in the White House worried that the government should not be in the business of telling homosexuals how to have sodomy. Even Dr. James Mason was heard complaining that since he had become CDC director, he found himself talking to complete strangers about sexual acts he would not discuss with his wife even in the privacy of his own home.

Liberal congressional aides struggled to interest reporters in these prosaic stories of federal sluggishness, but the media was unimpressed. Instead, stories dealt with celebrity AIDS cases or schoolchildren with AIDS or laboratory "breakthroughs." Just about every newspaper had also, by now, run a series of profiles following the life of an AIDS patient. And, of course, there were endless stories about the "spread of AIDS among heterosexuals." No hint that the disease might spread to straights, no matter how specious, was too small to put on page one.

Meanwhile, during most of 1986, anxious health officials within the administration desperately tried to turn the media's attention to the more significant story: the message that the AIDS challenge still was not being met. At one point, the Public Health Service held a meeting of its eighty-five top AIDS experts at the Coolfant Conference Center in Berkeley, West Virginia, to make recommendations on federal AIDS policy. Their stunning projections were covered by the press—that in five years the cumulative number of AIDS cases in the United States would be 270,000 and deaths would total 179,000. The recommendations—for massive public education, better coordination of the federal government's AIDS research and a blue-ribbon commission on AIDS to study whether enough money was being spent on research and treatment—were largely ignored.

Four months later, the prestigious Institute of Medicine of the National Academy of Sciences tried to direct the media's attention to the government's performance on AIDS with a 390-page report that called the administration's response to the epidemic "woefully inadequate." The academy report called for a permanent national AIDS commission and the start of coordinated planning, as well as scaling up of AIDS spending to $2 billion annually in research and education. Pointedly, the report also called for "presidential leadership to bring together all elements of society to deal with the problem." Again, congressional aides hoped the blast at the administration might prompt ambitious reporters to investigate the Reagan administration's AIDS efforts. To be sure, every major news organization gave the academy report serious news placement the day after its release, alongside assurances that AIDS was the administration's "number-one health priority." That, however, was the end of any investigation. After a few days, the report faded from the news altogether.

Ultimately, it was a report issued in October 1986 that turned the tale, galvanized the media and allowed AIDS to achieve the critical mass to make it a pivotal social issue in 1987.

Dr. C. Everett Koop had come to President Reagan's attention because of his leading role in the anti-abortion movement. His conservative religious fundamentalism horrified liberal, feminist, and gay leaders who had fiercely opposed his nomination as surgeon general in 1981. The administration prevailed, however, and few in the White House inner circle had any trepidations when Reagan went to the Hubert Humphrey Building the day after his 1986 State of the Union speech and asked Koop to write a report on the AIDS epidemic.

Koop spent much of 1986 interviewing scientists, health officials, and even suspicious gay community leaders. Once the text was prepared, he took the unusual step of having tens of thousands of copies printed – without letting the White House see it in advance. When Koop went public with the report, it was clear why. The "Surgeon General's Report on Acquired Immune Deficiency Syndrome" was a call to arms against the epidemic, complete with marching orders. For one of the first times, the problem of AIDS was addressed in purely public health terms, stripped of politics. AIDS education, Koop wrote, "should start at the earliest grade possible" for children. He bluntly advocated widespread use of condoms. Compulsory identification of virus carriers and any form of quarantine would be useless in fighting the disease, Koop concluded.

The surgeon general's research also had led him to some inescapable conclusions about AIDS antibody testing, which continued to be a controversial issue. Mandatory testing would do little more than frighten away from the public health establishment the people most at risk for AIDS, the people who most needed to be tested, Koop said. He reiterated what health officers had been saying for nearly two years – large-scale testing would not be feasible until people did not have to worry about losing their jobs or insurance policies if they took the test. A push for more testing should be accompanied by guarantees of confidentiality and nondiscrimination, Koop said.

Such safeguards proved an anathema to conservatives, who viewed them as coddling homosexuals. In California, conservative Republican Governor George Deukmejian vetoed anti-discrimination legislation for people with AIDS or the AIDS virus, not once but twice in 1986 alone. Koop, however, saw such laws as tools with which the epidemic could be fought.

The report proved an immediate media sensation. The calls for sex education and condom use at last gave journalists something titillating on which to hang their stories. This wasn't some tedious call for a blue-ribbon commission or bureaucratic coordination, this was about rubbers and sex education. At last, there was also a sensible explanation about why compulsory AIDS testing wasn't such a good idea. Uncorrupted by the language of AIDSpeak, Koop was able to talk in a way that made sense; at last, there was a public health official who sounded like a public health official. Not only that, he was able to utter words like "gay" without visibly flinching.

Koop's impact was due to archetypal juxtaposition. It took a square-jawed, heterosexually perceived actor like Rock Hudson to make AIDS something people could talk about. It took an ultra-conservative fundamentalist who looked like an Old Testament prophet to credibly call for all of America to take the epidemic seriously at last.

Unwittingly, the Reagan administration had produced a certifiable AIDS hero. From one corner of the country to the other, AIDS researchers, public health experts, and even the most militant of gay leaders hailed the surgeon general. Koop quickly became so in demand for speeches that he was called a "scientific Bruce Springsteen."

In the broader historical sense, Koop's role in the epidemic was a bit more ambiguous. After all, the surgeon general had managed to maintain a complete silence on the epidemic for over five years. By the time he spoke out, 27,000 Americans already were dead or dying of the disease; Koop's interest was historic for its impact, not its timeliness. There was no denying, however, that the report proved a watershed event in the history of the epidemic, and conservatives were stunned.

Anti-feminist leader Phyllis Schlafly decreed that the sex-ed recommendations represented little more than a call to institute grammar school sodomy classes. Anti-abortion groups went about the business of withdrawing their previous awards to Koop. President Reagan observed his ritualistic silence, though the PHS officials who had approved the report's printing without White House clearance quickly found themselves exiled to bureaucratic Siberia.

In the early weeks of 1987, conservatives retaliated with a call for AIDS testing, lots of it. The call for massive, even compulsory, AIDS testing carried a homophobic tenor; this was AIDSpeak with a new accent. Public health officials who opposed such testing, conservatives intimated, were patsies for homosexual militants. It was, of course, an ironic argument. Despite the early gay politicization of AIDS issues, it was also true just about anything done to fight AIDS for many years—whether in AIDS education or in lobbying for research—had come solely from the gay community. The new conservative concern in the epidemic belied the fact that conservatives had been entirely indifferent to the threat of the spreading pestilence. To be sure, the gay community's own obstructionism to early public health efforts, particularly on issues like bathhouses, had fueled the public conception that gays would flout the public health for their own interests. And public health officials hadn't helped by framing issues politically themselves. The public was used to hearing health officials sound like politicians, so it didn't sound jarring when politicians started talking like they were health officials.

The testing issue allowed conservatives to seize the AIDS issue as their own with rhetoric implicitly arguing that those thoughtless homosexuals were so awful that they should be forced to submit to testing, to protect all the good people who weren't infected with the virus. Public opinion polls showed most Americans favored massive AIDS testing, perhaps because most people were confident they wouldn't test positive for the virus and would not have to suffer the consequences of forced testing policies. With such popular support, conservative political theorists already were talking about what a good issue AIDS would be for Republicans in the next presidential election.

Meanwhile, the rest of the world was awakening to the AIDS threat.

While the disease had been reported in 51 countries in January 1986, by the spring of 1987 there were 113 countries, on every continent except Antarctica, reporting over 51,000 cases. Ultimately, WHO warned, the planet could expect 3 million AIDS cases internationally by 1991.

European countries rushed to provide nationwide educational efforts. English authorities launched a huge campaign of billboards, newspaper advertisements, and television commercials on AIDS education, hammering on one theme: "Don't die of ignorance." Indeed, by early 1987, the only major Western industrialized nation that had not launched a coordinated education campaign was the United States.

The various American controversies over AIDS education and antibody testing continued through the spring. As the international AIDS conference approached, pressure mounted on the Reagan administration. Though Reagan had at last uttered the word AIDS, he still had not given an address on the six-year-old epidemic. By now, his silence was thunderous. Even the hard-bitten White House press corps, which had never considered AIDS a serious issue, clamored for quotes. In his barnstorming for greater AIDS awareness, Dr. Koop met ever more frequently with embarrassing questions about why President Reagan refused to meet with him.

By the beginning of May, public attention forced the Senate, which had been far less active on AIDS issues than the House of Representatives, to pass unanimously a resolution calling on Reagan to appoint a national AIDS commission. The resolution, drafted by Senate Republican leader Senator Robert Dole, drew a remarkable array of Republican and Democratic co-sponsors.

Conservatives were no less anxious for Reagan to take a stand. Education Secretary William Bennett, a leading spokesman for conservatives on AIDS issues, was strident in his calls for mandatory testing and increasingly vocal in his criticism of Koop. Conservative opinion leaders and newspaper columnists joined the chorus; some called for Koop's resignation. Increasingly, all sides wanted to know where the president stood on AIDS.

As the AIDS conference approached, Reagan announced he would accede to the Senate's wishes and appoint an eleven-member presidential commission to advise him on the epidemic, and he would address an AIDS fund-raising dinner on the eve of the conference. By late May, it became clear that this would be more than just another scientific gathering. Here, at the hub of power in the United States, the science, the politics and the people of the AIDS epidemic would come together; these days would be remembered as the prologue to the future course of AIDS in America. The week would be one of those rare times when the past, the present and future converged. And everybody seemed to understand that as they trekked to their Washington hotel rooms on that cloudy, muggy Sunday afternoon.

Discussion Questions

1. How does Shilts's reference to the "sticky mugginess . . . over Washington" in the first sentence and "Washington . . . on that cloudy, muggy Sunday afternoon" in the final sentence create a frame for this account? Is it effective?

2. How does Shilts's description of the oppressiveness of the weather in the opening paragraph reinforce the emotions and attitudes of the people Shilts describes?

3. Why, according to Shilts, was Rock Hudson such a pivotal person in AIDS awareness? Did learning that Rock Hudson had AIDS cause you to view the disease differently?

4. How does Shilts describe the federal government's role, as well as the actions of President Reagan specifically, in fighting AIDS? Consider this sentence: "Initiatives for development of a vaccine and effective treatments puttered along at their usual speed."

Journal Entry

What made AIDS hit home for you? Has anything happened to make you realize that AIDS is not just a threat to someone you don't know but that it could directly affect you or someone close to you?

Writing Projects

1. Write an up-to-date account of the most promising AIDS research being done today. Why does this particular research seem the best? Is the government supporting it? What is needed to further develop this research?

2. Identify one of Shilts's major criticisms toward the government's involvement and support of (or the lack thereof) AIDS research, or AIDS education in the school, workplace, and community. Write a set of possible solutions to the problem. Then write a letter to an official who has the power to implement one of the solutions you offer. State clearly and firmly why and how the changes you propose should be brought about.

Collaborative Project

Working with one or two partners, read the entire book *And the Band Played On*. You could each read one-half or one-third, and summarize your section for the others. Together, write an analysis of the book as a whole to account for its success. What methods did Shilts use to collect his data? How does he interpret his data? Is his analysis of his findings objective or subjective? What are the most powerful parts of the book and why? Look carefully at Shilts's writing style. Does it reflect his training as a journalist, or is it literary?

Making Connections

Questions to Discuss

1. One of the characters in Amy Hempel's story refers to Elisabeth Kübler-Ross's book *On Death and Dying*. What ideas explored by Kübler-Ross enrich your reading of Hempel's story? Based on these writings and your own experience, what do you think we as a culture need to understand or change in order to reach an acceptable way of dealing with the role of medical machines in postponing death without improving health?

2. Carol Tavris uses numerous quotations from newspapers and magazine articles to illustrate how the media affects our understanding of PMS (premenstrual syndrome). What are the similarities and differences between Tavris's use of press references and Dorothy Nelkin's use of them (see Chapter 4)? How successful do you believe these writers are in supporting their theses? What methods do they use to construct effective arguments?

3. What is the potential of "technological fixes" — such as those described by Alvin Weinberg in Chapter 2 — to handle some of the social problems associated with the illness, infertility, and death highlighted by writers in this chapter or elsewhere?

Suggested Writing Projects

1. The excerpt from Randy Shilts's book reveals how politics influences funding for research. Write an essay exploring ways in which health issues and politics often become intertwined in our country, drawing on readings from this chapter to support your claims. Discuss why you think it is, or is not, possible to separate health issues from politics in our society.

2. Write an essay exploring the idea that in order for people to benefit from the latest advances in medical science and technology, they are often required to forfeit some degree of personal autonomy. Support your claims with references to readings in this text. For example, consider the similarities between Ruth Hubbard, who says that in vitro fertilization makes the women who elect it subservient to the medical establishment, and David Wheeler, who points out that genetic testing might place individuals at the mercy of the health care system, including health insurance companies.

3. Carol Tavris and Stephen Jay Gould (see Chapter 3) both seek to demonstrate how scientific research has been used to reinforce stereotypes and stigmatize groups. Write an essay assessing Gould's and Tavris's research methodologies, as well as the writing styles they use to present their research findings. What rhetorical strategies does each use to illustrate the main thesis? In what ways is each most successful? How would you have written these accounts differently? Describe and characterize the authorial voice that lends substance to the structure of each piece.

6

Controlling Nature with Technology

 Oil spills, acid rain, overfishing, destruction of tropical rain forests, depletion of the ozone layer, the greenhouse effect, poisoning of the food chain – all these, and more, reflect the marks humans have made on the environment. These marks provide evidence of our tendency to assume that the earth is ours to plunder for convenience, comfort, and profit. The writers in this chapter believe that such an assumption accounts for today's environmental crisis.

The goal of this chapter is not to solve the problem or outline specific actions, nor is it to lay blame at the feet of individuals or groups. However, the writers presented here *do* seek to identify issues that we must fully understand in order to live responsibly in today's world. A dominant theme of the following selections was fittingly expressed by Aldo Leopold in his *Sand County Almanac* (1966): "We abuse land because we regard it as a commodity belonging to us. When we see land as a community to which we belong, we may begin to use it with love and respect."

The *Exxon Valdez* oil spill in Prince William Sound, Alaska, in 1989 was just one example of the consequences of using the land as a commodity. Who is to blame for that particular environmental nightmare? The captain of the *Exxon Valdez*? The oil companies? The government? Or, as writer Richard Nelson has said, is it all of us as "members of a society that understood the risks and judged them acceptable"? Should we value short-term convenience and monetary profit more than the long-term health of our planet? Even if we agree that certain environmental tragedies should not happen, how are we to change?

Rachel Carson posed such questions, as we see in an excerpt from her landmark book, *Silent Spring* (1962). A master of poetic imagery in prose, Carson exposed the effects of using chemicals to control plants and animals while demonstrating how one concerned, knowledgeable writer can make a difference. Vice President Al Gore agreed with Carson in his book, *Earth in the Balance* (1992). To meet the situation head-on, we must resolve to see the world from an ecological perspective. Gore described it this way: "[It] begins with a view of the whole, an understanding of how the various parts of nature interact in patterns that tend toward balance and persist over time." Gore believes it is essential that we see ourselves as a part of the natural world rather than as separate from it.

Various writers have predicted dire consequences if we continue to upset the balance of nature. For example, Rick DeMarinis's short story "Weeds" presents a darkly comic fable about chemical warfare against plants.

People can be moved to action for various reasons. Sometimes outrage prompts individuals to become committed to an ideology. Joy Williams, in her essay entitled "Save the Whales, Screw the Shrimp," cries out against what she sees as environmental pillage, a circumstance she believes requires all of us to undergo a "deep change in personal consciousness."

Sometimes personal fear or a sense of threat can motivate a complete change in life-style. Life-threatening health problems were among the factors leading John Nichols, a writer, to embrace Henry David Thoreau's famous exhortation to "Simplify, simplify." Nichols has vastly simplified his own life. Now he eats only what he must in order to maintain his health; and he buys only a few second-hand clothes and bare essentials. He threatens to "punch out" anyone who turns on an air conditioner in his presence because it contributes to the greenhouse effect. Such an approach may seem extreme, even militant; yet Nichols has chosen to take a stand on what he views as a crisis situation.

Consider for a moment what you as an individual can do to help. Doing one's part to save the earth isn't always as simple as washing your clothes with laundry soap instead of detergent because soap is more biodegradable. Even choosing to use paper grocery bags is not a clear-cut solution. Paper might seem a better choice than plastic because it deteriorates faster; yet the destruction of trees and the pollution from paper mills make the issue of using paper over plastic a complicated one.

Perhaps, then, saving the environment cannot be strictly a matter of individual responsibility. There is a need for people in powerful positions to take a stand—this includes scientific writers like Rachel Carson and other scientific experts, as well as government officials. John C. Ogden, director of the Florida Institute of Oceanography, argues that environmental scientists must become activists. He explains: "Scientists studying environmental problems are beleaguered with demands for evidence and scientific proof that will justify complicated, expensive, and often politically sensitive decisions about managing our natural resources." Most of the time, according to Ogden, the information required relates to entire ecosystems. The necessary studies must be interdisciplinary, cover large geographical areas, and span many years, thereby making them quite expensive.

However, spending time and money to study entire ecosystems has not characterized our society's approach to the natural world to date. More typical is the combative stance recounted here by John McPhee in an excerpt from his book *The Control of Nature* (1989). McPhee, a widely recognized master of the literary essay, characterizes a civil engineering project on the Atchafalaya River as a battle between nature and the soldiers of commerce.

Theologian Rosemary Radford Ruether argues against the idea that humans stand at the pinnacle of the natural world. In her essay she asks us to re-examine the hierarchical notion that we are owners of the rest of nature and thus entitled to exploit and subdue it. Concluding the chapter is a selection by William Kittredge, writing from his unique point of view as a former rancher in Oregon who sought to exploit and subdue the land and water supply. He describes agriculture variously as an art, a craft, and as the management of an industrialized system.

The selections in this chapter raise questions about the idea of control. They suggest that using scientific research and technological methods to dominate nature reflects an attitude of arrogance rather than one of stewardship toward the environment. The readings also emphasize personal responsibility. They exhort us to embrace environmental preservation and protection as a moral issue, not just as a trendy pastime.

References

Al Gore, *Earth in the Balance* (New York: Penguin Books, 1992).
Aldo Leopold, *A Sand County Almanac* (New York: Oxford University Press, 1966).

Richard Nelson, "Oil and Ethics: Adrift on Troubled Waters," *Los Angeles Times*, April 9, 1989.

John Nichols, "Keep It Simple," *Buzzworm*, September/October, 1990.

John C. Ogden, "The Scientists Studying Environmental Issues Must Become Activists," *Chronicle of Higher Education*, September 15, 1993.

Rachel Carson

The Obligation to Endure

Rachel Carson *(1908–1964) worked as a marine biologist for the U.S. Fish and Wildlife Service before she became world-renowned as the author of* The Sea around Us *(1961). Her other books on marine life include* The Edge of the Sea *(1955) and* The Sense of Wonder *(1956). While working with government-sponsored agricultural control programs, Carson became deeply concerned about the widespread use of long-lasting insecticides. Carson's scientific research provided the data for* Silent Spring *(1962), but it is her own emotional response to nature and her literary command of language that account for the power of the book.* Silent Spring, *in which "The Obligation to Endure" appeared, provoked an extreme backlash from the chemical industry, whose representatives labeled Carson as a hysterical woman determined to turn the earth over to the insects. In this excerpt Carson calls for more investigation of the effects of chemicals used to control the living things we call pests, such as weeds and insects.*

Questions to Consider

☐ *Silent Spring* was published more than thirty years ago. As you read, consider what, if anything, seems out of date. What remains relevant today?

☐ As you read, notice whether Carson appeals more to reason, to emotion, or to both in this essay.

T HE history of life on earth has been a history of interaction between living things and their surroundings. To a large extent, the physical form and the habits of the earth's vegetation and its animal life have been molded by the environment. Considering the whole span of earthly time, the opposite effect, in which life actually modifies its surroundings, has been relatively slight. Only within the moment of time represented by the present century has one species — man — acquired significant power to alter the nature of his world.

During the past quarter century this power has not only increased to one of disturbing magnitude but it has changed in character. The most alarming of all man's assaults upon the environment is the contamination of air, earth, rivers, and sea with dangerous and even lethal materials. This pollution is for the most part irrecoverable; the chain of evil it initiates not only in the world that must support life but in living tissues is for the most part irreversible. In this now universal contamination of the environment, chemicals are the sinister and little-recognized partners of radiation in changing the very nature of the world—the very nature of its life. Strontium 90, released through nuclear explosions into the air, comes to earth in rain or drifts down as fallout, lodges in soil, enters into the grass or corn or wheat grown there, and in time takes up its abode in the bones of a human being, there to remain until his death. Similarly, chemicals sprayed on croplands or forests or gardens lie long in soil, entering into living organisms, passing from one to another in a chain of poisoning and death. Or they pass mysteriously by underground streams until they emerge and, through the alchemy of air and sunlight, combine into new forms that kill vegetation, sicken cattle, and work unknown harm on those who drink from once pure wells. As Albert Schweitzer has said, "Man can hardly even recognize the devils of his own creation."

It took hundreds of millions of years to produce the life that now inhabits the earth—eons of time in which that developing and evolving and diversifying life reached a state of adjustment and balance with its surroundings. The environment, rigorously shaping and directing the life it supported, contained elements that were hostile as well as supporting. Certain rocks gave out dangerous radiation; even within the light of the sun, from which all life draws its energy, there were short-wave radiations with power to injure. Given time— time not in years but in millennia—life adjusts, and a balance has been reached. For time is the essential ingredient; but in the modern world there is no time.

The rapidity of change and the speed with which new situations are created follow the impetuous and heedless pace of man rather than the deliberate pace of nature. Radiation is no longer merely the background radiation of rocks, the bombardment of cosmic rays, the ultraviolet of the sun that have existed before there was any life on earth; radiation is now the unnatural creation of man's tampering with the atom. The chemicals to which life is asked to make its adjustment are no longer merely the calcium and silica and copper and all the rest of the minerals washed out of the rocks and carried in rivers to the sea; they are the synthetic creations of man's inventive mind, brewed in his laboratories, and having no counterparts in nature.

To adjust to these chemicals would require time on the scale that is nature's; it would require not merely the years of a man's life but the life of generations. And even this, were it by some miracle possible, would be futile, for the new chemicals come from our laboratories in an endless stream; almost five hundred annually find their way into actual use in the United States alone. The figure is staggering and its implications are not easily grasped—500 new chemicals to which the bodies of men and animals are required somehow to adapt each year, chemicals totally outside the limits of biologic experience.

Among them are many that are used in man's war against nature. Since the mid-1940's over 200 basic chemicals have been created for use in killing insects, weeds, rodents, and other organisms described in the modern vernacular as "pests"; and they are sold under several thousand different brand names.

These sprays, dusts, and aerosols are now applied almost universally to farms, gardens, forests, and homes—nonselective chemicals that have the power to kill every insect, the "good" and the "bad," to still the song of birds and the leaping of fish in the streams, to coat the leaves with a deadly film, and to linger on in soil—all this though the intended target may be only a few weeds or insects. Can anyone believe it is possible to lay down such a barrage of poisons on the surface of the earth without making it unfit for all life? They should not be called "insecticides," but "biocides."

The whole process of spraying seems caught up in an endless spiral. Since DDT was released for civilian use, a process of escalation has been going on in which ever more toxic materials must be found. This has happened because insects, in a triumphant vindication of Darwin's principle of the survival of the fittest, have evolved super races immune to the particular insecticide used, hence a deadlier one has always to be developed—and then a deadlier one than that. It has happened also because, for reasons to be described later, destructive insects often undergo a "flareback," or resurgence, after spraying, in numbers greater than before. Thus the chemical war is never won, and all life is caught in its violent crossfire.

Along with the possibility of the extinction of mankind by nuclear war, the central problem of our age has therefore become the contamination of man's total environment with such substances of incredible potential for harm—substances that accumulate in the tissues of plants and animals and even penetrate the germ cells to shatter or alter the very material of heredity upon which the shape of the future depends.

Some would-be architects of our future look toward a time when it will be possible to alter the human germ plasm by design. But we may easily be doing so now by inadvertence, for many chemicals, like radiation, bring about gene mutations. It is ironic to think that man might determine his own future by something so seemingly trivial as the choice of an insect spray.

All this has been risked—for what? Future historians may well be amazed by our distorted sense of proportion. How could intelligent beings seek to control a few unwanted species by a method that contaminated the entire environment and brought the threat of disease and death even to their own kind? Yet this is precisely what we have done. We have done it, moreover, for reasons that collapse the moment we examine them. We are told that the enormous and expanding use of pesticides is necessary to maintain farm production. Yet is our real problem not one of *overproduction*? Our farms, despite measures to remove acreages from production and to pay farmers *not* to produce, have yielded such a staggering excess of crops that the American taxpayer in 1962 is paying out more than one billion dollars a year as the total carrying cost of the surplus-food storage program. And is the situation helped when one branch of the Agriculture Department tries to reduce production while another states, as it did in 1958, "It is believed generally that reduction of crop acreages under provisions of the Soil Bank will stimulate interest in use of chemicals to obtain maximum production on the land retained in crops."

All this is not to say there is no insect problem and no need of control. I am saying, rather, that control must be geared to realities, not to mythical situations, and that the methods employed must be such that they do not destroy us along with the insects.

The problem whose attempted solution has brought such a train of disaster in its wake is an accompaniment of our modern way of life. Long before the age of man, insects inhabited the earth—a group of extraordinarily varied and adaptable beings. Over the course of time since man's advent, a small percentage of the more than half a million species of insects have come into conflict with human welfare in two principal ways: as competitors for the food supply and as carriers of human disease.

Disease-carrying insects become important where human beings are crowded together, especially under conditions where sanitation is poor, as in time of natural disaster or war or in situations of extreme poverty and deprivation. Then control of some sort becomes necessary. It is a sobering fact, however, as we shall presently see, that the method of massive chemical control has had only limited success, and also threatens to worsen the very conditions it is intended to curb.

Under primitive agricultural conditions the farmer had few insect problems. These arose with the intensification of agriculture—the devotion of immense acreages to a single crop. Such a system set the stage for explosive increases in specific insect populations. Single-crop farming does not take advantage of the principles by which nature works; it is agriculture as an engineer might conceive it to be. Nature has introduced great variety into the landscape, but man has displayed a passion for simplifying it. Thus he undoes the built-in checks and balances by which nature holds the species within bounds. One important natural check is a limit on the amount of suitable habitat for each species. Obviously then, an insect that lives on wheat can build up its population to much higher levels on a farm devoted to wheat than on one in which wheat is intermingled with other crops to which the insect is not adapted.

The same thing happens in other situations. A generation or more ago, the towns of large areas of the United States lined their streets with the noble elm tree. Now the beauty they hopefully created is threatened with complete destruction as disease sweeps through the elms, carried by a beetle that would have only limited chance to build up large populations and to spread from tree to tree if the elms were only occasional trees in a richly diversified planting.

Another factor in the modern insect problem is one that must be viewed against a background of geologic and human history: the spreading of thousands of different kinds of organisms from their native homes to invade new territories. This worldwide migration has been studied and graphically described by the British ecologist Charles Elton in his recent book *The Ecology of Invasions*. During the Cretaceous Period, some hundred million years ago, flooding seas cut many land bridges between continents and living things found themselves confined in what Elton calls "colossal separate nature reserves." There, isolated from others of their kind, they developed many new species. When some of the land masses were joined again, about 15 million years ago, these species began to move out into new territories—a movement that is not only still in progress but is now receiving considerable assistance from man.

The importation of plants is the primary agent in the modern spread of species, for animals have almost invariably gone along with the plants, quarantine being a comparatively recent and not completely effective innovation. The United States Office of Plant Introduction alone has introduced almost 200,000 species and varieties of plants from all over the world. Nearly half of the 180 or so major insect enemies of plants in the United States are accidental imports from abroad, and most of them have come as hitchhikers on plants.

In new territory, out of reach of the restraining hand of the natural enemies that kept down its numbers in its native land, an invading plant or animal is able to become enormously abundant. Thus it is no accident that our most troublesome insects are introduced species.

These invasions, both the naturally occurring and those dependent on human assistance, are likely to continue indefinitely. Quarantine and massive chemical campaigns are only extremely expensive ways of buying time. We are faced, according to Dr. Elton, "with a life-and-death need not just to find new technological means of suppressing this plant or that animal"; instead we need the basic knowledge of animal populations and their relations to their surroundings that will "promote an even balance and damp down the explosive power of outbreaks and new invasions."

Much of the necessary knowledge is now available but we do not use it. We train ecologists in our universities and even employ them in our governmental agencies but we seldom take their advice. We allow the chemical death rain to fall as though there were no alternative, whereas in fact there are many, and our ingenuity could soon discover many more if given opportunity.

Have we fallen into a mesmerized state that makes us accept as inevitable that which is inferior or detrimental, as though having lost the will or the vision to demand that which is good? Such thinking, in the words of the ecologist Paul Shepard, "idealizes life with only its head out of water, inches above the limits of toleration of the corruption of its own environment . . . Why should we tolerate a diet of weak poisons, a home in insipid surroundings, a circle of acquaintances who are not quite our enemies, the noise of motors with just enough relief to prevent insanity? Who would want to live in a world which is just not quite fatal?"

Yet such a world is pressed upon us. The crusade to create a chemically sterile, insect-free world seems to have engendered a fanatic zeal on the part of many specialists and most of the so-called control agencies. On every hand there is evidence that those engaged in spraying operations exercise a ruthless power. "The regulatory entomologists . . . function as prosecutor, judge and jury, tax assessor and collector and sheriff to enforce their own orders," said Connecticut entomologist Neely Turner. The most flagrant abuses go unchecked in both state and federal agencies.

It is not my contention that chemical insecticides must never be used. I do contend that we have put poisonous and biologically potent chemicals indiscriminately into the hands of persons largely or wholly ignorant of their potentials for harm. We have subjected enormous numbers of people to contact with these poisons, without their consent and often without their knowledge. If the Bill of Rights contains no guarantee that a citizen shall be secure against lethal poisons distributed either by private individuals or by public officials, it is surely only because our forefathers, despite their considerable wisdom and foresight, could conceive of no such problem.

I contend, furthermore, that we have allowed these chemicals to be used with little or no advance investigation of their effect on soil, water, wildlife, and man himself. Future generations are unlikely to condone our lack of prudent concern for the integrity of the natural world that supports all life.

There is still very limited awareness of the nature of the threat. This is an era of specialists, each of whom sees his own problem and is unaware of or intolerant of the larger frame into which it fits. It is also an era dominated by industry, in which the right to make a dollar at whatever cost is seldom challenged. When the public protests, confronted with some obvious evidence of damaging results of pesticide applications, it is fed little tranquilizing pills of half truth. We urgently need an end to these false assurances, to the sugar coating of unpalatable facts. It is the public that is being asked to assume the risks that the insect controllers calculate. The public must decide whether it wishes to continue on the present road, and it can do so only when in full possession of the facts. In the words of Jean Rostand, "The obligation to endure gives us the right to know."

Discussion Questions

1. Consider Carson's choice of words. How many of Carson's readers, both in the 1960s and in the 1990s, would agree that humans "assault" the envi-

ronment, that pollution constitutes "a chain of evil," and that chemicals are "sinister" elements changing the "very nature of the world"? How are you, as a reader, affected by these phrases?

2. Carson identifies what she considers a life-threatening problem, and she describes its causes and effects. What solution does she offer, if any? What do you suggest as a feasible solution to the problem?

3. What is the meaning and significance of Carson's title for this essay? What do you think Jean Rostand meant when he said, "The obligation to endure gives us the right to know"? How does Carson appropriate Rostand's idea to suit her own message?

4. Discuss any relevant causes and effects, or problems and solutions, that Carson omits from this discussion. Which ones have developed during the years since Carson published her book?

Journal Entry

Write an entry explaining your attitude toward insects. Do you consider them fellow creatures or mainly a nuisance? Do you have any qualms about using insecticides in your home or yard? Why or why not?

Writing Projects

1. Analyze your own response to Carson's essay. After reading it did you want to take action, such as stop using any chemicals? What features of Carson's writing (for example, tone, organization, diction, choice and presentation of example) elicited a particular response from you?

2. Carson says that we live in an "era dominated by industry, in which the right to make a dollar at whatever cost is seldom challenged." Some of you will one day be employed by industries, if you aren't already. For example, chemistry majors may be working for chemical companies that produce insecticides. Investigate the point of view of the chemical industry toward reducing the use of chemicals to control insects and weeds. What steps are currently being taken to reduce both the short- and long-term harmful effects of pesticides on humans?

Collaborative Project

Working with one or two classmates, read about the reactions Carson's book provoked at the time it was published. Trace Carson's influence on established, and new, governmental policies as well as her success in raising the general population's awareness of the dangers of insecticide use. Work together to analyze your findings, and present a report to the class.

Rosemary Radford Ruether

Toward an Ecological-Feminist Theology of Nature

Rosemary Radford Ruether *(b. 1936) writes on feminism, Christianity, peace, and global justice, among other issues, and has been honored with numerous awards. A reviewer for the* New York Times *described Ruether as a writer who "challenges, irritates, stimulates, and inspires her readers to rethink . . . their own relationship to religious perception and experience." Ruether, currently a professor of theology, has been a contributing editor to* Christianity and Crisis *magazine and is the author of numerous other writings, among them* Mary: The Feminine Face of the Church *(1977) and* Gaia and God: Ecofeminist Theology of Earth Healing *(1992). The essay reprinted here is taken from Ruether's landmark book on women and Christianity,* Sexism and God-Talk: Toward a Feminist Theology *(1983). In "Toward an Ecological-Feminist Theology of Nature," Ruether questions the morality of the traditional hierarchical view that humans have dominion over nonhuman nature.*

Questions to Consider

☐ Ruether's essay is difficult for at least two reasons: her ideas are complex, and she challenges traditional views that most of us take for granted. The complex ideas require her to use terms with which you may be unfamiliar; therefore, have a dictionary handy to look up terms such as *ontological, theology, hierarchy,* and *dichotomize.*

☐ Ruether's argument challenges the idea of a "chain of being." For more information on this concept, consult a handbook of literary terms; refer also to the essay by Stephen Jay Gould in Chapter 3.

☐ The author's opening sentence serves as a strong thesis statement. As you read, notice how she develops her thesis structurally and contextually.

AN ecological-feminist theology of nature must rethink the whole western theological tradition of the hierarchical chain of being and chain of command. This theology must question the hierarchy of human over nonhuman nature as a relationship of ontological and moral value. It must challenge the right of the human to treat the nonhuman as private prop-

351

erty and material wealth to be exploited. It must unmask the structures of social domination, male over female, owner over worker, that mediate this domination of nonhuman nature. Finally, it must question the model of hierarchy that starts with nonmaterial spirit (God) as the source of the chain of being and continues down to nonspiritual "matter" as the bottom of the chain of being and the most inferior, valueless, and dominated point in the chain of command.

The God/ess who is primal Matrix, the ground of being–new being, is neither stifling immanence nor rootless transcendence. Spirit and matter are not dichotomized but are the inside and outside of the same thing. When we proceed to the inward depths of consciousness or probe beneath the surface of visible things to the electromagnetic field that is the ground of atomic and molecular structure, the visible disappears. Matter itself dissolves into energy. Energy, organized in patterns and relationships, is the basis for what we experience as visible things. It becomes impossible any more to dichotomize material and spiritual energy. Consciousness comes to be seen as the most intense and complex form of the inwardness of material energy itself as it bursts forth at that evolutionary level where matter is organized in the most complex and intensive way – the central nervous system and cortex of the human brain.

If we follow Teilhard de Chardin's interpretation of evolution, the radial energy of matter develops along the lines of increasing complexity and centralization. At certain "boiling points" of life energy, there is a critical leap to a new stage of being, from minerals to plant life, from plant life to animate life, moving through increasing stages of intelligence until the breakthrough to self-conscious intelligence.[1]

It becomes evident that one can no longer make the dichotomy between nature and history. Nature itself is historical. The universe is a great being that is born, grows and presumably will die. Critical moments of transformation appear at stages of the universe's growth, bringing into being new possibilities. These were latent in what existed before and yet represent something new, something that could not simply be expected from the pre-existing forms of being. Nature contains transcendence and freedom, as well as necessity. The change from mineral being to plant life, from plant life to animate life, and then to self-conscious intelligence is not just quantitative, but qualitative transformation. At each stage a qualitatively new dimension of life comes into being.

So far the evolutionary view of matter and radical energy in Teilhard de Chardin and others could lead simply to a new version of the chain of being. The chain of being has been laid on its side, so to speak. But this view still preserves the same presuppositions of the superiority of the "higher" over the "lower" forms and hence the domination of the "highest" form – namely, the human – over the rest, solely for human self-interest. Indeed, Teilhard does not question the racist assumptions that white western development is the privileged line of human development that has a right to control and reshape the rest of humanity.[2] This hierarchicalism of evolutionary theory has to be modified by several considerations.

We come to recognize the continuity of human consciousness with the radial energy of matter throughout the universe. Our intelligence is a special, intense form of this radial energy, but it is not without continuity with other forms; it is the self-conscious or "thinking dimension" of the radial energy of matter. We must respond to a "thou-ness" in all beings. This is not romanticism or an anthropomorphic animism that sees "dryads in trees," although there is truth in the animist view. The spirit in plants or animals is not anthropomorphic but biomorphic to its own forms of life. We respond not just as "I to it," but as "I to thou," to the spirit, the life energy that lies in every being in its own form of existence. The "brotherhood of man" needs to be widened to embrace not only women but also the whole community of life.

The more complex forms of life represent critical breakthroughs to new stages of existence that give them qualitatively more mobility and freedom for response. But they are radically dependent on all the stages of life that go before them and that continue to underlie their own existence. The plant can happily carry out its processes of photosynthesis without human beings, but we cannot exist without the photosynthesis of plants. The more complex forms of life are not the source and foundation of the less complex forms, just the opposite. An animal depends on a whole ecological community of life processes of plants, insects, other animals, water, air, and soil that underlie its existence. Still more, human beings cannot live without the whole ecological community that supports and makes possible our existence.

The privilege of intelligence, then, is not a privilege to alienate and dominate the world without concern for the welfare of all other forms of life. On the contrary, it is the responsibility to become the caretaker and cultivator of the welfare of the whole ecological community upon which our own existence depends. By what right are we the caretakers of nature when nonhuman nature takes care of its own processes very well and, in most cases, better without us? Human self-consciousness carries with it a danger that exists in no other form of creaturely life. Nonhuman creatures, to be sure, eat and are eaten by others. There is violence and bloodshed in nature, but it takes place within its own built-in balances. If one creature rapidly and drastically increases its population, it kills off its own life-support system and so dies off until it reaches a population back in balance with its ecological community.

Humans alone perpetuate their evolutionary advances primarily through cultural-social means. We don't grow our clothes on our bodies or our tools in the nails at the ends of our hands; we create these as artifacts. So we can continually change and develop them as part of our technology. More than that, we have the ability to create dysfunctional relationships with the earth, with our ecological community, and with each other, and to preserve them socially. We alone can "sin." We alone can disrupt and distort the balances of nature and force the price for this distortion on less fortunate humans, as well as the nonhuman community. We cannot do this forever. Finally, the universe will create inversions, under the weight of human distortion and oppression, that will undermine the whole human life-support system. But we may be able to bring the earth down with us in our downfall. We may destroy much of the work of evolutionary development back to the most primary level of minerals and photosynthesis, and leave even this deeply poisoned against the production of life. We are the rogue elephant of nature.

Thus we have not so much the privilege of intelligence, viewed as something above and against nonhuman nature, but the responsibility and necessity to convert our intelligence to the earth. We need to learn how to use intelligence to mend the distortions we have created and how to convert intelligence into an instrument that can cultivate the harmonies and balances of the ecological community and bring these to a refinement. We can turn the desert wilderness or the jungle into the garden. But we need to do that not simply by bulldozing what is and ignoring all other needs but our own, but by understanding the integrity of the existing ecological community and learning to build our niche in that community in harmony with the rest. We do this out of a genuine recognition of our interdependence. We cannot violate the ecological community without ultimately destroying our own life-support system. The notion of dominating the universe from a position of autonomy is an illusion of alienated consciousness. We have only two real options: either to learn to use our intelligence to become *servants* of the survival and cultivation of nature or to lose our own life-support system in an increasingly poisoned earth.

This conversion of our intelligence to the earth will demand a new form of human intelligence. The dominant white western male rationality has been based on linear, dichotomized thought patterns that divide reality into dualism: one is good and the other bad, one superior and the other inferior, one should dominate and the other should be eliminated or suppressed. The biological base of these patterns is specialization in left-brain, rational functions in a way that suppresses the right-brain, relational sense. This one-sided brain development seems more dominant in males than in females, possibly because of later verbal development in males.[3]

This biological tendency has been exaggerated by socialization into dominant and subordinate social roles. Dominant social roles exaggerate linear, dichotomized thinking and prevent the development of culture that would correct this bias by integrating the relational side. Women and other subordinate groups, moreover, have had their rational capacities suppressed through denial of education and leadership experience and so tend to be perceived as having primarily intuitive and affective patterns of thought. Thus socialization in power and powerlessness distorts integration further and creates what appears to be dichotomized personality cultures of men and women, that is, masculinity and femininity.

What we must now realize is that the patterns of rationality of left-brain specialization are, in many ways, ecologically dysfunctional. Far from this rationality being the mental counterpart of "natural law," it screens out much of reality as "irrelevant" to science and reduces scientific knowledge to a narrow spectrum fitted to dominance and control. But the systems it sets up are ecologically dysfunctional because they fail to see the larger relational patterns within which particular "facts" stand. This rationality tends toward monolithic systems of use of nature. Linear thinking, for example, directs agriculture, or even decorative planting, toward long rows of the same plant. This magnifies the plants' vulnerability to disease. Humans then compensate with chemical sprays, which in turn send a ripple effect of poisons through the whole ecological system. Nature, by contrast, diffuses and intersperses plants, so that each balances and corrects the vulnerabilities of the other. The inability to see the forest for the trees is typical of linear thinking.

Linear thinking simplifies, dichotomizes, focuses on parts, and fails to see the larger relationality and interdependence. Ecological thinking demands a different kind of rationality, one that integrates left-brain linear thought and right-brain spatial and relational thought. One has to disrupt the linear concept of order to create a different kind of order that is truly the way nature "orders," that is, balances and harmonizes, but that appears very "disorderly" to the linear, rational mind. One observes a meadow with many kinds of plants and insects balancing each other, each with their ecological niches, and then one learns to plant for human use in a way that imitates these same principles, in a more simplified and selective fashion. Converting our minds to the earth means understanding the more diffuse and relational logic of natural harmony. We learn to fit human ecology into its relation to nonhuman ecology in a way that maximizes the welfare of the whole rather than undermining and subverting (polluting) the life system.

Converting our minds to the earth cannot happen without converting our minds to each other, since the distorted and ecologically dysfunctional relationships appear necessary, yet they actually support the profits of the few against the many. There can be no ecological ethic simply as a new relation of "man" and "nature." Any ecological ethic must always take into account the structures of social domination and exploitation that mediate domination of nature and prevent concern for the welfare of the whole community in favor of the immediate advantage of the dominant class, race, and sex. An ecological ethic must always be an ethic of ecojustice that recognizes the interconnection of social domination and domination of nature.

Nonhuman nature, in this sense, is not just a "natural fact" to which we can "return" by rejecting human culture. Nature is a product not only of natural evolution but of human historical development. It partakes of the evils and distortions of human development. There is virtually no place on the planet where one can go to find "nature untouched by human hands." Even if humans have not been there before, their influence has been carried by winds, water, and soil, birds, insects, and animals, who bear within their beings the poisoning effects of human rapine of the globe. Nature, in this sense, can be seen as "fallen," not that it is evil itself but in that it has been marred and distorted by human misdevelopment. The remaking of our relation with nature and with each other, then, is a historical project and struggle of re-creation.

Nature will never be the same as it would have been without human intervention. Although we need to remake the earth in a way that converts our minds to nature's logic of ecological harmony, this will necessarily be a new synthesis, a new creation in which human nature and nonhuman nature become friends in the creating of a livable and sustainable cosmos.

NOTES

1. Pierre Teilhard de Chardin, *The Phenomenon of Man*, Harper & Row, New York, 1959, pp. 53–74.
2. Ibid., pp. 209–210.
3. Sally P. Springer and Georg Deutsch, *Left Brain, Right Brain*, Freeman, San Francisco, 1981, pp. 121–130.

Discussion Questions

1. Ruether states: "The privilege of intelligence, then, is not a privilege to alienate and dominate the world without concern for the welfare of all other forms of life." How does Ruether explain and defend this statement? Do you find her argument convincing? Why or why not? In what ways does intelligence confer privileges on humans? Are those privileges balanced with responsibilities? Why or why not?

2. Respond to the following statement by Ruether: "Spirit and matter are not dichotomized but are the inside and outside of the same thing." How does Ruether illustrate the concept of spirit and matter? What is your own reaction to Ruether's concept?

3. What is Ruether's view on the role technology has played in evolution? Do you agree? Why or why not?

4. What does Ruether mean when she refers to a traditional hierarchy in Western religion? Where did this belief originate? Explain why you do or do not think this tradition still has merit.

Journal Entry

If we all agreed with Ruether that "the brotherhood of man" needs to be expanded to include women and all living things, what kind of world would we live in? Describe specific changes that would take place in your daily life.

Writing Projects

1. Using the structural methods of definition and classification, explain Ruether's phrase "ecological-feminist theology of nature." Bring in examples from Ruether's text, and write your essay for an audience who is unfamiliar with Ruether's work.

2. Assume you are an editor in charge of making this selection more accessible to the general reader. It is your job to annotate the essay by providing footnotes that give further information about not only the meaning but also the significance of certain words within a particular context. Identify what terms, ideas, people, or other references you would annotate in this essay. Then, separately, write a series of statements justifying the choices you made.

Collaborative Project

Working with a partner, interview theologians in your community. Find out how many of them have read Ruether's work. What do they think of her ideas? Ask what they see as the connection between theology and ecology. How do they think the concept of stewardship extends to the natural environment? Write a report summarizing your findings. Draw conclusions about whether Ruether's work reflects mainstream theology of the 1990s.

John McPhee

Controlling the Atchafalaya River

John McPhee *(b. 1931) is one of the most widely admired contemporary writers of literary nonfiction. A fellow of the Geological Society of America, McPhee has received awards from the American Academy and Institute of Arts and Letters and the American Association of Petroleum Geologists, among others. A* New York Times *reviewer called him a "gifted liaison between specialist and layman reader." McPhee has written on a wide range of subjects.* Coming into the Country *(1977) presents an insider's view of the Alaskan frontier.* In Suspect Terrain *(1983) takes its title from a geologist's phrase that describes country with an ambiguous history.* Looking for a Ship *(1990) examines the decline of the Merchant Marine.* The Control of Nature *(1989) is a collection of three essays: "Cooling the Lava," "Los Angeles against the Mountains," and "Atchafalaya," from which the following selection is excerpted. In this essay, as elsewhere, McPhee characterizes his heroes as those who are not content to leave nature alone. His protagonists are compelled to attempt to manage and control natural forces.*

Questions to Consider

☐ As you read, consider McPhee's attitude toward the lockmaster he describes, and toward himself in relationship to the natives of this Cajun country. What phrases help you understand his position?

☐ Notice the kind of details McPhee focuses on and the types of images he selects to convey the geography of the place.

THREE hundred miles up the Mississippi River from its mouth—many parishes above New Orleans and well north of Baton Rouge—a navigation lock in the Mississippi's right bank allows ships to drop out of the river. In evident defiance of nature, they descend as much as thirty-three feet, then go off to the west or south. This, to say the least, bespeaks a rare relationship between a river and adjacent terrain—any river, anywhere, let alone the third-ranking river on earth. The adjacent terrain is Cajun country, in a geographical sense the apex of the French Acadian world, which forms a triangle in southern Louisiana, with its base the Gulf Coast from the mouth of the Mississippi almost to Texas, its two sides converging up here near the lock—and including neither New Orleans nor Baton Rouge. The people of the local parishes (Pointe Coupee Parish, Avoyelles Parish) would call this the apex of Cajun country in every possible sense—no one more emphatically than the lockmaster, on whose face one day I noticed a spreading astonishment as he watched me remove from my pocket a red bandanna.

"You are a coonass with that red handkerchief," he said.

A coonass being a Cajun, I threw him an appreciative smile. I told him that I always have a bandanna in my pocket, wherever I happen to be—in New York as in Maine or Louisiana, not to mention New Jersey (my home)—and sometimes the color is blue. He said, "Blue is the sign of a Yankee. But that red handkerchief—with that, you are pure coonass." The lockmaster wore a white hard hat above his creased and deeply tanned face, his full but not overloaded frame. The nameplate on his desk said RABALAIS.

The navigation lock is not a formal place. When I first met Rabalais, six months before, he was sitting with his staff at 10 A.M. eating homemade bread, macaroni and cheese, and a mound of rice that was concealed beneath what he called "smoked old-chicken gravy." He said, "Get yourself a plate of that." As I went somewhat heavily for the old chicken, Rabalais said to the others, "He's pure coonass. I knew it."

If I was pure coonass, I would like to know what that made Rabalais— Norris F. Rabalais, born and raised on a farm near Simmesport, in Avoyelles Parish, Louisiana. When Rabalais was a child, there was no navigation lock to lower ships from the Mississippi. The water just poured out—boats with it— and flowed on into a distributary waterscape known as Atchafalaya. In each decade since about 1860, the Atchafalaya River had drawn off more water from the Mississippi than it had in the decade before. By the late nineteen-forties, when Rabalais was in his teens, the volume approached one-third. As the Atchafalaya widened and deepened, eroding headward, offering the Mississippi an increasingly attractive alternative, it was preparing for nothing less than an absolute capture: before long, it would take all of the Mississippi, and itself become the master stream. Rabalais said, "They used to teach us in high school that one day there was going to be structures up here to control the flow of that water, but I never dreamed I was going to be on one. Somebody way back yonder—which is dead and gone now—visualized it. We had some pretty sharp teachers."

The Mississippi River, with its sand and silt, has created most of Louisiana, and it could not have done so by remaining in one channel. If it had, southern Louisiana would be a long narrow peninsula reaching into the Gulf of Mexico. Southern Louisiana exists in its present form because the Mississippi River has jumped here and there within an arc about two hundred miles wide, like a pianist playing with one hand—frequently and radically changing course, surging over the left or the right bank to go off in utterly new directions. Always it is the river's purpose to get to the Gulf by the short-est and steepest gradient. As the mouth advances southward and the river lengthens, the gradient declines, the current slows, and sediment builds up the bed. Eventually, it builds up so much that the river spills to one side. Major shifts of that nature have tended to occur roughly once a millennium. The Mississippi's main channel of three thousand years ago is now the quiet water of Bayou Teche, which mimics the shape of the Mississippi. Along Bayou Teche, on the high ground of ancient natural levees, are Jeanerette, Breaux Bridge, Broussard, Olivier—arcuate strings of Cajun towns. Eight hundred years before the birth of Christ, the channel was captured from the east. It shifted abruptly and flowed in that direction for about a thousand years. In the second century A.D., it was captured again, and taken south, by the now unprepossessing Bayou Lafourche, which, by the year 1000, was losing its hegemony to the river's present course, through the region that would be known as Plaquemines. By the nineteen-fifties, the Mississippi River had advanced so far past New Orleans and out into the Gulf that it was about to shift again, and its offspring Atchafalaya was ready to receive it. By the route of the Atchafalaya, the distance across the delta plain was a hundred and forty-five miles—well under half the length of the route of the master stream.

For the Mississippi to make such a change was completely natural, but in the interval since the last shift Europeans had settled beside the river, a nation had developed, and the nation could not afford nature. The consequences of the Atchafalaya's conquest of the Mississippi would include but not be limited to the demise of Baton Rouge and the virtual destruction of New Orleans. With its fresh water gone, its harbor a silt bar, its economy disconnected from inland commerce, New Orleans would turn into New Gomorrah. Moreover, there were so many big industries between the two cities that at night they made the river glow like a worm. As a result of settlement patterns, this reach of the Mississippi had long been known as "the German coast," and now, with B. F. Goodrich, E. I. du Pont, Union Carbide, Reynolds Metals, Shell, Mobil, Texaco, Exxon, Monsanto, Uniroyal, Georgia-Pacific, Hydrocarbon Industries, Vulcan Materials, Nalco Chemical, Freeport Chemical, Dow Chemical, Allied Chemical, Stauffer Chemical, Hooker Chemicals, Rubicon Chemicals, American Petrofina—with an infrastructural concentration equaled in few other places—it was often called "the American Ruhr." The industries were there because of the river. They had come for its navigational convenience and its fresh water. They would not, and could not, linger beside a tidal creek. For nature to take its course was simply unthinkable. The Sixth World War would do less damage to southern Louisiana. Nature, in this place, had become an enemy of the state.

Rabalais works for the U.S. Army Corps of Engineers. Some years ago, the Corps made a film that showed the navigation lock and a complex of associated structures built in an effort to prevent the capture of the Mississippi. The narrator said, "This nation has a large and powerful adversary. Our opponent could cause the United States to lose nearly all her seaborne commerce, to lose her standing as first among trading nations. . . . We are fighting Mother Nature. . . . It's a battle we have to fight day by day, year by year; the health of our economy depends on victory."

Rabalais was in on the action from the beginning, working as a construction inspector. Here by the site of the navigation lock was where the battle had begun. An old meander bend of the Mississippi was the conduit through which water had been escaping into the Atchafalaya. Complicating the scene, the old meander bend had also served as the mouth of the Red River. Coming in from the northwest, from Texas via Shreveport, the Red River had been a tributary of the Mississippi for a couple of thousand years—until the nineteen-forties, when the Atchafalaya captured it and drew it away. The capture of the Red increased the Atchafalaya's power as it cut down the country beside the Mississippi. On a map, these entangling watercourses had come to look like the letter "H." The Mississippi was the right-hand side. The Atchafalaya and the captured Red were the left-hand side. The crosspiece, scarcely seven miles long, was the former meander bend, which the people of the parish had long since named Old River. Sometimes enough water would pour out of the Mississippi and through Old River to quintuple the falls at Niagara. It was at Old River that the United States was going to lose its status among the world's trading nations. It was at Old River that New Orleans would be lost, Baton Rouge would be lost. At Old River, we would lose the American Ruhr. The Army's name for its operation there was Old River Control.

Rabalais gestured across the lock toward what seemed to be a pair of placid lakes separated by a trapezoidal earth dam a hundred feet high. It weighed five million tons, and it had stopped Old River. It had cut Old River in two. The severed ends were sitting there filling up with weeds. Where the Atchafalaya had entrapped the Mississippi, bigmouth bass were now in charge. The navigation lock had been dug beside this monument. The big dam, like the lock, was fitted into the mainline levee of the Mississippi. In Rabalais's pickup, we drove on the top of the dam, and drifted as well through Old River country. On this day, he said, the water on the Mississippi side was eighteen feet above sea level, while the water on the Atchafalaya side was five feet above sea level. Cattle were grazing on the slopes of the levees, and white horses with white colts, in deep-green grass. Behind the levees, the fields were flat and reached to rows of distant trees. Very early in the morning, a low fog had covered the fields. The sun, just above the horizon, was large and ruddy in the mist, rising slowly, like a hot-air balloon. This was a countryside of corn and soybeans, of grain-fed-catfish ponds, of feed stores and Kingdom Halls in crossroad towns. There were small neat cemeteries with ranks of white sarcophagi raised a foot or two aboveground, notwithstanding the protection of the levees. There were tarpapered cabins on concrete pylons, and low brick houses under planted pines. Pickups under the pines. If this was a form of battlefield, it was not unlike a great many battlefields—landscapes so quiet they belie their story. Most battlefields, though, are places where something happened once. Here it would happen indefinitely.

We went out to the Mississippi. Still indistinct in mist, it looked like a piece of the sea. Rabalais said, "That's a wide booger, right there." In the spring high water of vintage years—1927, 1937, 1973—more than two million cubic feet of water had gone by this place in every second. Sixty-five kilotons per second. By the mouth of the inflow channel leading to the lock were rock jetties, articulated concrete mattress revetments, and other heavy defenses. Rabalais observed that this particular site was no more vulnerable than almost any other point in this reach of river that ran so close to the Atchafalaya plain. There were countless places where a breakout might occur: "It has a tendency to go through just anywheres you can call for."

Why, then, had the Mississippi not jumped the bank and long since diverted to the Atchafalaya?

"Because they're watching it close," said Rabalais. "It's under close surveillance."

After the corps dammed Old River, in 1963, the engineers could not just walk away, like roofers who had fixed a leak. In the early planning stages, they had considered doing that, but there were certain effects they could not overlook. The Atchafalaya, after all, was a distributary of the Mississippi—the major one, and, as it happened, the only one worth mentioning that the Corps had not already plugged. In time of thundering flood, the Atchafalaya was useful as a safety valve, to relieve a good deal of pressure and help keep New Orleans from ending up in Yucatán. The Atchafalaya was also the source of the water in the swamps and bayous of the Cajun world. It was the water supply of small cities and countless towns. Its upper reaches were surrounded by farms. The Corps was not in a political or moral position to kill the Atchafalaya. It had to feed it water. By the principles of nature, the more the Atchafalaya was given, the more it would want to take, because it was the steeper stream. The more it was given, the deeper it would make its bed. The difference in level between the Atchafalaya and the Mississippi would continue to increase, magnifying the conditions for capture. The Corps would have to deal with that. The Corps would have to build something that could give the Atchafalaya a portion of the Mississippi and at the same time prevent it from taking all. In effect, the Corps would have to build a Fort Laramie: a place where the natives could buy flour and firearms but where the gates could be closed if they attacked.

Ten miles upriver from the navigation lock, where the collective sediments were thought to be more firm, they dug into a piece of dry ground and built what appeared for a time to be an incongruous, waterless bridge. Five hundred and sixty-six feet long, it stood parallel to the Mississippi and about a thousand yards back from the water. Between its abutments were ten piers, framing eleven gates that could be lifted or dropped, opened or shut, like windows. To this structure, and through it, there soon came a new Old River—an excavated channel leading in from the Mississippi and out seven miles to the Red-Atchafalaya. The Corps was not intending to accommodate nature. Its engineers were intending to control it in space and arrest it in time. In 1950, shortly before the project began, the Atchafalaya was taking thirty percent of the water that came down from the north to Old River. This water was known as the latitude flow, and it consisted of a little in the Red, a lot in the Mississippi. The United States Congress, in its deliberations, decided that "the distribution of flow and sediment in the Mississippi and Atchafalaya Rivers is now in desirable proportions and should be so maintained." The Corps was thereby ordered to preserve 1950. In perpetuity, at Old River, thirty percent of the latitude flow was to pass to the Atchafalaya.

The device that resembled a ten-pier bridge was technically a sill, or weir, and it was put on line in 1963, in an orchestrated sequence of events that flourished the art of civil engineering. The old Old River was closed. The new Old River was opened. The water, as it crossed the sill from the Mississippi's level to the Atchafalaya's, tore to white shreds in the deafening turbulence of a great new falls, from lip to basin the construction of the Corps. More or less simultaneously, the navigation lock opened its chamber. Now everything had changed and nothing had changed. Boats could still drop away from the river. The ratio of waters continued as before—this for the American Ruhr, that for the ecosystems of the Cajun swamps. Withal, there was a change of command, as the Army replaced nature.

In time, people would come to suggest that there was about these enterprises an element of hauteur. A professor of law at Tulane University, for example, would assign it third place in the annals of arrogance. His name was Oliver Houck. "The greatest arrogance was the stealing of the sun," he said. "The second-greatest arrogance is running rivers backward. The third-greatest arrogance is trying to hold the Mississippi in place. The ancient channels of the river go almost to Texas. Human beings have tried to restrict the river to one course—that's where the arrogance began." The Corps listens closely to things like that and files them in its archives. Houck had a point. Bold it was indeed to dig a fresh conduit in the very ground where one river had prepared to trap another, bolder yet to build a structure there meant to be in charge of what might happen.

Some people went further than Houck, and said that they thought the structure would fail. In 1980, for example, a study published by the Water Resources Research Institute, at Louisiana State University, described Old River as "the scene of a direct confrontation between the United States Government and the Mississippi River," and—all constructions of the Corps notwithstanding—awarded the victory to the Mississippi River. "Just when this will occur cannot be predicted," the report concluded. "It could happen next year, during the next decade, or sometime in the next thirty or forty years. But the final outcome is simply a matter of time and it is only prudent to prepare for it."

The Corps thought differently, saying, "We can't let that happen. We are charged by Congress not to let that happen." Its promotional film referred to Old River Control as "a good soldier." Old River Control was, moreover, "the keystone of the comprehensive flood-protection project for the lower Mississippi Valley," and nothing was going to remove the keystone. People arriving at New Orleans District Headquarters, U.S. Army Corps of Engineers, were confronted at the door by a muraled collage of maps and pictures and bold letters unequivocally declaring, "The Old River Control Structures, located about two hundred miles above New Orleans on the Mississippi River, prevent the Mississippi from changing course by controlling flows diverted into the Atchafalaya Basin."

No one's opinions were based on more intimate knowledge than those of LeRoy Dugas, Rabalais's upstream counterpart—the manager of the apparatus that controlled the flow at Old River. Like Rabalais, he was Acadian and of the country. Dugie—as he is universally called—had worked at Old River Control since 1963, when the water started flowing. In years to follow, colonels and generals would seek his counsel. "Those professors at L.S.U. say that whatever we do we're going to lose the system," he remarked one day at Old River, and, after a pause, added, "Maybe they're right." His voice had the sound of water over rock. In pitch, it was lower than a helicon tuba. Better to hear him indoors, in his operations office, away from the structure's competing thunders. "Maybe they're right," he repeated. "We feel that we can hold the river. We're going to try. Whenever you try to control nature, you've got one strike against you."

Dugie's face, weathered and deeply tanned, was saved from looking weary by the alertness and the humor in his eyes. He wore a large, lettered belt buckle that said TO HELP CONTROL THE MISSISSIPPI. "I was originally born in Morganza," he told me. "Thirty miles down the road. I have lived in Pointe Coupee Parish all my life. Once, I even closed my domicile and went to work in Texas for the Corps—but you always come back." (Rabalais also—as he puts it—"left out of here one time," but not for long.) All through Dugie's youth, of course, the Mississippi had spilled out freely to feed the Atchafalaya. He took the vagaries of the waters for granted, not to mention the supremacy of their force in flood. He was a naval gunner on Liberty ships in the South Pacific during the Second World War, and within a year or two of his return was astonished to hear that the Corps of Engineers was planning to restrain Old River. "They were going to try to control the flow," he said. "I thought they had lost their marbles."

Outside, on the roadway that crosses the five-hundred-and-sixty-six-foot structure, one could readily understand where the marbles might have gone. Even at this time of modest normal flow, we looked down into a rage of water. It was running at about twelve miles an hour—significantly faster than the Yukon after breakup—and it was pounding into the so-called stilling basin on the downstream side, the least still place you would ever see. The No. 10 rapids of the Grand Canyon, which cannot be run without risk of life, resemble the Old River stilling basin, but the rapids of the canyon are a fifth as wide. The Susitna River is sometimes more like it—melted glacier ice from the

Alaska Range. Huge trucks full of hardwood logs kept coming from the north to cross the structure, on their way to a chipping mill at Simmesport. One could scarcely hear them as they went by.

There was a high sill next to this one—a separate weir, two-thirds of a mile long and set two feet above the local flood stage, its purpose being to help regulate the flow of extremely high waters. The low sill, as the one we stood on was frequently called, was the prime valve at Old River, and dealt with the water every day. The fate of the project had depended on the low sill, and it was what people meant when, as they often did, they simply said "the structure." The structure and the high sill—like the navigation lock downstream—were fitted into the Mississippi's mainline levee. Beyond the sound of the water, the broad low country around these structures was quiet and truly still. Here and again in the fields, pump jacks bobbed for oil. In the river batture—the silt-swept no man's land between waterline and levee—lone egrets sat in trees, waiting for the next cow.

Dugie remarked that he would soon retire, that he felt old and worn down from fighting the river.

I said to him, "All you need is a good flood."

And he said, "Oh, no. Don't talk like that, man. You talk vulgar."

It was odd to look out toward the main-stem Mississippi, scarcely half a mile away, and see its contents spilling sideways, like cornmeal pouring from a hole in a burlap bag. Dugie said that so much water coming out of the Mississippi created a powerful and deceptive draw, something like a vacuum, that could suck in boats of any size. He had seen some big ones up against the structure. In the mid-sixties, a man alone had come down from Wisconsin in a small double-ended vessel with curling ends and tumblehome—a craft that would not have been unfamiliar to the Algonquians, who named the Mississippi. Dugie called this boat "a pirogue." Whatever it was, the man had paddled it all the way from Wisconsin, intent on reaching New Orleans. When he had nearly conquered the Mississippi, however, he was captured by the Atchafalaya. Old River caught him, pulled him off the Mississippi, and shot him through the structure. "He was in shock, but he lived," Dugie said. "We put him in the hospital in Natchez."

After a moment, I said, "This is an exciting place."

And Dugie said, "You've heard of Murphy—'What can happen will happen'? This is where Murphy lives."

Discussion Questions

1. What does McPhee accomplish by directly quoting Rabalais rather than simply paraphrasing Rabalais's point of view?

2. Why does McPhee include the historical background of the Atchafalaya River, going all the way back to 800 years before Christ?

3. McPhee explains that the Atchafalaya River draws water from the Mississippi, the "third-ranking river on earth." What similarities do you see between McPhee's treatment of the Mississippi as a subject for literary writing and other authors' writings about rivers—Mark Twain in *Huckleberry Finn*, for example?

4. What tone does McPhee achieve in the last sentence when he quotes Dugie saying, "You've heard of Murphy—'What can happen will happen'? This is where Murphy lives"? How does this quotation serve as a comment on the entire essay?

Journal Entry

How many river dams have you seen? What thoughts did you have when you visited? Why do you think river dams are often marked on maps and promoted as tourist attractions?

Writing Projects

1. Analyze how McPhee organized his account of the navigation lock construction around the metaphor of a battle, with nature as the "enemy of the state" and the U.S. Army Corps of Engineers as an army of soldiers engaged in combat.

2. This excerpt is only part of an essay about the Atchafalaya River. Read the entire essay, and then write an analysis of how McPhee uses characterization, traditionally a technique in fiction, to construct this factual account of humans and their efforts to control nature.

Collaborative Project

Writers of literary nonfiction research their subjects thoroughly because their writing must be based on fact. The source of the writer's information and how it was acquired is relevant to readers of literary nonfiction, who are usually interested in both the accuracy and the style of an essay. Writers of literary nonfiction collect data in various ways, just as do scientific researchers: through reading, interviewing, visiting a site, or becoming part of a professional or geographical community. Working with a partner, find published accounts in which McPhee explains how he collects the factual material for his literary nonfiction. Report to your class on how McPhee gained the knowledge and expertise to write authoritatively on subjects as diverse as geology and the Merchant Marine. Consider the role you think this type of writing plays in our society.

Joy Williams

Save the Whales, Screw the Shrimp

Joy Williams *(b. 1944) has been widely praised for her vivid writing style in such novels as* The Changeling *(1978) and* Breaking and Entering *(1989) and short story collections such as* Taking Care *(1982) and* Escapes *(1978). She has been awarded several fellowships for her writing, including a Guggenheim Fellowship (1974) and a Wallace Stegner Fellowship at Stanford University (1974–1975). She also received the National Endowment for the Arts Award (1973). Gail Godwin has described Williams's writing style as "distinctively sufficient. . . . laconic, austere, and luminously suggestive." The essay reprinted here, "Save the Whales, Screw the Shrimp," was first published in* Esquire *magazine and later selected for* The Best American Essays *(1990). Using a dramatic monologue to deliver her sentiments on our "greedy, selfish, expansionistic, industrialized society," Williams demands that we look at our own behavior and examine its consequences.*

Questions to Consider

☐ What expectations does Williams's title create in you before you actually read the piece?

☐ Watch Williams's use of imperative sentences; she confronts her audience with questions throughout. See how these sentence structures affect your reading experience.

I don't want to talk about *me*, of course, but it seems as though far too much attention has been lavished on *you* lately—that your greed and vanities and quest for self-fulfillment have been catered to far too much. You just want and want and want. You haven't had a mandala dream since the eighties began. To have a mandala dream you'd have to instinctively know that it was an attempt at self-healing on the part of Nature, and you don't believe in Nature anymore. It's too isolated from you. You've abstracted it. It's so messy and damaged and sad. Your eyes glaze as you travel life's highway past all the crushed animals and the Big Gulp cups. You don't even take pleasure in looking at nature photographs these days. Oh, they can be just as pretty, as always, but don't they make you feel increasingly . . . anxious?

Filled with more trepidation than peace? So what's the point? You see the picture of the baby condor or the panda munching on a bamboo shoot, and your heart just sinks, doesn't it? A picture of a poor old sea turtle with barnacles on her back, all ancient and exhausted, depositing her five gallons of doomed eggs in the sand hardly fills you with joy, because you realize, quite rightly, that just outside the frame falls the shadow of the condo. What's cropped from the shot of ocean waves crashing on a pristine shore is the plastics plant, and just beyond the dunes lies a parking lot. Hidden from immediate view in the butterfly-bright meadow, in the dusky thicket, in the oak and holly wood, are the surveyors' stakes, for someone wants to build a mall exactly there—some gas stations and supermarkets, some pizza and video shops, a health club, maybe a bulimia treatment center. Those lovely pictures of leopards and herons and wild rivers, well, you just know they're going to be accompanied by a text that will serve only to bring you down. You don't want to think about it! It's all so uncool. And you don't want to feel guilty either. Guilt is uncool. Regret maybe you'll consider. *Maybe.* Regret is a possibility, but don't push me, you say. Nature photographs have become something of a problem, along with almost everything else. Even though they leave the bad stuff out—maybe because you *know* they're leaving all the bad stuff out—such pictures are making you increasingly aware that you're a little too late for Nature. Do you feel that? Twenty years too late, maybe only ten? Not *way* too late, just a little too late? Well, it appears that you are. And since you are, you've decided you're just not going to attend this particular party.

Pascal said that it is easier to endure death without thinking about it than to endure the thought of death without dying. This is how you manage to dance the strange dance with that grim partner, nuclear annihilation. When the U.S. Army notified Winston Churchill that the first atom bomb had been detonated in New Mexico, it chose the code phrase BABIES SATISFACTORILY BORN. So you entered the age of irony, and the strange double life you've been leading with the world ever since. Joyce Carol Oates suggests that the reason writers—*real* writers, one assumes—don't write about Nature is that it lacks a sense of humor and registers no irony. It just doesn't seem to be of the times— these slick, sleek, knowing, objective, indulgent times. And the word *Environment.* Such a bloodless word. A flat-footed word with a shrunken heart. A word increasingly disengaged from its association with the natural world. Urban planners, industrialists, economists, and developers use it. It's a lost word, really. A cold word, mechanistic, suited strangely to the coldness generally felt toward Nature. It's their word now. You don't mind giving it up. As for *Environmentalist*, that's one that can really bring on the yawns, for you've tamed and tidied it, neutered it quite nicely. An environmentalist must be calm, rational, reasonable, and willing to compromise, otherwise you won't listen to him. Still, his beliefs are *opinions* only, for this is the age of radical subjectivism. Not long ago, Barry Commoner spoke to the Environmental Protection Agency. He scolded them. They loved it. The way they protect the environment these days is apparently to find an "acceptable level of harm from a pollutant and then issue rules allowing industry to pollute to that level." Commoner suggested that this was inappropriate. An EPA employee suggested that any other approach would place limits on economic growth and implied that Commoner was advocating this. Limits on economic growth! Commoner vigorously denied this. Oh, it was a healthy exchange of ideas, healthier certainly than our air and water. We needed that little spanking, the EPA felt. It was refreshing. The agency has recently lumbered into action in its campaign to ban dinoseb. You seem to have liked your dinoseb. It's been a popular weed killer, even though it has been directly linked with birth defects. You must hate weeds a lot. Although the EPA appears successful in banning the poison, it will still have to pay the disposal costs and compensate the manufacturers for the market value of the chemicals they still have in stock.

That's ironic, you say, but farmers will suffer losses, too, oh dreadful financial losses, if herbicide and pesticide use is restricted.

Farmers grow way too much stuff anyway. They grow surplus crops with subsidized water created by turning rivers great and small into a plumbing system of dams and canals. Rivers have become *systems*. Wetlands are increasingly being referred to as *filtering systems*—things deigned *useful* because of their ability to absorb urban run-off, oil from roads, et cetera.

We know that. We've known that for years about farmers. We know a lot these days. We're very well informed. If farmers aren't allowed to make a profit by growing surplus crops, they'll have to sell their land to developers, who'll turn all that *arable land* into office parks. Arable land isn't Nature anyway, and besides, we like those office parks and shopping plazas, with their monster supermarkets open twenty-four hours a day with aisle after aisle after aisle of *products*. It's fun. Products are fun.

Farmers like their poisons, but ranchers like them even more. There are well-funded predominantly federal and cooperative programs like the Agriculture Department's Animal Damage Control Unit that poison, shoot, and trap several thousand animals each year. This unit loves to kill things. It was created to kill things—bobcats, foxes, black bears, mountain lions, rabbits, badgers, countless birds—all to make this great land safe for the string bean and the corn, the sheep and the cow, even though you're not consuming as much cow these days. A burger now and then, but burgers are hardly cows at all, you feel. They're not all *our* cows in any case, for some burger matter is imported. There's a bit of Central American burger matter in your bun. Which is contributing to the conversion of tropical rain forest into cow pasture. Even so, you're getting away from meat these days. You're eschewing cow. It's seafood you love, shrimp most of all. And when you love something, it had better watch out, because you have a tendency to love it to death.

Shrimp, shrimp, shrimp. It's more common on menus than chicken. In the wilds of Ohio, far, far from watery shores, four out of the six entrées on a menu will be shrimp, for some modest sum. Everywhere, it's all the shrimp you can eat or all you *care* to eat, for sometimes you just don't feel like eating all you *can*. You are intensively *harvesting* shrimp. Soon there won't be any left and then you can stop. It takes that, often, to make you stop. Shrimpers shrimp, of course. That's their *business*. They put out these big nets and in these nets, for each pound of shrimp, they catch more than ten times that amount of fish, turtles, and dolphins. These, quite the worse for wear, they dump back in. There is an object called TED (Turtle Excluder Device), which would save thousands of turtles and some dolphins from dying in the nets, but the shrimpers are loath to use TEDs, as they say it would cut the size of their shrimp catch.

We've heard about TED, you say.

They want you, all of you, to have all the shrimp you can eat and more. At Kiawah Island, off the coast of South Carolina, visitors go out on Jeep "safaris" through the part of the island that hasn't been developed yet. ("Wherever you see trees," the guide says, "really, that's a lot.") The safari comprises six Jeeps, and these days they go out at least four times a day, with more trips promised soon. The tourists drive their own Jeeps and the guide talks to them by radio. Kiawah has nice beaches, and the guide talks about turtles. When he mentions the shrimpers' role in the decline of the turtle, the shrimpers, who share the same frequency, scream at him. Shrimpers and most commercial fishermen (many of them working with drift and gill nets anywhere from six to thirty miles long) think of themselves as an *endangered species*. A recent newspaper headline said, "Shrimpers Spared Anti-Turtle Devices." Even so, with the continuing wanton depletion of shrimp beds, they will undoubtedly have to find some other means of employment soon. They might, for instance, become part of that vast throng laboring in the *tourist industry*.

Tourism has become an industry as destructive as any other. You are no longer benign in your traveling somewhere to look at the scenery. You never thought there was much gain in just looking anyway, you've always preferred to *use* the scenery in some manner. In your desire to get away from what you've got, you've caused there to be no place to get away *to*. You're just all bumpered up out there. Sewage and dumps have become prime indicators of America's lifestyle. In resort towns in New England and the Adirondacks, measuring the flow into the sewage plant serves as a business barometer. Tourism is a growth industry. You believe in growth. *Controlled* growth, of course. Controlled exponential growth is what you'd really like to see. You certainly don't want to put a moratorium or a cap on anything. That's illegal, isn't it? Retro you're not. You don't want to go back or anything. Forward. Maybe ask directions later. Growth is *desirable* as well as being *inevitable*.

Growth is the one thing you seem to be powerless before, so you try to be realistic about it. Growth is—it's weird—it's like cancer or something.

Recently you, as tourist, have discovered your national parks and are quickly *overburdening* them. Spare land and it belongs to you! It's exotic land too, not looking like all the stuff around it that looks like everything else. You want to take advantage of this land, of course, and use it in every way you can. Thus the managers—or *stewards*, as they like to be called—have developed *wise* and *multiple-use* plans, keeping in mind exploiters' interests (for they have their needs, too) as well as the desires of the backpackers. Thus mining, timbering, and ranching activities take place in the national forests, where the Forest Service maintains a system of logging roads eight times larger than the interstate highway system. The national parks are more of a public playground and are becoming increasingly Europeanized in their look and management. Lots of concessions and motels. You deserve a clean bed and a hot meal when you go into the wilderness. At least your stewards think that you do. You keep your stewards busy. Not only must they cater to your multiple and conflicting desires, they have to manage your wildlife *resources*. They have managed wildfowl to such an extent that the reasoning has become, If it weren't for hunters, ducks would disappear. Duck stamps and licensing fees support the whole rickety duck-management system. Yes! If it weren't for the people who killed them, wild ducks wouldn't exist! Managers are managing all wild creatures, not just those that fly. They track and tape and tag and band. They relocate, restock, and reintroduce. They cull and control. It's hard to keep it all straight. Protect or poison? Extirpate or just mostly eliminate? Sometimes even the stewards get mixed up.

This is the time of machines and models, hands-on management and master plans. Don't you ever wonder as you pass that billboard advertising another MASTER-PLANNED COMMUNITY just what master they are actually talking about? Not the Big Master, certainly. Something brought to you by one of the tiny masters, of which there are many. But you like these tiny masters and have even come to expect and require them. In Florida they've just started a ten-thousand-acre city in the Everglades. It's a *megaproject*, one of the largest ever in the state. Yes, they must have thought you wanted it. No, what you thought of as the Everglades, the Park, is only a little bitty part of the Everglades. Developers have been gnawing at this irreplaceable, strange land for years. It's like they just *hate* this ancient sea of grass. Maybe you could ask them about this sometime. Roy Rogers is the senior vice president of strategic planning, and the old cowboy says that every tree and bush and inch of sidewalk in the project has been planned. Nevertheless, because the whole thing will take twenty-five years to complete, the plan is going to be constantly changed. You can understand this. The important thing is that there be a blueprint. You trust a blueprint. The tiny masters know what you like. You like *a secure landscape* and *access to services*. You like grass—that is, lawns. The ultimate lawn is the golf course, which you've been told has "some ecological value." You believe this! Not that it really matters, you just like to play golf. These golf courses require a lot of watering. So much that the more inspired of the masters have taken to watering them with effluent, *treated* effluent, but yours, from all the condos and villas built around the stocked artificial lakes you fancy.

I really don't want to think about sewage, you say, but it sounds like progress.

It is true that the masters are struggling with the problems of your incessant flushing. Cuisine is also one of their concerns. Advances in sorbets—sorbet intermezzos—in their clubs and fine restaurants. They know what you want. You want A HAVEN FROM THE ORDINARY WORLD. If you're A NATURE LOVER in the West you want to live in a $200,000 home in A WILD ANIMAL HABITAT. If you're eastern and consider yourself more hip, you want to live in new towns—brand-new reconstructed-from-scratch towns—in a house of NINE-TEENTH-CENTURY DESIGN. But in these new towns the masters are building, getting around can be confusing. There is an abundance of curves and an infrequency of through streets. It's the new wilderness without any trees. You can get lost, even with all the "mental bread crumbs" the masters scatter about as visual landmarks—the windmill, the water views, the various groupings of landscape "material." You *are* lost, you know. But you trust a Realtor will show you the way. There are many more Realtors than tiny masters, and many of them have to make do with less than a loaf—that is, trying to sell stuff that's already been built in an environment already "enhanced" rather than something being planned—but they're everywhere, willing to show you the path. If Dante returned to Hell today, he'd probably be escorted down by a Realtor, talking all the while about how it was just another level of Paradise.

> *When have you last watched a sunset? Do you remember where you were? With whom? At Loews Ventana Canyon Resort, the Grand Foyer will provide you with that opportunity through lighting which is computerized to diminish with the approaching sunset!*

The tiny masters are willing to arrange Nature for you. They will compose it into a picture that you can look at at your leisure, when you're not doing work or something like that. Nature becomes scenery, a prop. At some golf courses in the Southwest, the saguaro cacti are reported to be repaired with green paste when balls blast into their skin. The saguaro can attempt to heal themselves by growing over the balls, but this takes time, and the effect can be somewhat . . . baroque. It's better to get out the pastepot. Nature has become simply a visual form of entertainment, and it had better look snappy.

Listen, you say, we've been at Ventana Canyon. It's in the desert, right? It's very, very nice, a world-class resort. A totally self-contained environment with everything that a person could possibly want, on more than a thousand acres in the middle of zip. It sprawls but nestles, like. And they've maintained the integrity of as much of the desert ecosystem as possible. Give them credit for that. *Great* restaurant, too. We had baby bay scallops there. Coming into the lobby there are these two big hand-carved coyotes, mutely howling. And that's the way we like them, *mute*. God, why do those things howl like that?

Wildlife is a personal matter, you think. The attitude is up to you. You can prefer to see it dead or not dead. You might want to let it mosey about its business or blow it away. Wild things exist only if you have the graciousness to allow them to. Just outside Tucson, Arizona, there is a brand-new structure modeled after a French foreign legion outpost. It's the *International Wildlife Museum*, and it's full of dead animals. Three hundred species are there, at least a third of them – the rarest ones – killed and collected by one C. J. McElroy, who enjoyed doing it and now shares what's left with you. The museum claims to be educational because you can watch a taxidermist at work or touch a lion's tooth. You can get real close to these dead animals, closer than you can in a zoo. Some of you prefer zoos, however, which are becoming bigger, better, and bioclimatic. New-age zoo designers want the animals to *flow right out into your space*. In Dallas there will soon be a Wilds of Africa exhibit; in San Diego there's a simulated rain forest, where you can thread your way "down the side of a lush canyon, the air filled with a fine mist from 300 high-pressure nozzles"; in New Orleans you've constructed a swamp, the real swamp not far away on the verge of disappearing. Animals in these places are abstractions – wandering relics of their true selves, but that doesn't matter. Animal behavior in a zoo is nothing like natural behavior, but that doesn't really matter, either. Zoos are pretty, contained, and accessible. These new habitats can contain one hundred different species – not more than one or two of each thing, of course – on seven acres, three, one. You don't want to see *too much* of anything, certainly. An *example* will suffice. Sort of like a biological Crabtree & Evelyn basket selected with *you* in mind. You like things reduced, simplified. It's easier to take it all in, park it in your mind. You like things inside better than outside anyway. You are increasingly looking at and living in proxy environments created by substitution and simulation. *Resource economists* are a wee branch in the tree of tiny masters, and one, Martin Krieger, wrote, "Artificial prairies and wildernesses have been created, and there is no reason to believe that these artificial environments need be unsatisfactory for those who experience them. . . . We will have to realize that the way in which we experience nature is conditioned by our society – which more and more is seen to be receptive to responsible intervention."

Nature has become a world of appearances, a mere source of materials. You've been editing it for quite some time; now you're in the process of deleting it. Earth is beginning to look like not much more than a launching pad. Back near Tucson, on the opposite side of the mountain from the dead-animal habitat, you're building Biosphere II (as compared with or opposed to Biosphere I, more commonly known as Earth) – a 2 1/2-acre terrarium, an artificial ecosystem that will include a rain forest, a desert, a thirty-five-foot ocean, and several thousand species of life (lots of microbes), including eight human beings, who will cultivate a bit of farmland. You think it would be nice to colonize other worlds after you've made it necessary to leave this one.

Hey, that's pretty good, you say, all that stuff packed into just 2 1/2 acres. That's only about three times bigger than my entire *house*.

It's small all right, but still not small enough to be, apparently, useful. For the purposes of NASA, say, it would have to be smaller, oh much smaller, and energy-efficient too. Fiddle, fiddle, fiddle. You support fiddling, as well as meddling. This is how you learn. Though it's quite apparent the environment has been grossly polluted and the natural world abused and defiled, you seem to prefer to continue pondering effects rather than preventing causes. You want proof, you insist on proof. A Dr. Lave from Carnegie-Mellon—and he's an expert, an economist, and an environmental *expert*—says that scientists will have to prove to you that you will suffer if you don't become less of a "throw-away society." *If you really want me to give up my car or my air conditioner, you'd better prove to me first that the earth would otherwise be uninhabitable,* Dr. Lave says. *Me* is *you*, I presume, whereas *you* refers to them. You as in me—that is, *me, me, me*—certainly strike a hard bargain. Uninhabitable the world has to get before you rein in your requirements. You're a consumer after all, *the* consumer upon whom so much attention is lavished, the ultimate user of a commodity that has become, these days, everything. To try to appease your appetite for proof, for example, scientists have been leasing for experimentation forty-six pristine lakes in Canada.

They don't want to *keep* them, they just want to *borrow* them.

They've been intentionally contaminating many of the lakes with a variety of pollutants dribbled into the propeller wash of research boats. *It's one of the boldest experiments in lake ecology ever conducted.* They've turned these remote lakes into huge *real-world test tubes*. They've been doing this since 1976! And what they've found so far in these *preliminary* studies is that pollutants are really destructive. The lakes get gross. Life in them ceases. It took about eight years to make this happen in one of them, everything carefully measured and controlled all the while. Now the scientists are slowly reversing the process. But it will take hundreds of years for the lakes to recover. They think.

Remember when you used to like rain, the sound of it, the feel of it, the way it made the plants and trees all glisten. We needed that rain, you would say. It looked pretty too, you thought, particularly in the movies. Now it rains and you go, Oh-oh. A nice walloping rain these days means *overtaxing our sewage treatment plants*. It means *untreated waste discharged directly into our waterways*. It means . . .

Okay. Okay.

Acid rain! And we all know what this is. Or most of us do. People of power in government and industry still don't seem to know what it is. Whatever it is, they say, they don't want to curb it, but they're willing to study it some more. Economists call air and water pollution "externalities" anyway. Oh, acid rain. You do get so sick of hearing about it. The words have already become a white-noise kind of thing. But you think in terms of *mitigating* it maybe. As for *the greenhouse effect*, you think in terms of *countering* that. One way that's been discussed recently is the planting of new forests, not for the sake of the forests alone, oh my heavens, no. Not for the sake of majesty and mystery or of Thumper and Bambi, are you kidding me, but because, as every schoolchild knows, trees absorb carbon dioxide. They just soak it up and store it. They just love it. So this is the plan: you plant millions of acres of trees, and you can go on doing pretty much whatever you're doing—driving around, using staggering amounts of energy, keeping those power plants fired to the max. Isn't Nature remarkable? So willing to serve? You wouldn't think it had anything more to offer, but it seems it does. Of course these "forests" wouldn't exactly be forests. They would be more like trees. *Managed* trees. The Forest Service, which now manages our forests by cutting them down, might be called upon to evolve in their thinking and allow these trees to grow. They would probably be patented trees after a time. Fast-growing, uniform, genetically-created-to-be-toxin-eating *machines*. They would be *new-age* trees, because the problem with planting the old-fashioned variety to *combat* the greenhouse effect, which is caused by pollution, is that they're already dying from it. All along the crest of the Appalachians from Maine to Georgia, forests struggle to survive in a toxic soup of poisons. They can't *help* us if we've killed them, now can they?

All right, you say, wow, lighten up will you? Relax. Tell about yourself.
Well, I say, I live in Florida . . .
Oh my God, you say. Florida! Florida is a joke! How do you expect us to take you seriously if you still live there! Florida is crazy, it's pink concrete. It's paved, it's over. And a little girl just got eaten by an alligator down there. It came out of some swamp next to a subdivision and just carried her off. That set your Endangered Species Act back fifty years, you can bet.
I . . .
Listen, we don't want to hear any more about Florida. We don't want to hear about Phoenix or Hilton Head or California's Central Valley. If our wetlands—our *vanishing* wetlands—are mentioned one more time, we'll scream. And the talk about condors and grizzlies and wolves is becoming too de trop. We had just managed to get whales out of our minds when those three showed up under the ice in Alaska. They even had *names*. Bone is the dead one, right? It's almost the twenty-first century! Those last condors are *pathetic*. Can't we just get this over with?
Aristotle said that all living things are ensouled and striving to participate in eternity.
Oh, I just bet he said that, you say. That doesn't sound like Aristotle. He was a humanist. We're all humanists here. This is the age of humanism. And it has been for a long time.

You are driving with a stranger in the car, and it is the stranger behind the wheel. In the back seat are your pals for many years now—DO WHAT YOU LIKE and his swilling sidekick, WHY NOT. A deer, or some emblematic animal, something from that myriad natural world you've come from that you now treat with such indifference and scorn—steps from the dimming woods and tentatively upon the highway. The stranger does not decelerate or brake, not yet, maybe not at all. The feeling is that whatever it is *will get out of the way.* Oh, it's a fine car you've got, a fine machine, and oddly you don't mind the stranger driving it, because in a way, everything has gotten too complicated, way, way out of your control. You've given the wheel to the masters, the managers, the comptrollers. Something is wrong, *maybe*, you feel a little sick, *actually*, but the car is luxurious and fast and you're *moving*, which is the most important thing by far.

Why make a fuss when you're so comfortable? Don't make a fuss, make a baby. Go out and get something to eat, build something. Make *another* baby. Babies are cute. Babies show you have faith in the future. Although faith is perhaps too strong a word. They're everywhere these days, in all the crowds and traffic jams, there are the babies too. You don't seem to associate them with the problems of population increase. They're just babies! And you've come to believe in them again. They're a lot more tangible than the afterlife, which, of course, you haven't believed in in ages. At least not for yourself. The afterlife now belongs to plastics and poisons. Yes, plastics and poisons will have a far more extensive afterlife than you, that's known. A disposable diaper, for example, which is all plastic and wood pulp—you like them for all those babies, so easy to use and toss—will take around four centuries to degrade. Almost all plastics do, centuries and centuries. In the sea, many marine animals die from ingesting or being entangled in discarded plastic. In the dumps, plastic squats on more than 25 percent of dump space. But your heart is disposed toward plastic. Someone, no doubt the plastics industry, told you it was convenient. This same industry is now looking into recycling in an attempt to get the critics of their nefarious, multifarious products off their backs. That should make you feel better, because *recycling* has become an honorable word, no longer merely the hobby of Volvo owners. The fact is that people in plastics are born obscurants. Recycling (practically impossible) won't solve the plastic glut, only reduction of production will, and the plastics industry isn't looking into that, you can be sure. Waste is not just the stuff you throw away, of course, it's the stuff you use to excess. With the exception of *hazardous waste*, which you do worry about from time to time, it's even thought you have a declining sense of emergency about the problem. Builders are building bigger houses because you want bigger. You're trading up. Utility companies are beginning to worry about your constantly rising consumption. Utility companies! You haven't entered a new age at all but one of upscale nihilism, deluxe nihilism.

In the summer, particularly in *the industrial Northeast*, you did get a little excited. The filth cut into your fun time. Dead stuff floating around. Sludge and bloody vials. Hygienic devices—appearing not quite so hygienic out of context—all coming in on the tide. The air smelled funny, too. You tolerate a great deal, but the summer of '88 was truly creepy. It was even thought for a moment that the environment would become a political issue. But it didn't. You didn't want it to be, preferring instead to continue in your politics of subsidizing and advancing avarice. The issues were the same as always—jobs, defense, the economy, maintaining and improving the standard of living in this greedy, selfish, expansionistic, industrialized society.

You're getting a little shrill here, you say.

You're pretty well off. You expect to be better off soon. You do. What does this mean? More software, more scampi, more square footage? You have created an ecological crisis. The earth is infinitely variable and alive, and you are killing it. It seems safer this way. But you are not safe. You want to find wholeness and happiness in a land increasingly damaged and betrayed, and you never will. More than material matters. You must change your ways.

What is this? *Sinners in the Hands of an Angry God?*

The ecological crisis cannot be resolved by politics. It cannot be solved by science or technology. It is a crisis caused by culture and character, and a deep change in personal consciousness is needed. Your fundamental attitudes toward the earth have become twisted. You have made only brutal contact with Nature, you cannot comprehend its grace. You must change. Have few desires and simple pleasures. Honor nonhuman life. Control yourself, become more authentic. Live lightly upon the earth and treat it with respect. Redefine the word *progress* and dismiss the managers and masters. Grow inwardly and with knowledge become truly wiser. Make connections. Think differently, behave differently. For this is essentially a moral issue we face and moral decisions must be made.

A *moral issue!* Okay, this discussion is now toast. A *moral* issue . . . And who's this *we* now? Who are *you* is what I'd like to know. You're not me, anyway. I admit, someone's to blame and something should be done. But I've got to go. It's getting late. That's dusk out there. That is dusk, isn't it? It certainly doesn't look like any dawn I've ever seen. Well, take care.

Discussion Questions

1. Who are "me" and "you" in this essay? What conclusions do you reach about the speaker's own political views, level of education, and level of environmental awareness? As a reader, do you identify more with "you" or "me"? Why?

2. Do you think that Williams's argument is fair and objective? If so, how? If not, what do you think Williams's reaction would be to anyone who said her essay was biased?

3. Identify the author's transitions between paragraphs. How does she connect different perspectives into a unified theme?

4. What does the speaker mean by suggesting that the listener senses he or she is "a little too late for nature"? How can nature be like a party that you decide not to attend because you think it's just too late to go?

Journal Entry

What do you like or dislike about zoos? What are the pros and cons of having zoos? Link your own feelings to the larger issues presented in this essay.

Writing Projects

1. How does the author explore irony in this essay? What does she consider ironic about hunters' organizations claiming that without hunters the ducks would disappear? Which, if any, of Williams's own arguments are ironic?

2. Analyze how the author establishes tone and pacing in this essay. For example, how does diction (word choice) and sentence length establish a particular tone here? How does Williams achieve continuity between the various perspectives? Even though her essay is longer than most others, how does Williams sustain the reader's interest and conclude with a strong impact?

3. Write an essay for an issue of a periodical like *Farm Journal* in which you support or refute Williams's statement: "Farmers like their poisons, but ranchers like them even more."

Collaborative Projects

1. Working with a partner, investigate the biosphere project in Arizona that Williams mentions. On September 26, 1993, the crew of Biosphere II emerged after concluding its two-year experiment. What did the crew have to say about the experiment? What evaluations did the sponsors of the project offer of its success? What further experiments are going on? Is there a Biosphere III? You might work as a team throughout the stages of your research and follow-up analytical report. Or you could divide the research, one focusing on Biosphere II and the other on subsequent projects. Summarize your findings and conclusions for the class.

2. Working with a partner, research the Agriculture Department's Animal Damage Control Unit. Why was this division formed? When? What are the stated goals of the Control Unit? How does it go about achieving these goals? What is your evaluation of the goals? How would you rate the Unit's success in achieving them? Give an oral presentation in class explaining the Unit's history and effectiveness.

Rick DeMarinis

Weeds

Rick DeMarinis *(b. 1934) is the author of a number of prize-winning novels and short story collections. He has taught English at the University of El Paso since 1988. "Weeds" is from his collection of short stories* Under the Wheat *(1986), which was awarded the prestigious Drue Heinz Literature Prize. DeMarinis received critical acclaim for his novel* The Burning Women of Far Cry *(1986), a darkly humorous story of a young man growing up during the 1950s. More recent works by DeMarinis include a novel,* The Year of the Zinc Penny *(1991), and a collection of short stories,* Voice of America *(1991). "Weeds," a surrealistic version of the* Jack and the Beanstalk *fable, is typical of much of DeMarinis's fiction, which has been described as dark comedy.*

Questions to Consider

☐ As you read, watch for allusions to children's stories, fables, or well-known myths that DeMarinis has incorporated into this tale. These allusions could refer to characters, places, or events.

☐ Consult a glossary of literary terms or a good dictionary for a definition of *surrealism.* This will help you understand how the story operates on more than a surface level.

A black helicopter flapped out of the morning sun and dumped its sweet orange mist on our land instead of the Parley farm where it was intended. It was weedkiller, something strong enough to wipe out leafy spurge, knapweed and Canadian thistle, but it made us sick.

My father had a fatal stroke a week after that first spraying. I couldn't hold down solid food for nearly a month and went from 200 pounds to 170 in that time. Mama went to bed and slept for two days, and when she woke up she was not the same. She'd lost something of herself in that long sleep, and something that wasn't herself had replaced it.

Then it hit the animals. We didn't have much in the way of animals, but one by one they dropped. The chickens, the geese, the two old mules—Doc and Rex—and last of all, our only cow, Miss Milky, who was more or less the family pet.

Miss Milky was the only animal that didn't outright up and die. She just got sick. There was blood in her milk and her milk was thin. Her teats got so tender and brittle that she would try to mash me against the milk stall wall when I pulled at them. The white part of her eyes looked like fresh red meat. Her piss was so strong that the green grass wherever she stood died off. She got so bound up that when she'd lift her tail and bend with strain, only one black apple would drop. Her breath took on a burning sulphurous stink that would make you step back.

She also went crazy. She'd stare at me like she all at once had a desperate human mind and had never seen me before. Then she'd act as if she wanted to slip a horn under my ribs and peg me to the barn. She would drop her head and charge, blowing like a randy bull, and I would have to scramble out of the way. Several times I saw her gnaw on her hooves or stand stock-still in water up to her blistered teats. Or she would walk backward all day long, mewling like a lost cat that had been dropped off in a strange place. That mewling was enough to make you want to clap a set of noise dampers on your ears. The awful sound led Mama to say this: "It's the death song of the land, mark my words."

Mama never talked like that before in her life. She'd always been a cheerful woman who could never see the bad part of anything that was at least fifty percent good. But now she was dark and strange as a gypsy, and she would have spells of sheer derangement during which she'd make noises like a wild animal, or she'd play the part of another person – the sort of person she'd normally have nothing to do with at all. At Daddy's funeral, she got dressed up in an old and tattered evening gown the color of beet juice, her face painted and powdered like that of a barfly. And while the preacher told the onlookers what a fine man Daddy had been, Mama cupped her hands under her breasts and lifted them high, as if offering to appease a dangerous stranger. Then, ducking her head, she chortled, "Loo, loo, loo," her scared eyes scanning the trees for owls.

I was twenty-eight years old and my life had come to nothing. I'd had a girl but I'd lost her through neglect and a careless attitude that had spilled over into my personal life, souring it. I had no ambition to make something worthwhile of myself, and it nettled her. Toward the end, she began to parrot her mother: "You need to get yourself *established*, Jack," she would say. But I didn't want to get myself established. I was getting poorer and more aimless day by day, and I supposed she believed that "getting established" would put a stop to the downhill slide, but I had no desire to do whatever it took to accomplish that.

Shortly after Daddy died, the tax man came to our door with a paper in his hand. "Inheritance tax," he said, handing me the paper.

"What do you mean?" I asked.

"It's the law," he said. "Your father died, you see. And that's going to cost you some. You should have made better plans." He tapped his forehead with his finger and winked. He had a way of expressing himself that made me think he was country born and raised but wanted to seem citified. Or maybe it was the other way around.

"I don't understand this," I mumbled. I felt the weight of a world I'd so far been able to avoid. It was out there, tight-assed and squinty-eyed, and it knew to the dollar and dime what it needed to keep itself in business.

"Simple," he said. "Pay or move off. The government is the government, and it can't bend a rule to accommodate the confused. It's your decision. Pay or the next step is litigation."

He smiled when he said good-bye. I closed the door against the weight of his smile, which was the weight of the world. I went to a window and watched him head back to his green government car. The window was open and I could hear him. He was singing loudly in a fine tenor voice. He raised his right hand to hush an invisible audience that had broken into uncontrolled applause. I could still hear him singing as he slipped the car into gear and idled away. He was singing "Red River Valley."

Even though the farm was all ours, paid up in full, we had to give the government $7,000 for the right to stay on it. The singing tax man said we had inherited the land from my father, and the law was sharp on the subject.

I didn't know where the money was going to come from. I didn't talk it over with Mama because even in her better moments she would talk in riddles. To a simple question such as, "Should I paint the barns this year, Mama?" she might answer, "I've no eyes for glitter, nor ears for their ridicule."

One day I decided to load Miss Milky into the stock trailer and haul her into Saddle Butte where the vet, Doc Nevers, had his office. Normally, Doc Nevers would come out to your place, but he'd heard about the spraying that was going on and said he wouldn't come within three miles of our property until they were done.

The Parley farm was being sprayed regularly, for they grew an awful lot of wheat and almost as much corn, and they had the biggest haying operation in the county. Often, the helicopters they used were upwind from us and we were sprayed too. ("Don't complain," said Big Pete Parley when I called him up about it. "Think of it this way—you're getting your place weeded for *free!*" When I said I might have to dynamite some stumps on the property line and that he might get a barn or two blown away for free, he just laughed like hell, as if I had told one of the funniest jokes he'd ever heard.)

There was a good windbreak between our places, a thick grove of lombardy poplars, but the orange mist, sweet as a flower garden in full bloom, sifted through the trees and settled on our fields. Soon the poplars were mottled and dying. Some branches curled in an upward twist, as if flexed in pain, and others became soft and fibrous as if the wood were trying to turn itself into sponge.

With Miss Milky in the trailer, I sat in the truck sipping on a pint of Lewis and Clark bourbon and looking out across our unplanted fields. It was late – almost too late – to plant anything. Mama, in the state she was in, hadn't even noticed.

In the low hills on the north side of the property, some ugly looking things were growing. From the truck, they looked like white pimples on the smooth brown hill. Up close, they were big as melons. They were some kind of fungus, and they pushed up through the ground like the bald heads of fat babies. They gave off a rotten meat stink. I would get chillbumps just looking at them, and if I touched one, my stomach would rise. The bulbous heads had purple streaks on them that looked like blood vessels. I half expected to one day see human eyes clear the dirt and open. Big pale eyes that would see me and carry my image down to their deepest root. I was glad they seemed to prefer the hillside and bench and not the bottom land.

Justified or not, I blamed the growth of this fungus on the poison spray, just as I blamed it for the death of my father, the loss of our animals, and the strangeness of my mother. Now the land itself was becoming strange. And I thought, what about me? How am I being rearranged by that weedkiller?

I guess I should have gotten mad, but I didn't. Maybe I *had* been changed by the spray. Where once I had been a quick-to-take-offense hothead, I was now docile and thoughtful. I could sit on a stump and think for hours, enjoying the slow and complicated intertwinings of my own thoughts. Even though I felt sure the cause of all our troubles had fallen out of the sky, I would hold arguments with myself, as if there were always two sides to every question. If I said to myself, "Big Pete Parley has poisoned my family and farm and my father is dead because of it," I would follow it up with, "But Daddy was old anyway, past seventy-five, and he always had high blood pressure. Anything could have set off his stroke, from a wasp bite to a sonic boom."

"And what about Mama?" I would ask. "Senile with grief," came the quick answer. "Furthermore, Daddy himself used poison in his time. Cyanide traps for coyotes, DDT for mosquito larvae, arsenic for rats."

My mind was always doubling back on itself in this way, and it would often leave me standing motionless in a field for hours, paralyzed with indecision, sighing like a moonstruck girl of twelve. I imagined myself mistaken by passersby for a scarecrow.

Sometimes I saw myself as a human weed, useless to other people in general and maybe harmful in some weedy way. The notion wasn't entirely unpleasant. Jack Hucklebone: a weed among the well-established money crops of life.

On my way to town with Miss Milky, I crossed over the irrigation ditch my father had fallen into with the stroke that killed him. I pulled over onto the shoulder and switched off the engine. It was a warm, insect-loud day in early June. A spray of grasshoppers clattered over the hood of the truck. June bugs ticked past the windows like little flying clocks. The thirteen-year locusts were back and raising a whirring hell. I was fifteen the last time they came, but I didn't remember them arriving in such numbers. I expected more helicopters to come flapping over with special sprays meant just for them, even though they would be around for only a few weeks and the damage they would do is not much more than measurable. But anything that looks like it might have an appetite for a money crop brings down the spraying choppers. I climbed out of the truck and looked up into the bright air. A lone jet, eastbound, too high to see or hear, left its neat chalk line across the top of the sky. The sky itself was like hot blue wax, north to south. A giant hammerhead sat on the west horizon as if it were a creamy oblong planet gone dangerously off-course.

There's where Daddy died. Up the ditch about fifty yards from here. I found him, buckled, white as paper, half under water. His one good eye, his right (he'd lost the left one thirty years ago when a tractor tire blew up in his face as he was filling it), was above water and wide open, staring at his hand as if it could focus on the thing it gripped. He was holding on to a root. He had big hands, strong, with fingers like thick hardwood dowels, but now they were soft and puffy, like the hands of a giant baby. Water bugs raced against the current toward him. His body blocked the ditch and little eddies swirled around it. The water bugs skated into the eddies and, fighting to hold themselves still in the roiling current, touched his face. They held still long enough to satisfy their curiosity, then slid back into the circular flow as if bemused by the strangeness of dead human flesh.

I started to cry, remembering it, thinking about him in the water, he had been so sure and strong, but then—true to my changed nature—I began to laugh at the memory, for his wide blue eye had had a puzzled cast to it, as if it had never before seen such a crazy thing as the ordinary root in his forceless hand. It was an expression he never wore in life.

"It was only a weed, Daddy," I said, wiping the tears from my face.

The amazed puzzlement stayed in his eye until I brushed down the lid.

Of course he had been dead beyond all talk and puzzlement. Dead when I found him, dead for hours, bloated dead. And this is how I've come to be— blame the spray or don't: the chores don't get done on time, the unplanted fields wait, Mama wanders in her mind, and yet I'll sit in the shade of my truck sipping on Lewis and Clark bourbon, inventing the thoughts of a stone-dead man.

Time bent away from me like a tail-dancing rainbow. It was about to slip the hook. I wasn't trying to hold it. Try to hold it and it gets all the more slippery. Try to let it go and it sticks like a cocklebur to cotton. I was drifting somewhere between the two kinds of not trying: not trying to hold anything, not trying to let anything go.

Then he sat down next to me. The old man.

"You got something for me?" he said.

He was easily the homeliest man I had ever seen. His bald head was bullet-shaped and his lumpy nose was warty as a crookneck squash. His little, close-set eyes sat on either side of that nose like hard black beans. He had shaggy eyebrows that climbed upward in a white and wiry tangle. There was a blue lump in the middle of his forehead the size of a pullet's egg, and his hairy ear lobes touched his grimy collar. He was mumbling something, but it could have been the noise of the ditch water as it sluiced through the culvert under the road.

He stank of whiskey and dung, and looked like he'd been sleeping behind barns for weeks. His clothes were rags, and he was caked with dirt from fingernail to jaw. His shoes were held together with strips of burlap. He untied some of these strips and took off the shoes. Then he slid his gnarled, dirt-crusted feet into the water. His eyes fluttered shut and he let out a hissing moan of pleasure. His toes were long and twisted, the arthritic knuckles painfully bright. They reminded me of the surface roots of a stunted oak that had been trying to grow in hardpan. Though he was only about five feet tall, his feet were huge. Easy size twelves, wide as paddles.

He quit mumbling, cleared his throat, spit. "You got something for me?" he said.

I handed him my pint. He took it, then held it up to the sunlight and looked through the rusty booze as if testing for its quality.

"If it won't do," I said, "I could run into town to get something a little smoother for you. Maybe you'd like some Canadian Club or some twelve-year-old Scotch. I could run into town and be back in less than an hour. Maybe you'd like me to bring back a couple of fried chickens and a sack of buttered rolls." This was my old self talking, the hothead. But I didn't feel mad at him, and was just being mouthy out of habit.

"No need to do that," he said, as if my offer had been made in seriousness. He took a long pull off my pint. "This snake piss is just fine by me, son." He raised the bottle to the sunlight again, squinted through it.

I wandered down the ditch again to the place where Daddy died. There was nothing there to suggest a recent dead man had blocked the current. Everything was as it always was. The water surged, the quick water bugs skated up and down, inspecting brown clumps of algae along the banks; underwater weeds waved like slim snakes whose tails had been staked to the mud. I looked for the thistle he'd grabbed on to. I guess he thought that he was going to save himself from drowning by hanging on to its root, not realizing that the killing flood was *inside* his head. But there were many roots along the bank and none of them seemed more special than any other.

Something silver glinted at me. It was a coin. I picked it out of the slime and polished it against my pants. It was a silver dollar, a real one. It could have been his. He carried a few of the old cartwheels around with him for luck. The heft and gleam of the old solid silver coin choked me up.

I walked back to the old man. He had stuffed his bindle under his head for a pillow and had dozed off. I uncapped the pint and finished it, then flipped it into the weeds. It hit a rock and popped. The old man grunted and his eyes snapped open. He let out a barking snort, and his black eyes darted around him fiercely, like the eyes of a burrow animal caught in a daylight trap. Then, remembering where he was, he calmed down.

"You got something for me?" he asked. He pushed himself up to a sitting position. It was a struggle for him.

"Not any more," I said. I sat down next to him. Then, from behind us, a deep groan cut loose. It sounded like siding being pried off an old barn with a crowbar. We both turned to look at whatever had complained so mightily.

It was Miss Milky, up in the trailer, venting her misery. I'd forgotten about her. Horseflies were biting her. Her red eyes peered sadly out at us through the bars. The corners of her eyes were swollen, giving her a Chinese look.

With no warning at all, a snapping hail fell on us. Only it wasn't hail. It was a moving cloud of thirteen-year locusts. They darkened the air and they covered us. The noise was like static on the radio, miles of static across the bug-peppered sky, static that could drown out all important talk and idle music, no matter how powerful the station.

The old man's face was covered with the bugs and he was saying something to me, but I couldn't make out what it was. His mouth opened and closed, opened and closed. When it opened, he'd have to brush away the locusts from his lips. They were like ordinary grasshoppers, only smaller, and they had big red eyes that seemed to glow with their own hellish light. Then, as fast as they had come, they were gone, scattered back into the fields. A few hopped here and there, but the main cloud had broken up.

I just sat there, brushing at the lingering feel of them on my skin and trying to readjust myself to uncluttered air, but my ears were still crackling with their racket.

The old man pulled at my sleeve, breaking me out of my daydream or trance. "You got something for me?" he asked.

I felt blue. Worse than blue. Sick. I felt incurable – ridden with the pointlessness of just about everything you could name. The farm struck me as a pointless wonder, and I found the idea depressing and fearsome. Pointless bugs lay waiting in the fields for the pointless crops as the pointless days and seasons ran on and on into the pointless forever.

"Shit," I said.

"I'll take that worthless cow off your hands, then," said the old man. "She's done for. All you have to do is look at her."

"No shit," I said.

He didn't seem so old or so wrecked to me now. He was younger and bigger, somehow, as if all his clocks had started spinning backwards, triggered by the locust cloud. He stood up. He looked thick across the shoulders like he'd done hard work all his life and could still do it. He showed me his right hand and it was yellow with hard calluses. His beady black eyes were quick and lively in their shallow sockets. The blue lump on his forehead glinted in the sun. It seemed deliberately polished, as if it were an ornament. He took a little silver bell out of his pocket and rang it for no reason at all.

"Let me have her," he said.

"You want Miss Milky?" I asked. I felt weak and childish. Maybe I was drunk. My scalp itched and I scratched it hard. He rang his little silver bell again. I wanted to have it, but he put it back into his pocket. Then he knelt down and opened his bindle. He took out a paper sack.

I looked inside. It was packed with seeds of some kind. I ran my fingers through them and did not feel foolish. I heard a helicopter putt-putting in the distance. In defense of what I did, let me say this much: I knew Miss Milky was done for. Doc Nevers would have told me to kill her. I don't think she was even good for hamburger. Old cow meat can sometimes make good hamburger, but Miss Milky looked wormy and lean. And I wouldn't have trusted her bones for soup. The poison that had wasted her flesh and ruined her udder had probably settled in her marrow.

And so I unloaded my dying cow. He took out his silver bell again and tied it to a piece of string. He tied the string around Miss Milky's neck. Then he led her away. She was docile and easy, as though this was exactly the way things were supposed to turn out.

My throat was dry. I felt too tired to move. I watched their slow progress down the path that ran along the ditch. They got smaller and smaller in the field until, against a dark hedge of box elders, they disappeared. I strained to see after them, but it was as if the earth had given them refuge, swallowing them into its deep, loamy, composting interior. The only sign that they still existed in the world was the tinkling of the silver bell he had tied around Miss Milky's neck. It was a pure sound, naked on the air.

Then a breeze opened a gap in the box elders and a long blade of sunlight pierced through them, illuminating and magnifying the old man and his cow, as if the air between us had formed itself into a giant lens. The breeze let up and the box elders shut off the sun again, and I couldn't see anything but a dense quiltwork of black and green shadows out of which a raven big as an eagle flapped. It cawed in raucous good humor as it veered over my head.

I went on into town anyway, cow or no cow, and hit some bars. I met a girl from the East in the Hobble who thought I was a cowboy and I didn't try to correct her mistaken impression, for it proved to be a free pass to good times.

When I got home, Mama had company. She was dressed up in her beet juice gown, and her face was powdered white. Her dark lips looked like a wine stain in snow. But her clear blue eyes were direct and calm. There was no distraction in them.

"Hi boy," said the visitor. It was Big Pete Parley. He was wearing a blue suit, new boots, a gray felt Stetson. He had a toothy grin on his fat red face.

I looked at Mama. "What's *he* want?" I asked.

"Mr. Parley is going to help us, Jackie," she said.

"What's going on, Mama?" I asked. Something was wrong. I could feel it but I couldn't see it. It was Mama, the way she was carrying herself maybe, or the look in her eyes and her whitened skin. Maybe she had gone all the way insane. She went over to Parley and sat next to him on the davenport. She had slit her gown and it fell away from her thigh, revealing the veiny flesh.

"We're going to be married," she said. "Pete's tired of being a widower. He wants a warm bed."

As if to confirm it was no fantasy dreamed up by her senile mind, Big Pete slipped his meaty hand into the slit dress and squeezed her thigh. He clicked his teeth and winked at me.

"Pete knows how to operate a farm," said Mama. "And you do not, Jackie." She didn't intend for it to sound mean or critical. It was just a statement of the way things were. I couldn't argue with her.

I went into the kitchen. Mama followed me in. I opened a beer. "I don't mean to hurt your feelings, Jackie," she said.

"He's scheming to get our land," I said. "He owns half the county, but it isn't enough."

"No," she said. "I'm the one who's scheming. I'm scheming for my boy who does not grasp the rudiments of the world."

I had the sack of seed with me. I realized that I'd been rattling them nervously.

"What do you have there?" she asked, narrowing her eyes.

"Seeds," I said.

"Seeds? What seeds? Who gave you seeds? Where'd you get them?"

I thought it best not to mention where I'd gotten them. "Big Pete Parley doesn't want to marry *you*," I said. It was a mean thing to say, and I wanted to say it.

Mama sighed. "It doesn't matter what he wants, Jack. I'm dead anyway." She took the bag of seeds from me, picked some up, squinted at them.

"What is that supposed to mean?" I said, sarcastically.

She went to the window above the sink and stared out into the dark. Under the folds of her evening gown, I could see the ruined shape of her old body. "Dead, Jack," she said. "I've been dead for a while now. Maybe you didn't notice."

"No," I said. "I didn't."

"Well, you should have. I went to sleep shortly after your Daddy died and I had a dream. The dream got stronger and stronger as it went on until it was as vivid as real life itself. More vivid. When I woke up I knew that I had died. I also knew that nothing in the world would ever be as real to me as that dream."

I almost asked her what the dream was about, but I didn't, out of mean-ness. In the living room Big Pete Parley was whistling impatiently. The daven-port was squeaking under his nervous weight.

"So, you see, Jackie," said Mama. "It doesn't matter if I marry Pete Parley or what his motives are in this matter. You are all that counts now. He will en-sure your success in the world."

"I don't want to be a success, Mama," I said.

"Well, you have no choice. You cannot gainsay the dead."

She opened the window and dumped out the sack of seeds. Then Big Pete Parley came into the kitchen. "Let's go for a walk," he said. "It's too blame hot in this house."

They left by the kitchen door. I watched them walk across the yard and into the dark, unplanted field. Big Pete had his arm around Mama's shoulder. I wondered if he knew, or cared, that he was marrying a dead woman. Light from the half-moon painted their silhouettes for a while. Then the dark field absorbed them.

I went to bed and slept for what might have been days. In my long sleep I had a dream. I was canoeing down a whitewater river that ran sharply uphill. The farther up I got, the rougher the water became. Finally, I had to beach the canoe. I proceeded on foot until I came to a large gray house that had been built in a wilderness forest. The house was empty and quiet. I went in. It was clean and beautifully furnished. Nobody was home. I called out a few times be-fore I understood that silence was a rule. I went from room to room, going deeper and deeper toward some dark interior place. I understood that I was in-volved in a search. The longer I searched, the more vivid the dream became.

When I woke up I was stiff and weak. Mama wasn't in the house. I made a pot of coffee and took a cup outside. Under the kitchen window there was a patch of green shoots that had not been there before. "You got something for me?" I said.

A week later that patch of green shoots had grown and spread. They were weeds. The worst kind of weeds I had ever seen. Thick, spiny weeds, with broad green leaves tough as leather. They rolled away from the house, out across the fields, in a viny carpet. Mean, deep-rooted weeds, too mean to up-root by hand. When I tried, I came away with a palm full of cuts.

In another week they were tall as corn. They were fast growers and I could not see where they ended. They covered everything in sight. A smother-ing blanket of deep green sucked the life out of every other growing thing. They crossed fences, irrigation ditches, and when they reached the trees of a windbreak, they became ropy crawlers that wrapped themselves around trunks and limbs.

When they reached the Parley farm, over which my dead mother now presided, they were attacked by squadrons of helicopters which drenched them in poisons, the best poisons chemical science knew how to brew. But the poisons only seemed to make the weeds grow faster, and after a spraying the new growths were tougher, thornier, and more determined than ever to dominate the land.

Some of the weeds sent up long woody stalks. On top of these stalks were heavy seedpods, fat as melons. The strong stalks pushed the pods high into the air.

The day the pods cracked, a heavy wind came up. The wind raised black clouds of seed in grainy spirals that reached the top of the sky, then scattered them, far and wide, across the entire nation.

Discussion Questions

1. How does DeMarinis depict the characters in his story? As a class, outline the characteristics of all the people and animals. Why does he devote space to characterization of animals as well as people? How do you respond to his characters? Do you think yours is the response the author intended to elicit? Why or why not?

2. Do you think this story is funny? Why or why not? Point out a passage that made you laugh, and analyze how it works. Is it slapstick humor? A play on words? A mockery of some thing or idea you have contempt for? Does it deflate someone's pretensions? Poke fun at a stereotype?

3. At one point the narrator argues to himself over how much he can blame his troubles on Pete Parley's orange poison. How might the narrator's argument be interpreted as representing more than just two sides of his personal dilemma?

4. Who is the old man with the head that is "bullet-shaped" and the nose "warty as a crookneck squash"? Who or what does he represent?

Journal Entry

Try writing a descriptive passage that imitates DeMarinis's style. Incorporate color, smell, and other sensory images in a way similar to DeMarinis's.

Writing Projects

1. This story derives much of its effect from the author's construction of vivid analogies. Select particular passages and analyze how the images, analogies, and other figurative language work within the story.

2. At one point the narrator tells us that his Mama sometimes says, "It's the death song of the land, mark my words." Discuss to what extent this story is about the death of the land. Include an analysis of where the statement appears and why it is Mama who says it, as well as what it describes and how it fits into the whole story.

Collaborative Projects

1. Working with a partner, analyze how DeMarinis has adapted children's folk tales to his own story. Compare the story of Jack and the Beanstalk with other folk tales and parables, such as the one about the goose that laid the golden egg or the race between the tortoise and the hare. What are the common elements in these stories? How does Jack and the Beanstalk serve as a basis for DeMarinis's story? Would "Weeds" have the same impact for readers who are not familiar with folk tales as for those who have read them? You and your partner might work together, both reading the same tales and writing your final analysis together. Or you could each read different tales and draw your conclusions separately, then later synthesize them into a single article.

2. The comic elements of this story, along with its rich imagery, make it a likely candidate for illustration. Working with a partner, produce a set of illustrations to accompany this tale. They could be hand-drawn, painted, or produced with a computer graphics program. You don't need to have artistic talent for this project; simply concentrate on your concepts of the most compelling images suggested by the story. Try to create at least a sketch, and accompany each picture with a written statement explaining your concept. Show your annotated illustrations to your classmates.

William Kittredge

Owning It All

William Kittredge *(b. 1932) grew up on his family's ranch in southeastern Oregon. He spent a number of years of his adult life managing this ranch, which he refers to as an "agricultural machine." He obtained an undergraduate degree in agriculture from Oregon State University in 1953 and an M.F.A. in creative writing from the University of Iowa in 1969. He was a Wallace Stegner Fellow at Stanford University (1973–1974) and has received two grants from the National Endowment for the Arts (1974, 1981). Kittredge now teaches creative writing at the University of Montana. Some of his works include two short story collections,* The Van Gogh Field and Other Stories *(1979) and* We Are Not in This Together *(1984), and a memoir,* Hole in the Sky *(1992). The following excerpt is from his book* Owning It All *(1987), in which the author examines his roots, including his past actions and attitudes, and considers not just where he may have gone wrong but also how certain myths in Western culture seem to have come unraveled.*

Questions to Consider

☐ As you read, consider the appropriateness of Kittredge's title for this selection. What connotations (associations connected to a term) and denotations (literal definitions) of the term *owning* apply here?

☐ In the first paragraph, the author says he feels lucky to have grown up where and when he did. How do you feel about the time and place in which you grew up? As you read, consider whether you share with Kittredge any of the same ambiguous feelings he has about his roots.

I MAGINE the slow history of our country in the far reaches of southeastern Oregon, a backlands enclave even in the American West, the first settlers not arriving until a decade after the end of the Civil War. I've learned to think of myself as having had the luck to grow up at the tail end of a way of existing in which people lived in everyday proximity to animals on territory they knew more precisely than the patterns in the palms of their hands.

In Warner Valley we understood our property as others know their cities, a landscape of neighborhoods, some sacred, some demonic, some habitable, some not, which is as the sea, they tell me, is understood by fishermen. It was

392

only later, in college, that I learned it was possible to understand Warner as a fertile oasis in a vast featureless sagebrush desert.

Over in that other world on the edge of rain-forests which is the Willamette Valley of Oregon, I'd gone to school in General Agriculture, absorbed in a double-bind sort of learning, studying to center myself in the County Agent/Corps of Engineers mentality they taught and at the same time taking classes from Bernard Malamud and wondering with great romantic fervor if it was in me to write the true history of the place where I had always lived.

Straight from college I went to Photo Intelligence work in the Air Force. The last couple of those years were spent deep in jungle on the island of Guam, where we lived in a little compound of cleared land, in a quonset hut.

The years on Guam were basically happy and bookish: we were newly married, with children. A hundred or so yards north of our quonset hut, along a trail through the luxuriant undergrowth between coconut palms and banana trees, a ragged cliff of red porous volcanic rock fell directly to the ocean. When the Pacific typhoons came roaring in, our hut was washed with blowing spray from the great breakers. On calm days we would stand on the cliff at that absolute edge of our jungle and island, and gaze out across to the island of Rota, and to the endlessness of ocean beyond, and I would marvel at my life, so far from southeastern Oregon.

And then in the late fall of 1958, after I had been gone from Warner Valley for eight years, I came back to participate in our agriculture. The road in had been paved, we had Bonneville Power on lines from the Columbia River, and high atop the western rim of the valley there was a TV translator, which beamed fluttering pictures from New York and Los Angeles direct to us.

And I had changed, or thought I had, for a while. No more daydreams about writing the true history. Try to understand my excitement as I climbed to the rim behind our house and stood there by our community TV translator. The valley where I had always seen myself living was open before me like another map and playground, and this time I was an adult, and high up in the War Department. Looking down maybe 3,000 feet into Warner, and across to the high basin and range desert where we summered our cattle, I saw the beginnings of my real life as an agricultural manager. The flow of watercourses in the valley was spread before me like a map, and I saw it as a surgeon might see the flow of blood across a chart of anatomy, and saw myself helping to turn the fertile homeplace of my childhood into a machine for agriculture whose features could be delineated with the same surgeon's precision in my mind.

It was work which can be thought of as craftsmanlike, both artistic and mechanical, creating order according to an ideal of beauty based on efficiency, manipulating the forces of water and soil, season and seed, manpower and equipment, laying out functional patterns for irrigation and cultivation on the surface of our valley. We drained and leveled, ditched and pumped, and for a long while our crops were all any of us could have asked. There were over 5,000 water control devices. We constructed a perfect agricultural place, and it was sacred, so it seemed.

Agriculture is often envisioned as an art, and it can be. Of course there is always survival, and bank notes, and all that. But your basic bottom line on the farm is again and again some notion of how life should be lived. The majority of agricultural people, if you press them hard enough, even though most of them despise sentimental abstractions, will admit they are trying to create a good place, and to live as part of that goodness, in the kind of connection which with fine reason we call *rootedness*. It's just that there is good art and bad art.

These are thoughts which come back when I visit eastern Oregon. I park and stand looking down into the lava-rock and juniper-tree canyon where Deep Creek cuts its way out of the Warner Mountains, and the great turkey buzzard soars high in the yellow-orange light above the evening. The fishing water is low, as it always is in late August, unfurling itself around dark and broken boulders. The trout, I know, are hanging where the currents swirl across themselves, waiting for the one entirely precise and lucky cast, the Renegade fly bobbing toward them.

Even now I can see it, each turn of water along miles of that creek. Walk some stretch enough times with a fly rod and its configurations will imprint themselves on your being with Newtonian exactitude. Which is beyond doubt one of the attractions of such fishing—the hours of learning, and then the intimacy with a living system that carries you beyond the sadness of mere gaming for sport.

What I liked to do, back in the old days, was pack in some spuds and an onion and corn flour and spices mixed up in a plastic bag, a small cast-iron frying pan in my wicker creel and, in the late twilight on a gravel bar by the water, cook up a couple of rainbows over a fire of snapping dead willow and sage, eating alone while the birds flitted through the last hatch, wiping my greasy fingers on my pants while the heavy trout began rolling at the lower ends of the pools.

The canyon would be shadowed under the moon when I walked out to show up home empty-handed, to sit with my wife over a drink of whiskey at the kitchen table. Those nights I would go to bed and sleep without dreams, a grown-up man secure in the house and the western valley where he had been a child, enclosed in a topography of spirit he assumed he knew more closely than his own features in the shaving mirror.

So, I ask myself, if it was such a pretty life, why didn't I stay? The peat soil in Warner Valley was deep and rich, we ran good cattle, and my most sacred memories are centered there. What could run me off?

Well, for openers, it got harder and harder to get out of bed in the mornings and face the days, for reasons I didn't understand. More and more I sought the comfort of fishing that knowable creek. Or in winter the blindness of television.

My father grew up on a homestead place on the sagebrush flats outside Silver Lake, Oregon. He tells of hiding under the bed with his sisters when strangers came to the gate. He grew up, as we all did in that country and era, believing that the one sure defense against the world was property. I was born in 1932, and recall a life before the end of World War II in which it was possible for a child to imagine that his family owned the world.

Warner Valley was largely swampland when my grandfather bought the MC Ranch with no downpayment in 1936, right at the heart of the Great Depression. The outside work was done mostly by men and horses and mules, and our ranch valley was filled with life. In 1937 my father bought his first track-layer, a secondhand RD6 Caterpillar he used to build a 17-mile diversion canal to carry the spring floodwater around the east side of the valley, and we were on our way to draining all swamps. The next year he bought an RD7 and a John Deere 36 combine which cut an 18-foot swath, and we were deeper into the dream of power over nature and men, which I had begun to inhabit while playing those long-ago games of war.

The peat ground left by the decaying remnants of ancient tule beds was diked into huge undulating grainfields—Houston Swamp with 750 irrigated acres, Dodson Lake with 800—a final total of almost 8,000 acres under cultivation, and for reasons of what seemed like common sense and efficiency, the work became industrialized. Our artistry worked toward a model whose central image was the machine.

The natural patterns of drainage were squared into drag-line ditches, the tules and the aftermath of the oat and barley crops were burned—along with a little more of the combustible peat soil every year. We flood-irrigated when the water came in spring, drained in late March, and planted in a 24-hour-a-day frenzy which began around April 25 and ended—with luck—by the 10th of May, just as leaves on the Lombardy poplar were breaking from their buds. We summered our cattle on more than a million acres of Taylor Grazing Land across the high lava rock and sagebrush desert out east of the valley, miles of territory where we owned most of what water there was, and it was ours. We owned it all, or so we felt. The government was as distant as news on the radio.

The most intricate part of my job was called "balancing water," a night and day process of opening and closing pipes and redwood headgates and running the 18-inch drainage pumps. That system was the finest plaything I ever had.

And despite the mud and endless hours, the work remained play for a long time, the making of a thing both functional and elegant. We were doing God's labor and creating a good place on earth, living the pastoral yeoman dream—that's how our mythology defined it, although nobody would ever have thought to talk about work in that way.

And then it all went dead, over years, but swiftly.

You can imagine our surprise and despair, our sense of having been profoundly cheated. It took us a long while to realize some unnamable thing was wrong, and then we blamed it on ourselves, our inability to manage enough. But the fault wasn't ours, beyond the fact that we had all been educated to believe in a grand bad factory-land notion as our prime model of excellence.

We felt enormously betrayed. For so many years, through endless efforts, we had proceeded in good faith, and it turned out we had wrecked all we had not left untouched. The beloved migratory rafts of waterbirds, the green-headed mallards and the redheads and canvasbacks, the cinnamon teal and the great Canadian honkers, were mostly gone along with their swampland habitat. The hunting, in so many ways, was no longer what it had been.

We wanted to build a reservoir, and litigation started. Our laws were being used against us, by people who wanted a share of what we thought of as our water. We could not endure the boredom of our mechanical work, and couldn't hire anyone who cared enough to do it right. We baited the coyotes with 1080, and rodents destroyed our alfalfa; we sprayed weeds and insects with 2-4-D Ethyl and Malathion, and Parathion for clover mite, and we shortened our own lives.

In quite an actual way we had come to victory in the artistry of our playground warfare against all that was naturally alive in our native home. We had reinvented our valley according to the most persuasive ideal given us by our culture, and we ended with a landscape organized like a machine for growing crops and fattening cattle, a machine that creaked a little louder each year, a dreamland gone wrong.

One of my strongest memories comes from a morning when I was maybe 10 years old, out on the lawn before our country home in spring, beneath a bluebird sky. I was watching the waterbirds coming off the valley swamps and grainfields where they had been feeding overnight. They were going north to nesting grounds on the Canadian tundra, and that piece of morning, inhabited by the sounds of their wings and their calling in the clean air, was wonder-filled and magical. I was enclosed in a living place.

No doubt that memory has persisted because it was a sight of possibility which I will always cherish—an image of the great good place rubbed smooth over the years like a river stone, which I touch again as I consider why life in Warner Valley went so seriously haywire. But never again in my lifetime will it be possible for a child to stand out on a bright spring morning in Warner Valley and watch the waterbirds come through in enormous, rafting vee-shaped flocks of thousands—and I grieve.

My father is a very old man. A while back we were driving up the Bitterroot Valley of Montana, and he was gazing away to the mountains. "They'll never see it the way we did," he said, and I wonder what he saw.

We shaped our piece of the West according to the model provided by our mythology, and instead of a great good place such order had given us enormous power over nature, and a blank perfection of fields.

A mythology can be understood as a story that contains a set of implicit instructions from a society to its members, telling them what is valuable and how to conduct themselves if they are to preserve the things they value.

The teaching mythology we grew up with in the American West is a pastoral story of agricultural ownership. The story begins with a vast innocent continent, natural and almost magically alive, capable of inspiring us to reverence and awe, and yet savage, a wilderness. A good rural people come from the East, and they take the land from its native inhabitants, and tame it for agricultural purposes, bringing civilization: a notion of how to live embodied in law. The story is as old as invading armies, and at heart it is a racist, sexist, imperialist mythology of conquest; a rationale for violence—against other people and against nature.

At the same time, that mythology is a lens through which we continue to see ourselves. Many of us like to imagine ourselves as honest yeomen who sweat and work in the woods or the mines or the fields for a living. And many of us are. We live in a real family, a work-centered society, and we like to see ourselves as people with the good luck and sense to live in a place where some vestige of the natural world still exists in working order. Many of us hold that natural world as sacred to some degree, just as it is in our myth. Lately, more and more of us are coming to understand our society in the American West as an exploited colony, threatened by greedy outsiders who want to take our sacred place away from us, or at least to strip and degrade it.

In short, we see ourselves as a society of mostly decent people who live with some connection to a holy wilderness, threatened by those who lust for power and property. We look for Shane to come riding out of the Tetons, and instead we see Exxon and the Sierra Club. One looks virtually as alien as the other.

And our mythology tells us we own the West, absolutely and morally—we own it because of our history. Our people brought law to this difficult place, they suffered and they shed blood and they survived, and they earned this land for us. Our efforts have surely earned us the right to absolute control over the thing we created. The myth tells us this place is ours, and will always be ours, to do with as we see fit.

That's a most troubling and enduring message, because we want to believe it, and we do believe it, so many of us, despite its implicit ironies and wrongheadedness, despite the fact that we took the land from someone else. We try to ignore a genocidal history of violence against the Native Americans.

In the American West we are struggling to revise our dominant mythology, and to find a new story to inhabit. Laws control our lives, and they are designed to preserve a model of society based on values learned from mythology. Only after re-imagining our myths can we coherently remodel our laws, and hope to keep our society in a realistic relationship to what is actual.

In Warner Valley we thought we were living the right lives, creating a great precise perfection of fields, and we found the mythology had been telling us an enormous lie. The world had proven too complex, or the myth too simpleminded. And we were mortally angered.

The truth is, we never owned all the land and water. We don't even own very much of them, privately. And we don't own anything absolutely or forever. As our society grows more and more complex and interwoven, our entitlement becomes less and less absolute, more and more likely to be legally diminished. Our rights to property will never take precedence over the needs of society. Nor should they, we all must agree in our grudging hearts. Ownership of property has always been a privilege granted by society, and revokable.

Discussion Questions

1. Identify several instances in which the author describes something from a hilltop perspective, or from some other topographical high point. What is the purpose and effect of using this particular perspective?

2. Kittredge uses several richly suggestive terms in this selection, for example, *mythology, rootedness,* and *laws.* As a class, list on the board the personal associations you have for one or more of these terms. How does the author's use of such terms highlight the complexities of his dilemma?

3. Kittredge explains that his work on the ranch was craftsmanlike. What does he mean? Based on his description of his work and his attitude toward it, do you agree that he was a craftsman? Why or why not?

4. Identify the source of the allusion Kittredge makes when he says, "We look for Shane to come riding out of the Tetons, and instead we see Exxon and the Sierra Club. One looks virtually as alien as the other." What is the story of Shane? What is the Sierra Club? What associations does Exxon have now, as a consequence of the *Exxon Valdez* oil spill of 1989?

Journal Entry

More than once the author describes a certain place as "sacred." Describe a place that is, or was at one time, sacred to you.

Writing Projects

1. For this essay you will need to obtain some knowledge of daily agricultural life. Writing for an urban audience, explain and illustrate the concept of agriculture as an art. Drawing on your response to Discussion Question 3, distinguish between activities and products, identifying those that qualify as arts and those as crafts. What elements of work on a farm or ranch are analogous to an artist's work? What human qualities do farming and ranching require? What kind of language is used here, and in general, to describe the life and work of a farmer or rancher?

2. Analyze Kittredge's use of figurative language in this essay, focusing on his comparisons: analogies, metaphors, similes. See, for example, his comparison of "agricultural management" to the surgeon's work. How do these comparisons help you understand Kittredge's point of view? How do they illustrate his ambiguous feelings toward his work as a rancher? How do you respond to these images? Do they cause you to feel you understand more about Kittredge as a person and writer? Do they enable you to see farming and ranching in a new light? What other effects does his language produce?

Collaborative Project

Working with a partner, investigate current farming and irrigation methods. How has modern technology affected farming? What improvements have been made? What are the benefits? What is the price of these benefits? What side effects have accompanied the improvements? What measures are currently being taken to reverse the negative side effects? Work together or separately, synthesizing your findings and conclusions in an article.

Making Connections

Questions to Discuss

1. In "Controlling the Atchafalaya River," John McPhee mentions a college professor who thinks that the way the engineers battle the river is an example of extreme arrogance. Do you think McPhee himself agrees or disagrees with the professor? What passages can you cite to support your argument? Discuss other selections in this book in which authors point out our society's arrogant treatment of the natural environment.

2. Rachel Carson and Rosemary Radford Ruether both write about humans' attempts to control nature with chemicals. Do you think they would support or refute Sally Hacker's assertion that "chemical technologies [are used] for the exciting and often eroticized domination and control of nature" (see Chapter 2)? Which of Carson's and Ruether's arguments do you think Hacker would accept?

3. Writers sometimes draw attention to an opposing point of view in order to show flaws. Analyze one or two of the arguments presented in this chapter. Address how the authors used the opposing point of view to strengthen their own argument. Also point out instances in which the author ignored the opposing point of view, as in "Save the Whales, Screw the Shrimp."

Suggested Writing Projects

1. Drawing on the readings in this chapter and elsewhere in the text, write an essay exploring your view of a good relationship between humans and the environment. Is it our responsibility to preserve nature or to manage it? Must these two ideas be mutually exclusive?

2. Rick DeMarinis's story and Joy Williams's essay have several features in common: both writers use dialogue, humor (dark, cynical humor), and analogy to develop their themes. Compare the ways in which the two writers employ the same rhetorical strategies. Did the story or the essay affect you more, and why?

3. Both William Kittredge and Rachel Carson write about farmers' use of pesticides and their effect on the environment. After reviewing secondary sources and, if possible, speaking with people who work the land, write a report on current farming practices in terms of how pesticides are used. Include in your research some investigation of the role played by companies that produce chemicals used in farming.

4. Working with a partner, investigate at least two programs or policies – including ones at the county, state, or federal level – designed to preserve and

protect our environment. Classify these programs as either technological fixes or social engineering. Analyze your findings and draw conclusions, which you then present to a concerned audience. Discuss the success or failure of the programs. Explain why you concluded that either technological fixes or social changes work best at solving environmental problems.

7

Considering
Ethical Dilemmas

 *It's all a matter of opinion. It all depends on the situation. It will never get settled, so why keep arguing?* Statements such as these characterize the attitudes of some people whenever a discussion turns to ethics. The statements are not completely false; ethical behavior does reflect opinions, is often affected by circumstance, and is seldom decided by winning or losing an argument.

Nevertheless, reading, thinking, and discussing the complexities of moral dilemmas, as you will do here, does accomplish something important. Such activities allow each of us to explore our own judgments and thereby come to understand opposing judgments. By writing and talking about our values, we certify our positions as much for our own benefit as for the benefit of others. Through the public exposure and deliberation of moral issues we increase our sensitivity to others and heighten our intellectual awareness of the requirements for moral action.

There are countless moral choices you make as a student. The decision to write your own essays rather than plagiarize the work of others, to study for exams rather than purchase the answers—these are among the more clear-cut moral choices you face. Also, when you participate in the collaborative research and writing projects in this course, you demonstrate cooperativeness, sensitivity to others, knowledge, and strength of character, all of which philosopher Ronald D. Yezzi identifies as moral traits. Thus, you engage in ethical behavior.

As the selections in this chapter illustrate, in many situations it is difficult to determine if behavior is moral and ethical, or immoral and nonethical. Although we normally think of whistle-blowing (informing on colleagues, supervisors, or anyone else who breaks the law) as occurring in a business context, there are instances in scientific research when scientists speak out against what they see as immoral behavior by their colleagues. In some of these cases no clear ethical guidelines are specified; they are assumed. Issues directly related to scientific research and the development of technological products, such as the use of animals in laboratory experiments, can be seen as having a moral argument on both sides.

Issues specifically regarding the treatment of animals in experiments are presented from two different perspectives in this chapter. Ron Karpati, a pediatrician, outlines the many human benefits that animal experimentation makes possible—notably the saving of human lives owing to medical breakthroughs. Countering such arguments is Jean Bethke Elshtain, who challenges our Western belief that humans are entitled to dominate all other life forms. She wonders why the lives of animals are not considered as precious as human lives.

The selections in this chapter raise issues ranging from human rights to animal rights and publication rights. As a culture, we tend to trust that scientists and experimenters who work in areas affecting the general public's safety will not lose sight of certain basic values. When it comes to scientific theory, practice, and reporting, we feel we are entitled to ethical behavior and often assume that it occurs universally. After all, if you can't trust scientists to report the facts, how can you trust their conclusions?

"Some Thoughts on Ethics of Research," Diana Baumrind's critique of Stanley Milgram's experiments on obedience, examines the sacred relationship between those who perform experiments and those who are the subjects. Milgram's landmark study in 1963 was controversial, cited by numerous professionals as harmful to all subjects involved.

The ethics of scientific research is further explored in "A Search for Limits," an article from *Newsweek* displaying the pitfalls associated with fetal research and the harvesting of human organs for transplant. The authors put forward and then illustrate a very important assertion: "Science does not advance in a moral vacuum. Time and again it intrudes on the concerns of conscience."

Essays by Barbara Ehrenreich and Sharon Begley, two widely read columnists who often write about the interplay of culture and science, examine the ethics of disclosing scientific information to the public. Barbara Ehrenreich's lively, provocative article offers a specific example to illustrate what she believes is a problem threatening scientific integrity today. Because scientific research requires large amounts of money, the stakes are high and the pressure to produce results becomes intense. Consequently, scientists sometimes fall prey to the temptation to take dishonest shortcuts. Because many of us still believe in the sanctity of science, we feel particularly betrayed when scientists are shown to have lied to achieve fame and fortune.

Sharon Begley is concerned about the prevalence of censorship in the way scientific research findings are made available to the general public. She cites examples of studies that either were rejected for publication or were published in such a way as to downplay the potential for harm evidenced by the research findings. Begley asserts that such censorship poses a risk to science's reputation for probity, and ultimately a safety risk to us all.

Joyce Carol Oates's play, *Under/Ground*, dramatizes the complicated ethical questions related to bomb shelters and, by implication, the way in which certain technologies are developed that endanger many and benefit only a few. The existence of a sliding scale of ethical standards is another topic explored by Oates and other writers in this chapter.

These selections offer a rich array of material for thought and discussion about where you stand personally on numerous controversial issues. The readings highlight our need to do more than blindly place our trust in those who work in scientific and technological laboratories. We must all be involved in shaping the quality of our lives and the lives of all creatures around us.

Barbara Ehrenreich

Science, Lies, and the Ultimate Truth

Barbara Ehrenreich (b. 1941) is an outspoken Socialist and feminist who contributes regularly to a wide range of periodicals, including Nation, Esquire, Vogue, New Republic, Time, Ms., Mother Jones, *and the* Village Voice. *Ehrenreich has sharply criticized our country's health "empire"; she bases her critiques on observations made while working with the Health Policy Advisory Center in New York from 1969 to 1971. In several books co-written with Deirdre English—including* Complaints and Disorders: The Sexual Politics of Sickness *(1973), and* For Her Own Good: One Hundred Fifty Years of the Experts' Advice to Women *(1978)—Ehrenreich has exposed what she sees as the self-serving male domination of women's health issues. Recently, she has written her first novel,* Kipper's Game *(1993), about a mother's search for her missing son. In the essay that follows, Ehrenreich demonstrates her sharp wit as she points a finger at scientists who deliberately deceive the public.*

Questions to Consider

☐ Before reading, consider what Ehrenreich's title suggests. What connection do you see between science and lies? Between science and ultimate truth?

☐ Ehrenreich's opening sentence is quite lively and provocative. As you read, consider how, if at all, she sustains this colorful and irreverent style throughout the essay.

IF there is any specimen lower than a fornicating preacher, it must be a shady scientist. The dissolute evangelist betrays his one revealed Truth, but the scientist who rushes half-cocked into print or, worse yet, falsifies the data subverts the whole idea of truth. Cold fusion in a teacup? Or, as biologists (then at M.I.T.) David Baltimore and Thereza Imanishi-Kari claimed in a controversial 1986 article that the National Institutes of Health has now judged to be fraudulent, genes from one mouse mysteriously "imitating" those from another? Sure, and parallel lines might as well meet somewhere or apples leap back up onto trees.

Baltimore, the Nobel laureate and since 1990 president of Rockefeller University, has apologized, after a fashion, for his role in the alleged fraud, and many feel that the matter should be left to rest. He didn't, after all, falsify the data himself; he merely signed on as senior scientist to Imanishi-Kari's now discredited findings. But when a young postdoctoral fellow named Margot O'Toole tried to blow the whistle, Baltimore pooh-poohed O'Toole's evidence and stood by while she lost her job. Then, as the feds closed in, he launched a bold, misguided defense of the sanctity of science.

What does one more lie matter anyway? Politicians "mispeak" and are forgiven by their followers. Pop singers have been known to dub in better voices. Literary deconstructionists say there's no truth anyway, just ideologies and points of view. Lies, you might say, are the great lubricant of our way of life. They sell products, flatter the powerful, appease the electorate and save vast sums from the IRS. Imanishi-Kari's lie didn't even hurt anyone: no bridges fell, no patients died.

But science is different, and the difference does define a kind of sanctity. Although we think of it as the most secular of human enterprises, there is a little-known spiritual side to science, with its own stern ethical implications. Through research, we seek to know that ultimate Other, which could be called Nature if the term didn't sound so tame and beaten, or God if the word weren't loaded with so much human hope and superstition. Think of it more neutrally as the nameless Subject of so much that happens, like the It in "It is raining": something "out there" and vastly different from ourselves, but not so alien that we cannot hope to know Its ways.

When I was a graduate student in biology—at Rockefeller, where Baltimore also earned his Ph.D.—I would have winced at all this metaphysics. The ethos of the acolyte was humility and patience. If the experiment didn't succeed, you did it again and then scratched your head and tried a new approach. There were mistakes, but mistakes could be corrected, which is why you reported exactly how you did things, step by step, so others could prove you right or wrong. There were even, sometimes, corners cut: a little rounding off, an anomalous finding overlooked.

But falsifying data lay outside our moral universe. The least you could do as a scientist was record exactly what you observed (in ink, in notebooks that never left the lab). The most you could do was arrange the experimental circumstances so as to entrap the elusive It and squeeze out some small confession: This is how the enzyme works, or the protein folds, or the gene makes known its message. But always, and no matter what, you let It do the talking. And when It spoke, which wasn't often, your reward, as one of my professors used to say, was "to wake up screaming in the night"—at the cunning of Its logic and the elegance of Its design.

This was the ideal, anyway. But Big Science costs big bucks and breeds a more mundane and calculating kind of outlook. It takes hundreds of thousands of dollars a year to run a modern biological laboratory, with its electron microscopes, ultracentrifuges, amino-acid analyzers, Ph.D.s and technicians. The big bucks tend to go to big shots, like Baltimore, whose machines and underlings must grind out "results" in massive volume. In the past two decades, as federal funding for basic research has ebbed, the pressure to produce has risen to dangerous levels. At the same time, the worldly rewards of success have expanded to include fat paychecks (from patents and sidelines in the biotech business) as well as power and celebrity status. And these are the circumstances that invite deception.

Imanishi-Kari succumbed, apparently, to the desire to make a name for herself and hence, no doubt, expand her capacity for honest research. But Baltimore is a more disturbing case. He already had the name, the resources and the power that younger scientists covet. What he forgot is that although humans may respect these things, the truth does not. What he lost sight of, in the smugness of success, is that truth is no respecter of hierarchy or fame. It can come out of the mouths of mere underlings, like the valiant O'Toole.

And if no one was physically hurt, still there was damage done. Scientists worldwide briefly believed the bogus "findings" and altered their views accordingly or wasted time trying to follow the false lead in their labs. Then there is the inevitable damage from the exposure of the lie: millions of people, reading of the scandal, must have felt their deepest cynicism confirmed. If a Nobel laureate in science could sink to the moral level of Milli Vanilli or a White House spin doctor, then maybe the deconstructionists are right and there is no truth anywhere, only self-interest masked as objective fact.

Baltimore should issue a fuller apology, accounting for his alleged cover-up of the initial fraud. Then he should reflect for a week or two and consider stepping down from his position as president of Rockefeller University and de facto science statesman. Give him a modest lab to work in, maybe one in the old Rockefeller buildings where the microbe hunters toiled decades ago. I picture something with a river view, where it is impossible to forget that Manhattan is an island, that the earth is a planet, and that there is something out there much larger, and possibly even cleverer, than ourselves.

Discussion Questions

1. What is Ehrenreich's main point in this essay? Why does she target David Baltimore?

2. According to Ehrenreich, what is the most serious consequence of the scandal involving David Baltimore's research? Do you agree?

3. Do you believe in the sanctity of science? Who or what is the "It" that the author talks about midway through the essay?

4. In this selection Ehrenreich implicitly classifies individuals according to their profession. Do you think she has an adjustable set of ethical expectations based on a person's profession? Does she assume her readers share her opinion? Do you, like Ehrenreich, expect more honesty from scientists than you do from politicians? Why?

Journal Entry

As a student taking science courses at your university, how would you react if you learned that your professor was involved in the kind of fraud Ehrenreich discusses here? This essay explores factors, such as competition for scarce resources as well as large financial awards for success, that pressure researchers to get results. How does this pressure affect the quality of the instruction you receive in the classroom?

Writing Projects

1. Write an essay addressed to university science administrators in which you discuss the responsibility of the faculty and administration in preventing fraud in scientific research. Refer to Ehrenreich's account of the way in which David Baltimore treated the alleged fraud as well as his treatment of the postdoctoral fellow who blew the whistle. Include examples from your own research or personal experience.

2. Write a stylistic analysis of this essay. Focus on selected features, such as sentence length, use of first person, and colloquial terms. How do these features affect the tone and pacing of Ehrenreich's essay? How does the author's style influence your response to the subject? To the author personally?

Collaborative Projects

1. The author recalls her days as a graduate student in the biology lab, where she and her colleagues adhered to an ethical code that required careful observation and precise record keeping. Working with a classmate, observe and interview science majors in the lab and the classroom as they conduct a study. What ethical standards guide their procedures, interpretations, and attitudes? Share your findings and conclusions with one of your science professors, and record his or her reactions. Write a report on your research process and your findings, and discuss your conclusions about the role of a scientific code of ethics in the setting you observed.

2. Working with a partner, research the overlap between big business and big science today. You could both work together throughout the process, or each of you might focus on one particular industry/academic partnership. Investigate the impact of the competition for scarce resources and major financial rewards. Write an article on the benefits and dangers of the interdependence between science research and profit-oriented corporations. Include recommendations to assist academic researchers in preserving the integrity of their research while satisfying industry's desire for bottom-line results.

Diana Baumrind

Some Thoughts on Ethics of Research

Diana Baumrind *(b. 1927) is a developmental and clinical psychologist associated with the Institute of Human Development at the University of California at Berkeley. She is the winner of numerous awards from sources such as the National Institute for Child Health and Human Development and the MacArthur Foundation. Professor Baumrind has long been particularly interested in the ethics of research with human subjects. In the selection reprinted here, originally titled "Some Thoughts on Ethics of Research: After Reading Milgram's 'Behavioral Study of Obedience,'" Baumrind responds to Stanley Milgram's controversial study of human obedience to authority, which was published in 1963. Her article first appeared in* American Psychologist *in 1964.*

Questions to Consider

☐ As you read, consider the author's purpose in writing this article. Note features that demonstrate she is writing for an audience of professional peers.

☐ For background on Stanley Milgram's study, see his articles: "Behavioral Study of Obedience," *Journal of Abnormal Social Psychology* 67 (1963): 371–78; and "Some Conditions of Obedience and Disobedience to Authority," *Human Relations* 18, no. 1 (1965): 57–76.

C ERTAIN problems in psychological research require the experimenter to balance his career and scientific interests against the interests of his prospective subjects. When such occasions arise the experimenter's stated objective frequently is to do the best possible job with the least possible harm to his subjects. The experimenter seldom perceives in more positive terms an indebtedness to the subject for his services, perhaps because the detachment which his functions require prevents appreciation of the subject as an individual.

Yet a debt does exist, even when the subject's reason for volunteering includes course credit or monetary gain. Often a subject participates unwillingly in order to satisfy a course requirement. These requirements are of questionable merit ethically, and do not alter the experimenter's responsibility to the subject.

Most experimental conditions do not cause the subjects pain or indignity, and are sufficiently interesting or challenging to present no problem of an ethical nature to the experimenter. But where the experimental conditions expose the subject to loss of dignity, or offer him nothing of value, then the experimenter is obliged to consider the reasons why the subject volunteered and to reward him accordingly.

The subject's public motives for volunteering include having an enjoyable or stimulating experience, acquiring knowledge, doing the experimenter a favor which may some day be reciprocated, and making a contribution to science. These motives can be taken into account rather easily by the experimenter who is willing to spend a few minutes with the subject afterwards to thank him for his participation, answer his questions, reassure him that he did well, and chat with him a bit. Most volunteers also have less manifest, but equally legitimate, motives. A subject may be seeking an opportunity to have contact with, be noticed by, and perhaps confide in a person with psychological training. The dependent attitude of most subjects toward the experimenter is an artifact of the experimental situation as well as an expression of some subjects' personal need systems at the time they volunteer.

The dependent, obedient attitude assumed by most subjects in the experimental setting is appropriate to that situation. The "game" is defined by the experimenter and he makes the rules. By volunteering, the subject agrees implicitly to assume a posture of trust and obedience. While the experimental conditions leave him exposed, the subject has the right to assume that his security and self-esteem will be protected.

There are other professional situations in which one member—the patient or client—expects help and protection from the other—the physician or psychologist. But the interpersonal relationship between experimenter and subject additionally has unique features which are likely to provoke initial anxiety in the subject. The laboratory is unfamiliar as a setting and the rules of behavior ambiguous compared to a clinician's office. Because of the anxiety and passivity generated by the setting, the subject is more prone to behave in an obedient, suggestible manner in the laboratory than elsewhere. Therefore, the laboratory is not the place to study degree of obedience or suggestibility, as a function of a particular experimental condition, since the base line for these phenomena as found in the laboratory is probably much higher than in most other settings. Thus experiments in which the relationship to the experimenter as an authority is used as an independent condition are imperfectly designed for the same reason that they are prone to injure the subjects involved. They disregard the special quality of trust and obedience with which the subject appropriately regards the experimenter.

Other phenomena which present ethical decisions, unlike those mentioned above, *can* be reproduced successfully in the laboratory. Failure experience, conformity to peer judgment, and isolation are among such phenomena. In these cases we can expect the experimenter to take whatever measures are necessary to prevent the subject from leaving the laboratory more humiliated, insecure, alienated, or hostile than when he arrived. To guarantee that an especially sensitive subject leaves a stressful experimental experience in the proper state sometimes requires special clinical training. But usually an attitude of compassion, respect, gratitude, and common sense will suffice, and no amount of clinical training will substitute. The subject has the right to expect that the psychologist with whom he is interacting has some concern for his welfare, and the personal attributes and professional skill to express his good will effectively.

Unfortunately, the subject is not always treated with the respect he deserves. It has become more commonplace in sociopsychological laboratory studies to manipulate, embarrass, and discomfort subjects. At times the insult to the subject's sensibilities extends to the journal reader when the results are reported. Milgram's (1963) study is a case in point. The following is Milgram's abstract of his experiment:

> This article describes a procedure for the study of destructive obedience in the laboratory. It consists of ordering a naive S to administer increasingly more severe punishment to a victim in the context of a learning experiment. Punishment is administered by means of a shock generator with 30 graded switches ranging from Slight Shock to Danger: Severe Shock. The victim is a confederate of E. The primary dependent variable is the maximum shock the S is willing to administer before he refuses to continue further. 26 Ss obeyed the experimental commands fully, and administered the highest shock on the generator. 14 Ss broke off the experiment at some point after the victim protested and refused to provide further answers. The procedure created extreme levels of nervous tension in some Ss. Profuse sweating, trembling, and stuttering were typical expressions of this emotional disturbance. One unexpected sign of tension—yet to be explained—was the regular occurrence of nervous laughter, which in some Ss developed into uncontrollable seizures. The variety of interesting behavioral dynamics observed in the experiment, the reality of the situation for the S, and the possibility of parametric variation within the framework of the procedure, point to the fruitfulness of further study [p. 371].

The detached, objective manner in which Milgram reports the emotional disturbance suffered by his subjects contrasts sharply with his graphic account of that disturbance. Following are two other quotes describing the effects on his subjects of the experimental conditions:

> I observed a mature and initially poised businessman enter the laboratory smiling and confident. Within 20 minutes he was reduced to a twitching, stuttering wreck, who was rapidly approaching a point of nervous collapse. He constantly pulled on his earlobe, and twisted his hands. At one point he pushed his fist into his forehead and muttered: "Oh God, let's stop it." And yet he continued to respond to every word of the experimenter, and obeyed to the end [p. 377].

In a large number of cases the degree of tension reached extremes that are rarely seen in sociopsychological laboratory studies. Subjects were observed to sweat, tremble, stutter, bite their lips, groan, and dig their fingernails into their flesh. These were characteristic rather than exceptional responses to the experiment.

One sign of tension was the regular occurrence of nervous laughing fits. Fourteen of the 40 subjects showed definite signs of nervous laughter and smiling. The laughter seemed entirely out of place, even bizarre. Full-blown, uncontrollable seizures were observed for 3 subjects. On one occasion we observed a seizure so violently convulsive that it was necessary to call a halt to the experiment . . . [p. 375].

Milgram does state that,

After the interview, procedures were undertaken to assure that the subject would leave the laboratory in a state of well being. A friendly reconciliation was arranged between the subject and the victim, and an effort was made to reduce any tensions that arose as a result of the experiment [p. 374].

It would be interesting to know what sort of procedures could dissipate the type of emotional disturbance just described. In view of the effects on subjects, traumatic to a degree which Milgram himself considers nearly unprecedented in sociopsychological experiments, his casual assurance that these tensions were dissipated before the subject left the laboratory is unconvincing.

What could be the rational basis for such a posture of indifference? Perhaps Milgram supplies the answer himself when he partially explains the subject's destructive obedience as follows, "Thus they assume that the discomfort caused the victim is momentary, while the scientific gains resulting from the experiment are enduring [p. 378]." Indeed such a rationale might suffice to justify the means used to achieve his end if that end were of inestimable value to humanity or were not itself transformed by the means by which it was attained.

The behavioral psychologist is not in as good a position to objectify his faith in the significance of his work as medical colleagues at points of breakthrough. His experimental situations are not sufficiently accurate models of real-life experience; his sampling techniques are seldom of a scope which would justify the meaning with which he would like to endow his results; and these results are hard to reproduce by colleagues with opposing theoretical views. Unlike the Sabin vaccine, for example, the concrete benefit to humanity of his particular piece of work, no matter how competently handled, cannot justify the risk that real harm will be done to the subject. I am not speaking of physical discomfort, inconvenience, or experimental deception per se, but of permanent harm, however slight. I do regard the emotional disturbance described by Milgram as potentially harmful because it could easily effect an alteration in the subject's self-image or ability to trust adult authorities in the future. It is potentially harmful to a subject to commit, in the course of an experiment, acts which he himself considers unworthy, particularly when he has been entrapped into committing such acts by an individual he has reason to trust. The subject's personal responsibility for his actions is not erased because the experimenter reveals to him the means which he used to stimulate these actions. The subject realizes that he would have hurt the victim if the current were on. The realization that he also made a fool of himself by accepting the experimental set results in additional loss of self-esteem. Moreover, the subject finds it difficult to express his anger outwardly after the experimenter in a self-acceptant but friendly manner reveals the hoax.

A fairly intense corrective interpersonal experience is indicated wherein the subject admits and accepts his responsibility for his own actions, and at the same time gives vent to his hurt and anger at being fooled. Perhaps an experience as distressing as the one described by Milgram can be integrated by the subject, provided that careful thought is given to the matter. The propriety of such experimentation is still in question even if such a reparational experience were forthcoming. Without it I would expect a naive, sensitive subject to remain deeply hurt and anxious for some time, and a sophisticated, cynical subject to become even more alienated and distrustful.

In addition the experimental procedure used by Milgram does not appear suited to the objectives of the study because it does not take into account the special quality of the set which the subject has in the experimental situation. Milgram is concerned with a very important problem, namely, the social consequences of destructive obedience. He says,

> Gas chambers were built, death camps were guarded, daily quotas of corpses were produced with the same efficiency as the manufacture of appliances. These inhumane policies may have originated in the mind of a single person, but they could only be carried out on a massive scale if a very large number of persons obeyed orders [p. 371].

But the parallel between authority-subordinate relationships in Hitler's Germany and in Milgram's laboratory is unclear. In the former situation the SS man or member of the German Officer Corps, when obeying orders to slaughter, had no reason to think of his superior officer as benignly disposed towards himself or their victims. The victims were perceived as subhuman and not worthy of consideration. The subordinate officer was an agent in a great cause. He did not need to feel guilt or conflict because within his frame of reference he was acting rightly.

It is obvious from Milgram's own descriptions that most of his subjects were concerned about their victims and did trust the experimenter, and that their distressful conflict was generated in part by the consequences of these two disparate but appropriate attitudes. Their distress may have resulted from shock at what the experimenter was doing to them as well as from what they thought they were doing to their victims. In any case there is not a convincing parallel between the phenomena studied by Milgram and destructive obedience as that concept would apply to the subordinate-authority relationship demonstrated in Hitler Germany. If the experiments were conducted "outside of New Haven and without any visible ties to the university," I would still question their validity on similar although not identical grounds. In addition, I would question the representativeness of a sample of subjects who would voluntarily participate within a noninstitutional setting.

In summary, the experimental objectives of the psychologist are seldom incompatible with the subject's ongoing state of well being, provided that the experimenter is willing to take the subject's motives and interests into consideration when planning his methods and correctives. Section 4b in *Ethical Standards of Psychologists* (APA, undated) reads in part:

> Only when a problem is significant and can be investigated in no other way, is the psychologist justified in exposing human subjects to emotional stress or other possible harm. In conducting such research, the psychologist must seriously consider the possibility of harmful aftereffects, and should be prepared to remove them as soon as permitted by the design of the experiment. Where the danger of serious aftereffects exists, research should be conducted only when the subjects or their responsible agents are fully informed of this possibility and volunteer nevertheless [p. 12].

From the subject's point of view procedures which involve loss of dignity, self-esteem, and trust in rational authority are probably most harmful in the long run and require the most thoughtfully planned reparations, if engaged in at all. The public image of psychology as a profession is highly related to our own actions, and some of these actions are changeworthy. It is important that as research psychologists we protect our ethical sensibilities rather than adapt our personal standards to include as appropriate the kind of indignities to which Milgram's subjects were exposed. I would not like to see experiments such as Milgram's proceed unless the subjects were fully informed of the dangers of serious aftereffects and his correctives were clearly shown to be effective in restoring their state of well being.

REFERENCES

American Psychological Association. Ethical Standards of Psychologists: A summary of ethical principles. Washington, D.C.: APA, undated.

Milgram, S. Behavioral study of obedience. *J. abnorm. soc. Psychol.*, 1963, 67, 371–378.

Discussion Questions

1. Identify Baumrind's ethical stance. What is her view of Milgram's methods? According to Baumrind, what, if anything, could Milgram have done differently? Do you agree with her? Explain.

2. Baumrind asserts that the unethical treatment of human subjects in laboratory experiments is on the rise. Does she support this assertion in the rest of the article? If so, how?

3. Explain what you think Baumrind means when she says that researchers insult readers of their articles when they include evidence of mistreatment of their subjects. Do you agree? Why or why not?

4. It is not uncommon for college professors to make use of their students' work as data for their scholarly research. What ethical obligations do you think such teacher/researchers have to their students? Do you agree with Baumrind that researchers owe their human subjects a debt? Does it apply to classroom research conducted by teachers with students who are receiving course credit?

Journal Entries

1. Write an account of your experience as part of a research experiment, if you have had such experience. Describe the experiment. How did you feel about being a research subject in this study?

2. How would you have felt if you had been one of Milgram's subjects, both during the experiment and afterward when you found out the shocks administered were not real? Does the fact that the shocks were not actually administered change the guilt or other emotions you would feel?

Writing Projects

1. Write an essay on Baumrind's analysis of Milgram's abstract. Explain what purpose Baumrind accomplishes by quoting Milgram's entire abstract rather than simply summarizing it. How does she use passages from his abstract to make her point?

2. Obtain a copy of your university's policy regarding the use of human subjects in research projects. Interview the administrator in charge of overseeing the policy. Based on your study of the policy and information collected from your interview, write an essay directed to students and faculty in your school in which you outline the rights a student would have in any experiment on campus. State whether you support the current policy as providing the kind of protection students need, or whether you want to argue for changes to ensure the safety and well-being of human subjects.

Collaborative Project

With another student, ask a faculty member or other researcher in your college psychology department for permission to observe an experiment involving human subjects. With a supervisor's permission, interview the subjects to find out why they are participating. How do they see themselves benefiting from their participation? Present a report to your class on what you learned about the experiment process. What did you learn about the reasons people become human subjects? What did you learn about yourself from your role as observer? You worked as a research team, combining your perspectives; identify any important differences between the observations and responses each of you had as observers. How did the blending of your perspectives in this project produce a better understanding than if you each had worked alone?

Kenneth L. Woodward, with Mary Hager and Daniel Glick

A Search for Limits

Kenneth L. Woodward, with Mary Hager and Daniel Glick, *wrote this essay for the Society column in* Newsweek *(February 1993). These writers outline problems and raise questions about the ethical minefield of scientific research on human tissue, from aborted fetuses to organs harvested for transplant. Their article argues for more public information on biomedical research because no one can deny the complicated moral implications of this scientific research.*

Kenneth L. Woodward has been responsible for Newsweek*'s Religion section since 1964. Mary Hager has covered news in science, medicine, and the environment for* Newsweek *since 1978. Since joining* Newsweek*'s Washington bureau in 1989, Daniel Glick has contributed to cover stories on the men's movement, choosing death, and the future of gay America.*

Questions to Consider

☐ These authors have employed two conventional devices in their introduction: the shocking statement and the question. Consider whether you find the opening paragraph effective, and why.

☐ As you read, notice whether the authors show clearly where they acquired their information. What kinds of sources do they cite? Did they have access to sources you might have difficulty obtaining?

THERE are 1.5 million induced abortions every year. What's to be done with the remains? Bury them in a landfill or donate them to medical research, where organs and tissues may produce some good for others? The answer seems obvious. Or is it?

Science does not advance in a moral vacuum. Time and again it intrudes on the concerns of conscience. Consider: in 1973 a team of Finnish and American scientists decapitated a dozen human fetuses, each aborted live through hysterotomy, and kept the heads alive artificially for study. The ghoulish experiment – partially funded by the National Institutes of Health – was designed to measure fetal metabolism. At about the same time, another research team kept a batch of aborted fetuses alive in saline solution in order to find out if they could absorb oxygen. One fetus survived for nearly a day.

When word of these experiments reached the public, the outcry was such that NIH halted all federally funded fetal research except that which directly benefited the fetus. Those rules still hold. But now that the NIH is free to fund research using aborted human tissue for transplantation, the public – no less than politicians, physicians and science researchers – still faces profound moral questions. What limits, if any, should be observed when experimenting with human fetuses? Does a mother who aborts her fetus have the moral right to then donate that fetus to science – or have any say at all about the disposition of the body? Will the opportunity to donate their fetuses to research that might help others influence more women to elect abortion?

Now factor in the profit motive. Why not allow fetuses to be sold, like blood, or imported from poorer countries? Should society allow the stockpiling of spare fetal parts for nonmedical purposes, such as replacement therapy for sagging cheeks and aging stomach muscles? Will fetal research lead to a bioengineering industry that, in turn, will require more and more fetuses as raw material for pharmaceutical and other products? Could there – should there – be a futures market in precious fetal organs? Who will police ethics guidelines – and who will punish violators?

No one denies the pertinence of such questions. Difficult in their own right, they also illuminate the confounding ambiguity that still haunts the issue of abortion. It's been 20 years since the U.S. Supreme Court's decision in *Roe v. Wade*. In legalizing abortion, the court ruled that the fetus has no constitutional right to protection by the law. Legally, the fetus is now a nothing. And yet, as public-policy analyst Andrew Kimbrell argues in his forthcoming book, "The Human Body Shop" (*357 pages. Harpers. $20*), the fetus is clearly a growing *human* organism; a *human* nothing. That is why it is so highly prized as a source for tissue and organ transplantation. And that is also why, Kimbrell believes, the morality of using fetal materials is too important to leave to scientists alone.

Many ethicists who specialize in biomedical issues believe that fetal research and transplantation can, and should, be regulated. Indeed, much of the legislation now moving through Congress is based on the recommendations issued by an NIH ethics advisory panel in 1988. In essence, the panel suggested a series of procedural guidelines aimed at erecting a wall of separation between the scientific use of fetal remains and the means – induced abortion – by which they are obtained. In its report, which passed 17–4, the panel insisted that abortion counselors should not even discuss the donation of fetuses to science until *after* clients have decided to undergo an abortion. In other words, pregnant women should not allow the possible scientific benefit to others to influence their decision whether to abort or carry their child. Similarly, physicians should not alter the means or methods of abortion in order to produce better specimens for subsequent experiment. In short, women should not be morally or physically coerced into providing fetal tissue for scientific or therapeutic purposes. Both decisions – to abort and to donate – should be hers alone and made independently of each other.

In addition, once a woman chooses to abort her fetus, the panel urged that she not be permitted to designate the beneficiary of the aborted tissue. This regulation would thus prevent women from conceiving and aborting in order to provide fetal tissue for transplantation for an ailing relative or friend. Further, in keeping with laws in some states, the proposed guidelines would disallow the *sale* of fetal tissue or organs for transplantation, in an effort to prevent both physicians and women, here or abroad, from seeking abortions for profit. But they would permit payment of reasonable fees to companies and other third parties for the retrieval, preparation and storage of fetal materials. Finally, the panel declared that at all stages everyone involved in fetal research and transplantation should "accord human fetal tissue the same respect accorded other cadaveric human tissues entitled to respect." That's a curious rule that only a committee could love. Cadavers were once human beings and hence worthy of respect. But fetuses, what were they? In life, nothing. In death, deserving a modicum of care.

Even though the panel achieved an ethical majority, the testimony they heard made clear that Americans are far from agreement on the morality of fetal-tissue transplantation. In general, representatives of the diabetes and other advocacy associations judged the ethics of using fetal tissue solely by the hoped-for end of finding cures. They make a powerful case: extract some good from tragedy by easing those who are suffering. The medical researchers themselves, while welcoming procedural guidelines, bristled at the notion that their intentions could be regarded as anything other than altruistic. Just as predictably, pro-life spokespersons maintained that intentionally aborted fetuses should not be "harvested" for medical research.

The majority of the panelists concluded that, regardless of how one judges the morality of abortion, researchers in fetal transplantation "could be ethically isolated" from physicians who do abortions. But in a vigorous minority report, moral theologian James T. Burtchaell of Notre Dame University and James Bopp, Jr., an attorney for the National Right to Life Committee, challenged this conclusion. On the contrary, they argued, both procedures are so intertwined – materially, financially and technologically – that "a symbiotic relationship between the abortion industry and fetal-tissue transplantation therapy" cannot be avoided. Further, they wrote, everyone involved in an elective abortion – especially the mother – is morally disqualified from deciding how the fetal remains should be disposed, "as the man who has killed his wife is morally disqualified from acting as her executor." In this respect, they insisted, the donation of aborted fetal tissue is ethically different from the choice facing the guardian of an accident victim whose organs are suitable for transplant.

There are some pro-choice feminists, too, who nonetheless worry about the implications of fetal research. In the worst-case scenarios, they see the specter of dehumanized women, whose bodies have become fetal factories. "The role of women in fetal-tissue research is, after all, to provide the raw material," says Janice Raymond, a professor of Women's Studies and Medical Ethics at the University of Massachusetts. "One primary effect of fetal-tissue research and transplants," Raymond writes in On the Issues, a liberal women's quarterly, "has been to turn women into fetal-tissue containers; mere material environments for the fetus."

Even with the adoption of the panel's guidelines, Raymond and other critics doubt that they can be enforced or properly policed. Though long on ethical procedures, the panel had no advice on corresponding penalties. Just as physicians could and did do abortions when they were illegal, so could they privately arrange to have fetal tissue supplied to relatives of the donor. Laws proposed by Congress, however, criminalize the sale of fetal tissue across state lines; state laws will have to do the rest. But the NIH itself has no power to police free-standing abortion clinics in order to ensure that counselors do not advocate abortions for the sake of science, or use abortion methods that are medically riskier for women in order to obtain better fetal specimens.

Yet without some sort of ethical standards, fetal-tissue transplantation threatens to become an unsupervised private industry. In many ways it already is. Kimbrell charges that at least a half dozen companies supply fetal tissues to clients and estimates annual sales of several million dollars. "A fetal-tissue transplant industry," warns economist Emanuel Throne, coauthor of a report for Congress's Office of Technology Assessment, "could dwarf the present organ-transplant industry."

Worse, argues Kimbrell, there currently are few legal barriers to prevent private firms and hospitals from using fetal transplantation for cosmetic and other nonmedical purposes. For example, he cites researchers in Canada who have found that injections from fetal tissue accelerate the healing of muscles in animals. What works for animals could help humans as well. The next step, he suggests, could be the use of fetal injections to enhance – like steroids – the ability of athletes, thus raising the specter of Olympic competitors running on "baby power."

Although such scenarios may seem farfetched, even ethicists who support fetal-tissue research warn that the research and medical communities need to take action to keep emerging biotechnologies in check. Unlike drugs or medical devices, which are regulated by the Food and Drug Administration, fetal-tissue transplantation is a surgical procedure that can be regulated only by each hospital's research ethics committees. "These committees have institutional loyalties and a heavy medical membership," observes Arthur Caplan of the Center for Biomedical Ethics at the University of Minnesota, "and may not always be able to give independent assessments." Bioethicist LeRoy Walters of Georgetown University thinks the only practical solution is for the federal government to fund a fetal-tissue bank to keep "research and transplantation carefully insulated against commercialization."

Clearly, society should foster research to alleviate human suffering. Just as clearly, it must also protect itself against the callous use of human material, even in its early stages of development. Even though human fetuses have been thrust into a legal limbo, they still elicit feelings of protection and respect. The question society still has not resolved is: how much?

Discussion Questions

1. In the second paragraph the authors present details of research experiments with live human fetuses. Why do they describe these experiments at this point in the article? What is your reaction as a reader: Are you more or less likely to continue reading? How do the authors view the research they describe, and on what do you base your conclusions?

2. Identify and discuss sentences or passages in this article where the authors succinctly yet successfully illustrate the irony of the issue involved. For example: "But fetuses, what were they? In life, nothing. In death, deserving a modicum of care." How does the use of irony help further the argument?

3. Controversial ethical issues are often quite difficult to write about objectively. Keeping in mind that journalists pride themselves on objective reporting, discuss the degree to which you think this article succeeds or fails to be objective.

4. Why do you think there is ambiguity regarding the rights of a human fetus? Is it, or is it not, contradictory to view the fetus as having no constitutional rights regarding abortion but having rights regarding the manner of its disposition?

Journal Entry

Write an entry in which you explore your own attitudes and feelings regarding abortion. Include your thoughts on whether aborted fetuses should be used for research.

Writing Projects

1. The authors ask a number of important and difficult questions about such issues as the overlap between scientific research and morality, the rights of a fetus, and the sale of human organs and tissue for profit. Select one and write an essay in which you offer an answer to the question. Support your views with examples from the text and from your own experience. Explain how your answer agrees with or differs from the authors' views.

2. Examine the analogies in this article in which the authors compare a woman who elects abortion to "the man who has killed his wife" and to "the guardian of an accident victim whose organs are suitable for transplant." Are these strong or weak analogies? Discuss your own stance on the ethical issues involved, and offer your own set of analogies. Explain how each analogy reflects certain aspects of your viewpoint.

Collaborative Project

Working with a partner, research the current policies and practices regarding the use of human tissue. Find out what agencies are currently involved in "harvesting" human tissue and organs for science and profit. Describe any difficulties you faced in finding the information you sought, and explain why you think you had them. Report your findings and conclusions to the class.

Jean Bethke Elshtain

Why Worry about the Animals?

Jean Bethke Elshtain *(b. 1941) writes, "We have lost a sense of community and of the dignity of caring and being of service." She has also expressed particular concern for the way children are too often mistreated in our society. A Ph.D. who has taught political science at the university level, Elshtain has written numerous books, including* Public Man, Private Woman: Women in Social and Political Thought *(1981),* Meditations on Modern Political Thought *(1986), and* Power Trips and Other Journeys: Essays in Feminism as Civic Discourse *(1990). Her essays have appeared in periodicals such as the* Nation, Dissent, *and the* Progressive, *which published the following selection in March 1990. Here Elshtain argues for a more humane treatment of all animals, but she is particularly appalled by the abuse of animals in research experiments.*

Questions to Consider

☐ Do you believe animals are used and abused unnecessarily in scientific research? If so, what do you think should be done about it? Have you worked on any science experiments in school during which you were expected to bring harm to animal subjects? Do you take any kind of action to protect animals? Do you boycott products (cosmetics, for example) made by companies that use animal testing?

☐ What effect on the reader does Elshtain hope to achieve by beginning her essay with the list of examples she uses? What kind of account do you expect to follow such an opening?

These things are happening or have happened recently:

☐ The wings of seventy-four mallard ducks are snapped to see whether crippled birds can survive in the wild. (They can't.)

☐ Infant monkeys are deafened to study their social behavior, or turned into amphetamine addicts to see what happens to their stress level.

☐ Monkeys are separated from their mothers, kept in isolation, addicted to drugs, and induced to commit "aggressive" acts.

☐ Pigs are blowtorched and observed to see how they respond to third-degree burns. No pain-killers are used.

424

- ☐ Monkeys are immersed in water and vibrated to cause brain damage.
- ☐ For thirteen years, baboons have their brains bashed at the University of Pennsylvania as research assistants laugh at signs of the animals' distress.
- ☐ Monkeys are dipped in boiling water; other animals are shot in the face with high-powered rifles.

The list of cruelties committed in the name of "science" or "research" could be expanded endlessly. "Fully 80 percent of the experiments involving rhesus monkeys are either unnecessary, represent useless duplication of previous work, or could utilize nonanimal alternatives," says John E. McArdle, a biologist and specialist in primates at Illinois Wesleyan University.

Growing awareness of animal abuse is helping to build an increasingly militant animal-welfare movement in this country and abroad – a movement that is beginning to have an impact on public policy. Secretary of Health and Human Services Frederick Goodwin complained recently that complying with new Federal regulations on the use – or abuse – of animals will drain off some 17 percent of the research funds appropriated to the National Institutes of Health. (It is cheaper to purchase, use, and destroy animals than to retool for alternative procedures.) One of the institutes, the National Institute of Mental Health, spends about $30 million a year on research that involves pain and suffering for animals.

The new animal-welfare activists are drawing attention in part because of the tactics they espouse. Many preach and practice civil disobedience, violating laws against, say, breaking and entering. Some have been known to resort to violence against property and – on a few occasions – against humans.

Some individuals and groups have always fretted about human responsibility toward nonhuman creatures. In the ancient world, the historian Plutarch and the philosopher Porphyry were among those who insisted that human excellence embodied a refusal to inflict unnecessary suffering on all other creatures, human and nonhuman.

But with the emergence of the Western rationalist tradition, animals lost the philosophic struggle. Two of that tradition's great exponents, René Descartes and Immanuel Kant, dismissed out of hand the moral worth of animals. Descartes's view, which has brought comfort to every human who decides to confine, poison, cripple, infect, or dismember animals in the interest of human knowledge, was the more extreme: He held that animals are simply machines, devoid of consciousness or feeling. Kant, more sophisticated in his ethical reasoning, knew that animals could suffer but denied that they were self-conscious. Therefore, he argued, they could aptly serve as means to human ends.

To make sure that human sensibilities would not be troubled by the groans, cries, and yelps of suffering animals – which might lead some to suspect that animals not only bleed but feel pain – researchers have for a century subjected dogs and other animals to an operation called a centriculocordec-tomy, which destroys their vocal chords.

Still, there have long been groups that placed the suffering of animals within the bounds of human concern. In the Nineteenth and early Twentieth Centuries, such reform movements as women's suffrage and abolitionism made common cause with societies for the prevention of cruelty to animals. On one occasion in 1907, British suffragettes, trade-unionists, and their ani-mal-welfare allies battled London University medical students in a riot trig-gered by the vivisection of a dog.

Traditionally, such concern has been charitable and, frequently, highly sentimental. Those who perpetrated the worst abuses against animals were de-nounced for their "beastly" behavior – the farmer who beat or starved his horse; the householder who chained and kicked his dog; the aristocratic hunter who, with his guests, slew birds by the thousands in a single day on his private game preserve.

For the most part, however, animals have been viewed, even by those with "humane" concerns, as means to human ends. The charitable impulse, therefore, had a rather condescending, patronizing air: Alas, the poor creatures deserve our pity.

The new animal-welfare movement incorporates those historic concerns but steers them in new directions. Philosophically, animal-rights activists seek to close the gap between "human" and "beast," challenging the entire Western rationalist tradition which holds that the ability to reason abstractly is *the* defin-ing human attribute. (In that tradition, women were often located on a scale somewhere between "man" and "beast," being deemed human but not quite rational.)

Politically, the new abolitionists, as many animal-welfare activists call themselves, eschew sentimentalism in favor of a tough-minded, insistent claim that animals, too, have rights, and that violating those rights constitutes op-pression. It follows that animals must be liberated – and since they cannot lib-erate themselves in the face of overwhelming human hegemony, they require the help of liberators much as slaves did in the last century.

Thus, the rise of vocal movements for animal well-being has strong historic antecedents. What is remarkable about the current proliferation of efforts is their scope and diversity. Some proclaim animal "rights." Others speak of animal "welfare" or "protection." Still others find the term "equality" most apt, arguing that we should have "equal concern" for the needs of all sentient creatures.

When so many issues clamor for our attention, when so many problems demand our best attempts at fair-minded solution, why animals, why now? There is no simple explanation for the explosion of concern, but it is clearly linked to themes of peace and justice. Perhaps it can be summed up this way: Those who are troubled by the question of who is or is not within the circle of moral concern; those who are made queasy by our use and abuse of living be-ings for our own ends; those whose dreams of a better world are animated by some notion of a peaceable kingdom, *should* consider our relationship with the creatures that inhabit our planet with us—the creatures that have helped sustain us and that may share a similar fate with us unless we find ways to deflect if not altogether end the destruction of our earthly habitat.

Dozens of organizations have sprung up, operating alongside—and sometimes in conflict with—such older mainline outfits as the Humane Society, the Anti-Vivisection League, and the World Wildlife Fund. Among the new groups are People for the Ethical Treatment of Animals (PETA), Trans-Species Unlimited, In Defense of Animals, the Gorilla Foundation, Primarily Primates, Humane Farming Association, Farm Animal Reform, Alliance for Animals, Citizens to End Animal Suffering and Exploitation (CEASE), Whale Adoption Project, Digit Fund—the list goes on and on.

Some organizations focus on the plight of animals on factory farms, especially the condition of anemic, imprisoned veal calves kept in darkness and unable to turn around until they are killed at fourteen weeks. Others are primarily concerned with conditions in the wild, where the habitat of the panda, among others, is being destroyed or where great and wonderful creatures like the black rhinoceros and the African elephant or magnificent cats like the snow leopard or the Siberian tiger are marching toward extinction, victims of greedy buyers of illegal tusks or pelts.

Another group of activists clusters around the use of animals in such profitable pursuits as greyhound racing, where dogs by the hundreds are destroyed once they cease "earning their keep," or in tourist attractions where such wonderfully intelligent social beings as the orca and the dolphin are turned into circus freaks for profit. In the wild, orcas can live for up to one hundred years; in captivity, the average, sadly misnamed "killer whale" lasts about five.

Those wonderful chimpanzees that have been taught to speak to us through sign-language also arouse concern. If the funding ends or a researcher loses interest, they are sometimes killed, sometimes turned over to the less-than-tender mercies of laboratory researchers to be addicted to cocaine, infected with a virus, or subjected to some other terrible fate. Eugene Linden describes, in his study *Silent Partners*, chimps desperately trying to convey their pain and fear and sadness to uncomprehending experimenters.

Use of animals in war research is an industry in itself, though one usually shielded from public view. Monkeys are the most likely subjects of experiments designed to measure the effects of neutron-bomb radiation and the toxicity of chemical-warfare agents. Beginning in 1957, monkeys were placed at varying distances from ground zero during atomic testing; those that didn't die immediately were encaged so that the "progress" of their various cancers might be noted.

Radiation experiments on primates continue. Monkeys' eyes are irradiated, and the animals are subjected to shocks of up to twelve hundred volts.

Junior researchers are assigned the "death watch," and what they see are primates so distressed that they claw at themselves and even bite hunks from their own arms or legs in a futile attempt to stem the pain. At a government proving ground in Aberdeen, Maryland, monkeys are exposed to chemical-warfare agents.

Dolphins, animals of exquisite intelligence, have been trained by the military in such scenarios as injecting carbon dioxide cartridges into Vietnamese divers and planting and removing mines. The Navy announced in April 1989 that it would continue its thirty-million-dollar clandestine program, expanded in the Reagan years, to put dolphins to military use. The aim, the *New York Times* reported, is to use dolphins captured in the Gulf of Mexico to guard the Trident Nuclear Submarine Base at Bangor, Washington.

Several years ago, when I was writing a book on women and war, I came across references to the use of dogs in Vietnam. When I called the Pentagon and was put through to the chief of military history, Southeast Asia Branch, he told me that no books existed on the subject, but he did send me an excerpt from the *Vietnam War Almanac* that stated the U.S. military "made extensive use of dogs for a variety of duties in Vietnam, including scouting, mine detecting, tracking, sentry duty, flushing out tunnels, and drug detecting." Evidently, many of these dogs were killed rather than returned home, since it was feared their military training ill-suited them for civilian life.

Much better known, because of an increasingly successful animal-rights campaign, is the use of animals to test such household products as furniture polish and such cosmetics as shampoo and lipstick.

For years, industry has determined the toxicity of floor wax and detergents by injecting various substances into the stomachs of beagles, rabbits, and calves, producing vomiting, convulsions, respiratory illness, and paralysis. The so-called LD (lethal dose) 50 test ends only when half the animals in a test group have died. No anesthesia or pain killers are administered.

Dr. Andrew Rowan, assistant dean of the Tufts University School of Medicine, has offered persuasive evidence that such testing methods are crude and inaccurate measures of a product's safety. For one thing, a number of potentially significant variables, including the stress of laboratory living, are not taken into account, thus tainting any comparison of the effect of a given substance on human consumers.

The LD50 is notoriously unreproducible; the method for rating irritation is extremely subjective; and interspecies variations make test results highly suspect when applied to the human organism.

Most notorious of the "tests" deployed by the multibillion-dollar cosmetics industry is the Draize, which has been used since the 1940s to measure the potential irritative effects of products. Rabbits—used because their eyes do not produce tears and, therefore, cannot cleanse themselves—are placed into stocks and their eyes are filled with foreign substances. When a rabbit's eyes ulcerate—again, no pain killers are used—the cosmetics testers (who are usually not trained laboratory researchers) report a result. To call this procedure "scientific" is to demean authentic science.

Curiously, neither the LD50 test nor the Draize is required by law. They continue in use because manufacturers want to avoid alarming consumers by placing warning labels on products. More accurate methods available include computer simulations to measure toxicity, cell-culture systems, and organ-culture tests that use chicken-egg membranes.

The disdainful response by corporate America to animal-protection concerns seems, at least in this area, to be undergoing a slow shift toward new laboratory techniques that abandon wasteful, crude, and cruel animal testing. Several large cosmetics manufacturers, including Revlon, have only recently announced that they will phase out animal testing, confirming the claim of animal-welfare groups that the tests are unnecessary.

Among the nastier issues in the forefront of the "animal wars" is the controversy over hunting and trapping.

It's estimated that about seventeen million fur-bearing animals (plus "trash" animals—including pets—the trapper doesn't want) are mangled each year in steel-jaw leg-hold traps that tear an animal's flesh and break its bones. Many die of shock or starvation before the trapper returns. Some animals chew off part of a limb in order to escape. More than sixty countries now ban the leg-hold trap, requiring the use of less painful and damaging devices.

Protests against the manufacture, sale, and wearing of fur coats have been aggressively—and successfully—mounted in Western Europe. In Holland, fur sales have dropped 80 percent in the last few years. Radical groups in Sweden have broken into fur farms to release minks and foxes. An effort to shame women who wear fur has had enormous impact in Great Britain.

Similar campaigns have been mounted in the United States, but the fur industry is waging a well-financed counterattack in this country. Curiously, the industry's efforts have been tacitly supported by some rights-absolutists within feminism who see wearing a fur coat as a woman's right. It's difficult to think of a greater *reductio ad absurdum* of the notion of "freedom of choice," but it seems to appeal to certain adherents of upwardly mobile, choice-obsessed political orthodoxy.

Hunting may be the final frontier for animal-welfare groups. Because hunting is tied to the right to bear arms, any criticism of hunting is construed as an attack on constitutional freedoms by hunting and gun organizations, including the powerful and effective National Rifle Association. A bumper sticker I saw on a pickup truck in Northampton, Massachusetts, may tell the tale: MY WIFE, YES. MY DOG, MAYBE. BUT MY GUN, NEVER.

For some animal protectionists, the case against hunting is open and shut. They argue that the vast majority of the estimated 170 million animals shot to death in any given year are killed for blood sport, not for food, and that the offspring of these slaughtered creatures are left to die of exposure or starvation. Defenders of blood sports see them as a skill and a tradition, a lingering relic of America's great frontier past. Others – from Nineteenth Century feminists to the Norman Mailer of *Why Are We in Vietnam?* – link the national mania for hunting with a deeper thirst for violence.

I am not convinced there is an inherent connection between animal killing and a more general lust for violence, but some disquieting evidence is beginning to accumulate. Battered and abused women in rural areas often testify, for example, that their spouses also abused animals, especially cows, by stabbing them with pitchforks, twisting their ears, kicking them, or, in one reported incident, using a board with a nail in it to beat a cow to death.

But even people who recoil from hunting and other abuses of animals often find it difficult to condemn such experiments as those cited at the beginning of this article, which are, after all, conducted to serve "science" and, perhaps, to alleviate human pain and suffering. Sorting out this issue is no easy task if one is neither an absolute prohibitionist nor a relentless defender of the scientific establishment. When gross abuses come to light, they are often reported in ways that allow and encourage us to distance ourselves from emotional and ethical involvement. Thus the case of the baboons whose brains were bashed in at the University of Pennsylvania prompted the *New York Times* to editorialize, on July 31, 1985, that the animals "seemed" to be suffering. They *were* suffering, and thousands of animals suffer every day.

Reasonable people should be able to agree on this: that alternatives to research that involves animal suffering must be vigorously sought; that there is no excuse for such conditions as dogs lying with open incisions, their entrails exposed, or monkeys with untreated, protruding broken bones, exposed muscle tissue, and infected wounds, living in grossly unsanitary conditions amidst feces and rotting food; that quick euthanasia should be administered to a suffering animal after the conclusion of a pain-inducing procedure; that pre- and post-surgical care must be provided for animals; that research should not be needlessly duplicated, thereby wasting animal lives, desensitizing generations of researchers, and flushing tax dollars down the drain.

What stands in the way of change? Old habits, bad science, unreflective cruelty, profit, and, in some cases, a genuine fear that animal-welfare groups want to stop all research dead in its tracks. "Scientists fear shackles on research," intones one report. But why are scientists so reluctant to promote such research alternatives as modeling, in-vitro techniques, and the use of lower organisms? Because they fear that the public may gain wider knowledge of what goes on behind the laboratory door. Surely those using animals should be able to explain themselves and to justify their expenditure of the lives, bodies, and minds of other creatures.

There is, to be sure, no justification for the harassment and terror tactics used by some animal-welfare groups. But the scientist who is offended when an animal-welfare proponent asks, "How would you feel if someone treated your child the way you treat laboratory animals?" should ponder one of the great ironies in the continuing debate: Research on animals is justified on grounds that they are "so like us."

I *do* appreciate the ethical dilemma here. As a former victim of polio, I have thought long and hard for years about animal research and human welfare. This is where I come down, at least for now:

First, most human suffering in this world cannot be ameliorated in any way by animal experimentation. Laboratory infliction of suffering on animals will not keep people healthy in Asia, Africa, and Latin America. As philosopher Peter Singer has argued, we already know how to cure what ails people in desperate poverty; they need "adequate nutrition, sanitation, and health care. It has been estimated that 250,000 children die each week around the world, and that one quarter of these deaths are by dehydration due to diarrhea. A simple treatment, already known and needing no animal experimentation, could prevent the deaths of these children."

Second, it is not clear that a cure for terrible and thus far incurable diseases such as AIDS is best promoted with animal experimentation. Some American experts on AIDS admit that French scientists are making more rapid progress toward a vaccine because they are working directly with human volunteers, a course of action Larry Kramer, a gay activist, has urged upon American scientists. Americans have been trying since 1984 to infect chimpanzees with AIDS, but after the expenditure of millions of dollars, AIDS has not been induced in any nonhuman animal. Why continue down this obviously flawed route?

Third, we could surely agree that a new lipstick color, or an even more dazzling floor wax, should never be promoted for profit over the wounded bodies of animals. The vast majority of creatures tortured and killed each year suffer for *nonmedical* reasons. Once this abuse is eliminated, the really hard cases having to do with human medical advance and welfare can be debated, item by item.

Finally, what is at stake is the exhaustion of the Eighteenth Century model of humanity's relationship to nature, which had, in the words of philosopher Mary Midgley, "built into it a bold, contemptuous rejection of the nonhuman world."

Confronted as we are with genetic engineering and a new eugenics, with the transformation of farms where animals ranged freely into giant factories where animals are processed and produced like objects, with callous behavior on a scale never before imagined under the rubric of "science," we can and must do better than to dismiss those who care as irrational and emotional animal-lovers who are thinking with their hearts (not surprisingly, their ranks are heavily filled with women), and who are out to put a stop to the forward march of rationalism and science.

We humans do not deserve peace of mind on this issue. Our sleep should be troubled and our days riddled with ethical difficulties as we come to realize the terrible toll one definition of "progress" has taken on our fellow creatures.

We must consider our meat-eating habits as well. Meat-eating is one of the most volatile, because most personal, of all animal-welfare questions. Meat-eaters do not consider themselves immoral, though hard-core vegetarians find meat-eating repugnant – the consumption of corpses. Such feminist theorists as Carol Adams insist that there is a connection between the butchering of animals and the historic maltreatment of women. Certainly, there is a politics of meat that belongs on the agenda along with other animal-welfare issues.

I, for one, do not believe humans and animals have identical rights. But I do believe that creatures who can reason in their own ways, who can suffer, who are mortal beings like ourselves, have a value and dignity we must take into account. Animals are not simply a means to our ends.

When I was sixteen years old, I journeyed on a yellow school bus from LaPorte, Colorado, to Fairbanks, Iowa, on a 4-H Club "exchange trip." On the itinerary was a visit to a meat-packing plant in Des Moines. As vivid as the day I witnessed it is the scene I replay of men in blood-drenched coats "bleeding" pigs strung up by their heels on a slowly moving conveyer belt. The pigs – bright and sensitive creatures, as any person who has ever met one knows – were screaming in terror before the sharp, thin blade entered their jugular veins. They continued to struggle and squeal until they writhed and fell silent.

The men in the slaughter room wore boots. The floor was awash in blood. I was horrified. But I told myself this was something I should remember. For a few months I refused to eat pork. But then I fell back into old habits – this was Colorado farm country in the late 1950s, after all.

But at one point, a few years ago, that scene and those cries of terror returned. This time I decided I would not forget, even though I knew my peace of mind would forever be disturbed.

Discussion Questions

1. Describe the type and structure of Elshtain's argument. Does she intend to evoke a rational or emotional response? What does this reveal about her view of her audience?

2. Analyze Elshtain's use of historical background in tracing various attitudes and movements over the years regarding animal rights. How does Elshtain incorporate the historical material to reinforce her main argument?

3. What are three or four different practices in scientific research that concern people about the plight of the animals used? Give examples of acceptable

methods of protecting these animals. Suggest ways in which the research data might still be obtained without abusing the animals.

4. Do you agree with Elshtain that hunting animals today is not simply for sport but reflects a deep and pervasive compulsion for violence in our country? Do you feel there is a moral distinction between killing animals for sport versus killing them for food? Why or why not?

Journal Entry

What rights do you think animals have when being used for scientific research? To what extent do you think it is morally acceptable to view animals as a necessary means toward the goal of improving human health and safety? What moral distinction do you make between using animals for medical research versus cosmetic research?

Writing Projects

1. Elshtain points out that some animal-welfare activists engage in violence, sometimes breaking the law. Write an essay on what you consider effective and appropriate means of protecting animals from mistreatment in the name of scientific research. What methods and actions of protest do you deem inappropriate? Why? Which of Elshtain's ideas about the tactics of animal-welfare activists do you accept? Which do you reject? Did Elshtain provide any new information or present any arguments that changed your mind about the use of animals in research?

2. What similarities and differences do you see between research using animal subjects and research using aborted fetuses (discussed previously in the essay by Kenneth Woodward et al.)? Investigate one company that uses animal subjects in its research lab and one company that uses aborted fetuses. How does each view its research? What role does commercial profit have in either type of research?

Collaborative Projects

1. Elshtain lists some fifteen different organizations concerned with the plight of animals. Working with a partner, select two or more that agree that animals are mistreated, but disagree on issues such as why and how animals are abused and what should be done about it. Study the policy statements and other writings published by each group, and write a report comparing the ideologies and methodologies of the different groups.

2. Working with two classmates, write three letters to the editor of the *Progressive*, where Elshtain's piece was originally published. One letter should agree strongly with Elshtain; one should strongly disagree with Elshtain; and one should agree to some extent but take issue with some of her points. When you present your letters to the class, discuss the difficulties each of you faced in writing a letter in which both the topic and your opinion were dictated to you. What kind of professional situation might require you to adopt a persona (an assumed identity) that expresses views that are not the same as your own?

Ron Karpati

A Scientist: "I Am the Enemy"

Ron Karpati *(b. 1961) is a pediatric oncologist (a children's doctor who treats cancer) practicing at Sunrise Children's Hospital in Las Vegas, Nevada. Dr. Karpati is currently specializing in bone marrow transplant therapy. As a doctor who treats terminally ill children, Karpati finds himself defending the use of animals in medical research. His own experience as a researcher leads him to oppose certain animal rights arguments, like those presented by Jean Bethke Elshtain in this chapter. The following essay first appeared in the "My Turn" column of* Newsweek *in December 1989.*

Questions to Consider

☐ This essay was submitted to *Newsweek* as a personal opinion piece, similar to the way in which people write letters to the editor. What do you think motivates people who are not professional writers to submit letters to the editor or essays for the "opinion page" of a newspaper or magazine? Does the fact that such letters are written by nonjournalists usually influence your response in any way? If so, how?

☐ Karpati supports his argument mainly with reference to his own experience. As you read, consider whether the support he offers is convincing and effective.

I am the enemy! One of those vilified, inhumane physician-scientists involved in animal research. How strange, for I have never thought of myself as an evil person. I became a pediatrician because of my love for children and my desire to keep them healthy. During medical school and residency, however, I saw many children die of leukemia, prematurity and traumatic injury—circumstances against which medicine has made tremendous progress, but still has far to go. More important, I also saw children, alive and healthy, thanks to advances in medical science such as infant respirators, potent antibiotics, new surgical techniques and the entire field of organ transplantation. My desire to tip the scales in favor of the healthy, happy children drew me to medical research.

My accusers claim that I inflict torture on animals for the sole purpose of career advancement. My experiments supposedly have no relevance to medicine and are easily replaced by computer simulation. Meanwhile, an apathetic public barely watches, convinced that the issue has no significance, and publicity-conscious politicians increasingly give way to the demands of the activists.

We in medical research have also been unconscionably apathetic. We have allowed the most extreme animal-rights protesters to seize the initiative and frame the issue as one of "animal fraud." We have been complacent in our belief that a knowledgeable public would sense the importance of animal research to the public health. Perhaps we have been mistaken in not responding to the emotional tone of the argument created by those sad posters of animals by waving equally sad posters of children dying of leukemia or cystic fibrosis.

Much is made of the pain inflicted on these animals in the name of medical science. The animal-rights activists contend that this is evidence of our malevolent and sadistic nature. A more reasonable argument, however, can be advanced in our defense. Life is often cruel, both to animals and human beings. Teenagers get thrown from the back of a pickup truck and suffer severe head injuries. Toddlers, barely able to walk, find themselves at the bottom of a swimming pool while a parent checks the mail. Physicians hoping to alleviate the pain and suffering these tragedies cause have but three choices: create an animal model of the injury or disease and use that model to understand the process and test new therapies; experiment on human beings—some experiments will succeed, most will fail—or finally, leave medical knowledge static, hoping that accidental discoveries will lead us to the advances.

Some animal-rights activists would suggest a fourth choice, claiming that computer models can simulate animal experiments, thus making the actual experiments unnecessary. Computers can simulate, reasonably well, the effects of well-understood principles on complex systems, as in the application of the laws of physics to airplane and automobile design. However, when the principles themselves are in question, as is the case with the complex biological systems under study, computer modeling alone is of little value.

One of the terrifying effects of the effort to restrict the use of animals in medical research is that the impact will not be felt for years and decades: drugs that might have been discovered will not be; surgical techniques that might have been developed will not be; and fundamental biological processes that might have been understood will remain mysteries. There is the danger that politically expedient solutions will be found to placate a vocal minority, while the consequences of those decisions will not be apparent until long after the decisions are made and the decision makers forgotten.

Fortunately, most of us enjoy good health, and the trauma of watching one's child die has become a rare experience. Yet our good fortune should not make us unappreciative of the health we enjoy or the advances that make it possible. Vaccines, antibiotics, insulin and drugs to treat heart disease, hypertension and stroke are all based on animal research. Most complex surgical procedures, such as coronary-artery bypass and organ transplantation, are initially developed in animals. Presently undergoing animal studies are techniques to insert genes in humans in order to replace the defective ones found to be the cause of so much disease. These studies will effectively end if animal research is severely restricted.

In America today, death has become an event isolated from our daily existence—out of the sight and thoughts of most of us. As a doctor who has watched many children die, and their parents grieve, I am particularly angered by people capable of so much compassion for a dog or a cat, but with seemingly so little for a dying human being. These people seem so insulated from the reality of human life and death and what it means.

Make no mistake, however: I am not advocating the needlessly cruel treatment of animals. To the extent that the animal-rights movement has made us more aware of the needs of these animals, and made us search harder for suitable alternatives, they have made a significant contribution. But if the more radical members of this movement are successful in limiting further research, their efforts will bring about a tragedy that will cost many lives. The real question is whether an apathetic majority can be aroused to protect its future against a vocal, but misdirected, minority.

Discussion Questions

1. Karpati says he and his colleagues have been labeled "inhumane," "malevolent," and "sadistic." Consider how these terms are at odds with the usual adjectives used to describe physicians and scientists. How does this affect your understanding of the situation and your own conclusions?

2. If your feelings and attitudes changed toward the use of animals in medical research as a result of reading Karpati's essay, what arguments does he present that changed your mind?

3. Karpati classifies those involved in the medical research versus animal rights controversy into three main categories. What are they? Is his summary of the views held by those in each category informative and objectively presented?

4. Which of Karpati's suggestions for how to handle animal rights activists do you accept? Which do you reject? Why?

Journal Entry

Following Karpati's example, write an informal essay about the ethical issues of a topic of special concern to you. It should be a topic that you believe generally receives biased treatment in the media. Contrast how the media portrays the ethical issues with what you see as the real situation.

Writing Projects

1. Write a response to Karpati's essay. Cite passages in his essay and support or refute them with your own ideas. Use essays throughout this text and your own experience to back up your argument.

2. Write an analysis of the structure of Karpati's argument. How does he define the key points of his main argument? How does he refer to the opposition? How do you know when he is presenting his view and when he is laying out the opposition's view just prior to refuting it? Does his argument use appeals that are based mainly on reason, emotion, his own ethical stance, or a combination? How does his use of language reinforce his use of examples to lend support to his argument?

Collaborative Project

Design one of the following panel presentations on animal rights in medical and scientific research. One panel could be comprised of representatives from different organizations and companies who are willing to speak to your class. In this case, the members of your team should prepare a set of questions to ask each representative, and select one group member to act as moderator. Your questions should provide the groundwork for stimulating discussion. Another panel could be comprised of students from class who assume the roles of representatives from various organizations and companies. As a team the students would research the organizations, survey their literature, and interview the researchers or the activists opposing the companies. Again, prepare a set of questions and assign a moderator. In both cases, try to set up a panel of people or groups with opposing viewpoints to spark discussion.

Joyce Carol Oates

Under/Ground

Joyce Carol Oates *(b. 1938) possesses the literary genius to produce an astonishing quantity of outstanding work in many literary genres, including fiction, poetry, drama, and literary criticism. The winner of numerous prestigious literary awards, Oates is the Roger S. Berlind Distinguished Professor in the Humanities at Princeton University. Tagged a "gothic novelist" by some, Oates writes fiction that is, indeed, at times grotesque and lurid; typical events in her stories and plays include rape, murder, suicide, and mental breakdown. Her approach can be described as unflinching and clinical, but also tender without sentimentality. Her recent novels include* Because It Is Bitter and Because It Is My Heart *(1990) and* Foxfire *(1993).* Under/Ground *is from* Twelve Plays, *a collection of recent works, most of which have been performed since 1990.* Under/Ground *is a one-act play with only three characters, which Oates says "begins in apparent realism and moves gradually toward surrealism." The play explores the personality shifts of these three characters as their descent into an underground bomb shelter affects their behavior and outlook.*

Questions to Consider

☐ This play treats various ethical problems, as do the other selections in this chapter. As you read, consider how the playwright is able to use her characters to explore conflicting views and interpretations as compared to the way in which essay writers present and support their points.

☐ At the beginning of the play, the characters are described in some detail. As you read, think about how the characters change and why.

☐ If *surrealism* is a new term for you, consult a glossary of literary terms.

A Play in One Act

CHARACTERS
NOLA HARVEY: twenty-eight years old
MILES HARVEY: forty to fifty years old
KEITH: thirty to thirty-five years old

Lights up. Extreme stage right, KEITH, NOLA, *and* MILES *are standing preparatory to entering the underground bomb shelter. Most of the stage is dark.* KEITH, NOLA, *and*

MILES *may be standing on a raised platform to indicate "ground level"—a sidewalk—outside the shelter. There are double doors leading into the shelter; stairs, a landing, more stairs, corridors, doors to rooms, etc. The shelter need not be represented realistically but should be suggestive in its labyrinthine, gloomy, sinister, surreal complexity. The play itself begins in apparent realism and moves gradually toward surrealism.*

KEITH *is a foreign-service officer of modest rank at the American embassy of this capital city of an unnamed European country: seemingly upbeat, optimistic, ebullient, "patriotic" in the professional manner of foreign-service employees abroad.* NOLA HARVEY *is the young wife of* DR. MILES HARVEY, *an American historian of some reputation. The* HARVEYS *are attractively dressed:* NOLA *in a tasteful, "feminine" dress or suit;* MILES *more conservatively.* KEITH *wears regulation diplomatic attire—a dark blue suit, conservatively cut, a plain necktie. As these three descend into the bomb shelter, their personalities gradually shift—from their "daylight" or "social" personae to deeper, more primitive personalities.*

As the lights come up, KEITH, NOLA, *and* MILES *are laughing companionably.* KEITH *fumbles for his wallet and extracts two small plastic card-keys to unlock the shelter doors. The locks on the doors are prominent.*

NOLA: Oh, I've had too much to drink—that luncheon went on and *on*. Is it always like that at the embassy?

KEITH *(suavely, boyishly)*: Only when our visitors are VIPs.

MILES: We weren't treated half so well in Frankfurt after my lecture.

KEITH: That's because it was Frankfurt—a major post. Here— *(lowering his voice, smiling)*—well, things are sort of *minor*, as maybe you've noticed.

NOLA: This is a lovely country. The people are so—warm, and curious, and *interested* in us.

KEITH: Yes, they adore Americans—at least to our faces. *(As he peers at the card-keys and fits one into the lock of the outer door, without success)* They're eager for visas to "study"—to get scholarships to pay their way to the States. *(Smiling)* Wait'll you see this place—as the ambassador was saying, they lost most of the capital city's historic architecture in the war, so they've poured money into government buildings. *(Fussing with key-cards, still pleasant, but getting impatient)* This bomb shelter is quite something, y'know, for a country so—limited in resources as this.

NOLA *(a bit apprehensive)*: This—bomb shelter—is it big?

KEITH: Mammoth!

NOLA: I've never been in a bomb shelter before.

MILES: Nor have I, come to think of it. They've lost popularity, back home.

KEITH *(sly smile)*: They still exist, back home—but they're reserved for VIPs, you bet!

NOLA *(uneasily)*: Well. I guess we don't like to think about that.

KEITH: That's the idea.

NOLA *(to MILES)*: I—I'm wondering whether I really want to go in here. It's such a lovely, sunny day.

MILES: Certainly you're coming along. We want to "share everything," don't we? (*Gives her a significant look, squeezes her hand*)

KEITH (*as a guide; "booster" voice*): When it was built in 1964, this was as modern as any shelter in the world, even the Kremlin's—even our own leaders'. Now, I guess it's outmoded in certain respects, like for instance a chemical attack—toxic chemicals *sink*, y'know—but in case of a conventional nuclear war, it should be adequate. Ah! (*Succeeds in unlocking the door; turns the knob and pushes the door in, producing a sharp, creaking, jarring noise*)

NOLA (*startled by the noise, laughs nervously*): I—I think I—

MILES (*displeased*): Nola, dear, don't be silly.

NOLA: —I'd rather wait in the car.

KEITH (*like a salesman*): Oh, the shelter is perfectly safe, Mrs. Harvey. (*Joking, with a gesture toward the sky*) Much safer than "reality."

NOLA (*apologetic, but willful*): My head aches, I must have drunk too much champagne.

MILES (*pulling gently but firmly at her arm*): We are not going to leave you in the car, and *I* want to see the shelter. If Ken says it's safe—

KEITH: Keith.

MILES: —if he's taken visitors through before—

KEITH: Dozens of American VIPs! The most distinguished, last year, was Vice-President Quayle! And he loved it.

NOLA: Loved it?

KEITH: Mr. Quayle is *appreciative*.

(NOLA *acquiesces. The three step through the first doorway into a small vestibule.* KEITH *is enjoying his role as guide.*)

KEITH (*playful finger to lips*): The existence of this shelter is a state secret, so we'll close the door—quickly. (*Shuts outer door;* NOLA *makes an involuntary gesture, as of distress at being locked in.*)

MILES (*bemused*): A state secret? This gigantic door, in a wall fronting a street? Behind Parliament?

KEITH: An open secret, for sure. But—it isn't spoken of. (*To* NOLA) Are you all right, Mrs. Harvey?

NOLA: Oh—yes.

MILES (*overlapping with* NOLA): My wife is *fine*.

KEITH (*familiar, solicitous*): Gee, I used to be claustrophobic too, as a kid. Even through college. Had dreams about being buried alive, choking for air, trapped—brrrr! (*Shudders, but reverts easily to cheerful tone as he inserts the second card in the inner door*) They say it's a basic human phobia—fear of being buried alive.

(NOLA *hugs herself, shudders; sniffs as if smelling something unpleasant.*)

MILES (*professorial, pedantic*): No doubt because in the past, people often *were* buried alive—poor souls who were believed to be dead but weren't. Before modern medical technology. Before embalming.

NOLA (*nervous laugh*): That's what it smells like!

MILES: What smells like—?

NOLA: The air in here smells like formaldehyde.

MILES (*disapproving*): *I* don't smell anything.

KEITH (*cheerfully*): Oh, this is nothing, yet.

NOLA (*accommodating*): Of course, it could be my—imagination.

(KEITH *continues to try to fit the card into the lock, turning it upside-down, jamming it in harder or more gently, etc., but without success. To cover his annoyance, he begins to whistle.*)

MILES (*to* KEITH): Do many people have access to this shelter?

KEITH: Naturally not. This is *the* bomb shelter in the country. The prime minister—high-ranking government officials and members of Parliament—a select number of diplomats and visitors. (*Smiles*) Everyone at the U.S. Embassy, for sure. They wouldn't keep *us* out. (*Muttering*) Damn this lock, I *know* it works.

NOLA (*an edge to her voice; schoolgirl sort of manner*): And what about the others?

KEITH: What others?

NOLA: The seventy million others in this country.

KEITH (*vaguely, blandly*): Oh, I'm sure they'd be taken care of. There are lots of bomb shelters, more conventional ones, built during the war. (*Pause*) Anyway, ordinary folks wouldn't expect to be included in *this* shelter.

MILES: I should think not.

NOLA (*stubbornly*): I thought this was a "parliamentary democracy"—an "egalitarian" society.

KEITH: So? That doesn't affect their tradition.

MILES (*to* KEITH): Keith—it *is* Keith, isn't it?—how long have you been posted here?

KEITH (*shrugging, pleasant*): Oh, forever! . . . Naw, only a few years. They rotate us around. Prevent us from getting "attached." Before this I was stationed in Norway. Before that, Canada. (*Yawns*) Places where nothing much happens. Or if it does, you don't notice. (*An old joke*) Like—tree rings growing. (*Pause, more seriously*) Almost, y'know, you wish for some kind of action—"history"—in backwaters like this. Gee, I envy my colleagues in the Mideast—I *do*.

NOLA (*incensed*): You wouldn't want bombings, would you? Missiles? *War?*

KEITH (*quickly*): Oh, no, of course not. (*Reverts to an earnest, official voice*) The goal of all U.S. diplomacy is global peace.

(KEITH *has managed to unlock the door, with a cracking, creaking sound, as before. As the three step through the inner door,* MILES *takes a small camera out of his pocket.*)

KEITH (*with sudden authority*): Uh, Dr. Harvey—better not.

MILES: Not even for private use?

KEITH: This *is* an official classified zone.

MILES: But who would know?

KEITH: It's just forbidden.

MILES (*smiling*): Yes, but who would know?

NOLA (*embarrassed*): Oh, Miles, put it away. Please.

MILES (*reluctantly*): Well. All right. But I don't see—

KEITH: It's all right that we're here so long as it isn't *known* we're here. Y'know—diplomacy.

MILES: I understand. Sorry. (*Slips camera back into pocket*)

KEITH: Thanks! (*Switches on fluorescent lights, shuts second door, with a little difficulty.*)

NOLA: What if we're locked in here?

KEITH: Impossible, Mrs. Harvey. (*Waving cards*) What got us in will get us out. Also—there are plenty of telephones.

(NOLA *nudges herself against* MILES, *who slips an arm around her.* KEITH *begins to lead them down the stairs, which are steep.*)

KEITH (*ebulliently*): Hmmmm! It *does* smell a bit, doesn't it? But you get used to it quickly. Nothing to be worried about—it's perfectly empty, and it's perfectly safe. In fact, I find it comforting. I feel so *privileged.*

(*Lights out.*)

(*Lights up.*)

(KEITH, NOLA, MILES *are standing on a landing, illuminated brightly while the rest of the stage remains darkened.* NOLA *and* MILES *glance up behind them a bit edgily, as if to indicate that they've descended a considerable distance.*)

(*Here, we see a large, glossy—though faded—poster giving numbered instructions in a foreign language, an invented language suggestive of Finnish and Russian: "Kyväuoppyio"—"Hyvmespheere"—"Janisijäaratiaj"—"Vytirkborg"—"Svenszeri"—"Vääjivilya"—"Reostrov"—"Ostrykyr"—etc. There is a life-sized mannequin in full nuclear defense gear: khaki jacket and trousers, gas mask, boots, gloves.*)

NOLA (*girlish reaction, seeing mannequin*): Oh! It's so—lifelike.

KEITH (*tapping mannequin on head*): Yeah, he's my buddy. Hiya, pal! (*To the* HARVEYS) He's wearing your basic issue, for when the bomb falls. I mean—uh, if—*if* the bomb falls. (*Chuckles*) I've had the gear on—actually, it's a lot more comfortable than it looks.

NOLA: A gas mask can suffocate you, if it's defective.

KEITH: Nah, more likely people put them on wrong. The human factor—no matter how they're educated, some people for sure are going to goof up in times of emergency.

(*A deep, subterranean, near-inaudible throbbing and vibrating has begun.*)

MILES *(cupping hand to ear)*: What's that?

KEITH: Generator, ventilation system, hydraulic pumps—everything running constantly, of course. Twenty-four hours a day.

NOLA: So—everything is ready. *(Shivers)*

KEITH: Absolutely! There's a maintenance crew, for sure. And the whole thing is in the process of being computerized.

NOLA *(glancing back up behind her, uneasy)*: How deep *is* this place?

KEITH: Oh, we've hardly begun. We're down about twenty-five feet is all. The lowermost level is one hundred seventy-five feet. *(Gesturing expansively)* A regular metropolis!

MILES *(has been examining poster)*: What a language! I know German, and Russian, and some Swedish, but this hardly seems Indo-European.

KEITH: Yeah, it's like Hungarian—a real linguistic challenge.

(MILES stumbles through some of the words on the poster, mispronouncing them; KEITH rattles them off with surprising fluency.)

KEITH: It's just directions in time of emergency. Routine stuff—schoolchildren are drilled in it.

(Fluorescent lights flicker subtly. NOLA, KEITH, MILES notice but say nothing. Lights then stabilize.)

MILES *(an air of profundity)*: How—strange! After millions of years of evolution, and the progress of civilization, a man doesn't know—*really* know—what he's made of. Until he's put to the test.

NOLA *(lightly ironic)*: And a woman?

MILES: By "man" I include woman. As in "mankind."

KEITH: It's true, Dr. Harvey! And for entire nations, too. Entire nations can be courageous, or cowardly.

MILES: It's a process of evolution, I suppose.

KEITH: Survival of the fittest!

MILES: I'm a historian, not a scientist, but I've always seen the basic pattern—adaptation or death.

NOLA *(shivering)*: It *is* cold.

MILES: Would you like my coat, dear? To drape over your shoulders?

NOLA: No, I'll be all right.

(KEITH leads NOLA and MILES down another flight of stairs; or the action is simulated. Lights behind them go out; others come on. The throbbing and vibrating sound is more pronounced. We come to an area of several shut doors; a television monitor; an old-fashioned wall telephone, its receiver dangling loose. Signs on the wall "Út Ysskräjivak-Ylla"—"Czijillo Bvtthliomez.")

KEITH *(chattering)*: Above us—four-ton steel reinforced shields. On all sides—steel and concrete. Tons of dirt. *(Pointing)* Down that corridor, the communications center; down here, the infirmary; and this corridor *(pointing)* is a secret passageway connecting the shelter with the prime minister's residence. *(Turns on light switch, but corridor remains dark)*

MILES: Say, can we see that?

KEITH: Well, Doctor, it's, uh, *dark*.

MILES *(peering into corridor)*: I believe I hear — dripping?

KEITH: *I* don't hear anything.

NOLA *(wrinkling her nose)*: That smell . . .

MILES: How far down are we now?

KEITH: Approximately one hundred feet. *(Cheerfully, glancing up)* You can feel it, sort of, can't you? — eardrums, eyeballs — a sort of *—force?*

NOLA: . . . like stagnant water.

MILES *(primly)*: Leakage in here could be dangerous.

KEITH *(stiffly)*: The shelter has *never* leaked, Dr. Harvey, in its entire history.

(NOLA has wandered to the telephone, lifts the receiver to her ear, out of curiosity. She catches MILES' eye, mouths the words "It's dead," shakes her head, and returns the receiver to its cradle.)

(KEITH, oblivious of NOLA, has gone to a door to open it, switch on lights. The room is cell-like, very small. A single cot.)

KEITH: Here we have a typical room: a bit compact, but not bad, eh? And a single, if you like privacy.

NOLA *(holding her nose)*: Oh, dear! The smell!

(MILES too reacts, but enters the room; bends to peer under the cot; recoils in disgust.)

MILES: *Ugh!*

NOLA *(frightened)*: What is it?

MILES: Uh — nothing.

NOLA *(dreading)*: Something — dead?

KEITH *(quickly)*: Oh, I'm sure it's — nothing.

NOLA *(voice rising)*: Something dead?

MILES *(professorial irony, dry wit)*: Darling, it isn't any danger to us in the condition it's in — let's put it that way.

KEITH *(peering under the cot too, similarly revolted; turns off lights, firmly shuts the door; apologetic, chagrined)*: Whew! That's most unusual, I swear.

MILES *(pedantic)*: Decomposition would be very slow in here, of course — no flies, very little bacteria. More likely, since the air is so dry, the process would be like — mummification.

(A pause.)

NOLA *(frightened)*: A rat?

KEITH *(whistling)*: *Most* unusual.

(NOLA *looks around, alarmed, listening to the throbbing, vibrating sound.*)

NOLA: My God, isn't this—madness! This! Down here! How long could human beings survive down here, if there *was* a war?

MILES: Now, Nola.

KEITH: Now, Mrs. Harvey.

NOLA (*pulling away from* MILES*'s touch*): Think of the terror, the disorientation, the hopelessness—

KEITH (*ticking off on his fingers, matter-of-fact*): The alert sounds—you report to your station—the shelter is sealed—you wait out the results of the attack: what's so hopeless about that? Anyway, what's the alternative?

NOLA (*angry*): You don't seem to realize, either of you, that we are surrounded by *earth*. This is a tomb, it's for burial—burial alive.

KEITH (*smiling*): Why, no. It's for surviving. Surviving alive.

NOLA: I can feel the earth—the weight of it. The pressure. (*Swaying, hands to eyes*) It's horrible.

MILES (*embracing* NOLA, *addressing* KEITH *over her shoulder*): My poor darling interprets everything so *personally*.

KEITH: My wife was the exactly same way, Dr. Harvey! I guess that's how women are.

MILES: They lack the gift of abstraction. Of detaching yourself from experience.

KEITH: Exactly!

MILES: Nola, dear, it's just your imagination, whatever you're thinking of. Mmm? (*Whispers in her ear*)

KEITH: Shall we continue?

NOLA (*easing away from* MILES, *with an expression of dread yet resignation*): There's more?

KEITH: The best is yet to come.

(NOLA *stares at him, laughs incredulously.*)

KEITH (*politely*): I gather you are a disarmament person, Mrs. Harvey? An "ecology" person?

NOLA (*pertly*): And you are a war person?

KEITH (*laughing pleasantly*): I don't care to be reduced to a political stance, Mrs. Harvey, any more than you do. I'm a realist. Americans are realists. Of course, the shelter isn't a luxury hotel, but the fact is, it *exists*. And if there's a nuclear war, you're either *in* or you're *out*.

(*A pause.* MILES *nods professorially.* NOLA *glares at* KEITH, *then turns away, to continue down the stairs.*)

NOLA (*grimly*): Let's get this over with.

(KEITH *hurries to accompany* NOLA; *takes her arm on the steep stairs.* MILES *holds back, surreptitiously removes his camera from his pocket, takes two quick photographs of the secret passageway and the room. Neither* KEITH *nor* NOLA *notices.*)

Lights out.

Several beats. "Shelter" sounds—rustlings, scuttlings, echoes of footsteps, distorted voices, distant laughter or cries. An eerie sort of music, underlaid by the throbbing, vibrating pulse.

Lights up.

KEITH *and* NOLA *are on the next level. There is a new rapport between them, as if their outburst has linked them emotionally.* MILES *in background.)*

KEITH: All sorts of Americans come through here, and the cultural attaché foists them off on—I mean, entrusts them to—me. But it's a lonely post.

NOLA: Is it? You seem so sociable.

KEITH: You and the professor are leaving tomorrow?

NOLA: Yes. For Stockholm.

KEITH: Were you—a student of his?

NOLA: Does it show?

KEITH: It's the best kind of marriage, I'm sure. Marriage between equals never works. *(As* NOLA *looks at him, startled)* I mean—somebody always wants to be more equal than the other.

NOLA *(stiffly)*: I have an advanced degree too—I'm just not using it right now. I'm *(pause)* . . . just not using it right now.

KEITH: No kids, eh?

NOLA: Miles has two sons, already grown. *(Pause)* He doesn't want more.

KEITH: He dumped his old wife for you, eh? I don't blame him.

NOLA *(offended)*: What did you say?

KEITH: *I* was married, but it didn't last. Marriages sort of fall apart in the foreign service.

NOLA: That's—too bad.

KEITH: My wife hung on through Ottawa pretty well, just about made it through Oslo; but here *(laughs)* she started speaking their language, suddenly!—like, y'know, the words would—*erupt*—in the midst of other things, in her sleep, or in—uh—intimate moments with me. *(*KEITH *emits harsh, crowing sounds, his eyes shut.)* "Kuhvavalaji!"—"Pyajuddik-ut!"— "Uzkavajjikyyo!"

NOLA *(staring at him)*: How—

KEITH *(when we think he has finished)*: "Hyvskyygizkyi!"

NOLA: —awful.

KEITH *(wiping forehead)*: It was awful. I'd hafta pacify her, like— *(a gesture as of pressing the flat of his hand over someone's mouth; then pause)* Poor li'l Bobbie went back to Tulsa, where she's from, with the kids. Got remarried to some ol' high-school sweetheart. *(Yawns)* That's how it is.

NOLA: You must miss your children.

KEITH *(leaning closer to her)*: I get lonely, but not for my children.

NOLA *(uneasy)*: You—uh—must go back home occasionally, to the States?

KEITH *(shrugs)*: Once you leave, and live in other countries, you sort of forget about home. *(Slight sneer)* That's another secret everybody knows.

NOLA *(stiffly)*: I wouldn't forget my home. My birthplace. *(Pause, as if a bit vague)* My family . . .

KEITH *(with a sudden, curious ardor, seizing NOLA's hand)*: In a place like this, *(drawing out word)* underground, you forget your own name. It's easier that way.

(Pause. NOLA and KEITH stare at each other. NOLA slowly withdraws her hand. MILES, out of breath, joins them.)

MILES: Wait for me! *(Pulling at necktie)* It's a little – close in here, isn't it?

(KEITH, NOLA, and MILES descend stairs to another, lower level. The sounds of the shelter are more evident here, especially to MILES, who glances about with increasing unease. KEITH whistles cheerfully, intermittently, in short outbursts.

NOLA loses her footing momentarily, grips KEITH's arm; he steadies her. MILES, grown querulous, seems not to notice.)

MILES: Is the air fresh, coming in these vents? It smells like mold.

KEITH *(as if a direct, ingenuous reply)*: Mold manufactures oxygen, doesn't it, doctor? "The action of friendly bacteria in fungus." *(Chuckles)*

(MILES stares at him.)

MILES *(tugging at tie)*: I – I'm thirsty.

(During the following dialogue, while KEITH continues his tour, MILES wanders off, toward stage right, to get water from a water cooler. He has some difficulty getting the water to come out the spout. His hands tremble as he lifts the paper cup to his mouth. Then, when he drinks, he reacts immediately to the water – spitting it out, gagging, crying, "Ugh! – ugh!" He has spilled water on himself and dabs at it with a handkerchief, muttering. KEITH and NOLA do not notice.)

KEITH *(expansive, ebullient)*: Yessir! This is one of many nations with a "tragic history." Hitler punished them for their neutrality – Stalin killed hundreds of thousands in slave labor camps – and the Allies, I'm afraid, bombed the hell out of them – couldn't be helped. That's how history is – cruel to losers. *(Chuckles)*

NOLA *(sympathetic)*: The soil of Europe is drenched in blood . . . World War II seems so *recent.*

KEITH: Yeah. People hang on to their history, even when it's fucked them up. *(Shakes head, bemused)* It's an old-fashioned concept, like that's how they know who they *are.*

NOLA *(looking around, indicating door)*: What's in here?

KEITH: Medical supplies. But the door's locked.

(NOLA nonetheless tries the door, which opens, startling them.)

KEITH: Oops! Guess I'm wrong.

(It is a closet, with shelves of bottles, vials, first-aid equipment, bedpans, enemas, rolls of gauze, etc. There is a sudden scuttling noise, as of rodents fleeing, and one of the enema bags is knocked to the floor.)

NOLA: Oh!

KEITH: God*damn. (Kicks enema bag)*

NOLA: What was that?

KEITH: What was what?

NOLA: Some – things – creatures – were in there. I could see them running.

KEITH: A roach, maybe. A mouse.

NOLA *(weakly)*: There were more than one. They were bigger than mice.

KEITH: Nah, this shelter is vermin-proof.

MILES *(clutching at* KEITH'S *arm)*: Excuse me, is there maybe – distilled water in there?

KEITH *(shutting door firmly; officiously)*: We can't be breaking into the supplies, doctor. We aren't even citizens of this country.

NOLA *(dismayed, to* MILES*)*: Miles, you look so –

MILES *(querulous, self-pitying)*: I don't feel well. It's this impure air. *(To* KEITH*)* What about oxygen – is there, maybe, oxygen in there?

KEITH: Pure oxygen is a depressant – you don't want that, doctor.

MILES: I'm having difficulty – breathing.

KEITH: Nah, you'll get used to it.

NOLA: If you didn't – talk – so much, Miles, dear. I mean – *(as if genuinely solicitous of him, like a concerned wife, even as he stares at her in disbelief)* – if you didn't take up so much *space.*

MILES: So much space? *(Looking down at himself)* This is all I have.

NOLA *(poking fingers in ears, experimentally)*: Oh – something feels so strange! Like – champagne bubbles!

KEITH: It's the pressure – on the brain. Makes the brain cells sort of fizzle and pop – feel it? *(Giddy, he too pokes fingers in his ears and wriggles them playfully.)*

NOLA *(giggling)*: So straaange – !

MILES: Nola, Ken – I – I don't feel well. I –

NOLA *(to* KEITH*)*: Where are we now? How far underground?

KEITH: What's it matter? We're here.

MILES *(as they ignore him, as if he were invisible)*: I – I'd like to go back to the hotel. I don't feel well. *(Reeling backward, to stare up at the stairs they've descended)* But, my God, how can I ever climb . . . ?

NOLA: I've never felt like this before. *(Sniffing)* I think there's something in the air. *(Sly smile)*

KEITH: The best is yet to come.

NOLA *(pointing at door, childlike, mischievous)*: Uh-oh, *that* door – what's behind it?

KEITH: Better not open it!

NOLA: Why not?

KEITH: Mmmm – it's forbidden, that's why.

NOLA: Yes, but why?

KEITH: Maybe it's locked. Maybe there's nothing behind it.

(NOLA tiptoes to the door, daringly.)

MILES *(pleading)*: Nola, Ken—*please*—I need oxygen—

(NOLA opens the door, and a figure tumbles out. It is dressed in a gas mask, khakis, etc.: but is it a dummy, or a corpse? NOLA shrieks and leaps back into KEITH's arms; MILES nearly faints.)

KEITH *(seems seriously alarmed, disapproving, crouches over the figure)*: It's a—dummy. Like the other.

NOLA *(frightened)*: Oh, *who* is—?

KEITH *(insistent)*: A dummy. Like the other. *(KEITH tries to lift the figure to push it back through the doorway; though lifeless, it seems to be resistant.)*

NOLA: I'm so sorry! Let me help you.

MILES *(backing off, swaying, weakly)*: Don't touch it, Nola. It's contaminated.

(KEITH and NOLA struggle to lift the bulky figure. With some effort, they push it back through the doorway, and KEITH quickly shuts the door.)

KEITH *(panting, wiping at forehead with handkerchief)*: Only a dummy. We all saw.

MILES *(a bit wildly)*: *I* saw! I saw what that was!

KEITH *(incensed)*: The prime minister will hear about this. Things are getting shamefully lax. *(To NOLA)* Are you all right, Nola? Mrs. Harvey?

NOLA: A little—out of breath.

KEITH *(staring at her)*: Your eyes! Dilated like a cat's.

NOLA: I'm so sorry I—interfered.

KEITH: *I'm* sorry. Perhaps we should wash up.

MILES *(accusing, cowering at stage right)*: Nola, how could you? You touched it. That thing. I saw.

NOLA: Wash up? Is the guided tour over?

KEITH: Almost.

NOLA: I want to see everything.

MILES *(faintly)*: I want to go back to the hotel.

KEITH: Well! Let's see! *(Opens another door, resuming his official manner; switches on lights, which flicker)* Here is one of the jewels of the shelter—the parliamentary assembly room, with a seating capacity of three hundred.

NOLA *(looking in)*: Goodness, it's vast. I can't see the walls.

KEITH *(cups hands to mouth, makes a yodellike sound)*: Halloo! Halloo in there! Syvkrikkoya omphysikr!

(Low, rippling, booming echo of KEITH's words)

KEITH *(whistles, yodels)*: Pskyooyiala-ptimi! *(To NOLA)* Hear 'em? The P.M. and the M.P. debating what to do, now the Big One got dropped, that everybody said never would, and Northern Europe is zapped. *(As if listening)*

Nothing left aboveground, but down here, chatterchatterchatter, gobbly-gook talk—Jeezuz.

(We seem to hear low, murmurous, contentious voices.)

NOLA: Oh, dear. Is it—?
KEITH: Yeah, it's sad. But, y'know—history. *(Shuts door, and the sounds vanish.)*
MILES *(cowering at stage right, almost inaudible)*: Help—can't breathe—

(KEITH kisses NOLA, somewhat grossly, on the mouth. NOLA stiffens in resistance but does not shove him away.)

NOLA *(as if incensed)*: You're—crude, that's what you are.
KEITH: *You're* nice.
NOLA: Oh!
KEITH: Some meat on your bones, the way I like 'em. *(Pinches her buttocks)*

(NOLA slaps at him, shocked.)

NOLA: How dare you! You know I'm married!
KEITH *(gripping her wrist)*: Every American cunt who comes through here is married, for sure.
NOLA: I'll report you to the ambassador!

(KEITH advances upon NOLA, who retreats toward stage left. It is as if she were mesmerized by him, backing away, arms extended gropingly behind her. MILES watches helplessly, in anguish.)

MILES: Nola—Nola! Help me! Can't breathe! *(Opens shirt, sinks to knees)*
KEITH *(in his earlier, ebullient tone)*: The luxury rooms come equipped with saunas. But it's a state secret.

(Lights out.
In the darkness, sinister sounds: vibrating, throbbing, echoes as of voices, laughter, erotic/anguished murmurs, cries.
Lights up. MILES alone, stage right, sitting dazed on the floor. He has taken his camera out of his pocket, raises it with shaking fingers, to take a flash shot of the audience.)

MILES: The only evidence. All the dead. No one will believe, otherwise. *(He is breathing hoarsely; perspiration gleams on his face.)*

(Lights out on MILES; Lights up on KEITH and NOLA, entering from stage left. They are wearing dazzling white terrycloth robes and are barefoot; seemingly naked beneath the robes. Their hair is damp: KEITH's is slicked back, and NOLA is combing hers. They are amorous, playful; oblivious of MILES, who, under cover of darkness, crawls to exit stage right.)

KEITH *(as they enter, arms around each other's waist, nuzzling NOLA's neck)*: Toldja, eh? What'd I tellya?
NOLA: That hurts!

KEITH: Eh, sweetheart! What'd I tellya?

NOLA *(glancing around nervously)*: Not *here.* Goodness, this is a public place!

KEITH: So? Everybody's *fried,* nobody's *left.*

NOLA: You shouldn't have sealed that door. I can't believe you so selfishly *sealed that door.*

KEITH: We can repopulate, you and me. *(Whistles cheerfully)*

NOLA *(pouting)*: I don't know if I—if I love you that much. In that way.

KEITH *(grabbing* NOLA*'s hips playfully, roughly)*: That's what all the cunts say.

NOLA *(trying to slap him, but he restrains her)*: I hate that kind of talk, I really do. I *do.*

KEITH *(discovering camera on floor, whistling sharply)*: What's this? *(He snatches it up, opens it, takes out the roll of film and pitches it into the darkness)*

NOLA *(closing robe at throat, as if her modesty were being threatened)*: Oh, is that a *camera?*

*(*KEITH *stuffs the camera into his pocket. Offstage, in the darkness stage right, an ominous chewing and crunching sound has begun, nearly inaudible at first, then building.)*

NOLA: What's that?

KEITH: What's what?

*(*KEITH *goes to fetch a bottle of wine and two glasses.* NOLA *approaches the darkness at stage right but holds back, fearfully.)*

NOLA: I hear something—strange.

KEITH *(pouring wine into glasses)*: I don't hear anything. Just the generator. *(Pause)* When that goes out, *we* go out. *(Amorous, cheerful, handing* NOLA *her glass)* But not for billions of years!

NOLA *(distracted by sounds offstage)*: Oh, dear, it sounds like—something eating? chewing? *(Listens)* Or being chewed. *(Squints into darkness)*

KEITH: Aw, it's all dark there. It's oblivion. "The darkness upon the face of the deep." *(Smirks)* But the Spirit of God isn't coming this time. *Zap.*

NOLA *(listening, blinking)*: Hear it? Little jaws, teeth—so many—grinding. Brrr! *(Turning to* KEITH*)* Oh, protect me!

*(*KEITH *slides an arm around* NOLA*; she rests her head against his shoulder; after a moment, they raise their glasses, clink them together, drink.)*

KEITH: It's great, eh? From the P.M.'s private cellar. *(Chuckles)* We're *in* the cellar.

NOLA: I'm so ashamed, I seem to have forgotten your name.

KEITH: Nah, it's all right.

NOLA: But it isn't like me at all.

KEITH: Down here, honey, we don't have names.

NOLA: Don't?

KEITH: It's easier that way.

(Lights flicker and dim, but remain steady.)

NOLA: And if the generator goes out?

KEITH: It never has, yet.

NOLA *(gazing up at him, urgently)*: But — if it does?

KEITH *(firmly, ebulliently)*: We still have each other. There's always — love. And — I have this. *(Takes from his pocket a candle, which he lights)*

Lights slowly out. Noises of chewing, etc., in background. Finally only the candle flame remains, illuminating the lovers' radiant faces.

(THE END)

Discussion Questions

1. If you could assign a societal issue to each character in the play, what would it be? Do you think that the playwright has used any stereotypes? If so, what are they?

2. How does Keith handle the questions the Harveys raise about the various sounds and smells? Why does he respond in this way?

3. Both men in the play seem excited about the prospect of entering the bomb shelter, but the woman in the play is not. Why does Oates set up this differentiation? What statement do you think she is making on societal values regarding war and destruction?

4. Keith, the guide, talks early in the play about phobias, claiming that the fear of being buried alive is an innate human phobia. How does this phobia get played out? What kind of ironic tension gets established by the exploitation of this phobia?

5. Fear of being buried alive and fear of falling are phobias that writers and filmmakers commonly exploit to create suspense. What are other examples of common phobias that are used to produce thrills? How does Oates play on both our fear and our love of suspense?

Journal Entries

1. Consider what it would be like to live in a bomb shelter. What would your concerns be? What would be the hardest part of the experience for you? How would you spend your time?

2. Discuss your own phobias. What do you fear in an overwhelming way? What strategies have you devised for dealing with your phobias?

Writing Projects

1. Write an essay exploring the way in which the characters' reactions represent a collective American conscience on the issue of nuclear war. Can you determine in what year this play is set? Why does Oates use characters to illuminate only three different perspectives on the issue?

2. Analyze how Oates creates tension between eroticism and fear in this play. How does fear and the sense of being entombed bring about changes in the personalities of the three characters? How does Oates indicate an increase in sexual tension the further the characters descend into the shelter?

Collaborative Project

Working with one or two partners (one theater major would help), explore different ways to direct and stage this play. First, read reviews of any productions of the play. Then read a critical analysis of the play, including production notes Oates has written herself. How would the set be designed to show the downward movement? How would the gradual shift from apparent realism toward surrealism be accomplished? What specific directions would you give each of the characters so they could convey a certain interpretation that you choose? How would you use lighting or sound to create effects? Report your conclusions, or stage a demonstration for the class. Or, for the ambitious, perform the play in class.

Sharon Begley

Is Science Censored?

Sharon Begley *has been a senior writer in* Newsweek*'s science department since 1990. The recipient of numerous journalism awards, Begley has written such cover stories as "Loved to Death" (September 1993), a look at conservation efforts that may ultimately cause more harm than good, and "Cures from the Womb" (February 1993), which examines the use of fetal tissue to correct various genetic disorders prior to birth. In the following essay from* Newsweek *(September 1992), Begley illustrates that not all scientific findings have an equal chance of publication. Her article suggests that the editorial boards of scientific journals are sometimes biased and that some have acted as censors, deciding what scientific findings the public deserves to know and is capable of handling.*

Questions to Consider

☐ What is your definition of censorship, and what are some of the forms it commonly takes?

☐ Do you assume that all significant scientific discoveries that are made are published? If they are not, who do you think decides which ones will be published and which will not? Do you believe that the general public cannot be trusted to deal with some kinds of information? What kinds of information that might have a direct impact on your life would you prefer not to know about, if any? Why?

P UBLICITY . . . would certainly follow," fretted the editor of one top journal. "A possible general panic," predicted a researcher. Both were explaining why a study linking childhood leukemia to fluorescent lights should not be published. That fear trumped the conclusion of other reviewers – scientists who evaluate whether a manuscript should be published in a journal – who called the paper "intriguing" and an "extraordinary piece of deductive reasoning." The paper was rejected.

This is how science works? Despite its objective face, science is as shot through with ideology as any political campaign, and now that dirty secret is coming out. The party line is that papers submitted to journals are rejected only for reasons of substance – the methodology is suspect, the data don't support the conclusions, the journal has better papers to use. But lately scientists

455

have been privately fuming over rejections they blame on censorship. And this summer, the issue exploded in public. Dr. Thomas Chalmers of the Harvard School of Public Health charged that a paper he co-authored, which concluded that chlorine in drinking water raises the risk of bladder and rectal cancers, had been rejected by three journals partly because reviewers "were uneasy about informing people about this problem." (Chlorination kills microbes that cause typhus and other diseases.) Before the American Journal of Public Health accepted the paper, Chalmers says, his data had been "suppressed. Papers are rejected all the time based on the biases of reviewers." The bias he sees is the conviction that the wares of technology, from pesticides to radiation, pose little risk.

"Vitriolic reviews": Some scientists and journal editors angrily deny that ideology colors decisions on whether to print a study. "Editors like to *publish* innovative work, not suppress it," says Dr. Drummond Rennie, deputy editor of the Journal of the American Medical Association. "On the subject of peer review, people can easily get dreadfully paranoid." But others acknowledged the problem. "There are many examples of bias on the part of my reviewers," says Mervyn Susser, an epidemiologist at Columbia University and editor of the journal that published the chlorination paper. "We had a recent experience in which vitriolic reviews revealed very powerful preconceptions that low doses [of radiation] can't possibly cause cancer. They felt that if you get such a result you should throw it out the window [and not tell the public about it]."

That mind-set runs through the peer-review documents obtained by NEWSWEEK. One assessment of the chlorination study calls it "conducted carefully and rigorously," but feared that "the casual reader [might get] the impression that . . . [chlorination] is a potential problem with respect to cancer risk." That, of course, was exactly the point. The paper linking fluorescent lights to childhood leukemia met similar resistance. The New England Journal of Medicine reviewer called it "an intriguing idea that can be readily tested," but NEJM rejected it "because it does not warrant the publicity." The Lancet feared a "general panic in which nurseries are plunged into semi-darkness." (The paper finally was accepted by Cancer Causes and Control.) "There was clearly a discrepancy between the reviewers' favorable comments and the reluctance to publish," says Shmuel Ben-Sasson of Hebrew University in Jerusalem, the paper's lead author.

To be sure, science is not routinely censored. Several researchers who work in areas that stir controversy—lead's effects on intelligence, toxicity of chemicals—say they have never had a paper rejected for political reasons. And it is "reasonable," as Columbia's Susser argues, to be more careful with papers on health issues than on, say, a new species of nematode. "You don't want to press the panic button unless the work is very strong," he says. What many scientists object to is what they perceive as a double standard that welcomes studies that conclude all is well but erects barriers to those that raise alarms. One leading cancer journal, for instance, recently published an industry study concluding that the fluoride added to drinking water does not increase the risk of cancer in lab animals. That same journal rejected a government study, by researchers at the National Institute of Environmental Health Sciences, that reported an increase in rare bone cancers among male rats fed fluoride. The journal explained that it does not publish lab-animal studies anymore. "No one wants to touch this," says toxicologist James Huff of NIEHS about the persistent evidence that fluoride poses some hazard.

Tiny risk: Bias doesn't end with publication, Harvard's Chalmers says. In the year of the spinmeister, science gets spun, too. The New York Times called the cancer risk from chlorination "tiny," even though the 38 percent and 21 percent elevated risks for bladder and rectal cancers, respectively, are 380,000 and 210,000 times higher than the level the government defines as a "negligible" risk. The National Cancer Institute began its press release on the study, "Chlorinated drinking water offers immense health benefits."

Chalmers hasn't made many friends at science journals by opening this debate, but some researchers applaud him. "He's made statements about something that is very, very disturbing," said toxicologist Ellen Silbergeld of the University of Maryland. "[Suppression of studies] is particularly vicious when they concern public-health issues." But the risk that censorship poses to public health may be the least of it. If science loses its reputation for probity, its conclusions will carry no more weight than any interest group's.

Discussion Questions

1. What kind of focus and tone are established by the quotations the author includes in her opening paragraph?

2. Begley's second paragraph contains what could be identified as a thesis statement. Analyze this statement and discuss how it guides the reader toward a particular conclusion regarding the publication of scientific research findings.

3. Does Begley seem to have carefully checked her background information and presented the credentials of those on whom she relies for information? Do you believe she has performed any kind of censorship herself in what or whom she chooses to discuss? Where do you see holes indicating she may have omitted details of the opposing arguments?

4. Summarize Begley's chief concerns about censorship in science. How does she illustrate the seriousness of the problem? Does she offer any solution or suggest any course of action to reverse the trend of censorship in science?

5. What is your response to learning that certain scientific findings regarding threatening or unsafe conditions have been suppressed from publication?

What is your reaction to the opinion held by some media executives as well as editors of scholarly journals that the public is not able to handle the truth calmly and rationally when it involves threats to public safety?

Journal Entry

Write about a personal experience wherein you felt you were expected to censor your true opinions, or wherein your writing was censored by someone else who considered it inappropriate. Describe the situation and relate your feelings.

Writing Projects

1. Write a letter in which you agree or disagree with the idea that technology poses little risk, whether in regard to radiation, pesticides, or some other hazardous substance. Do you think there is a prevailing view about technological products that constitutes a bias that is ultimately dangerous to the general public? Address your letter to public officials who are entrusted to ensure people's health and safety.

2. Write an essay exploring the idea that Begley has censored herself in her essay. What kind of details might she have omitted? Why? Given the fact that professional writers who wish to sell their work must please a paying audience, how likely do you think it is that they manage to avoid self-censorship? Does Begley's essay seem to reflect her own bias in any way? Do you think it is possible to write a thought-provoking essay that does not reflect some of the writer's personal bias? Why or why not?

Collaborative Project

Working with a partner, find at least two different versions of the same scientific discovery or technological product or event. Look in trade magazines, professional journals, general news magazines, daily newspapers, and radio or television, for example. Compare these versions to determine which details were omitted in each case. Then draw conclusions regarding whether the omissions represent censorship. Do you find evidence to suggest that certain details were highlighted to reflect the bias of the editorial boards of the particular media? Summarize your findings and conclusions for the class, offering examples from the media sources you examined.

Making Connections

Questions to Discuss

1. Barbara Ehrenreich asserts that scientific fraud threatens our culture's belief in the "sanctity of science." Sharon Begley claims that censoring research findings in science threatens what she calls the "probity of science." Why, according to Ehrenreich and Begley, are these attributes so important? Discuss ways in which several authors in this text portray the scientist and the scientific method in the terms highlighted by Ehrenreich and Begley.

2. Discuss why you do, or do not, believe that ethical issues in science and technology ought to be investigated and debated by everyone, including people who do not possess much expert knowledge in either area. Refer to readings in this text for specific examples to support your claims.

3. Do you believe that professionals who conduct scientific research and those who make practical applications of this research are generally guided by a code of ethics? What are the main tenets of such a code? Which examples of ethical behavior and practice, or the lack thereof, that are mentioned by authors in this book do you think are most important? For example, do you agree with Stephen Jay Gould (Chapter 3) that both conscious and unconscious fraud occur in science and that it is just as important to expose one as the other? Do you agree with Barbara Ehrenreich that a scientist's falsification of research data is the lowest form of dishonesty, even if no one actually gets hurt?

Suggested Writing Projects

1. The doctor/patient relationship is interesting to most of us because we all have experiences as patients at one time or another. Write an essay on what patients and physicians are entitled to expect from each other. Refer to the examples of doctors' attitudes toward their patients as described in this chapter (by Diana Baumrind and Ron Karpati, for example) or in other chapters (by Richard Selzer and Oliver Sacks in Chapter 8 or Elisabeth Kübler-Ross in Chapter 5, for example). Consider the exchange of knowledge. How much should patients know about the details of their own physical condition? How much should doctors know of their patients while still respecting their privacy? What kind of individualized care can a patient expect? How emotionally intimate with a patient should a doctor become while still protecting his or her professional objectivity, particularly in regard to terminally ill patients?

2. Choose one of the selections from this chapter and write a letter to the editor of the publication in which the essay originally appeared. You may ei-

ther agree or disagree with the main argument of the article you select, supporting your argument with references to the text itself. Assume that your letter will be published and that among your audience will be the editor-in-chief of the publication, the staff of the magazine, a devoted subscriber audience, and, most likely, the author. Consider how addressing this audience affects what you say and how you say it. As you write, consider whether you are censoring yourself in any way because you think your audience might reject one of your ideas. Does your letter to the editor reflect your own bias in any way? If so, was it intentional?

3. The status of those who create technology of destruction, and the issue of who decides whom to save from destruction, comes up in both Joyce Carol Oates's play and Langston Hughes's story (Chapter 4). Analyze how these authors use two different literary genres, a play and a story, to treat the same subject. Extend your discussion to explore how literary interpretations of any given issue or subject usually differ from nonfiction treatments of those same subjects.

4. Five of the essays from this chapter were published in general interest periodicals (the essays by Barbara Ehrenreich, Jean Bethke Elshtain, Ron Karpati, Sharon Begley, and Kenneth Woodward et al.). Write an analysis in which you compare these magazine pieces in terms of their stylistic features: diction, tone, organizational structure, and writer's stance. Contrast the style in these with Diana Baumrind's style in her article, which was originally published in a professional journal.

8

Writing to Construct Science and Technology

 Writing can be seen as a tool by which we apply technological developments and construct scientific facts. Accordingly, this chapter considers the motivations and consequences of the writing that scientists and engineers produce.

First, we take a look at physicians who write. It seems reasonable to wonder why a doctor would want—or need—to be a writer as well. Isn't it enough to be a healer, a savior? Two surgeons, Richard Selzer and Oliver Sacks, tell us why they feel compelled to write. According to Selzer, ". . . the poet . . . heals with his words." Selzer demonstrates his own affinity to the poetic with his essay's command of language that is descriptive and heartfelt.

Selzer has said in an interview that everything he writes is produced "in accordance with the First Law of the Imagination: The moment an artist picks up his pen, he is no longer himself nor entirely of this world." Perhaps it was a call of the imagination, a desire to escape the ordinary and move beyond himself, that motivated Selzer to teach himself to write at the age of 40. In the midst of a career that revolved around a demanding surgery schedule, he would set his alarm for 1:00 A.M., get up and boil a pot of tea, and sit at the kitchen table to write for two hours in the middle of each night.

Unlike Selzer, Oliver Sacks claims he never yearned to be a poet. In fact, he told one reviewer, "I have no literary aspirations and don't regard myself as a writer." Although Sacks rejects the label of writer, preferring to call himself a "reporter, transcriber, and witness," in an interview he once acknowledged the personal importance of writing: "There's something about words, and the written word in particular, which is almost necessary for my own processes of thought."

Apparently, both these men of science write not primarily for their audiences but for themselves, for the self-fulfillment they experience from the act of writing. It is the same fulfillment each of us can derive from putting our thoughts on paper.

More often, however, scientists write for public as well as personal reasons. This chapter includes the article that James D. Watson and Francis H. C. Crick published in 1953 in the scientific journal *Nature*, in which they announced the discovery of how deoxyribose nucleic acid (DNA) is structured as a double helix. Their article has prompted considerable interest of late among experts in rhetorical theory; it has been analyzed in terms of its organization, language, and tone. An example of such revealing analysis is provided by S. Michael Halloran in "An Essay in the Rhetorical Criticism of Scientific Discourse." From this essay we can see how crafted scientific language is, and how carefully we must read the work of all scientists.

Watson and Crick themselves commented on the writing of their article; their perspective can enrich our sense of the context in which scientific writing is constructed. In his book *The Double Helix* (1968), Watson recounts how the structure of DNA was worked out and how he and Crick circulated a draft of their article among various colleagues. He relates how he and Crick stood over the shoulder of Watson's sister as she typed the 900-word paper, which they told her represented "the most famous event in biology since Darwin's book."

Crick has said that he and Watson negotiated the phrasing of their paper, explaining how the opening sentence was "a compromise, reflecting a difference of opinion." Though Crick and Watson disagreed on how the paper should be written, they settled on wording that served, according to Crick, as "a claim to priority." Thus we see that for the two scientists, writing an account of their major discovery was not simply a matter of presenting the bare facts in an objective manner. Writing the article involved a process of negotiation and compromise, with one of their objectives being a bid for credit.

The final two selections in this chapter direct our attention to the fact that scientific and technological writing, which many people assume to be objective and unbiased, can be laden with prejudiced ideas and assumptions. For example, gender issues often play a role in technical and scientific writing. Although the two selections are separated by forty-five years, Ruth Herschberger's "Society Writes Biology" (1948) and Beverly A. Sauer's "Sense and Sensibility in Technical Documentation" (1993) both qualify as feminist critiques. In recent years gender scholarship has spread into wide and varied arenas, but one consistent element of gender study is criticism of the way in which technical and scientific writing often emphasizes dualities – between male and female, culture and nature, objective and subjective – in such a way as to promote a hierarchical arrangement that privileges the masculine.

Ruth Herschberger, writing in a vivid and entertaining style, offers a feminist revision of the human reproductive process. From her viewpoint the egg plays a role of "courage and acumen," whereas the sperm "plays a very small and hesitant part" in the creation of life. Does this sound like the traditional perspective on reproduction?

Beverly Sauer, writing in a more scholarly style, directs a feminist look at mining accident reports. She strives to show how technical writing often gives precedence to the "rational (male) objective voice" and thereby "excludes women's experiential knowledge." Sauer believes these reports proceed according to assumptions that put at risk the "health, safety, and lives of miners – and in a broader sense – all of those who are dependent on technology for their personal safety." Sauer's essay makes us realize how carefully we should pay attention to the wording of many different kinds of forms and reports.

This book concludes, then, by emphasizing that because language has a social dimension, writing is never merely an innocent vehicle for transcribing and conveying technical and scientific knowledge – or, indeed, any particular kind of knowledge. Rather, through writing we can all – professionals and novices alike – communicate our fascination with the wonders of science and our pride in technological achievement.

Reference

Francis H. C. Crick, "The Double Helix: A Personal View," *Nature*, April 26, 1974.

Richard Selzer

The Exact Location of the Soul

Richard Selzer *(b. 1928) has been the recipient of numerous prestigious awards, among them a National Magazine Award in 1975, an American Medical Writer's Award in 1984, and a Guggenheim Award in 1985. Dr. Selzer, who has taught both surgery and writing at Yale, was a surgeon in private practice until he retired in 1984 to write full-time. His widely read essays have been published in* Literature and Medicine, Esquire, *and* Vanity Fair, *among others. "The Exact Location of the Soul" illustrates Selzer's talent for transforming his experience as a surgeon into literary meditations; it originally appeared in his collection of autobiographical essays,* Mortal Lessons *(1976). Selzer believes that his essays, many of which are directed to young physicians in training, might not necessarily make his readers better surgeons in terms of technique, but that they might make them better healers. Selzer's other collections include* Rituals of Surgery *(1974), a collection of short stories; two essay collections,* Letters to a Young Doctor *(1982) and* Taking the World in for Repairs *(1986); and two books of memoirs,* Down from Troy: A Doctor Comes of Age *(1992) and* Raising the Dead *(1994).*

Questions to Consider

☐ Who do you think is more likely to know where to find the soul, the poet or the physician? As you read this essay, consider why Selzer believes the poet can be a healer. Does Selzer think of himself as a poet in any way?

☐ As you read, note Selzer's use of metaphor and other figurative language. What effect does Selzer achieve with imagery? How do you respond to these images?

SOMEONE asked me why a surgeon would write. Why, when the shelves are already too full? They sag under the deadweight of books. To add a single adverb is to risk exceeding the strength of the boards. A surgeon should abstain. A surgeon, whose fingers are more at home in the steamy gullies of the body than they are tapping the dry keys of a typewriter. A surgeon, who feels the slow slide of intestines against the back of his hand and is no more alarmed than were a family of snakes taking their comfort from such an indolent rubbing. A surgeon, who palms the human heart as though it were some captured bird.

Why should he write? Is it vanity that urges him? There is glory enough in the knife. Is it for money? One can make too much money. No. It is to search for some meaning in the ritual of surgery, which is at once murderous, painful, healing, and full of love. It is a devilish hard thing to transmit—to find, even. Perhaps if one were to cut out a heart, a lobe of the liver, a single convolution of the brain, and paste it to a page, it would speak with more eloquence than all the words of Balzac. Such a piece would need no literary style, no mass of erudition or history, but in its very shape and feel would tell all the frailty and strength, the despair and nobility of man. What? Publish a heart? A little piece of bone? Preposterous. Still I fear that is what it may require to reveal the truth that lies hidden in the body. Not all the undressings of Rabelais, Chekhov, or even William Carlos Williams have wrested it free, although God knows each one of those doctors made a heroic assault upon it.

I have come to believe that it is the flesh alone that counts. The rest is that with which we distract ourselves when we are not hungry or cold, in pain or ecstasy. In the recesses of the body I search for the philosophers' stone. I know it is there, hidden in the deepest, dampest cul-de-sac. It awaits discovery. To find it would be like the harnessing of fire. It would illuminate the world. Such a quest is not without pain. Who can gaze on so much misery and feel no hurt? Emerson has written that the poet is the only true doctor. I believe him, for the poet, lacking the impediment of speech with which the rest of us are afflicted, gazes, records, diagnoses, and prophesies.

I invited a young diabetic woman to the operating room to amputate her leg. She could not see the great shaggy black ulcer upon her foot and ankle that threatened to encroach upon the rest of her body, for she was blind as well. There upon her foot was a Mississippi Delta brimming with corruption, sending its raw tributaries down between her toes. Gone were all the little web spaces that when fresh and whole are such a delight to loving men. She could not see her wound, but she could feel it. There is no pain like that of the bloodless limb turned rotten and festering. There is neither unguent nor anodyne to kill such a pain yet leave intact the body.

For over a year I trimmed away the putrid flesh, cleansed, anointed, and dressed the foot, staving off, delaying. Three times each week, in her darkness, she sat upon my table, rocking back and forth, holding her extended leg by the thigh, gripping it as though it were a rocket that must be steadied lest it explode and scatter her toes about the room. And I would cut away a bit here, a bit there, of the swollen blue leather that was her tissue.

At last we gave up, she and I. We could no longer run ahead of the gangrene. We had not the legs for it. There must be an amputation in order that she might live—and I as well. It was to heal us both that I must take up knife and saw, and cut the leg off. And when I could feel it drop from her body to the table, see the blessed *space* appear between her and that leg, I too would be well.

Now it is the day of the operation. I stand by while the anesthetist administers the drugs, watch as the tense familiar body relaxes into narcosis. I turn then to uncover the leg. There, upon her kneecap, she has drawn, blindly, upside down for me to see, a face; just a circle with two ears, two eyes, a nose, and a smiling upturned mouth. Under it she has printed SMILE, DOCTOR. Minutes later I listen to the sound of the saw, until a little crack at the end tells me it is done.

So, I have learned that man is not ugly, but that he is Beauty itself. There is no other his equal. Are we not all dying, none faster or more slowly than any other? I have become receptive to the possibilities of love (for it is love, this thing that happens in the operating room), and each day I wait, trembling in the busy air. Perhaps today it will come. Perhaps today I will find it, take part in it, this love that blooms in the stoniest desert.

All through literature the doctor is portrayed as a figure of fun. Shaw was splenetic about him; Molière delighted in pricking his pompous medicine men, and well they deserved it. The doctor is ripe for caricature. But I believe that the truly great writing about doctors has not yet been done. I think it must be done *by* a doctor, one who is through with the love affair with his technique, who recognizes that he has played Narcissus, raining kisses on a mirror, and who now, out of the impacted masses of his guilt, has expanded into self-doubt, and finally into the high state of wonderment. Perhaps he will be a nonbeliever who, after a lifetime of grand gestures and mighty deeds, comes upon the knowledge that he has done no more than meddle in the lives of his fellows, and that he has done at least as much harm as good. Yet he may continue to pretend, at least, that there is nothing to fear, that death will not come, so long as people depend on his authority. Later, after his patients have left, he may closet himself in his darkened office, sweating and afraid.

There is a story by Unamuno in which a priest, living in a small Spanish village, is adored by all the people for his piety, kindness, and the majesty with which he celebrates the mass each Sunday. To them he is already a saint. It is a foregone conclusion, and they speak of him as Saint Immanuel. He helps them with their plowing and planting, tends them when they are sick, confesses them, comforts them in death, and every Sunday, in his rich, thrilling voice, transports them to paradise with his chanting. The fact is that Don Immanuel is not so much a saint as a martyr. Long ago his own faith left him. He is an atheist, a good man doomed to suffer the life of a hypocrite, pretending to a faith he does not have. As he raises the chalice of wine, his hands tremble, and a cold sweat pours from him. He cannot stop for he knows that the people need this of him, that their need is greater than his sacrifice. Still . . . still . . . could it be that Don Immanuel's whole life is a kind of prayer, a paean to God?

A writing doctor would treat men and women with equal reverence, for what is the "liberation" of either sex to him who knows the diagrams, the inner geographies of each? I love the solid heft of men as much as I adore the heated capaciousness of women – women in whose penetralia is found the repository of existence. I would have them glory in that. Women are physics and chemistry. They are matter. It is their bodies that tell of the frailty of men. Men have not their cellular, enzymatic wisdom. Man is albuminoid, proteinaceous, laked pearl; woman is yolky, ovoid, rich. Both are exuberant bloody growths. I would use the defects and deformities of each for my sacred purpose of writing, for I know that it is the marred and scarred and faulty that are subject to grace. I would seek the soul in the facts of animal economy and profligacy. Yes, it is the exact location of the soul that I am after. The smell of it is in my nostrils. I have caught glimpses of it in the body diseased. If only I could tell it. Is there no mathematical equation that can guide me? So much pain and pus equals so much truth? It is elusive as the whippoorwill that one hears calling incessantly from out the night window, but which, nesting as it does low in the brush, no one sees. No one but the poet, for he sees what no one else can. He was born with the eye for it.

Once I thought I had it: Ten o'clock one night, the end room off a long corridor in a college infirmary, my last patient of the day, degree of exhaustion suitable for the appearance of a vision, some manifestation. The patient is a young man recently returned from Guatemala, from the excavation of Mayan ruins. His left upper arm wears a gauze dressing which, when removed, reveals a clean punched-out hole the size of a dime. The tissues about the opening are swollen and tense. A thin brownish fluid lips the edge, and now and then a lazy drop of the overflow spills down the arm. An abscess, inadequately drained. I will enlarge the opening to allow better egress of the pus. Nurse, will you get me a scalpel and some . . . ?

What happens next is enough to lay Francis Drake avomit in his cabin. No explorer ever stared in wilder surmise than I into that crater from which there now emerges a narrow gray head whose sole distinguishing feature is a pair of black pincers. The head sits atop a longish flexible neck arching now this way, now that, testing the air. Alternately it folds back upon itself, then advances in new boldness. And all the while, with dreadful rhythmicity, the unspeakable pincers open and close. Abscess? Pus? Never. Here is the lair of a beast at whose malignant purpose I could but guess. A Mayan devil, I think, that would soon burst free to fly about the room, with horrid blanket-wings and iridescent scales, raking, pinching, injecting God knows what acid juice. And even now the irony does not escape me, the irony of my patient as excavator excavated.

With all the ritual deliberation of a high priest I advance a surgical clamp toward the hole. The surgeon's heart is become a bat hanging upside down from his rib cage. The rim achieved—now thrust—and the ratchets of the clamp close upon the empty air. The devil has retracted. Evil mocking laughter bangs back and forth in the brain. More stealth. Lying in wait. One must skulk. Minutes pass, perhaps an hour. . . . A faint disturbance in the lake, and once again the thing upraises, farther and farther, hovering. Acrouch, strung, the surgeon is one with his instrument; there is no longer any boundary between its metal and his flesh. They are joined in a single perfect tool of extirpation. It is just for this that he was born. Now—thrust—and clamp—and *yes*. Got him!

Transmitted to the fingers comes the wild thrashing of the creature. Pinned and wriggling, he is mine. I hear the dry brittle scream of the dragon, and a hatred seizes me, but such a detestation as would make of Iago a drooling sucktit. It is the demented hatred of the victor for the vanquished, the warden for his prisoner. It is the hatred of fear. Within the jaws of my hemostat is the whole of the evil of the world, the dark concentrate itself, and I shall kill it. For mankind. And, in so doing, will open the way into a thousand years of perfect peace. Here is Surgeon as Savior indeed.

Tight grip now . . . steady, relentless pull. How it scrabbles to keep its tentacle-hold. With an abrupt moist plop the extraction is complete. There, writhing in the teeth of the clamp, is a dirty gray body, the size and shape of an English walnut. He is hung everywhere with tiny black hooklets. Quickly . . . into the specimen jar of saline . . . the lid screwed tight. Crazily he swims round and round, wiping his slimy head against the glass, then slowly sinks to the bottom, the mass of hooks in frantic agonal wave.

"You are going to be all right," I say to my patient. "We are *all* going to be all right from now on."

The next day I take the jar to the medical school. "That's the larva of the botfly," says a pathologist. "The fly usually bites a cow and deposits its eggs beneath the skin. There, the egg develops into the larval form which, when ready, burrows its way to the outside through the hide and falls to the ground. In time it matures into a full-grown botfly. This one happened to bite a man. It was about to come out on its own, and, of course, it would have died."

The words *imposter, sorehead, servant of Satan* spring to my lips. But now he has been joined by other scientists. They nod in agreement. I gaze from one gray eminence to another, and know the mallet-blow of glory pulverized. I tried to save the world, but it didn't work out.

No, it is not the surgeon who is God's darling. He is the victim of vanity. It is the poet who heals with his words, stanches the flow of blood, stills the rattling breath, applies poultice to the scalded flesh.

Did you ask me why a surgeon writes? I think it is because I wish to be a doctor.

Discussion Questions

1. Look closely at Selzer's sentence construction, noting any distinctive patterns. Consider, for example, the opening paragraph, which includes three sentences in a row, each beginning with "A surgeon, who[se]. . ." How

does Selzer's deliberate manipulation of language and rhythm influence your response to his ideas?

2. Selzer presents two reasons, phrased as questions, that readers may believe he has for writing. What are these two reasons, and how does he dismiss them? Do you think these two reasons could pertain to other writers you have read in this book? Explain.

3. How many one- or two-word statements (such as "No" and "What?") does Selzer use in this essay? How do these constructions convey meaning, and how do they establish a certain tone?

4. How does Selzer describe men and women? Does his identification of the unique characteristics of each give precedence to one or the other? To what extent does Selzer seem in awe of men's and women's defects as well as their glory?

5. Discuss Selzer's title, "The Exact Location of the Soul." What does it mean? How does his essay provide a context that illustrates the meaning of his title? Can you think of an alternative title that conveys the same sense of mystery and spiritual feeling?

Journal Entries

1. Describe how you view your own doctor. Which of Selzer's types of doctors does yours come closer to: the one who believes that no harm will come to the patient as long as he or she depends on the doctor, or the one who sits sweating and afraid in his or her office after the patient has gone?

2. Selzer says it is not the surgeon but the poet who is "God's darling." Explain what he means, and tell whether you agree or disagree. How would Cynthia Ozick (see Chapter 1) respond to Selzer's claim? Is "God's darling" the poet, the surgeon, or someone else altogether?

Writing Projects

1. Analyze the methods Selzer employs to unfold the story of the diabetic woman whose leg he had to amputate. Why does he choose her case to describe? How does he develop her as a character in his story, or is she just a typical patient? What kind of physician does Selzer portray himself to be through this account? How does Selzer convey his own feelings about his patient and about himself?

2. Write an essay, directed at an audience of medical students, in which you discuss the status of doctors in American society today. Explain the cultural attitudes at the basis of the prestige we afford physicians. Do you think the

status of doctors will remain the same as in the past two or three decades? What changes do you foresee, and why?

Collaborative Project

Working with a partner (perhaps a pre-med or health science major from your class), read passages written by two other physician-writers, such as François Rabelais, Anton Chekhov, William Carlos Williams, or Oliver Sacks (in this chapter). Compare their various writing genres and styles. Do any discuss their attitudes toward their own writing? Why do they write? Why do they find medicine and writing compatible?

Oliver Sacks

On the Level

Oliver Sacks *(b. 1933), a professor of clinical neurology at Albert Einstein College of Medicine, has been described by a writer for the* New York Times Book Review *as "one of the great clinical writers of the 20th century." The essay reprinted here, "On the Level," originally appeared in* The Sciences *(1985). In this tale Sacks describes how he and one of his patients collaborated in creating a relatively simple invention to deal with the patient's own perceptual difficulties. The essay is preceded by part of the preface to* The Man Who Mistook His Wife for a Hat *(1987), a collection of true clinical tales about people experiencing various neurological dysfunctions. In the preface Sacks explains why he chose a narrative structure to tell his patients' stories. Sacks's writing is characterized by expert knowledge, compassion, and wit, thus making him a widely read and respected author. His other books include* Awakenings *(1974), which is based on Sacks's own efforts to help patients suffering from "sleeping sickness" by administering the controversial drug L-dopa;* A Leg to Stand On *(1984), which grew out of his own experience as a patient with an injured leg; and* Seeing Voices *(1989), in which Sacks explores the world of the deaf.*

Questions to Consider

☐ Sacks opens the preface with a quotation from Pascal. Consider how this quotation affects your understanding of the essay.

☐ Sacks says that sickness is an essential condition, that we couldn't get along without it. Why might he think this? Do you believe this?

☐ As you read "On the Level," notice how machines and tools are used to diagnose and treat physiological difficulties in perception.

From the Preface of *The Man Who Mistook His Wife for a Hat*

To talk of diseases is a sort of *Arabian Nights* entertainment.
—WILLIAM OSLER

> The physician is concerned [unlike the naturalist] . . . with a single organism, the human subject, striving to preserve its identity in adverse circumstances.
>
> –IVY MCKENZIE

"The last thing one settles in writing a book," Pascal observes, "is what one should put in first." So, having written, collected and arranged these strange tales, having selected a title and two epigraphs, I must now examine what I have done – and why.

The doubleness of the epigraphs, and the contrast between them – indeed, the contrast which Ivy McKenzie draws between the physician and the naturalist – corresponds to a certain doubleness in me: that I feel myself a naturalist and a physician both; and that I am equally interested in diseases and people; perhaps, too, that I am equally, if inadequately, a theorist and dramatist, am equally drawn to the scientific and the romantic, and continually see both in the human condition, not least in that quintessential human condition of sickness – animals get diseases, but only man falls radically into sickness.

My work, my life, is all with the sick – but the sick and their sickness drives me to thoughts which, perhaps, I might otherwise not have. So much so that I am compelled to ask, with Nietzsche: "As for sickness: are we not almost tempted to ask whether we could get along without it?" – and to see the questions it raises as fundamental in nature. Constantly my patients drive me to question, and constantly my questions drive me to patients – thus in the stories or studies which follow there is a continual movement from one to the other.

Studies, yes; why stories, or cases? Hippocrates introduced the historical conception of disease, the idea that diseases have a course, from their first intimations to their climax or crisis, and thence to their happy or fatal resolution. Hippocrates thus introduced the case history, a description, or depiction, of the natural history of disease – precisely expressed by the old word "pathology." Such histories are a form of natural history – but they tell us nothing about the individual and *his* history; they convey nothing of the person, and the experience of the person, as he faces, and struggles to survive, his disease. There is no "subject" in a narrow case history; modern case histories allude to the subject in a cursory phrase ("a trisomic albino female of 21"), which could as well apply to a rat as a human being. To restore the human subject at the center – the suffering, afflicted, fighting, human subject – we must deepen a case history to a narrative or tale; only then do we have a "who" as well as a "what," a real person, a patient, in relation to disease – in relation to the physical.

The patient's essential being is very relevant in the higher reaches of neurology, and in psychology; for here the patient's personhood is essentially involved, and the study of disease and of identity cannot be disjoined. Such disorders, and their depiction and study, indeed entail a new discipline, which we may call the "neurology of identity," for it deals with the neural foundations of the self, the age-old problem of mind and brain. It is possible that there must, of necessity, be a gulf, a gulf of category, between the psychical and the physical; but studies and stories pertaining simultaneously and inseparably to both—and it is these which especially fascinate me, and which (on the whole) I present here—may nonetheless serve to bring them nearer, to bring us to the very intersection of mechanism and life, to the relation of physiological processes to biography.

The tradition of richly human clinical tales reached a high point in the nineteenth century, and then declined, with the advent of an impersonal neurological science. Luria wrote: "The power to describe, which was so common to the great nineteenth-century neurologists and psychiatrists, is almost gone now. . . . It must be revived." His own late works, such as *The Mind of a Mnemonist* and *The Man with a Shattered World,* are attempts to revive this lost tradition. Thus the case-histories in this book hark back to an ancient tradition: to the nineteenth-century tradition of which Luria speaks; to the tradition of the first medical historian, Hippocrates; and to that universal and prehistorical tradition by which patients have always told their stories to doctors.

Classical fables have archetypal figures—heroes, victims, martyrs, warriors. Neurological patients are all of these—and in the strange tales told here they are also something more. How, in these mythical or metaphorical terms, shall we categorize the "lost Mariner," or the other strange figures in this book? We may say they are travelers to unimaginable lands—lands of which otherwise we should have no idea or conception. This is why their lives and journeys seem to me to have a quality of the fabulous, why I have used Osler's *Arabian Nights* image as an epigraph, and why I feel compelled to speak of tales and fables as well as cases. The scientific and the romantic in such realms cry out to come together—Luria liked to speak here of "romantic science." They come together at the intersection of fact and fable, the intersection which characterizes (as it did in my book *Awakenings*) the lives of the patients here narrated.

But what facts! What fables! To what shall we compare them? We may not have any existing models, metaphors or myths. Has the time perhaps come for new symbols, new myths?

"On the Level"

I T is nine years now since I met Mr. MacGregor, in the neurology clinic of St. Dunstan's, an old-people's home where I once worked, but I remember him—I see him—as if it were yesterday.

"What's the problem?" I asked, as he tilted in.

"Problem? No problem—none that I know of. . . . But others keep telling me I lean to the side: 'You're like the Leaning Tower of Pisa,' they say. 'A bit more tilt, and you'll topple right over.'"

"But *you* don't feel any tilt?"

"I feel fine. I don't know what they mean. How *could* I be tilted without knowing I was?"

"It sounds a queer business," I agreed. "Let's have a look. I'd like to see you stand and take a little stroll—just from here to that wall and back. I want to see for myself, *and I want you to see too*. We'll take a videotape of you walking and play it right back."

"Suits me, Doc," he said, and, after a couple of lunges, stood up. What a fine old chap, I thought. Ninety-three—and he doesn't look a day past seventy. Alert, bright as a button. Good for a hundred. And strong as a coal-heaver, even if he does have Parkinson's disease. He was walking, now, confidently, swiftly, but canted over, improbably, a good twenty degrees, his center of gravity way off to the left, maintaining his balance by the narrowest possible margin.

"There!" he said with a pleased smile. "See! No problems—I walked straight as a die."

"Did you, indeed, Mr. MacGregor?" I asked. "I want you to judge for yourself."

I rewound the tape and played it back. He was profoundly shocked when he saw himself on the screen. His eyes bulged, his jaw dropped, and he muttered, "I'll be damned!" And then, "They're right, I *am* over to one side. I *see* it here clear enough, but I've no sense of it. I don't *feel* it."

"That's it," I said. "That's the heart of the problem."

We have five senses in which we glory and which we recognize and celebrate, senses that constitute the sensible world for us. But there are other senses—secret senses, sixth senses, if you will—equally vital, but unrecognized, and unlauded. These senses, unconscious, automatic, had to be discovered. Historically, indeed, their discovery came late: what the Victorians vaguely called "muscle sense"—the awareness of the relative position of trunk and limbs, derived from receptors in the joints and tendons—was only really defined (and named "proprioception") in the 1890s. And the complex mechanisms and controls by which our bodies are properly aligned and balanced in space—these have only been defined in our own century, and still hold many mysteries. Perhaps it will only be in this space age, with the paradoxical license and hazards of gravity-free life, that we will truly appreciate our inner ears, our vestibules and all the other obscure receptors and reflexes that govern our body orientation. For normal man, in normal situations, they simply do not exist.

Yet their absence can be quite conspicuous. If there is defective (or distorted) sensation in our overlooked secret senses, what we then experience is profoundly strange, an almost incommunicable equivalent to being blind or being deaf. If proprioception is completely knocked out, the body becomes, so to speak, blind and deaf to itself—and (as the meaning of the Latin root *proprius* hints) ceases to "own" itself, to feel itself as itself.

The old man suddenly became intent, his brows knitted, his lips pursed. He stood motionless, in deep thought, presenting the picture that I love to see: a patient in the actual moment of discovery – half-appalled, half-amused – seeing for the first time exactly what is wrong and, in the same moment, exactly what there is to be done. This *is* the therapeutic moment.

"Let me think, let me think," he murmured, half to himself, drawing his shaggy white brows down over his eyes and emphasizing each point with his powerful, gnarled hands. "Let me think. You think with me – there must be an answer! I tilt to one side, and I can't tell it, right? There *should* be some feeling, a clear signal, but it's not there, right?" He paused. "I used to be a carpenter," he said, his face lighting up. "We would always use a spirit level to tell whether a surface was level or not, or whether it was tilted from the vertical or not. Is there a sort of spirit level in the brain?"

I nodded.

"Can it be knocked out by Parkinson's disease?"

I nodded again.

"Is *this* what has happened with me?"

I nodded a third time and said, "Yes. Yes. Yes."

In speaking of such a spirit level, Mr. MacGregor had hit on a fundamental analogy, a metaphor for an essential control system in the brain. Parts of the inner ear are indeed physically – literally – like levels; the labyrinth consists of semicircular canals containing liquid whose motion is continually monitored. But it was not these, as such, that were essentially at fault; rather, it was his ability to *use* his balance organs, in conjunction with the body's sense of itself and with its visual picture of the world. Mr. MacGregor's homely symbol applies not just to the labyrinth but also to the complex *integration* of the three secret senses: the labyrinthine, the proprioceptive, and the visual. It is this synthesis that is impaired in Parkinsonism.

The most profound (and most practical) studies of such integrations – and of their singular *dis*integrations in Parkinsonism – were made by the late, great Purdon Martin and are to be found in his remarkable book *The Basal Ganglia and Posture* (originally published in 1967, but continually revised and expanded in the ensuing years; he was just completing a new edition when he died recently). Speaking of this integration, this integrator, in the brain, Purdon Martin writes "There must be some centre or 'higher authority' in the brain . . . some 'controller' we may say. This controller or higher authority must be informed of the state of stability or instability of the body."

In the section on "tilting reactions" Purdon Martin emphasizes the threefold contribution to the maintenance of a stable and upright posture, and he notes how commonly its subtle balance is upset in Parkinsonism – how, in particular, "it is usual for the labyrinthine element to be lost before the proprioceptive and the visual." This triple control system, he implies, is such that *one* sense, *one* control, can compensate for the others – not wholly (since the senses differ in their capabilities) but in part, at least, and to a useful degree. Visual reflexes and controls are perhaps the least important – normally. So long as our vestibular and proprioceptive systems are intact, we are perfectly stable with our eyes closed. We do not tilt or lean or fall over the moment we close our eyes. But the precariously balanced Parkinsonian may do so. (One often sees Parkinsonian patients sitting in the most grossly tilted positions, with no awareness that this is the case. But let a mirror be provided, so they can *see* their positions, and they instantly straighten up.)

Proprioception, to a considerable extent, can compensate for defects in the inner ears. Thus patients who have been surgically deprived of their labyrinths (as is sometimes done to relieve the intolerable, crippling vertigo of severe Ménière's disease), while at first unable to stand upright or take a single step, may learn to employ and to *enhance* their proprioception quite wonderfully; in particular, to use the sensors in the vast latissimus dorsi muscles of the back – the greatest, most mobile muscular expanse in the body – as an accessory and novel balance organ, a pair of vast, winglike proprioceptors. As the patients become practiced, as this becomes second-nature, they are able to stand and walk – not perfectly, but with safety, assurance, and ease.

Purdon Martin was endlessly thoughtful and ingenious in designing a variety of mechanisms and methods that made it possible for even severely disabled Parkinsonians to achieve an artificial normality of gait and posture – lines painted on the floor, counterweights in the belt, loudly ticking pacemakers – to set the cadence for walking. In this he always learned from his patients (to whom, indeed, his great book is dedicated). He was a deeply human pioneer, and in his medicine understanding and collaborating were central: patient and physician were coequals, on the same level, each learning from and helping the other and *between them* arriving at new insights and treatment. But he had not, to my knowledge, devised a prosthesis for the correction of impaired tilting and higher vestibular reflexes, the problem that afflicted Mr. MacGregor.

"So that's it, is it?" asked Mr. MacGregor. "I can't use the spirit level inside my head. I can't use my ears, but I *can* use my eyes." Quizzically, experimentally, he tilted his head to one side: "Things look the same now – the world doesn't tilt." Then he asked for a mirror, and I had a long one wheeled before him. "*Now* I see myself tilting," he said. "*Now* I can straighten up – maybe I could stay straight. . . . But I can't live among mirrors, or carry one round with me."

He thought again deeply, frowning in concentration – then suddenly his face cleared, and lit up with a smile. "I've got it!" he exclaimed. "Yeah, Doc, I've got it! I don't need a mirror – I just need a level. I can't use the spirit levels *inside* my head, but why couldn't I use levels *outside* my head – levels I could *see*, I could use with my eyes?" He took off his glasses, fingering them thoughtfully, his smile slowly broadening.

"Here, for example, in the rim of my glasses. . . . This could tell me, tell my eyes, if I was tilting. I'd keep an eye on it at first; it would be a real strain.

But then it might become second-nature, automatic. Okay, Doc, so what do you think?"

"I think it's a brilliant idea, Mr. MacGregor. Let's give it a try."

The principle was clear, the mechanics a bit tricky. We first experimented with a sort of pendulum, a weighted thread hung from the rims, but this was too close to the eyes, and scarcely seen at all. Then, with the help of our optometrist and workshop, we made a clip extending two nose-lengths forward from the bridge of the spectacles, with a miniature horizontal level fixed to each side. We fiddled with various designs, all tested and modified by Mr. MacGregor. In a couple of weeks we had completed a prototype, a pair of somewhat Heath Robinsonish spirit spectacles: "The world's first pair!" said Mr. MacGregor, in glee and triumph. He donned them. They looked a bit cumbersome and odd, but scarcely more so than the bulky hearing-aid spectacles that were coming in at the time. And now a strange sight was to be seen in our Home—Mr. MacGregor in the spirit spectacles he had invented and made, his gaze intensely fixed, like a steersman eyeing the binnacle of his ship. This worked, in a fashion—at least he stopped tilting: but it was a continuous, exhausting exercise. And then, over the ensuing weeks, it got easier and easier; keeping an eye on his "instruments" became unconscious, like keeping an eye on the instrument panel of one's car while being free to think, chat, and do other things.

Mr. MacGregor's spectacles became the rage of St. Dunstan's. We had several other patients with Parkinsonism who also suffered from impairment of tilting reactions and postural reflexes—a problem not only hazardous but also notoriously resistant to treatment. Soon a second patient, then a third, were wearing Mr. MacGregor's spirit spectacles, and now, like him, could walk upright, on the level.

Discussion Questions

1. What is Sacks's attitude toward writing and toward himself as a writer? How does he convey his attitude, both directly and indirectly?

2. What explanation does Sacks give for presenting his neurological studies as stories? What elements of fiction has he implemented? How does he use dialogue?

3. All writers write about subjects and people they know. How do you suppose the patients and the patients' families feel about these stories? Do writers like Sacks, who have a special professional relationship with their patients, have any special obligations to their patients or clients, such as respecting their privacy? Explain your views.

4. Sacks says that Mr. MacGregor "had hit on a fundamental analogy, a metaphor for an essential control system in the brain." How is metaphor used to help us understand sickness? What is the role of metaphor in healing?

Journal Entry

Sacks points out that patients have always told stories to their doctors. Describe the last time you told your doctor the story of your problem or illness. How did he or she respond? Was the response what you expected? Explain.

Writing Projects

1. In his preface Sacks identifies several dualities in his life. Analyze Sacks's illustration of his idea of doubleness. Can you relate this sense of doubleness to your own life? Are the dualities you experience conflicting ones, or, as in Sacks's case, do they complement each other?

2. Sacks refers at one time or another to "studies," "cases," "stories," "tales," and "fables," all of which are forms of narrative. Which of these types of narrative best describes "On the Level"? What are the key features of the essay that establish its form? Explore how Sacks's account reveals his own life while narrating his patients' experiences.

Collaborative Project

Working with a partner, read Sacks's book *Awakenings* and view the movie version. Analyze the significant differences between the original text and the movie. Point out advantages and disadvantages of each genre. Explore the methods each uses to portray the characters in the story. If time allows, you might show the movie in class and present your analysis.

James D. Watson and Francis H. C. Crick

A Structure for Deoxyribose Nucleic Acid

James D. Watson (b. 1928) and Francis H. C. Crick (b. 1916), along with their colleague Maurice Wilkins, received the 1962 Nobel Prize in Medicine for discovering the helical structure of deoxyribose nucleic acid (DNA), the molecule that transmits genetic information. The following paper, originally published in Nature (1953), marks the pivotal point in establishing molecular biology as a science. The paper also represents Watson and Crick's statement claiming credit for solving the puzzle of DNA construction.

Watson obtained his Ph.D. at age 22 from Indiana University in 1950 and began teaching at Harvard in 1956. His book The Double Helix: A Personal Account of the Discovery of the Structure of DNA *(1968) caused a sensation with its frank and gossipy style. Watson gloated that he had deliberately attached himself to the research group most likely to make him famous. Watson is also the author of* Recombinant DNA *(1992) and co-editor of* Origins of Human Cancer *(1977).*

Crick received his doctorate from Cambridge University in 1954 and worked in the Cambridge Cavendish Laboratory from 1949 to 1977. He later joined the faculty at the Salk Institute in San Diego, where he still conducts research. Crick's other writings include Life Itself: Its Origin and Nature *(1981) and* What Mad Pursuit: A Personal View of Scientific Discovery *(1988).*

Questions to Consider

☐ Because this article was written for an audience of experts, some of the terminology and scientific details may be unfamiliar to you. Nevertheless, a thorough understanding of the topic is not required for you to be able to analyze the persuasive techniques the authors use. Consider what their purpose is in writing this article, and notice how they make their purpose evident.

☐ Considering the importance of this article, both in terms of its content and timing, note the authors' understated style. Why do you think Crick and Watson adopt this tactic? Watch how they use it to manipulate the reader's experience.

WE wish to suggest a structure for the salt of deoxyribose nucleic acid (D.N.A.). This structure has novel features which are of considerable biological interest.

A structure for nucleic acid has already been proposed by Pauling and Corey.[1] They kindly made their manuscript available to us in advance of publication. Their model consists of three intertwined chains, with the phosphates near the fibre axis, and the bases on the outside. In our opinion, this structure is unsatisfactory for two reasons: (1) We believe that the material which gives the X-ray diagrams is the salt, not the free acid. Without the acidic hydrogen atoms it is not clear what forces would hold the structure together, especially as the negatively charged phosphates near the axis will repel each other. (2) Some of the van der Waals distances appear to be too small.

Another three-chain structure has also been suggested by Fraser. . . . In his model the phosphates are on the outside and the bases on the inside, linked together by hydrogen bonds. This structure as described is rather ill-defined, and for this reason we shall not comment on it.

We wish to put forward a radically different structure for the salt of deoxyribose nucleic acid. This structure has two helical chains each coiled round the same axis [see Figure 8-1]. We have made the usual chemical assumptions, namely, that each chain consists of phosphate diester groups joining β-D-deoxyribofuranose residues with 3′,5′ linkages. The two chains (but not their bases) are related by a dyad perpendicular to the fibre axis. Both chains follow right-handed helices, but owing to the dyad the sequences of the atoms in the two chains run in opposite directions. Each chain loosely resembles Furberg's[2]

FIGURE 8-1   The Double Helix. This figure is purely diagrammatic. The two ribbons symbolize the two phosphate–sugar chains, and the horizontal rods the pairs of bases holding the chains together. The vertical line marks the fibre axis.

model No. 1; that is, the bases are on the inside of the helix and the phosphates on the outside. The configuration of the sugar and the atoms near it is close to Furberg's "standard configuration," the sugar being roughly perpendicular to the attached base. There is a residue on each chain every 3·4 A, in the z-direction. We have assumed an angle of 36° between adjacent residues in the same chain, so that the structure repeats after 10 residues on each chain, that is, after 34 A. The distance of a phosphorus atom from the fibre axis is 10 A. As the phosphates are on the outside, cations have easy access to them.

The structure is an open one, and its water content is rather high. At lower water contents we would expect the bases to tilt so that the structure could become more compact.

The novel feature of the structure is the manner in which the two chains are held together by the purine and pyrimidine bases. The planes of the bases are perpendicular to the fibre axis. They are joined together in pairs, a single base from one chain being hydrogen-bonded to a single base from the other chain, so that the two lie side by side with identical z-co-ordinates. One of the pair must be a purine and the other a pyrimidine for bonding to occur. The hydrogen bonds are made as follows: purine position 1 to pyrimidine position 1; purine position 6 to pyrimidine position 6.

If it is assumed that the bases only occur in the structure in the most plausible tautomeric forms (that is, with the keto rather than the enol configurations) it is found that only specific pairs of bases can bond together. These pairs are: adenine (purine) with thymine (pyrimidine), and guanine (purine) with cytosine (pyrimidine).

In other words, if an adenine forms one member of a pair, on either chain, then on these assumptions the other member must be thymine; similarly for guanine and cytosine. The sequence of bases on a single chain does not appear to be restricted in any way. However, if only specific pairs of bases can be formed, it follows that if the sequence of bases on one chain is given, then the sequence on the other chain is automatically determined.

It has been found experimentally[3,4] that the ratio of the amounts of adenine to thymine, and the ratio of guanine to cytosine, are always very close to unity for deoxyribose nucleic acid.

It is probably impossible to build this structure with a ribose sugar in place of the deoxyribose, as the extra oxygen atom would make too close a van der Waals contact.

The previously published X-ray data[5,6] on deoxyribose nucleic acid are insufficient for a rigorous test of our structure. So far as we can tell, it is roughly compatible with the experimental data, but it must be regarded as unproved until it has been checked against more exact results. Some of these are given in the following communications. We were not aware of the details of the results presented there when we devised our structure, which rests mainly though not entirely on published experimental data and stereo-chemical arguments.

It has not escaped our notice that the specific pairing we have postulated immediately suggests a possible copying mechanism for the genetic material.

Full details of the structure, including the conditions assumed in building it, together with a set of co-ordinates for the atoms, will be published elsewhere.

We are much indebted to Dr. Jerry Donohue for constant advice and criticism, especially on interatomic distances. We have also been stimulated by a knowledge of the general nature of the unpublished experimental results and ideas of Dr. M. H. F. Wilkins, Dr. R. E. Franklin and their co-workers at King's College, London. One of us (J. D. W.) has been aided by a fellowship from the National Foundation for Infantile Paralysis.

NOTES

1. Pauling, L., and Corey, R. B., *Nature*, 171, 346 (1953); *Proc. U.S. Nat. Acad. Sci.*, 39, 84 (1953).
2. Furberg, S., *Acta Chem. Scand.*, 6, 634 (1952).
3. Chargaff, E., for references see Zamenhof, S., Brawerman, G., and Chargaff, E., *Biochim. et Biophys. Acta*, 9, 402 (1952).
4. Wyatt, G. R., *J. Gen. Physiol.*, 36, 201 (1952).
5. Astbury, W. T., Symp. Soc. Exp. Biol. 1, Nucleic Acid, 66 (Camb. Univ. Press, 1947).
6. Wilkins, M. H. F., and Randall, J. T., *Biochim. et Biophys. Acta*, 10, 192 (1953).

Discussion Questions

1. To what extent is viewing Watson and Crick's diagram of DNA essential to understanding their main point?

2. Notice the authors' acknowledgment of outside sources, in particular the work of Pauling and Corey, as well as that of Wilkins and Franklin. What advantages did Watson and Crick gain by having access to their colleagues' writing prior to its publication? Do you think it is ethical to borrow in this way to stay on the cutting edge of research?

3. Crick has written that their fellow scientists found the wording of the twelfth paragraph to be "coy." Do you agree that "coy" is an apt word to describe the sentence that begins, "It has not escaped our notice that the specific paring we have postulated. . ."? Why do you suppose other scientists remarked on the style of that paragraph?

4. In what important ways is the writing style and structure of this article both similar to and significantly different from the kind of research reports you have been taught to write? How do you account for the differences?

Journal Entries

1. Write a journal entry in which you identify what you consider to be a serious problem today, one that can be solved through scientific research. If a crucial discovery were made, how would the public be informed? What would be a quicker and more efficient way of publishing than by mailing an article to a scientific journal, as Watson and Crick did? What might be the disadvantages of using the quickest form of publication?

2. One technique of active critical reading that students sometimes use is outlining an article they wish to comprehend more fully, either with words alone or a combination of words and diagrams (e.g. a flowchart). Construct an outline of the Watson-Crick article, summarizing its organization and content. Feel free to refer to Halloran's article in this chapter for an example of such a summary, but make yours both shorter and easier to use than Halloran's.

Writing Projects

1. Analyze tactics and phrases these authors employ to establish their proprietary relationship to DNA research.

2. Analyze how Watson and Crick first review selected published studies on their topic and then proceed to refute their colleagues' arguments. What is the basis of their rejection of others' research findings? How do Watson and Crick go about establishing they have discovered the key structure for DNA?

Collaborative Projects

1. Working with a partner, research the contributions of Rosalind Franklin to the discovery of DNA. What was her area of specialty? Where did she work? What crucial element of DNA structure did her work reveal? How did Watson and Crick make use of her work? Why did she not receive a Nobel Prize along with Watson, Crick, and Wilkins? Write an essay presenting findings and interpretations.

2. Writing an article collaboratively, as Watson and Crick did, can be even more difficult than jointly conducting the study itself. In fact, in an article published in *Nature* (April 26, 1974) approximately twenty years after Watson and Crick's first article on the structure of DNA appeared, Crick explains that the wording of paragraph twelve represents a compromise between himself and Watson. Select a classmate with whom you have already collaborated, turn on a tape recorder, and then discuss the special difficulties, as well as the rewards, of writing a jointly-authored essay. Transcribe your tape recording (with some editing) as a dialogue on the topic of collaborative writing.

S. Michael Halloran

An Essay in the Rhetorical Criticism of Scientific Discourse

S. Michael Halloran *(b. 1939) is a professor of rhetoric at Rensselaer Polytechnic Institute, where he has also served as director of graduate studies and associate dean of humanities and social sciences. Professor Halloran has published a wide variety of articles on rhetorical theory, criticism, and history. His particular interests include the language of civic discourse and the rhetoric of scientific discourse. Originally entitled "The Birth of Molecular Biology: An Essay in the Rhetorical Criticism of Scientific Discourse," the following article was first published in* Rhetoric Review *(1984). A substantial portion of it analyzes Watson and Crick's "A Structure for Deoxyribose Nucleic Acid." The audience of* Rhetoric Review *comprises professionals in the field of rhetoric; but despite the use of difficult terms, Halloran's message is clear: scientific writing reflects a characteristic understanding of the scientific enterprise and binds the scientific community together.*

Questions to Consider

☐ Before beginning Halloran's article, refer once more to Watson and Crick's article. Also, review for a moment Thomas Kuhn's essay in Chapter 3, because Halloran draws extensively on Kuhn's theories.

☐ Because Halloran assumes his specialized audience is already familiar with standard rhetorical terms such as *ethos, logos*, and *topos*, he does not fully define them. If these terms are new to you, consult your dictionary or a glossary of rhetorical terms before you begin.

I N his introduction to the Norton Critical Edition of *The Double Helix*, Gunther Stent assigns a birthday to the science of molecular biology: April 25, 1953, the publication date of James Watson and Francis Crick's paper sketching the double helical structure they had devised for the DNA molecule.[1] Others have confirmed the view that this paper was pivotal in establishing molecular biology as a science. The editors of the journal *Nature* carried a series of papers under the collective title "Molecular Biology Comes of Age" just twenty-one years and a day after its publication, and they used a facsimile of it as the title page for the retrospective.[2] Horace Freeland Judson's ex-

haustive history of the field quotes from scores of scientific papers but reproduces *in toto* only this one.[3] More clearly than any single scientific paper in recent years, this one stands near if not precisely *at* the center of what Thomas
Kuhn would call a scientific revolution.

I have written elsewhere of the rhetorical implications of Kuhn's view of
the nature of science, and in a general way of the rhetorical dimensions of
Watson and Crick's work.[4] This essay might be regarded as a sequel to that
earlier one, but I don't intend to pursue further the theoretical implications of
Kuhn's ideas for developing a rhetorical analysis of science. I want instead to
develop a more thorough critical analysis of Watson and Crick's 1953 paper.
Rhetoric has traditionally been a strongly empirical field of study in that it
places great emphasis on the particular case. The job of the rhetorical critic is
to discover what in the particular case were the available means of persuasion,
and judge whether the rhetor managed them well or badly. The particular
case commands his or her attention as something worth knowing in itself,
apart from any general principles that might be abstracted from it. But while a
number of scholars have been arguing theoretically that science is rhetorical,
very little attention has been paid to particular cases of scientific rhetoric.[5]

This essay comes at the rhetoric of science from a critical perspective; I
want to explicate a particular case that is surely worth the effort. Ultimately, I
hope to show that the Watson-Crick paper establishes an *ethos*, a characteristic
manner of holding and expressing ideas, rooted in a distinctive understanding
of the scientific enterprise.

I am here consciously echoing lines from an essay by Edwin Black in
which, while he does not use the term *ethos* as I am using it, he develops a very
similar concept in connection with nineteenth-century American oratory:

> Groups of people become distinctive as groups sometimes by their habitual
> patterns of commitment—not by the beliefs they hold, but by the manner in
> which they hold them and give them expression. Such people do not neces-
> sarily share ideas; they share rather stylistic proclivities and the qualities of
> mental life of which those proclivities are tokens.[6]

The most general point I hope to make in this paper is that scientific communities can be bound together in this fashion. While the specific beliefs they
hold—the *logos* of the discipline—may be crucial to a scientific community,
their identity as a community may rest equally on "stylistic proclivities and the
qualities of mental life of which those proclivities are tokens," that is, on what
I am calling *ethos*. I will begin by concentrating rather closely on a single scientific paper, then try to place it in a larger context.

"A Structure for Deoxyribose Nucleic Acid" was the first published announcement of the double-helical structure Watson and Crick had devised for
DNA, the molecule that had by the early 1950s been identified as the transmit-
ter of genetic information.[7] While the story of how Watson and Crick arrived
at their discovery has been told elsewhere,[8] certain facts bear retelling here, by

way of outlining the rhetorical situation. First, there was a degree of competition surrounding the work: Linus Pauling in California was known to be working on the problem of DNA's structure; Maurice Wilkins and Rosalind Franklin at King's College in London were also working on it, and there was a vague sense in England that the problem belonged to them; Watson and Crick were supposed to be working on other matters at Cambridge, but they hoped to be first to the solution of the DNA molecule. Second, while the structure of the DNA molecule was regarded as an important research problem, no one knew beforehand just how important its solution would turn out to be. No one knew or even hoped that genetic information would turn out to be transmitted by a straightforward mechanical process, and that knowing the structure of DNA would therefore suggest the possibility of mastering and ultimately manipulating the process.

Because of the competitiveness of the situation and of the unanticipated significance of the discovery, Watson and Crick chose to publish their discovery in *Nature*, a journal that would publish the article promptly and reach a broad scientific audience. *Nature* is published weekly and, like the U.S. journal *Science*, is not specialized in a particular discipline. An arrangement was made for Wilkins and Franklin to publish simultaneously with Watson and Crick results of their most recent x-ray diffraction studies, which tended to support the proposed model. What appeared in *Nature*, then, was a trilogy of articles under the collective title "Molecular Structure of Nucleic Acids." The first is Watson and Crick's paper; the second is "Molecular Structure of Deoxypentose Nucleic Acids," signed M. H. F. Wilkins, A. R. Stokes and H. R. Wilson; the third is "Molecular Configuration in Sodium Thymonucleate," signed Rosalind E. Franklin and R. H. Gosling.[9] This apparent attempt to portray the discovery of the double helix as a broad-based team effort failed. The Watson-Crick paper is reprinted in three places that I know of with the title "Molecular Structure of Nucleic Acids," but without the Wilkins and Franklin papers that properly go with it under that title.[10]

The paper consists of fourteen paragraphs totaling just over 900 words. It contains one figure—a "purely diagrammatic" representation of two helices wound around a central axis—and no formulas. The text is organized as follows:

Paragraph 1—introduction: "We wish to suggest a structure for the salt of . . . (DNA). This structure has novel features which are of considerable biological interest."

Paragraphs 2–3—review of selected literature: Models of DNA proposed by Pauling and Corey (paragraph 2) and Fraser (paragraph 3) are considered and rejected.

Paragraphs 4–12—body of the paper:

Paragraphs 4–5 sketch the broad outlines of the model (two helical chains wound around each other).

Paragraphs 6–8 describe the "novel feature" of the structure, the mechanism by which the two chains are bound together. Each chain contains four bases in a sequence that "does not appear to be restricted in any way." The bases on one chain form hydrogen bonds with those on the other according to a fixed pattern (adenine bonds only to thymine, guanine only to cytosine), so that the sequence of bases on one chain automatically determines the sequence on the other.

Paragraph 9 notes that experimentation has shown adenine equal to thymine and guanine equal to cytosine in DNA.

Paragraph 10 speculates that the structure will not be found in RNA.

Paragraph 11 considers the status of the proposed model relative to available x-ray data. The model is "roughly compatible" with the data, "but it must be regarded as unproved. . . . Our structure . . . rests mainly though not entirely on published experimental data and stereo-chemical arguments."

Paragraph 12: "It has not escaped our notice that the specific pairing we have postulated immediately suggests a possible copying mechanism for the genetic material."

Paragraphs 13–14 – conclusion: Paragraph 13 promises a more detailed picture of the structure to be published elsewhere; paragraph 14 acknowledges the help of a few other scientists, including Wilkins and Franklin.

There are, as I see it, three substantial arguments put forward in support of their model by Watson and Crick. The most important is the great elegance of the model, particularly the base-pairing mechanism (described in paragraphs 6–8) that holds the two helical chains together. This argument is in their paper left entirely implicit, as it probably had to be. They assume that the description in paragraphs 4–8 will appeal strongly to the reader's sense of theoretical elegance. The argument is in effect an enthymeme whose missing premise is a scientific *topos* so basic and powerful that it would be gauche in the extreme to state it openly in a technical paper. But in *The Double Helix* Watson makes the argument from elegance explicit: "a structure this pretty just had to exist."[11] (Future developments in the history of molecular biology would demonstrate that a structure could be extraordinarily "pretty" and still not exist. The story of the comma-free code – "an idea of Crick's that was the most elegant biological theory ever to be proposed and proved wrong" – is too intricate to warrant retelling here, and it is told with appropriate elegance by Judson.[12] I mention it to underscore my point that for the scientist elegance functions not as an absolute principle, but as a rhetorical *topos*, a premise for argument in contingent cases.)

The second argument offered by Watson-Crick is that the proposed model provides a very precise theoretical explanation for what before had been simply a curious fact – the observed ratios of adenine to thymine and guanine to cytosine, referred to in paragraph nine. Given the base-pairing mechanism that holds the DNA molecule together according to the model, the ratios become inevitable rather than just curious. What is interesting rhetorically about this argument is that Watson and Crick leave it implicit just as they had the argument from elegance, though in this case they might have made their point explicit without any impropriety. Instead they merely juxtapose a statement of the observed ratios immediately following the description of the base-pairing mechanism, and expect the reader to make the connection. The argument is another enthymeme resting on the *topos* of explanatory power.

The third argument is negative: the proposed model is not inconsistent with any available experimental data. Unlike the first two arguments, this one is laid out explicitly, in paragraph 11. But notice how carefully qualified the statement is.

Argumentatively, then, the paper is understated, and the rhetorical effect is to communicate a sense of supreme confidence. The claim that the proposed model is of "considerable biological interest" is advanced boldly in the first paragraph, and the arguments in support of the model are assumed to be so persuasive that they need no bolstering or emphasis.

Stylistically, the most striking quality of the paper is its genteel tone. Note, for example, the diction of the introductory paragraph: "We *wish* to *suggest* a structure for the salt of deoxyribose nucleic acid (D.N.A.). This structure has *novel* features which are of *considerable* biological *interest*." (italics added) Note too the delicate fashion in which they reject the model that had been proposed by Linus Pauling and his colleague: "*In our opinion*, this structure is *unsatisfactory* for two reasons: (1) *We believe* that the material which gives the X-ray diagrams is the salt, not the free acid. Without the acidic hydrogen atoms *it is not clear* what forces would hold the structure together. . . . (2) Some of the van der Waals distances *appear to be* too small." (Paragraph 2; italics again mine) That this is a consciously contrived style becomes apparent in light of *The Double Helix*, from which we know that Watson and Crick regarded the Pauling-Corey model as an incredible blunder, a violation of the most elementary fact of chemistry. They were astonished and jubilant to find the great Pauling guilty of what they regarded as a gross error. If we can believe *The Double Helix*, the genteel style of Watson and Crick's first published paper reflects a rhetorical persona, perhaps fabricated with a bit of intentional, tongue-in-cheek irony; in the flesh they were obstreperous and irreverent.

Note finally the one sentence paragraph that concludes the body of the paper, a sentence in which the genteel style becomes a transparent burlesque: "It has not escaped our notice that the specific pairing we have postulated immediately suggests a possible copying mechanism for the genetic material." One can almost feel the elbow in one's ribs.

The effect of Watson-Crick's self-consciously genteel style is to give the paper a highly personal tone that is somewhat unusual in scientific prose. There are a number of conventional devices by which scientific prose is depersonalized. Simplest and most frequently noted by critical readers is the passive voice construction: "It was observed that . . ." Rather than "I observed . . ." Somewhat more subtle and rhetorically interesting is a device that one finds with increasing frequency in academic writing across the disciplines, a device that amounts to the manufacture of abstract rhetors: "*The data show that . . .*" Or "*This paper* will argue that . . ." The effect of the device is to suppress human agency, to imply that what are essentially rhetorical acts – arguing, showing, demonstrating, suggesting – can be accomplished without human volition. Watson and Crick are noteworthy in that they generally avoid this convention, particularly in putting forward their own case. They claim the argument quite explicitly as their own: "We wish to suggest" "In our opinion" "We believe" "We wish to put forward" "It has not escaped our notice" "We have postulated." By contrast, the Wilkins et al. paper that appears immediately following Watson-Crick in the April 1953 *Nature* is bloodless and impersonal in the manner more typical of scientific prose: "The purpose of this communication is . . ." "It may be shown that . . ." "It must be decided whether . . ." "The . . . significance of a two chain nucleic acid unit has been shown . . ."

Both argumentatively and stylistically, then, Watson and Crick put forward a strong proprietary claim to the double helix. What they offer is not *the* structure of DNA or *a* model of DNA, but Watson and Crick's structure or model. Moreover, in staking their claim they enact a distinctive way of adhering to ideas in public; they dramatize themselves as intellectual beings in a particular style. The paper articulates a recognizable public persona, an *ethos*. The Watson-Crick *ethos* does not necessarily overturn established conventions of scientific rhetoric, though we shall see that it offends at least one authoritative sensibility. What I believe it does is shape a particular image of *the scientist speaking*, within a broader set of more vague and general norms that apply to all scientific discourse. And this *ethos* I contend is an important aspect of what Kuhn would call the paradigm offered to the broader scientific community.

This claim is a rather large critical speculation based on my general sense of how rhetorical norms operate in scientific communities. Some evidence in its support can be found by comparing Watson and Crick's rhetoric with that of other biologists, and I will turn now briefly to a paper without which Watson and Crick's own work might not have been possible.

The effort devoted to discovering the structure of DNA – not just by Watson and Crick, but by Wilkins, Franklin, Pauling and a great number of others – was of course based upon a consensus that DNA is indeed the substance that transmits genetic information from one generation of cells to the next. The first published demonstration of this crucial fact was a paper by Oswald Avery and two associates that appeared in 1944 in the *Journal of Experimental Medicine*.[13] Avery and his colleagues had used a well-known experimental procedure in which one strain of Pneumococcus bacteria is transformed into a genetically distinct strain. By a series of tortuously executed procedures, they isolated the "active principle" involved in the transformation and identified it as DNA. Prior to the publication of their work, DNA was thought to be a genetically irrelevant substance, and most biologists assumed that genes consisted of some form of protein. In a sense, then, one might date the "revolution" in molecular biology from the appearance of their paper rather than Watson and Crick's. The simplest reason for not doing so is that Avery's work did not have an immediate revolutionary effect. Although it is now regarded as an air-tight demonstration of DNA's role in heredity, scientists were slow to accept it as such and focus on DNA's structure as a biologically important problem. According to Gunther Stent, Avery's discovery was "premature" because it could not at the time be connected with canonical knowledge in the field.[14]

An obvious feature of the Avery et al. paper is that by comparison with Watson and Crick's on the double helix, it is much longer and more dense with technical detail. Whereas Watson and Crick simply sketch in broad outline the results of their work, Avery and his colleagues rehearse in painstaking detail the experimental technique by which the "active principle" was isolated and then the analytic techniques by which it was identified as DNA. In effect they present their case according to the method of residues, recording a sequence of technical procedures that gradually narrows the explanatory possibilities down to the single conclusion that the substance responsible for the phenomenon in question is DNA. A characteristic point of their argumentative strategy is that the paper does not state its thesis in the introductory section and in fact does not even mention the substance DNA until roughly half-way through its 7500 word length. They make no strong claims about the importance of their discovery, and in fact introduce the paper as simply a "more detailed analysis" of the already well-known transformation phenomenon. They observe all the conventions of depersonalization: events transpire in the passive voice, data suggest conclusions without human assistance, and Avery and his colleagues take on that ultimate *nom de plume*, "the writers."

I am tempted to suggest that the "prematurity" of Avery's work was owing in part to his rhetoric in presenting it to the scientific community.[15] But while I think that a persuasive case could be made for such a claim, I am more concerned here simply to point up the contrast between Avery's *ethos* and that of Watson and Crick. The character that speaks to us from Avery's paper is that of a cautious skeptic who is forced somewhat unwillingly to certain conclusions. That of the Watson-Crick paper is quietly confident, so much so that "he" can indulge in a gentle bit of leg-pulling. I put quotation marks around "he" for the obvious reason that the voice in which the paper speaks is in a sense that of two men speaking in unison, a fact that points up the corporate, conventional, public nature of the phenomenon I am trying to capture. What interests me here is not the unique personality of an Oswald Avery or a Francis Crick, but the public role of *scientist* as dramatized by them. They offer two sharply contrasting versions of that role, two images of a fitting way for scientists to hold ideas.

A larger view of the contrast comes into focus if we consider the notions of form and strategy. At a simple level, the Watson and Crick paper offers something very close to a textbook illustration of Burkean form: the "arrows of desire" are pointed in the opening sentences,[16] which promise that the proposed structure has *novel features* which are of *considerable biological interest.* The promise of novel features is satisfied by paragraphs 6–8, which describe the crucial base-pairing mechanism, introducing it with the phrase, "The novel feature of the structure is . . ." The promise of biological interest is partially satisfied by the last substantive paragraph (12), which hints at an explanation of the genetic process. But of course this is simply a further pointing of arrows, and the appetite so aroused is in turn satisfied by a second paper that appeared in *Nature* just five weeks later, this one speculating on how the DNA molecule (as described in "our model") might transmit genetic information by means of an essentially mechanical process.[17] And, since neither of these two brief papers develops a sufficiently detailed picture of the model for other scientists to begin working with it, both together serve to create an appetite for two more technically elaborate papers that followed in more specialized journals.[18] Finally, just eighteen months after the publication of the original brief paper in *Nature,* Crick published an essay in *Scientific American* reviewing the state of the art in molecular biology and placing his work with Watson in this larger context.[19]

The April 1953 paper, then, is really just the initial move in a rhetorical strategy aimed at gaining and holding the attention of an audience. As such, it presumes an understanding of science as a human community in which neither facts nor ideas speak for themselves, and the attention of an audience must be courted. By contrast, Avery and his colleagues present their work in a single technical paper structured in a reportorial pattern which implies that facts *do* speak for themselves. Their strategy seems to presume that the work of the scientist is simply to give oneself up to the facts. Avery speaks from within an essentially positivistic, pre-Kuhnian view of science, Watson and Crick from within what Frederick Suppe calls a *Weltanschauungen* view.[20] They recognize that a discipline includes tacit assumptions about what is and what is not a legitimate question, and that in order to gain a hearing for a new theory, one may have to suggest what use the theory might have, what new questions it might both pose and answer, what new lines of research it might open up.

The success of the Watson-Crick strategy is indicated by the publication of Crick's essay in *Scientific American,* a periodical that addresses the entire scholarly community and carries a very substantial weight of authority. In this piece, Crick is no longer speaking only for himself and Watson, but for the community of specialists in molecular biology as well. When he writes of what "we" know to be the case and what "we" regard as an important research problem, he speaks for an international scientific community, defining their view of the world to an audience that embraces scholars and scientists in all disciplines. The essay does not yet speak of the double-helical model of DNA as one of the established facts of biology; the model is still in effect the private property of Watson and Crick. But as "owner" of that theory, Crick has gained the authority to say what the facts are in biology and to place the theory before the entire scholarly community in the context of those facts. The implication is that the theory is a strong candidate for admission to the canon of established knowledge in biology.

Perhaps I should be explicit here on a point that I hope would go without saying: none of this is meant to deny the importance of Watson and Crick's model in its technical particulars. To say with Perelman that a *fact* is defined by its claim to the adherence of the universal audience is not to deny that a fact must also correspond to an observation of the world.[21] The double-helix and its attendant explanation of genetic information transfer would not have survived as a theory had it failed to work in predicting experimental observations. My point is to bring into focus another aspect of Watson and Crick's work, a rhetorical aspect that falls under the heading of *ethos*. In offering their model of DNA to the scientific world, they simultaneously offered a model of the scientist, of how he ought to hold ideas and present them to his peers. I believe that this ethical aspect of Watson and Crick's work contributed to the speed with which their model of DNA gained prominence as a theory, but I have been more concerned simply to explicate the *ethos*.

One question remaining is whether the confident, personal, rhetorically adept *ethos* of Watson and Crick was effective *as a model*, whether it was adopted by other scientists. A strongly persuasive answer to that question would have to rest upon close rhetorical analysis of the work of later biologists. That analysis remains to be done. In the meanwhile, I can offer two somewhat weaker arguments in support of my belief that Watson and Crick *have* become a rhetorical-ethical model for others.

First, there is today an adventuresome, entrepreneurial, slightly irreverent spirit associated with the field of molecular biology and genetic engineering, a spirit that on its face strikes me as a recognizable offspring of the Watson-Crick *ethos*. The irreverence is apparent in the breezy, somewhat whimsical terminology current in the field: "gene splicing" is done with the assistance of a "gene machine"; segments of "genetic gibberish" on the DNA molecule are thought by some to act as "genetic errand boys."[22] I am inevitably reminded of the touches of delicate irony in the original Watson-Crick paper. The entrepreneurial spirit is evident in the enthusiasm with which researchers have welcomed opportunities for commercial exploitation of knowledge, even to the possible detriment of traditional academic values. According to an article in a recent issue of *Science 81*,

> Currently there is not a single top-ranking molecular biologist at an American university who has not signed up with one of the new genetics companies. The development dismays some biology watchers. One of science's brighter points as a human endeavor has been the traditional willingness of scientists to share time, information, and even specimens and equipment. That scientific knowledge should be considered private property is a concept repugnant to many scientists.[23]

I would contend that this notion of scientific knowledge as private, profit-making property is simply a logical extension of the manner in which Watson and Crick laid proprietary claim to their original discovery.

It is also a reduction to a peculiarly simple form of a tendency present generally in modern science. In an essay on the nature of scientific discovery, Kuhn points out that "to make a discovery is to achieve one of the closest approximations to a property right that the scientific career affords."[24] In her study of the cultural effects of print technology, Elizabeth Eisenstein makes a similar point about the importance of clarifying the proprietary claims of authors as a condition for the development of modern science: the incremental building of knowledge – science – presumes a certain niceness in identifying the individual components in the developing structure.[25] Heretofore the scientist's claim to a discovery was a rather inexact approximation of a property right, in that one exercised this right most fully by having others make free use of the property; a discovery became a "contribution" in the very moment that it became one's own property. There was, perhaps, some residue of the much older rhetorical tradition, within which all knowledge was in a sense *commonplace* – available for use by anyone – and such notions as plagiarism, copyright, and product patent would consequently have made little sense.

My second argument rests on the testimony of one of the original actors in the revolution in molecular history. The chemical ratios in DNA which Watson and Crick offered as evidence for their model (paragraph 9 of the paper) had been established in the laboratory and documented in the literature by Erwin Chargaff. These equalities were in fact known as "Chargaff's ratios," and Watson and Crick's failure to mention his name (except as a footnote) in connection with this crucial piece of evidence might be regarded as a slight. It is perhaps worth noting that while Watson and Crick generally avoid the passive voice, in paragraph 9 they use it with the result that Chargaff's contribution becomes anonymous: "It has been found experimentally that . . . ." In any event, Chargaff has become a strong critic of the direction that biology has taken since the discovery of DNA's structure, and the tenor of his critique tends to support my view that the Watson-Crick *ethos* has been adopted by others. For example, in the 1974 *Nature* retrospective, "Molecular Biology Comes of Age," he recalls reading the original Watson and Crick papers in this way: "The tone was certainly unusual: somehow oracular and imperious, almost decalogous. Difficulties were brushed aside in *the Mr. Fix-it spirit that was to become so evident in our scientific literature.*"[26] (italics added) In Chargaff's mind, Watson and Crick have influenced not just the ideational content of biology, but the manner in which ideas are pursued, the spirit in which science is done. The "Mr. Fix-it spirit" that he deplores is what I have been calling an *ethos*.

Assuming that my analysis of the Watson-Crick *ethos* is at all persuasive, it has one very important implication for rhetorical studies of scientific discourse: except at the most general level, it may be misleading to speak of *the* rhetoric of science. While there is a sense in which what Oswald Avery was doing rhetorically is "the same as" what Watson and Crick were doing, the contrasts are profound, and they suggest the possibility that other particular cases of scientific rhetoric will exhibit their own peculiarities. A detailed understanding of the rhetoric of science will have to include some sense of the permissible range of variation. To achieve this sense, we need a body of critical literature on particular cases of scientific discourse.

I am suggesting the need for a program of what Black calls "emic" criticism, criticism that begins with the particular instance and aims toward the development of theories comprehending more general principles that operate across larger bodies of discourse.[27] To do this with scientific discourse is particularly difficult simply because the discourse is specialized and highly demanding. It is a daunting experience to take up a technical paper in, say, molecular biology equipped with an education in the hard sciences that ends somewhere around the time of Matthew Arnold and T. H. Huxley. That it can be done responsibly is demonstrated by Horace Freeland Judson, who started as a journalist and wrote what is generally regarded as a definitive history of molecular biology. That it should be done by scholars in rhetoric is suggested by the increasing importance of scientific matters in the arena of public affairs, the traditional realm of rhetoric. Science is itself an increasingly public enterprise, both in the sense that the public supports it financially and in the sense that it offers monumental threats and promises to our well-being. Science also serves as warrant for many of the arguments about traditionally non-specialized, civic questions—war and peace, ways and means for promoting the public welfare. To understand public discourse in the closing decades of this century, we must have some understanding of scientific discourse.

NOTES

1. James D. Watson, *The Double Helix: A Personal Account of the Discovery of the Structure of DNA*—Text, Commentary, Reviews, Original Papers, ed. by Gunther S. Stent (New York: W. W. Norton & Company, 1980), xi.

2. "Molecular Biology Comes of Age," *Nature*, 248 (April 26, 1974), 765–88.

3. Horace Freeland Judson, *The Eighth Day of Creation: Makers of the Revolution in Biology* (New York: Simon and Schuster, 1979), 196–98.

4. "Technical Writing and the Rhetoric of Science," *Journal of Technical Writing and Communication*, 8 (Spring 1978), 77–88; reprinted in *Technical Communication* (fourth quarter 1978), 7–10, 13.

5. Here follow some of the more interesting studies of scientific rhetoric: John Angus Campbell, "Charles Darwin and the Crisis of Ecology: A Rhetorical Perspective," *QJS*, 60 (Dec. 1974), 442–49; Paul Newell Campbell, "The *Personae* of Scientific Discourse," *QJS*, 61 (Dec. 1975), 391–405; Joseph Gusfield, "The Literary Rhetoric of Science: Comedy and Pathos in Drinking Driver Research," *American Sociological Review*, 41 (Feb. 1976), 16–34; Carolyn R. Miller, "Technology as a Form of Consciousness; A Study of Contemporary Ethos," *CSSJ*, 29 (Winter 1978), 223–36; Michael A. Overington, "The Scientific Community as Audience: Toward a Rhetorical Analysis of Science," *Philosophy and Rhetoric*, 10 (Summer 1977), 143–64; Herbert W. Simons, "Are Scientists Rhetors in Disguise? An Analysis of Discursive Processes Within Scientific

Communities," in Eugene F. White (ed.), *Rhetoric in Transition: Studies in the Nature and Uses of Rhetoric* (Univ. Park: Penn. State U. Press, 1980), 115–30; Philip C. Wander, "The Rhetoric of Science," *Western Speech Communication*, 40 (Fall 1976), 226–35; Walter B. Weimer, "Science as a Rhetorical Transaction: Toward a Nonjustificational Conception of Rhetoric," *Philosophy and Rhetoric*, 10 (Winter 1977), 1–29. Of these, only Campbell's paper on Darwin, and Gusfield's on drinking driver research are *critical* essays in the sense that they include close analysis of particular rhetorical transactions.

6. Edwin Black, "The Sentimental Style as Escapism, or The Devil with Dan'l Webster," in Karlyn Kohrs Campbell and Kathleen Hall Jamieson (eds.), *Form and Genre: Shaping Rhetorical Action* (Falls Church, Va.: SCA, n.d.), 85.

7. J. D. Watson and F. H. C. Crick, "A Structure for Deoxyribose Nucleic Acid," *Nature*, 171 (April 25, 1953), 737–38.

8. In addition to *The Double Helix* and *The Eighth Day of Creation*, see Robert Olby, *The Path to the Double Helix* (London: Macmillan, 1974).

9. *Nature*, 171 (April 25, 1953), 738–41; both papers are reprinted in the Norton Critical Edition of *The Double Helix*, 247–57.

10. Both the 1974 *Nature* retrospective and Judson's *Eighth Day* reprint the Watson-Crick paper in this somewhat misleading way. The same error is committed by Mary Elizabeth Bowen and Joseph A. Mazzeo (eds.), *Writing About Science* (New York: Oxford University Press, 1979). Stent's Norton edition of *The Double Helix* includes the Wilkins et al. and Franklin-Gosling papers, but it places them following a second Watson-Crick paper that appeared in *Nature* more than a month after the original trilogy of DNA papers.

11. *The Double Helix*, 120.

12. *The Eighth Day of Creation*, 318 ff.

13. Oswald T. Avery, Colin M. MacLeod and Maclyn McCarty, "Studies on the Chemical Nature of the Substance Inducing Transformation of Pneumococcal Types," *Journal of Experimental Medicine*, 79 (1944), 137–58; reprinted in Harry O. Corwin and John B. Jenkins (eds.), *Conceptual Foundations of Genetics: Selected Readings* (Boston: Houghton Mifflin Company, 1979), 13–27.

14. Gunther S. Stent, "Prematurity and Uniqueness in Scientific Discovery," *Scientific American*, 227 (Dec. 1972), 84–93.

15. Judson speaks of the Avery et al. paper as "a model of reasoning from and about experiment." (*The Eighth Day of Creation*, 37) I see no conflict between this view and my own belief that the paper is *rhetorically* weak.

16. I am thinking of Kenneth Burke's notion of form, as developed in the essays "Psychology and Form" and "Lexicon Rhetoricae," both in *Counter-Statement* (Berkeley: University of California Press, 1968), 29–44 and 123–83. My belief that Watson and Crick make use of what Burke calls the psychology of form in presenting their model of DNA would require some qualification of the views Burke expresses about science in these essays.

17. J. D. Watson and F. H. C. Crick, "Genetical Implications of the Structure of Deoxyribonucleic Acid," *Nature*, 171 (May 30, 1953), 964–67; reprinted in the Norton Critical Edition of *The Double Helix*, 241–47, and in Corwin and Jenkins, *Conceptual Foundations of Genetics*, 52–55.

18. J. D. Watson and F. H. C. Crick, "The Structure of DNA," *Cold Spring Harbor Symposia on Quantitative Biology*, 18 (1953), 123–31; F. H. C. Crick and J. D. Watson, "The Complementary Structure of Deoxyribonucleic Acid," *Proceedings of the Royal Society*, A, 223 (1954), 80–96. Both papers are reprinted in the Norton Critical Edition of *The Double Helix*, 257–74 and 274–93.

19. F. H. C. Crick, "The Structure of the Hereditary Material," *Scientific American*, 191 (Oct. 1954), 54–61.

20. Frederick Suppe (ed.), *The Structure of Scientific Theories* (Urbana: University of

Illinois Press, 1974), 125–220. In addition to Kuhn, Suppe identifies Stephen Toulmin, N. R. Hanson, Paul Feyerabend, Karl Popper, and David Bohn as proponents of *Weltanschauungen* views of science.

21. Ch. Perelman and L. Olbrechts-Tyteca, *The New Rhetoric: A Treatise on Argumentation*, trans. by John Wolkinson and Purcell Weaver (Notre Dame: University of Notre Dame Press, 1969), 67–70.

22. Graham Chedd, "Genetic Gibberish in the Code of Life," *Science 81*, 2 (Nov. 1981), 50–55.

23. Boyce Rensberger, "Tinkering with Life," *Science 81*, 2 (Nov. 1981), 47–48.

24. Thomas S. Kuhn, "Historical Structure of Scientific Discovery," *Science*, 136 (1 June 1962), 760.

25. Elizabeth L. Eisenstein, *The Printing Press as an Agent of Change: Communications and Cultural Transformation in Early-modern Europe* (Cambridge: Cambridge University Press, 1979), 119 ff.

26. Erwin Chargaff, "Building the Tower of Babel," *Nature*, 248 (April 26, 1974), 778. See also Chargaff's "A Quick Climb Up Mount Olympus: A Review of *The Double Helix*," *Science*, 159 (29 March 1968), 1448–49. According to Stent, Chargaff refused permission for this piece to be reprinted together with other reviews in the Norton Critical Edition of *The Double Helix* (p. 168).

27. Edwin Black, "A Note on Theory and Practice in Rhetorical Criticism," *Western Journal of Speech Communication*, 44 (Fall 1980), 331–36. *Communication*, 44 (Fall 1980), 331–36.

Discussion Questions

1. Why does Halloran include a paragraph-by-paragraph outline of the original Watson-Crick article? How does he use this to reinforce his argument?

2. What evidence can you find in Halloran's analysis of the Watson-Crick *Nature* article that he bases his reading on additional works by Watson and Crick?

3. Why, according to Halloran, is examination of a particular case an appropriate method to reach general conclusions? Outline step by step Halloran's method, pointing out where and when he moves from the specific to the general and how he accomplishes it.

4. Why, according to Halloran, is it important for the nonscientist to understand scientific discourse? How important do you think the analysis of scientific discourse is? In what ways does practicing critical examination of scientific discourse equip you to function better as a member of society?

Journal Entry

What is your personal response to the quotation Halloran includes from *Science 81:* "Currently there is not a single top-ranking biologist at an American university who has not signed up with one of the new genetics companies"? Do you have any qualms about university scientists, who are paid with tax dollars, also being employed by commercial genetics companies? What are the benefits for the scientists as well as for the companies? What are the pitfalls of this type of affiliation?

Writing Projects

1. Halloran contrasts a paper by Oswald Avery with the paper by Watson and Crick to illustrate two different types of scientific approach—not just different writing styles, but different ways for "scientists to hold ideas." Analyze Halloran's treatment of the two. How does he use each? Why?

2. Imitating Halloran's method, analyze a scientific article. You could limit your discussion to features such as overall tone, which would include use of the passive voice and what Halloran refers to as "abstract rhetors," or you could examine organization and structure of the argument. Alternatively, you could concentrate on the language used for expressing the issues themselves.

Collaborative Project

With a classmate, examine the earlier article by Halloran that he mentions in the second paragraph of this article. How does that article lay the groundwork for this one? In what way is it appropriate to view this article as a sequel to the earlier one? Share your analysis with the class.

Ruth Herschberger

Society Writes Biology

Ruth Herschberger *(b. 1917) grew up in Chicago and attended the University of Chicago and Black Mountain College in North Carolina; she now lives in New York City. Several of her plays have been produced, and she received critical acclaim for her book of poems* A Way of Happening *(1948). Another book of her poems,* Nature & Love Poems *(1969), received the Midland Authors Poetry Award. Herschberger's work has also been recognized with a Rockefeller Foundation grant, the Hopwood Award, and the Harriet Monroe Memorial Prize. The following excerpt is from her book* Adam's Rib *(which is no longer in print). First published in 1948, the book offers a feminist perspective on the position of women in society, although it predated the women's movement by several decades.* Adam's Rib *was described in the* New Yorker *as "a clever, literate, and coldly logical analysis." In the following excerpt Herschberger rewrites biology from a matriarchal point of view to illustrate the patriarchal bias in our accepted understanding of conception. The end result is funny, illuminating, and engrossing.*

Questions to Consider

☐ Herschberger refers to the "lingo of Science." Before reading this excerpt, consider what Herschberger might mean by this phrase. Do you currently believe the terminology of science is completely objective?

☐ As you read, consider the source and reliability of the evidence Herschberger uses to support her claim that much writing about biology has a patriarchal slant.

---

well) here's looking at ourselves
—E. E. CUMMINGS

There is a prevalent belief that scientists are unprejudiced. It is true that they of all citizens make the most stirring attempt at objectivity, but in realms close to the social structure, as in the biological sciences, it is easy for the scientist and popularizer of science to slip into hidden evaluations in their reports on organic fact. If we like their bias, we contentedly ignore it. In accounts of sexual processes, however, there is a painfully persistent tendency to award the female a derogatory role.

By capturing the mood, and an occasional phrase, from various widely selling sex books, we shall piece together a typical account entitled *A Patriarchal Society Writes Biology*. The outstanding device for entering opinion under the guise of objective fact, we will see, is consistently to animate one portion of a process and *de*animate the other. The male cell acts, voluntarily, yet with a teleological sense of destiny, while the female reacts, involuntarily, taking her cues from him.

For in the patriarchal account, the male sperm is by all odds the central character. We watch his actions with breathless suspense. He is an independent little creature, single-minded, manly, full of charm, resourcefulness and enterprise, who will make his own minute decision to swim toward the egg.

The female egg is portrayed as the blushing bride, ignorant but desirable, who awaits arousal by the gallant male cell. The egg, like the human female, is receptive. In most accounts of the physiology of sex, the writer becomes rhapsodic over the relaxed and nutritious condition of the waiting ovum. Since the egg is not known to be capable of self-motion, it is regarded as helpless.

The sperm is the purposeful agent in reproduction; the egg learns direction and purpose only after union with the sperm. Thus the human ovum is a country cousin until entered by the worldly male cell; the human female is only half alive until she is pregnant.

In choice of terms the patriarchal biologist makes liberal use of the word *vestigial*, as applied to any organ in the female which is similar to an organ in the male but not quite like it. The uterus escapes being called a vestigial prostate because it bears sons, but the clitoris has never thrown off the label of vestigial penis.

The patriarchal biologist employs *erection* in regard to male organs and *congestion* for female. Erection of tissue is equivalent to the filling of the local blood vessels, or congestion; but erection is too aggressive-sounding for women. Congestion, being associated with the rushing of blood to areas that have been infected or injured, appears to scientists to be a more adequate characterization of female response.

While robbing us of some of our illusions about father science, the discussion may have a salutary effect upon poets, who have expressed fears that the language was losing its flavor and its myth-creating qualities. Opinions are still hiding out among us, but less often in such naïve adjectives as *good* and *bad*, *superior* and *inferior*. Opinion finds just as adequate shelter, and a wider market, by adopting the dress of the times — the lingo of Science, its vocabulary and its accent.

A Patriarchal Society Writes Biology

EMBRYOLOGY

Male. The human embryo first passes through an indifferent or asexual stage in which it is not possible to distinguish male from female. In the second month, however, nature prepares for the great differentiation which is to come.

The genital projection, later the penis, is joined by a large genital fold, a sort of collar. This collar later becomes the scrotum.

Along the genital projection is a cleft, a median slit which leads to the kidneys and internal genital glands.

As development proceeds, the penis grows rapidly, and the genital cleft closes to form the urethra which opens temporarily at the base of the glans.

In the third month the glans splits and forms a groove which recloses, continuing the urethra to its proper place at the tip of the penis.

Just before or after birth the testes progress from their position within the pelvic region to their definitive place in the scrotum.

Thus the male human being has utilized the asexual embryonic projection (or genital tubercle) to develop the organs of penis and scrotum.

Female. The female, we find, does not develop in any important way from the asexual or early embryonic state. Her sexual organs remain in an infantile condition, displaying an early arrest of development.

Whereas in the male the genital tubercle progresses rapidly toward the mature penis form, the genital tubercle in the female embryo slowly regresses until it forms the clitoris, or vestigial penis, a minute glans hidden in an upper depression of the vulva.

Similarly, the genital cleft which successfully closes in the male remains as a pronounced unsealed slit in the female, forming the inner lips of the vulva. The outer lips are the vestigial scrotum; the inner are the vestigial raphe.

Biologically the woman occupies an intermediate position between the man and the child.

She remains related to the child in order to be able to serve better as a mother.

Various malformings of the female system may take place, due to embryonic development suddenly ceasing. This leads to many kinds of infantilisms in the organic construction of the female.

The conditions of female development are negative rather than positive — that is to say . . . they depend on the absence of male hormone rather than the presence of female hormone . . . The female may therefore be regarded as the basic type of the mammalian species, and the male as the more highly differentiated type derived from it by the action of the male hormone.

PHYSIOLOGY

The Male Sexual Mechanism. The simple and elementary fact behind human reproduction is that a fertile female egg awaits impregnation in the fallopian tube, and the active male sperm must find this egg and penetrate it.

The female sex apparatus is a depression to receive the sex cells; the male organs are advanced in order to expel the cells.

When the male becomes sexually excited by internal stimuli, his sexual mechanism is called into play. There is a spontaneous erection of the penis, and the passageway from the testicles is thrown open. The sperm has a long way to travel through the vas deferens, through the penis, through vagina and uterus, and finally into the tiny tube where the female egg is waiting.

Nature has provided for this purpose an aggressive and active male cell. Each sperm manufactured in the complex tissues of the testes is composed of very rich and highly specialized material, and is equipped with a fine wriggling tail which gives it the power of self-locomotion.

No less than 225,000,000 cells are emitted from the man's body with each ejaculation—and every cell is a human being!*

The male seminal fluid, which accompanies the sperm, has a characteristic faint odor, remarkably like that of the flowers of the Spanish chestnut.†

When coitus and ejaculation take place, the male sperm, millions in number and each one swimming like a fish, begin their concentrated search for the female egg.

The instant that one of the sperm penetrates a receptive egg, the creation of a new human being has occurred.

The male system differs markedly from that of the female, for the male produces billions of sperm without interruption for forty or fifty years, whereas the girl child is born with ova already present. It merely follows that each month one ovum is discharged from an ovary.

It is of the utmost importance to make clear that reproduction and the sex act are far more closely allied in the man's case than in the woman's, for in the normal man the sex act is by Nature's design specifically a reproductive act as well.

A woman produces an egg usually only once a month, and it may be viable—capable of being fertilized—for perhaps no more than twenty-four hours. . . . Intercourse at all other times has no reproductive significance to the female.††

The Female Reproductive Function. The coordinated system of the female is merely the negative reflection of the positive features of the male. It functions to receive the male sperm, and to provide shelter for the growing embryo. When the male has sufficiently aroused the female, the organs of vulva and vagina become flushed and congested, while various glands secrete mucus in order to permit the entrance of the erect penis. This moisture is the signal that the female is ready to receive the male cells.

---

*The sperm itself is only ½ a human being, but such fractional qualification would ruin the esthetic veracity of the statement.
†From Van de Velde's description of semen, quoted by Parshley.
††If we assume, and one would not like to assume otherwise, that the male in question is monogamous as well as normal, intercourse at times other than when his wife is fertile will have no reproductive significance for him either.

The female egg is incapable of self-motion. It is dependent on mechanical means for transportation from the ovary to the fallopian tube, where it is fertilized by the male sperm. It is significant that only one egg is provided each month in the female, while billions of active sperm are produced in the male for the purposes of reproduction.

If an egg is not fertilized, the currents of moisture that are always present in the female sweep it out of the body.

As an inducement to sexual union and procreation, nature has provided both men and women with sensitive pleasure-producing zones. In the male the source of pleasure is outside of his body, whereas in the female it is inside. In a fully developed woman, the strongest sexual feeling will be in the vagina. The female's vestigial penis, the clitoris, has its function in the transmission of external stimuli to the internal generative organs.

Many women say that they do not experience either pleasure or orgasm, and some have come to regard orgasm as a luxury.

And from the point of view of function, it may be said that they are right; an orgasm is for them a luxury. Whereas for the satisfactory discharge of the male function of fertilization an ejaculation, and therefore an orgasm, is indispensable, for the female function of conception an orgasm is unnecessary.

Frigidity. Frigidity is a condition in females in which sexual desire or the ability to reach a climax is lacking. This is very frequent, and the theory may be advanced that the cause of this, more frequently than usually realized, is an actual organic inadequacy in the human female, perhaps resulting from the rigors of evolution. The frigidity of a wife should not interfere any more than necessary with the normal gratification of the man's sexual impulse.

Impotence. Impotence is the occasional inability of a man to obtain an erection or to carry out intercourse, either because of revulsion to the woman, indifference, or because of a psychological barrier.

We will now watch the Matriarchal biologist take over the facts of biology, producing a mirror-image of the Patriarchal account, as true and as false.

Through patriarchal eyes we observed the Tom Mix bravado of the male cell and the flower-like receptivity of the female egg. In the matriarchal account, we are not surprised to discover that the egg has become overnight the smart little administrator of fertilization, ringleader and lion-tamer, led on by destiny and a sense of right.

The male semen, on the other hand, is laboriously put together by one doubtful function after another. It begins to seem a miracle that it stays intact as long as it does, in time for the capable egg to extend a helping hand to the faltering sperm that comes so reluctantly to the bridal hour.

The matriarchal account is by no means a fair account. It is invented for the purpose of illustrating the emotional connotations of words thought by science to be objective and unprejudiced. Since the matriarchal version has not found previous expression, we will allow it a little more space and a louder grasp of adjectives.

A Matriarchal Society Writes Biology

EMBRYOLOGY

Female. The human embryo first passes through an indifferent or asexual stage in which it is not possible to distinguish female from male. In the second month, however, nature prepares for the great differentiation that is to come.

The genital projection, later the clitoris, is joined by a large genital fold, a sort of collar. This collar later becomes the outer lips of the vulva.

Along the genital projection is a cleft, a median slit which leads to the kidneys and internal genital glands. This cleft widens to form the inner lips of the vulva.

As development proceeds, the vestigial human tail, which projects from the body just as the genital tubercle does, begins to recede, taking its proper place at the base of the spine.

In like manner—but only in the female—the genital tubercle also progresses to its proper place at the head of the labia minora, or inner lips of the vulva. This interesting development of the clitoris is accompanied in the female by an extensive development of the genital fold, which becomes the pubis and outer lips of the vulva.

Thus the female human being utilizes the asexual embryonic projection (or genital tubercle) to develop the distinctive organs of clitoris and vulva.

Male. The male, we find, does not develop in any important way from the asexual or early embryonic state. His sexual organs remain in an infantile condition, displaying an early arrest of development.

Whereas in the female the genital tubercle becomes the complex and highly differentiated organ, the clitoris, in the male the infantile genital projection remains, merely thickening and growing larger. The penis is best described as a vestigial clitoris which has lost much of its sensitivity.

The genital cleft, which normally remains open to form the vulva, closes regressively in the male. During the third month nature, as though dissatisfied with her work, rips out the stitches of the original seam and begins again; that is to say, the glans splits and forms a groove which closes so that the urethra opens at the top of the penis.

The so-called raphe is the gathering line (almost like a sewn thread) which runs longitudinally down penis and scrotum. The raphe is the vestigial vulva, here functionless.

Before or after birth, the male scrotum descends outside of the body, since sperm are incapable of tolerating the high body temperatures that the female ova find congenial. The scrotum, in which the testes reside, is the vestigial labia majora.

Biologically the male occupies an intermediate position between the woman and the child, or—embryonically—between the fish and the human being (for the young embryo very much resembles an amphibious animal).

Various malformings of the male system may take place, due to embryonic development suddenly ceasing. This leads to many kinds of infantilisms in the organic construction of the male.

When the sealing of the genital cleft ceases prematurely, leaving the urethral opening somewhere between the glans and the base of the penis, an abnormality called *hypospadias* is produced. If the inguinal canals fail to close, a part of the intestine may find its way through in later life, causing *hernia*. Sometimes one or both testes fail to descend. The testis retained in the body is then sterile: *cryptorchidism*, a relatively common condition.*

The conditions of male development are derivative rather than positive, dependent rather than independent. This is scientifically proven by the fact that if ovaries are removed from new-born mammals, the development of the female organs is not perceptibly affected; the female retains her sexual identity.

But if we remove the testicles of young rats, we find not only the growth of all the male structures in the body arrested, but female traits soon begin to appear.

It is clear that the female is the dominant human form, while the male is a more or less anomalous and accidental variation on that of the female.

Physiology

The Female Sexual Mechanism. The simple and elementary fact behind human reproduction is that the active female egg must obtain a male sperm before it can create new life.

The male sex apparatus is a tiny factory which continually manufactures sex cells for the female reproductive system.

When the female becomes sexually excited by internal stimuli, the pressure of hormones and mental images, her highly coordinated sexual mechanism is called into full play. There is a spontaneous erection of the clitoris, and a flow of blood into the fine sensitive tissues of the vagina. This causes a similar erection of this region and of the vulva, while the involuntary musculature of the vagina begins rhythmically to contract.

Secretions begin to flow which have a characteristic faint odor remarkably

---

*The matriarchal biologist realizes that it is not necessary to state that the male system is more *likely* to have disorders than the female. She simply restricts her interest to the disorders of the opposite sex, communicating the impression that they are somehow more fallible.

like that of the peach-tree blossoms of Mara, a small island off the coast of New Zealand.

Because of its central importance in reproduction, the female egg has been provided with a size much greater than that of the male sperm. This contributes to its greater resistance and independence. The female egg is actually visible to the naked eye, and is the largest cell in the female body and larger than any cell in the male body. The male germ cells are unbelievably tiny, and must be magnified one hundred times in order to be visible at all.

The male sperm is produced in superfluously great numbers since the survival of any one sperm or its contact with an egg is so hazardous, and indeed improbable. The egg being more resilient, and endowed with solidity, toughness, and endurance, can be produced singly and yet effect reproduction.

In the complex tissues of the ovary one egg each month attains maturity. The ovum is composed of very rich and highly specialized material. By the active pressure of its growth, it produces a slit in the wall of the ovary and escapes into the abdominal cavity. From here it works its way into the fallopian tube aided by active cilia and moisture.

The sperm are provided with a continuous enclosed passageway from the testes to the penis, thus making their conveyance as simple as possible. For the female, however, there is a remarkable gap between ovary and tube, a gap which the egg must traverse alone. When we consider that an egg never gets lost on its route, we realize the striking efficiency of the female sexual mechanism.

When the female's impulse inclines her to sexual intercourse, she must arouse the male in order to produce distension of the male organ of reproduction, the penis. This organ is composed of three sacks whose walls are riddled with blood vessels. When the male has been sufficiently stimulated, the vessels relax, thus receiving blood which causes congestion and a consequent swelling of the organ.

This response serves as a signal to the female that the male is ready for coitus. In a fully developed male, moisture will be present at the time of erection, but if this does not occur, adequate secretion is supplied by the numerous specialized glands of the female, particularly the well-known Bartholin's glands.

It is essential that the female take the initiative in the sex act, since she may have multiple orgasms and must secure contact for the clitoris. The male, on the other hand, needs only the rhythmic contractions of the vagina. If the woman obtains an orgasm before he obtains his, it is absolutely essential that she see that he too receives an orgasm. This is especially true if fertilization is desired (and the time of month propitious), but also for humanitarian reasons, in order to relieve the congestion of the penis.

At the height of the orgasm the uterus contracts maximally, becomes erect, prolongs its neck downwards, and now the external os, which, owing to the prolongation of the neck, dips into the seminal fluid, carries out snapping movements like the mouth of a fish. By means of these movements it laps up the semen. . . .

While the external os thus draws certain spermatozoa into the uterus, it leaves still others in the vagina. These are killed by the acids of the vagina and then swept out of the body.

The weakened or dead sperm cells are ingested by scavenger cells that creep out of the vaginal walls.

After the sperm are drawn to the vicinity of the egg, the egg by some little-known mechanism selects one cell from the many present. Sometimes none of the sperm suits the egg, in which case there is no fertilization.

When an egg does select a male sperm, the sperm is required to shed its wisp-like tail. Whatever temporary means the male cell had for locomotion, it is no longer to be retained. Nature seems to be insisting that the sperm sacrifice its independence for the larger destiny of the female egg.

For the future of the new human being now depends wholly upon the courage and acumen with which the egg establishes its placenta and obtains food for the active embryo.

It is clear that the sperm plays a very small and hesitant part in this larger panorama of the creation of life. We must not assume, however, that the sperm is any less essential than the egg; it is a difference in function. There is no question of superiority or inferiority.

The female system differs from that of the male in that the female egg is produced once each month with timely regularity and therefore with greater chance of being fertilized, while a margin of several million sperm is required for the fertilization of one mature egg.

Reproduction and the sex act are more closely allied in the female than in the male, because no matter how many male sperm are present, unless the female provides an ovum the sex act cannot result in fertilization. Only once each month, when the female egg is present, does intercourse have any reproductive significance for the male.

The Male Reproductive Function. The coordinated system of the male is merely the negative reflection of the positive features of the female. The male functions to produce sperm to give to the female.

The sperm are manufactured by the testes and stored away. At this time they have wispy thread-like projections but are totally incapable of any motion. When the female induces a sexual response in the male, passive sperm are forced up the tubes and receive a milky secretion from the prostate. It is this secretion which gives the sperm a limited capacity for self-locomotion.

The motility of the sperm should not be exaggerated. It is the contractions of muscular tissues which force the semen from the penis. The sperm have no capacity for motion until they are supplied with the milky fluid from the prostate during ejaculation; under this influence they move jerkily about. So abortive are their movements, however, that it is no wonder millions of spare sperm are necessary.

The movement of the sperm is neither swift nor certain. Not all sperm have effective tails, and if the prostatic secretion is deficient, there may be no movement whatever. Those sperm which do move cover about one millimeter in three minutes or one centimeter in a half hour.

The mature female egg is obliged to bide its time, not without impatience, until one of the tiny snail-like cells manages to reach it. No wonder the complicated sexual system of the female undertakes as one of its principal tasks the helpful encouragement of the dependent male cell. The fatal acids of the vagina are neutralized as much as possible by sexually stimulated glands. Active moistures supply a milieu without which the sperm would soon dry up and die.

Nature, in order to induce the male to consent to sexual union, has provided him with a sensitive pleasure-producing zone. This zone is the penis, especially the glans. The male differs from the female in that his source of pleasure is only outside the body, while the female's is both outside and inside.

Many men say that they do not experience pleasure during orgasm, and some have come to regard pleasure as a luxury.

From the point of view of function, it may be said that they are right; pleasure for men is indeed a luxury. No woman in a matriarchal society will consent to intercourse unless pleasure is involved, and therefore there can be no conception without female pleasure and satisfaction. But for the male function of supplying sperm, an emission, whether accompanied by pleasure or not, will serve to supply the egg with its needed fertilization.

Frigidity. Frigidity is a condition in males in which sexual desire or the ability to reach a climax is lacking. This is very frequent, and the theory may be advanced that the cause of this, more frequently than usually realized, is an actual organic inadequacy in the human male, perhaps resulting from the rigors of evolution. The frigidity of a husband should not interfere any more than necessary with the normal gratification of the woman's sexual impulse.

Impotence. Impotence is the occasional inability of a woman to obtain erection or to enjoy intercourse, either because of revulsion to the man, indifference, or because of a psychological barrier.

Someday, perhaps, a democratic account of the physiology of sex will be written, an account that will stress both the functional and organic aspects of reproduction. . . .

Discussion Questions

1. Do you think Herschberger's writing two contrasting versions of a biological process represents a more or less effective way to make her point than a

typical argumentative essay would? How does Herschberger capture your attention and sustain your interest in her presentation?

2. How and why do scientists and writers animate and de-animate accounts of the life process?

3. Why do many people believe scientists are unbiased? Explain why you do or do not agree with Herschberger that scientists usually reflect prejudice. Do you believe that there is no way to use language without reflecting some type of bias? Explain.

4. Evaluate how the author informs her argument with figurative language. Do you think her use of metaphor strengthens or weakens her main point?

Journal Entry

Describe and account for any emotional response you had to this essay. Did you identify more with the patriarchal or matriarchal version? How much of your response do you think was determined by your own sex?

Writing Projects

1. Compare and contrast the patriarchal and matriarchal versions in Herschberger's sections on frigidity and impotence. Which version seems more reasonable to you? What details in each version conflict with your view? What elements of each version confirm your own ideas on the subject?

2. With an audience of biologists in mind, write an essay that synthesizes Herschberger's two opposing views to create a unified perspective on the process of reproduction. Attach a brief account of the difficulties you faced and how you dealt with them.

Collaborative Project

Working in pairs, find an article on science or technology (try looking in one of your textbooks) that you consider to be gender-biased. Together, rewrite the article from the opposite perspective, imitating Herschberger's structure.

Beverly A. Sauer

Sense and Sensibility in Technical Documentation

Beverly A. Sauer *is an associate professor of English at the University of Maine. Recently she received a grant from the National Science Foundation to work on ethics and value studies in science and technology. Professor Sauer has published in several scholarly journals, such as* IEEE Transactions on Professional Communication *and the* Journal of Business and Technical Communication. *The following article demonstrates the author's interest in feminist perspectives on technical writing, the rhetoric of disaster, and communication standards for the Occupational Safety and Health Administration (OSHA). Here Sauer illustrates how technical documents sometimes marginalize and even exclude voices that, if heard, would increase the safety of the people involved.*

Questions to Consider

☐ The original title of Sauer's article is "Sense and Sensibility in Technical Documentation: How Feminist Interpretation Strategies Can Save Lives in the Nation's Mines." What are the sources for the "sense and sensibility" allusion? As you read, consider why Sauer incorporated this allusion.

☐ As Sauer's subtitle suggests, she believes that the way in which we use language to communicate can have life-and-death consequences. Watch how she proves this point in her article.

Abstract: *This article analyzes postaccident investigation reports from a feminist perspective to show (a) how the conventions of public discourse privilege the rational (male) objective voice and silence human suffering, (b) how the notion of expertise excludes women's experiential knowledge, (c) how the conventions of public discourse sanction the exclusion of alternative voices and thus perpetuate salient and silent power structures, and (d) how interpretation strategies that fail to consider unstated assumptions about gender, power, authority, and expertise seriously compromise the health, safety, and lives of miners—and in a broader sense—all of those who are dependent on technology for their personal safety.*

I N her preface to *The Poetics of Gender*, Nancy K. Miller argues that "the social construction of sexual difference" affects the production, reception, and history of texts as well as the conventions and categories of critical discourse within which we all operate (xi). In short, she argues, "the acts of interpretation we perform and which come to embody us, are inextricably involved with the conventions and categories of identity itself" (xi). Many feminists, in fact, question whether we can interpret anything at all without a consideration of gender, class, and race (N. Miller; Sherwin; Von Morstein; Wittig; Mullett; Jardine; Berg; Code).

From a feminist point of view, writing is *gendered* to the extent that writers use signs or clues in the text that reveal the sex, class, or status of the writing subject. For feminist theorists, gender reveals itself in the subject's voice – not merely in the choice of pronouns, but in the very attempt to arrange words (Wittig 65–66). Whether feminists believe in an *essential* difference between male and female writing or in a *socially constructed* difference, they generally agree that there are structural differences in the way men and women – and in particular, men and women in power – arrange their words, orient their ideas, and construct the subject underlying the text's meaning. A feminist analysis thus questions the writer's ability to produce an exact account of any event without a consideration of the gendered assumptions that govern the construction of the text.

In articulating the silent codes and unarticulated assumptions in a text, moreover, a feminist analysis reveals both the hidden power structures that govern the construction of a text and the silent and salient privileging of one voice over another. A feminist interpretation is thus overtly iconoclastic to the extent that the reader (a) challenges attempts to reduce discourse to a single image or representation of truth and (b) fails to accept the codes embedded in the text (Berg 208).

In scientific and technical discourse, a feminist analysis challenges the unacknowledged power relations implicit in the traditional Cartesian model of science based on the concept of the objective, interchangeable knower (Harding 58). From this point of view, scientific discourse – with its traditional notions of expertise and authority – excludes the feminine perspective and employs what Lorraine Code calls the double standard of knowledge in which experience is considered second class to "knowledge" (64). This hierarchical distinction between knowledge and experience, Code argues, confines women within narrowly circumscribed private spheres of knowledge and expertise (64). In the public sphere, Catharine MacKinnon contends, the conventions of scientific or objective discourse simply rationalize male power and enforce women's powerlessness in socially constructed legal norms and structures. Thus she argues that

> the state will appear most relentless in imposing the male point of view when it comes closest to achieving its highest formal criterion of distanced aperspectivity. When it is most ruthlessly neutral, it will be most male. . . . When it most closely conforms to precedent, to "facts," to legislative intent, it will most closely enforce socially male norms and most thoroughly preclude questioning their content as having a point of view at all. . . . (qtd. in Hanen 31)

Von Morstein uses the archetype Cassandra to concretize the exclusion of women's voices from public discourse. According to Von Morstein, "Cassandra's story is the story of her *angst* because she was condemned to be alive in the face of blindness, of disbelief. She could not choose not to 'see.'" But if she spoke from the ground of her own experiences, she was necessarily bound to "break, abandon, or expand some of the rules that govern our common language and behavior," and she risked the animosity and aggression of others. To conform, she had to relinquish her freedom and speak the language of what Von Morstein calls *Ubereinstimmungssucht,* or "agreement-addiction" – socially constructed discourse that does not challenge or threaten the status quo (56–57).

Technology and the Feminist Perspective

Although researchers have considered the impact of gender on communication practices such as collaboration, sexual harassment, and conversation in the workplace (see Lay, "Interpersonal Conflict"; Tebeaux; Lay, "Feminist Theory"; Allen; Flynn et al.; Baker and Goubil-Gambrell; Carrell; Halterman, Dutkiewicz, and Halterman), recent studies in the social construction of knowledge in organizations have not used feminist theory to analyze miscommunication in large-scale technological disasters and have not analyzed documents outside the traditional research and development framework (see Winsor; Dombrowski; Herndl, Fennell, and Miller; Nelkin; Petroski; Perrow).

A feminist ethic raises questions about the rhetorical function of technical reports that document a single version of events "for the record." Instead, a feminist ethic demands that readers use a double standard for judging texts: the standard of historical, or representational, truth (the standard of historical accuracy) and the additional standard of performative truth – the ability of a text to change reality or events. From this perspective, technical documentation that merely records events "for the record," in the historical sense, may fail when judged by the standards of performance – how documents function to solve problems or prevent disaster in the future.

In this article, I will show how a feminist interpretation can change the way that technical writers look at expertise and evidence in technical writing. By comparing formal documentation of mine inspection reports with women's testimony about conditions in the mines, I will show how

1. the conventions of public discourse privilege the rational (male) objective voice and silence human suffering;
2. the notion of expertise excludes women's experiential knowledge[1];
3. the conventions of public discourse sanction the exclusion of alternative voices and thus perpetuate salient and silent power structures;
4. interpretation strategies that fail to consider unstated assumptions about gender, power, authority, and expertise seriously compromise the health, safety, and lives of miners and, in a broader sense, of all those who are dependent on technology for their personal safety.

The Rhetorical Function of Postaccident Investigation Reports

The Mine Safety and Health Administration (MSHA) prescribes specific formats and procedures for postaccident investigation reports in the *Manual for Investigation of Coal Mining Accidents* (United States, Department of the Interior). According to the manual, the purpose of a postaccident investigation is "to determine how and why an accident occurred in order that remedial actions may be taken to prevent a recurrence in the same or in another mine" (7). According to one official at MSHA, however, postaccident investigation reports are "pretty much fill in the blank, pro forma" operations. Writers learn to look for a single, technical cause of the accident and closely imitate the style and syntax of regulations to construct findings and conclusions.[2]

Like other reports, the *Report of Investigation: Underground Mine Coal Dust Explosion* for the No. 11 Mine (ID No. 15-02290) Adkins Coal Company, Kite, Knott County, Kentucky, 7 December 1981, follows a standard format (Luxmore and Elam):

☐ The abstract summarizes the factual findings of the report and sets the tone for the report that follows: passive verbs, objective findings, and technical details within a legal framework.

☐ Part I includes (a) two pages of general information, including the organizational structure of the mine, a list of mine-management officials, company data, location of the mine, sample methods and tests, and the date of the last inspection, 7–22 October 1981, when seven citations were issued, four in the underground workings of the 007 section (where the explosion occurred) and (b) eight pages describing "Mining Methods, Conditions, and Equipment."

☐ Part III of the report (investigation, discussion, and evaluation) describes the explosion and recovery operations in great detail, almost hour to hour.

☐ Part IV lists 31 findings of fact and eight contributing violations, including data from postaccident laboratory analyses and observations and statements from miners employed at the mine prior to the accident. The findings note that tests taken *after* the accident reveal that the volatile ratio of the coal in the face area of the no. 1 entry of the 007 section was 0.39 (indicating that the coal dust at this mine was highly explosive).

☐ Part V (conclusion) lists six "conditions and practices that contributed to the explosion and its propagation" (28).

☐ Appendix A lists the names and social security numbers of the dead miners, as well as their ages, sex, job classifications, experience at the job, and total mining experience.

☐ Appendix F contains copies of inspection citations (for safety violations) issued following the explosion.

Viewed from a feminist perspective, the inspection report demonstrates how the categories and conventions of public discourse reflect industry assumptions about blame and responsibility and masculinist notions of credibility, expertise, and scientific objectivity. Both the format and conventions of the investigation report encourage inspectors to record and document findings for the record without directly blaming operators or mine supervisors for problems in the mines, but, as the following analysis reveals,

1. the objective language and scientific format of postaccident investigation reports privilege industry assumptions about risk and safety in the mines;
2. the scientific format, chronological ordering of evidence, and regulatory language obscure lines of authority and responsibility and silence the firsthand experience of women, who measure danger in domestic terms (the amount of dust in the washing machine rather than in ppm's [parts per million], for example).

Industry Assumptions About Mine Safety and Health

Industry and labor agree that the mining industry in this country has an appalling safety record, but they disagree about the cause of accidents and the effectiveness of MSHA's enforcement under the Mine Safety and Health Act of 1969 (Drury; *Federal Coal Mine Health and Safety Act of 1969*; Levy, "Rhetoric of Disaster"; Spicer; U.S. Congress, House; U.S. Congress, Senate; United States, Department of the Interior, "Coal"; United States, President's Commission on Coal). Whereas industry blames miners for poor work habits and carelessness, miner advocates blame management for willful violation of the law.

In a 1977 report, the National Coal Association Bituminous Coal Operators' Association, Inc. (BCOA) admitted that although the industry had experienced a reduction in the total number of disabling injuries, it had not been as successful in reducing injuries as it had been in reducing fatalities. But the BCOA challenged the assumption that more inspections and increased regulation would improve mine safety and health. Citing a government-funded Bendix Corporation report, the BCOA report concludes, among other findings, that

1. the causes of violations usually have little relationship to the causes of accidents;
2. the level of disabling accidents in underground coal mines that can be prevented by current enforcement efforts has reached a relatively fixed plateau;
3. insufficient attention has been given to the fact that accidents are most often caused by deficiencies in worker attitudes, habits, and skills that can only be corrected by training and direction (*Federal Coal Mine Health and Safety Act of 1969* 2).

Moreover, according to Louis H. Hunter, executive vice president of the National Independent Coal Operators' Association, enforcement and inspection have little relationship to safety:

> There were two MSHA inspectors in the mine when they had a belt catch on fire. Luckily, no one was injured. But if you would have had 19 inspectors in there, it wouldn't have prevented the fire. (304)

Miner advocates such as J. Davitt McAteer and L. Thomas Galloway challenge these claims, arguing that MSHA investigation reports show that management negligence was at least a contributing cause in 76% of the cases in 1975 and that poor work habits and/or insufficient training was one of a number of factors in only 58% of the cases (559–60). In the Scotia disaster alone (which killed 26 men), they argue,

> at least the first explosion was a direct result of repeated violations of law, especially of the ventilation regulations. Scotia was issued 62 citations for ventilation in two years, yet the intentional disregard of the law shows that the enforcement effort was inadequate, not that it was misdirected. The same holds true for the Hyden explosion. (562–63)

Feminist Analysis of the Report

A feminist analysis reveals how the conventions of public discourse privilege the rational objective voice and exclude expression of the human suffering of the miners. Although one agency official acknowledged that report writers were sensitive to the fact that widows would read the report—and thus, he claimed, he was careful not to describe the condition of the dead miners in detail—the report's language reflects industry assumptions about blame and responsibility in mining accidents. The feminist analysis that follows demonstrates how salient and silent power structures influence the construction of evidence even in theoretically objective technical investigation reports.

Workers' names appear only in an appendix, where data categories reflect industry's contention that experience and worker error cause accidents. Despite 19 years total mining experience, for example, Bobby Slone, the section foreman at Adkins No. 11, had only one month's experience at the job. The data thus suggests that Slone's inexperience at the job site may have caused the accident, but data on *victims* excludes information on others responsible for rock dusting, testing, inspection, and management. By using only data from the now-dead victims of the explosion, moreover, the appendix directs attention away from operators' legislated responsibility to provide a safe working environment. Prior to the accident, according to the report, at least one miner – a scoop operator – left the working section and was thus not injured; the appendix does not include his name, age, mining experience, or experience on the job, or other such information on miners not injured in the explosion (Luxmore and Elam).

The subject focus of the report and ensuing investigation is technical rather than human. The coldly objective language of the Adkins report documents a series of unpreventable events, practices, and conditions precipitated by a technical failure for which no remediation seems possible: "A coal dust explosion occurred. . . ." "The accident resulted in. . . ." "The accident occurred. . . ." "The investigation revealed. . . ." "Evidence indicated. . ." (Luxmore and Elam i). No responsible human agent appears in the chain of causes that led to the accident: "A train of explosives . . . failed to detonate. This failure provided too much burden for the rib hole to pull. . ." (i). The objective scientific discourse thus reinforces the industry's fatalistic notion that accidents occur regardless of human agency or intent.

Passive verbs conceal the subject of the text as well as the agent in the disaster and conflate worker error with management negligence. MSHA investigators are taught to use the "negative" of the regulation in listing the technical causes of the accident (personnel interviews). Thus they imitate closely the agency-free language of the regulations in describing the chain of events leading up to the accident: "Each blast hole was charged . . . ; water . . . was not applied; coal dust . . . was permitted to accumulate . . . ; line brattices . . . were not installed and maintained in the working places to remove the coal dust that was dispersed into suspension when coal was being blasted. . ." (Luxmore and Elam 28). A feminist analysis (as well as good management practice) raises questions about the silences in the text: Who permitted dust to accumulate? Who failed to install and maintain line brattices?

Quasi-passive adjectives conflate technical descriptions with possibly causative actions. The report contains two references to the fact that the paper wrapping surrounding the explosives was slit. The following examples reveal how subtle editing can change a deliberate violation into a simple technical description. In the first example, the language implies that the cartridges were deliberately slit by an unnamed human agent:

> The paper wrapping that contained the explosive cartridges was deliberately deformed by slitting with a razor blade so that it could be compacted in the holes. (Luxmore and Elam 23)

In the conclusion, however, the writer changes the verb to an adjective. The ambiguous language conceals the deliberate human action responsible for slitting the cartridges:

> Miners employed at the mine stated that the paper wrappings around the cartridges of explosives were slit before inserting the cartridges into the blast holes and that the deformed cartridges were tamped into the hole and blasted without stemming. (28)

The document is a five-part research report rather than a problem-oriented report (problem/solution report) or a recommendation report. The *Report of Investigation* (Luxmore and Elam) follows a format prescribed by the *Manual for Investigation of Coal Mining Accidents* (United States, Department of the Interior). The carefully formatted categories, careful recording of detail, and standard headings imply a careful investigation of the event, but the authors make no recommendations to improve risk management and assessment in the future. The document is an informational report that provides a single narrative of the accident from a single point of view. Recommendations are inappropriate to the genre. The document functions as a historical record of the event from a single point of view but fails as a performative document: To use the report's technical findings to improve mine safety and health in the future, readers must reinterpret evidence in the text.

The report is a report of an investigation rather than a report to a responsible agency—whether government, management, or labor. The *Manual for Investigation of Coal Mining Accidents* prescribes a wide distribution for accident reports (United States, Department of the Interior), with multiple copies for each district office and the MSHA administrator's office. MSHA district managers must reanalyze data in the report to construct an action plan to prevent accidents in the future. As the following example illustrates, however, the lack of a clear audience dilutes the sense of responsibility and mediates against responsible risk management and risk-reduction strategies. In a memorandum to William Querry, Joseph A. Lamonica, administrator for Coal Mine Safety and Health, asks Querry to formulate an action plan to deal with the "dismal record" of repeated accidents at the mines (243). In the memorandum, he notes that two fatalities have occurred within a seven-month period and that 10 fatalities have occurred in less than five years. Seven of the ten fatalities involved roof fall. Like the Adkins investigation report (Luxmore and Elam), report after report repeats a formulaic sentence describing the cause of the accident in the passive voice with no recommendations and no clear sense of audience:

> The accident and resultant fatality occurred when the victim proceeded into
> an area of known loose roof before the roof was supported or taken down.
> (Lamonica 250)

Only two accident reports, written by Ronnie Brock in 1984, indicate that management played a role in the accident. His reports attract Querry's attention – the cause is circled in the testimony – and prompt a call for an action plan to prevent further disasters.

Although the document reveals that several violations existed prior to the accident, it leaves an ambiguous record of blame and/or responsibility. The final conclusion (number 31) notes that "smoking articles were found in jacket pockets and in lunch buckets of several of the victims" (Luxmore and Elam 26). The conclusion carefully itemizes the number of cigarettes and summarizes the pathologist's statement that "2 victims had smoking materials in their clothing pockets" (26). Although the report acknowledges that "smoking was not considered a factor in the explosion" the concluding remark that "it was apparent that smoking was a practice underground" shifts blame for the accident from mining practices to worker habits (reflecting industry assumptions about mine safety and health) (26).

The technical language of the document silences the horror of human suffering and the loss of human life in a mine explosion. In describing the explosion and propagation of the accident, the authors tell the story of the flame and forces as *they* moved through the mine, in a traditional technical narrative description. Although the report notes that the forces damaged a jeep parked on the surface near the mine opening, it fails to mention the miners, who were burned – and killed – in the explosion:

> Flame and major forces of the explosion traveled out the No. 1 entry and
> across the last open crosscut and then out all 6 entries. When the flame and
> forces reached the entries developed to the left off the No. 1 entry, the evi-
> dence indicated that they traveled into the left side of these entries until they
> reached the face. The flame and forces then traveled out the right side of these
> entries back to the south main entries. The explosion developed enough pres-
> sure and velocity to damage the stoppings 12 crosscuts, or 700 feet, outby [sic]
> the face to the south main on the intake and return side, except the stoppings
> in the Nos. 27 and 28 crosscuts on the return side which remained intact. . . .
> Other forces also traveled outby [sic] in the south main entries and damaged a
> concrete block stopping at the intersection of the east main and south main en-
> tries. Debris blown by the explosion forces damaged a jeep automobile parked
> on the surface near the drift openings. (Luxmore and Elam 19)

The "Findings of Fact" section of the report also lists technical details of the explosion but silences the human death and suffering in the disaster. Finding No. 22 reports the results of tests on clothing, safety hats, and lunch buckets, but not on the bodies of miners:

22. Samples of clothing, safety hats, lunch buckets and other articles present in the explosion area were tested to determine the melting point of each. The tests indicated that a temperature of at least 553 degrees Fahrenheit existed in the last open crosscut. (Luxmore and Elam 24)

The Impact of MSHA's Rhetorical Conventions on Risk Analysis and Assessment in the Nation's Mines

Ironically, the passive language and nominalized structures in the report also prevent accurate data analysis. MSHA personnel frequently complained that they needed to "read a great deal into the report" to derive data for accident analysis on a larger scale (personnel interviews). They claimed that silences in the report—about technical details as well as human responsibility—prevented accurate analysis, particularly for new technologies such as longwall and deep-cut mining.

Agency personnel frequently complained that archaic data categories that forced inspectors to categorize accidents as "electrical" or "haulage" thwarted accurate data gathering and statistical analysis (personnel interviews). One official, for example, noted that he developed his own system to interpret key words in the text to derive statistical information for analysis only to discover the same statistics repeated in other reports with significant figures to three or four digits. Another agency analyst noted that researchers were frequently unable to verify data derived from reports because each analyst interpreted clues in the text differently and thus produced different numbers (personnel interviews). In short, the conventions established by the manual undercut effective risk management and assessment.

Women's Narratives

Women's testimonies in the oversight hearings contrast sharply with the highly technical public discourse of the investigation reports and technical analyses. Although only nine women testified in the 1982 hearings, their voices speak clearly of the daily danger in the mines and the refusal of management to deal with imminent danger. The following is the testimony of Jewelene Centers, widow of Tommy Centers:

> I can recall Tommy telling me what bad shape the mines was in, and that if things weren't changed, in his words, "they're going to get a bunch of us killed." As you know, that is exactly what happened.
>
> Tommy was a bolting machine operator. He told me that the company did not want him to take the time to set the safety jacks on the bolter, because then they couldn't run as much coal. The company was always pushing the men for more production on coal. Tommy also told me that Harold Baldrige,

the superintendent, wouldn't provide him with dust bags for his bolting machine. This meant that more coal dust was left to float in the air. This is the same coal dust that led to the explosion. (249)

The women have their own standards for judging danger. Centers testifies:

When Tommy worked at Irishman, he never came home as tired or dirty or upset as he did when he worked for Adkins Coal Co. While he worked for Adkins, he constantly kept a headache, and he couldn't even walk across the floor without leaving a trail of coal dust. He told me he had to find another job because the company just didn't care about the men's safety and it was too dangerous to work there. (250)

Annis Ashley measured the amount of rock dust in her wash cycles; her own domestic evidence represents truth for her, in contrast to mine employees, who must lie to save their jobs:

Dillard [Ashley] would come home filthy from the mines, and his work clothes always required two or three wash cycles to get all the coal dust out of them. . . . And had the mines been properly rock dusted the explosion would never have happened. While the employees at the State hearings in Martin, Ky., said that the mines weren't dusty, they have to worry about their jobs. They knew if they told the truth, that they would probably be replaced. (247)

The women's testimonies reveal a keen awareness that "they are not experts," but they have a clear agenda and motivation for solving problems in the nations' mines. Jennifer Boggs explains:

Every time a coal miner dies because of unsafe practices, I die a little more inside, too. These men have got to be protected.
     When my husband Dennis was killed, I had no idea that the mine was unsafe. When MESA [Mining Enforcement and Safety Administration] held the hearings in Whitesburg I sat there day after day, I couldn't believe my ears. I was actually stunned to think those men had died for no reason that made any sense to me. . . .
     Why do we have MSHA inspectors? They cite a mine for violations and within a few hours they are running coal again. If the inspectors would shut these mines down for a week or so and let them lose some of that precious money, then just maybe they would see how important it is for our men to come home to us.
     MSHA should hire widows for inspectors, [she concludes]. They would get the job done and without pay. (259)

A formal statement of the Adkins Widows and Families and the Council of the Southern Mountains, Inc., challenges MESA to translate the lessons of the past into accident-prevention strategies for the future. Despite the awkwardness of their language and the lack of parallel structure, the statement reveals a clear plan for improving mine safety and health:

1. Only allowing a minimal work force underground at the time;
2. punching out two entries nearly simultaneously;
3. increase the rock dusting requirements;
4. wear or have on hand SCSRs [self-rescuer devices];
5. required notification of MSHA; and
6. increased requirements and monitoring of ventilation. ("Summary" 271)

Their report challenges the assumption that individuals cause accidents, yet encourages MSHA to design mine safety programs with human as well as technical factors in mind:

> Noting the increase in multiple fatal accidents, the testimony pointed out the need to design mines for safety around human error (whether that error be management or labor) although noting that in 1980 and 1981 a review of MSHA fatal reports indicated that in roughly 80% of the cases management negligence was a contributing factor; as compared to only 35 to 40% of all fatals which included an employee-contributing factor. The multiple fatals point out the *flaw* in pointing to *individuals* as causes, but strongly suggests the need to design the workplace and machinery with the past safety lessons in mind. ("Summary" 271)

Despite their losses, the widows speak in the clear voice of survivors looking to the future rather than as victims. The summary concludes with homely advice not to "set back" but to keep moving forward in the face of tragedy:

> Mine safety . . . lies in common sense practical answers. Not in setting [sic] back bemoaning the accidents, but in using present reserves to prevent tragedies. It is a question of committment [sic] to mine safety, a question of translating accidents into prevention. ("Summary" 272)

Sense and Sensibility in Technical Documentation

If the women's voices make such sense, why are they not heard?

First, the women in mining communities have not learned the language of *Übereinstimmungssucht*, agreement addiction—the unarticulated code beneath the carefully categorized data in the inspection reports—a code that intentionally or unintentionally operates to maintain power structures within mining communities. When Jennifer Boggs testifies that her husband lacked effective safety training, for example, Eugene Johnston, representative from North Carolina, challenges the authority of her testimony. As the following excerpt reveals, J. Davitt McAteer answers Johnston's challenges—the male voices usurping the female testimony in the quest for a single representation of truth:

MR. JOHNSTON: I note in your statement "training should be mandatory before a man steps in the mines." That is in fact the case now.

MR. MCATEER: Mr. Chairman, for the record it is the training requirement and the whole discussion of the training requirement, and Chairman Gaydos' information grew out of the Scotia disaster.

MR. JOHNSTON: We are aware of that, but her statement "training should be mandatory" is not in accordance with the facts, is it, Mr. McAteer? . . . Don't you think we should be very, very concerned with truth in this hearing in noting moving a training center to another location does not mean it is being closed? . . .

MR. JOHNSTON: What you are saying is in your opinion training is now being deemphasized?

MR. MCATEER: That is correct.

MR. JOHNSTON: Anything else, Mrs. Boggs? (United States, Cong. 260)

In their home communities and in the oversight hearings, women lack the elements of credibility that give weight to their evidence: technical expertise, favorable reputation, corporate status, values similar to the reader, and "characteristics in [their] writing which show them to be understanding, well-informed, carefully organized, articulate, and fair minded" (Burnett 221; see also Stanford).

Second, as a result of their lack of expertise, women are excluded from the salient and silent power structures that control discourse in mining communities. Evidence in 1977 congressional oversight hearings, for example, suggests that inspectors soon learned not to mess with "the boys of Hazard" (anonymous, cited in Potter 222). In a handwritten memo, for example, Henry Stanford tells Paul Scaff that Gene Greenlee wants him taken off the investigation. Stanford tells Scaff to reclassify violations as Class II rather than Class I to keep the mines operating. If inspectors failed to cooperate or issued too many citations, they were transferred to Washington. In one case, a federal inspector served on the board of directors of a small Kentucky mine.

Third, as this analysis suggests, conventions of discourse maintain power structures within the mining community. Even the best inspectors slavishly followed models in the *Manual for Investigation of Coal Mining Accidents* and thus gave passive forms an authority that prevented active risk reduction strategies in the mines (United States, Department of Interior).

Finally, Steven Lukes's analysis of power suggests a more generalized explanation for women's exclusion from discourse in mining communities. According to Lukes, philosophers have described one-, two-, and three-dimensional models of power relationships. John Gaventa develops the argument in his study of power and powerlessness in an Appalachian community. In the one-dimensional relationship, according to Gaventa, power reveals itself visibly in situations of conflict and decision making (5–8). In simplest terms, powerful people make decisions and prevail in power struggles. Political silence, then, reflects "consensus" (7). In the two-dimensional model of power developed by Bachrach and Baratz, the powerful not only prevail in active conflicts but determine the agenda of the struggle itself (cited in Gaventa 10; see also Bachrach and Baratz, *Power and Poverty*, "Two Faces"). Political silence in this model reflects the suppression of options and alternatives in the conflict. In the "three-dimensional" model of power that Lukes proposes, the powerless internalize the beliefs, myths, symbols, and values that preserve unequal power structures. Gaventa writes:

> The culture of silence may preclude the development of consciousness among the powerless thus lending to the dominant order an air of legitimacy. As in the sense of powerlessness, it may also encourage a susceptibility among the dependent society to internalization of the values of the dominant themselves. (18)

Beula Gibson's testimony reveals the degree to which women have internalized the silent power structures of the mining community. Although her responses demonstrate a clear understanding of the technical details of rock dusting, the role of inspectors, the difference between union and nonunion mines, and the influence of Ford B. Ford as head of the MSHA, Gibson depreciates the value of her testimony and claims that she speaks only as the vehicle of her dead husband's voice:

> I realize that since I actually was never inside the mines in which my husband lost his life, and since I did not work on that particular shift, that Bert Combs, the attorney for Adkin Coal Co., might say that anything I can relate has nothing to do with what occurred at the mine. However, my husband cannot speak for himself, and I do know things that he told me and things that I observed. (245)

Implications for Technical Writing

A feminist perspective allows researchers to analyze the symbols, formats, and processes that silence the human element in objective scientific discourse, not merely to alter power relationships but to improve the lives and safety of workers. In this sense, feminism forces us to acknowledge the moral and ethical power of language as well as the political power of language. As Sheila Mullett argues, until we listen to the alternative voices and acquire a painful awareness of suffering, we inadvertently perpetuate it:

> "Good" people, nice people, [she writes] people of good will, whom I do not hesitate to call "moral" in the ordinary sense of that term, myself included, all participate in and perpetuate, even extend and legitimate violence against women simply by going about our business in an ordinary way. We do so primarily by our quotidian participation in social patterns and institutions which make up the bulk of everyday life. (115)

To counter this perpetuation, she urges that we must "experience the suffering of women . . . experience the shock of seeing the 'normal' categories of interpretation shift before a perception of almost inchoate possibilities of social transformation" (115).

From this perspective, the silencing of women's testimony raises fundamental issues for technical writers about texts excluded from traditional corporate communication networks. A feminist analysis

- ☐ forces us to reconsider questions of literacy, knowledge, and expertise
- ☐ raises issues about what counts as evidence in a closely controlled corporate structure
- ☐ raises issues about how we value information when it comes from sources outside the network of experts and those credentialed to speak in corporate networks
- ☐ raises questions about how we structure information to achieve political, social, and economic ends
- ☐ raises questions about the genres we admit and those that we exclude
- ☐ raises questions about the practice—and costs—of documentation and report writing for historical purposes
- ☐ raises questions about the gendered assumptions that structure the prescriptions and recommendations of the texts we use and the practices we teach
- ☐ raises questions about how discourse reflects both the salient and silent power structures in discourse communities
- ☐ raises questions about how that silencing prevents successful risk management and assessment.

By all standards of technical writing, the discourse these women speak is inarticulate, unstructured, and unobjective, but like Cassandra, they speak the truth in the face of agreement addiction. When we shift perspectives, however, objective scientific discourse reveals its own inadequacies.

A feminist analysis demands that technical writers acknowledge the silent power structures that govern public discourse, not because we are interested in theoretical constructs about language but because those power structures affect the fabric of technology on which we all depend. As the examples in the mine disasters show, the silenced voices may already know the answers to problems that continue to puzzle experts.

NOTES

1. In limiting the scope of this article to the exclusion of women's experiential knowledge, I do not mean to suggest that (male) miners' experiential knowledge is not also silenced or potentially significant. I have written elsewhere how the concept of imminent danger erects arbitrary distinctions between the engineer as "Rational Man" and the miners he (sic) must protect. Such arbitrary distinctions also obstruct effective risk management and assessment (Sauer, "Engineer").

2. In February, 1992, I conducted interviews with agency personnel at the Mine Safety and Health Administration, Arlington, VA, as part of an ethnographic research project under a grant from the National Science Foundation. Agency personnel graciously consented to interviews but could not be identified by name in this article. I am grateful to Rachelle Hollander, National Science Foundation and the Program in Ethics and Values Studies in Science and Technology of the National Science Foundation for their generous support of this project.

REFERENCES

Allen, Jo. "Gender Issues in Technical Communication Studies: An Overview of the Implications for the Profession, Research, and Pedagogy." *JBTC* 5.4 (1991): 371–92.

Ashley, Annis. Testimony. United States. Cong. House. Subcommittee on Health and Safety of the Committee on Education and Labor. *MSHA Oversight Hearings on Coal Mine Explosions During December 1981 and January 1982.* 97th Cong., 2nd sess. Washington, DC: GPO, 1982.

Bachrach, Peter, and Morton S. Baratz. *Power and Poverty: Theory and Practice.* New York: Oxford University Press, 1970.

——."The Two Faces of Power." *American Political Science Review* 56 (1962): 947–52.

Baker, Margaret Ann, and Patricia Goubil-Gambrell. "Scholarly Writing: The Myth of Gender and Performance." *JBTC* 5.4 (1991): 412–43.

Berg, Elizabeth L. "Iconoclastic Moments: Reading the *Sonnets for Helene,* Writing the *Portuguese Letters." The Poetics of Gender.* Ed. Nancy K. Miller. New York: Columbia University Press, 1986. 208–21.

Boggs, Jennifer. Testimony. United States. Cong. House. Subcommittee on Health and Safety of the Committee on Education and Labor. *MSHA Oversight Hearings on Coal Mine Explosions During December 1981 and January 1982.* 97th Cong., 2nd sess. Washington, DC: GPO, 1982.

Brock, Ronnie. "Abstract of Investigation, Fatal Roof Fall Accident, February 15, 1985, No. 1 Mine, Manalapan Mine Company, Inc., Highsplint, Harlan County, Kentucky." United States. Cong. Senate. Committee on Labor and Human Resources. *Oversight of the Mine Safety and Health Administration.* 100th Cong. 1st sess. Washington: GPO, 1987. 250.

Burnett, Rebecca. *Technical Communication.* 2nd ed. Belmont, CA: Wadsworth, 1990.

Carrell, David. "Gender Scripts in Professional Writing Texts." *JBTC* 5.4 (1991): 463–68.

Centers, Jewelene. Testimony. United States. Cong. House. Subcommittee on Health and Safety of the Committee on Education and Labor. *MSHA Oversight Hearings on Coal Mine Explosions During December 1981 and January 1982.* 97th Cong., 2nd sess. Washington, DC: GPO, 1982.

Code, Lorraine. "Credibility: A Double Standard." *Feminist Perspectives: Philosophical Essays on Methods and Morals.* Ed. Lorraine Code, Sheila Mullett, and Christine Overall. Toronto: University of Toronto Press, 1988. 64–88.

Dombrowski, Paul M. "A Comment on 'The Construction of Knowledge in Organizations: Asking the Right Questions about the *Challenger.'* " JBTC 6.1 (1992): 123–27.

Drury, Doris. *The Accident Records in Coal Mines of the United States: A Study of the Literature with Comparisons of the Records in Other Coal-Producing Countries.* Bloomington: Indiana University Press, 1964.

Federal Coal Mine Health and Safety Act of 1969: A Constructive Analysis with Recommendations for Improvements. National Coal Association/Bituminous Coal Operators' Association. June 9, 1977. United States. Cong. House. Subcommittee on Labor Standards of the Committee on Education and Labor. *Oversight Hearings on the Coal Mine Health and Safety Act of 1969 (Excluding Title IV).* 95th Cong., 1st sess. Washington, DC: GPO, 1977.

Flynn, Elizabeth A. et al. "Gender and Modes of Collaboration in a Chemical Engineering Course." *JBTC* 5.4 (1991): 444–62.

Gaventa, John. *Power and Powerlessness: Quiescence and Rebellion in an Appalachian Valley.* Champaign: University of Illinois Press, 1980.

Gibson, Beula. Testimony. United States. Cong. House. Subcommittee on Health and Safety of the Committee on Education and Labor. *MSHA Oversight Hearings on Coal Mine Explosions During December 1981 and January 1982.* 97th Cong., 2nd sess. Washington, DC: GPO, 1982.

Halterman, Carroll, Jody Dutkiewicz, and Eve Halterman. "Men and Women on the Job: Gender Bias in Work Teams." *JBTC* 5.4 (1991): 469–81.

Hanen, Marsha P. "Feminism, Objectivity and Legal Truth." *Philosophical Essays on Method and Morals.* Ed. Lorraine Code, Sheila Mullett, and Christine Overall. Toronto: University of Toronto Press, 1988. 29–45.

Harding, Sandra. *Whose Science? Whose Knowledge? Thinking from Women's Lives.* Ithaca, NY: Cornell University Press, 1991.

Heilbrun, Carolyn. Foreword. *The Poetics of Gender.* Ed. Nancy K. Miller. New York: Columbia University Press, 1986. vii–x.

Herndl, Carl C., Barbara A. Fennell, and Carolyn R. Miller. "Understanding Failures in Organizational Discourse: The Accident at Three Mile Island and the Shuttle *Challenger* Disaster." *Textual Dynamics of the Professions.* Ed. Charles Bazerman and James Paradis. Madison: University of Wisconsin Press, 1991. 279–305.

Hunter, Louis. Statement. United States. Cong. House. Subcommittee on Health and Safety of the Committee on Education and Labor. *MSHA Oversight Hearings on Coal Mine Explosions During December 1981 and January 1982.* 97th Cong., 2nd sess. Washington, DC: GPO, 1982.

Jardine, Alice. "Opaque Texts and Transparent Contexts: The Political Difference." *The Poetics of Gender.* Ed. Nancy K. Miller. New York: Columbia University Press, 1986. 96–116.

Lamonica, Joseph A. "Memorandum for William E. Querry Re: Fatalities at the No. 1 Mine, Manalapan Mining Company, Inc., Highsplint, Harlan County, KY, June 20, 1985." United States. Cong. Senate. Committee on Labor and Human Resources. *Oversight of the Mine Safety and Health Administration.* 100th Cong., 1st sess. Washington, DC: GPO, 1987. 243–51.

Lay, Mary M. "Feminist Theory and the Redefinition of Technical Communication." *JBTC* 5.4 (1991): 348–70.

——. "Interpersonal Conflict in Collaborative Writing: What We Can Learn from Gender Studies." *JBTC* 3.2 (1989): 5–28.

Levy, Beverly Sauer. "The Rhetoric of Disaster." Modern Language Association Conference. Chicago, 27–30 Dec. 1990.

Lukes, Steven. *Power: A Radical View.* London: Macmillan, 1974.

Luxmore, Charles E., and Robert Elam. *Report of Investigation: Underground Mine Coal Dust Explosion. No. 11 Mine (ID No. 15-02290). Adkins Coal Company. Kite, Knott County, Kentucky. December 7, 1981.* Arlington, VA: Mine Safety and Health Administration, 1981.

McAteer, J. Davitt. "Statements on Behalf of Beulah Gibson, Annis Mae Ashley, Jewelene Centers, Ora Slone, Sandra Perry, Verna Perry, Ralph and Clara Slone, Widows and Families of Miners Killed in an Explosion December 7, 1981, and the Council of Southern Mountains," United States. Cong. House. Subcommittee on Health and Safety of the Committee on Education and Labor. *MSHA Oversight Hearings on Coal Mine Explosions During December 1981 and January 1982.* 97th Cong., 2nd sess. Washington, DC: GPO, 1982. 194–243.

McAteer, J. Davitt, and L. Thomas Galloway. "Testimony . . . on Behalf of the Council of Southern Mountains, Inc., June 29, 1977." United States. Cong. House. Subcommittee on Labor Standards of the Committee on Education and Labor. *Oversight Hearings on the Coal Mine Health and Safety Act of 1969 (Excluding Title IV).* 95th Cong., 1st sess. Washington, DC: GPO, 1977. 554–715.

Miller, Carolyn. "The Rhetoric of Decision Science: Or Herbert A. Simon Says." *Science, Technology, & Human Values* 14.1 (1989): 43–46.

Miller, Nancy K., ed. *The Poetics of Gender.* New York: Columbia University Press, 1986.

Mullett, Sheila. "Shifting Perspective: A New Approach to Ethics." *Feminist Perspectives: Philosophical Essays on Methods and Morals.* Ed. Lorraine Code, Sheila Mullett, and Christine Overall. Toronto: University of Toronto Press, 1988. 109–26.

Nelkin, Dorothy, ed. *The Language of Risk.* Newbury Park, CA: Sage, 1989.

Perrow, Charles. *Normal Accidents.* New York: Basic Books, 1984.

Petroski, Henry. *To Engineer Is Human.* New York: St. Martin's, 1985.

Potter, Herschel H. "Memorandum for J. L. Spicer, January 19, 1982. Subject: Code-A-Phone Message No. 11." United States. Cong. Senate. Committee on Labor and Human Resources. *Oversight of the Mine Safety and Health Administration.* 100th Cong., 1st sess. Washington, DC: GPO, 1987. 222–23.

Sauer, Beverly. "The Engineer as Rational Man: The Problem of Imminent Danger in Non-Rational Environment." *IEEE Transactions on Professional Communication* 35.4. Forthcoming.

Sherwin, Susan. "Philosophical Methodology and Feminist Methodology: Are They Compatible?" *Feminist Perspectives: Philosophical Essays on Methods and Morals.* Ed. Lorraine Code, Sheila Mullett, and Christine Overall. Toronto: University of Toronto, 1988. 13–28.

Spicer, Jerry. Testimony. United States. Cong. Senate. Committee on Labor and Human Resources. *Oversight of the Mine Safety and Health Administration.* 100th Cong., 1st sess. Washington, DC: GPO, 1987.

Stanford, Henry. Handwritten Memo from Henry Stanford to "Paul" (Scaff), 16 March 1981. United States. Cong. Senate. Committee on Labor and Human Resources. *Oversight of the Mine Safety and Health Administration.* 100th Cong., 1st sess. Washington, DC: GPO, 1987. 221.

Stimpson, Catharine R. "Gertrude Stein and the Transposition of Gender." *The Poetics of Gender.* Ed. Nancy K. Miller. New York: Columbia University Press, 1986. 1–18.

"Summary of Adkins Widows and Families and the Council of the Southern

Mountains, Inc." United States. Cong. House. Subcommittee on Health and Safety of the Committee on Education and Labor. *MSHA Oversight Hearings on Coal Mine Explosions During December 1981 and January 1982.* 97th Cong., 2nd sess. Washington, DC: GPO, 1982. 270–75.

Tebeaux, Elizabeth. "Toward an Understanding of Gender Differences in Written Business Communications: A Suggested Perspective for Further Research." *JBTC* 4.1 (1990): 25–43.

United States. Cong. House. Subcommittee on Labor Standards. *To Amend the Federal Coal Mine Health and Safety Act.* Washington, DC: GPO, 1977.

——. Cong. Senate. Committee on Labor and Human Resources. *Oversight of the Mine Safety and Health Administration.* Washington, DC: GPO, 1987.

——. Department of the Interior. Mine Safety and Health Administration. *Coal Mine Injury and Employment Experience by Occupation, 1972–75.* Washington, DC: GPO, 1978.

——. Department of the Interior. Mine Safety and Health Administration. *Manual for Investigation of Coal Mining Accidents and Other Occurrences Relating to Health and Safety.* Washington, DC: GPO, 1977.

——. The President's Commission on Coal. *Coal: A Data Book.* Washington, DC: GPO, 1979.

Von Morstein, Petra. "A Message from Cassandra–Experience and Knowledge: Dichotomy and Unity." *Feminist Perspectives: Philosophical Essays on Methods and Morals.* Ed. Lorraine Code, Sheila Mullett, and Christine Overall. Toronto: University of Toronto Press, 1988. 46–63.

Winsor, Dorothy. "The Construction of Knowledge in Organizations: Asking the Right Questions about the *Challenger.*" *JBTC* 4.2 (1990): 7–21.

Wittig, Monique. "The Mark of Gender." *The Poetics of Gender.* Ed. Nancy K. Miller. New York: Columbia University Press, 1986. 63–73.

Discussion Questions

1. Sauer's article here is preceded by an abstract, just as originally published. From this example, what can you assume about the accepted structure of an abstract? How does it begin and conclude? How are the points made? What is the overall structure?

2. Define Sauer's concept of a hierarchical distinction between knowledge and experience. How is this significant for our understanding of scientific and technological issues?

3. Consider the question Sauer poses: "If women's voices make such sense, why are they not heard?" What does this reveal about Sauer's own bias? How does this question direct her argument? How would you answer the question?

4. Do you believe, as Sauer does, that the way language is used in public discourse is sometimes harmful because the power structures that govern tech-

nological decisions employ language that conceals the presence of danger? Why or why not?

Journal Entry

Sauer speaks of "masculinist notions of credibility, expertise, and scientific objectivity." Explain what you think those masculinist notions are. What do you consider to be feminist notions of credibility, expertise, and scientific objectivity?

Writing Projects

1. Analyze the structure of Sauer's article. What constitutes her main source of examples and illustrations? How is it like or different from her opening abstract? How do the abstract and the article complement each other?

2. Sauer makes several references to Cassandra. Who was Cassandra, and what is the myth surrounding her? Write an essay exploring why Sauer links the myth of Cassandra with her study. What connections does Sauer want her readers to make? How does the myth reinforce her argument?

Collaborative Projects

1. Working with a partner, obtain a sample of an accident report that you believe reflects certain assumptions about the definition of responsibility and the assignment of blame. Notice, for example, whether the directions on the accident report form ask the victim to describe what he or she did to contribute to the accident, but fail to ask what else may have accounted for the accident. Analyze the rhetorical elements of the accident report. With your partner, rewrite the accident report to reflect a more inclusive account of the accident situation.

2. In the final section of Sauer's article, she identifies nine issues revealed by her feminist analysis of "texts excluded from traditional corporate communication networks." Working with one or more classmates, analyze one or several of these issues. Consider, for instance, the possibility that ignoring certain points of view and kinds of testimonies allows risks and dangers to go unnoticed and hence unmanaged. Share your analysis with the class.

Making Connections

Questions to Discuss

1. How do physicians Oliver Sacks and Richard Selzer use narrative structure as a method for probing their patients' cases and for exploring what their own work means to them personally? What parallels do you see with essays by other physicians in the book, such as Ron Karpati in Chapter 7 and Elisabeth Kübler-Ross in Chapter 5?

2. This chapter explores the notion that we can exert control over science and technology through writing. Chapter 7 focuses on ethical issues arising from our use of science and technology. Develop connections between Chapters 7 and 8 by discussing ethical issues that face those who write about scientific and technological topics. Consider, for example, the ethical implications of Beverly Sauer's assertion that the way in which mining accident reports are written sometimes fails to emphasize dangers that workers face.

3. The articles by James Watson and Francis Crick, Michael Halloran, and Beverly Sauer were all originally published in professional journals (*Nature, Rhetoric Review,* and *Journal of Business and Technical Communication*). Based on your study of these articles, what can you surmise about the readers of each journal? What features stemming from the writers' assumptions about their audience do the three articles have in common? What significant differences can you find among them?

Suggested Writing Projects

1. Both of the narratives by physicians, "The Exact Location of the Soul" and "On the Level," are striking in their overall style and rich imagery. Write an essay analyzing how each writer uses figurative language. Compare and contrast the two writers' use of figurative language with that of writers from other chapters (Loren Eiseley in Chapter 3, for example).

2. The essay by Ruth Herschberger and the article by Beverly Sauer might both be described as feminist interpretations. Even so, they were written for widely different audiences, Herschberger's in 1948 and Sauer's in 1993. Compare and contrast the two pieces in terms of the methods and style used to examine male and female biases in language.

3. All six essays in this chapter acknowledge a rhetoric of scientific and technical language. Write an essay in which you compare and contrast specific writings in this chapter, explaining ways in which the authors implicitly or explicitly acknowledge this rhetoric. Analyze how the rhetoric suits the purposes of even those who distrust it.

530

Ozick, Cynthia. "Science and Letters: God's Work—and Ours." First published in *The New York Times Book Review*, September 27, 1987. Reprinted as "Crocodiled Moats in the Kingdom of Letters" in *Metaphor and Memory* by Cynthia Ozick. Copyright © 1989 by Cynthia Ozick. Reprinted by permission of Alfred A. Knopf, Inc.

Postman, Neil. "Invisible Technologies." From *Technopoly* by Neil Postman. Copyright © 1992 by Neil Postman. Reprinted by permission of Alfred A. Knopf, Inc.

Ruether, Rosemary Radford. "Toward and Ecological-Feminist Theology of Nature." From *Sexism and God Talk* by Rosemary Radford Ruether. Copyright © 1983 by Rosemary Radford Ruether. Reprinted by permission of Beacon Press.

Rybczynski, Witold. "Mirror, Mirror on the Wall," from *Taming the Tiger* by Witold Rybczynski. Copyright © 1983 by Witold Rybczynski. Used by permission of Viking Penguin, a division of Penguin Books USA Inc.

Sacks, Oliver. "On the Level" from *The Man Who Mistook His Wife for a Hat.* Copyright © 1970, 1981, 1984, 1985 by Oliver Sacks. Reprinted by permission of Summit Books, a division of Simon & Schuster, Inc.

Samuelson, Robert J. "Technology in Reverse." From Newsweek, July 20, 1992, © 1992, Newsweek, Inc. All rights reserved. Reprinted by permission.

Sauer, Beverly A. "Sense and Sensibility in Technical Documentation." Reprinted from *Journal of Business and Technical Communication*, vol. 7, no. 1, January 1993, pp. 63–83. Copyright © 1993. Reprinted by permission of Sage Publications, Inc.

Selzer, Richard. "The Exact Location of the Soul" from *Mortal Lessons.* Copyright © 1974, 1975, 1976, 1987 by Richard Selzer. Reprinted by permission of Simon & Schuster, Inc.

Shilts, Randy. "Reunion," from *And the Band Played On.* Copyright © 1987 by Randy Shilts, reprinted with permission of St. Martin's Press, Inc., New York, NY.

Snow, C. P. "The Moment." From *The Search.* Copyright © C. P. Snow 1958, reproduced by permission of Curtis Brown Ltd., London.

Tavris, Carol. "The Manufacture of 'PMS.'" From *The Mismeasure of Woman*, copyright © 1992 by Carol Tavris. Reprinted by permission of Simon & Schuster, Inc.

Thomas, Lewis. "The Hazards of Science," copyright © 1977 by Lewis Thomas, from *The Medusa and the Snail* by Lewis Thomas. Used by permission of Viking Penguin, a division of Penguin Books USA Inc.

Tilghman, Shirley M. "Science vs. the Female Scientist." Part I, January 25, 1993. Copyright © 1993 by The New York Times Company. Reprinted by permission.

Watson, James D. and Francis H. C. Crick. "A Structure for Deoxyribose Nucleic Acid." Reprinted with permission from *Nature*, April, 1953. Copyright © 1953 Macmillan Magazines Limited.

Weinberg, Alvin M. "Can Technology Replace Social Engineering?" Reprinted with permission of the author.

Wheeler, David L. "Scientists Worry About the Implications of Genetic Testing for Inherited Diseases." Copyright © 1993, *The Chronicle of Higher Education.* Reprinted with permission.

Williams, Joy. "Save the Whales, Screw the Shrimp." Reprinted by permission of International Creative Management, Inc. Copyright © 1988 by Joy Williams.

Woodward, Kenneth L., Mary Hager, and Daniel Glick. "A Search for Limits" from Newsweek, February 22, 1993. Copyright © 1993, Newsweek, Inc. All rights reserved. Reprinted by permission.

Index